teach yourself...

Word 97 for Windows

teach yourself...

Word 97 for Windows

Jan Weingarten and Colin Bay

A Subsidiary of
Henry Holt and Co., Inc.

MIS:Press
A Subsidiary of Henry Holt and Company, Inc.
115 West 18th Street
New York, New York 10011
http://www.mispress.com

Printed in the United States of America

This book is based on Betas 2 and 3 of Microsoft Office 97, not final code. Although the product we declared is stable, and the majority of the features enabled and finalized, there may be some differences between these builds and final product. For the latest information on Microsoft Office 97 differences, please visit http://www.microsoft.com.

First Edition—1997

Library of Congress Cataloging-in-Publication Data

ISBN 1-55828-524-5

MIS:Press and M&T Books are available at special discounts for bulk purchases for sales promotions, premiums, and fundraising. Special editions or book excerpts can also be created to specification. For details contact the Special Sales Director at the address listed above.

10 9 8 7 6 5 4 3 2 1

Associate Publisher: *Paul Farrell*
Executive Editor: *Cary Sullivan*
Editor: *Rebekah Young*

Copy Edit Manager: *Shari Chappell*
Production Editor: *Anne Incao*
Technical Editor: *Kristy Clason*

ACKNOWLEDGMENTS

As with the previous edition, this book would not have been possible without the support and dedication of the following team members:

Rebekah Young, my editor at MIS:Press. Thanks for putting up with me, Rebekah! You dealt remarkably well with all the delays, last minute changes, and inevitable ups-and-downs of the production cycle.

Kristy Clason, my trusty technical editor. I really appreciate your dedication and friendship. Thanks for hanging in through all the projects we've worked on together, Kristy. And thanks for making me look good by catching those oh-so-unavoidable errors before they could make it into the book.

The rest of the MIS:Press team: Anne Incao, Senior Production Editor, and Shari Chappell, Copy Edit Manager.

And last but never least, my agent at Waterside Productions, Matt Wagner. Thanks, Matt. You keep getting me into gigs and out of trouble.

CONTENTS

Section III: Dressing Up: Fonts and Graphic Elements 269

SECTION IX: CUSTOMIZING WORD 593

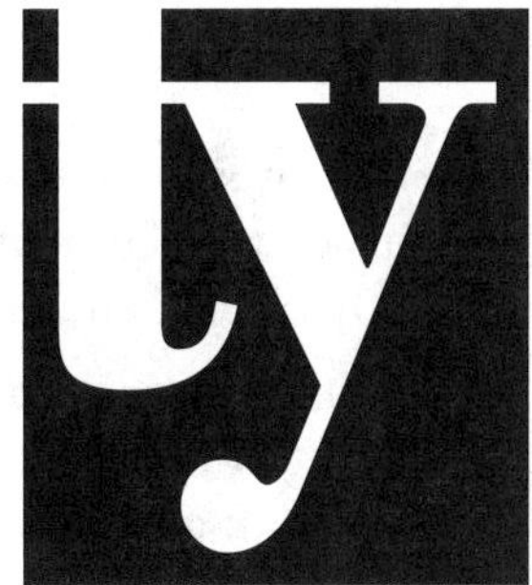

Introduction

If you already own Word 97, give yourself a pat on the back—you made a wise decision. Word's user-friendly approach and impressive collection of features have secured its position among the most popular word processing programs on the market.

With Word's vast potential, it's easy to become overwhelmed and intimidated. Where do you start? Which features do you really need? *Teach Yourself... Word 97* has the answers. You don't need to have any experience with computers or word processing; this book takes you by the hand and makes sense out of the maze of features. I won't throw a lot of jargon at you—I'll use real English and examples you can relate to to introduce the necessary computer terminology. Stick with me and you'll be speaking computerese and producing impressive-looking documents in no time.

Where You Should Start

Even if you are totally new to computers, Chapter 1, "Jumpstart," will have you creating an actual document right away. I'll walk you through the process of starting Word. Then you'll create, save, spell check, and print your first document.

If you've never used a mouse or are new to Windows or Windows 95, you might want to look at Chapter 2, "Getting Started with Word," before you do Chapter 1. I'll give you mouse and keyboard techniques, talk in more detail about starting and exiting Word, and explain the Word screen.

If you're an old hand with mice and Windows 95 (or even a medium hand), you can probably skip right to Chapter 3, "Power Tools." Even if you've used an earlier version of Word for Windows, look through this chapter; Word has made several additions to its arsenal of power tools.

Chapter 4, "Using Help," is probably the most important chapter in the whole book. Word is so feature-rich that no single book can possibly cover every nook and cranny. Word's online Help system provides the tools you need to figure out how to do just about anything. Even if you only skim through the rest of the book, make sure you're comfortable navigating through Help.

How This Book Is Organized

Section I: "Getting Started" takes you through the basics. After the "Jumpstart" chapter, Chapters 2 through 9 give you essential tools for creating and working with Word. You'll start Word and learn to recognize the different parts of the Word screen. Then you'll learn how to navigate your way around the document screen, move and copy text from one place to another, and recover when you make a mistake (such as accidentally pressing the wrong key). Chapters 7, 8, and 9 teach you essential skills for creating and formatting Word documents. You'll learn how to center, bold, and underline text; set tabs; change margins and line spacing; and work with other elements of character, paragraph, and page formatting.

Section II: "Beyond the Basics" covers more advanced material. You'll use Word's powerful find and replace feature to locate text or formatting anywhere in a document. And you'll learn how to use Word's proofreading tools.

In Section III: "Dressing It Up—Fonts and Graphic Elements," you'll learn how to spice up your documents by adding graphic images, lines, and borders. And you'll use different fonts (type styles) to add impact. This section also covers

Word's WordArt feature, which allows you to perform all sorts of contortions with your text—you can stretch or twist lines of text into different shapes and styles.

In Section IV: "File Management and Printing," you'll learn how to use Word's file management tools to find files in different folders, create new folders, and move or copy files. You'll also learn how to make the most of Word's printing capabilities: printing a whole document or selected parts of it, canceling print jobs, and more.

In Section V: "Tables and Columns," you'll work with the Tables feature to easily arrange text and numbers in columns and rows. You'll learn to adjust table formatting, and I'll introduce Word's spreadsheet features, which enable you to use tables for complex calculations. Then I'll show you how to work with newspaper-style columns and mailing labels.

Section VI: "Automation Tools" covers Word's powerful collection of tools that can save you time by automating the process of document creation. AutoText, macros, styles, and templates can all be used to keep you from having to enter the same text and codes over and over. In addition to saving time, these features will help you achieve consistency in your formatting. And you'll see how the merge feature makes short work of creating form letters.

Section VII: "Organizational and Referencing Tools" teaches you how to organize material and how to work efficiently with long documents. This section covers outlines, tables of contents, indexing, and working with several documents at once.

Look Out for These

Throughout this book, I'll point out additional information, tips, and shortcuts, and I'll tell you what to watch out for. Look for the following:

When you see this, it means there's some information that you should pay particular attention to. It might be a tip or some additional information that will help you make sense of what's being discussed.

I've used this icon primarily in Chapter 1. Because this chapter takes you through many features very quickly, the roadmaps point you to the chapter in this book where you can learn about specific features in more detail. I've also used this icon throughout the book as a cross-referencing tool.

I use this icon to let you know when there's an easier way to do something.

Pay attention when you see this. I'll tell you what to watch out for when you're working with certain features.

This icon points out keyboard shortcuts.

SECTION I

Getting Started

CHAPTER 1

Jumpstart

Let's talk about:

- Starting Word
- Entering text
- Saving a document
- Spell checking a document
- Making minor editing changes
- Printing a document
- Exiting Word

Jump Right in, the Water's Fine

This chapter is for all you Type-A personalities who can't be bothered with a lot of details—"just give it to me straight." And that's exactly what you'll get here. No frills, no tricks, just the basics. By the end of the chapter you'll be able to create, save, spell check, and print a simple document. You'll also know how to get into and out of Word.

Obviously, there's much more to mastering Word (or they wouldn't have paid me to write this book), but it all builds on the basics of typing, saving, and printing. If you can do that, you can start to produce real documents right away.

I'm not going to get into any shortcuts in this chapter. You'll have to stick with me a little longer to get those. (Yes, that *was* a blatant attempt to get you to keep reading.) I'm also not going to give you a lot of explanations and tell you why things are the way they are. What you will get in this chapter are bare-bone techniques to get you started until you learn all about neat stuff like toolbars, which streamline the process of choosing commands.

ROADMAP

As we create the sample document, I'll point out Roadmaps along the way, directing you to areas of this book where you can get more information.

Ready? Let's do it.

Starting Word

I'm assuming that you have Windows 95 up and running. It doesn't matter whether you have any other programs open—you can use the technique shown in Figure 1.1 to open Word even if another program is currently active.

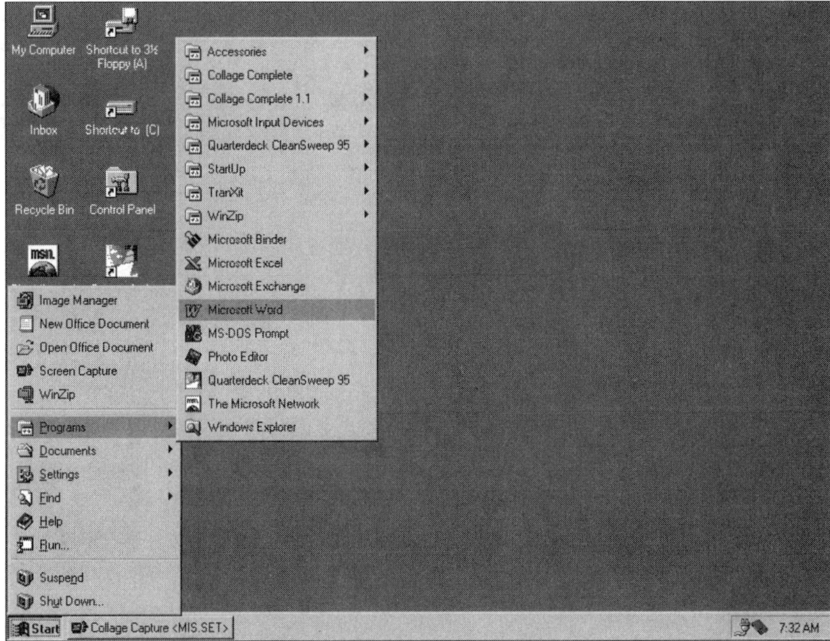

*Figure 1.1 Click **Microsoft Word** from the Programs menu.*

To start Word:

1. Click the **Start** button on your Taskbar.
2. Click **Programs** (this should be just below the dividing line on your Start menu).
3. Click **Microsoft Word** from the Programs menu.

Depending on how fast your computer is, this might take a little time, but pretty soon you should see the Word screen shown in Figure 1.2.

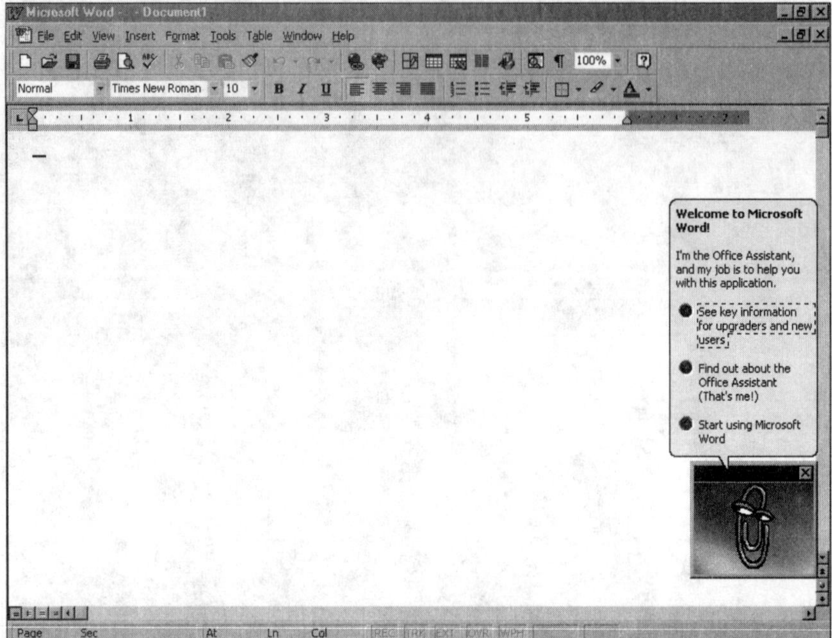

Figure 1.2 When you first start Word, this is what you should see.

Just Type

That's all you have to do now. There's a whole bunch of stuff on the screen, but you don't really have to deal with it to create a simple document. You can just start typing.

But wait—maybe you can't just start typing. If your computer refuses to follow your orders and beeps at you when you try to type, take a look at the right side of the screen. If a goofy-looking paperclip like the one in Figure 1.2 is asking you a bunch of questions, you have to click **Start using Microsoft Word** before you can actually type stuff in Word.

That cartoon paperclip is your Office Assistant, and he's there to help you. We're just getting him (or her, I can't quite figure out its gender) out of the way in this chapter so we can cut to the chase and quickly create a document. You'll learn all about Mr./Ms. Office Assistant in Chapter 4, "Getting Help."

To enter text:

1. Type today's date and press the **Enter** key twice.
2. Type the following name and address, pressing **Enter** after each line:

```
Ms. Florence Fellows
682 Fallible Point
Federal Way, WA 98107
```

3. Press **Enter** once more to add an extra line between the address and the salutation.
4. Type **Dear Ms. Fellows** and press **Enter** twice.
5. Type the following text, mistakes and all (and if you make a few more of your own, no problem—you can fix them later). Don't press **Enter** at the end of each line. The only time you need to press **Enter** is at the end of a paragraph.

```
I enjoyed are conversashun yesterday and am am pleased that
you will represent our new line of waterproof sundresses.
I know that these will be hot items in the damp Northwest.
Now women will be able to venture out in their summer best,
confidunt that they will not be caught unawares by our
changeable weather.

I will call you as soon as I have more information abot the
shipping schedule.

Sincerely


Sarah Sewell

Marketing Manager
```

Your letter should look like Figure 1.3.

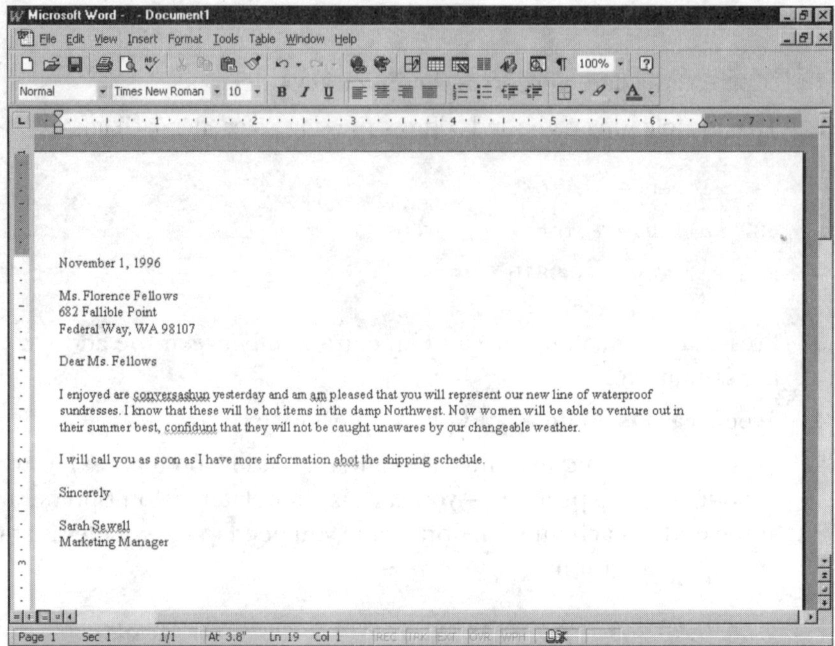

Figure 1.3 *Hey, you just typed your first letter!*

Don't worry about the squiggly red lines under some of the words—they're part of a nifty spelling shortcut that allows you to check spelling automatically as you type. We'll talk about it (and other spelling feats) in Chapter 11, "Proofreading Tools."

Saving Your Masterpiece

Saving should always be the first thing you do after creating a document. Until you save your document to disk, it only exists in the computer's temporary memory. If the power goes out or you turn off your computer without saving, all your work could be lost. In fact, if your document is much longer than the one we just created, you should save it while you're in the middle of creating it and then save it frequently while you're working. This is something I'll keep bugging you about throughout the book; saving documents often is one of the best habits you can get into (unless you really like to type the same stuff over and over).

To save your file:

1. Click on the word **File** on the menu line (just below where it says Microsoft Word at the very top of your screen). Or press **Alt+F**. That opens the File menu (see Figure 1.4).

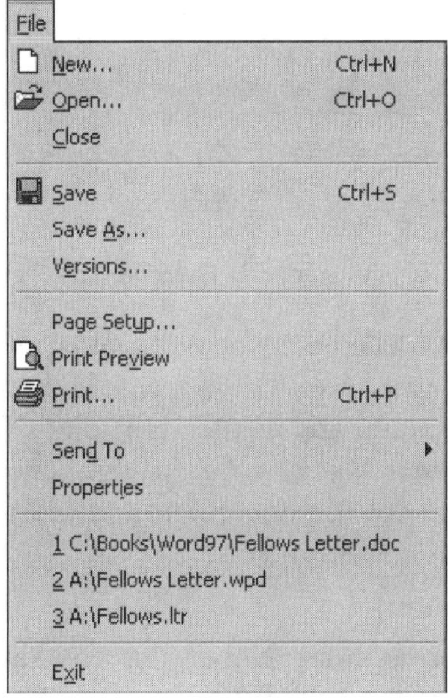

Figure 1.4 *This is the File menu.*

KEYBOARD

To press **Alt+F**, hold down the **Alt** key while you press the letter **F**, then release both keys. For any menu selection, the letter that's underlined is the one you press, either on its own or in combination with the **Alt** key.

2. Click on **Save As...** (or press the letter **A**). Any time a menu item has an ellipsis (...) after it, you'll see a window or dialog box when you choose that item. The ellipsis is Word's way of saying it needs more information—in this case, it needs to know what name you want to give your file (see Figure 1.5).

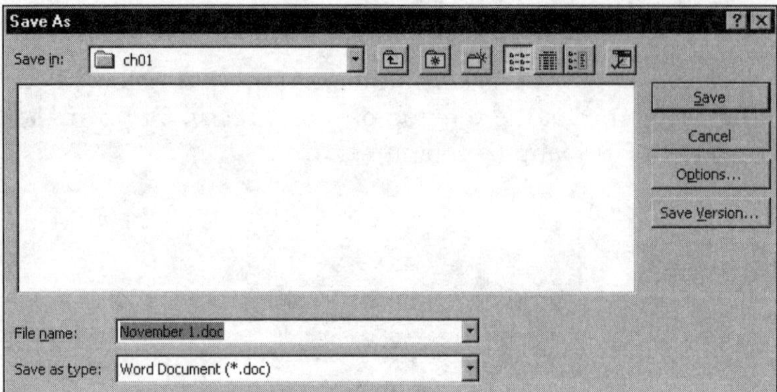

Figure 1.5 *Choosing **Save As** opens the Save As dialog box.*

When the Save As dialog box opens, it looks like there are a lot of choices to make, but all you have to do is type a name for the document—the insertion point is already in the right place for you to start typing. Notice that the text *November 1.doc* is highlighted. Word took that text from the first line of the document and will use it as the filename if you don't specify something else.

3. Type **Fellows Letter**.
4. Click **Save** or press **Enter**. Notice that the **Save** button has a darker border around it than the other buttons. That tells you that it's the *default button*; its action will be executed if you press **Enter**. So, pressing **Enter** in this case is just like clicking on **Save**.

After you choose **Save,** the Save As window disappears and you're back at the main Word screen.

Once you've used **Save As** to save a document for the first time, you can choose **Save** from the File menu at any time to save the document. Word won't ask any questions—it'll just do it. It's very fast, and it's a good idea to do this on a regular basis—any time you've made major changes to your document or added a lot of text.

Go to Chapter 5, "Editing 101," to learn more about saving documents.

Spell It Right

After you've entered your text and saved the document, the next step is to make sure everything's spelled right. Wait—don't pull out your dictionary and start looking up every word. Word has a built-in feature that automatically checks your document. You might be wondering why we didn't spell check the document before saving it. That would've saved some time, right? Well, yeah, but there's a method here.

Any time you run a spell check or send a document to the printer (or do other complex things like running a mail merge) there's a slight possibility that something could go wrong or your computer could freeze up. If that happens before you save, you could lose all your work. I don't want to scare you; it's not going to happen often, but I'd rather be safe than sorry. (How's that for a tired but true cliché?)

To spell check a document:

1. With **Fellows Letter** on the screen, click on the **Tools** menu (or press **Alt+T**).
2. Click on **Spelling and Grammar** (see Figures 1.6 and 1.7).

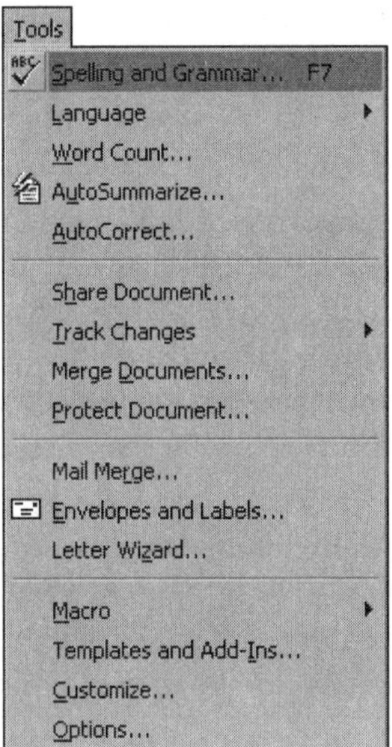

Figure 1.6 *Choose* ***Spelling and Grammar*** *from the Tools menu.*

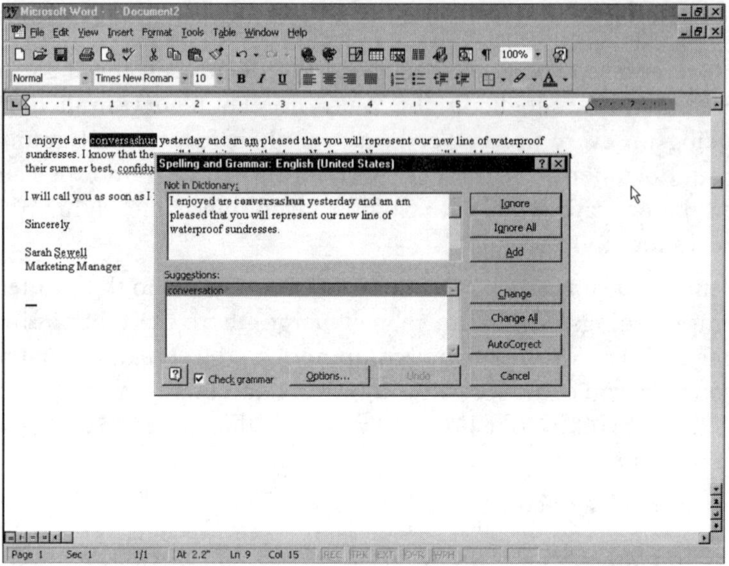

Figure 1.7 The Spelling and Grammar dialog box is displayed.

Word highlights the first word it finds that's not in its dictionary (in this case, *conversashun*) and waits for your action.

3. When the spelling and grammar checker stops on a word, there are several choices you can make. Most of them are covered in Chapter 11—you just need to deal with a couple for now:

   ✦ If the spelling and grammar checker stops on a word that's spelled correctly but isn't in Word's dictionary (a good example of this would be someone's name), you can choose **Ignore** to skip over the word without making any changes (with **Ignore**, the spell checker stops the next time it sees the same word). Choose **Ignore All** to skip the word every time the spell checker sees it until you close Word.

   ✦ If the word is misspelled, look at the Suggestions list. If you see the correct spelling there, click on that word and then click the **Change** button. For example, to replace *conversashun* with *conversation*, just click on **conversation**, then click **Change**. You can also use your **Up Arrow** and **Down Arrow** keys to highlight the correct word and then press **Enter**.

If the word you want isn't in the Suggestions list, you can edit the spelling manually. You'll know more about this after reading Chapter 11, "Proofreading Tools."

4. Go through the letter, skipping or replacing words as necessary.
5. Click the **OK** button (or press **Enter**) to close the spelling and grammar checker (see Figure 1.8).

Figure 1.8 *You'll see this dialog box when the spell check is completed.*

6. Click on **File**, then **Save**, to save the document.

All the changes you make during the spell check are stored in the computer's temporary memory (RAM) until you save the document again. You should always save your work right after spell checking.

Fixing Mistakes

What, you're not perfect? You mean there are still some problems with your letter even after running the spell check? Well, join the club. Fortunately, Word gives you multiple ways to clean up your work. For now, I'll give you a basic tool that will let you change a word or letter here and there.

The word *are* in the first sentence should be *our*. Why didn't that get caught during the spell check? Okay, I'll give you the brief version of minilecture #3248 (which will be repeated at length in Chapter 11): A spell checker (even one that's supposed to check grammar) does not take the place of proofreading your work. *Are* is a real word, and it's spelled correctly, even though it's not the word you meant to use. 'Nuff said for now.

To fix a mistake:

1. Move the mouse pointer (which is now a thin vertical line that looks like the capital letter "I") so that it's anywhere in the word *are*, and click the left mouse button. The insertion point (the flashing vertical line) is displayed where you click the mouse.
2. Get rid of the word *are* by pressing **Delete** or **Backspace** a total of three times. The key you press depends on where the insertion point is:
   - ✦ If the insertion point is just after the letter you want to delete, press **Backspace**.
   - ✦ If the insertion point is just in front of the letter you want to delete, press **Delete**.
3. Type **our**. Until you learn more techniques for deleting and changing text, you can always delete one character at a time with **Backspace** or **Delete**, then type whatever you want to replace it with.
4. Don't forget to save again.

ROADMAP

You've probably already noticed that the mouse pointer changes shape depending on what's happening. Chapter 2, "Getting Started with Word," explains the different shapes and when they're displayed.

The Last Step—Printing

Finally, you're ready to print the letter and get the boss off your back! Again, no details here—just the basic tools you need to print a document until you get a chance to delve into printing in more depth.

To print your document:

1. With the letter on your screen, click on **File** (or press **Alt+F**).
2. Click on **Print** (or press **P**).

   Take a look at Figure 1.9. Notice that in the Page Range section of the dialog box, the button next to **All** is selected. That means that Word will print the whole document unless you make another selection. For now, you don't have to worry about the other choices in the dialog box.

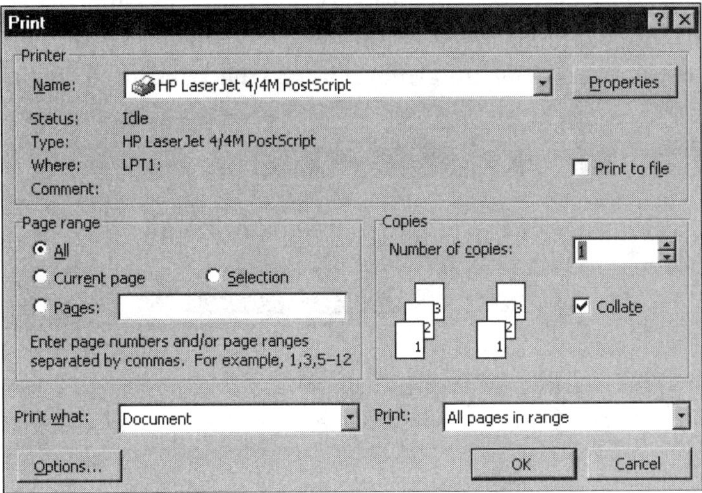

Figure 1.9 Here's the Print dialog box.

3. Click **OK** to start printing (or press **Enter**).

If Windows 95 and Word have been set up properly on your computer, you shouldn't have to worry about selecting a printer. But if you can't get the letter to print, don't worry. It's probably just a matter of changing a couple of settings. Take a look at Chapter 15, "Printing," to find out more.

Exiting Word

Let's pretend that letter was the only thing you needed to do today (we can dream, can't we?), so it's time to get out of Word and turn off the computer.

To exit Word:

1. Click on **File** (or press **Alt+F**).
2. Choose **Exit** from the File menu (or press the letter **X**).

If you haven't made any changes to your document since the last time you saved it, choosing **Exit** from the File menu takes you right out of Word and back to the Windows 95 desktop.

If any changes have been made, you'll see the dialog box shown in Figure 1.10. If you want to save the changes, choose **Yes**; otherwise, choose **No**. After you click **Yes** or **No**, Word closes and you're back at the Windows 95 desktop.

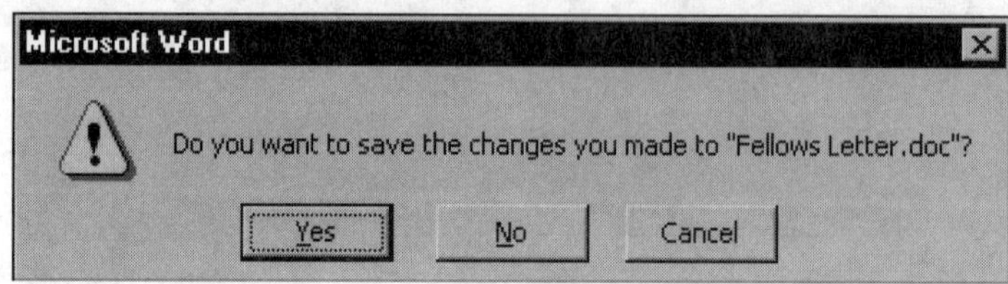

Figure 1.10 *If any changes have been made to your document, this dialog box is displayed when you try to exit Word.*

THE END... AND THE BEGINNING

Give yourself a pat on the back. You got in and out of Word; you created a document, saved it, checked the spelling, made an editing change, and printed it. Whew! There's a lot more to learn, but you've got the basic ingredients. Everything else will build on the basic elements you learned in this chapter.

In the next chapter, "Getting Started with Word," you'll learn techniques for using the mouse and keyboard. Then you'll learn how to recognize and work with different elements of the Word screen: dialog boxes, scroll bars, pull-down menus, and much more.

CHAPTER 2

Getting Started with Word

Let's talk about:

- ✦ Why Windows 95?
- ✦ Using a mouse
- ✦ Using the keyboard
- ✦ Starting Word
- ✦ Understanding the Word screen
- ✦ What's WYSIWYG?

Windows 95 Warmup

Wait! Don't turn the page yet. I can hear you thinking, "I didn't buy this book to learn about Windows 95. I'll just skip to the Word stuff." Well, hold on a minute. I'm only going to talk about "Windows 95 stuff" that you actually need to know to use Word 97. In fact, I'll use Word as an example, so you can use this chapter to start getting familiar with the Word screen. So, stick with me for a little while (unless you're an old hand with Windows 95 and really don't need this introduction, in which case you have my permission to skip ahead).

Why Windows 95?

Okay, everyone's talking about Windows 95, and your best friend finally convinced you that you absolutely had to buy Windows 95 and Word or Office 97. So you did. But was it the right thing to do? The answer is an unequivocal *yes.* Why, you may ask? In a word: *standardization.*

What that means is that once you learn techniques for working with any Windows 95 program (in this case, Word 97, hereinafter referred to simply as Word), you have the basic tools for working in any other Windows 95 program. For example, you use the same method to save files and close documents or applications no matter which program you're using.

Windows 95's standardization extends to printing. Instead of having to set up a printer every time you install a new program, when you install a Windows 95 application, it *knows* what printer you have by looking at your Windows 95 setup. If you get a new printer, all you have to do is set it up in Windows 95, and all your Windows 95 programs can automatically use it.

There are many more advantages to Windows 95, which you'll discover as you delve further into it. For now, just be aware that a lot of what you learn in this book will apply to the next Windows 95 program you decide to master.

If You're New to Windows or Windows 95

I'm going to assume that Windows 95 is already installed on your computer (if you're smart, you got that friend who talked you into buying it to install it for you). If it's not, refer to the documentation that came with your Windows 95 software.

Windows 95 comes with a couple of tours to help you get started. The *Ten Minutes to Using Windows* tour is the one for you if you're completely new to Windows. It helps you with starting programs, finding files, switching between different windows, and using the help system. If you've used Windows 3.1 but are new to Windows 95, check out the *If You've Used Windows Before* tour, which quickly updates you on the major differences between Windows 3.1 and Windows 95.

Both of these tours can be accessed from Windows 95's Help dialog box. To get there, choose **Help** from the Start menu and follow the on-screen instructions. If that last sentence sounded like Greek, don't worry for now. Just keep reading; I'll tell you how to access the Start menu and what it's for.

Using a Mouse

Before we go any further, I have one question: Do you have a mouse? No? You mean you went out and got Windows 95 *and* Word, and you *still* don't have a mouse?? Well, go get one. A mouse is very important (if not crucial) to Windows 95 and Windows 95 applications. You can use Windows 95 and Word without a mouse (just barely), but you won't be able to take advantage of a lot of nifty shortcuts, and some things will be downright cumbersome to accomplish.

Got your mouse now? Good. Let's go. Just rest your hand lightly on that little critter with your index finger over the left button and your middle finger over the right button. Both of those mouse fingers will get plenty of exercise. The left button is the one you'll use to open menus and select items, and the right mouse button will get you to all sorts of shortcut menus. If your mouse has three buttons, ignore the middle one; you won't use it at all in Word.

NOTE

If you do have a three-button mouse, take a look at the documentation that came with it. In most cases, you can program the middle button to perform certain actions. I have mine programmed to double-click, so whenever I'm supposed to double-click something, all I have to do is click the middle button once. This may sound trivial, but if you do a lot of double-clicking over the course of a day, eliminating that extra click each time can be a real time-saver.

Lefties Unite!

All you lefties out there, don't fret. Microsoft thought of you when they designed Windows 95. You can swap the left and right mouse buttons to make it easier to operate the mouse.

To change the mouse buttons for left-handed use:

1. Click the **Start** button on your Taskbar.

2. Click **Settings** on the Start menu, then click **Control Panel** from the Settings menu.
3. Double-click **Mouse** in the **Control Panel** folder to open the Mouse Properties dialog box.
4. Click **Left-handed** in the Button configuration section of the **Buttons** tab, then click **OK** to close the Mouse Properties dialog box, and click the **Close** button in the upper right corner to close the Control Panel.

If some of these instructions seem a bit cryptic, skip over them until you've read the rest of this chapter. By then you'll know how to double-click and what a tabbed dialog box is.

NOTE

If you've swapped the mouse buttons, you'll have to mentally reverse any instructions I give for using the mouse. When I write "click the left mouse button," you'll click the right one.

Click, Click, Click... What a Drag

Click and drag. There, you just learned most of the mouse lingo you need to know. What's the rest? Pointing. That's all there is to it. You point, you click, or you drag. There are some fancy combinations, like double-clicking, quadruple-clicking, and dragging and dropping, but they're just extensions of the basic techniques:

- **Point**. This means that you move the mouse pointer (the little arrow that moves around on your screen when you move the mouse) to a particular spot. If I write "point to the **Save** button," move the mouse until the arrow is on the **Save** button.
- **Click**. If I write "click on the **File** menu," point to the File menu, press down on the mouse button (in this case it would be the left button), and then let go. It's called *clicking* because with most mice you'll hear a little click when you let go of the button.
- **Double-click**. Double-clicking is something you'll be doing a lot. All it means is that you point at the item in question and click the left mouse button (press and let go) twice in fairly rapid succession. This action might seem awkward at first, but with a little practice you'll be double-clicking with the best of them. (Here's where you might get

some use out of that middle button if you have one. Depending on what kind of mouse it is, you can probably set up the middle button to do the double-clicking for you. So, instead of having to click the left mouse button twice, you would just click the middle button once. Check your mouse documentation for more info.)

- **Drag**. This is a technique in which you point at the item and hold down the left mouse button while you move the mouse to a new location. When the object you're dragging is where you want it, release the mouse button.

The mouse pointer is a tricky little devil—it actually changes its shape depending on what you're doing. The two shapes you'll see most of the time are an arrow (or some variation of an arrow) and an I-beam (sort of like a capital letter "I"). A regular arrow means that you can make a selection from a menu or dialog box; the arrow changes to a double-arrow to let you know you can change the size of a window or dialog box. The I-beam lets you know you're in an area where text can be entered. Throughout this book, I'll use the term *mouse pointer* when I tell you to do something with the mouse, and I'll explain what's happening to the shape when it's important.

Using the Keyboard

There isn't much I need to tell you about the keyboard. When you're entering text, you can type the same way you would on a typewriter. But I do want to point out a few added attractions.

Special Keys

Your computer keyboard contains special keys that Word uses for different purposes at different times. How's that for a vague statement? All it means is that Word takes advantage of all the extra keys to give you shortcut methods for accomplishing tasks.

I emphasize mouse use in this book, because in most cases the mouse is the easiest way to do things. But I'll give you keyboard alternatives for most procedures and let you know when the keyboard method is actually a shortcut. Sometimes using the keyboard can save you time. As you become more familiar with Word, experiment with the mouse and keyboard in various situations. The whole idea is to use whichever method feels most comfortable and efficient to you.

I'll point out specific keyboard alternatives as we go along. For now, here are the basics:

- **Function keys**. These are the strange-looking keys numbered **F1** through **F12** (your keyboard might only go up to **F10**). Depending on what kind of keyboard you have, these keys are at the top of your keyboard or in a block to the left of the main typing area. As the name implies, *function keys* are assigned specific functions. For example, pressing **F7** starts a spelling and grammar check in Word.
- **Ctrl, Alt, and Shift**. These keys are used in combination with other keys to extend their power or change what they do. For example, pressing **F7** by itself starts a spelling and grammar check, but **Shift+F7** opens the thesaurus. If I write "press **Shift+F7**," hold down the **Shift** key while you press the **F7** key and release both keys at the same time. Don't worry if using these combination keystrokes seems awkward at first; it takes practice, and you'll get plenty of that throughout this book.
- **Esc**. This is the cancel key. If you open a menu or dialog box by mistake, just press **Esc** to back out of it.
- **The Windows key**. If you're lucky enough to have one of those keyboards that has special Windows 95 keys, you can press the **Windows** key (the one with the little Windows logo) to open the Start menu, and you can use the **Menu** key (the one with the little menu and mouse pointer arrow) instead of the right mouse button to open shortcut menus.
- **Other special keys**. As we work through Word's features, I'll point out other keys that can be used as mouse alternatives (and, in some cases, shortcuts). The **Home**, **End**, **Page Up**, and **Page Down** keys make it easy to move around in a document or dialog box. You'll use the **Delete** key to delete text and other objects and the **Insert** key to change your typing mode.

The Windows 95 Desktop

When you turn on your computer, Windows 95 starts up automatically. Before you open any programs, your screen should look something like Figure 2.1. Don't worry if your screen doesn't look exactly like this. One of the neat (and initially confusing) things about Windows 95 is that you can change just about everything, including the arrangement of the screen. Even if your screen has a different number of icons or they're arranged differently, you still have access to the same features and you use them the same way.

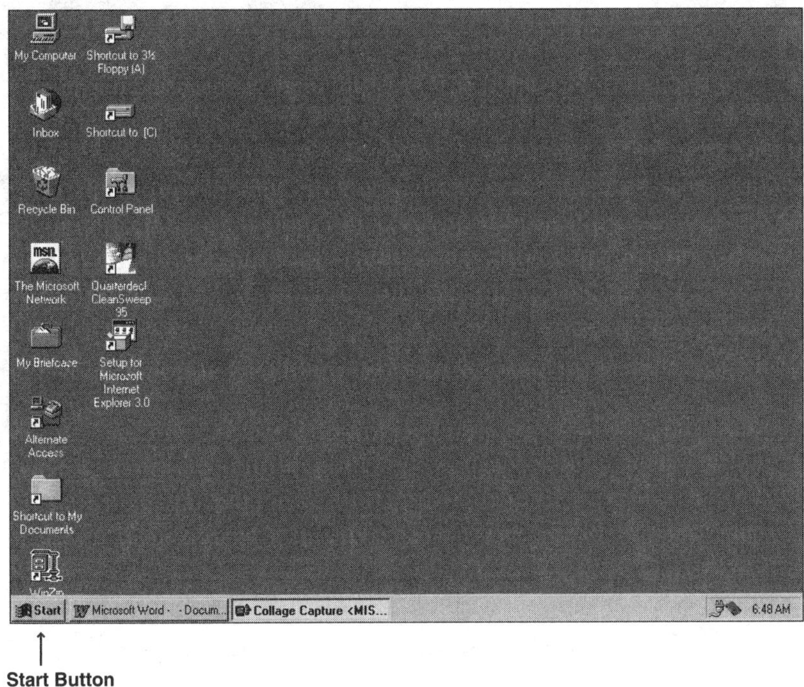

Figure 2.1 The Windows 95 desktop.

What you see when Windows 95 starts up is called the *desktop*. You can think of this virtual desktop just like your real desktop. Your desk is still there (believe it or not) no matter how many papers, pop bottles, and chewing gum wrappers you pile on top of it. And no matter how many programs you have running on top of the desktop, the Windows desktop is still there. The important thing to know is that the desktop is your starting point for getting where you want to go in Windows 95.

Starting Word

You start a Windows 95 program by making a selection from the Start menu or by double-clicking a program icon on the desktop. Sounds simple enough, right? Figure 2.2 shows you my Start menu with **Microsoft Word** highlighted.

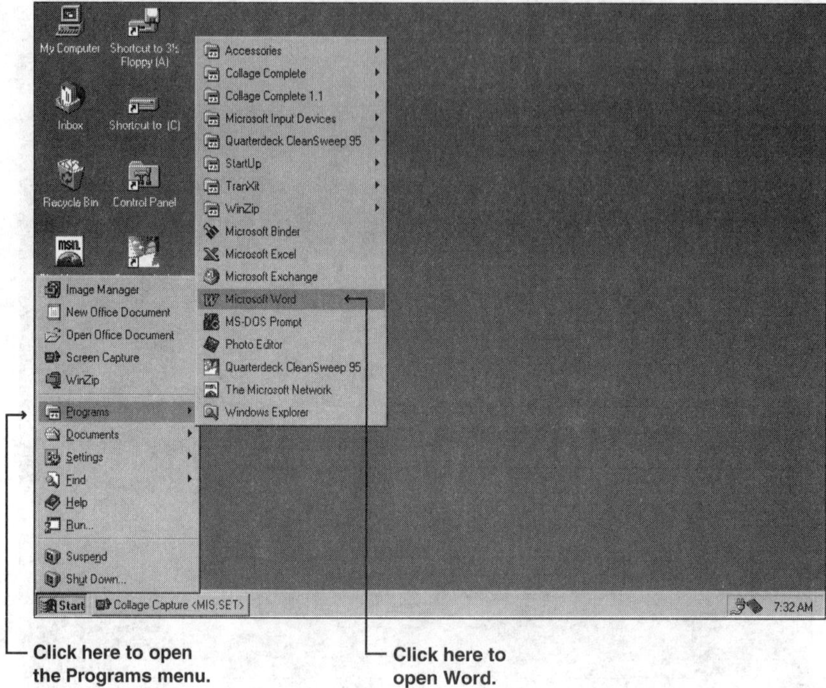

Figure 2.2 Click on ***Microsoft Word*** *from the Programs menu.*

To open Word:

1. Click the **Start** button on your Taskbar.
2. Point to **Programs** (this should be in the bottom half of your Start menu) to open a menu like the one shown in Figure 2.2 that lists most of the programs installed on your computer. The items on your Start and Programs menus won't be exactly the same as mine; they vary depending on what programs are installed.
3. Click **Microsoft Word** from the Programs menu. With any luck, you will soon see the opening Word screen, which should look like Figure 2.3.

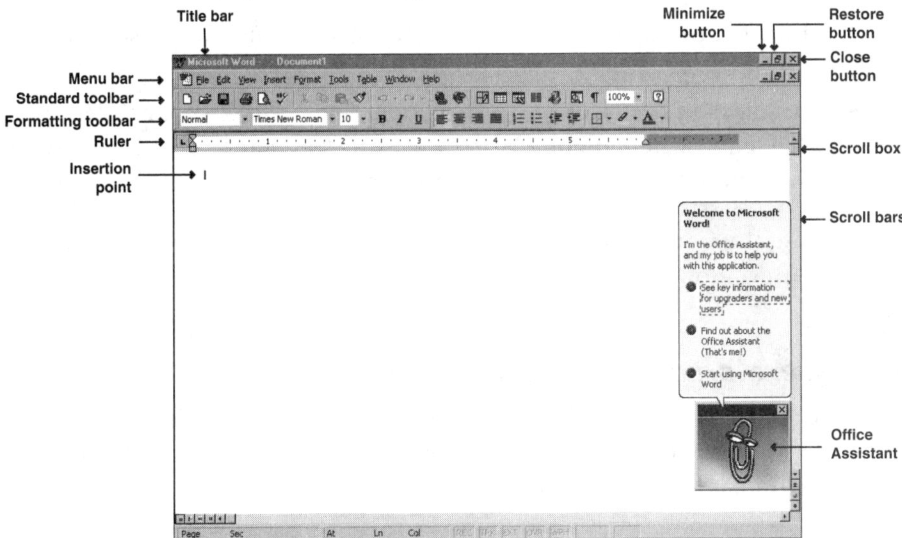

Figure 2.3 The opening Word screen.

Anatomy of the Word Screen

Get used to looking at this screen—it's the starting point for everything you'll do in Word. Don't be intimidated by all the buttons and icons. You can hide many of them and leave yourself with an almost blank screen, but they're there to give you quick access to many of Word's features. Let's get acquainted with the Word screen by going over the elements shown in Figure 2.3.

Control Menus

The little Word logos in the upper-left corner of the screen are actually icons that open *Control menus.* The one on top is for Word, and the one underneath is for your current document. If you're using a mouse, you don't need to use these menus, but they provide handy keyboard shortcuts for minimizing and maximizing your program or document window. You can open either Control menu by clicking on a logo icon, but because there's really no reason to use these icons with a mouse, I'll give you instructions for opening them with the keyboard.

- To open Word's Control menu, press **Alt+Spacebar**.
- To open the Control menu for the active document, press **Alt+** -(the hyphen key).
- To select an item from a Control menu, type the underlined letter for that item. So, to minimize Word using your keyboard, press **Alt+Spacebar** to open the Control menu and then press **n** to minimize the window.

You can use the Control menus to close, move, resize, minimize, or maximize the current window.

Minimize, Maximize, and Close Buttons

The three buttons at the far right end of the title bar are (from left to right) the **Minimize**, **Maximize/Restore**, and **Close** buttons for Word. The identical buttons on the menu bar are for the document window.

- Click the **Minimize** button (the button with a line near the bottom) to hide the program or document. If you minimize Word, it disappears from your screen but remains on the Taskbar so you can open it at any time by clicking its button on the Taskbar. If you minimize the document window, the document is reduced to an button at the bottom of your program window. You can open the document by clicking the **Restore** or **Maximize** button on the document's icon. The minimized document also remains on the Window menu, so you can switch to it at any time by choosing it from the Window menu.
- Click the **Maximize/Restore** button to change the size of the program or document window. The **Maximize** button has a picture of a folder in it; when a program or document is already maximized, the **Maximize** button turns into a **Restore** button, which has a picture of two overlapping folders.
- When you maximize the program window, it enlarges to take up the entire screen. When you maximize the document window, the document takes up all the space inside the program window. When you restore either the program or document window, the window returns to its previous size—whatever it was before you last maximized it.

- Click the **Close** button to close the program or document. Clicking the **Close** button on the title bar closes Word; clicking the **Close** button for the document closes the active document but leaves Word open. If you have any unsaved documents when you click **Close**, word will prompt you to save the documents before it clses the program.

Title Bar

The *title bar* is the highlighted strip at the top of the window. It tells you what program is running (in this case, Microsoft Word), and after you save a document, the document name is displayed in the title bar.

Toolbars

Word comes with several different toolbars that allow you quick access to common commands. By default, Word displays the Standard and Formatting toolbars (but you can tell it not to).

The *Standard toolbar* includes buttons for several basic features like opening, saving, printing, spell checking, and copying and pasting. The *Formatting toolbar* lets you take care of most of your formatting needs without having to open a dialog box. With the click of a button, you can change your font style or size, apply bold or italic, align text, create bulleted or numbered lists, and more.

The Ruler

The *ruler* shows margin, tab, and indent settings. You can change these settings by dragging markers on the ruler.

Insertion Point

The *insertion point* is the blinking vertical line near the top of your screen. It's where text will appear when you start typing. Go ahead, try it. Just type a word or two and notice that the insertion point moves to reflect the new text location. Always make sure your insertion point is where you want it to be before you type.

Office Assistant

The *Office Assistant* (that silly paper clip you were introduced to in Chapter 1) is one of Word's many help features, and you'll learn all about it in Chapter 4, "Getting Help."

Scroll Bars

Because your computer screen is smaller than a standard piece of paper, parts of your text are usually hidden, even if your document is only one page long. And in a longer document, of course, you can only see a small part of it at a time. You'll learn different techniques for moving around in documents in Chapter 5, "Editing 101." For now, I just want you to be familiar with the scroll bars. The vertical and horizontal *scroll bars* make it easy to view different parts of your document. I'll use the vertical scroll bar for the following examples. The horizontal scroll bar does the same thing, except it moves you left and right instead of up and down.

- Click on the black up or down arrow at the top or bottom of the vertical scroll bar to move up or down a line at a time. Hold the arrow down to move continuously.
- The *scroll box* reflects your location in the document. For example, when the scroll box is at the top of the scroll bar, you're at the beginning of the document. If the scroll box is in the middle, you're somewhere in the middle of the document. To scroll to an approximate position in your document, just drag the scroll box up or down. If your document is longer than one page, an information box to the left of the scroll bar displays the current page number.
- The little circle button between the double up and down arrow buttons at the bottom of the vertical scroll bar is called the **Browse Object** button; it lets you tell Word what the double up and down arrows should do. When you click on the **Browse Object** button, you get the palette shown in Figure 2.4.

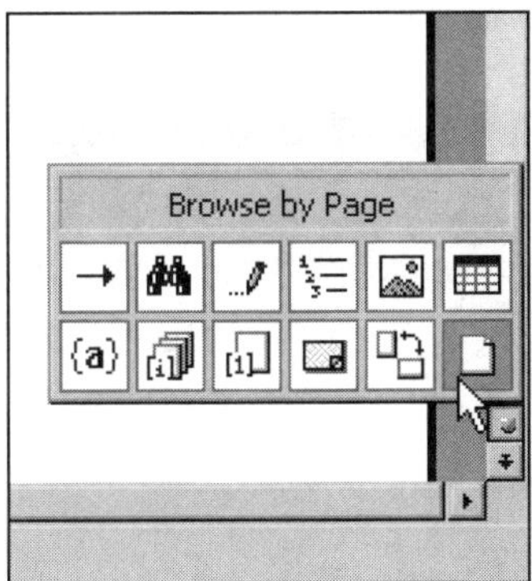

Figure 2.4 *The Select Browse Object palette.*

As you move your mouse pointer over a button, the palette's title bar tells you what the button does. In Figure 2.4, my mouse pointer is on the button that looks like a piece of paper, and the title bar says *Browse by Page.* If I click on this button, the double-arrow buttons will allow me to move through my document a page at a time.

The scroll bars change your view of the document, but they don't have anything to do with where text appears when you type. For example, if you're typing text at the beginning of a document and you use the vertical scroll bar to move to the bottom of the document and start typing, the new text will be inserted at the top of the document. You have to move your insertion point before you can type in a new location. After you use the scroll bar to bring a different part of the document into view, move your mouse pointer to the place in the document window where you want to enter text and click the left mouse button. That repositions your insertion point.

The Menu Bar

The *menu bar* is right under the title bar. You open a menu by clicking on its name.

To open a menu with the keyboard, hold down the **Alt** key while you press the underlined letter for the item you want. Alternatively, you can press the **Alt** key to activate the menu bar, then use the **Left Arrow** or **Right Arrow** key to highlight your menu choice and press **Enter**.

In Figure 2.5, I clicked on **Format** to pull down (or open) the Format menu.

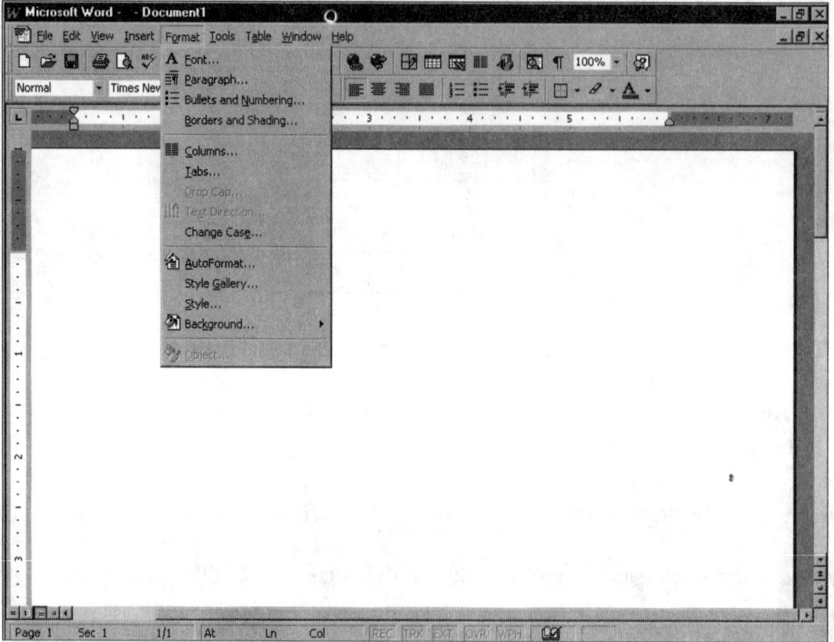

Figure 2.5 *The Format menu is pulled down.*

Once you've opened a menu, you can choose an item by either clicking on it or typing the underlined letter for the item. You can also use the **Up Arrow** and **Down Arrow** keys to highlight the item you want and then press **Enter**.

For now, don't worry about what the features actually *do*. In this chapter we're concentrating on *how* the menus and dialog boxes work. We'll get to all the specific features later.

You will notice that some of the menu items have three little dots after them, and some of them have right-pointing triangles. Why? The symbols tell you what will happen if you choose that item:

- An ellipsis (...) tells you that choosing the item opens a dialog box. The dialog box gives you options or asks for more information before it executes the command. I'll talk about dialog boxes in a separate section in this chapter.

- A right-pointing triangle lets you know that choosing the item opens a *cascading menu*, which gives you another set of commands to choose from. In Figure 2.6, I clicked on **Language** from the Tools menu. This gave me a cascading menu with choices related to Word's language options. Notice that there are ellipses after some of the items on the cascading menu. A dialog box is displayed when you choose an item followed by an ellipsis, whether it is on the main menu or a cascading one.

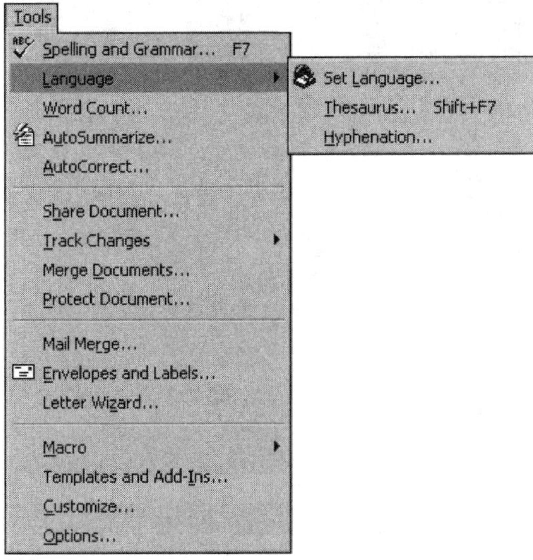

Figure 2.6 *The cascading Language menu.*

Have you noticed the key combinations listed next to some of the menu items? Those are keystroke alternatives or shortcuts you can use instead of choosing the item from a menu. For example, I can press **Shift+F7** to open the thesaurus instead of choosing **Thesaurus** from the cascading Language menu.

In addition to ellipses, triangles, and shortcut keys, there are two more items you might see on menus:

- **Check marks**. When you see a check mark next to an item, as shown in Figure 2.7, it means that it's turned on, or activated. Items with check marks are called toggles—you choose the same item to turn the feature on or off. For example, in Figure 2.7, the Standard and Formatting toolbars are activated. To turn them off and remove the check marks, I would click on their names in the menu.

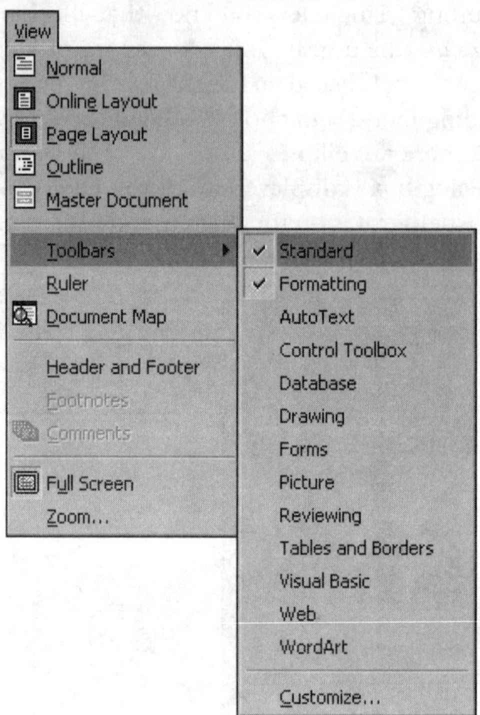

Figure 2.7 The Toolbars menu with check marks next to Standard and Formatting.

- **Dimmed items**. If a menu item is dimmed, the command is not currently available. For example, in the Edit menu shown in Figure 2.8, **Cut** and **Copy** are dimmed. In this case, there's nothing to cut or copy because I don't have any text selected.

If a menu item is displayed without an ellipsis or triangle, choosing the item causes an action to happen. For example, choosing **Select All** from the Edit menu shown in Figure 2.8 selects everything in the document without any further input from you.

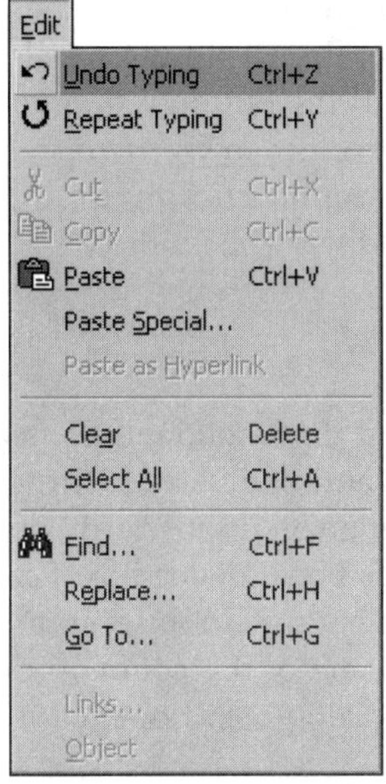

Figure 2.8 *The Edit menu.*

Closing a Menu

You can close a menu by clicking anywhere outside it. (You can also close a menu by clicking on the menu's name, but the entire screen is a much bigger target.)

To close a menu with the keyboard, press **Esc** twice. Pressing **Esc** the first time closes the menu, but the menu bar is still active. You have to press **Esc** again to move your insertion point back into the document area.

The Status Bar

The *Status Bar* (at the bottom of the document window) gives you information about what's going on in your document. You can also double-click on some of the Status Bar items to make things happen:

- The left half of the Status Bar gives information about where you are in the document: page number, section number, how many pages the document contains (1/1 means you're on the first page of a one-page document), etc.

- The dimmed buttons in the middle are both informational and functional. For example, the *OVR* button tells you whether or not you're in Overtype mode. If the button is dimmed, you're in Insert mode. If the button is active, you're in Overtype mode. You can switch between the two modes by double-clicking on the **OVR** button. (Chapter 5 explains Insert and Overtype modes.)

Dialog Boxes

Choosing a menu command that's followed by an ellipsis opens a dialog box. Dialog boxes are the meat and potatoes of Word: except for some very basic commands, almost everything you do in Word happens through a dialog box. As you'll see throughout this book, dialog boxes come in many guises and can contain all sorts of different options. In this section, I'll use a few representative dialog boxes to show you some of the common elements you will encounter. Figure 2.9 shows the Font dialog box. I opened it by choosing **Font** from the Format menu.

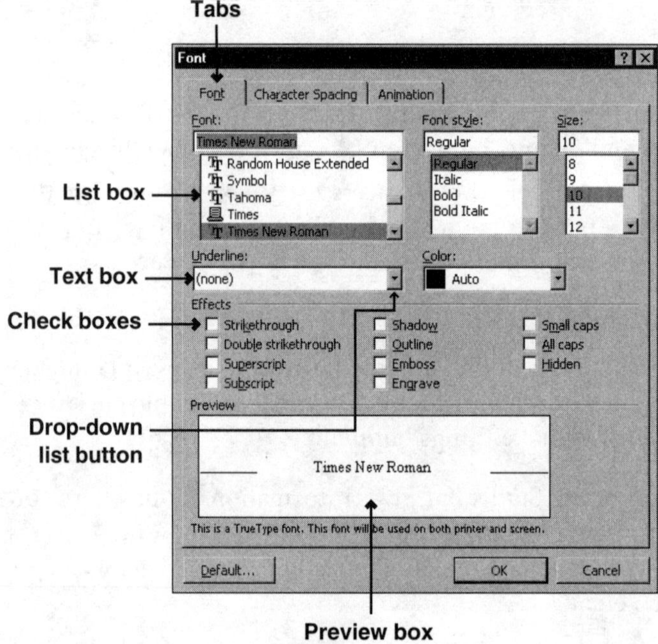

Figure 2.9 The Font dialog box.

Command Buttons

Look at the buttons at the bottom of the dialog box. These are called *command buttons*; you press them to make something happen. If there's an ellipsis after the name in the command button, choosing it opens another dialog box with more options.

Most dialog boxes have **OK** and **Cancel** buttons. Choose **OK** to execute your commands after you've entered all the required information or made whatever choices you want to make in the dialog box. Choose **Cancel** to close the dialog box without executing any commands.

NOTE

Command buttons can be anywhere in the dialog box. They're not always neatly lined up on the bottom.

Check Boxes

All the options in the Effects area have check boxes next to them. Notice that there are **X**es in the boxes next to **Shadow** and **Small caps**. Chose those options by clicking on them or pressing the **Alt** key and the underlined letter. Check boxes are toggles; you select a check box item by clicking on it, and clicking the same item again deselects it. You can select as many check boxes as you want. For example, I could choose to apply **Shadow**, and **Small caps** to the same section of text.

Text Boxes

A *text box* is an area where you can type specific information in a dialog box. In the Font dialog box, there are text boxes just above the Font, Font style, and Size lists. (Font size has to do with the size of your text.) To enter information in a text box, press the **Tab** key until the box you want is highlighted (pressing the **Tab** key in a dialog box moves you among the different sections of the box). Or just click to place your insertion point in the text box. At that point, you can just start typing. When text is highlighted (or selected) in your document or in a text box, that text will automatically be deleted as soon as something else is typed. You'll see text boxes in dialog boxes where you need to enter specific information, such as a number or the name of a file.

List Boxes

A *list box* is just a box that has a bunch of choices. In the Font dialog box, there are list boxes for Font, Font style, and Size. You choose an item from a list box by clicking on it or by using your **Up Arrow** and **Down Arrow** keys to highlight the item. (Size is an example of a situation where you can either type your choice in the text box or select an item from the list box.) If all the choices don't fit in the list box, there are scroll bars that let you move through the list.

Drop-Down Lists

Notice that there are down arrows next to the Underline and Color boxes. That means you'll get a *drop-down list* when you click on the arrow or the box next to it. Make choices from a drop-down list exactly the way you do from a list box.

Tabs

In Figure 2.9, take a look at the Font, Character Spacing, and Animation tabs near the top of the Font dialog box. They're just like the divider tabs you use in a binder—clicking on a tab takes you to a different section of the binder. Selecting a tab in a dialog box takes you to a different section of the dialog box that gives you different options related to the general purpose of the dialog box. To select a tab, just click on it. In Figure 2.10, I clicked on the **Character Spacing** tab to get a set of options that allow me to work precisely with text spacing and position. Notice that I'm still in the Font dialog box; I'm just on a different "page."

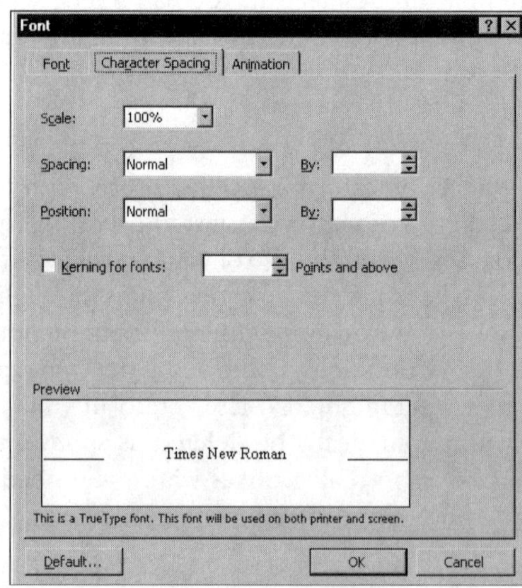

Figure 2.10 *The* ***Character Spacing*** *tab in the Font dialog box.*

You can move between tabs in a dialog box by pressing **Ctrl+Tab**.

Radio Buttons

There are two more buttons we haven't talked about. Take a look at Figure 2.11. This is the Zoom dialog box, which I opened by choosing **Zoom** from the View menu.

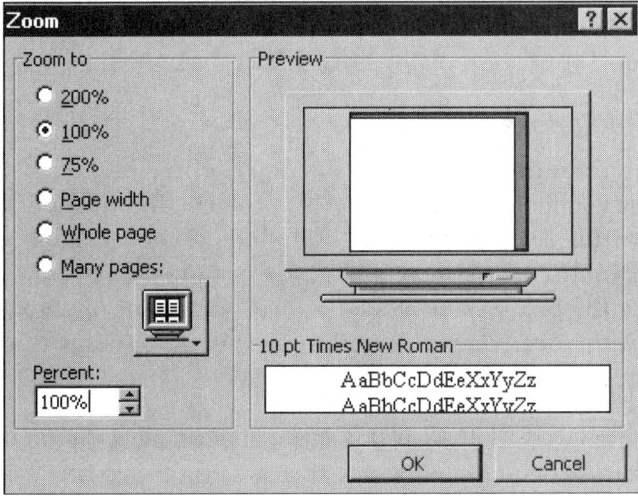

Figure 2.11 *The Zoom dialog box.*

We haven't seen those little round buttons before. They're like check boxes, only different.

The buttons next to the choices in the Zoom dialog box are called *radio buttons.* Unlike check boxes, you can only choose one radio button at a time. Think of it like the buttons on your car radio—you can only tune in one station at a time. When you click on a choice to select a radio button, the previous choice is automatically deselected. Even though you can only select one radio button in each group, a dialog box can contain more than one group of radio buttons. When there is more than one group of radio buttons, you can select one radio button from each group.

Increment Buttons

The up and down arrows next to the Percent text box in the Zoom dialog box are examples of *increment buttons.* These buttons are displayed next to most text boxes where you're supposed to type in a number. Increment buttons are an alternative to typing a number in the text box. You can click on the **up arrow** to increase the number or the **down arrow** to decrease the number. If the number is already as high as it can go for that option, the number won't change. For example, you can't zoom any lower than 10%, so if you try to click on the **down arrow** with **10%** selected, nothing will happen.

Now you've seen a few examples of dialog boxes. Each has a different purpose, but you use the same techniques to work with them. By the time you finish this book, you'll be a dialog box expert.

Moving Dialog Boxes

Dialog boxes can sometimes pop up where you don't want them. They might end up hiding text that you need to see. No problem. Did you notice that dialog boxes all have title bars, just like the Word window? You can move a dialog box anywhere on your screen by positioning your mouse pointer over the title bar and dragging the box. As you drag, a dotted outline of the box is displayed and moves with you. When the outline is where you want the box to be, release the mouse button.

ROADMAP

You can work with several documents at one time, and you can change the size of the document window to see more than one document on-screen. See Chapter 23, "Working with Multiple Documents," for information on moving, sizing, and minimizing documents. That chapter also has information on switching between documents and other programs.

WYSIWHAT???

Windows 95 (and most Windows 95 programs, including Word) use what's called a WYSIWYG display. *WYSIWYG* stands for *what you see is what you get,* and it means that what you see on the screen is a close approximation of what you'll see on the printed page. For example, if you change the size of your type or add a graphics image or footnote, you'll see all those elements on your screen. In a non-WYSIWYG environment, a graphics image might appear as an empty box, and your text always appears the same size, which makes it hard to tell how the document will look when it's printed.

Word's Page Layout view is a full WYSIWYG display—what you see on the screen should translate closely to your printed documents. There's also a Normal view, which is a partial WYSIWYG display. You may prefer to work in different views at different times, depending on how much formatting and information you want to see. Each view has its own advantages, as shown in Table 2.1.

Table 2.1 *Different ways of looking at documents.*

VIEW	WHAT IT SHOWS
Normal	This view shows text, character formatting, graphics, and paragraph formatting. It doesn't show columns or frames (which allow you to wrap text around a graphic or other paragraph). Normal view also doesn't show headers or footers, which contain information (like page numbers) that can automatically be carried over from page to page. Normal view is the fastest view option. Because Normal view doesn't display as many different screen elements, you can move through a document more quickly, and it doesn't use up as much of your computer's resources. Normal view is the default view, which means it's what you get when you start Word the first time. Unless you've chosen another view, what you're probably looking at right now is Normal view.
Page Layout	In Page Layout view, everything in your document is displayed and positioned exactly as it will appear on the printed page. You see headers and footers, footnotes, page numbers, columns, graphics and frames, and just about every other formatting feature (too many to list here). Page Layout view is good for editing headers and footers and working with frames and columns, but my preference is to do most of my work in Normal view and switch to Page Layout view when I want a more complete view of my document. It's so easy to switch back and forth that you don't have to restrict yourself to one view.
Online Layout	This view is new to Word 97, and it's designed specifically to make documents easier to read on-screen. Word increases the size of your text and wraps lines of text so you can see everything on the screen without having to scroll horizontally. Online Layout view includes a new feature called a *document map* that gives you an outline view of your document's structure and allows you to easily navigate to

continued

Table 2.1 continued

	different portions of the document. (You can turn off the document map in Online Layout view by choosing **Document Map** from the View menu.) As you'll see in Chapter 22, "Working with Long Documents," the document map feature can be quite helpful when you're dealing with lengthy documents.
Outline	This view shows the document in outline form if you are using the built-in heading numbered styles. This lets you see the document in hierarchical form, where you can collapse or expand various parts of the document. If you're used to working in outlines, this can be a handy way of viewing a document, but graphics and full paragraph formatting are not shown. The Outline feature is much more than just a different way of viewing your document—you can use it to manipulate text in ways that aren't possible in the other views. In Chapter 21, "Creating Lists and Outlines," I'll show you how to use Outline view to create and work with outlines.
Print Preview	This view shows you how the document will look when printed. In Print Preview, you can also view thumbnails of several pages at one time, which gives you a great bird's-eye view of your document: whether the pages look even, how big the headings appear, and where the page breaks fall. In Chapter 15, "Printing," I'll fill you in on the details of Print Preview.

ROADMAP

Take a look at Chapter 5, "Editing 101," for more information about working in different views and zooming in on parts of your document.

Changing the View

Open the View menu by clicking on **View** or pressing **Alt+V**. Then choose the view option you want. You can also change the view by clicking the View buttons in the lower-left corner of the Word screen (just above the Status Bar, as you can see in Figure 2.12). The button that represents your current view has a darker border around it.

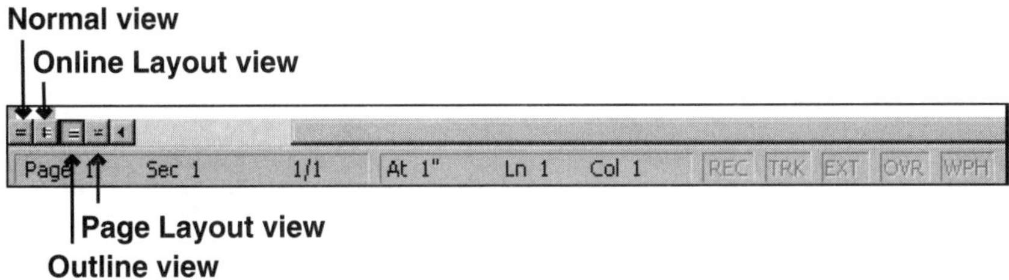

Figure 2.12 *Use these buttons to change your view.*

I've used Page Layout view for all the figures in this book (except where I'm specifically talking about another view option. If you're using another view, sometimes your screen won't quite match what you see in the book.

Exiting Word

Close Word by clicking the **Close** button (the **X** in the upper-right corner of the Word window). You can also exit Word by pressing **Alt+F4** or choosing **Exit** from the File menu.

If you have any documents that aren't saved, a dialog box is displayed that asks if you want to save them. Choose **Yes** to save or **No** to close the documents without saving them. You'll be returned to the Windows 95 desktop.

From Here...

Let's see, we've opened and closed Word. We've talked about menus, scroll bars, and dialog boxes. Are we done yet? Is it lunch time? Nope. There just one more thing I want you to do before you take a break.

Did you notice that I didn't say much about the toolbars or the ruler? Well, that's not because they're insignificant; it's because they're important enough to get their own chapter (which they have to share with a couple of other features). The next chapter zeros in on Word's arsenal of power tools that will speed up and simplify your work.

CHAPTER 3

Power Tools: Toolbars, Shortcut Menus, Wizards, and Templates

Let's talk about:

- Toolbars
- Shortcut menus
- Wizards
- Templates

I don't know about you, but I'm really lazy. If there's an easy way to do something, I'm all for it. And even then, I'll usually try to find an even easier way. Well, those friendly Microsoft programmers busted their you-know-whats so that we wouldn't have to. This chapter introduces a bunch of cool tools that put most of Word's features just a mouse click away. And wizards and templates take all the work out of creating and formatting several types of documents, from letters to calendars (unfortunately, you still have to come up with the content yourself).

ROADMAP

This chapter focuses on using the toolbars and shortcut menus "out of the box." But most of them can be customized in various ways (such as moving them to different parts of the screen, changing how they look, or displaying different items). You'll find information on customization in Chapter 25.

Toolbars

Toolbars are the rows of buttons that you see just below the menu bar (see Figure 3.1). When you start Word the first time, the Standard and Formatting toolbars are displayed by default, but you can hide them if you choose. They're so handy that I can't think of a good reason to turn them off (unless you don't have a mouse), but let's turn them off and back on just for the heck of it.

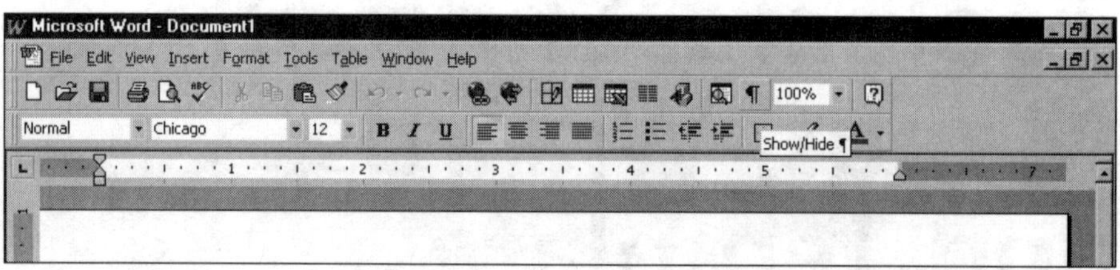

Figure 3.1 *Toolbars and the ruler give you quick access to a bunch of commonly used features.*

ROADMAP

The ruler is covered in a separate section in this chapter.

Toolbars consist of buttons that you click on to make something happen. You can have as many different toolbars as you want, and you can move the current toolbar to different locations on the screen. Check out Chapter 25 if you want to create your own toolbars or move them around.

To hide or display toolbars:

1. To activate or hide a toolbar, choose **Toolbars** from the View menu (or press **Alt+V, T**) to open the Toolbars menu shown in Figure 3.2.

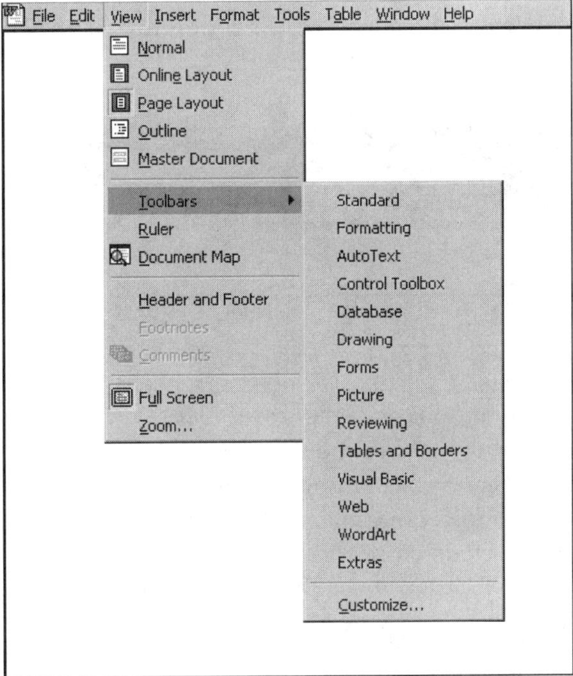

Figure 3.2 *The Toolbars menu.*

2. Click the toolbar you want to display or hide. If there's a check mark next to a toolbar's name, that toolbar is activated and should appear on your screen. To hide a toolbar, just click its name, making sure the check mark no longer appears.

At this point, make sure the Standard and Formatting toolbars are displayed.

What Do the Buttons Do?

Good question. Those toolbar pictures are pretty cryptic, aren't they? But no problem—Word thought of us here, too. If you move the mouse pointer to any of the buttons (don't click—just point), and hold it there for a moment, you'll see a box that tells you what the button does. Word calls these boxes *ScreenTips.*

To display ScreenTips, move your mouse pointer over any of the toolbar buttons—you don't have to click on anything; just move the mouse. Check out the ScreenTip just below the mouse pointer. Play around with this a bit and get a sense of the different options you can access. In Figure 3.3 my mouse pointer's on the button with a picture of a floppy disk. The ScreenTip tells me that this button's for saving the document.

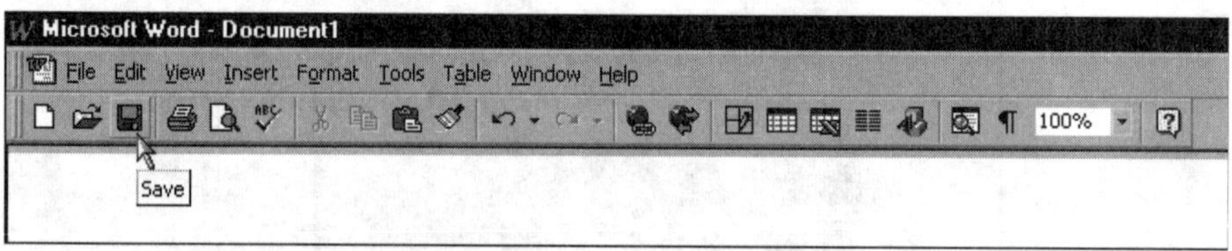

Figure 3.3 *Mouse pointer on the Save button.*

Why are some of the buttons grayed out (or *dimmed*)? Think back to Chapter 2. Any time an item is dimmed in a menu or dialog box, it means that item is not currently available. Usually something else needs to happen before the feature can be used. For example, the **Cut** and **Copy** buttons are dimmed because you have to have text selected before you can perform either of these actions.

How Do I Use the Buttons?

Okay, you know how to figure out what the buttons do, but how do you use them? Click. That's it. Just click once on any of the buttons to get to the feature.

Depending on the feature, clicking on a button might give you a dialog box or a list of choices, or it might simply implement the feature. That all depends on whether there are further choices that need to be made. Don't worry about what the individual buttons actually accomplish for now. The goal here is to be able to use them. As we get into different features throughout the book, we'll make extensive use of the toolbars and you'll find out what the specific buttons do.

It's time to test-drive the toolbar. Let's use the **Open** button as an example:

1. Move your mouse pointer to the **Open** button on the Standard toolbar and look at the ScreenTip that tells you that this button is for opening a document.
2. Click the left mouse button on the **Open** button. That's all there is to it. The Open dialog box is displayed, as you can see in Figure 3.4.

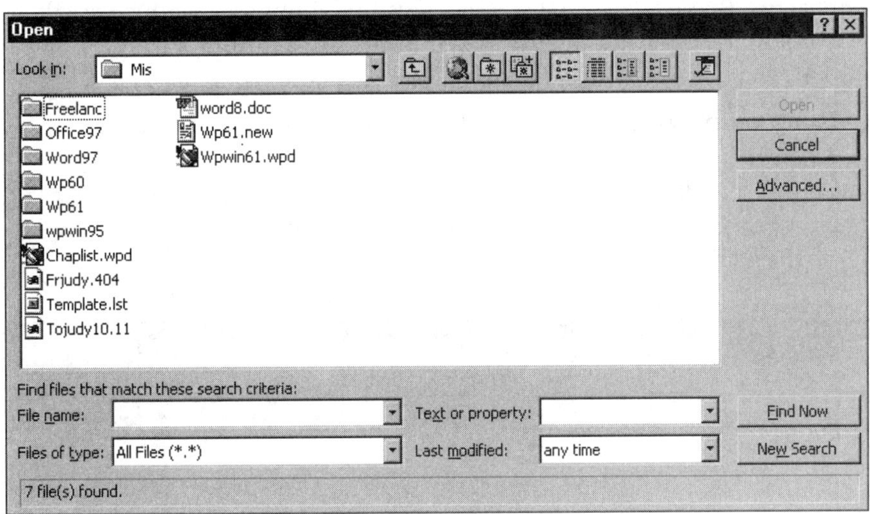

*Figure 3.4 The **Open** button takes you right to the Open dialog box.*

3. Because we're just using this as an example, click on the **Cancel** button (or press **Esc**) to close the Open dialog box.

You can also open the Open dialog box by opening the File menu and choosing the **Open** command. With the toolbar button, one click and you're there.

Displaying Different Toolbars

Word comes with more than 14 predefined toolbars. If you're working with a particular feature, you can choose a special toolbar to streamline your efforts. For example, there's a Tables and Borders toolbar that makes it easier to get to table options that might otherwise be buried in menus and dialog boxes.

The Standard and Formatting toolbars are displayed unless you make another choice. They include options that Word decided would apply to most general situations. Some of the other toolbars automatically appear when you use a particular feature. Throughout the book, we'll use different toolbars as appropriate.

How do you choose a different toolbar? You could choose **Toolbars** from the View menu and then click on the toolbar you want to display, as mentioned earlier. But there's even a shortcut for choosing toolbars. And speaking of shortcuts, that exactly what the shortcut I'm about to introduce is called: a *shortcut menu.* That's the next power tool I'll discuss in this chapter, but for now let's just use one without a bunch of explanation.

Using a shortcut menu to display toolbars:

1. Move your mouse pointer so that it's anywhere on one of the toolbars.
2. Click the right mouse button. A list of available toolbars is displayed (see Figure 3.5).

Figure 3.5 *The currently displayed toolbars (in this case, Standard and Formatting) have check marks next to them.*

3. Click on the toolbar you want.

When you're finished playing with the different toolbars, make sure the Standard and Formatting toolbars are displayed before you move on to the next section.

Shortcut Menus

Word's menu system is designed to make it easy to get to the features you need, but it can be confusing and intimidating if you have to wade through layers of menus to get to the right one.

Shortcut menus to the rescue! You saw an example in the last section, when we used a shortcut menu to change toolbars. When you clicked the right mouse button anywhere on a toolbar, you got a menu that gave you options specifically related to toolbars. That's the whole idea behind shortcut menus: to narrow down the possible choices. With a shortcut menu, you get only those menu items that relate to the specific feature or document area in which you're working.

Where Are the Shortcut Menus?

Shortcut menus are all over the place. Unlike toolbars, you don't turn on a shortcut menu by selecting it from a menu. The neat thing about shortcut menus is that you don't even have to know what you want or what features are available in a particular area—just click the right mouse button, and if a shortcut menu pops up, it will tell you which features are appropriate for that section of the document.

Word has hidden shortcut menus throughout the program. Some of them are available when you're working on a particular feature or have a graphic image on your screen. We'll talk about and use most of them as we work our way through the features.

Are Shortcut Menus Different from Regular Menus?

Nope. When you choose an item from a shortcut menu, it's the same as choosing it from a pull-down menu or dialog box. Shortcut menu items are no different from regular pull-down menu items. If an item is followed by an ellipsis (...), choosing that item activates a dialog box. If there's a check mark next to an item, that item is turned on or selected. If there's nothing next to an item, clicking on it causes an action to happen without any further input.

To create the shortcut menus, Word grouped items from the pull-down menus for easier access and copied them to shortcut menus. So it doesn't matter how you get to a feature—the end result is the same.

The best way to practice using shortcut menus is to start clicking your right mouse button in different areas of the screen and see what happens. I'll give you a few basic instructions, and then I'd like you to take a few minutes to explore shortcut menus before we move on to the ruler:

- To trigger a shortcut menu, click the right mouse button. The shortcut menu you get depends on where your mouse pointer is when you click.
- To choose a shortcut menu item, click on it with either mouse button.
- To turn off a shortcut menu, click the left mouse button anywhere outside the menu or press **Esc**.

If you don't get the shortcut menu you wanted, try clicking in a slightly different location.

THE RULER

With toolbars and shortcut menus, virtually all of Word's features are a mouse click away. Can it get any easier than that? Sure it can. How about changing margin and tab settings without having to select a feature at all?

The ruler is displayed just below the toolbars; it gives you visible margin, indent, and tab markings (Figure 3.6). The markings aren't just window dressing: you can change a tab, indent, or margin setting just by dragging the appropriate marker to a new location on the ruler.

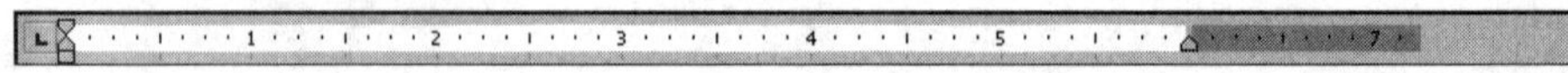

Figure 3.6 When the ruler is displayed, you can see all margin and tab settings.

For now, I'll just show you how to activate the Ruler. In Chapter 8, "Paragraph Formatting," you'll learn how to make it do your bidding.

To activate or deactivate the Ruler:

1. Click on **View** (or press **Alt+V**).
2. Choose **Ruler** from the View menu.

If there's a check mark next to this item, the ruler is already on. Just like the toolbar menus, the **Ruler** command is a toggle—choosing it turns it on if it's off or off if it's on.

WIZARDS

The power tools we've discussed so far are great, but they all require you to know what you want to do to your document. Wizards don't just make it easier to access features—they can actually create a professionally formatted document for you. All you have to do is answer some questions, and a Word wizard takes it from there. Once the wizard creates the basic document, you can edit it just like any other Word document.

The basic techniques for working with wizards are the same no matter which wizard you're working with. The best way to show you how wizards work is to jump right in and use a couple.

Creating a Polished Memo in a Flash

Before you can use a wizard, you have to find it. No problem—wizards are located in the New dialog box, the same place you go whenever you create a new document.

1. Choose **New** from the File menu to open the New dialog box. Take a look at the tabs just below the title bar. We talked about tabbed dialog boxes in Chapter 2—the tabs are like folders inside a compartment. When you click on a tab, you move to a different folder (referred to simply as a *tab*) in the dialog box.
2. Select the tab that contains the wizard you want to use. For this example, click on the **Memos** tab. Figure 3.7 shows the available templates and wizards in the **Memos** tab.

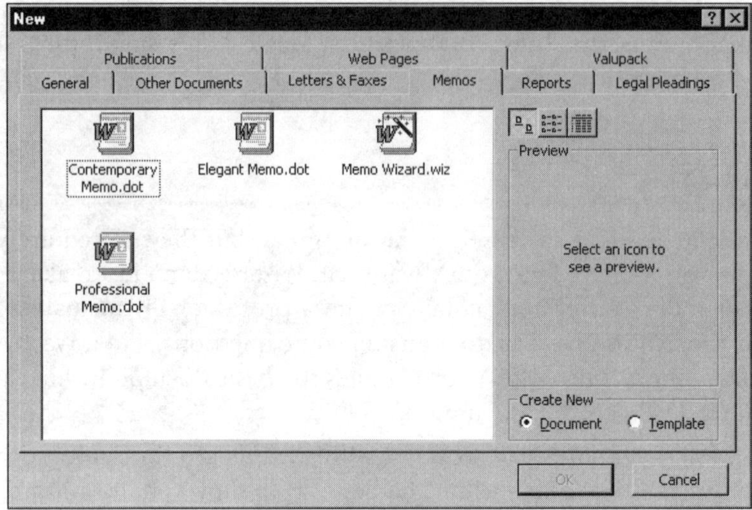

*Figure 3.7 The **Memos** tab in the New dialog box.*

3. Select the wizard you want to use (in this case, **Memo Wizard.wiz**) and click **OK**. This takes you to the first Memo Wizard screen, as shown in Figure 3.8.

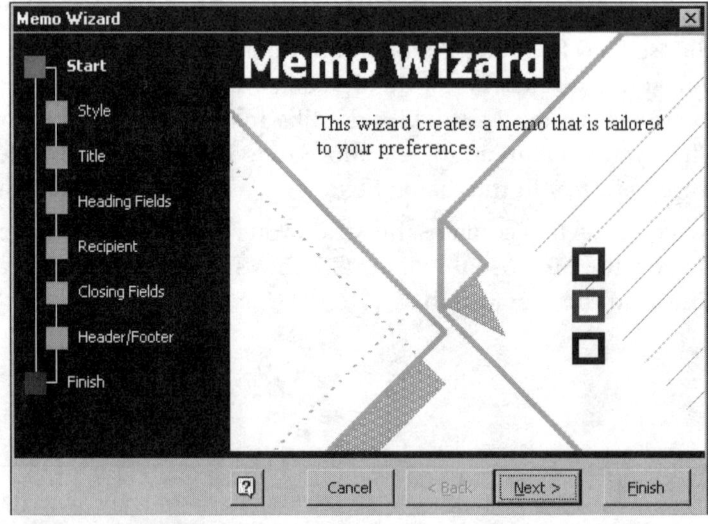

Figure 3.8 The first Memo Wizard screen.

To move through the wizard, click the **Next** button when you're ready to advance to the next screen. If you want to go back a step, click the **Back** button. You can leave the wizard at any time without completing it by clicking the **Cancel** button, or skip any remaining screens but still complete the wizard by clicking the **Finish** button.

4. Click **Next**. The window shown in Figure 3.9 asks you to choose a style for your memo.

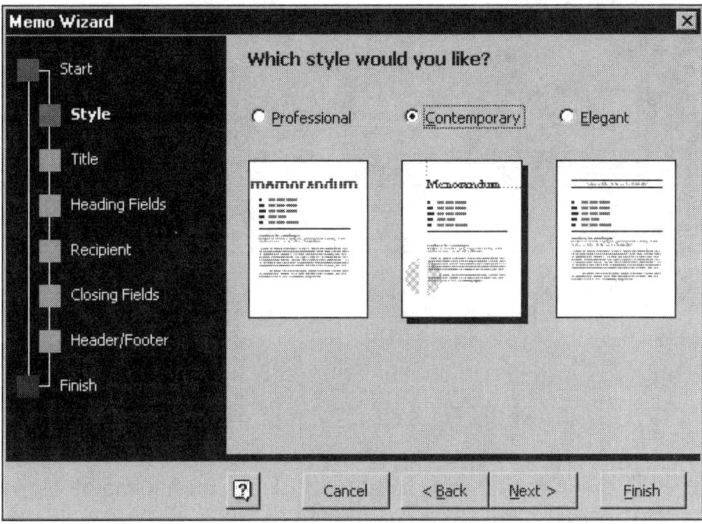

Figure 3.9 Choose a memo style from this screen.

5. Click to select a style, then click **Next**.
6. If you want to use Word's suggested title, *Interoffice Memo*, just click **Next**. Otherwise, type the title you want (Figure 3.10). Notice that as soon as you start typing, *Interoffice Memo* disappears and is replaced by what you type.

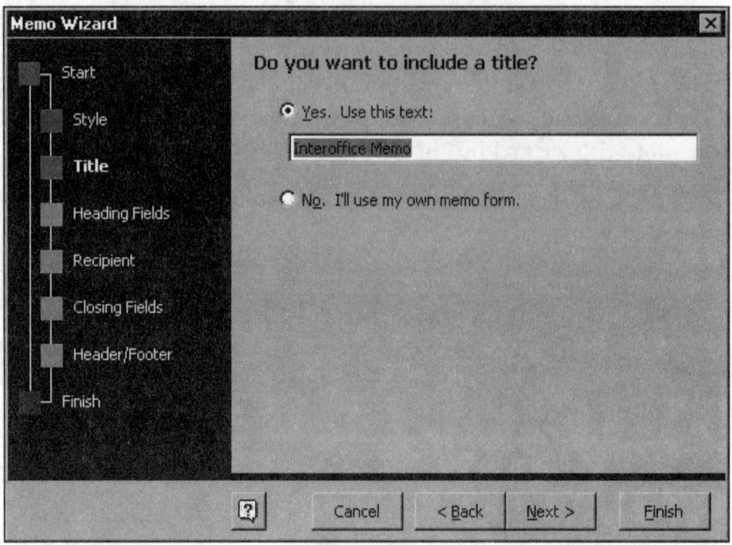

Figure 3.10 Here's where you can give your memo a title.

If you have your own preprinted memo stationery, click **No**.

7. The screen shown in Figure 3.11 contains several items that are commonly used in memos. If you don't want to include the item at all, click on the item's name to get rid of the check mark (conversely, if you want to include an item that doesn't have a check mark, clicking on the item adds the check mark). For the items you want to include, type the information you want in the appropriate text boxes, then click **Next**.

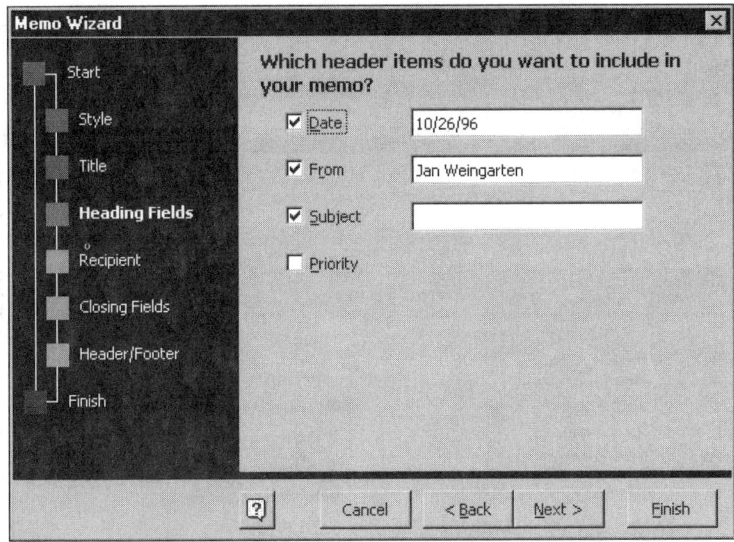

Figure 3.11 *Enter standard memo header information here.*

8. When you're finished with the wizard, click the **Finish** button. Word produces a memo that uses the information you specified, as shown in Figure 3.12.

The remaining screens in the Memo Wizard allow you to tell Word who should get the memo (you can use names from your Address Book if you want), what information you want at the end of the memo (like the writer's or typist's initials), and what items you want in a header or footer. Because this is just an example of how to use wizards, I won't go through every screen. Just realize that the wizard's purpose is to make your life easier. All you have to do is check items you want to include, uncheck those you don't want, and enter information in the appropriate text boxes.

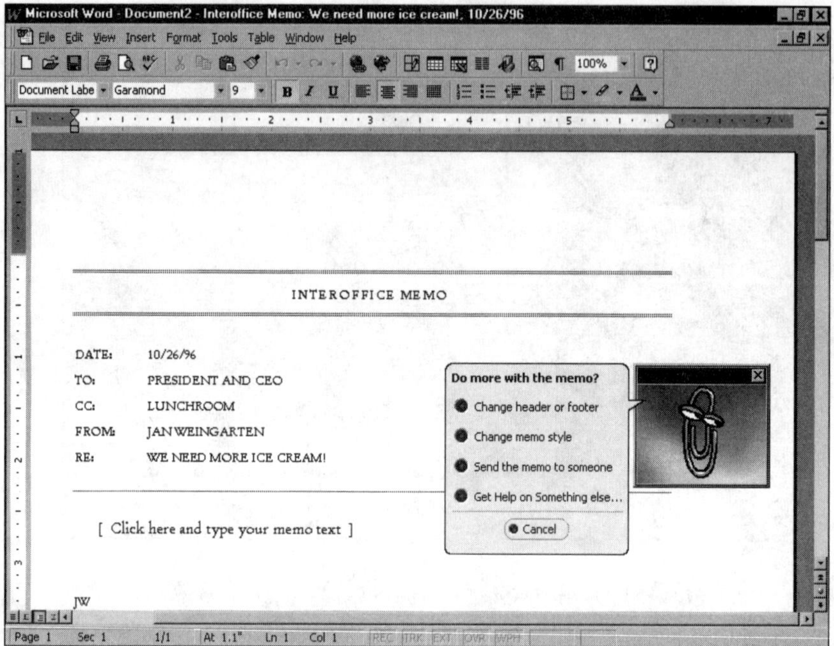

Figure 3.12 *The completed memo with the Office Assistant asking what you need help with.*

The Office Assistant pops up at this point, ready to help you edit the memo. To get more assistance with one of the items on the Office Assistant list, just click on it. Or, if you want to proceed on your own, you can ignore the Office Assistant and keep working. To get rid of the Office Assistant's questions, click **Cancel**.

NOTE

You can click **Finish** from any wizard screen—you don't have to go through all the screens if you don't need them.

Notice where it says *[click here and type your memo text]*. Whenever you see a **Click here** prompt in a completed wizard, clicking anywhere in the text selects the whole phrase. This means that as soon as you click in the **click here** phrase and start typing, the *click here* phrase is replaced by your text.

TEMPLATES

Templates are an integral part of Word. Every time you create a new document and choose **Blank Document** from the New dialog box, you're really opening a document that uses a template called *Normal*. This template controls the options that are available. Almost everything you see on the screen (and a lot of things you don't see) is part of a template. The toolbars and available styles are attached to the template.

As you learned in the last section, a wizard asks questions and then produces a formatted document that uses the options you selected and the information you supplied. A template, on the other hand, gives you a sample document that includes styles and formatting and lets you take it from there.

In most of the templates included with Word, you simply select the text you want to replace and type over it. Most templates include in their body text instructions on how to use the template, so even if you don't understand all the formatting and features, you can still use them.

Creating a Document from a Template

Remember how in the Memo Wizard you decided whether you wanted a Contemporary, Elegant, or Professional memo style? Well, take a look at the **Memos** tab in Figure 3.13. To get to it, I chose **New** from the File menu and clicked on the **Memos** tab.

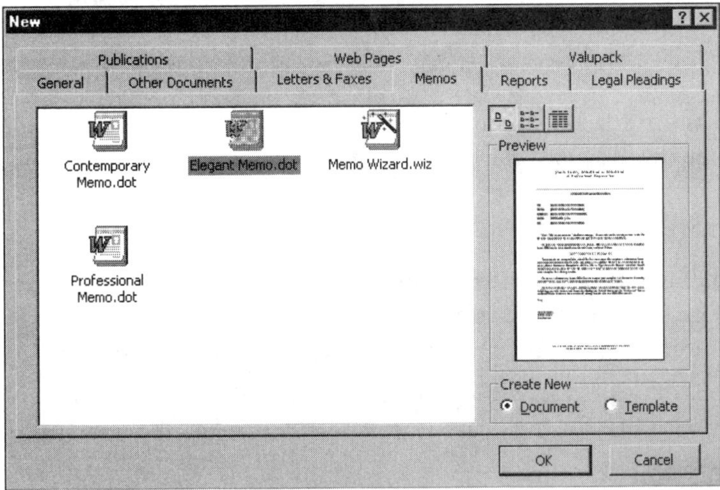

Figure 3.13 *The* **Memo** *tab in the New dialog box.*

In addition to the Memo Wizard (**Memo Wizard.wiz**), you have three templates: **Contemporary Memo.dot**, **Elegant Memo.dot**, and **Professional Memo.dot**. If you choose one of these templates, you get a preformatted document without going through all the questions the wizard asks. To get Figure 3.14, I selected **Elegant Memo.dot** and clicked **OK**.

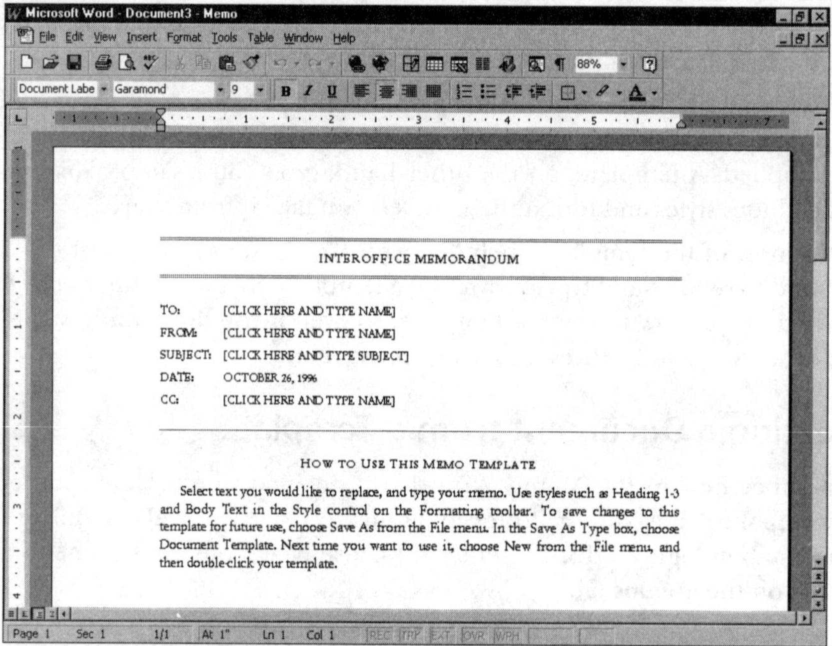

*Figure 3.14 The document that results from choosing **Elegant Memo.dot**.*

NOTE

As you select different items in the New dialog box, notice that the Preview box gives an idea of what the finished product will look like.

As with the memo you created from the wizard, the memo template includes **click here** prompts. Just click anywhere in a **click here** phrase to select the entire phrase and start typing. Your text automatically replaces the existing text.

The rest of the text (anything that's not in a **click here** prompt) is just regular text. If any of it fits, you can leave it in. Otherwise, select the text and replace it with your own.

See Chapter 6 for information about selecting text.

Before you delete the sample text, make sure you look at any instructions it contains. Look at the sample body text in Figure 3.14—it's actually instructions on using the template.

Be sure you save the document—remember, what's on your screen is a regular Word document that can be edited and saved just like any other document.

If you want to replace the sample text but would still like to refer to the instructions, print the sample document before you make changes. Choose **Print** from the File menu and click **OK**.

Customizing a Template

What you did with the Memo template was create a document based on it and customize the text of the document. The next time you create a new document based on the template, you'll have to make those same customization changes again. However, if you save your changes to the template itself, every time you create a document based on it, your customized information will already be there. There's no need to repeat your work.

All you have to do is save the document as a template. Once you do this, your customized template will appear in the New dialog box with the rest of your templates.

To customize a template:

1. Choose **New** from the File menu.
2. Click the tab that contains the template you want to modify, and select the template you want.
3. Select **Template** in the Create New section in the lower-right part of the dialog box and click **OK** (Figure 3.15). Now, instead of creating a new document, you'll be creating a new template. Notice that the title bar says *Template1* instead of *Document1*. This lets you know you're working with a template.

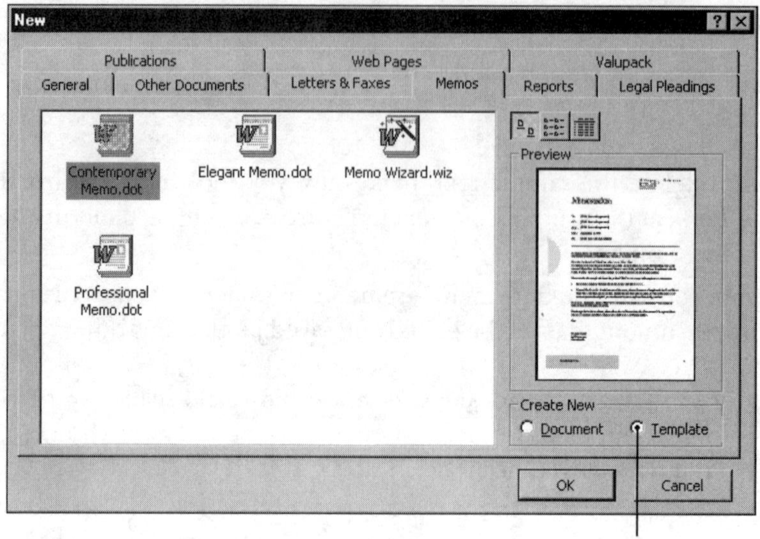

Figure 3.15 The New dialog box with Template selected.

4. Customize the template to include any text and formatting you want.
5. Choose **Save As** from the File menu to open the Save As dialog box shown in Figure 3.16.

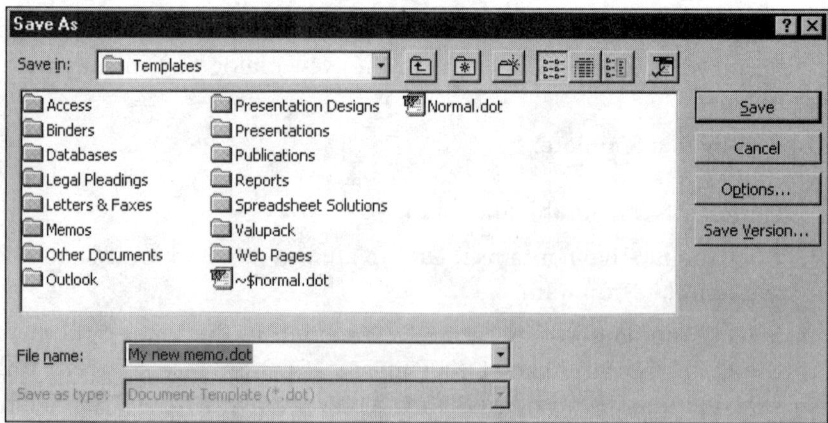

Figure 3.16 The Save As dialog box.

In the Save in box, notice that Word automatically selected the **Templates** folder. Word knows you're saving a template, and it knows where the template should be stored.

6. Double-click on the folder in which you want to store the template. For example, if you want the template to be stored with the other memo templates, double-click on **Memos**. If you save the template in the main **Templates** folder, it will appear in the **General** tab. Otherwise, it will appear on the tab that matches the folder name, as in Figure 3.17.

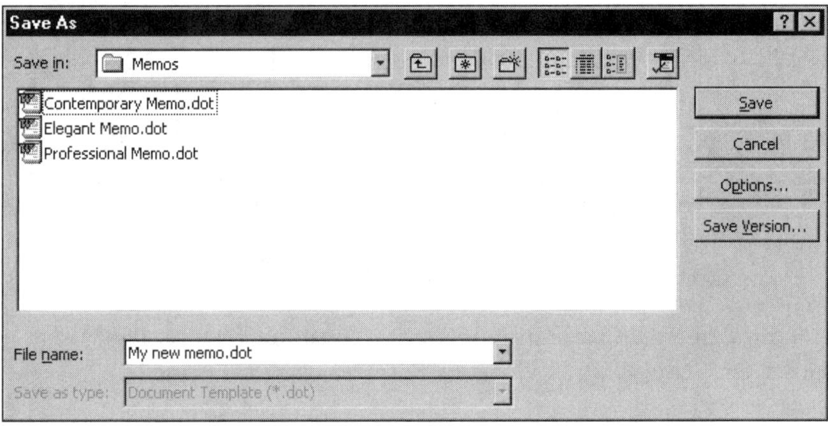

Figure 3.17 *Save the template here to display it in the* ***Memos*** *tab.*

7. Enter a name in the File name box.
8. Click **Save**.

That's it. Your new customized template now appears with the other templates and wizards in the New dialog box. You can verify this by choosing **New** from the File menu and selecting the appropriate tab, as shown in Figure 3.18.

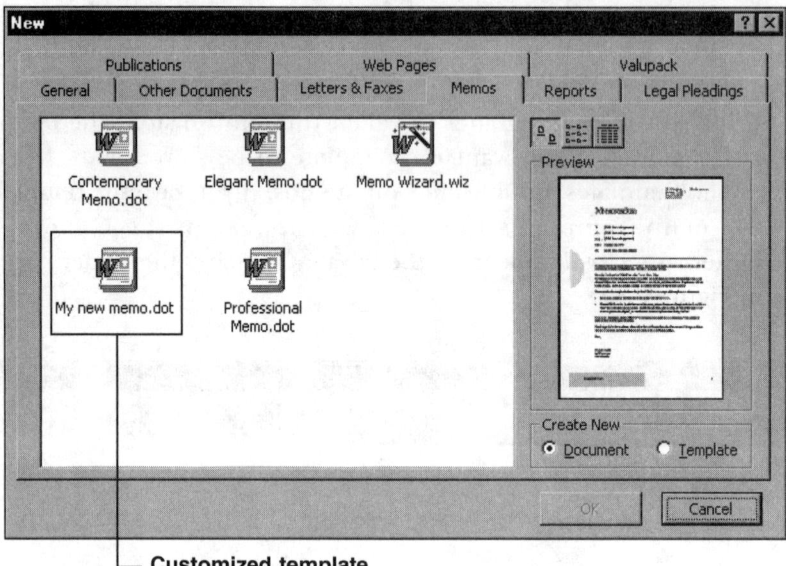

Figure 3.18 The New dialog box with the customized template.

You can now create documents based on this customized template, just as with any other template.

FROM HERE...

The power tools you learned about in this chapter are heavily used throughout this book. From now on, when I tell you about a feature, I'll emphasize the easiest method, and that'll usually mean using toolbars or shortcut menus. You've also seen how wizards and templates can take the drudgery out of formatting and setting up documents, leaving you free to concentrate on what you want to say.

The next chapter, "Getting Help," will make you even more self-sufficient (uh-oh, I better stop with this self-sufficiency stuff or I'll be out of a job). I'll give you resources that will help you figure out any Word problem on the spot.

CHAPTER 4

Getting Help

Let's talk about:

- ✦ Using the Office Assistant
- ✦ Using Word's Help system
- ✦ Searching for help on a specific topic
- ✦ Getting help from the World Wide Web
- ✦ Using Help to get information about your system

I know you're chomping at the bit—you want to use Word, not take detours to learn about useless stuff like the Help system. Well, it's far from useless. In fact, if this is the only chapter you read, you'll have all the resources you need to navigate your way through Word's features. Word's online help is a great way to get fast information that can lead you through whatever feature you're working on.

Although this chapter won't teach you about producing documents, it may prove to be the most valuable chapter of the book. That's because it shows how you can continue learning about Word long after you've finished this book. This book doesn't attempt to cover every single feature in Word—there's just too much. For example, you'll learn nothing about writing Visual Basic code in macros or manipulating information in custom fields. Nor does this book explain every possible aspect of the features that it does cover. When you come across a feature that's not covered or if you want to delve into greater detail on a feature that's introduced in this book, it's time for online help.

All it takes is knowing how to reach the information and practicing so it doesn't seem intimidating. Instead of having just a single help file, help of various kinds is embedded throughout Word. When you finish this chapter, you'll find it easy to take advantage of not one but several kinds of assistance. You can search for help on a specific topic, ask the Office Assistant questions in plain English, or use the Show Me feature to have Word walk you through a procedure.

We'll take a brief tour of the available help options. I don't need to go into great detail or cover all the things you can do; because the main purpose of the help system is to assist you, most of its options are fairly self-explanatory.

Meet Mr./Ms. Office Assistant

The first thing you probably saw when you started Word for the first time was that goofy-looking paper clip asking what you wanted to do next. That's when you met our gender-neutral (as far as I can tell) Office Assistant, whose purpose is to guide you through the potentially murky waters of Word. As you work, the Office Assistant keeps an eye on what you're doing and offers assistance when it thinks you might need some help.

If the Office Assistant isn't visible, open it by doing one of the following:

- ✦ Click the **Office Assistant** button on the Standard toolbar (the button on the far right with a question mark).
- ✦ Choose **Microsoft Word Help** from the Help menu.
- ✦ Press **F1.**

Even if the Office Assistant isn't, it will still pop up at variouse times. For example, here's what happens when Word thinks I might need some help. If I type a date, followed by an address block and a salutation like *Dear Sue,* the Office Assistant figures out that I'm probably typing a letter, and asks if I want help, as shown in Figure 4.1.

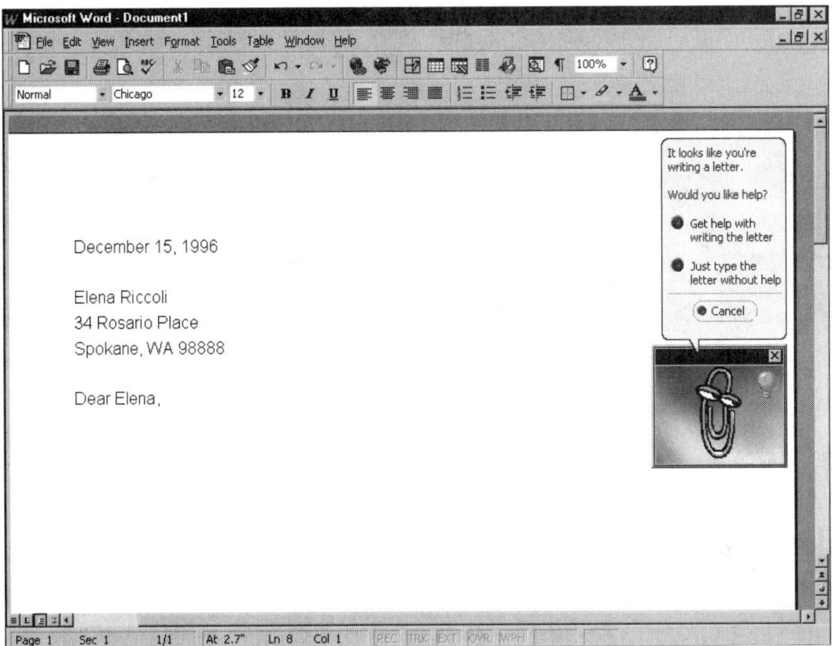

Figure 4.1 *The Office Assistant is ready to help me with my letter.*

If I don't need any help, I can click on **Just type the letter without help**, and the Office Assistant will leave me alone for a while. If I do want help, I can click on **Get help with writing the letter** to open the Letter Wizard, shown in Figure 4.2.

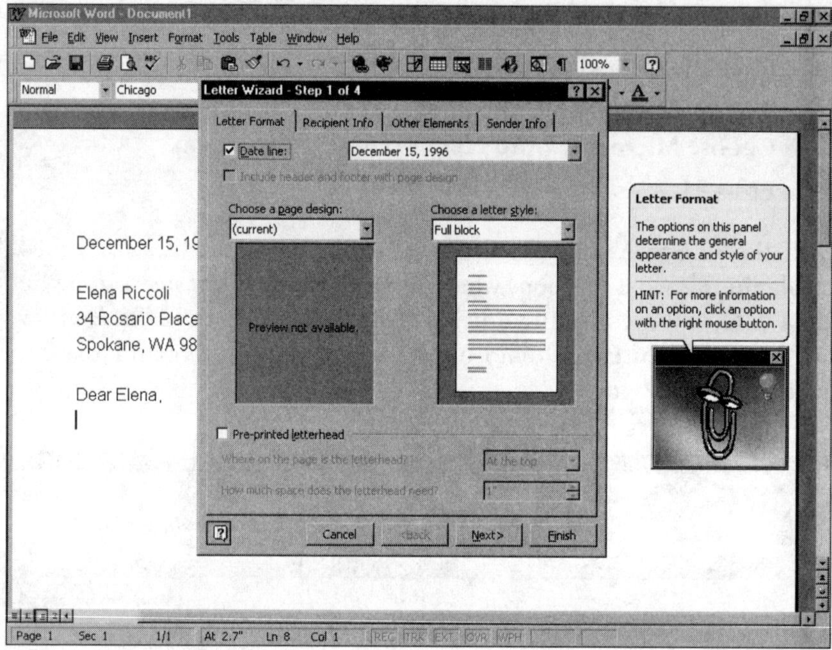

Figure 4.2 The Letter Wizard can walk me through the process of creating a letter.

As you saw in Chapter 3, wizards are a great way of setting up and formatting documents. The Letter Wizard takes you step by step through the letter-creation process (of course, *you* still have to figure out what to say in the letter).

Depending on the type of help offered by the Office Assistant, you may end up in a wizard or help screen that provides additional information.

Asking a Question

The Office Assistant can't always figure out what you're trying to do, but it *is* always ready to answer your questions. If the Office Assistant is just sitting there minding its own business, as in Figure 4.3, just click anywhere on it to open a bubble like the one in Figure 4.4.

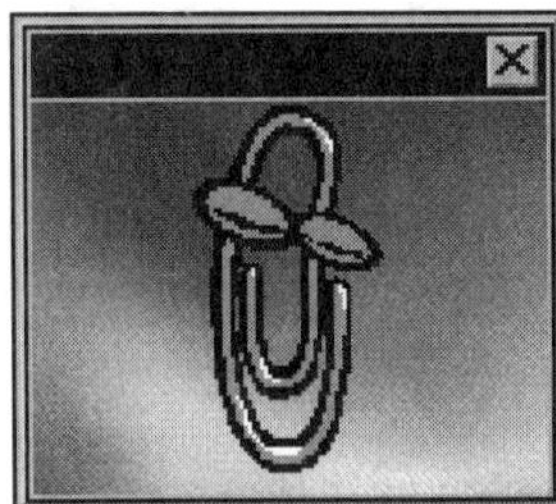

Figure 4.3 The Office Assistant at rest.

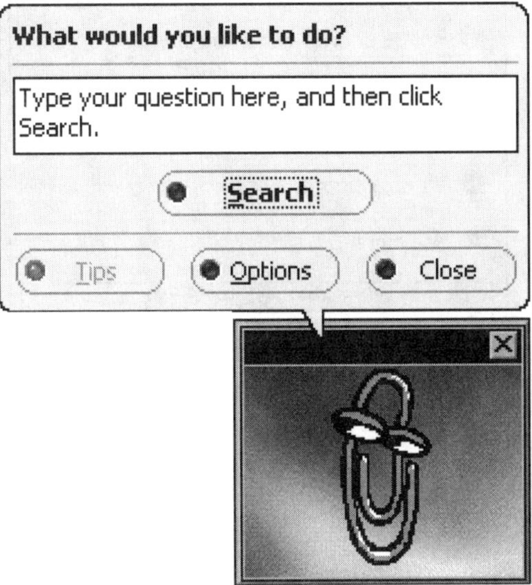

Figure 4.4 The Office Assistant ready for a question.

Depending on what you're doing, the Office Assistant might make some assumptions about the kind of help you need. If what you're looking for is listed, click on it to get more help. If not, here's what you need to do:

- Type your question in the text box (the insertion point's already in it, so all you have to do is start typing). The more specific your question, the better your chances of getting the response you need. For example, if you want help changing the size of graphic images, type *change the size of graphic images,* not just *graphics.*

✦ Click the **Search** button. As you can see in Figure 4.5, the Office Assistant came up with several possibilities. Because I want to know how to resize graphics, I'm going to click **Resize or crop a drawing object**. This takes me directly to a Word help screen with the information I need.

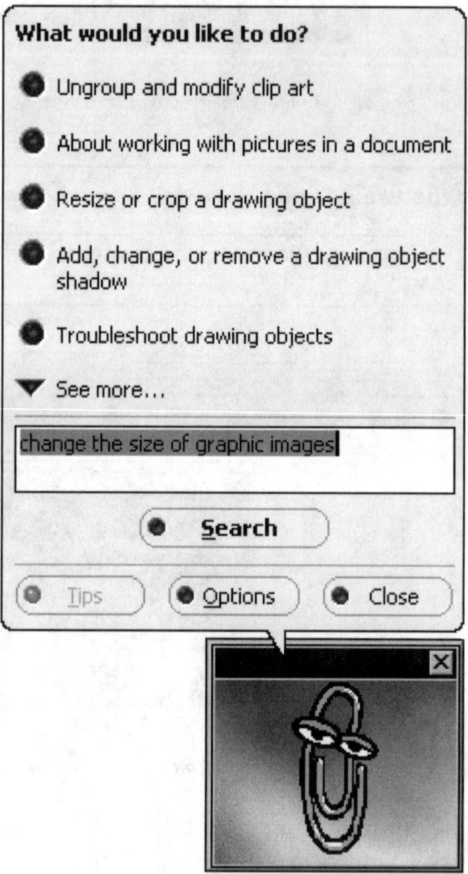

Figure 4.5 Answers to my question.

NOTE

The Office Assistant uses technology called *IntelliSense* that intelligently digests phrases and distills from them the topics you want to see.

Getting Tips

When Word has a tip it thinks might be useful to you, a light bulb appears on the Office Assistant.

- To display the tip, just click on the light bulb.
- If you've closed the Office Assistant, you can still get tips—the light bulb will appear on the Office Assistant button on the Standard toolbar. When you see a light bulb there, click the button to open the Office Assistant, then click the light bulb in the Office Assistant to display the tip.

Getting Rid of the Office Assistant

The Office Assistant can be an annoying little beastie, always hanging out and watching your every move. To get rid of it temporarily, just click the **Close** button in the Office Assistant window. This only solves the immediate problem, however. It's still lurking in the background, and the next time it thinks you need help, up it pops again. Read the next section on changing the Office Assistant's options to find out how to kill it entirely.

Changing the Office Assistant Options

The Office Assistant is set up to respond to certain commands and to provide certain kinds of help, but you can control the extent of its helpfulness.

To change how the Office Assistant works, click **Options** from any Office Assistant bubble. This opens the Office Assistant dialog box shown in Figure 4.6. (If the bubble isn't visible, click anywhere in the Office Assistant screen to display it.)

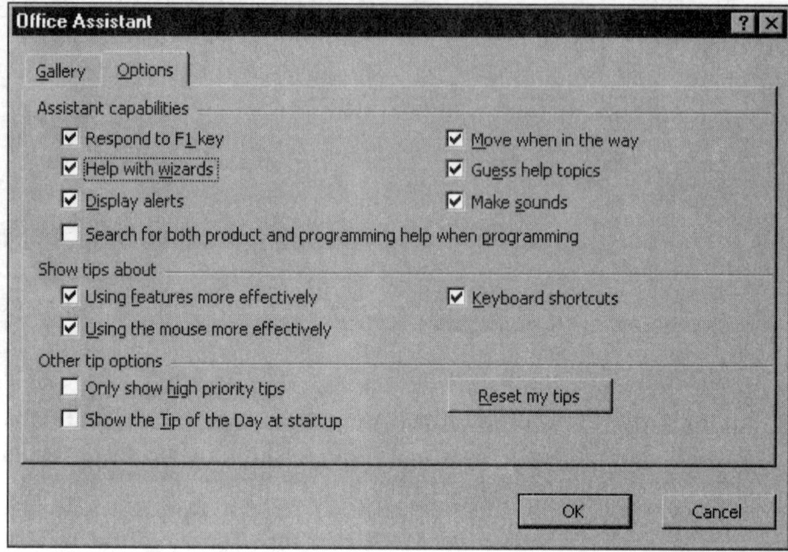

***Figure 4.6** The Options tab in the Office Assistant dialog box.*

If there's a check mark next to an item, clicking the item deselects it. If there's no check mark, clicking selects the item. Here's what the different options do:

- **Respond to F1 key** tells Word to display the Office Assistant when you press **F1**. If you deselect this, pressing **F1** opens the Help Topics dialog box instead of the Office Assistant.
- Deselect **Help with wizards** if you don't want the Office Assistant to pop up whenever you use a wizard.
- Deselect **Display alerts** if you don't want the Office Assistant to display messages when it thinks there's something you need to know.
- **Move when in the way** causes Word to move the Office Assistant so it's not blocking dialog boxes or other important screen elements. This option also shrinks the Assistant if you don't use it for five minutes.
- If you don't want the Office Assistant to try to figure out what you're doing and provide help, deselect **Guess help topics**.
- The Office Assistant makes various sounds depending on what it's doing. If you prefer a silent assistant, deselect **Make sounds**.

- ✦ The Show tips about and Other tip options sections let you decide what kind of tips you want the Office Assistant to provide.

Changing the Way the Office Assistant Looks

If you don't like that goofy paper clip (called *Clippit*), you can select from several other options. To choose a different Office Assistant, click **Options** from an Office Assistant bubble and click on the **Gallery** tab (shown in Figure 4.7).

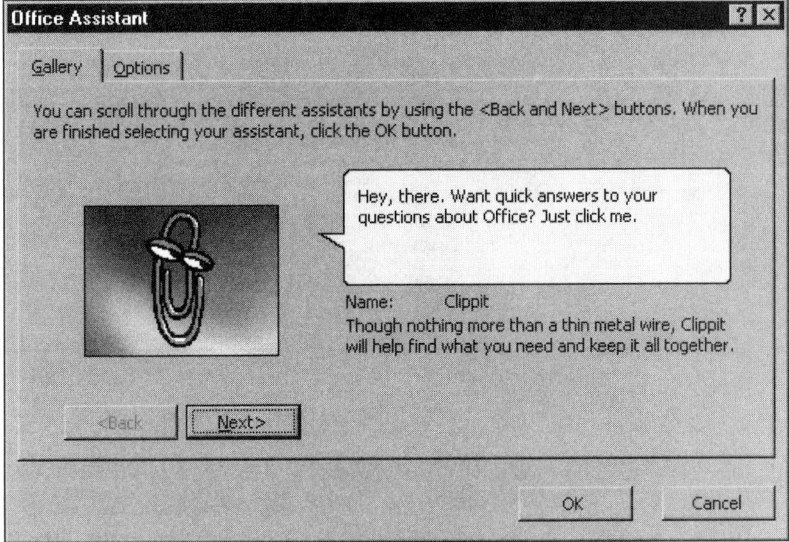

***Figure 4.7** The **Gallery** tab in the Office Assistant dialog box.*

The instructions for choosing a different assistant are right there on the **Gallery** tab, so I don't have to tell you what to do. Just find an assistant you like and click **OK**.

If you didn't install the additional assistants when you installed Word, the Office Assistant will prompt you for the original CD.

USING HELP

The Office Assistant is there on the front lines, ready to help even when you don't know what kind of help you need. But dig a little deeper into the Office Assistant, and you'll usually end up in a Help window. So without further ado, let's get some serious help.

Opening Help:

1. Open the Help menu by clicking on **Help** or pressing **Alt+H**. Figure 4.8 shows the Help menu. We'll get into most of the items on this menu in a bit.

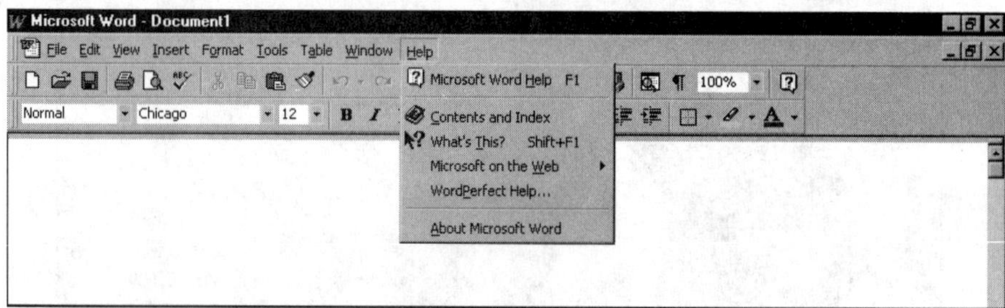

Figure 4.8 The Help menu.

2. Choose **Contents and Index**, which opens the dialog box shown in Figure 4.9, and make sure the **Contents** tab is selected. Notice that there's a closed book icon to the left of each topic. The closed book tells you that the topic contains additional subtopics.

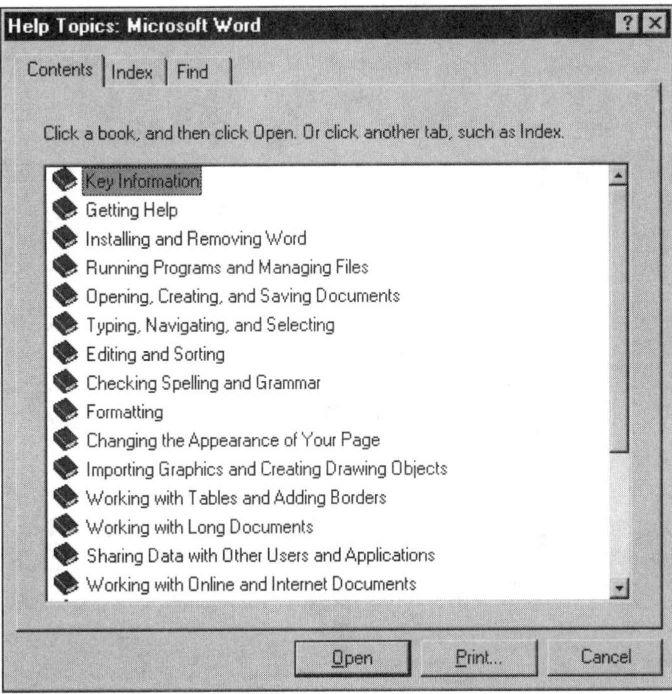

Figure 4.9 *The Contents tab in the Help Topics dialog box.*

3. Double-click on **Opening, Creating, and Saving Documents**. The closed book icon changes to an open book, and a bunch of subtopics are displayed. Notice that all the subtopics in **Opening, Creating, and Saving Documents** have closed book icons next to them. That means that each of them contains additional subtopics, which can be viewed by double-clicking the item. Let's dig down through the topics until we get to an actual help file.
4. Double-click on **Creating Documents**. As you can see in Figure 4.10, the items under **Creating Documents** all have question mark icons next to them. The question mark tells you that there's a help file associated with the item.

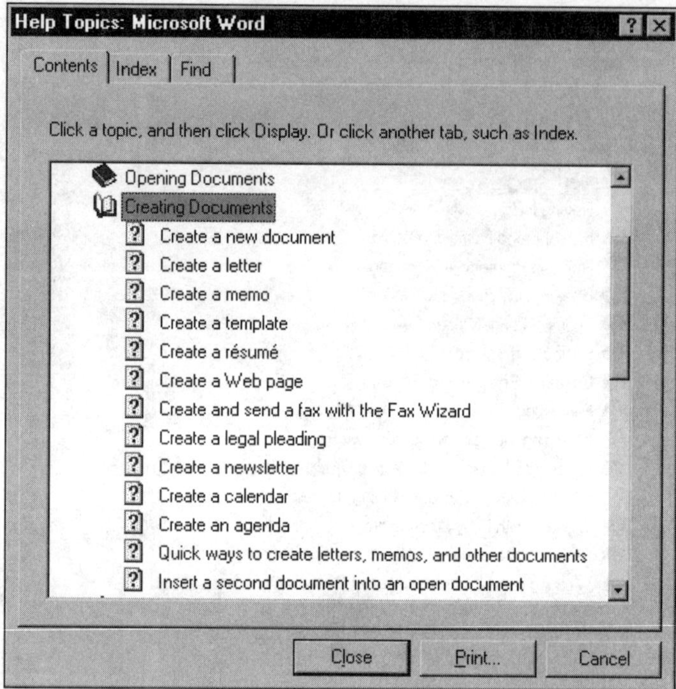

Figure 4.10 The Help items for creating documents.

This is a great place to start with Help. By playing around in this area, you can experiment with the different elements of Word's help system and learn more about Word at the same time. Double-click on any item to get more information.

5. Double-click on **Create a New Document**. This opens the Microsoft Word Help dialog box shown in Figure 4.11. Notice that the Help Topics dialog box has disappeared.

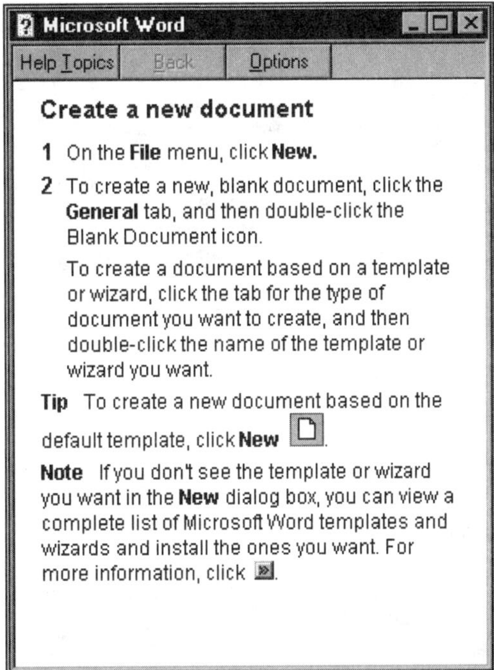

Figure 4.11 Get help with the basics of document creation.

6. When you're finished reading the Help information, click the **Help Topics** button in the Word Help dialog box. This returns you to the Help Topics dialog box, right where you left off.

USING THE INDEX

The Help Index contains an alphabetical index of all the Word features. But if Help just presented a list, you'd have to do an awful lot of scrolling to find what you want, because there are about a kazillion features. So Help helps you by giving you a way to search through the index and get the specific help you need. Suppose you want to find out how to add the date to a document.

1. Click on the Index tab in the Help Topics dialog box to display the index shown in Figure 4.12. Notice that your insertion point is inside the text box at the top of the dialog box, ready for you to start typing.

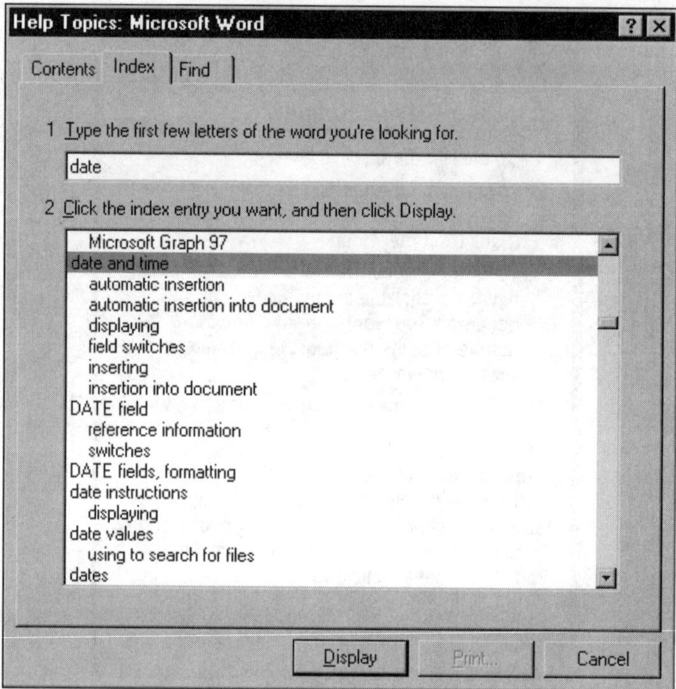

Figure 4.12 *The Help Index.*

2. Type the word you want to search for. For this example, type **date**. As you type, notice that the selection bar moves through the index to highlight the word you type.
3. When the main topic (in this case, date) is highlighted, use the arrow keys to highlight the subtopic you want to find out about (or just click on the item).
4. Click the **Display** button to open the Help window for the selected item.

Navigating through Help

Here are a few tips that will help you get around in Help:

- Click the **Help Topics** button from any Help window to return to the main Help Topics dialog box.

- You can move backward through the Help topics you've used in the current Help session by clicking on the **Back** button.
- You can get a printout of a Help topic by clicking the **Options** button and choosing **Print Topic** from any Word Help window.
- If you want the Help window to remain visible while you work on your document, click on the **Options** button and choose **On Top** from the cascading Keep Help On Top menu. Just click in your document window to work on the document, and click in the Help window if you want to look up another topic. Click on the **Close** button when you're finished using Help.

Context-Sensitive Help

Sometimes you want specific help on the feature you're trying to use, and it would be really nice if you could just tell Word, "I want help on what I'm doing right now—you figure it out for me." Well, you can. In fact, there are a couple of ways to get context-sensitive help. **Context-sensitive** just means that Word figures out what you're trying to do based on the context (which dialog box you're in, which button you're pointing to, or which menu item is highlighted).

- Press **Shift+F1** in any document window. Notice that a question mark attaches itself to your mouse pointer. When you point at a menu item, a button, or a particular area of the window and click the left mouse button, you'll get a ScreenTip help window for the item or feature.
- You can also use **Shift+F1** to find out what a particular keystroke will do. For example, if you press **Shift+F1** and then press **Ctrl+O**, a ScreenTip tells you that this keystroke is for opening a file.
- When you're in a dialog box, click the **?** button (just to the left of the **Close** button in the upper-right corner), then click on a dialog box item to display a box with a description of the item's purpose.
- When you're in a dialog box, press **F1** to open the Office Assistant with a list of options pertaining to the dialog box. Click any of the options for more help.

Show Me

Several Word help screens contain a **Show Me** button that walks you through some common procedures. Let's say you want to change the size of some text, but you've never done it before, so a little assistance is in order:

1. Open the **Contents** tab in the Help Topics dialog box (choose **Contents and Index** from the Help menu and click on the **Contents** tab.
2. Double-click on **Formatting**, then double-click on **Formatting Characters**. The topic list shown in Figure 4.13 should be displayed.

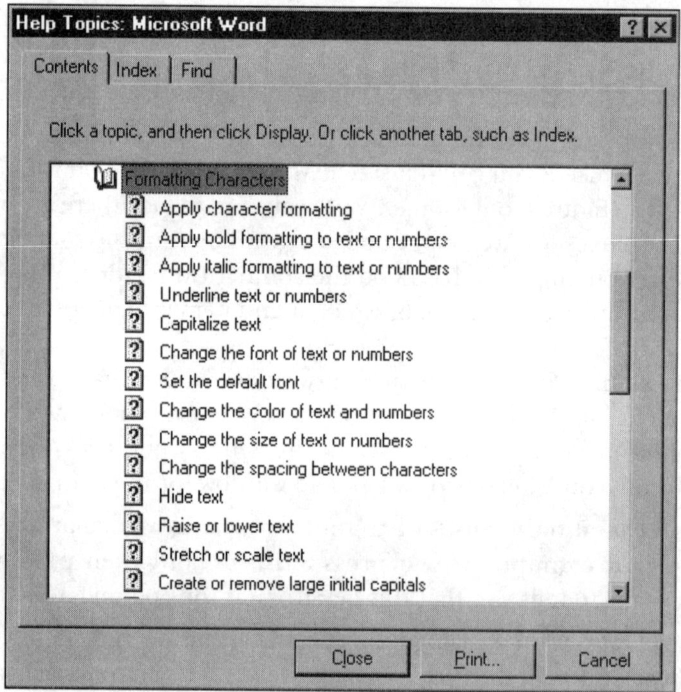

Figure 4.13 *This Help screen should be displayed now.*

3. Double-click on **Change the size of text or numbers** to open the Help screen shown in Figure 4.14. The information in the Help screen tells you what you need to do—the Show Me button just gives you some extra help.

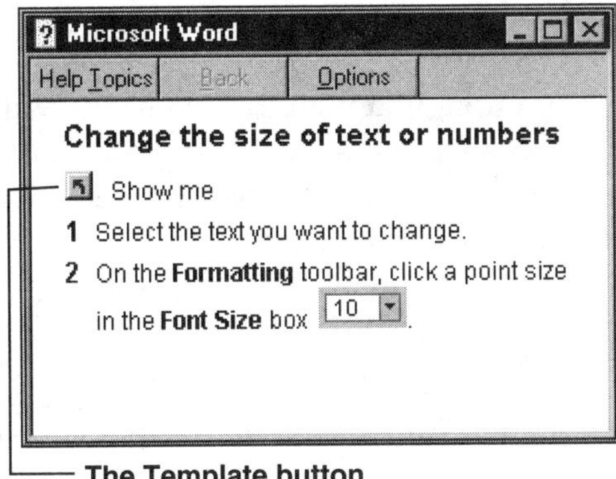

Figure 4.14 *A Help screen with a Show Me button.*

4. Click the **Show Me** button. Notice that the mouse pointer moves all by itself over to the Font Size box on the Formatting toolbar and (after a brief pause) Word displays a ScreenTip that tells you how to proceed (see Figure 4.15).

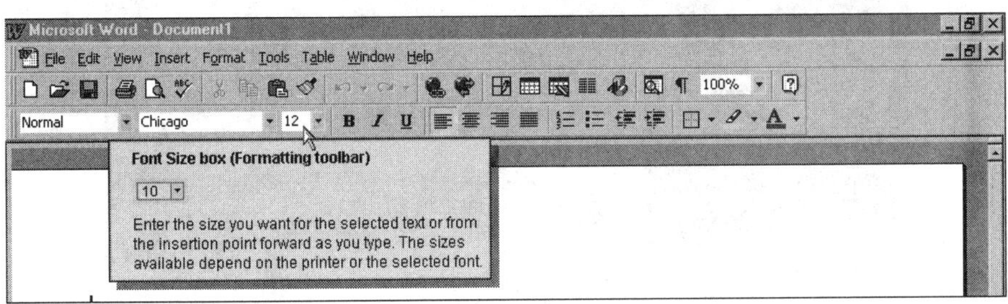

Figure 4.15 *The result of clicking a Show Me button.*

NOTE

Whenever you see a **Show Me** button in a Help screen, click it if you want Word to walk you through the procedure.

USING HELP'S FIND TOOL

If you don't already have enough help tools at your disposal, here's one more. You can create a database that contains all the words and phrases in all the help topics. Once you create the database (which is really easy—a wizard walks you through it), you can search through the help topics for any item that contains the word or phrase you want.

To use the Find Setup Wizard:

1. Choose **Contents and Index** from the Help menu and select the **Find** tab. The first time you select the **Find** tab, Word opens the Find Setup Wizard shown in Figure 4.16.

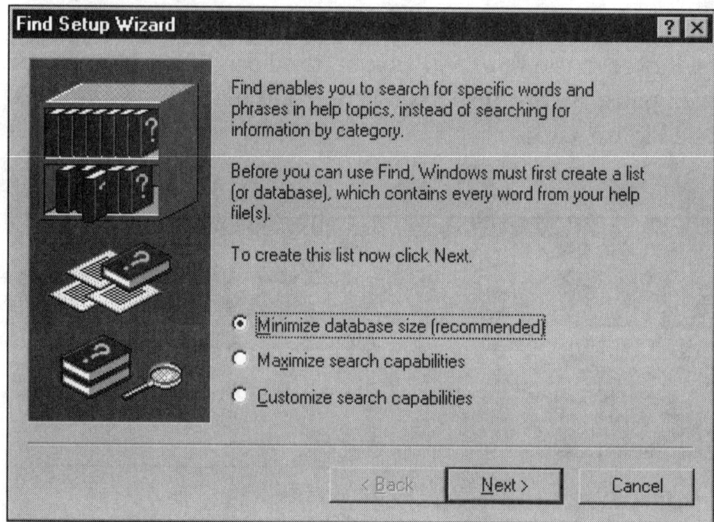

Figure 4.16 The Find Setup Wizard.

2. Choose one of the database options. The default selection is **Minimize database size**, which gives you a perfectly adequate database but conserves disk space. If you have tons of disk space, choose **Maximize search capabilities**. Or, if you want more control over how the database is set up, choose **Customize search capabilities**.

3. Click the **Next** button. If you chose **Customize search capabilities**, you get a few additional wizard screens. Just select the options you want and keep clicking the **Next** button until you get to the screen shown in Figure 4.17. If you chose either of the other options, you go right to the screen shown in Figure 4.17.

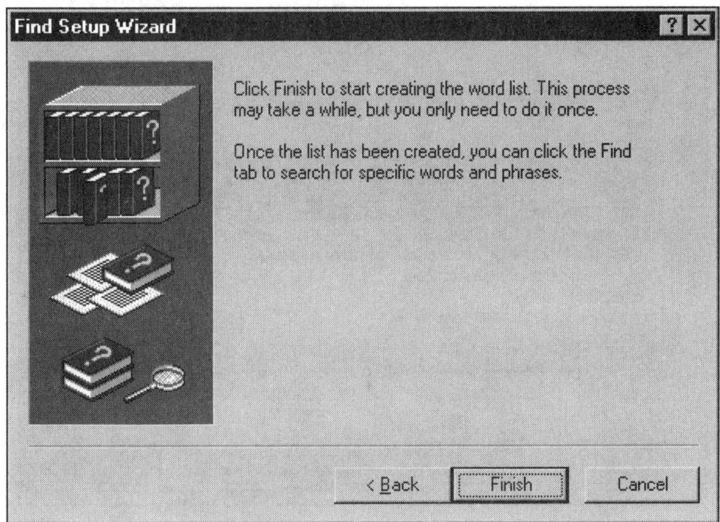

Figure 4.17 The final Find Setup Wizard screen.

4. Click **Finish**. Depending on the options you selected and the speed of your computer, it may take a while to build the database. When it's finished, your **Find** tab should look like Figure 4.18.

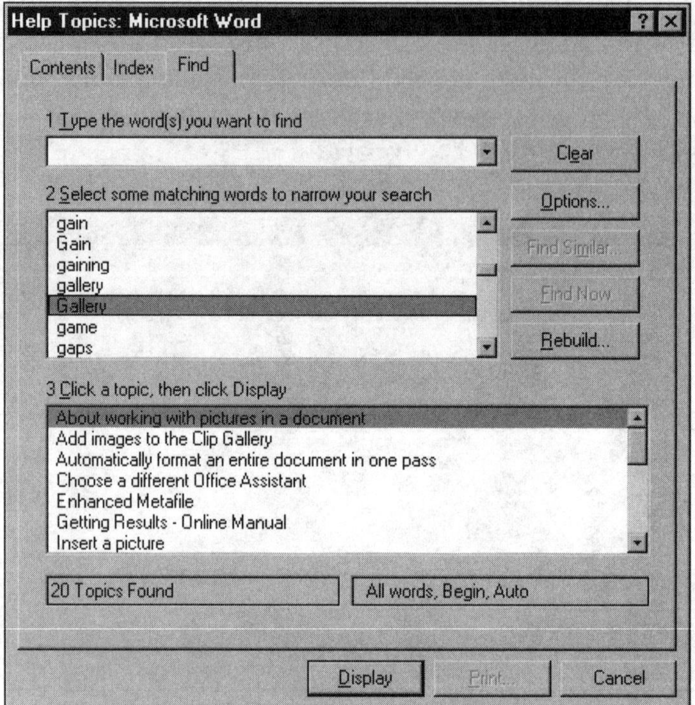

Figure 4.18 The Find tab in the Help Topics dialog box.

5. Type what you want in the Type the word(s) you want to find text box.
6. In the topics list at the bottom, click to place check marks in the boxes next to the topics you want to display, then click **Display**.

If the topics list doesn't contain what you want, try selecting different items in the matching words list (the list in the middle of the dialog box).

You can change the way Find performs searches by clicking **Options** and making selections in the Find Options dialog box shown in Figure 4.19.

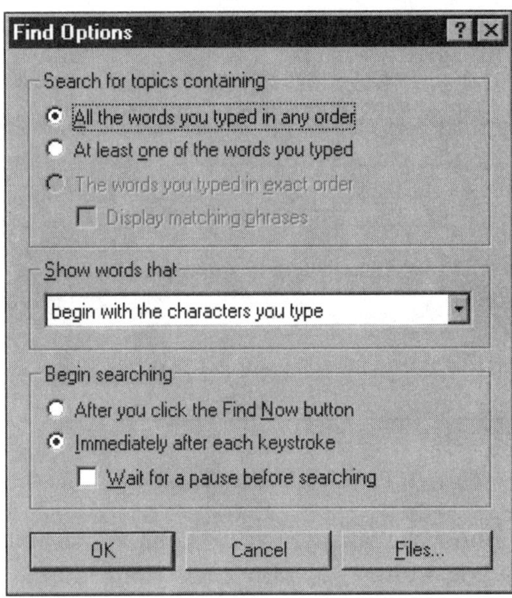

Figure 4.19 *The Find Options dialog box.*

You can use the Find Setup Wizard to rebuild your database with different options by clicking the **Rebuild** button.

GETTING HELP THROUGH THE WEB

If you have Internet access and a Web browser, you can get help directly from Microsoft's Web site. Just choose **Microsoft on the Web** from the Help menu to open the menu shown in Figure 4.20.

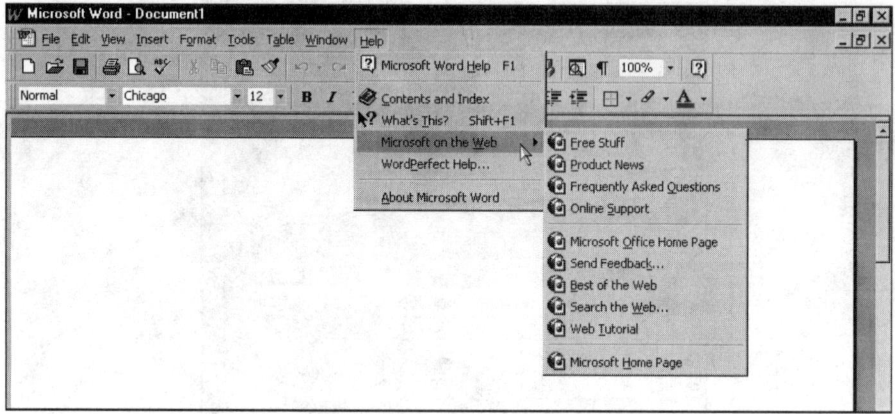

Figure 4.20 The Microsoft on the Web menu.

Just click on the option you want to connect directly to that Web site. What happens next depends on how your Internet connection is set up, but clicking on an option should open your Web browser and initiate a connection.

Getting System and Word Version Information

It is often helpful to know how Word and Windows are using your system's resources. In addition, if you call Word's telephone support line, they'll want to know the date on your Word program and your license number. All this information is available in one place:

- Choose **About Microsoft Word** from the Help menu to display the dialog box shown in Figure 4.21.

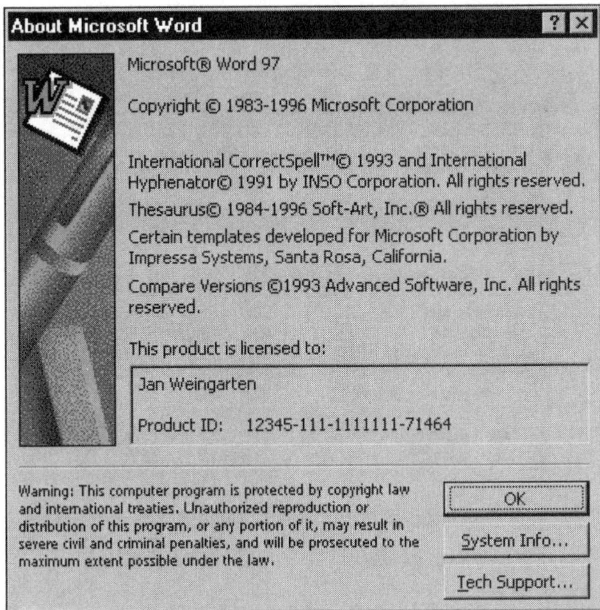

Figure 4.21 *The About Microsoft Word dialog box.*

- For additional information about your system, click **System Info** to open Microsoft System Information, as shown in Figure 4.22. To find out about different parts of your system, click the appropriate item in the list on the left. Many of the information screens are fairly cryptic and are meant to be used only by people who need to "get under the hood." You probably won't need to go much farther than the main System screen, which is the one that's displayed by default.

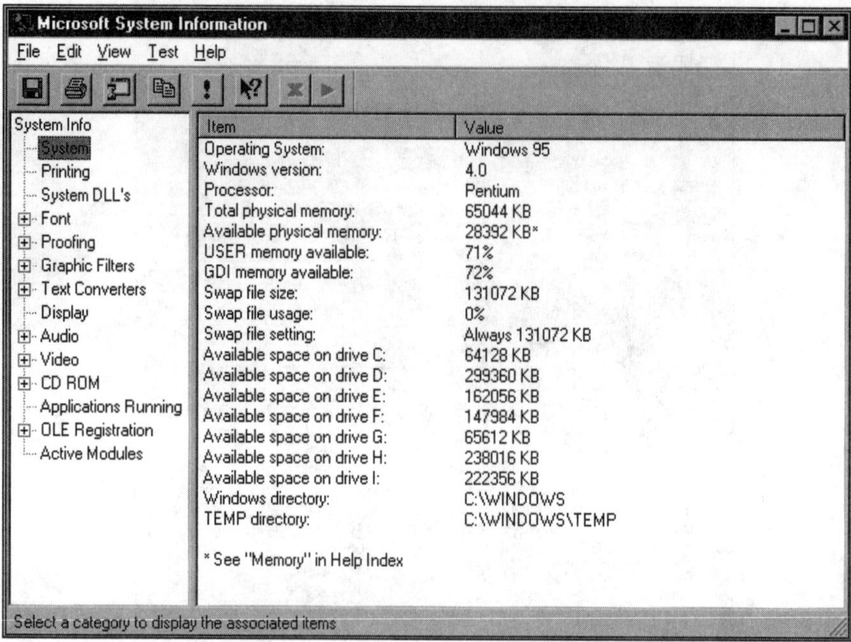

Figure 4.22 *Microsoft system information.*

- If you click **Tech Support** from the About Microsoft Word dialog box, Word opens a Help screen with information about Microsoft's support options. This works just like the other Help screens we've used in this chapter—double-click on a closed book icon to open its subtopics; double-click on a question mark icon to open a help topic.

FROM HERE...

As you work through this book and begin creating your own documents, don't forget that Help is near. If you want to review something I've talked about or get a different perspective on it, try Help. I can't cover every detail about every feature in this book, so use Help when you're ready to delve a little deeper.

In the next chapter, "Editing 101," you'll learn more about the basics of opening, creating, and saving documents. We'll make some changes to the document you created in Chapter 1, and you'll learn techniques for efficiently moving around in a document. I'll even show you how to recover when you do something you didn't mean to do.

CHAPTER 5

Editing 101

Let's talk about:

- ✦ Opening a document
- ✦ Moving around in a document
- ✦ Adding text
- ✦ Deleting text
- ✦ Undoing (the Oops! features)
- ✦ Closing a document without saving
- ✦ Saving a document

Pop quiz time. What's the first thing that happens after you finish creating a document? Give up? Come on, think about it—as soon as you're done and the document's no longer on your screen, you remember something that needs to be added. (Or am I the only one that happens to?)

In the bad old typewriter days, this meant either starting over or scrawling a note in the margin before you mailed the letter. Even a minor error could cause you to have to retype a lengthy document. Well, as far as I'm concerned, one of the greatest things about computers is that I *never* have to retype. I can bring that document back to the screen, get rid of what I don't want, add what I do, and move the rest of it around in any order I desire.

In this chapter, you'll bring a document you already created back to the screen and learn how to make simple changes. Then, in Chapter 6, "Moving and Copying Text," you'll learn how to take chunks of text and move them around.

It's Not a Typewriter!

Most of us grew up with typewriters and developed habits that work great with those mechanical monsters but can get you in trouble with a word processing program. Many people who have been using computers for years still fall into these traps, so by heeding the Don'ts in this section, you'll be way ahead of the game.

- **Don't press the Enter key after every line**. On a typewriter, you have to press a carriage return to move to the next line so you can keep typing. A computer does the work for you—as soon as you type the beginning of a word that won't fit on a line the computer automatically wraps the word to the next line. If you press the **Enter** key at the end of a line, it may look fine now but can cause formatting problems when you add or delete text or do anything that changes the way the line would wrap.
- **Don't use spaces to line things up**. If you type a series of spaces to line up columns or start a line at a certain horizontal position, you're doing things the hard way. You're also setting yourself up for trouble if you have to change anything (like the type size). You'll find that after a change, your columns and indents no longer line up. It's much more efficient and effective to use tabs and margin settings.

- **Don't press the Tab key repeatedly**. One habit that even many professional word processors find themselves getting into is pressing the **Tab** key repeatedly to move the insertion point to where they want to start typing. For example, at the beginning of a letter, you might press the **Tab** key six or seven times to move the insertion point to the middle of the page so you can type the date. The better way is to use Word's **Align Center** feature, which allows you to accomplish your task with the click of a button. Or, if you want to position text at a horizontal position that's not centered, consider setting a tab stop where you want it so you can position the text by pressing the **Tab** key only once. You may not understand alignment options and margin and tab settings yet. Just remember that if you're pressing the **Tab** key lots of times to get where you want to go, there's probably a better way.
- **Don't use underscores**. Although Word and most word processors have an underlining feature, it's best not to use it (unless you're doing it for a specific purpose and know what you're doing). You'll have much more classy-looking documents if you remember that italic and bold are the preferred typographical ways of emphasizing text. And with the proliferation of computers and laser printers, readers have come to expect professional-looking documents in all but the most casual settings (and sometimes even there).

Opening an Existing Document

When you're staring at an empty Word screen, you have two choices: You can start creating a new document (that's what we did in Chapters 1 and 3), or you can open a document that's already been created.

ROADMAP

If you click the **New** button on the Toolbar (or press **Ctrl+N**), you get a blank document screen like the one you used in Chapter 1. But if you choose **New** from the File menu, you get the New dialog box, which allows you to choose a template or use a wizard to give your document a basic layout. In case you skipped past it, take a look back at Chapter 3, "Working with Toolbars, Templates, and Wizards," for a bunch of information on this subject.

To open the document you created in Chapter 1:

1. Click on the **Open** button on the Toolbar. The Open dialog box, shown in Figure 5.1, is displayed. You can also choose **Open** from the File menu or press **Ctrl+O**.

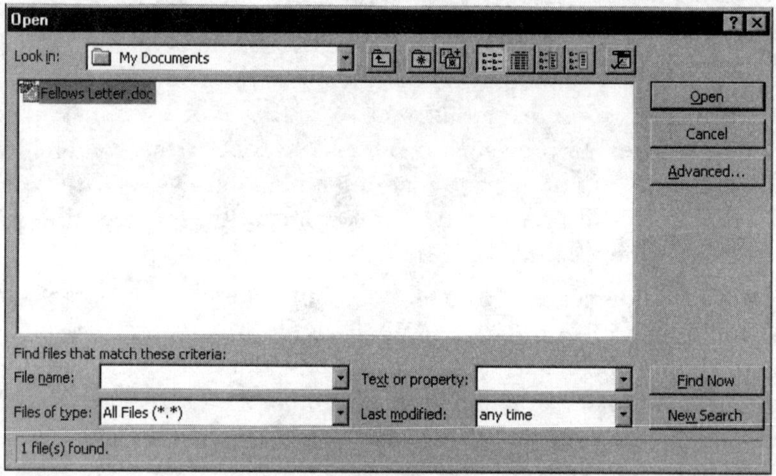

Figure 5.1 The Open dialog box.

2. Double-click on the file you want to open (in this case, **Fellows Letter**). If necessary, use the vertical scroll bar to bring the file you want to open into view.

KEYBOARD

If you know the name of the file you want, just type its name in the File name text box and press **Enter**. Otherwise, press **Shift+Tab** to move into the list area, then use the **Up Arrow** and **Down Arrow** keys to select the file you want. Then press **Enter** to open the file.

ROADMAP

Fellows Letter should be back on your screen at this point. If you had a problem opening it, refer to Chapter 14, "Managing Files and Folders," for help. Take a look at the sections on understanding and changing folders. It's possible that you inadvertently saved **Fellows Letter** in a different folder. We're not going to get into all that folder stuff now—just hang in there and it'll all become clear.

SHORTCUT

If you've worked on a document recently, there's an even easier way to open it. By default, Word keeps track of the last four documents you've opened, and they're listed on the bottom of the File menu (as shown in Figure 5.2). To open one of the documents, just open the File menu and click on the file you want. Or, if you're using the keyboard, press the number next to the name. (Note: Word can keep track of up to nine of your recently opened documents. For info about how to change Word's default settings, see Chapter 25, "Making Word Work the Way You Do.")

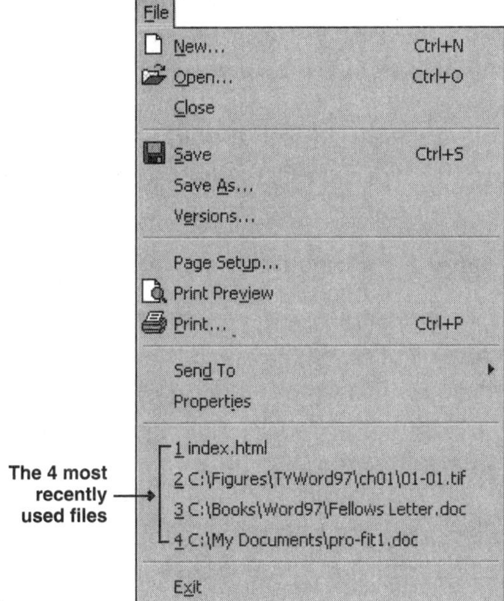

***Figure 5.2** The File menu with the four most recently opened documents listed at the bottom.*

Moving Around in a Document

Okay, the document's on your screen. Now what? How do you move your insertion point to the part of the document you want to change? As usual, there are several answers. You can always just click the left mouse button anywhere on the screen to move your insertion point to a new location. But what if your document is several pages long and you want to get to a particular page or the end of the document? I'll give you a whole list of shortcut methods for moving to different parts of a document.

A lot of the movement shortcuts use keyboard combinations, and this is one situation where I'm going to encourage you to use the keyboard. When you're typing and editing, your hands are on the keyboard, and a keyboard shortcut can be a lot quicker than reaching for the mouse.

NOTE

You can't move your insertion point past the area that has text and formatting codes. To Word, the blank area beyond where you've entered text or codes doesn't exist until you type something or add some formatting. If you try to move beyond the current document area, the insertion point will just move to the last text or object in the document. For example, if you click the mouse button anywhere below the signature lines in **Fellows Letter**, the insertion point moves to the end of *Marketing Manager*, because that's the end of the document.

Before I give you the navigation tips, let's add a bit to your letter to give you more to work with. In the process, I'll show you a couple of keyboard shortcuts that, in my humble opinion, beat the heck out of the mouse alternatives.

To add to your letter for navigation practice:

1. With **Fellows Letter** on the screen, click to place your insertion point somewhere near the middle of the letter.
2. Now press **Ctrl+End** to move your insertion point to the end of the document. How's that for a slick shortcut? **Ctrl+End** always takes you to the very end in an instant, even if the document is 100 pages long. The mouse alternative in this case would involve pointing to the vertical scroll box and dragging it all the way to the bottom of the scroll bar, then clicking inside the document. Reminder: Scrolling does not move the insertion point.
3. Press **Shift+F5**. Notice that your insertion point moves back to where it was in step 1. Another indispensable shortcut, **Shift+F5** takes you back to the last place you were working. And this shortcut works even after you've closed Word and gone home. The next time you activate Word and open a document, just press **Shift+F5** to move your insertion point to wherever it was when you closed the document.
4. Now we'll add a couple of pages so you have a longer document to play with. Press **Ctrl+Enter** to insert a hard page break. Notice that the status bar changes to show that you're on page 2.
5. Type **Page Two** on the second page so you'll have a frame of reference.
6. Add one more page break (by pressing **Ctrl+Enter**) and type **Page Three** on the third page.

7. Press **Ctrl+Home** to move your insertion point back to the top of the document.

Table 5.1 contains a list of keyboard shortcuts that will get you where you want to go. Don't try to memorize these, just refer to them and use them as you work with Word. The ones you find yourself using frequently will quickly find their way into your memory bank. In Table 5.1, a plus sign (+) between the keys means that you hold down the first key while you press the second and then release both keys. A comma means that you press and release the first key before you press the second.

Table 5.1 *Moving the insertion point with the keyboard.*

TO GET HERE	PRESS THESE KEYS
One character to the right	**Right Arrow**
One character to the left	**Left Arrow**
Beginning of next word	**Ctrl+Right Arrow**
Beginning of current or previous word	**Ctrl+Left Arrow**
Beginning of current line	**Home**
End of current line	**End**
Up one line	**Up Arrow**
Down one line	**Down Arrow**
Next Paragraph	**Ctrl+Down Arrow**
Previous paragraph	**Ctrl+Up Arrow**
Previous screen	**Page Up**
Next screen	**Page Down**
Top of current screen	**Ctrl+Page Up**
Bottom of current screen	**Ctrl+Page Down**
First line of previous page	**Alt+Ctrl+Page Up**
First line of next page	**Alt+Ctrl+Page Down**
Beginning of the document	**Ctrl+Home**

Take a few minutes to move through your letter using these keystroke combinations. Try moving word by word (you can hold down the **Ctrl** key and keep pressing the **Left Arrow** or **Right Arrow** key to move several words at a time).

Then move up and down through the paragraphs, move between the pages, and move to the beginning and end of lines. In other words, just play around for a bit.

Are you finished playing? It's time to use the mouse. As I said before, the keystroke combinations are quick, but you have to know which to use in a particular situation. The main advantage to using the mouse is that you don't have to remember all those keystrokes—you just click or drag, either in the document window or on the scroll bars.

I'm not going to give you the mouse information in a table, because it takes a little more explaining:

- To move the insertion point to any location visible on the screen, just click the left mouse button where you want the insertion point to be positioned. If you're used to using the mouse a lot anyway, this can be easier than dealing with all those keystroke combinations.
- If you can't see the area you want to move to, use the scroll bars to bring the text into view, and then click inside the document window to move the insertion point.

NOTE

Remember that the scroll bars just change your *view* of the screen—they don't move the insertion point.

Adding Text

Now that you can move around your document, adding text where you want is simple. Just move your insertion point to the location where you want the new text and start typing.

Insert and Overtype Modes

When you first start Word, you are in *Insert mode.* This means that when you type, the characters are inserted to the left of your insertion point, and the text that follows is pushed to the right to make room for the added text. Most of the time, Insert mode works fine; your existing text automatically reformats as you add new text.

Sometimes, though, you don't want to push the existing text out of the way; you want to replace it. That's where *Overtype mode* comes in handy. Overtype does exactly what it sounds like—in Overtype mode, you are typing over your existing text, and the existing text does not move to make way for new text.

So why use Overtype? There's a good example in your letter. In Chapter 1, you replaced the word *are* with *our*. Because we were using only basic techniques, you deleted *are* and then typed in the word **our**. Because both words have the same number of letters, it would have been quicker to just turn Overtype on and type the correct word right over the wrong one.

Let's add some text to your letter, using both Insert and Overtype modes. We'll start by adding a sentence in Insert mode, and then switch to Overtype mode to make a correction.

To understand Insert and Overtype modes:

1. Move your insertion point just in front of the word *Now*, as shown in Figure 5.3. As you type new text, it will be inserted in front of the insertion point, and the rest of the text will move over to make room.

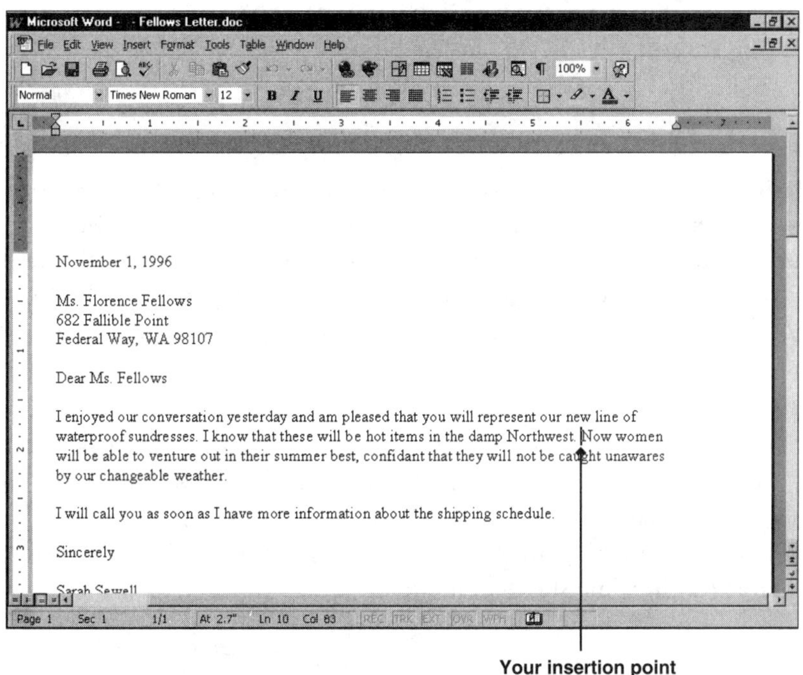

Figure 5.3 *The insertion point is in front of the word Now.*

2. Type **Because of our new fashion breakthrough**, and press the **Spacebar** once. Turn Overtype mode on by pressing the **Insert** key (or double-clicking on **OVR** on the Status Bar).

NOTE

The **Insert** key is a toggle: If Overtype is on, pressing **Insert** turns it off; if Overtype is off, pressing **Insert** turns it on. The same goes for the **OVR** button on the Status Bar. Double-clicking turns Overtype on if it's off and off if it's on. You can tell when Overtype is on because the **OVR** button becomes active (the letters aren't dimmed).

3. Your insertion point should still be in front of the letter *N* in the word *Now*. Because *Now* is no longer the beginning of the sentence, the first letter shouldn't be capitalized. We're just replacing one letter with another, so this is a perfect use for Typeover.
4. Type a lowercase **n**. Notice that it replaces the capital *N*, and the rest of the text stays put.
5. Save the letter by clicking on the **Save** button on the Toolbar (or pressing **Ctrl+S**).

Deleting Text

In Chapter 1, you learned how to delete one character at a time using the **Delete** and **Backspace** keys. **Backspace** deletes the character to the left of the insertion point, and **Delete** gets rid of the character to the right of the insertion point. Well, that's okay, but it could get pretty tedious if you have a lot to delete.

Fortunately, Word is no slouch in this area, either. There are several methods for deleting text—you'll probably end up using different ones depending on your needs.

You can delete text using the keyboard or the mouse. As with moving the insertion point, using keystrokes can often be easier and faster than switching to the mouse. The main advantage of the mouse methods is that you don't have to remember a particular keystroke combination. For now, we'll try a little of both. (I'll even throw in some shortcut menu action.)

To delete text:

1. Place your insertion point just past the word *now.*
2. Press **Ctrl+Backspace** to delete the entire word. **Ctrl+Backspace** always deletes an entire word when the insertion point is located just past the word. If the insertion point is in the middle of a word, pressing **Ctrl+Backspace** deletes from your insertion point to the beginning of the word. You can delete several words by holding down the **Ctrl** key while you press the **Backspace** key as many times as you want. Doing this deletes words from the insertion point backward. For example, if you held down the **Ctrl** key after you deleted the word *now* and pressed the **Backspace** key four more times, you would delete the words *our new fashion breakthrough.*

   To delete words from the insertion point forward, use **Ctrl+Delete** instead of **Ctrl+Backspace**. **Ctrl+Delete** works just like **Ctrl+Backspace** in reverse. If your insertion point is in the middle of a word, **Ctrl+Delete** deletes the remainder of the word from the insertion point forward. If the insertion point is between words, **Ctrl+Delete** deletes the next word. Using the example in the previous paragraph, if you used **Ctrl+Delete** to delete the word *now* and then held down the **Ctrl** key while you pressed the **Delete** key four times, you would delete the words *women will be able.*
3. Move your mouse pointer into the left margin area next to the sentence that begins *I will call you,* and click the left mouse button. (You can tell you're in the margin when the mouse pointer changes from an I-beam to an arrow.) Notice that the entire sentence is selected: it has a dark box around it, and the letters appear in reverse color, as shown in Figure 5.4. Clicking in the left margin next to a line of text selects the entire line.

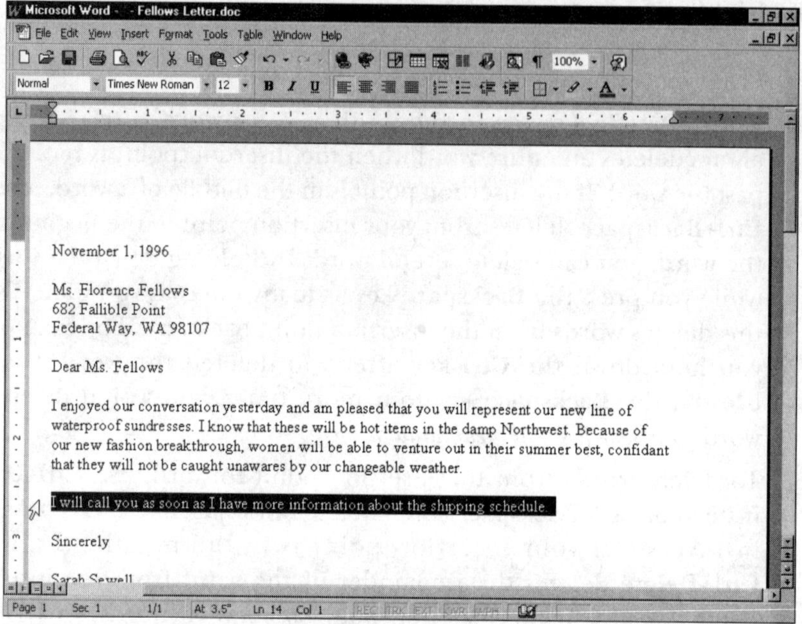

Figure 5.4 *The entire line is selected.*

5. Press the **Delete** key. The entire sentence is deleted. But notice there's some empty space where the sentence used to be. That's because the paragraph that contained the sentence is still there. Press the **Delete** key again to delete the paragraph.

ROADMAP

Chapter 6, "Moving and Copying Text," gets into a lot more detail on different methods of selecting text. The main thing to note here is that, once text has been selected, you can always delete it by pressing **Delete**.

Undo and Redo (Or Oops! I Didn't Mean to Do That)

So, you selected a bunch of text, and just as your finger hit the **Delete** key, you said to yourself, "I didn't want to delete that sentence!" Happens all the time. That's why those lovely Word folks gave you **Undo**. Whenever you say Oops!, think *Undo*.

Undo doesn't just undelete text, it can reverse almost any editing change, including fancy formatting stuff. For example, if you delete a sentence and then type a new word, choosing **Undo** *deletes the new word* rather than undeleting the sentence, because entering the new word was your last editing change. And if you add a border to a page and then decide you don't want it, **Undo** does the job for you. Anything that changes the contents or formatting of your document can be undone.

SHORTCUT

You can actually use **Undo** as a deletion shortcut. For example, if you've just typed a sentence and change your mind, choose **Undo** and the sentence is gone.

Because **Undo** reverses your most recent editing actions, it can be used to delete or restore text or formatting codes—it all depends on what you did last. And if you want to undo the **Undo**, there's a **Redo** feature.

To undo or redo editing actions:

1. Type a few words so that you can see what happens when you choose **Undo**.
2. Click the **Undo** button on the Standard toolbar. Voilá! The text you just typed is gone. You can also choose **Undo** from the Edit menu or press **Ctrl+Z**. Notice that the **Undo** command on the Edit menu and the ToolTip for the **Undo** button both say *Undo Typing* instead of just *Undo.* The menu and ToolTip text for **Undo** and **Redo** change to reflect the type of action you're undoing or redoing. The command name changes to *Can't Undo* if Word can't undo your most recent action.

   Typing a bunch of text counts as a single action unless you interrupt your typing by clicking somewhere else in the document or performing another action like making a word bold or italic.

NOTE

Don't forget—you can always figure out what a toolbar button does by positioning your mouse pointer over the button and looking at the ToolTip.

3. Now what if you want those pearls of wisdom you typed back on-screen? Simple. Just click the **Redo** button on the Standard toolbar. You can also choose **Redo** from the Edit menu or press **Ctrl+Y**).

Undoing More than One Action

If you find that you've really messed up and want to undo or redo everything you did back to a certain point, no problem:

- Each time you click on the **Undo** button (or choose **Undo** from the Edit menu or press **Ctrl+Z**), Word undoes an additional action in sequence. For example, if you typed the word **important** and then applied bold formatting to the word, choosing **Undo** once would undo the bold formatting because that's the most recent action. Choosing **Undo** again would delete the word *important,* because that's the next most recent action. You can continue choosing **Undo** until you get back to the point you want. (If you want to redo, substitute the **Redo** command for **Undo** in the preceding instructions.) When there's nothing more to undo or redo, the menu command or button ToolTip will tell you *Can't Undo* or *Can't Redo.*
- You can undo or redo several actions at one time by clicking the arrow next to the **Undo** or **Redo** button on the Standard toolbar. This opens a list like the one in Figure 5.5, which shows the actions available for undoing or redoing. Scroll down the list and select the command that's as far back as you want to go. Before you release the mouse button, the list shows how many actions you'll be undoing.

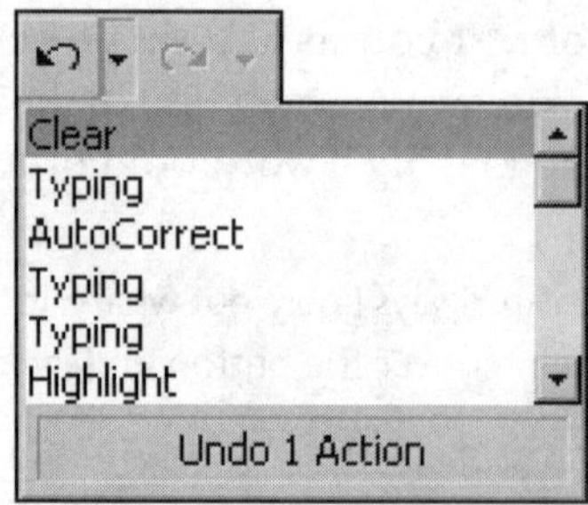

Figure 5.5 *This list allows you to undo multiple actions.*

Don't rely on **Undo** to solve all your problems. A change you made ten minutes ago may or may not be available for undoing. And even if it is, getting back to it may require you to undo a lot of stuff you'd rather keep. Saving frequently and undoing right away when you make a mistake are the best options.

To undo multiple actions at once:

1. Type a couple of lines of text.
2. Delete several words or phrases, add some additional text (a few words will do), and then make a couple more deletions.
3. Click the arrow next to the Undo button on the Standard toolbar to open the list shown in Figure 5.5. Your list won't look exactly like mine, but it should have several actions listed.
4. Move your mouse pointer to one of the actions in the Undo list (any action but the first one), but don't click before you notice that all the actions above the one you selected are also highlighted. That's because Word can't undo or redo something you did several steps ago without also undoing or redoing the actions that brought you to that point.

Closing a Document without Saving

In the Delete and Undo sections, you probably messed around with your document quite a bit. Sometimes a document gets so messed up that you just wish you could start over. Well, you can. Remember that everything you type exists only in the computer's temporary memory until you save it. That means you can close the document without saving at any time, and any changes you've made will be lost. That can sometimes be a good thing. The next time you open the document, it'll be just the way it was before you made all those changes. Let's try this with **Fellows Letter**.

To close a document without saving:

1. Choose **Close** from the File menu (or press **Ctrl+F4**).
2. If the dialog box shown in Figure 5.6 displays, choose **No** to close the document without saving the changes.

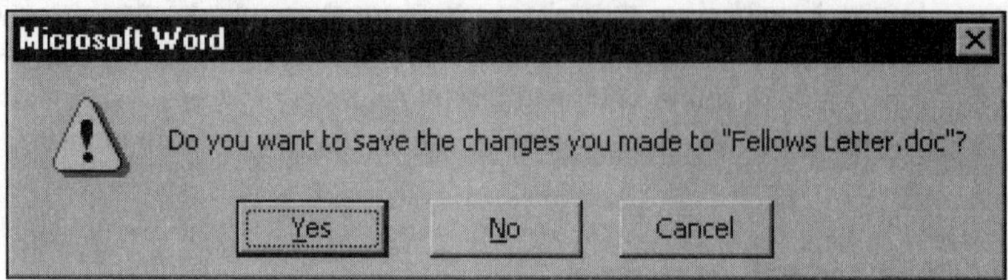

Figure 5.6 *This dialog box is displayed if any changes have been made since the last time the document was saved.*

3. Open **Fellows Letter** again. (If you need a little help, refer to the section on opening a document earlier in this chapter.) Notice that all the stuff you did since the last time you saved is gone.

Saving

We talked briefly about saving in Chapter 1. Now it's time to jump in a little further. As I've mentioned (and will probably mention many more times), frequent saving is very, very important. In fact, now that you know how to close a document without saving, you have a pair of tools that can really free you to experiment with Word without fear. As long as you save your document before you do anything drastic or try a feature you're not sure of, you can always close the document without saving and go back to the original version if things don't turn out.

Where do My Documents Go?

When you install Word, it creates a folder called **My Documents**. Unless you specify something else, that's where your documents go when you save them. If you haven't changed Word's default location for documents, all the files you create in this book will end up in the **My Documents** folder. Both the Open and Save dialog boxes should automatically default to that folder. If you have a problem finding your documents, you (or some trying-to-be-helpful friend) may have switched folders. For more information about finding documents in different folders, read Chapter 14, "Managing Files and Folders."

Naming Documents

For **Fellows Letter**, I told you what to name the file, but I didn't give you any information to help you name your own files. As I told you earlier, you can include up to 255 characters in a filename, so you have room to be quite descriptive. There are only a couple of rules to follow:

- You can use any symbol except the following:

  `* / < > ? " : |`

  Don't worry too much about which symbols you can and can't use. If you try to use a symbol that Word won't accept as part of a valid filename, the **Save** operation won't be completed and you'll be left with your insertion point in the Name text box, where you can try again.

- Avoid using the following extensions: **COM**, **EXE**, **BIN**, **SYS**, and **BAT**. These are extensions that DOS and other programs use for special files, such as the ones that start programs.

NOTE

You can type a filename in either uppercase or lowercase letters or even mix up the cases; it doesn't make any difference.

Suggestions

As long as you follow the rules, anything goes as far as naming files. It's a good idea to develop a file-naming system that works for you. When you look at a list of files, it should be easy to find the one you want. The following suggestions might help:

- You can use numbers in a filename. You might want to use numbers to identify filenames by date. For example, you could identify a series of meetings as **Board Meeting 3-12-96**, **Board Meeting 4-18-96**, etc.
- Be consistent with your filenames. For example, don't name one meeting file **11-12 Meeting** and the next one **Meeting December**.

Word uses a default extension of **DOC**. This extension is used for your documents unless you specify something else. With the ability to have 255-character filenames, you don't really need to add your own file extensions. Leaving the **DOC** extension enables Windows 95 to recognize the document as a Word file.

Saving an Existing Document

Earlier in this chapter, I had you save **Fellows Letter** by clicking the **Save** button on the toolbar. In Chapter 3, I told you that the toolbars are usually the quickest way to access features, and clicking on the **Save** icon is definitely quick. When you're typing along, however, it may be easier to press a couple of keys than to reach for the mouse.

Ctrl+S is the keystroke shortcut for **Save**. It can become almost automatic to press **Ctrl+S** every so often without missing a beat. Whichever method you prefer, get in the habit of saving often.

Saving a Document with a Different Name

Sometimes you might want to use a document for a different purpose. Let's say you really like **Fellows Letter**, and you want to use it as a sort of blueprint for another letter. There are methods for copying part of the text to another document, but it can be easier just to give the document a different name and then make the changes you want.

To give a document a different name:

1. Choose **Save As** from the File menu. The Save As dialog box is displayed with the current filename selected in the File name text box, as shown in Figure 5.7.

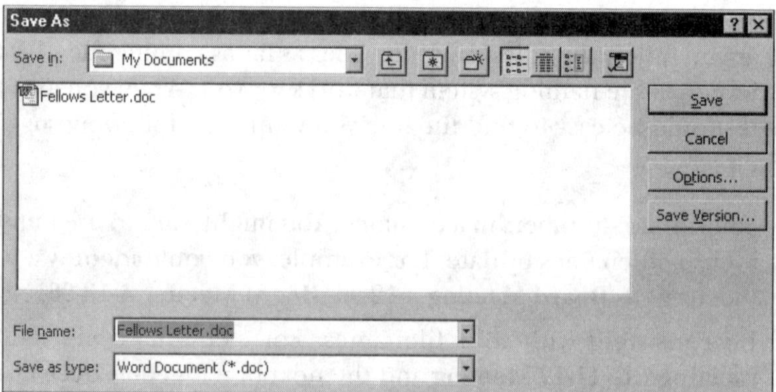

***Figure 5.7** The Save As dialog box.*

2. As soon as you start typing, the old filename disappears. You could type in the new name, but in this case we just want to change the name slightly, so there's no need to retype the whole thing. Click inside the

text box to deselect (remove the highlighting from) the filename. Move the insertion point just past the word *Letter*, then press the **Spacebar** and type the number **1**. The text in the File name text box should now read *Fellows Letter 1.doc.*

3. Click **Save** (or press **Enter**).

You now have a new document that contains the text from **Fellows Letter**. You can change the new document in any way you like without affecting the original **Fellows Letter**.

Open as Copy

The **Save As** procedure I just told you about works great, but in Word there's an even better way to accomplish the same thing. You can make a copy of the document directly from the Open dialog box. That way you never even have to touch the original document, so you can't inadvertently mess it up.

To make a copy of a document:

1. Choose **Open** from the File menu to display the Open dialog box.
2. Select the file you want to copy. For this example, select **Fellows Letter**.
3. Click the **Commands and Settings** button (at the right end of the dialog box toolbar) to open the menu shown in Figure 5.8.

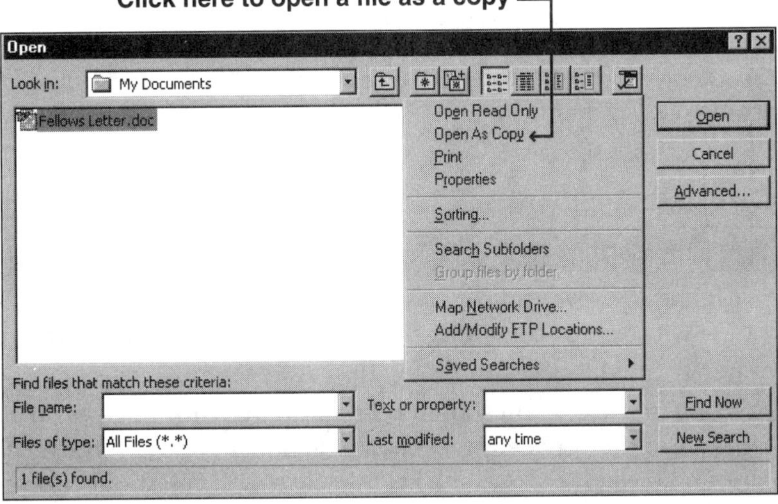

Figure 5.8 *The Open dialog box with the Commands and Settings menu opened.*

4. Choose **Open As Copy**.

When the document opens, notice that its name on the Word title bar appears as *Copy of Fellows Letter.* That is the new document's actual name, so you can edit the file without affecting the original **Fellows Letter**. If you want to change the file's name, use the techniques I just gave you for saving a file with a different name.

Open Read-Only

If you choose **Open Read Only** instead of **Open As Copy** from the Commands and Settings menu in the Open dialog box, Word opens the document in *read-only mode.* That means you can edit the document, but Word won't let you save it with its original name. This is another great way of keeping yourself from inadvertently saving over a file you didn't mean to change. If you choose **Save** with a file that's been opened as a copy, you get a message like the one in Figure 5.9.

Figure 5.9 This message tells you the file is read-only.

When you choose **OK**, the Save As dialog box opens and you are forced to give the document a new name.

FROM HERE...

We're about to move into deeper waters (but not too deep). In the next chapter, you'll learn how to move and copy blocks of text to different locations, and in Chapter 7, "Character Formatting," we'll start adding some pizzazz to the page with tabs, indents, bold, and underline.

Before you move on, you should be comfortable with what we covered in this chapter. You should be able to open a document, move through it using the mouse and the keyboard, and add and delete text. You should also be able to recover (remember the Oops! feature) when you delete text by mistake or want to reverse an editing action. And you can close a document without saving if you've made changes that you can't recover from with **Undo**. Finally, you learned more about saving: you understand filenames, you know how to save a document while you're working on it, and you know how to save a document with a different name and open it as a copy or in read-only mode.

CHAPTER 6

Moving and Copying Text

Let's talk about:

- Selecting text
- Understanding the Clipboard
- Cutting, copying, and pasting
- Using drag and drop

So, you can add new text and delete text you don't want; in this chapter, you'll start to see the real power of Word. Selecting (*highlighting*) text is the springboard for innumerable nifty tricks. When you want to delete text, format a word, or make other changes, the first thing you have to do is tell Word which text you want to change—you do that by selecting the text. Once the text is selected, you can do all sorts of things to it. We'll talk about all the cool things you can do with selected text, and you'll move and copy blocks of text all over the place.

Before You Start

Open **Fellows Letter 1** to give yourself something to play with in this chapter. As I show you how to use various selection, move, and copy techniques, try them on this document. Go ahead—mess it up. If you practice every time I give you a set of steps or a new way to do something, you'll be a pro in no time. Then, at the end of the chapter, you can close the document without saving it, and your original **Fellows Letter 1** will still be intact.

ROADMAP

See the "Open Read-Only" section in Chapter 5 for another alternative.

Selecting Text

Pay attention here. Once you learn about selecting text, you'll use this skill throughout the book. After you select a block of text, you can apply almost any Word feature to that block. For example, you can change the *font* (type style) for a particular section of text, or you can choose to spell check only a selected block of text (this can come in handy when you've added text to a document and don't want to spell check what you've already done).

As you progress through Word's features, you'll rely heavily on selecting. And because selecting text is a major component of moving and copying, I figure this is as good a place as any to show you the basics.

NOTE

So far we've just worked with text, so that's what we'll talk about in this chapter. But anything that can be put into a Word document can be selected, moved, or copied. That includes formatting, graphic images, tables, and columns. The selection techniques in this chapter work for any Word object.

As with deleting text and moving around in a document, selecting can be done with both the keyboard and the mouse, and one method might be better than the other at various times. I'll show you both methods, and where appropriate, I'll give you my preferences. (Actually, I'll probably give you my preferences whether or not it's appropriate.)

Selecting Text with the Mouse

The basic method for selecting text with the mouse is really easy, but it's not necessarily the most efficient. You just hold down the left mouse button and drag it across the text you want to select. When you've selected what you want, release the mouse button. This method works, and its main advantage is that you don't have to remember any special techniques, but it's not very precise. You have to pay close attention as you move the mouse; it's easy to select too much or too little. I'm not saying you shouldn't use this technique—just that the other methods are usually quicker and even easier.

When you do drag to select text, Word automatically selects word by word rather than character by character. Here's what happens. Say you position your mouse pointer in the middle of a word and begin to drag. At first, only the portion of the word following your insertion point is selected. But as soon as you drag past the end of the word, Word selects the entire word. If you then drag onto another word, that whole word will be selected. The selection highlight appears to jump from word to word as you drag.

If you want to be able to select character by character, hold down the **Alt** key as you drag. Table 6.1 shows mouse shortcuts for selecting text.

Table 6.1 Mouse shortcuts for selecting text.

To select	Do this
A word	With the insertion point anywhere in the word, double-click on the word.
A sentence	Hold down the **Ctrl** key while you click anywhere in the sentence.
A line	Click in the left margin area next to the line. When you're in the margin area, the mouse pointer changes from an I-beam to a right-pointing arrow.
A paragraph	Double-click in the left margin area next to the paragraph.
Several paragraphs	Double-click in the left margin next to the first paragraph you want to select and continue to hold down the mouse button while you drag up or down in the margin area to select additional paragraphs.
The whole document	Quadruple-click anywhere in the left margin area (make sure to move the mouse pointer until it turns into a right-pointing arrow).

WARNING

If you start typing with text selected, what you type replaces the selected text. This can save time by eliminating the need to delete the existing text. But it can also be a gotcha. If you select a bunch of text and then start typing without putting your brain in gear, that text is gone. If that's not what you intended, choose **Undo** immediately to bring back the text that was selected.

The Best Shortcut of All: The Shift+Click Trick

That heading's not too opinionated, is it? Anyway, in my (maybe not so humble) opinion, if you don't remember any other methods for selecting text, remember this one. It can be used for any chunk of text, and it doesn't involve fancy moves like quadruple-clicking while standing on your head and rubbing your tummy. Here it is:

1. Place your insertion point where you want the selection to begin.
2. Move your mouse pointer to where you want the selection to end (but don't click yet). You can use any of the movement shortcuts you

learned in the last chapter; it doesn't matter how you move to the end—just get there.

3. Hold down the **Shift** key while you click the left mouse button.
4. If you didn't select quite enough, just move the mouse pointer down to where you want it and **Shift+click** again. It's easy to extend the selection. This also works in reverse—to decrease the size of your selection, position your mouse pointer in the middle of the selected area (where you want the selection to end) and **Shift+click**

   You can also increase or decrease the size of a selection by holding down the **Shift** key while you drag the mouse pointer to the right or left.

That's it. I probably use this method more than any other. I don't have to worry about whether I want to select a sentence, a paragraph, or some other chunk of text. Having categorically stated that this is absolutely the best way to select text, I must admit that there are a couple of situations where another method works better.

Shift+clicking works great for most text chunks, with one exception that I can think of: selecting the whole document. If you know you want to select the entire document, there's no need to go through the process of moving the mouse pointer just so you can **Shift+click** at the end of the document. In this situation, the simplest and quickest technique is a keystroke shortcut: **Ctrl+A**.

Selecting Text with the Keyboard

If you don't have a mouse, you've still got many options for selecting text. In fact, you mousers might want to take heed of some of these shortcuts.

The key (and I mean that literally) to selecting with the keyboard is **Shift**. Use the **Shift** key in conjunction with other keyboard combinations to select various portions of text. Table 6.2 lists several keystroke combinations you can use to select text.

NOTE

You can use **F8** or the **EXT** button on the Status Bar instead of the **Shift** key. Pressing **F8** or double-clicking the **EXT** button turns **Extend Selection** mode on. With **Extend Selection** mode active, you can use any of the keystrokes in Table 6.2 (without holding down the **Shift** key). To turn **Extend Selection** mode off, press the **Esc** key or double-click the **EXT** button again.

Table 6.2 Keyboard shortcuts for selecting text.

To select	Use these keys
One character to the right	**Shift+Right Arrow**
One character to the left	**Shift+Left Arrow**
One word to the right	**Shift+Ctrl+Right Arrow**
One word to the left	**Shift+Ctrl+Left Arrow**
From the insertion point down one line	**Shift+Down Arrow**
From the insertion point up one line	**Shift+Up Arrow**
From the insertion point to the end of the current line	**Shift+End**
From the insertion point back to the beginning of the current line	**Shift+Home**
From the insertion point to the end of the current paragraph	**Shift+Ctrl+Down Arrow**
From the insertion point to the beginning of the current paragraph	**Shift+Ctrl+Up Arropw**
From the insertion point to the end of the document	**Shift+Ctrl+End**
From the insertion point to the beginning of the document	**Shift+Ctrl+Home**
The entire document	**Ctrl+A**

WARNING

If Word keeps selecting text whenever you press an arrow key or click a mouse button, you probably have **Extend Selection** mode turned on. Just press the **Esc** key or double-click the **EXT** button on the Status Bar to turn it off. You can tell when **Extend Selection** mode is on because the **EXT** button on the Status Bar is active—when **Extend Selection** mode is off, the button is dimmed.

Deselecting Text

No matter how large an area of text you've selected, you can deselect it by clicking anywhere in the document. If you don't have a mouse, you can press one of the arrow keys.

WHAT CAN YOU DO WITH SELECTED TEXT?

Here are a few of the operations you can perform on a block of selected text. You can:

- Save it
- Spell check it
- Delete it
- Move or copy it
- Change its formatting
- Print it
- Change the text from uppercase to lowercase (or vice versa)

To do any of these, just select the text you want the change to apply to and then implement the feature. As you've already seen, to delete text you select it and press the **Delete** key. It's just as easy to use selected text with other features; you'll see for yourself as we get to the different features in the following chapters. Now, let's do some selecting, moving, and copying.

Moving and Copying Text

Word makes it easy to shuffle text around to your heart's content. You can take a block of text and put it wherever you want, even in another document. Word calls the process of copying and moving text *cutting* (or *copying*) and *pasting*.

These terms come from the old days of manual page layout and paste-up, when you literally had to cut out a piece of text using an X-acto knife. Then you took that piece and used rubber cement or wax to paste it in a new location. You had to use rulers and stuff to make sure you pasted it in straight. Fun, huh? And not very practical, except in a commercial environment.

ROADMAP

For more about copying text between documents, see Chapter 23, "Working with Multiple Documents."

But now, through the magic of modern technology, cutting and pasting are yours to command with just a few mouse clicks or keystrokes.

Before we get into the mechanics of cutting, copying, and pasting, you need to know what happens to the text when you cut or copy it.

The Clipboard

Windows has a special area that stores the last thing you cut or copied. When you cut or copy something from Word for Windows, it goes into the Windows *Clipboard.* Because the Clipboard is shared by all Windows programs, anything in the Clipboard can be pasted into any Windows program.

The Clipboard can hold only one thing at a time. Whenever you cut or copy something, it replaces whatever was in the Clipboard before. When you choose the **Paste** command, whatever is in the Clipboard is moved back into your document.

ROADMAP

Even though the Clipboard holds only one thing at a time, Word has a special feature called the *Spike* that allows you to cut chunks of text from different areas or even from different documents and then paste them back into a document as a unit. The Spike can be useful if you want to compile different sections of a document and put them in a new location. (The Spike is covered a little later in this chapter.)

Cutting vs. Copying vs. Deleting

Once you select a block of text, you can choose to either cut or copy it to the Clipboard. When you cut text, it is removed from the document and placed in the Clipboard. When you copy text, the original text stays where it is and a copy of it is placed in the Clipboard. That's the only difference. And it's important to mention deleting here, because it's easy to confuse deleting text with cutting it. When you delete text, it's gone—the only way to get it back is with the **Undo** feature. When you cut text, it's not really gone; it's just taken a trip to the Clipboard.

Drag and Drop

Drag and drop is a Windows technique that makes moving and copying super simple. With this technique, pasting isn't a separate step; it's part of the same process. Dragging and dropping works best when the selection you're cutting or copying and the place you want to move it to are both visible in your editing window.

To move text with drag and drop:

1. Select the text.
2. Hold down the left mouse button while you drag the text to a new location. Notice that a box with a dotted border attaches itself to the mouse pointer.
3. Release the mouse button, and the text is pasted at the insertion point.

To copy text with drag and drop:

1. Select the text.
2. Hold down the **Ctrl** key while you drag the text to its new location. Notice that a box with a plus sign is added to the box icon attached to the mouse pointer.
3. Release the mouse button; a copy of the text is pasted at the insertion point, and the original text remains where it was.

Move and Copy Methods

Dragging and dropping is usually the easiest way to move or copy text. There are a few situations, however, when other methods might work better. The most obvious, of course, is if you don't have a mouse—you can't drag and drop with the keyboard. In addition, if you're working in a long document and you want to move or copy some text to a location several pages away or if you are selecting a really large block of text, it can be a pain to drag the selection over that distance. Instead, try the techniques that follow. I'm not going to tell you which of the following three methods is best—it's a matter of preference.

If you have a mouse, the shortcut menu and toolbar are both good choices. With the shortcut menu, you have to activate the menu and then make a selection. With the toolbar, you just click on an icon. On the other hand, you have to move the mouse farther to get to the toolbar. I suggest you try both methods and see which works better for you. The third method, using the keyboard, is the obvious choice if you don't have a mouse. And if you're a speedy typist and you like to keep your hands on the keyboard, the keyboard shortcuts can save you time even if you have a mouse.

Using the shortcut menu to cut and paste:

1. Select the text.
2. Click the right mouse button anywhere in the selected text to display the shortcut menu shown in Figure 6.1.

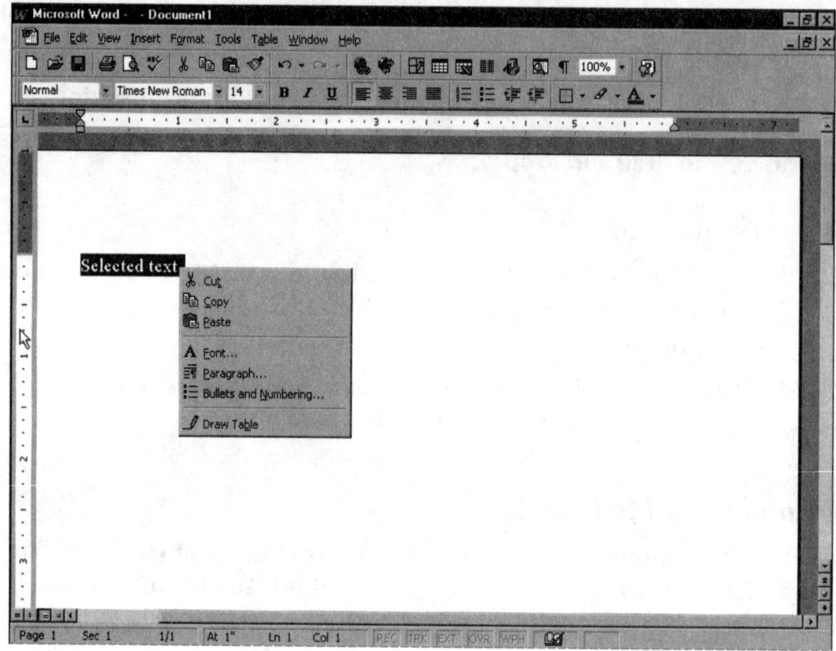

Figure 6.1 This Shortcut menu is displayed when you click the right mouse button in the document window when text is selected.

3. Choose **Cut** if you want to move the text to the Clipboard or **Copy** to leave the text where it is and place a copy in the Clipboard.
4. Move the insertion point to where you want the text to be inserted.
5. Activate the shortcut menu by clicking the right mouse button anywhere in the document window.
6. Choose **Paste**.

Using the toolbar to cut and paste:

1. Select the text.
2. Click on the **Cut** button on the Standard toolbar (the button looks like a pair of scissors) to move the text to the Clipboard or click on the

Copy button (looks like two little pieces of paper) to leave the text where it is and place a copy in the Clipboard.

3. Move the insertion point to where you want the text to be inserted.
4. Click on the **Paste** button (a little clipboard with a piece of paper attached).

Using the keyboard to cut and paste:

1. Select the text.
2. Press **Ctrl+X** to move the text to the Clipboard or **Ctrl+C** to leave the text where it is and place a copy in the Clipboard.
3. Move the insertion point to where you want the text to be inserted.
4. Press **Ctrl+V** to paste the text into your document.

Ctrl+X, **Ctrl+C**, and **Ctrl+V** are all keyboard shortcuts for items that can also be accessed through the pull-down menu. Any time you don't remember the shortcuts, you can choose **Cut**, **Copy**, or **Paste** from the Edit menu.

Here's another quick keystroke shortcut for moving an entire paragraph. Just place your insertion point anywhere in the paragraph and press **Alt+Shift+Up Arrow** key to move the paragraph up or **Alt+Shift+Down Arrow** key to move the paragraph down. This shortcut also works for multiple paragraphs if you select them first.

Using the Spike

As mentioned earlier, the Spike allows you to cut text from separate parts of a document or different documents and to insert them as a group somewhere else.

To move text using the Spike:

1. Select the text.
2. Press **Ctrl+F3**. Word cuts the selected text and places it in the Spike.
3. To add additional items to the Spike, repeat steps 1 and 2. Word continues adding items to the Spike until you clear it.

To insert the Spike's contents:

1. Position your insertion point where you want the text.

2. Press **Ctrl+Shift+F3** or begin typing the word **spike**. As you type, notice the ScreenTip containing a sample of the Spike's contents that appears above the word. As soon as you see the ScreenTip, press **Enter** to insert the contents of the Spike at your insertion point location.

You can't copy items into the Spike. If you select text and press **Ctrl+F3,** the text is immediately cut and placed in the Spike. To get it back if you didn't intend to cut it, use the **Undo** feature.

To empty the Spike:

1. Choose **AutoText** from the Insert menu, then choose **AutoText** from the cascading menu.
2. Select **Spike** in the AutoText list, as shown in Figure 6.2, and click the **Delete** button.

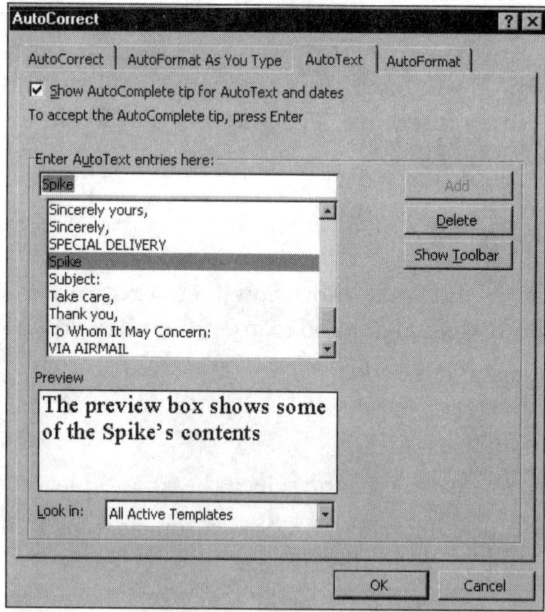

Figure 6.2 *Select the **Spike** entry from the AutoText list.*

When you move text to the Spike, Word actually creates an AutoText entry called *Spike*. Emptying the Spike just means deleting the AutoText entry. AutoText, a great way of automating the process of entering text that you would normally have to type over and over, is covered in Chapter 18.

From Here...

In the next chapter, we'll add some formatting to your text. Before you move on, make sure you feel comfortable selecting text. Think of selecting as your base camp; you'll always come back to it and branch out from there. The cutting, copying, and pasting techniques you learned in this chapter will also stand you in good stead. All the elements that you add to your document can be dragged, dropped, cut, copied, and pasted.

SECTION II

Beyond the Basics

CHAPTER 7

Character Formatting

Let's talk about:

- ✦ Changing text appearance
- ✦ Changing text to uppercase or lowercase
- ✦ Applying multiple formatting effects
- ✦ Using Word's highlighter
- ✦ Changing character spacing options

In this chapter, you'll learn all sorts of ways to make your text look pretty. You can add emphasis with bold or italic formatting, change the text's size or style, adjust the spacing of characters, and even add a splash of color.

ROADMAP

Chapter 12, "A Look at Fonts," covers the concepts of text formatting in more depth. It gets into design considerations and describes fonts and font families. For now, all you need to know is that a *font* is a set of characters in a particular type style and size.

Changing Text Appearance

There are any number of ways you can change the appearance of your text. We'll start with bold, underline, and italic, because they're all fairly common—and all just a click away on the Formatting toolbar. Move your mouse pointer over the Formatting toolbar and see if you can pick out the **Bold**, **Italic**, and **Underline** buttons. (If the Formatting toolbar isn't turned on, choose **Toolbars** from the View menu and click on **Formatting**.)

You can turn on any of these formatting options before you type, or you can apply them to selected text. We'll try it both ways.

NOTE

You use the same techniques for any of the character formatting options. So when I talk about turning off italic formatting, for example, I'm not just talking about italic. You would do exactly the same thing to turn off bold or underline.

To apply character formatting with the toolbar as you type:

1. Place your insertion point where you want to begin applying the formatting.
2. Click the button for the format you want. For this example, click the **Bold** button on the Formatting toolbar.
3. Start typing. As you type, notice that your text is bold and that the **Bold** button on the toolbar looks like it's pressed in. For this example, type **This text is bold**.

4. To turn off the formatting, just click the button again. For this example, click the **Bold** button and notice that the button is no longer depressed.
5. Type **This text is not bold** and notice that the text you type after turning off the formatting is back to normal.

KEYBOARD

Word has built-in keyboard shortcuts for bold, italic, and underline. To turn on bold formatting, press **Ctrl+B**. For italic, it's **Ctrl+I**, and underline is **Ctrl+U**. The keyboard shortcuts work just like the toolbar buttons. To turn on the formatting, press the keystroke combination; to turn off the formatting, press the same keystroke combination again.

To apply character formatting to selected text with the toolbar:

1. Select the text to which you want to apply the formatting.
2. Click the appropriate button—**Bold**, **Italic**, or **Underline**. Notice that only the selected text takes on the formatting. Any text before or after the selected text retains its normal appearance.

Applying More than One Effect

What if you want to bold, underline, and italicize the same word or phrase? You could select the text and then click on the **Bold**, **Underline**, and **Italic** buttons in succession, but there's an easier way. The Font dialog box lets you change all the appearance items you want at once. Not only that, the dialog box gives you access to even more appearance options.

WARNING

Be careful when applying effects and changing type sizes and styles. Your document can easily end up looking like a ransom note. Use your own judgment, but don't overdo it with too many different options. For a good example of going too far, take a look at Figure 12.8 in Chapter 12. Normally you wouldn't use this many type styles and sizes and apply bold, italic, and underline in these combinations and to this extent (unless you really are writing a ransom note).

To apply multiple formatting effects:

1. Choose **Font** from the Format menu to open the Font dialog box. The complete Font dialog box is shown in Figure 7.2 in the following section. Figure 7.1 just shows the Effects check boxes.

Effects
Strikethrough
Double strikethrough
Superscript
Subscript
Shadow
Outline
Emboss
Engrave
Small caps
All caps
Hidden

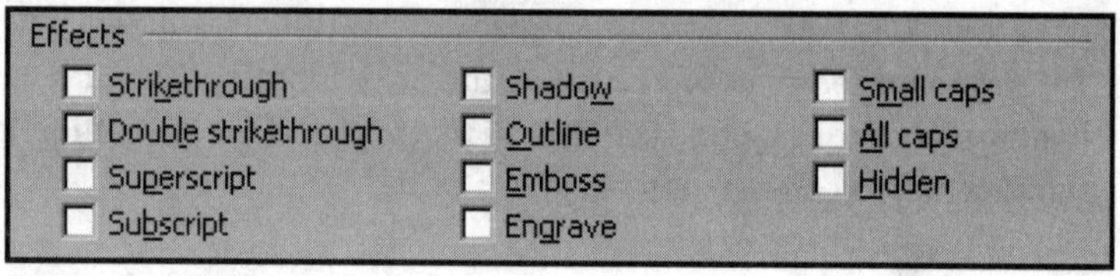

Figure 7.1 The Effects check boxes in the Font dialog box.

2. Select the items you want to use, then click **OK**.

Descriptions and examples of the font effects are given later in this chapter. The main thing to note is that everything's in one place. You can check as many of the boxes as you want and then click **OK**—it's a one-step process.

Applying Fonts

Just like bold, italic, and underline, you can change your type style and size from the Formatting toolbar. The advantage of the Formatting toolbar is quick access to the most common font variations. The advantages of the Fonts dialog box are being able to apply several variations at once and having access to the less common formatting options not found on the Formatting toolbar.

You can apply fonts and other character formatting as you type a document, or you can type the document in the default font and apply the formatting later. Most often, you'll do a combination of these, going over the document later and changing the fonts or sizes of individual selections for the effect you want. Table 7.1 shows how to apply formatting in a document.

Table 7.1 Formatting a document.

To do this	Do this
Format a selection	Select the text and then change the font, size, or other character formatting.
Change formatting as you type	Apply a new format without selecting any text. Nothing in the document changes visibly, but as soon as you start typing, the text uses the new font formatting.
Format a word	Place your insertion point anywhere in the word (without selecting any characters) and make a formatting change. The change is applied to the whole word.

NOTE

What if you apply a formatting change and nothing happens? Here's a possible scenario: if you make a formatting change without any text selected and click somewhere else before returning to the original place and typing, your formatting change is forgotten. If you begin typing immediately after making the formatting change, however, the formatting is applied to your newly typed text.

To change fonts with the Font dialog box:

1. Select the text you want to change or place your insertion point where you the font change to take effect.
2. Choose **Font** from the Format menu to open the Font dialog box shown in Figure 7.2.

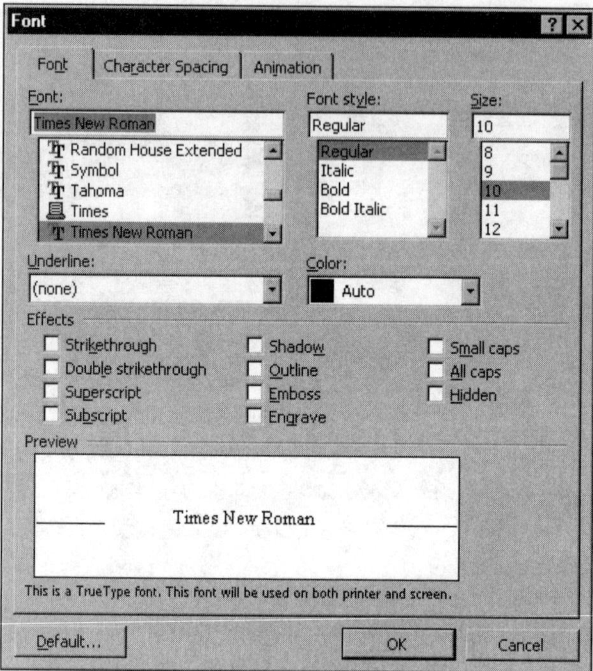

Figure 7.2 The Font dialog box.

3. From the Font list, select the type style you want to use. The font and any other changes you select are reflected immediately in the Preview box. You can get a quick preview of what all your fonts look like by pressing the **Down Arrow** key to move through the fonts in the Font list .
4. Make a selection from the Font Style list.
5. From the Size list, select the point size you want. If the font size you want isn't displayed in the list, you can simply type it in the text box.
6. Apply any other formatting choices and click **OK**. The rest of the formatting options in the dialog box are covered throughout this chapter.

To change fonts with the toolbar:

1. Select the text you want to change or position your insertion point where you want the change to start. If your insertion point is positioned in the middle of a word without anything selected, the change applies to the whole word.

2. Click the **down arrow** next to the Font box on the Formatting toolbar and select a type style from the list shown in Figure 7.3.

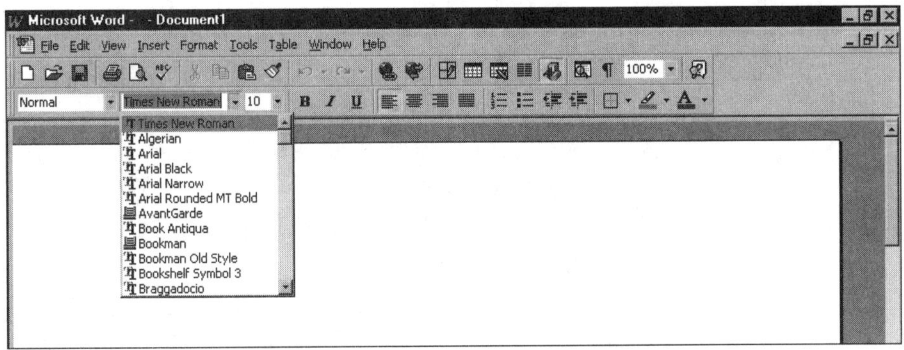

Figure 7.3 *The Font drop-down list.*

All of your fonts are included in this list; the last five fonts you used are listed at the top for quick access.

3. Click the **down arrow** next to the Font Size box and pick a size.

What do the Font Effects do?

Table 7.2 shows a brief description of the different font effects, and Figure 7.4 contains examples of some of the effects.

Table 7.2 *What font effects do.*

THIS EFFECT	DOES THIS
Strikethrough	Places a horizontal line through the middle of the text. In academic writing, strikethroughs are used to indicate material that was crossed out or deleted in revisions of a piece of writing.
Double strikethrough	Same as strikethrough, except a double line is inserted through the text.
Superscript	Makes the character (or selected characters) slightly smaller and places it above the regular text, as in $e = mc^2$.

continued

Table 7.2 continued

THIS EFFECT	DOES THIS
Subscript	Shrinks and lowers the selected characters, as in H_2O.
Shadow	Adds a shadow effect to the text.
Outline	Turns the text into an outline, so all you see is the inner and outer border of each character.
Embossed	Gives the text a 3-D effect, making it look like it's raised off the page.
Engraved	Like embossed in reverse, makes text look like it's pressed into the page.
Small Caps	Makes lowercase text all capital letters and decreases its size. In professional typography, acronyms such as *USA* are generally put in small caps so that their appearance in all capitals won't be of such overwhelming size compared to the text around them. Applying **Small Caps** to letters that are already uppercase has no effect, and **Small Caps** doesn't change numbers, punctuation marks, or other nonalphabetic characters (like @ or %).
All Caps	Displays and prints the text in all capital letters. The text itself is not changed to capital letters: it simply appears and is printed as all capital letters. If you turn off the **All Caps** option, the text returns to whatever combination of upper- and lowercase letters it originally had.
Hidden	Choosing this effect hides the text so it doesn't appear on the screen or in the printed document. If you choose to display hidden text, it appears with a dotted underline. More about controlling hidden text and its uses a little later in this chapter.

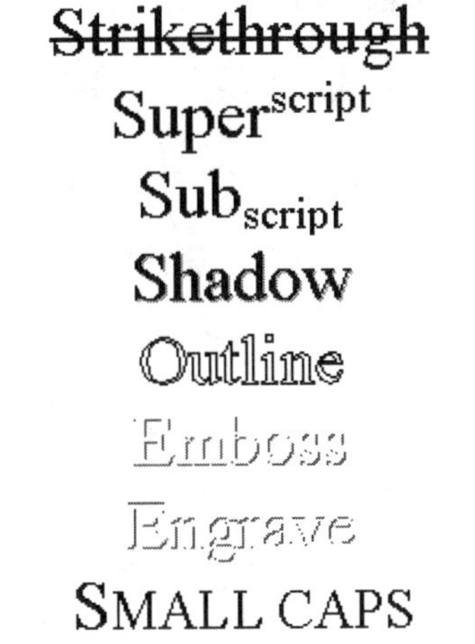

Figure 7.4 *Examples of font effects.*

KEYBOARD

Ctrl+Shift+A	All caps
Ctrl+B	Bold
Ctrl+Shift+H	Hidden
Ctrl+I	Italic
Ctrl+Shift+K	Small caps
Ctrl+=	Subscript
Ctrl+Shift+=	Superscript

Underlining Options

The **Underline** button on the Formatting toolbar places a single line under the selected text. If you want to use a different underline style, open the Font dialog box and make a selection from the Underline drop-down list shown in Figure 7.5.

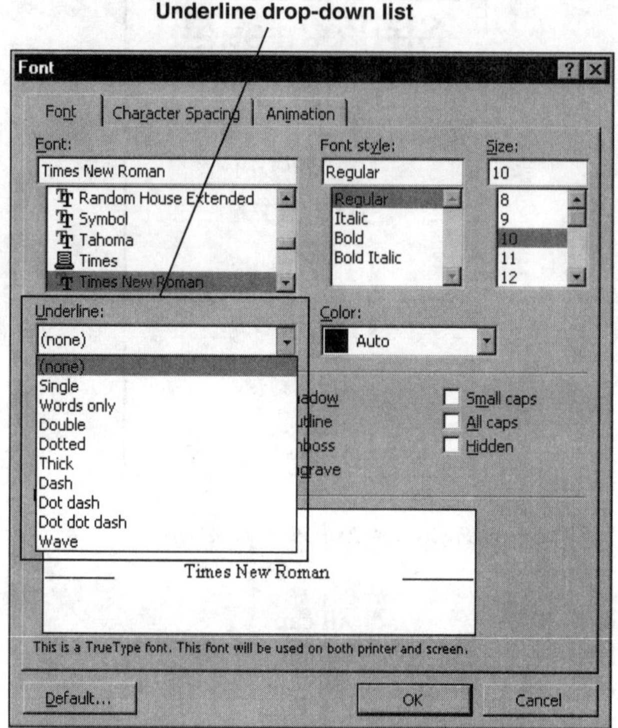

Figure 7.5 The Font dialog box with the Underline drop-down list.

Word has keyboard shortcuts for the following underline options. All of these shortcuts are toggles, which means that the same keystroke turns the option on or off:

Ctrl+U	Single underline
Ctrl+Shift+U	Double underline
Ctrl+Shift+W	Underline words only (no line under spaces)

In most cases, whatever you think you want to underline should probably be made bold or italic for a more professional, polished appearance. There are, however, a few legitimate uses for underlining (Table 7.3 and Figure 7.6).

Table 7.3 Uses for underlining.

UNDERLINE TYPE	PURPOSE
Single	Meets someone else's formatting requirements if their style sheet calls for underlining.
Words Only	Underlines only the text of a selection, but not the spaces or tabs between words.
Double	Marks subtotals or totals in invoices or similar forms, where sums are traditionally marked with a double underline.
Dotted, Dashed, Thick, Dot dash, Dot dot dash, and Wave	Draws attention to a word or selection for some special meaning you want to assign to the marking.

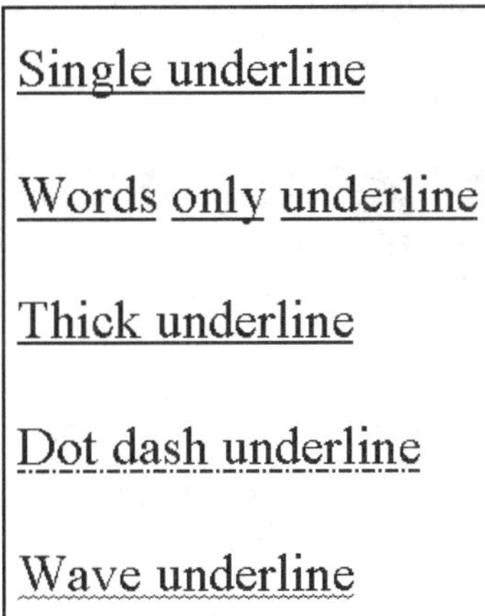

Figure 7.6 Examples of underlining styles.

Animating Text

If you create fancy screen presentations, you might want to take a look at Word's **Animation** feature, which can make your text shimmer, sparkle, or blink.

WARNING

Think about what you're trying to accomplish before you add animation effects to your text. Judicious use of a lighted marquee can add splash to a presentation's title page, but blinking or shimmering text can rapidly drive a person bonkers if they have to look at it for any period of time. If a page contains more than a couple of sentences or will remain visible for more than a few moments, don't annoy your viewers with bouncy text just because you can.

Animation works just like any other font effect—if you turn animation on and start typing, anything you type uses the effect until you turn it off; if you select text and then turn animation on, the effect applies only to the selected text.

To animate text:

1. Place your insertion point where you want the animation to begin or select the text you want to animate.
2. Choose **Font** from the Format menu and select the **Animation** tab in the Font dialog box (Figure 7.7).
3. Select the effect you want to use and click **OK**. Notice that the Preview box shows the result of the selected animation effect, so you can try before you buy.

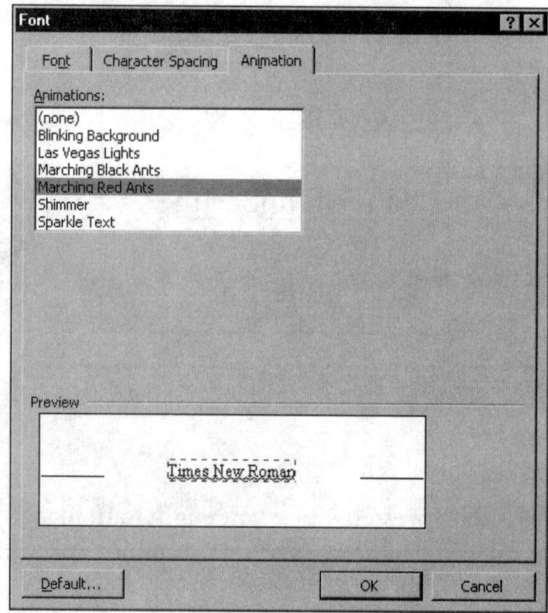

***Figure 7.7** The **Animation** tab in the Font dialog box.*

Highlighting Text

Throw out those yellow markers—with Word's **Highlighting** feature, you can just drag your mouse pointer over text to highlight it in any color you want.

To highlight text:

1. Click the **Highlight** button on the Formatting toolbar. A little highlighting pen attaches itself to your mouse pointer, and the **Highlight** button looks like it's pressed in.
2. Drag the mouse pointer over the text you want to highlight.
3. You can highlight as many sections of text as you want. To turn highlighting off, just click the **Highlight** button again or press the **Esc** key.

You can also select text before you click the **Highlight** button. When you do it this way, the selected text is highlighted, and highlighting is automatically turned off.

By default, Word highlights text in yellow. **To change the highlighter color**:

1. Click the **down arrow** next to the **Highlight** button on the Formatting toolbar.
2. Click on a color in the color palette. Notice that the color splash on the **Highlight** button changes to reflect the color you select.

If you plan to print highlighted text, make sure you use a light highlighter color so that the highlighting doesn't obscure the text (unless you have a color printer).

Getting Rid of Character Formatting

Sometimes you just want to start over—you may have gone way overboard applying different formatting to text and wish you could just wipe the slate clean. Well, you can. Select the text from which you want to remove the formatting and press **Ctrl+Spacebar**.

This returns the text selection to whatever character formatting is specified in your Normal template. But this keystroke won't get rid of highlighting or any character formatting that's part of a paragraph style (see Chapter 20, "Working with Styles," for more information about paragraph styles).

Of course, if you apply formatting and decide right away that it's not what you want, just choose **Undo** from the Edit menu or press **Ctrl+Z**.

Changing Text to Uppercase or Lowercase

Have you ever turned on **Caps Lock** by mistake and typed several lines of text before you realized it? No? You mean I'm the only one again? Oh, well. Anyway, whether you need to change text that's all in caps to lowercase or you decide to change a title to uppercase text, Word can handle that chore with ease.

To change the case of text:

1. Select the text you want to change.
2. Choose **Change Case** from the Format menu to open the Change Case dialog box shown in Figure 7.8.

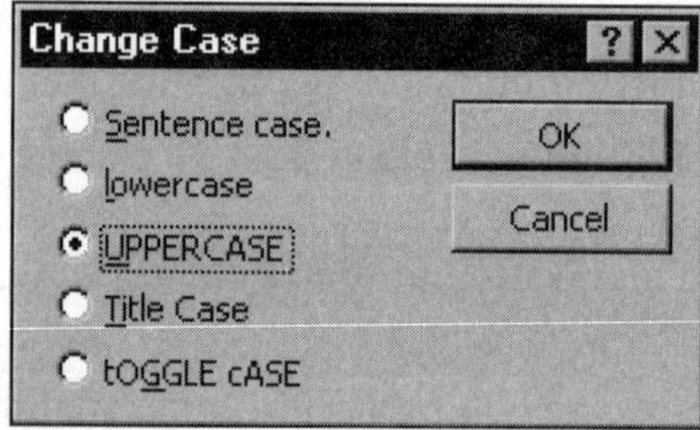

Figure 7.8 The Change Case dialog box.

3. Select the option you want and click **OK**. Lowercase and uppercase are self-explanatory, but here's what the other options do:
   - **Sentence case** capitalizes the first letter of the first word in each sentence in the selection.
   - **Title case** capitalizes the first letter of each word in the selection.
   - **Toggle case** reverses the case of each letter in the selection. This one's great for those occasions when you turn Caps Lock on without realizing it.

KEYBOARD

Select text and then press **Shift+F3** to cycle between sentence case, uppercase, and lowercase. Stop when the text is the way you want it.

Changing Character Spacing Options

Word's character spacing options take us into somewhat advanced territory, but I'll cover them in case you ever need to use them. Without these options, you would have to manually insert a space character between each letter to increase the spacing between characters or shrink the size of the font to reduce the spacing between characters. Word gives you three separate features that allow you to adjust character spacing:

- Increase or decrease the space between all the selected characters, making them look cramped or loose, depending on your setting.
- Raise or lower the characters in relation to the rest of the characters in a line of text.
- Kern the text, which adjusts the spacing between individual pairs of letters, depending on the letter shape.

Loosening or Tightening Text

You may have seen memos where a heading across the top of the page, perhaps the word *MEMORANDUM*, was expanded to put extra space between the letters. The hard (and inefficient) way to do this is to press the **Spacebar** as many times as necessary between each character. The easy way is just to select the whole word and apply a spacing option. If you don't like the way it looks, you can easily adjust the spacing option to suit your preferences. It's hard to make adjustments if you've inserted spaces manually.

You can also condense characters to make sure they fit into a given space. Be careful with this option—it's usually better to have a document that's a few pages longer if the alternative is condensing your text to the point that it's hard to read. However, if you're typing something that will be copied onto a form where it must fit or there's absolutely no choice but to make the text fit, the option to condense text can come in handy.

To loosen or tighten text:

1. Select the text you want to change or place your insertion point where you want the change to begin.
2. Choose **Font** from the Format menu and select the **Character Spacing** tab (shown in Figure 7.9).

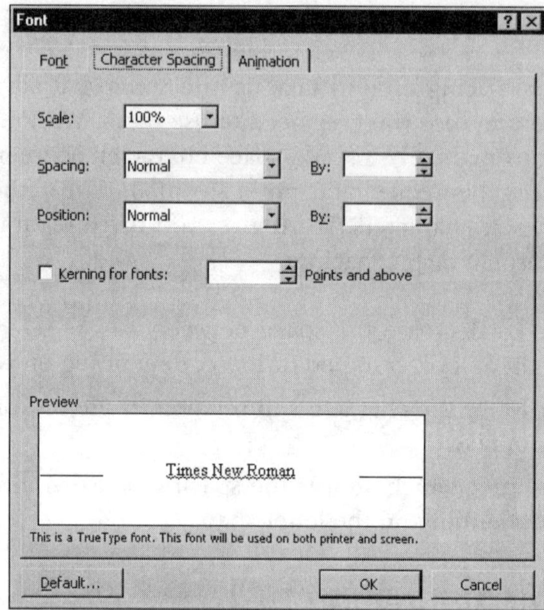

*Figure 7.9 The **Character Spacing** tab in the Font dialog box.*

3. Make a selection from the Spacing drop-down list. **Expanded** loosens the text by adding space between characters. **Condensed** tightens the text by decreasing the space between characters.
4. In the By box next to the Spacing box, specify in points how much you want the text expanded or condensed.
5. Check the Preview box to make sure the effect is what you want, then click **OK**. See Figure 7.10 for examples.

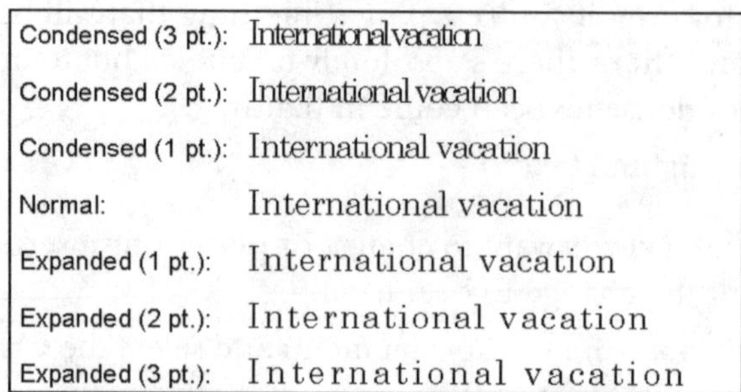

Figure 7.10 Examples of different spacing options.

Raising or Lowering Text on the Line

The option to raise or lower text may seem redundant. Aren't there already subscript and superscript options? Well, this is slightly different. The **Subscript** and **Superscript** options are for standard superscripts and subscripts, where the characters are automatically shrunk in size and raised or lowered to a preset height. When you raise or lower the text with the **Position** option, you have control over exactly how much the characters are raised or lowered, and the character size doesn't change. You can change the font size to exactly what you want, rather than using the preset size and height combinations of the **Subscript** and **Superscript** options.

Don't use this option to get extra space between paragraphs. In the next chapter, "Paragraph Formatting," you'll see that there are better ways to add space between paragraphs.

To raise or lower text on a line:

1. Select the text you want to change or place your insertion point where you want the change to begin.
2. Choose **Font** from the Format menu and select the **Character Spacing** tab.
3. Select **Raised** or **Lowered** from the Position drop-down list.

The text is raised or lowered relative to the rest of the text on the line. If you select an entire line, there's no effect because all the text on the line is raised or lowered to the same extent.

4. In the By box next to the Position box, specify in points how far you want the text raised or lowered.
5. Check the Preview box to make sure the effect is what you want, then click **OK**. Figure 7.11 shows raised and lowered text.

Are you getting dizzy yet?

Figure 7.11 *Raised and lowered text.*

Using Font Kerning

Kerning is a typesetting term that refers to the process of adjusting the amount of space between specified pairs of characters. You can turn on automatic kerning if you want Word to automatically adjust the spacing between character pairs. For each font and point size, only certain pairs of letters are predefined for kerning.

Kerning may sound a bit like the condensed spacing option we just discussed, but it's quite a different animal. When you apply condensed spacing to a selection, everything is tightened up by the same amount, no matter what characters you apply it to. Kerning uses built-in font information to adjust the spacing between particular pairs of letters to make them look more natural.

For example, take the word *Tools*. If the characters were spaced exactly the same distance apart between the left and right edges of each character, the *T* would look funny because the *o* could fit nicely under the *T* without any parts of the letters touching. However, in the word *boar*, the *b* and the *o* can't get much closer together without touching. Many fonts have built-in kerning information so that each kerned character pair is spaced for optimal readability and appearance.

However, you may not necessarily want to have kerning turned on all the time for everything. When you have text at very small sizes, pulling certain letter pairs closer with kerning may make the text harder to read because the characters are already so small. Word lets you specify at which size you want kerning to begin to take effect.

To turn on kerning:

1. Select the text you want to change or place your insertion point where you want kerning to begin.
2. Choose **Font** from the Format menu and select the **Character Spacing** tab.
3. Select the **Kerning for Fonts** check box.
4. In the **Points and Above box**, specify the size at which you want kerning to take effect. This setting may depend on what kind of printer you are using. If you have a high-resolution 1200-dpi printer, for example, you could safely use a small setting here. If you have only a 300-dpi printer, you might want to use kerning for only 12 or 14 points and above.

NOTE

When you turn the **Kerning** option on and off, you're unlikely to notice a difference in the Preview box, because kerning differences can be subtle.

Applying Colors

You may be one of the growing number of lucky souls with a color printer. If you are, you can use Word's color options to add zing to your documents. Even if you don't have a color printer, you can still assign colors to text to change the way the text is displayed on-screen. Just remember that if you don't have a color printer, none of the color changes will translate to the printed page—you're stuck with boring old black and white.

To change text color:

1. Select the text you want to change or place your insertion point where you want the change to begin.
2. Choose **Font** from the Format menu and make sure the **Font** tab is selected.
3. Select a color from the Color drop-down list shown in Figure 7.12, then click **OK**.

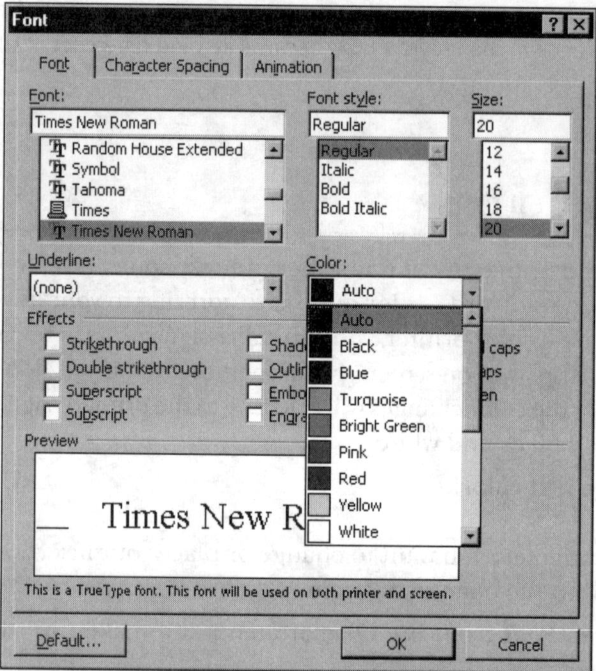

Figure 7.12 Selecting a color in the Font dialog box.

The colors in the list are self-explanatory, except for **Auto**. When you select **Auto**, Word uses your default Windows 95 text color, which is black unless you've changed it.

Changing the Default Font for New Documents

If you want Word to use a particular font whenever you start a new document, no problem. I'll show you how to change Word's defaults so that all your new documents start with exactly the font, size, and character formatting you want.

To change default character formatting:

1. Choose **New** from the File menu and select the **General** tab in the New dialog box, as shown in Figure 7.13.

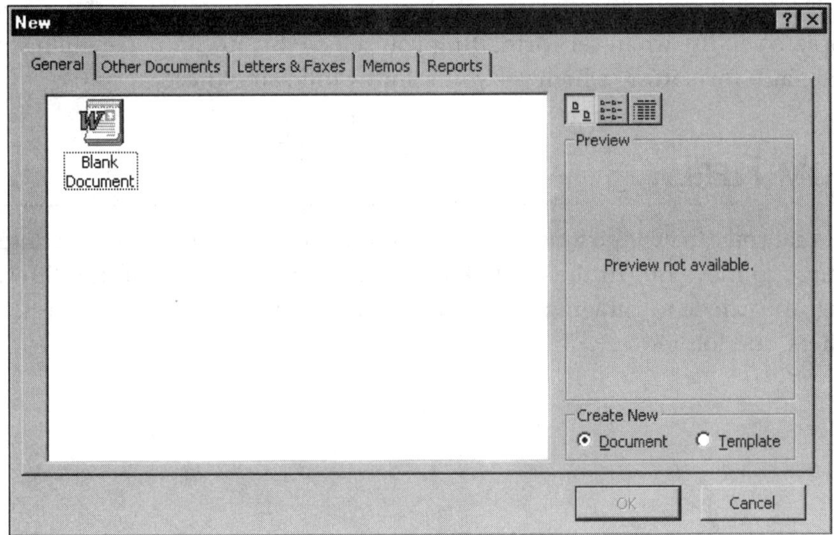

*Figure 7.13 The **General** tab in the New dialog box.*

2. Select the **Blank Document** icon and click **OK**. This opens a new document based on the Normal template.
3. Choose **Font** from the Format menu.
4. Make any changes you want in the Font dialog box.
5. Click the **Default** button in the lower-left corner of the Font dialog box. As you can see in Figure 7.14, Word asks you to confirm that you want this change to affect all new documents that use the Normal template.

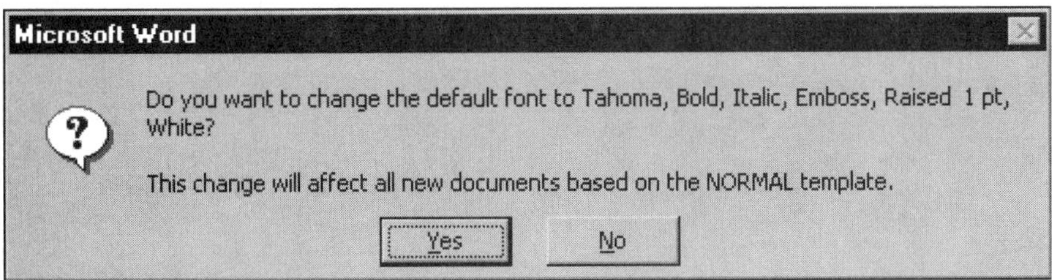

*Figure 7.14 Click **Yes** if you want to change the formatting for all your new documents.*

6. Click **Yes** to confirm the change.

That's it. From now on, any new documents you create using the Normal template will use whatever formatting you selected. You can make changes to the default formatting whenever you want by following these steps.

From Here...

Now that you can change fonts and character formatting to your heart's content, it's time to move on. In the next chapter, we'll take a look at all the different things you can do to paragraphs: adjust the line spacing, change tab settings, add borders, and lots more.

CHAPTER 8

Paragraph Formatting

Let's talk about:

- Displaying formatting information
- Indenting lines
- Aligning paragraphs
- Adjusting line spacing
- Adding borders and shading
- Setting tabs
- Using AutoFormat and the Format Painter

How a document looks is often as important as the information it contains. Cramped, hard-to-read text or anonymous hard-to-find headings can put up obstacles that obscure the meaning of your brilliant words. Remember the old adage: neatness counts! In this chapter, you'll learn how to make the most of Word's paragraph formatting tools. The result will be documents that not only look better, but communicate better.

What Is a Paragraph?

Yeah, I know you know what a paragraph is. But you may not know everything about how Word treats paragraphs. Hence this short paragraph primer.

In Word, the *paragraph* is one of the basic units of a document. Every time you press the **Enter** key while typing, you create a new paragraph. If you press **Enter** every time the text nears the end of a line instead of letting Word wrap the text, you end up with a paragraph for each line rather than a single paragraph with several lines in it.

A paragraph doesn't have to have multiple lines of text—it can contain only one line, and it may not even include any text. For example, a two-word heading is a paragraph. So is a blank line consisting only of a paragraph mark. Every time you press the **Enter** key, Word starts a new paragraph.

NOTE

Sometimes you might want to start a new line without starting a new paragraph. For example, you probably want all of the signature lines for a letter to be part of the same paragraph so that formatting changes to any signature line will automatically apply to all of them. To start a new line but keep it part of the same paragraph, just press **Shift+Enter**.

When you use any of Word's paragraph formatting features, Word applies the formatting to the whole paragraph (or multiple paragraphs, if you select a bunch of paragraphs before you apply the formatting). This means that when you add paragraph formatting, you don't need to have the whole paragraph selected. All you have to do to apply paragraph formatting to a paragraph is place the insertion point anywhere in the paragraph.

Remember that the paragraph mark contains the paragraph formatting. If you delete that mark, the paragraph loses its formatting and takes on the formatting of the next paragraph. The paragraph mark is always the last character in any paragraph, whether or not it's displayed. To display paragraph marks, just click the **Show/Hide** button on the Standard toolbar (the button has a paragraph symbol on it). For more information about what happens when you click this button and why you would want to, read the "Displaying Paragraph Marks" section a little later in this chapter.

Displaying Formatting Information

Word gives you several ways to check on your formatting. If you don't know what formatting has been applied to a particular paragraph, just look at the ruler or use the **What's This** tool (described a little later) to display the format settings. You can also tell Word to display paragraph marks, tabs, spaces, and a few other formatting elements. You probably won't use all these tools all the time, but it's good to be familiar with them so you can check your formatting when you need to. Of course, because Word provides a *WYSIWYG* (what you see is what you get) display, you usually have a good idea just by looking at the document. But formatting changes can come from different sources, so it's useful to get feedback. For example, text that appears centered between the margins could be formatted with the **Center Alignment** feature or it could just be moved over with tabs or indents.

Displaying the Ruler

When you're setting up paragraph formatting and styles, the ruler can be invaluable. A quick glance tells you exactly where your margins, indents, and tabs are for the selected paragraph. Furthermore, if something weird happens—for example, if inserting a tab moves the text to an unexpected place—the ruler shows the exact location of any tabs and indents you might have forgotten.

ROADMAP

The ruler and most dialog boxes that allow you to change measurement settings are set up to use inches as the unit of measurement. If you don't like to work with inches, you can set up the ruler and other settings to use some other unit of measure. The same unit appears in the Format Paragraph dialog boxes and other dialog boxes that normally specify measurements in inches. You can choose inches, centimeters, *picas* (a printer's measure, 6 per inch), or *points* (72 per inch). See Chapter 25 for more information about changing Word's default settings.

To display the ruler:

1. Choose **Ruler** from the View menu.

NOTE

If the ruler is already displayed, you'll see a check mark next to the **Ruler** command on the View menu.

In Normal view, the ruler looks like it does in Figure 8.1. In Page Layout view, you get a vertical ruler in addition to the horizontal one, as shown in Figure 8.2. And in Outline view, the ruler doesn't appear at all, and the **Ruler** command on the View menu is dimmed.

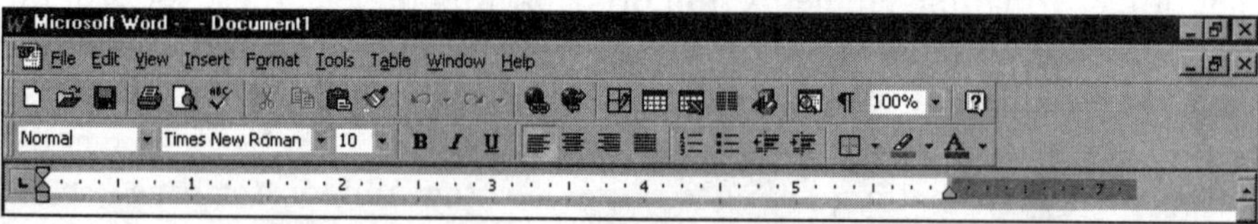

Figure 8.1 The ruler in Normal view.

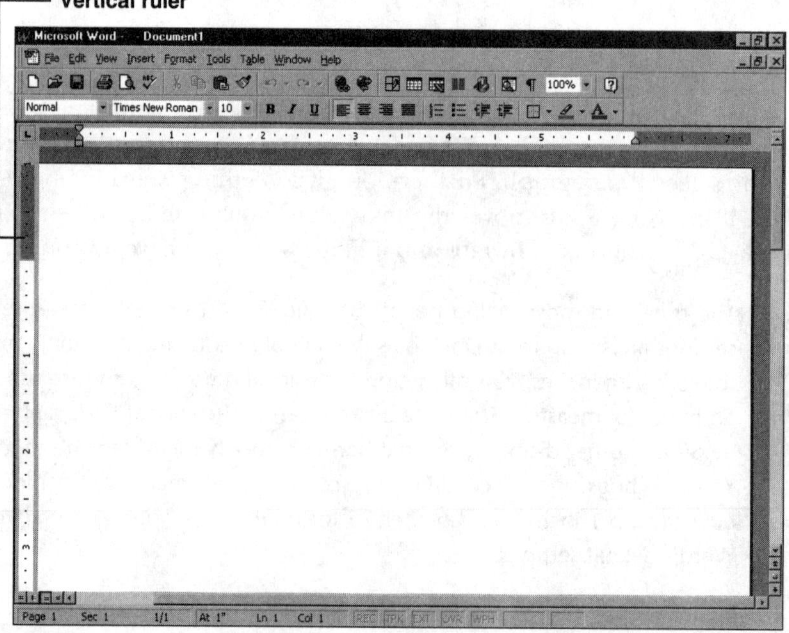

Figure 8.2 The ruler in Page Layout view.

The ruler is more than just a pretty face—in addition to using it to see your formatting for the current paragraph, you can use the ruler to change the formatting. Throughout this chapter, I'll show you techniques that allow you to change paragraph formatting just by dragging items on the ruler.

Displaying Paragraph Marks

By default, all you see on-screen is the text and pictures that will appear on the printed document—spaces, tabs, and paragraph marks appear as white space. Figure 8.3 contains all these elements, but you can't tell by looking whether an empty spot is a series of spaces, a tab, or a paragraph mark.

The ClipArt Gallery gives you access to hundreds of professionally designed images—everything from maps to people to buildings and scenic backgrounds. Here are a few examples:

Maps Italy, France, Belgium
People Engineers, drivers, pedestrians

Figure 8.3 *In this text, the paragraph marks are hidden.*

Most of the time this isn't a problem, but if you run into formatting problems, or a paragraph just doesn't line up the way you think it should, you need to get to the bottom of the situation. And when you're performing heavy-duty formatting, it can really help to see what you're working with.

To display paragraph marks, tabs, and spaces, click the **Show/Hide ¶** button on the Standard toolbar. As you can see in Figure 8.4, the paragraph marks, spaces, and tabs now appear in the document window.

The·ClipArt·Gallery·gives·you·access·to·hundreds·of·professionally·designed· images—everything·from·maps·to·people·to·buildings·and·scenic· backgrounds.·Here·are·a·few·examples:¶
¶
Maps → Italy,·France,·Belgium¶
People → Engineers,·drivers,·pedestrians¶

Figure 8.4 *Now you can see paragraph marks, spaces, and tabs.*

It's important to understand that the text in a paragraph belongs to the paragraph mark at the end of that paragraph. The paragraph mark contains the style and paragraph formatting (for example, the vertical spacing) as well as the carriage return. When you delete a paragraph mark, you're deleting the paragraph formatting as well as the carriage return. When this happens, the text in the paragraph gets thrown into the next paragraph and acquires its paragraph formatting.

NOTE

If you accidentally delete a paragraph mark, click the **Undo** button right away to reverse the action.

If you want to hide the paragraph marks , just click the **Show/Hide ¶** button again.

Displaying a Formatting Summary

You can apply a variety of formatting options to a paragraph. One way to find out what formatting options are in use is to choose **Paragraph** from the Format menu and look at all the boxes and settings in the two parts of that dialog box. But there's a much easier way—just display a formatting summary that shows you everything at a glance.

To display a summary of paragraph formatting:

1. Press **Shift+F1** or choose **What's This** from the Help menu. Notice that a question mark attaches itself to your mouse pointer.
2. Click anywhere in paragraph whose formatting you want to see (Figure 8.5).

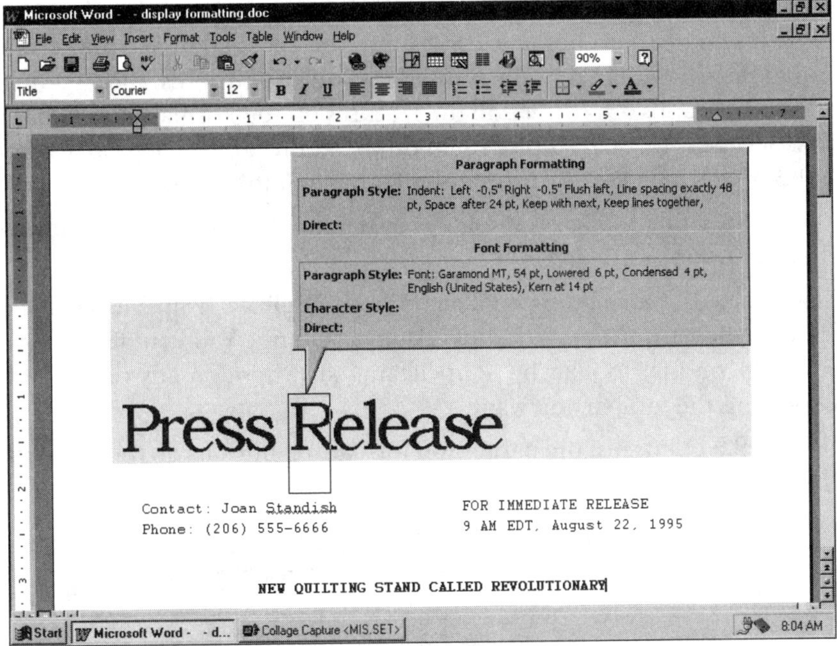

Figure 8.5 Everything you want to know about this paragraph.

3. You can continue clicking on different paragraphs to see their formatting. The question mark that tells you the **What's This** tool is active remains attached to your mouse pointer until you either press **Esc** or choose **What's This** from the Help menu again.

ROADMAP

The *Paragraph Style* sections for both paragraph and font formatting tell you which formatting options are part of a style. You'll learn about styles in Chapter 20, "Working with Styles." The *Direct* sections show any formatting that you've added manually (without making it part of a style). Everything we do in this chapter is considered *direct formatting.*

Displaying the Formatting Toolbar

The Formatting toolbar is split about equally between buttons for font formatting and buttons for paragraph formatting. You can't do everything from this toolbar, but it puts several of the most commonly used formatting options within easy reach. With a click on one of the buttons, you can change the paragraph alignment, start bulleted or numbered lists, change a paragraph's indentation, or display a toolbar that lets you assign lines and shading to selected paragraphs. Of course, all the features on the Formatting toolbar can also be accessed through Word's pull-down menus and dialog boxes. You'll learn both ways of accessing formatting features in this chapter.

The Formatting toolbar is displayed by default, but in case you've turned it off, here's how to get it back.

To display the formatting toolbar, choose **Toolbars** from the View menu and **Formatting** from the cascading Toolbars menu. You can also open the Formatting (or any) toolbar by right-clicking anywhere on any visible toolbar and selecting the toolbar you want.

Figure 8.6 points out the paragraph formatting buttons on the Formatting toolbar.

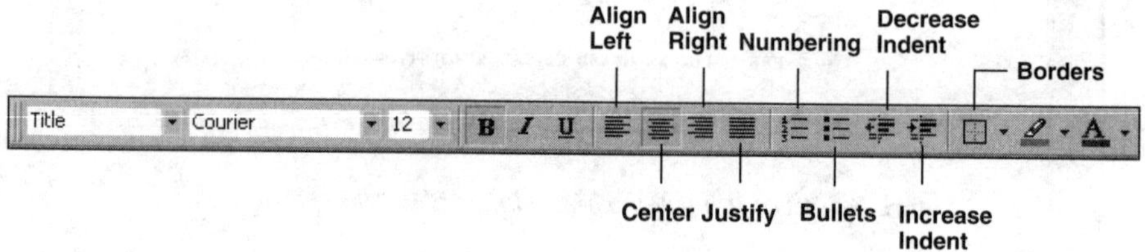

Figure 8.6 *Use the Formatting toolbar for quick access to paragraph formatting options.*

INDENTING LINES

You can indent lines or paragraphs to make your text more readable or more appropriate to the kind of document you're producing in several ways. For example, many academic guidelines call for bibliography entries with a *hanging indent*—that is, paragraphs in which the first line is further to the left than the other lines in the paragraph.

What makes indenting lines particularly easy in Word is that the Paragraph dialog box shows a preview of all the options you select. Even if you don't know what a first-line indent or a hanging indent is, you can immediately see what its effect will be. You can also use the ruler to change most of the indent options.

Indenting the First Line of Each Paragraph

One common formatting style has the first line of each paragraph indented a few characters, as shown in Figure 8.7.

Ivor Richards once declaimed, in an attack of hyperbole, that translation is "probably the most complex type of event yet produced in the evolution of the cosmos" (qtd. in Nida 79). The translator's task is intricate, especially with French, and especially with written literature, for as Charles Bally said, "*Le français est une langue faite pour l'oeil*" (qtd. in Rickard 138). ("French is a language made for the eye.") This is not to say that one language is better than the other; but I contend that beyond the difficulties already inherent in translation in general, French is difficult to translate into English because of both its similarites and dissimilarites with English. Jean Paris put it simply: "French and English are so obviously antagonistic" (62).

The most obvious difference that might cause problems is the way the words are combined: sentence construction and idiom. Translation is not a mere matching up of words that need only to be found in a dictionary, just seeing that *chien* = dog and *traverser* = to cross. Although a literary genius like Vladimir Nabokov holds that "the clumsiest literal translation is a thousand times more useful than the prettiest paraphrase" (496), paraphrase cannot be avoided when translating from French.

Figure 8.7 *Indented first lines.*

Word has a feature that allows you to indent just the first line of each paragraph, which means you don't have to type a tab at the beginning of every paragraph. When you go on to the next paragraph of your document, those same indenting options continue until you change the formatting. Not pressing the **Tab** key at the beginning of each paragraph may not seem like much of a time-saver, but it frees you from having to worry about formatting as your novel is unfolding. And using Word's built-in formatting features helps to ensure consistency—you don't have to remember to press the **Tab** key—Word does the work for you.

In Figure 8.7 the first line is indented and the rest of the lines of the paragraph wrap back to the left margin. What would happen if you reversed the indents? That is, what if the first line started at the left margin, but the rest of the paragraph's lines were indented? The result is a hanging indent, shown in Figure 8.8.

Milton, John. *Paradise Lost.* Vol. 2, part 1 of *The Works of John Milton.* Ed. Frank Allen Patterson. 18 vols. New York: Columbia UP, 1931.

Pope, Alexander. *The Rape of the Lock.* Vol. 2 of *The Poems of Alexander Pope.* Ed. Geoffrey Tillotson. Rev. ed. 11 vols. London: Methuen, 1954.

Rousseau, G. S., ed. *Twentieth Century Interpretations of* The Rape of the Lock: *A Collection of Critical Essays.* Englewood Cliffs, NJ: Prentice-Hall, 1969.

Spenser, Edmund. *The Faerie Queene.* Vols. 1-7 of *The Works of Edmund Spenser.* Ed. Edwin Greenlaw, Charles Grosvenor Osgood, and Frederick Morgan Padelford. 9 vols. Baltimore: Johns Hopkins UP, 1933.

Figure 8.8 *Paragraphs with hanging indents.*

Some cases where you might want to use a hanging indent: numbered or bulleted lists (which, as you'll learn in Chapter 21, "Creating Lists and Outlines," Word can take care of automatically), bibliography entries, and glossary-type paragraphs where a term is on the left and a description is on the right (like the example in Figure 8.9).

Start Menu	The Windows 95 equivalent of Windows 3.1's Task Manager. Unlike the Task Manager, the Start menu is configurable and supports multiple layers of cascading menus.
Explorer	The new File Manager. From Explorer, you can manage your files in a variety of views and see file types by their distinctive icons rather than by their filename extensions.

Figure 8.9 *Another type of hanging indent.*

To indent the first line of each paragraph:

1. Click in the paragraph you want to format (or select multiple paragraphs).
2. Choose **Paragraph** from the Format menu and make sure the **Indents and Spacing** tab is visible (as in Figure 8.10).

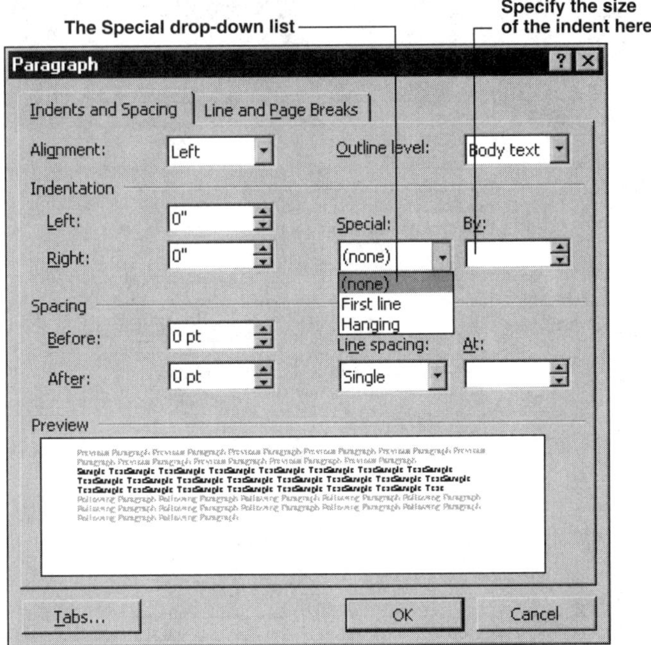

*Figure 8.10 The **Indents and Spacing** tab in the Paragraph dialog box.*

3. Choose **First Line** or **Hanging** from the Special drop-down list. The **First Line** option pushes the first line in, while the **Hanging** option leaves the first line out and pushes the rest of the paragraph in.
4. Use the **By** box to specify how large an indent you want, then click **OK**. As you select different options, the Preview box shows what the formatting will look like on the page.

Indenting the Entire Paragraph

What if you want to indent the entire paragraph? An example of this might be a direct quotation that you want set off from the rest of the text. In Figure 8.11, the first quotation is indented only from the left, and the second quotation is indented from both the left and right.

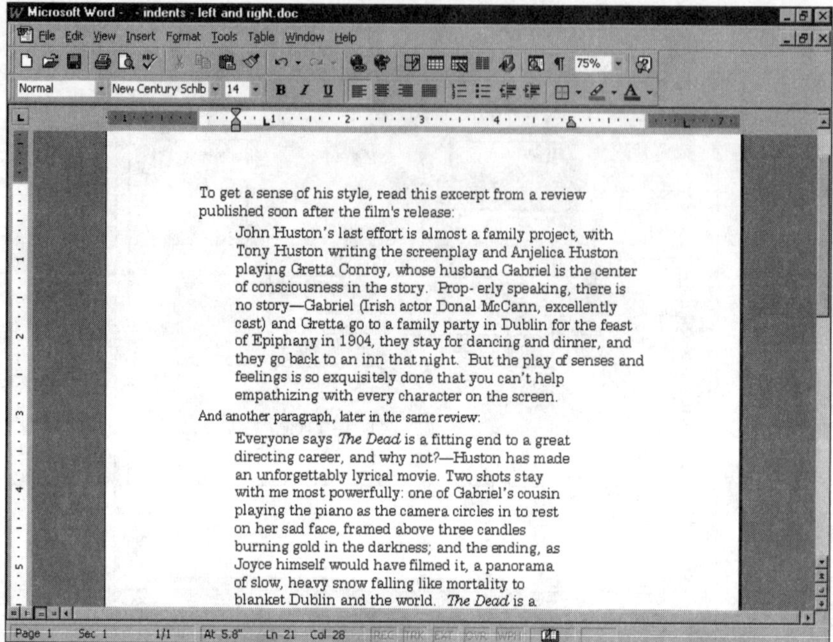

Figure 8.11 *Left and right indents.*

Another type of indent is sometimes called *outdenting*. If you indent a paragraph by a negative amount, the paragraph wraps past the left or right margin and sticks out into the empty margin of the page. One use for a negative indent is section headings.

To indent an entire paragraph using the Paragraph dialog box:

1. Click in the paragraph that you want to apply formatting to (or select multiple paragraphs).
2. Choose **Paragraph** from the Format menu and click the **Indents and Spacing** tab (shown in Figure 8.12).

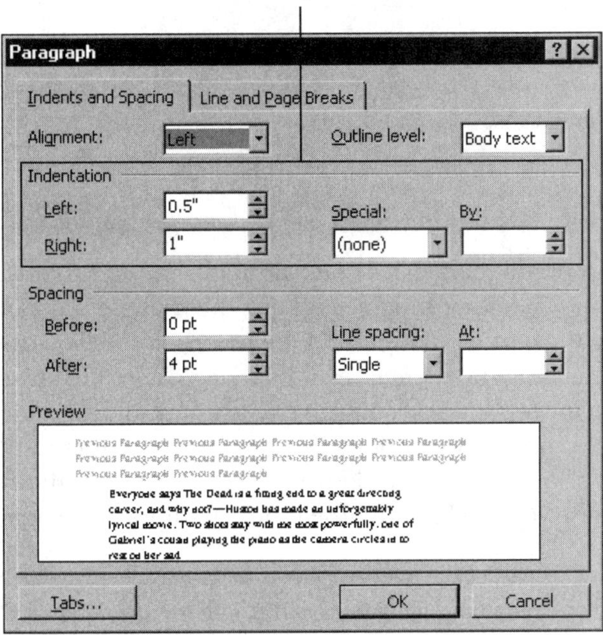

*Figure 8.12 The **Indents and Spacing** tab in the Paragraph dialog box.*

3. In the Left box, specify how far to indent the paragraph from the left. If you specify a negative measurement, you'll extend the paragraph into the left margin by that amount.
4. In the Right box, specify how far to indent the right side of the paragraph and click OK. Once again, the Preview box shows the effect of your changes.

Indenting Paragraphs with the Ruler

You can use the dialog box or the ruler (Figure 8.13) to set paragraph indentation. Using the ruler can be quicker, but using the dialog box lets you specify measurements with more precision.

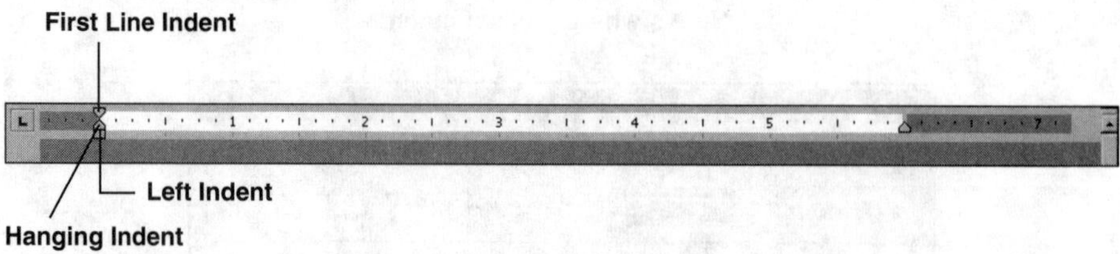

Figure 8.13 You can use the ruler to change paragraph indents.

Drag the appropriate marker to a new position on the ruler. If you drag the top triangle (the First Line Indent marker), the triangle is the only thing that moves, leaving the bottom triangle and the box behind. If you drag the bottom triangle (the Hanging Indent marker), the triangle and the box move together. That's because the top triangle controls only the first line's indentation and the bottom triangle controls the indentation for the remainder of the paragraph. If you drag the square box (the Left Indent marker), all the markers move together because you're changing the indentation for the whole paragraph.

The white part of the ruler represents the part of the page within the margins you set. If you drag an indent marker into the gray area of the ruler, you're outdenting, or using negative indents.

Aligning Paragraphs

The edges of paragraphs come in two flavors: justified and ragged. *Justified* means lined up evenly, while *ragged* means just what you'd guess—ending wherever the last word in the paragraph ends, with each line a slightly different length. In Word, you can have any combination of justified and ragged edges for the left and right sides of the paragraph.

Most of your writing will probably be left-aligned, that is, with the left side justified and the right side ragged. For a more polished, business-like look, you may want to fully justify your text—that is, align both the left and right sides of each paragraph. And you might want to center titles or graphics. In a few cases, like with page numbers of the top of a multipage letter, you'll want to use right alignment.

To change the alignment of a paragraph:

1. Click anywhere in the paragraph you want to format (or select multiple paragraphs).

2. Click one of the paragraph alignment buttons on the Formatting toolbar (shown in Figure 8.14).

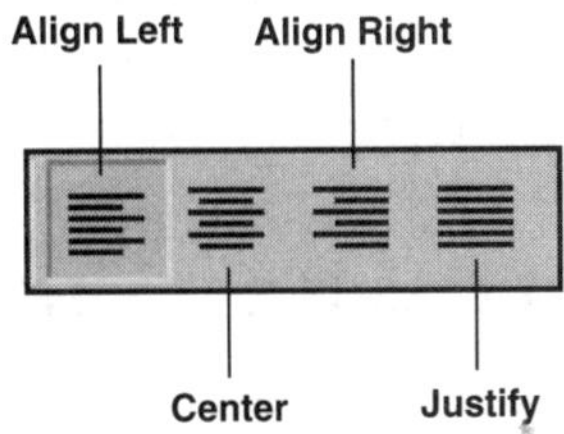

Figure 8.14 *Click one of these buttons to align the selected paragraphs.*

You can choose **Align Left**, **Align Right**, **Center**, or **Justify**. The currently applied alignment button appears pressed in. If none of the four buttons looks like it's pressed in, it means you have multiple paragraphs selected and they don't all have the same alignment.

Figure 8.15 shows examples of the four types of alignment. When you click the **Justify** toolbar button to align both sides of the paragraph, Word automatically adds as much space as necessary between each word to make the ends come out even. If a long word can't fit and wraps to the next line, the spaces between words can be large, creating distracting white "rivers" in the text.

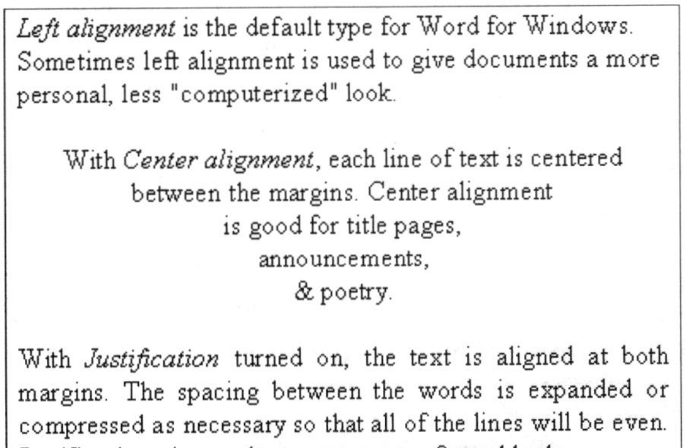

Left alignment is the default type for Word for Windows. Sometimes left alignment is used to give documents a more personal, less "computerized" look.

With *Center alignment*, each line of text is centered
between the margins. Center alignment
is good for title pages,
announcements,
& poetry.

With *Justification* turned on, the text is aligned at both margins. The spacing between the words is expanded or compressed as necessary so that all of the lines will be even. Justification gives a document a more formal look.

With *Right alignment,*
your text is aligned at the right margin,
leaving the left margin ragged.
This might typically be used for a name
and return address on a letter.

Figure 8.15 *Left-aligned, centered, right-aligned, and justified paragraphs.*

NOTE

Even though the easiest way to align text is with the Formatting toolbar buttons, you can also choose alignment options from the **Indents and Spacing** tab in the Paragraph dialog box (choose **Paragraph** from the Format menu and select the **Indents and Spacing** tab). If you're changing several formatting options at once, using the dialog box can make more sense.

Adjusting Vertical and Line Spacing

By default, documents that you create in Word are single-spaced, and that's what we've worked with so far. But what if you need to give your boss a double-spaced draft so she can mark it up with her red pencil? By now you probably have the idea that this'll be a piece of cake, and you're right. You can change your line spacing in almost infinite increments, and you can use Word's other vertical spacing options to make more sophisticated spacing adjustments.

NOTE

Word uses *points* to measure line spacing. We'll talk more about points in Chapter 12, "A Look at Fonts," but for now all you need to know is that a *point* is 1/72 inch.

Changing Line Spacing

By default, documents that you create in Word are single-spaced, and that's what we've worked with so far. But what if you need to give your boss a double-spaced draft so she can mark it up with her red pencil? By now you probably have the idea that this'll be a piece of cake, and you're right. Word makes it easy to adjust your line spacing using the Paragraph dialog box.

To set line spacing:

1. Click in the paragraph you want to format (or select multiple paragraphs).
2. Choose **Paragraph** from the Format menu and click the **Indents and Spacing** tab.
3. Select an option from the Line spacing drop-down list shown in Figure 8.16.
4. If you select **At Least**, **Exactly**, or **Multiple**, specify the number of points or lines in the At box.
5. When you're finished, click **OK**.

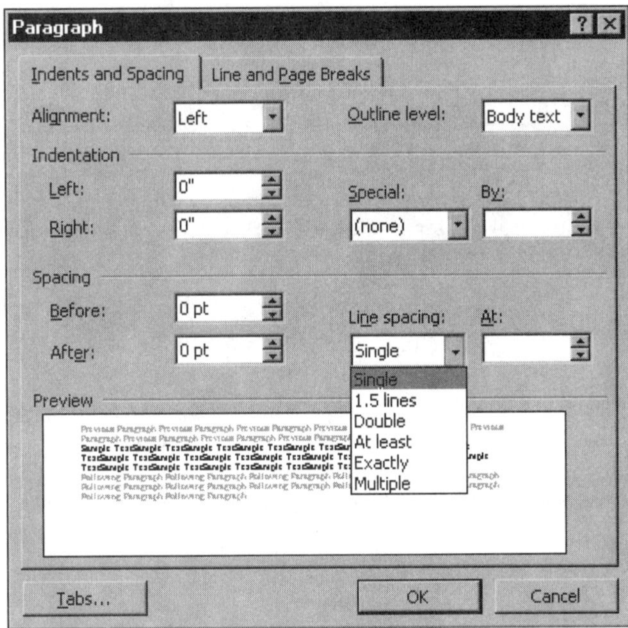

*Figure 8.16 The **Indents and Spacing** tab with the Line spacing drop-down list.*

The spacing options are given in Table 8.1.

***Table 8.1** Spacing options.*

THIS SPACING OPTION	DOES THIS
Single	The default option, which means it's what you get automatically unless you tell Word to do something else.
1.5 lines or Double	Gives you an extra half or whole space between lines.
At Least	Allows you to set a specific line height for the paragraph. **At Least** guarantees that if you set the line spacing to 12 points and later change the paragraph to an 18-point font, for example, the tops of the lines won't be cut off.

continued

Table 8.1 continued

THIS SPACING OPTION	DOES THIS
Exactly	Gives you the exact amount of spacing you specify in the At box. This option can get you in trouble if you later change the font size or add superscripted or subscripted text.
Multiple	Lets you specify spacing in multiples of single. For example, if you enter **3.5** in the At box, you'll get spacing that's 3-1/2 times the amount of single spacing.

KEYBOARD

Use these keystroke shortcuts to change line spacing:

Ctrl+1	Single spacing
Ctrl+2	Double spacing
Ctrl+5	1.5-line spacing
Ctrl+0 (zero)	Adds or removes 1 unit of spacing. Example: With single-spaced text, pressing **Ctrl+0** once changes the selected text to double-spaced, and pressing **Ctrl+0** again returns it to single-spaced.

Adding Space Before or After a Paragraph

In general, the amount of space between paragraphs for body text depends on whether the first lines of each paragraph are indented. In a document that's nearly all body text, like a novel, the first lines of paragraphs will probably be indented, so you don't need much extra space between paragraphs. However, in work that is broken up by frequent headings (like a report), first lines are usually not indented. Paragraphs then need space between them to give readers visual cues. In either case, apply your paragraph settings to a series of paragraphs and scan them to make sure you can easily catch the breaks between paragraphs as you read. In Figure 8.17, each paragraph except the address is formatted to add 11 points of space before the paragraph. Notice that there's only one paragraph mark after each paragraph.

Kay·Howton¶
13409·183rd·SE¶
Bellevue,·WA·98052¶

Dear·Ms.·Howton:¶

Your·November·2,·1996·letter·regarding··the·delivery·of·damaged·merchandise·was·forwarded·to·me.·I·am·looking·into·the·situation·and·I·hope·to·resolve·it·quickly.·When·I·have·finished·my·investigation,·I·will·write·or·call·you·with·a·response.·You·might·check·to·make·sure·our·logo·appears·on·the·package,·just·in·case.¶

I·assure·you·that·we·are·taking·your·complaint·very·seriously.·You·are·a·valuable·customer,·and·any·dissatisfaction·on·your·part·indicates·an·opportunity·for·improvement·on·our·part.¶

If·I·need·more·information·from·you·to·help·me·resolve·this·matter,·I·will·contact·you.·Thank·you·for·your·patience.¶

Sincerely,¶

***Figure 8.17** Paragraphs formatted with 11 points of space before.*

NOTE

Want to know the big advantage of using the **Spacing Before** and **Spacing After** options over pressing the **Enter** key twice at the end of each paragraph? Simple. Using the spacing options allows you to change your mind without paying a penalty. If you decide that you want a little more space between the paragraphs, just change one setting and it's done.

Headings should already stand out from body text by virtue of their larger size, bold formatting, or different font style. However, to keep a heading from looking like it's crushed by the paragraphs above, you need to give it a few points of space above and below. The amount should increase with the size of the heading. For example, a heading using a 16-point font should probably have at least 8 points of empty space before it. An easy guideline is from 1/2 to 1 times the point size of the heading as extra space before it.

You need some space after the heading too, so it doesn't get jammed against the following paragraph, but not too much. If there's too much, the heading looks like it's been abandoned instead of being a part of the section that it's supposed to lead into. A good guideline for the space after a heading is 1/3 or less of the extra space before the heading. See Figure 8.18 for an example, and notice again that there's only one paragraph mark between each paragraph—the paragraph formatting is all done with Word's built-in spacing options.

▪Introduction¶

It's·not·that·no·one·is·proposing·any·solutions.·People·get·excited·for·awhile·about·Japanese·management·techniques·and·institute·a·few·quality·circles·as·experiments,·usually·without·the·passionate·support·of·upper-level·management.··Companies·give·lip·service·to·the·need·to·transform·themselves·beyond·the·quarterly·report·mentality.·Books·about·corporate·excellence·have·long·lives·on·the·New·York·Times·bestseller·list·and·make·their·way·into·business·school·classes.·Politicians·pontificate·about·growth·and·meeting·the·foreign·challenge,·all·within·existing·economic·structures·and·ideas.¶

▪The·Company·as·Person¶

But·regardless·of·pressures·from·every·direction·and·regardless·of·a·consensus·on·what·should·be·done·in·a·general·way,·there·is·very·little·change:·American·business·is·a·hapless·Gulliver,·tied·down·by·its·own·traditions·and·inefficient·habits·so·that·a·few·fingers·move,·maybe·a·knee·jerks·and·an·arm·stretches,·giving·the·illusion·of·evolution·and·adaptation,·while·the·huge·trunk·moves·only·when·the·ground·under·it·erodes.·We·need·real,·not·illusory·change:·a·change·of·paradigm,·not·of·external·image.¶

Figure 8.18 *Appropriate space before and after headings.*

A third type of paragraph that can use extra space before and after is special material set off from body text. This might be a picture embedded in a document, a long quotation, or a table in the midst of body paragraphs. In these cases, it's a good idea to put roughly equal space before and after the paragraph and enough to keep the eye from confusing the paragraph with the body text around it (see Figure 8.19 for an example). Half the line height of the surrounding text is a good guideline.

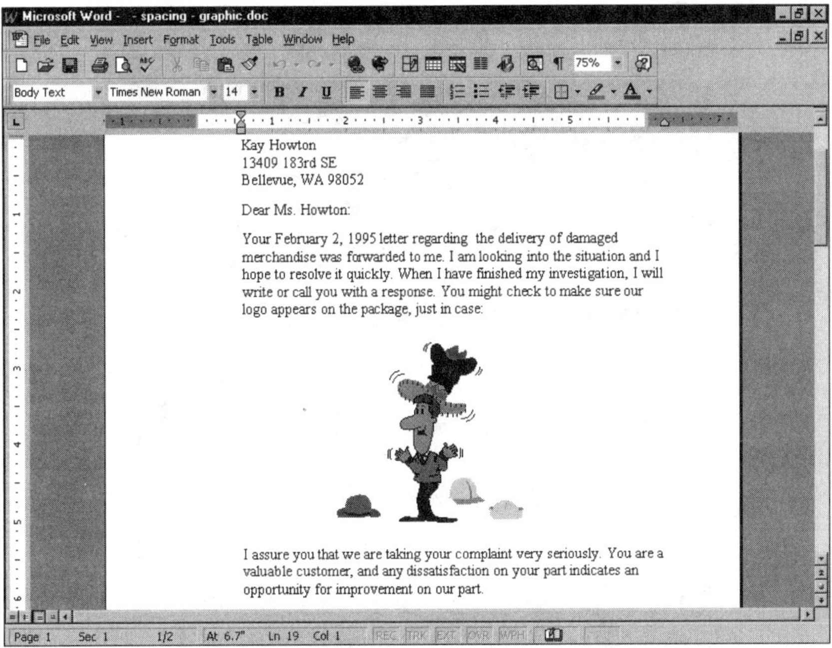

Figure 8.19 *A graphic requires extra space, both above and below.*

To add space before or after a paragraph:

1. Click in the paragraph you want to format (or select multiple paragraphs).
2. Choose **Paragraph** from the Format menu and click the **Indents and Spacing** tab (shown in Figure8.20).

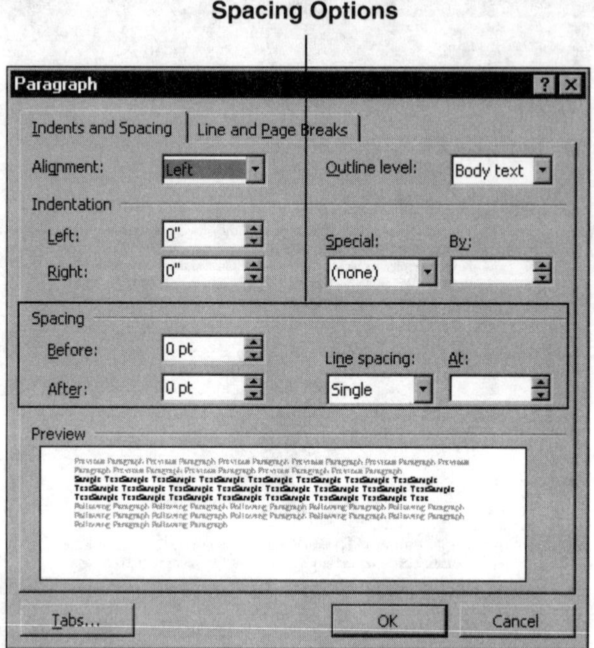

Figure 8.20 *Notice the Spacing options in the* ***Indents and Spacing*** *tab.*

3. Specify the spacing you want in the Before and After boxes, then click **OK**. As usual, the Preview box shows the effect of your changes.

KEEPING TEXT TOGETHER

As you're typing along, Word moves the text to the next page as soon as you get to the bottom margin. It doesn't care whether it's breaking a two-line paragraph or ripping a heading from its accompanying text—it just does it. But there are four different features that put you in control of how text gets split between pages. The first, *hard page breaks,* are inserted with a keystroke or by choosing **Page Break** from the Break dialog box. You get to the other three through the **Line and Page Breaks** tab in the Paragraph dialog box, shown in Figure 8.21. To access this dialog box, choose **Paragraph** from the Format menu, then select the **Line and Page Breaks** tab.

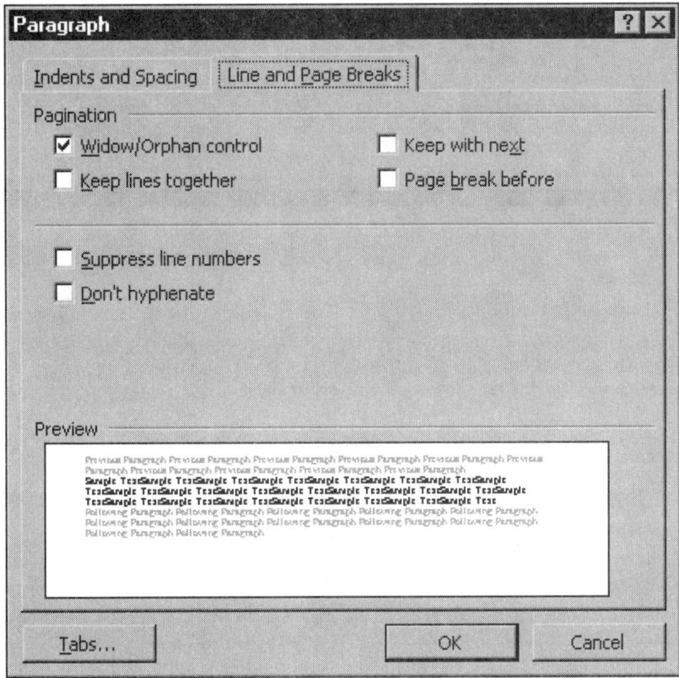

Figure 8.21 *The* ***Line and Page Breaks*** *tab in the Paragraph dialog box.*

Preventing Widows and Orphans

Widows are single lines of text that get stranded all by themselves at the top of a page, while their *orphans* are left alone at the bottom of a page (Figure 8.22). Let's take pity on those poor widows and orphans by using Word's widow/orphan protection. (Bet you didn't know Word was such a civic-minded program.)

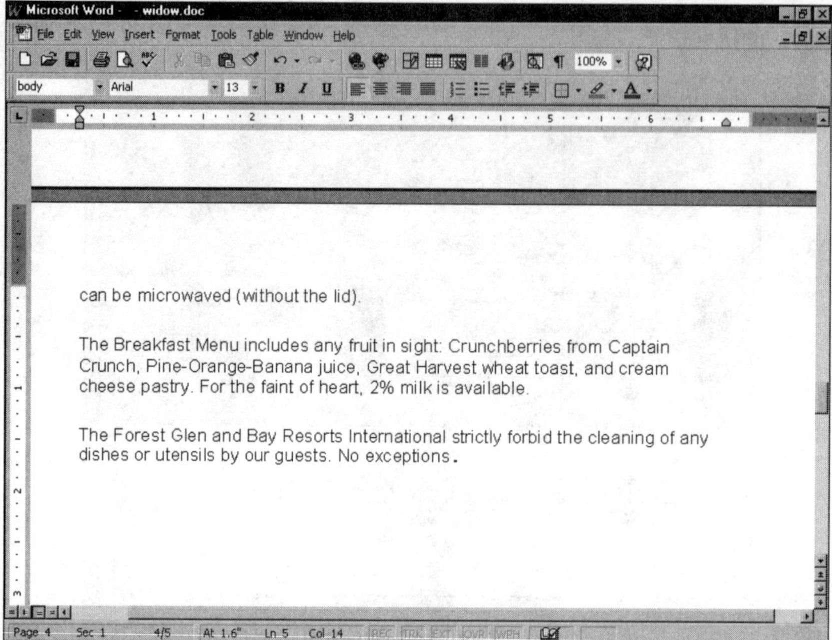

Figure 8.22 *A lonely orphan at the top of the page.*

Fortunately, the option that prevents widows and orphans from showing up is turned on by default in Word. You can allow widows and orphans for an entire document by selecting the whole document and turning off the option or turn it off a paragraph at a time (but I can't think of a reason to turn it off).

When widow and orphan control is turned on, a line that would ordinarily be alone at the bottom of a page is pushed to the next page, leaving the first page slightly shorter. Where a single line would stand alone at the top of a page, Word borrows a line from the previous page to give the orphan a companion.

To control widows and orphans:

1. Click in the paragraph you want to format (or select multiple paragraphs).
2. Choose **Paragraph** from the Format menu and select the **Line and Page Breaks** tab.

3. Select or clear the **Widow/Orphan Control** check box and click **OK**. When the check box is selected, as it is by default, Word prevents widows and orphans.

Preventing a Paragraph from Splitting between Pages

Where you have a long series of text paragraphs, you may not care whether two or three lines of a paragraph are at the bottom of a page and the other three lines are on the top of the next page. In some circumstances, however, you want to make sure an entire paragraph stays together on the same page. For example, if a long heading runs onto a second line, you certainly don't want the heading to be split across pages. Or if you have a quotation that you want readers to be able to see all together, you can apply an option to make sure this paragraph stays together on a page. If the paragraph is too long to fit on the current page, the whole paragraph is moved to the top of the next page.

To prevent a paragraph from splitting:

1. Click in the paragraph you want to format (or select multiple paragraphs).
2. Choose **Paragraph** from the Format menu and select the **Line and Page Breaks** tab.
3. Select the **Keep lines together** check box and click **OK**. The paragraph will now remain intact, no matter where the page break would normally fall.

Keeping Two Paragraphs on the Same Page

Authors and designers often want to keep two or three paragraphs together on the same page. If you think about it, it's not so unreasonable. Some paragraphs just don't make sense when separated from what follows. For example, consider the heading at the bottom of the page in Figure 8.23. It's separated from the text it's supposed to introduce.

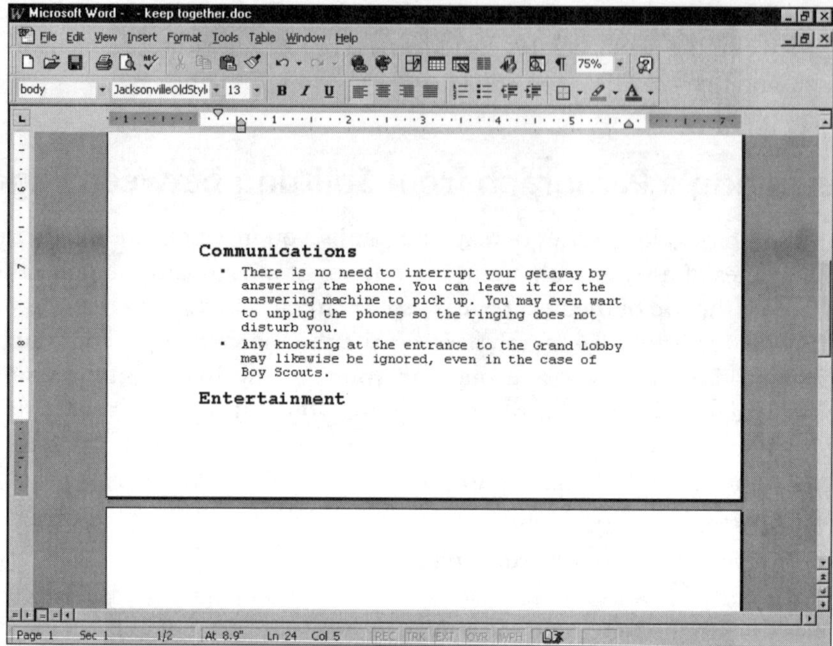

Figure 8.23 *The Entertainment heading is all alone at the bottom of the page.*

A heading should nearly always be kept together with at least the beginning of next paragraph. The same goes for a phrase that introduces a list. For example, as you'll notice that in this book, the text that precedes sets of instructions (such as *To keep two paragraphs on the same page*) is always on the same page with at least the first step that follows.

In Word, the way to keep two paragraphs together is to select an option for the first paragraph that tells Word to keep it with the next paragraph. If you have three paragraphs that must all stay together, apply this option to the first two paragraphs, and so on.

To keep two paragraphs on the same page:

1. Click in the paragraph you want to format (or select multiple paragraphs).
2. Choose **Paragraph** from the Format menu and select the **Line and Page Breaks** tab.
3. Select the **Keep with next** check box, then click **OK**.

Making a Paragraph Start on a New Page

There's one last way of determining where a page break will fall relative to a paragraph: by guaranteeing that a certain paragraph is always the first paragraph on a new page. An obvious example is the heading for a chapter title. If you apply this option to the paragraph containing a chapter's title, that chapter will always begin on a new page, no matter how much text is before it and no matter where on a page the preceding text ends.

To make a paragraph start on a new page:

1. Click anywhere in the paragraph.
2. Choose **Paragraph** from the Format menu and select the **Line and Page Breaks** tab.
3. Select the **Page break before** check box, then click **OK**. When the background pagination catches up with this paragraph, an automatic page break appears just before the paragraph.

WARNING

If you apply the **Page break before** option here and there throughout a document, you may forget later what you've done. If you find a page break in a place that makes no sense, take a look at the first paragraph after the page break and make sure this option hasn't been applied.

Adding Borders and Shading

In the not-too-distant past, adding a bold line above a heading, placing a box around a paragraph, or adding gray shading behind a block of text required careful measuring and several extra steps in the process of creating printing plates. But never fear—you lucky Word users can accomplish all of this without breaking a sweat. There's even a special toolbar that gives instant access to these and other features.

Putting a Box Around a Paragraph

A box grabs the reader's attention. For example, if you want to make sure readers notice a particular block of text, putting a box around it as in Figure 8.24 will do the trick. Just be careful not to overdo the border bit—if you have several boxes on every page, they no longer perform the function of drawing attention to themselves.

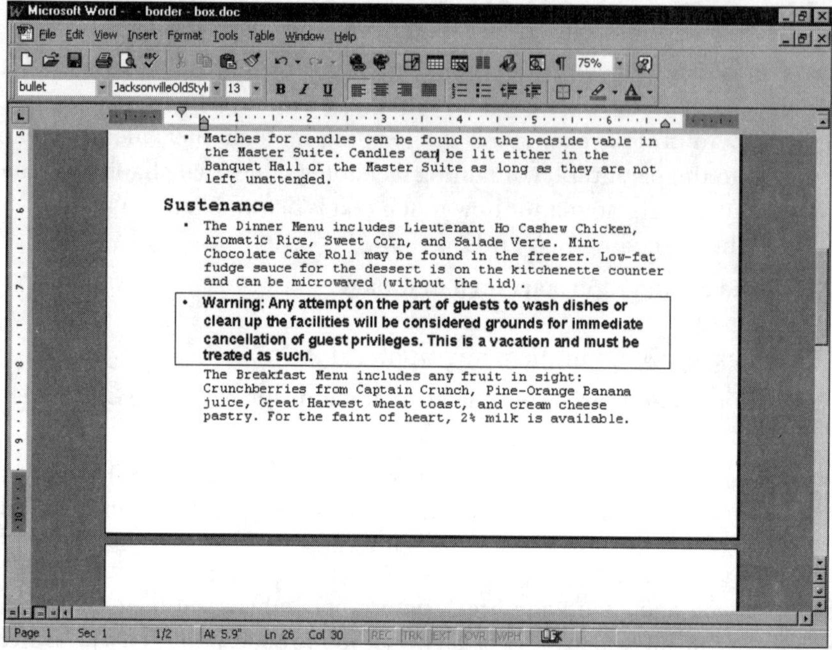

Figure 8.24 A boxed paragraph.

By default, if you select three paragraphs and apply a border, one box goes around all three paragraphs. rather than having a separate box around each paragraph.

Marking a Paragraph with a Top or Bottom Border

A line (sometimes called a *rule*) above or below a paragraph can help to set off headings or introductory lines from the rest of the text and can add an elegant effect that makes you look like a professional. Figure 8.25 shows an example of a rule above heading paragraphs.

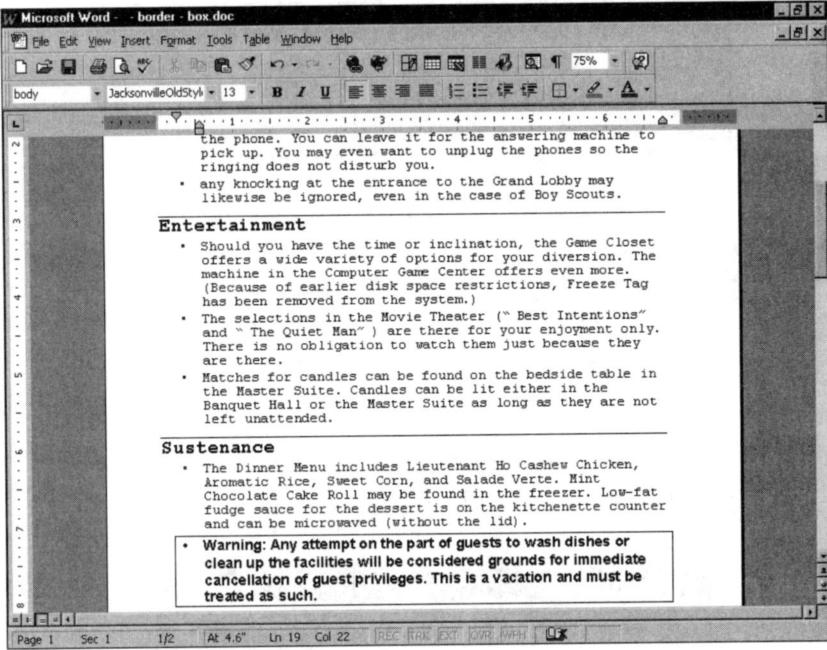

Figure 8.25 Heading with top rules.

Rules can also add emphasis to margin notes, tables of contents, and in the running text repeated at the tops or bottoms of pages (*headers* and *footers*), which often includes chapter titles or page numbers. You'll learn more about headers and footers in Chapter 9.

To add a border to a paragraph using the toolbar:

1. Place your insertion point in the paragraph you want to add a border to (or select multiple paragraphs).
2. Click the **Tables and Borders** button on the Standard toolbar to open the Tables and Borders toolbar shown in Figure 8.26.

Figure 8.26 The Tables and Borders toolbar.

Don't worry about all the different buttons on the Tables and Borders toolbar for now. Most of them are for working with tables, which we'll get to in Chapter 16, "Working with Tables."

3. Click the **down arrow** next to the Line Style button and select a style from the list shown in Figure 8.27.

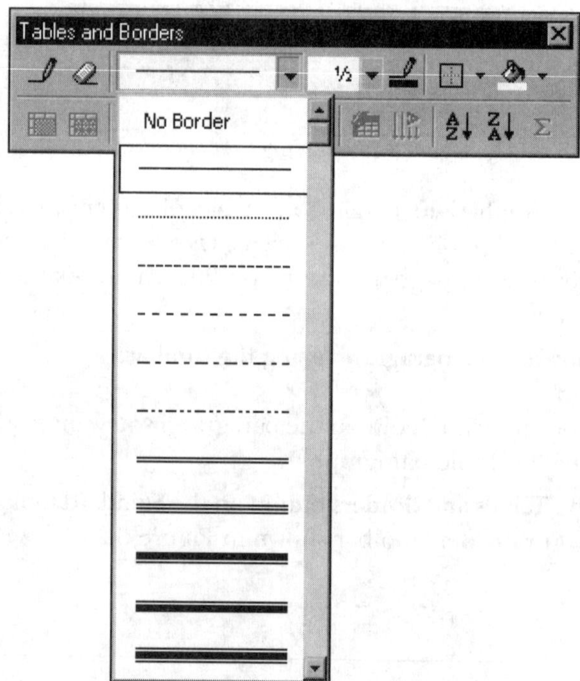

Figure 8.27 The Line Style drop-down list.

4. Click the **down arrow** next to the Line Weight button and select a line thickness from the list shown in Figure 8.28.

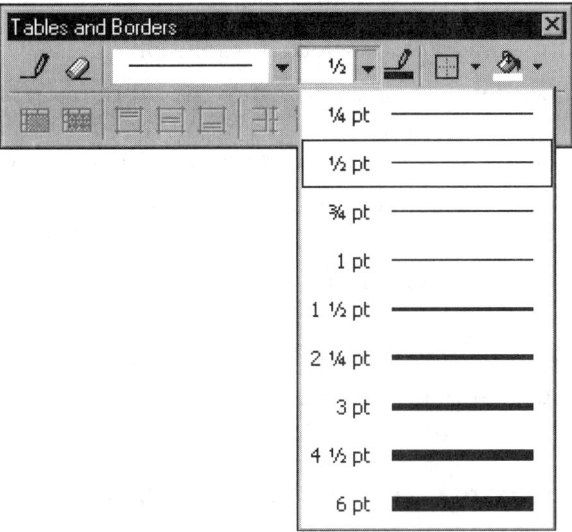

***Figure 8.28** The Line Weight drop-down list.*

5. Click the **down arrow** next to the Borders button to open the palette shown in Figure 8.29. (It's the second button from the left on the top row, the one that looks like a little box split in four quarters.)

***Figure 8.29** Choose one of these border options.*

6. Click to select a border option. As you move your mouse pointer over the different options, notice the ScreenTip that tells you what the option does:

- **Outside Border** puts a box around the paragraph or selected paragraphs.
- **Top Border**, **Bottom Border**, **Left Border**, or **Right Border** puts a line (or rule) on the top, bottom, left, or right side, respectively, of the paragraph or selected paragraphs.
- **All Borders** puts a box around the entire paragraph or selected paragraph and puts borders around the individual paragraphs in the selection and between columns (if there are any).
- **Inside Border** puts horizontal lines between each paragraph and vertical lines between each column in the selection.
- **Inside Horizontal Border** or **Inside Vertical Border** puts horizontal lines between each paragraph or vertical lines between each column in the selection, respectively.
- **No Border** removes any existing borders from the selection.

Using the Borders and Shading Dialog Box

You can also add borders through the Borders and Shading dialog box. The dialog box makes it easy to work with all the border options on the toolbar, and it gives you some additional options. You can increase the white space between the box and the text, create a shadowed or 3-D box, or create a box that uses custom borders.

To use the Borders and Shading dialog box:

1. Place your insertion point in the paragraph you want to format (or select multiple paragraphs.
2. Choose **Borders and Shading** from the Format menu to open the Borders and Shading dialog box shown in Figure 8.30. Select the **Borders** tab if it isn't already visible.
3. Make any selections you want from the Style, Color, and Width lists.

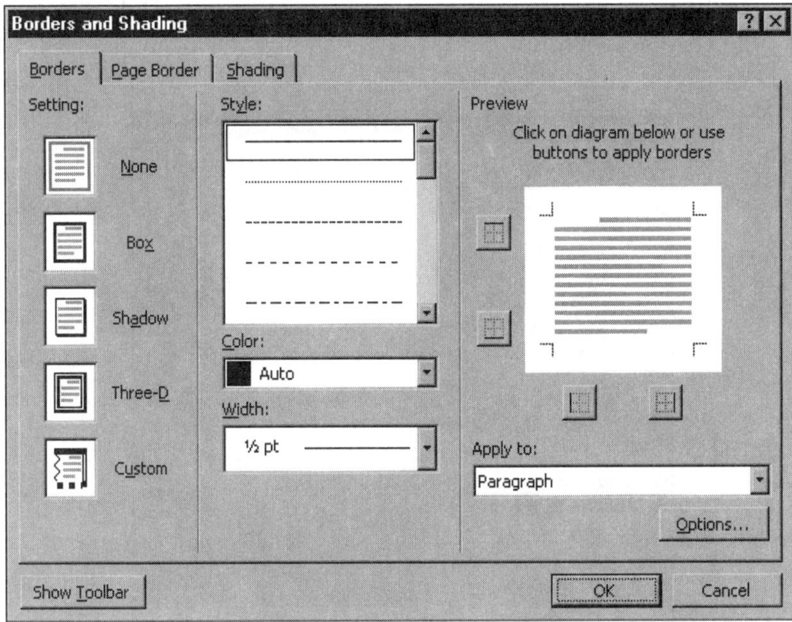

Figure 8.30 The ***Borders*** *tab in the Borders and Shading dialog box.*

4. Click one of the Setting buttons:

   - **None** gives you no border at all. Use this option to get rid of existing borders on selected text.
   - **Box** gives you a standard box that uses whatever style, color, and width settings you select.
   - **Shadow** applies a shadow effect (a dark, thicker border to the bottom and right sides of the box). The shadow effect only works if you have a box with all four borders.
   - **Three-D** gives you a three-dimensional effect. This option only works when one of the asymmetric line styles is selected (like the thick/thin line combinations).
   - **Custom** creates a box using the options you click in the Preview diagram. You can click the different buttons to mix and match various border options. If you use the **Preview** button to change border options, Word automatically changes the setting to **Custom**.

5. To change the amount of space between the text and the border, click the **Options** button to open the dialog box shown in Figure 8.31.

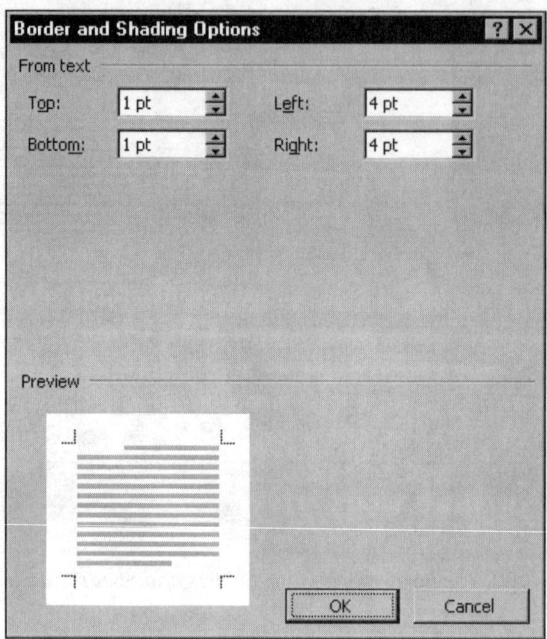

Figure 8.31 *The Border and Shading Options dialog box.*

6. Make any changes you want, then click **OK** to return to the Borders and Shading dialog box.
7. When you finish selecting options, click **OK**.

Applying Shading Behind a Paragraph

As with putting boxes around a paragraph, a little shading goes a long way. Infrequently used, shading can mark a paragraph as being outside the flow of the rest of the body text. For example, you've probably seen sidebars in magazines with short pieces related to the main story but not directly a part of it. Sidebars often have gray or colored shading behind the text. Another use might be occasional tips or gossipy tidbits to enliven a nonfiction book, as shown in Figure 8.32.

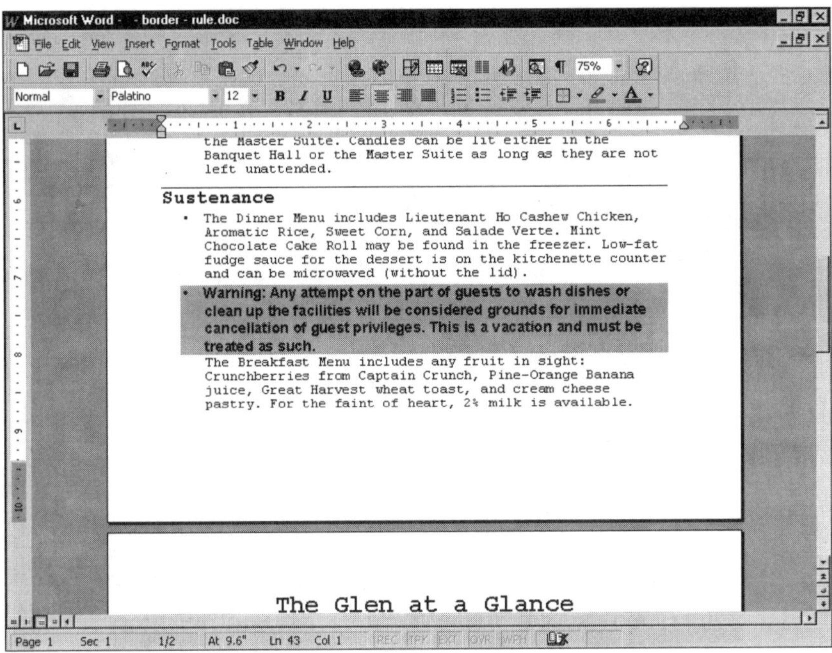

Figure 8.32 A paragraph with shading.

In most cases, shading looks better with a border. In Figure 8.32 the effect would be much crisper with a border around the shaded text.

If you're using gray shading, don't make it too dark. 20% gray is a good shading to start with. A background that's too dark gray can make the paragraph text difficult to read. As always, print a draft if there's any question.

To put shading behind a paragraph:

1. Position your insertion point in the paragraph you want to shade (or select multiple paragraphs).
2. Choose **Borders and Shading** from the Paragraph menu and select the **Shading** tab (shown in Figure 8.33).

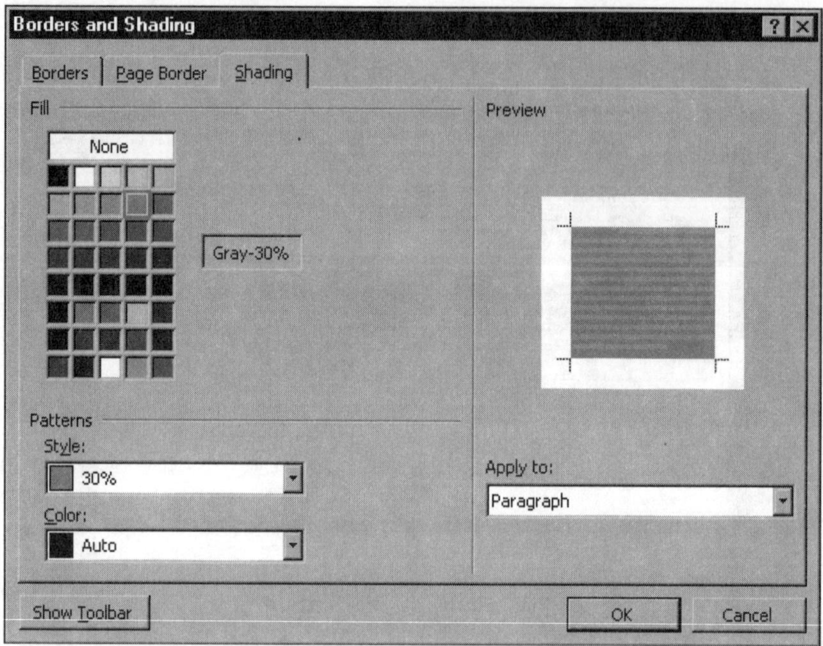

*Figure 8.33 The **Shading** tab in the Borders and Shading dialog box.*

3. Choose a fill amount or color from the Fill palette.
4. Choose a pattern from the Style drop-down list shown in Figure 8.34. In the figure, I've scrolled down a bit in the list to show you some of the available patterns.
5. Choose a color from the Color list.
6. Click **OK** when you've made all your selections.

Some of the shading styles can make it difficult to read the text. Don't forget that no matter how pretty the shading, someone needs to read the text.

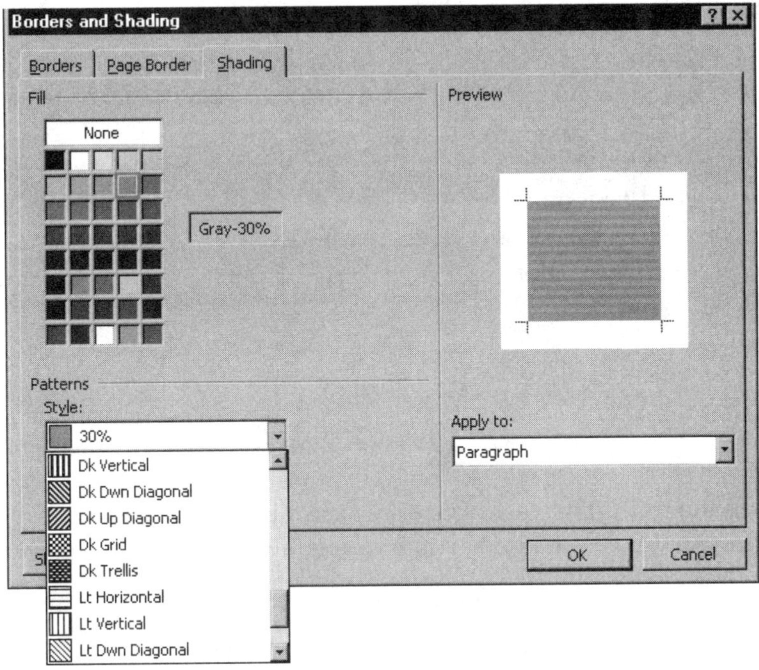

Figure 8.34 *The Style drop-down list.*

USING TABS

As long as people have been typing, tab settings have been used to align columns or indent paragraphs. Oddly enough, the most important thing to remember about tabs in Word is when *not* to use them. A lot of the previous reasons for using tabs are now taken care of with nearly automatic methods. Table 8.2 shows former reasons for using tabs and the feature in Word that now take care of the problem much more easily.

Table 8.2 Old reasons to use tabs and how to accomplish in Word.

To do this	Use this feature instead of tabs
Line up items in a table format	Table feature (see Chapter 16).
Indent the first line of a paragraph	**First line indent** option covered earlier in this chapter.
Separate numbers from text in a numbered list	The **Bullets and Numbers** feature (see Chapter 21).

Four Types of Tab Stops

Word has four different types of tabs, and the tab markers on the ruler change so you can see what kind of tabs you have. Figure 8.35 shows examples of each tab type and points out the different tab markers.

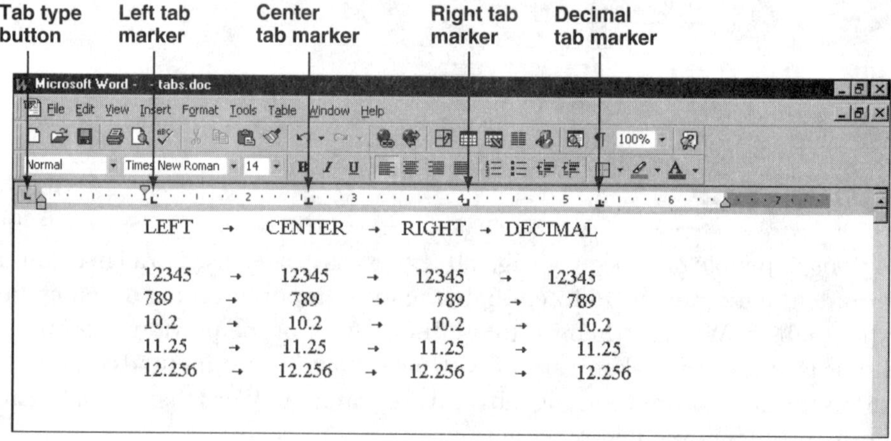

Figure 8.35 Examples of tab-types in Word.

The different tab types are:

- **Left tabs** are the default. With a *left tab*, the left edge of the text lines up at the tab stop and the text moves over to the right as you type.

- With *right tabs*, the right edge of the text lines up at the tab stop and the text moves to the left as you type.
- With *center tabs*, the text is centered over the tab stop.
- With *decimal tabs*, the text lines up on a decimal point. The text in front of the decimal point acts like it's right-aligned (moving to the left as you type). The text after the decimal point is left-aligned (it moves to the right as you type). If the text doesn't contain a decimal point, a decimal tab acts like a right-aligned tab.

One thing to remember in times of tab confusion is that tabs can be submerged. That is, if you have a line of text that goes beyond the first tab setting and then you press the **Tab** key, that first tab setting is ignored. For example, suppose you have a tab set at one inch, another at three inches, and two inches of text on that line. If you press the **Tab** key at this point, you'll go straight to the second tab, ignoring the first.

Setting Tabs with the Ruler

Depending on your needs, you can set tabs quickly from the ruler or set them precisely by entering measurements in a dialog box.

To set a tab with the ruler:

1. Click anywhere in the paragraph for which you want to set a tab (or select multiple paragraphs to apply the tab settings to).
2. Make sure the ruler is displayed. If necessary, choose **Ruler** from the View menu.
3. Click the tab alignment button to the left of the ruler until the tab type you want is displayed. A ScreenTip shows you the current tab type.
4. Click in the ruler where you want the tab to be, holding down the mouse button and dragging left or right until it's positioned correctly.

If the ruler doesn't seem to respond to your click, make sure you click in the bottom half of the ruler, below the marks for inches and fractions of an inch. If you accidentally move an indent mark instead, release the mouse button and choose **Undo**. To set a tab in a difficult spot, such as at the right margin, first click in an open part of the ruler and then drag the tab marker to the new position.

To delete a tab, just drag it off the ruler. To move a tab, position your mouse pointer on the tab you want to move and drag it to a new location.

To set tabs with the Tabs dialog box:

1. Click anywhere in the paragraph where you want to set the tab (or select multiple paragraphs).
2. Choose **Tabs** from the Format menu to open the Tabs dialog box shown in Figure 8.36.

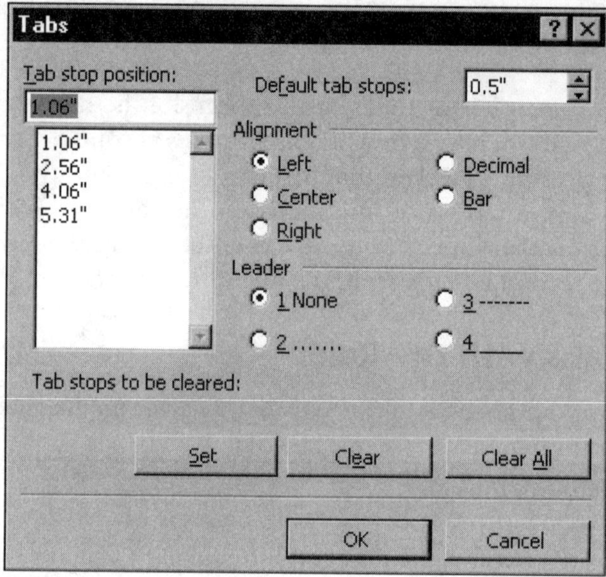

Figure 8.36 *The Tabs dialog box.*

3. Enter a measurement in the Tab stop position box. The number you enter tells Word how far to position the tab stop from the left margin. The Tab stop position list shows any other tabs that have been set, including tabs that you set using the ruler.
4. Choose the alignment option you want for this tab and click the **Set** button. If you want to set more tabs during this session, don't click **OK** or press **Enter**. Taking either of these actions closes the dialog box.
5. When you've set all the tabs you want, click **OK** or press **Enter**.

You can get rid of one tab setting by selecting it from the Tab stop position list and clicking the **Clear** button or delete all the existing tabs by clicking the **Clear All** button.

Setting Default Tabs

Word comes with default tab settings every half-inch. When you insert a custom tab setting, Word deletes all of the preset tabs to the left of the new tab.

In the Tabs dialog box, enter a setting in the Default tab stops text box. For example, if you want tabs every inch instead of every half-inch, type a **1** in the text box (or click on the **up arrow** next to the text box until **1"** is displayed in the box).

Changing the default settings won't affect any tabs you may have set for existing paragraphs.

Setting Tab Leaders

One of the few formatting options you can't do with a table but can with tabs is *dot leaders.* You see these most often in tables of contents and price lists. The purpose of dotted tab leaders is to connect an item on the left with another item (usually a number) on the right. This reduces the problem of not being able to tell, for example, which heading in a table of contents goes with which page number. If you let Word build your table of contents (you'll learn how to do this in Chapter 22), the dot leader tab is set automatically.

To add leaders to your tab settings:

1. Click in the paragraph where you want the leaders.
2. Choose **Tabs** from the Format menu to open the Tabs dialog box.
3. Select the tab setting to which you want to add a leader from the Tab stop position list. Or, to add a new tab setting, enter a measurement in the Tab stop position box.
4. Select an alignment option. In most cases, you'll want to use right-aligned tabs with dot leaders to make sure the text after the leader (usually a page number) ends at the same spot on each line.
5. Select a Leader option and click **OK.** Option 2 is the most common leader style, a series of small dots.
6. Type some text, press the **Tab** key, and then type a number. As soon as you press the **Tab** key, notice that the leader dots or lines appear. Figure 8.37 shows the different leader styles.

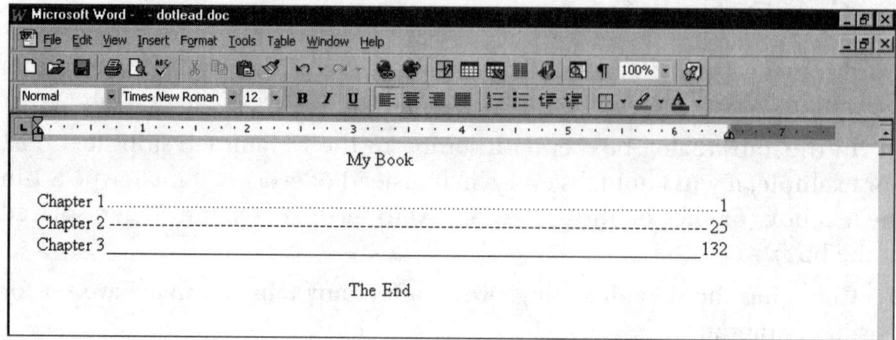

Figure 8.37 Samples of each leader style.

From Here...

In this chapter you've learned all the basic options (and some advanced ones) for formatting paragraphs. You can adjust the space before, after, and between lines of a paragraph. You can apply borders and shading to set off paragraphs from the rest of a document. With indenting and outdenting, you can make headings and body paragraphs easy to read. Now it's time to learn about all the stuff you can do to format pages.

CHAPTER 9

Page and Section Formatting

Let's talk about:

- Page breaks
- Section breaks
- Working with margins
- Creating headers and footers
- Adding page numbers
- Changing the paper size and orientation

In the preceding chapters, you learned how to format characters and paragraphs and how to change font formatting and such paragraph properties as indents and vertical spacing. In this chapter, you'll how to work with pages and sections.

Word's page formatting options include margins, paper size, page break, page numbers, and headers and footers. And what's the scoop with sections? Well, you need a way to tell Word when you want to apply page formatting options to a specific part of a document. Otherwise, your top and bottom margin settings or page numbers would have to be used on every single page. Read on to learn more about pages and sections.

PAGE BREAKS

With Word, you usually don't have to worry about where to end a page. As soon as you type more text than will fit on a page, Word inserts an automatic page break and starts a new page for the text that follows. But there are times when you may want to force a page break at a certain place.

Suppose you have a questionnaire and want to leave blank space at the bottom of a page for notes or responses. Or what if you're writing a book and want each chapter to begin on a new page. No problem—just insert a manual page break.

NOTE

If you find that you're inserting manual page breaks in consistent, predictable places (like at the end of every chapter), you would probably be better off using one of Word's section or formatting options that will create the page breaks automatically. Using these features means that your page breaks will always occur where you want them even when you add or delete text.

To insert a manual page break, press **Ctrl+Enter** or choose **Break** from the Insert menu, select **Page break** in the Break dialog box, and then click **OK**.

In Normal view, it's easy to tell a manual page break from an automatic one, but in Page Layout view, both types of page breaks look the same. To display manual page breaks in Page Layout view, click the **Show/Hide ¶** button on the Standard toolbar.

Understanding Pages and Sections

With primitive word processors, you could have many different kinds of font formats in the document, but some settings had to remain the same for the whole document. Page formats were among these. In Word, you can have many kinds of page formats in the same document. For example, you can have a page that prints to an envelope, followed by several pages that print to normal 8.5x11-inch paper, followed by pages with a different top margin setting, followed by another part of the page that prints the document sideways and uses three columns of text instead of one. In older word processors, each of these parts would have to be a separate document.

If you never need to change page formatting options part way through a document, you don't need to know about sections. However, if you will ever want to mix single-column and multicolumn layouts in the same document, use running chapter titles at the top of each page, or use Roman numerals for page numbers in one part of a document and Arabic numerals in another, keep reading.

What's a Section?

Sections allow you to divide a Word document into parts that each have their own page formatting options. A section is divided from the rest of the document by a *section break*, an on-screen marker that looks similar to a manual page break (see Figure 9.1).

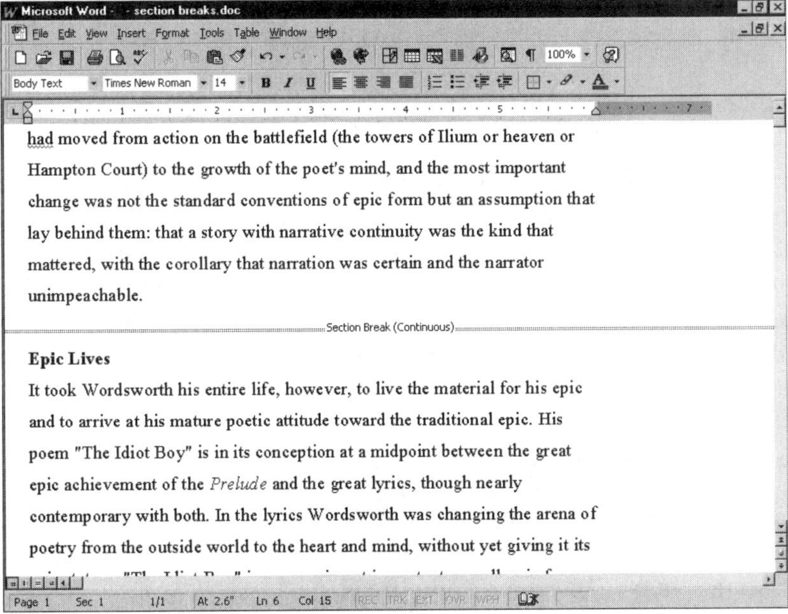

Figure 9.1 *A section break in Normal view.*

Like manual page breaks, section breaks are not normally visible in Page Layout view. To see section breaks in Page Layout view (see Figure 9.2), click the **Show/Hide ¶** button on the Standard toolbar.

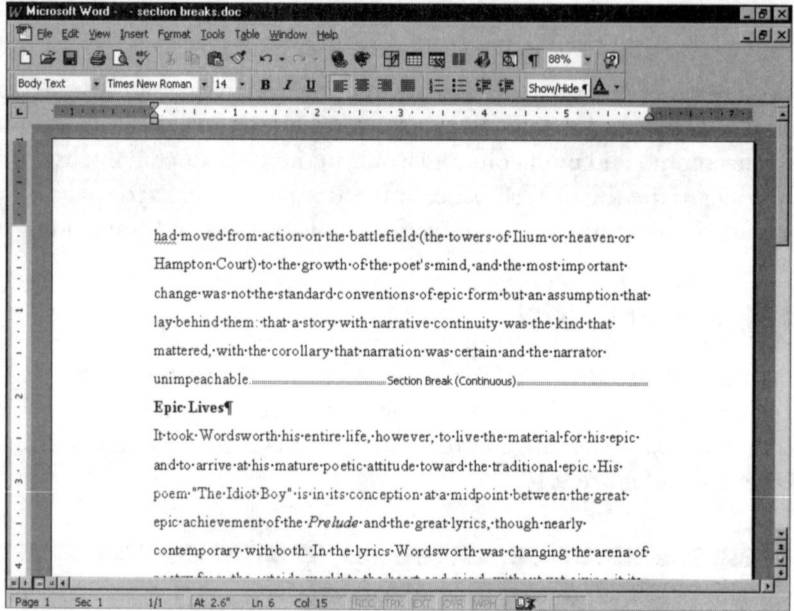

Figure 9.2 *A section break in Page Layout view.*

A section mark contains the page formatting options for that section. As with a paragraph mark, deleting a section mark causes the two sections to run together and acquire the same page formatting. The last paragraph mark in any document contains the section formatting for the final section. Section breaks can occur midway through a page, as when a page changes from one to three columns of text, or a section break can be automatically followed by a break for a new page.

Inserting a Section Break

A simple document with no section breaks is a single section. No matter where you go in the document, the status bar reads *Sec 1.* To add a new section or to split a section in two, insert a section break.

When you insert a section break, you get to decide what happens between one section and the next. You can make the new section begin right where the old section leaves off, at the top of a new page, or at the top of the next even or odd page. If you insert a section break in the middle of text that's formatted in more than one column, you can also have the section begin at the top of the next column instead of immediately.

Why bother with a special kind of section break rather than just inserting a page break or two to make sure the next section starts in the right place? The answer is that it's easier to do something once than many times. If you insert a couple of page breaks to make a chapter start on an odd page, you're all set—for the moment. But as soon as you do some editing, the chapter heading could end up on an even page. If anything is consistently true in writing, it's that documents change. And when you think they're all ready to go, they change again.

To insert a section break:

1. Place the insertion point at the beginning of the line that should start the new section.
2. Choose **Break** from the Insert menu to open the Break dialog box shown in Figure 9.3.

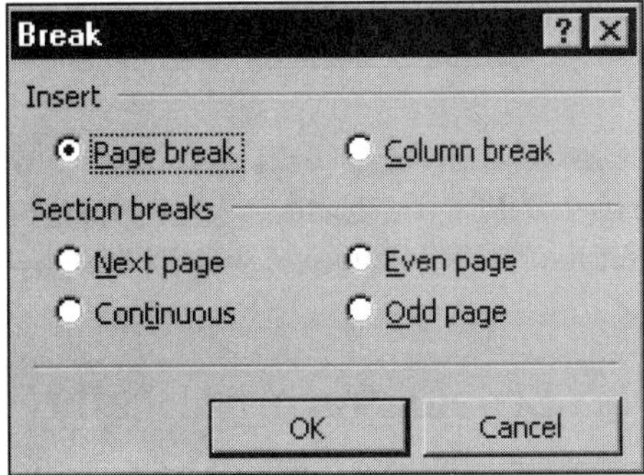

Figure 9.3 *The Break dialog box.*

3. Select the kind of section break (see Table 9.1) you want and click **OK**.

Table 9.1 *What different section breaks do.*

THIS SECTION BREAK	DOES THIS
Next Page	Inserts a page break at the section break and begins the following text at the top of the next page.
Continuous	Continues, on the same page, the text that follows the section break. For example, if you want a page that has one text column and then three columns, the section break should be continuous. You can have multiple sections on the same page.
Even Page	Begins the text following the section break at the top of the next even page. For example, if the section break is in the middle of page 13, the new section begins at the top of page 14. If the section break is at the middle of page 12, the new section still begins at the top of page 14. This is useful when you want chapters to always begin on the left-hand (even) page.
Odd Page	Begins the text following the section break at the top of the next odd-numbered page. This is useful if you want each chapter or section to begin on a right-hand (odd) page.

NOTE

After you've inserted a section break, you can select, copy, or delete it as you can any character. Before you delete a section break, however, make sure you know what formatting it contains and what will happen when you delete it.

Inserting Section Breaks Automatically

Now you know how to insert a new section break. It's easy, but in most cases you don't even have to take that simple action. Word can automatically insert appropriate section breaks as you change your page formatting, saving you an extra step.

Depending on whether text is selected and whether your document already contains multiple sections, you can apply page formatting in a variety of ways. You can apply page formatting to only the text you have selected, to the selected section, to the whole document, or from the insertion point to the next section break. When you choose to apply formatting from this point forward, Word automatically inserts section breaks at the appropriate locations.

To insert a section break automatically:

1. Position your insertion point at the beginning of the area you want to format or select the text you want to format if you want the formatting applied to a particular section of text.
2. Choose **Page Setup** from File menu to open the Page Setup dialog box shown in Figure 9.4.

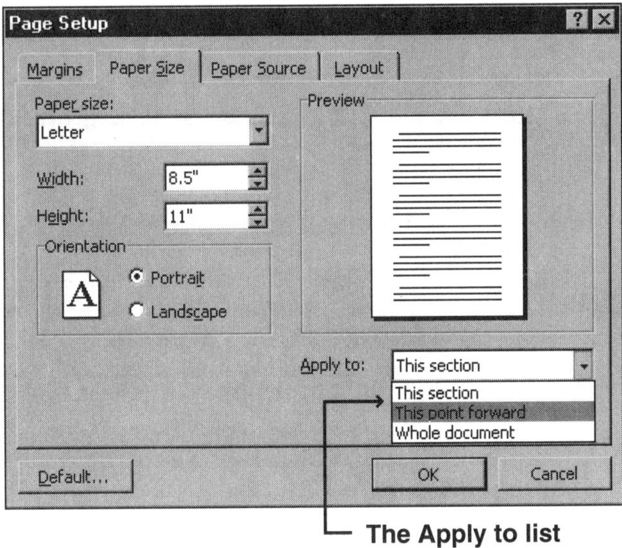

Figure 9.4 The Page Setup dialog box with the Apply to drop-down list opened.

3. Choose **This point forward** or **Selected text** from the Apply to drop-down list. The options in this list vary, depending on whether text is selected and whether your document contains more than one section already. If you don't have text selected, the **Selected Text** option isn't available, and if you do have text selected, the **This point forward** option isn't available.

4. Select the page formatting changes you want and click **OK**. Word inserts any section breaks necessary to apply page formatting changes to the text that you selected or otherwise specified.

For example, suppose you want to leave your 1-inch margins for the beginning of your document but change to a 3-inch left margin starting in the middle of page 2. To do this, just place your insertion point at the beginning of the line where you want the margin change to begin and follow the steps just listed.

Word automatically inserts a section break at the insertion point and changes the page formatting. In Normal view, you can't see the effect of the margin change, but when you select **Page Layout** view it becomes apparent, as shown in Figure 9.5.

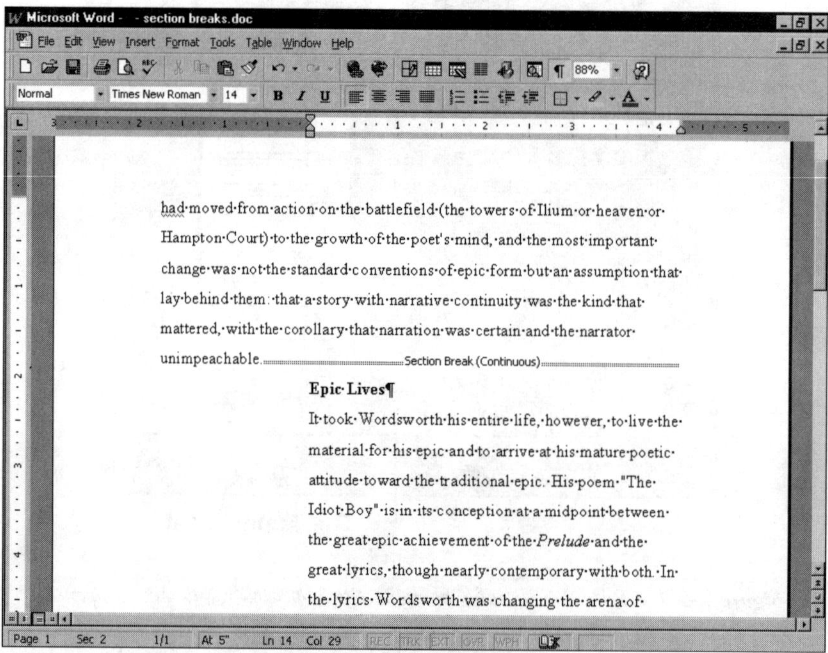

Figure 9.5 *The text after the section break has a 3-inch left margin.*

If you had made this change by selecting an area of text in the middle of the document and applying the change to the selected text, Word would automatically insert section breaks at the beginning and end of your selected text.

Now that you know how to create new sections and apply formatting to different parts of a document, it's time to dive into the actual formatting options.

WORKING WITH MARGINS

Word gives you default margins of 1 inch at the top and bottom and 1.25 inches on the left and right. If these defaults work for you, you don't have to do anything. But if you want to change the margins, Word lets you accomplish the task either by using the Page Setup dialog box or the ruler. Before we get into the actual techniques for changing margins, here's a brief primer on margins and indents.

Margins vs. Indents

Margins, not to be confused with paragraph indents, determine the basic working space of a page. There are several things that can go outside the page margins, however. These include headers and footers (which can include page numbers or running chapter titles), paragraphs with negative indents that stick out into the margins, and framed text or graphics (like the icons in this book) that can be placed anywhere on the page, inside or outside the margins. You'll learn more about frames in Chapter 13.

Distinguishing between margins and indents can be confusing because in typewriter terms, what we normally think of as margins are closer to what Word calls *indents.* Perhaps the easiest way to think of margins is as guidelines that tabs or indents are measured from. In the previous chapter, you learned that you could set a paragraph's left indent to half an inch to narrow the paragraph's width, bringing it in from the left. But half an inch narrower than what? Narrower than the margins. Margins are what left and right indents are measured from.

It's easy to see this graphically by looking at the ruler. The white part of the ruler shows the usable width of the page defined by your margins. Within that usable space, you can set paragraph indents. By setting the paragraph indents outside the white space, you're setting negative indents that go into the margins. For example, if you're using 8.5x11-inch paper with 1.25-inch left and right margins (Word's default setting), you're left with 6 inches for the main body of the document. With unindented paragraphs, the ruler looks like Figure 9.6.

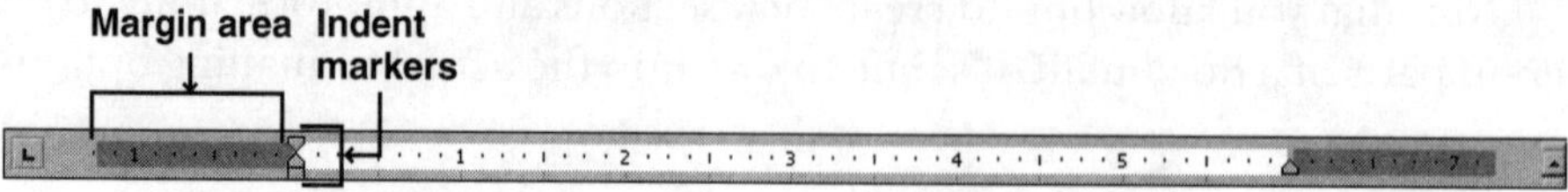

Figure 9.6 The ruler in Page Layout view with default margins and no indents.

If the whole paragraph is indented half an inch from the left, with the first line indented an extra quarter of an inch, the ruler looks like Figure 9.7.

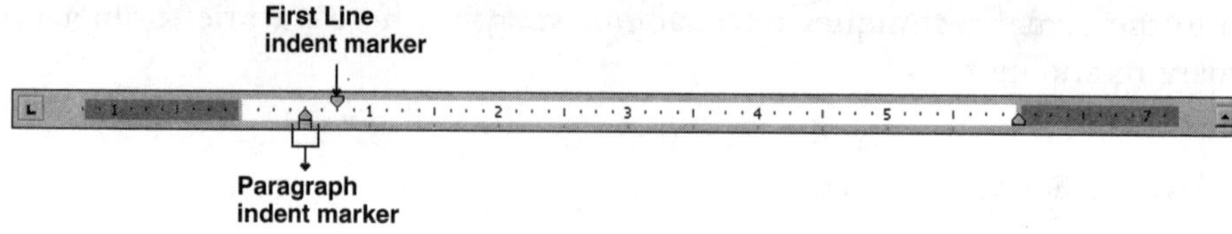

Figure 9.7 The ruler with a first line indent.

A paragraph that extends into both the left and right margins by a quarter inch looks like Figure 9.8 on the ruler.

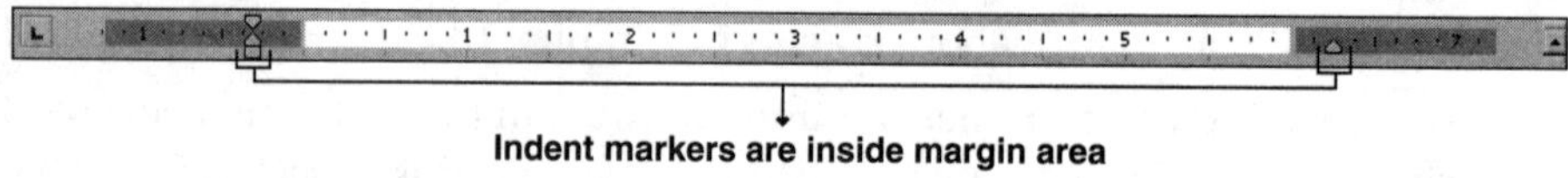

Figure 9.8 The ruler with outdented settings.

An 8.5x11-inch page with 2-inch margins on each side leaves a narrower space for body text, as shown in Figure 9.9.

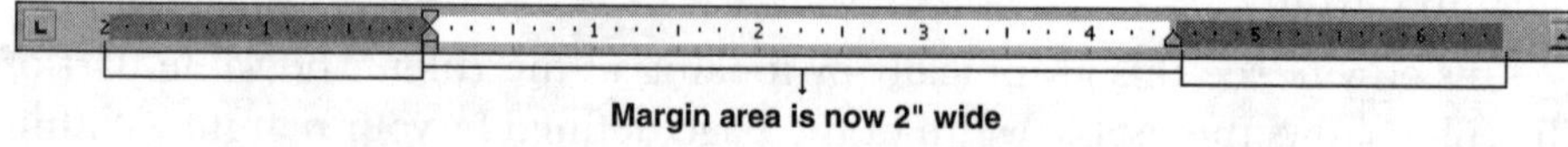

Figure 9.9 Two-inch margins.

In Page Layout view, the vertical ruler shows the top and bottom margins in a similar way. By increasing the top margin, you push the text further down the page, and by increasing the bottom margin, you move the lower limit further up the page.

Setting Page Margins

Even though you may want to add some elements outside the main text area, plan to set your margins to reflect where you want *most* of your text to fall. Then you can put certain items in the margin by using negative indents. You can extend headings into the margins this way, for example. To put icons or other objects in the margins, you can use text boxes, which are covered in Chapter 13.

As for top and bottom margins, the default settings do very well for most documents such as letters, memos, and reports. But suppose you have special stationery with a logo at the top or extra printing on the side. Increasing the margin on the top or side is the best way to make sure your document text doesn't overrun the logo.

Like many of the formatting options in Word, you can set page margins directly from the ruler or with precise measurements in a dialog box.

To set margins using the Page Setup dialog box:

1. Choose **Page Setup** from the File menu and select the **Margins** tab, as shown in Figure 9.10.

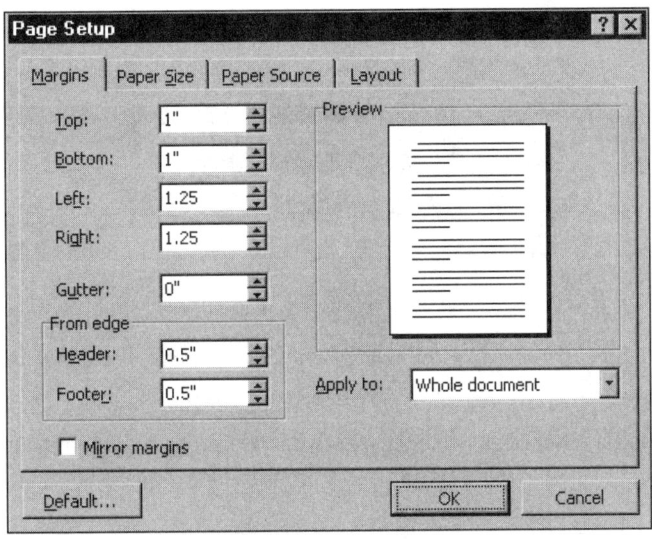

Figure 9.10 *The* ***Margins*** *tab in the Page Setup dialog box.*

2. Enter settings in the Top, Bottom, Left, and Right text boxes. Check the **Preview** box to make sure the margins are the way you want them.
3. From the Apply To list, select **Whole document** or **This point forward**. If you choose **Whole document**, Word applies your margin settings to the entire document. If you choose **This point forward**, Word applies the margin setting to the rest of the document, starting with the location of your insertion point and adds a new section break.
4. Click **OK**.

To set margins from the ruler:

1. Make sure the ruler is displayed and you are in Page Layout view. Choose **Ruler** from the View menu, if necessary, and switch to Page Layout view by choosing **Page Layout** from the View menu.
2. Position the mouse pointer at the edge of the white space at either end of the ruler. When you move the mouse pointer over the correct part of the ruler, the pointer changes to a small, two-headed arrow (Figure 9.11) and a ToolTip says *Left Margin* or *Right Margin* (or *Top* or *Bottom Margin* on the vertical ruler). You can then drag the margin left or right (on the horizontal ruler) or up and down (on the vertical ruler).

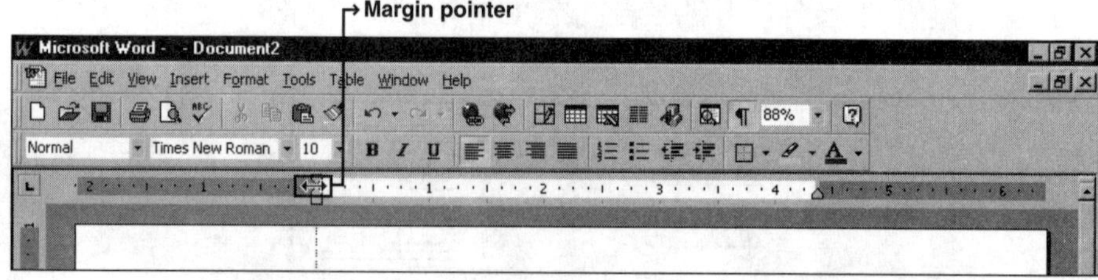

Figure 9.11 When you see this double-arrow, you're ready to change margins.

If nothing happens when you try to change a margin, you may not be in Page Layout view. Choose **Page Layout** from the View menu and try again.

3. Drag the margin to the width you want. As you drag, a dashed vertical line shows what's happening on the page.

Using Mirror Margins to Distinguish Left and Right Pages

The margin settings you've applied so far assume that each page in the document will have the same margins, regardless of whether it's an odd-numbered or an even-numbered page. In some situations, that may not be what you want. Suppose your printed pages will be bound into a book or printed on both sides of paper with punched holes for a three-ring binder. In these cases, you need extra space on the inside margin, but which side is inside depends on the page. On the left-hand (even-numbered) page, the inside edge is on the right. For the right-hand (odd-numbered) page, the inside edge is on the left. For outside edges, it's the opposite (see Figure 9.12).

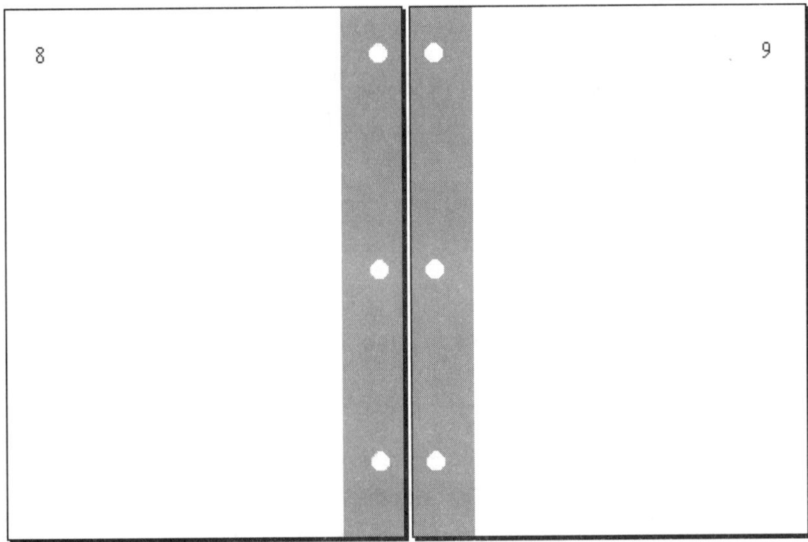

Figure 9.12 *With three-hole punched paper, you need different margins for odd and even pages.*

The solution is to use *mirror margins*. This option tells Word to distinguish between left and right pages, ensuring consistent margin measurements regardless of whether you have an odd-numbered or an even-numbered page.

In addition, when you create headers or footers (covered later in this chapter), you can specify different information on the even-numbered and odd-numbered pages. Many books take advantage of this capability to print the book's title on even pages, for example, and the chapter title on odd pages.

When you set aside extra space on the inside margins for binding or hole-punched paper, the area you don't want anything printed on is called the *gutter.* Word lets you specify how wide you want the gutter area to be. If you're using mirror margins only to allow separate odd and even headers, you don't need to specify a gutter width.

To set mirror margins:

1. Choose **Page Setup** from the File menu and make sure the **Margins** tab is selected.
2. Click the **Mirror Margins** check box. As you can see in Figure 9.13, the Preview box now shows both left and right (even and odd) pages, and the Left and Right boxes change to Inside and Outside.

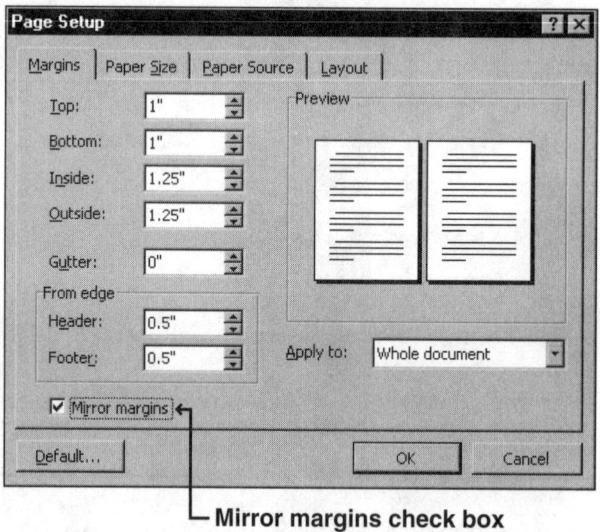

*Figure 9.13 The **Margins** tab with **Mirror Margins** selected.*

3. Enter settings in the Inside and Outside text boxes.
4. In the Gutter box, specify how much space you want to add to the inside margins.
5. Select **Whole Document** from the Apply To drop-down list (unless you have a reason not to use mirror margins for the entire document) and then click **OK**.

REPEATING INFORMATION IN HEADERS AND FOOTERS

Headers and footers make it easy to repeat the same text on every page (or on selected pages) of your document. What's the difference between headers and footers? C'mon, take a wild guess. That's right; *headers* appear at the top of a page and *footers* at the bottom. That's the *only* difference. Other than that, everything I say about headers can be applied to footers (and vice versa).

Why use headers and footers? Have you ever typed a title and page number at the bottom of every page of a document? You have? Then I bet you can guess what's coming next. You end up adding a couple of lines of text to the first page, and the text that used to be at the bottom of each page is now somewhere in the middle. So you have to adjust the position of every title and page number. Imagine this process repeated every time a small change is made to the document (maybe you don't have to imagine—maybe you've been there).

Headers and footers let you completely bypass this time-wasting nightmare. If you use these features, you only enter the information once, and the text stays where it's supposed to be no matter how many changes you make to your document. In addition, if you want to change something about the header or footer itself, you only do it once.

What You Can Put in a Header or Footer

Almost anything you can put in a document—text, numbers, graphic images, lines, borders—can go in headers and footers. If you can do it in a document, you can probably do it in a header or footer. You can use all the techniques you've already learned to move the insertion point and make formatting changes. Any features that aren't available in headers or footers are dimmed on the pull-down menus.

To get an idea of the practical usage of headers and footers, take a look at this book. The top of every page contains the page number and the chapter number or the chapter name. All the chapter information, including the line, is part of an automatic header that repeats on each page.

Creating a Header or Footer

In a simple document such as a long business letter, you probably need only one header. But in books or other complex documents, you may want to change the header information throughout the document. For example, the chapter number and title are different in each chapter. To create a different header or footer for different sections of a document, all you need to do is insert a section break each time you want to change the header.

These instructions just cover the basics of creating a header or footer; the Header and Footer toolbar includes several options to automate the process (like adding automatic page numbering). I'll cover those options in a bit.

1. Place your insertion point anywhere in the section where you want the header or footer.
2. Choose **Header and Footer** from the View menu. As you can see in Figure 9.14, Word switches to Page Layout view, dims the document text area (so you can see that it's currently unavailable), displays the Header and Footer toolbar, and puts your insertion point inside the Header editing box. If you want to create a footer instead of a header, click the **Switch Between Header and Footer** button.
3. Type the text for your header or footer and format it however you want.
4. When you're finished, click the **Close** button on the Header and Footer toolbar. Word returns to the editing view you were using previously.

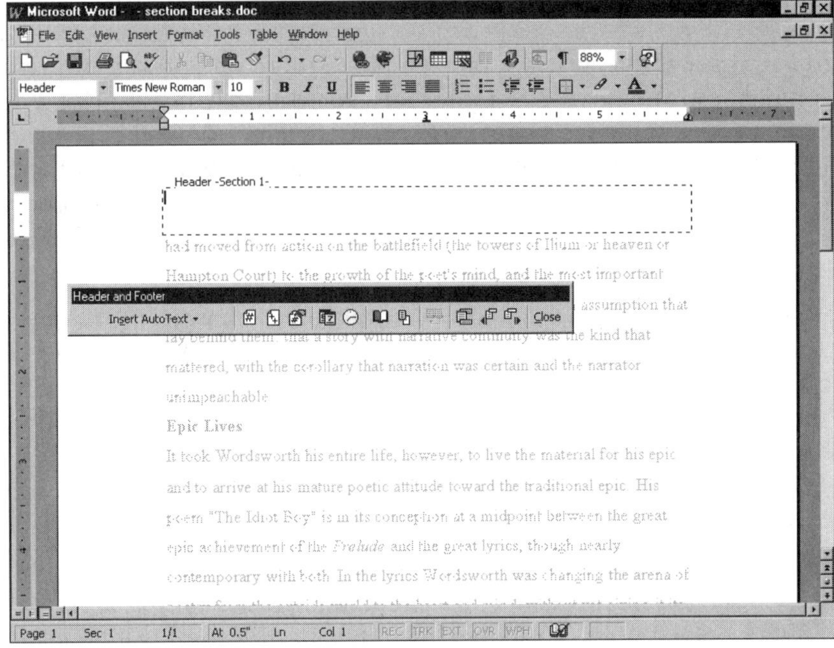

Figure 9.14 *You're ready to create a header.*

The Header and Footer toolbar contains options for just about anything you might want to include in a header or footer. Figure 9.15 shows the toolbar, and the following sections show how to use the different options.

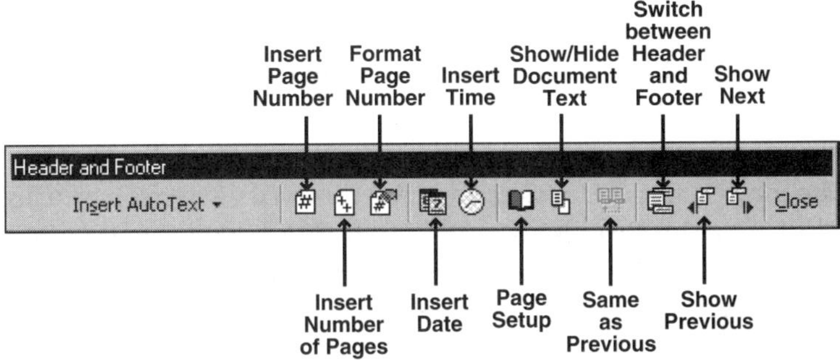

Figure 9.15 *The Header and Footer toolbar.*

Adding Page Numbers in the Header or Footer

Word automatically keeps track of what page you're on and can display that page number in the header or footer for each page when you print a document. The page number that Word inserts in a header or footer isn't an actual number, but a special code, called a *field*. This is how Word keeps the page number updated. The page number field is treated as a single unit, so that when you select the page number for formatting, the whole page number is selected, even if it's several digits long.

The page number field is treated like any other character. You can align the paragraph it's in, put a tab in front of it, delete it, and format it with any font, size, or font effect you want.

To display page numbers in a header or footer:

1. Make sure the Header and Footer toolbar is visible and your insertion point is in a header or footer editing box.
2. Set the page number position by pressing the **Tab** key. Word has two preset tabs in the header and footer editing areas. If you press the **Tab** key once, the page number (or other header text) will be centered between the margins. If you press the **Tab** key again, the page number will be aligned at the right margin.
3. Click the **Page Numbers** button on the Headers and Footers toolbar. Word inserts the page number field in the header or footer. It appears simply as the number of the current page. When selected, the page number has a gray background; this identifies it as a field rather than regular text.
4. To include the total number of pages in the document, click the **Insert Number of Pages** button. I'm sure you've seen documents where a header or footer says something like *Page 6 of 10.* To do this in a Word header or footer, you could type the word **Page** followed by a space and click the **Page Numbers** button. Then type the word **of** followed by a space and click the **Insert Number of Pages** button. That's pretty slick, but there's an even easier way. Check out the **Page X of Y** option in the next section.
5. To format the page number, click the **Format Page Number** button to open the Page Number Format dialog box shown in Figure 9.16. Select the options you want and click **OK**.

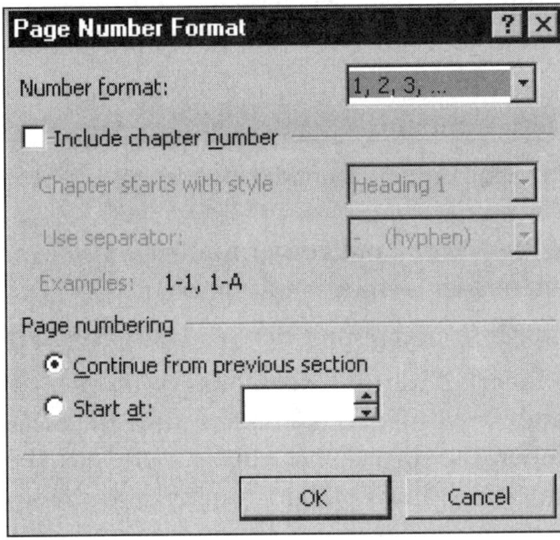

Figure 9.16 *The Page Number Format dialog box.*

- Use the Number Format drop-down list to select Arabic numeral, uppercase or lowercase letters, or uppercase or lowercase Roman numerals.
- Select the **Include chapter number** check box if you want to include chapter numbers along with the page number. With this option, page 3 of chapter 4 would appear like this: *IV-3.*
- By default, the page numbering continues sequentially from section to section. If you want to restart the numbers from a different point for this section, deselect **Continue from previous section** and enter a number in the Start at text box.

Adding Other Information to a Header or Footer

In addition to page numbers, you can add other automatic information to a header or footer: the date, time, filename, file size, author, date last printed, date created, and more. The date and time have their own buttons on the Header and Footer toolbar. The other items can be selected from the Insert AutoText drop-down list.

What is the advantage of this over simply typing the information by hand? Simple. Word keeps track of field information rather than forcing you to do so. If the filename changes, for example, the name is automatically updated in the field. If the number of pages changes, that too is updated. The same goes for the date, time, and other kinds of field information.

If you're not sure whether a word is regular text or part of a field, click it. If it's a field, its background turns gray.

To insert the date or time in a header or footer:

1. Make sure the Header and Footer toolbar is visible and your insertion point is in a header or footer editing box.
2. Position your insertion point where you want to insert the date or time.
3. Click the **Insert Date** or **Insert Time** button on the Headers and Footers toolbar. Word inserts a date or time field that is updated each time you open the document. This is useful for keeping track when you print multiple drafts of a document as you're working on it.

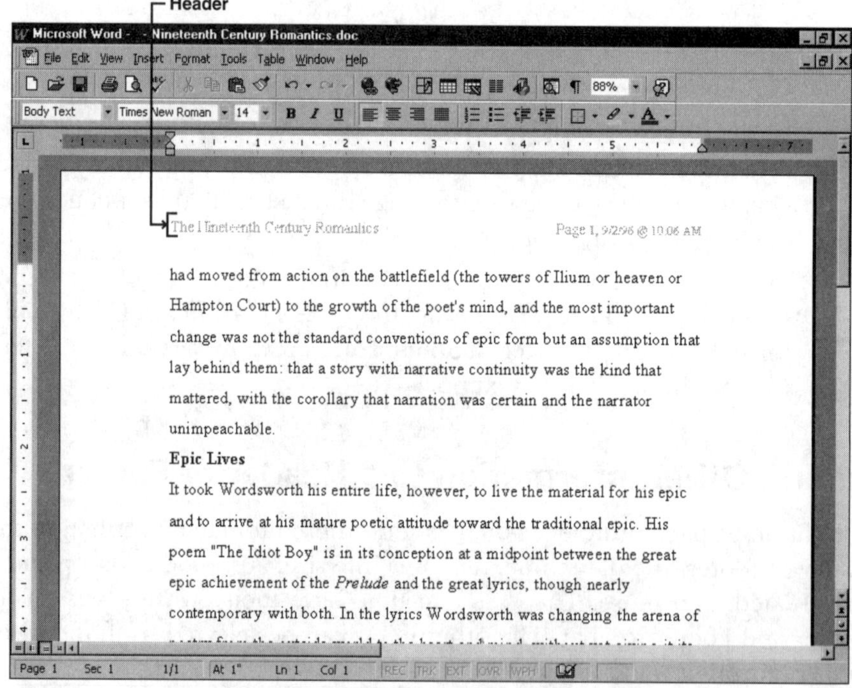

Figure 9.17 A header with date, time, and page number fields.

To insert AutoText entries in a header or footer:

1. Make sure the Header and Footer toolbar is visible and your insertion point is in a header or footer editing box.
2. Position your insertion point where you want to insert the entry.
3. Click the **Insert AutoText** button to open the drop-down list shown in Figure 9.18.

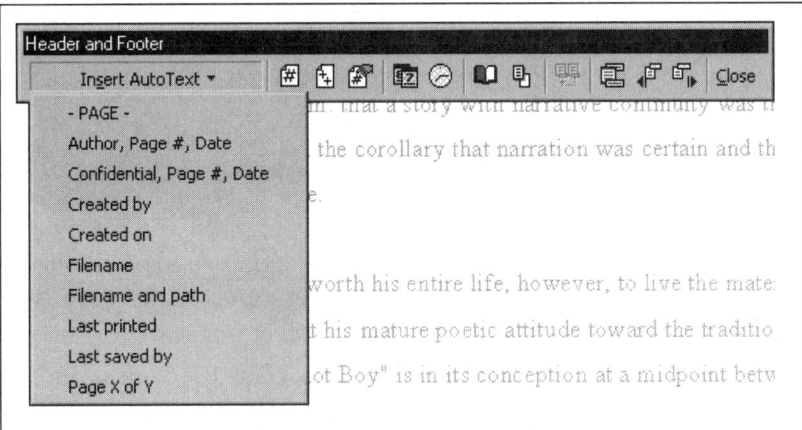

Figure 9.18 The Insert AutoText drop-down list.

The AutoText feature is covered in Chapter 18, "An Introduction to AutoText and Macros."

4. Click to select the item you want to insert. If you're not sure what a particular selection will do, insert it and see if it's what you want. If not, you can always delete it. You can insert more than one AutoText entry in a header or footer. Just repeat steps 2 and 3 for each entry.

Figure 9.19 shows a header that uses the Filename entry on the first line and the Author, Page #, Date entry on the second line. I pressed the **Tab** key to center the Filename, but the Author, Page #, Date entry automatically formats the text so the author is at the left margin, the page number is centered, and the date is right-aligned. I didn't have to make any formatting changes to the second line.

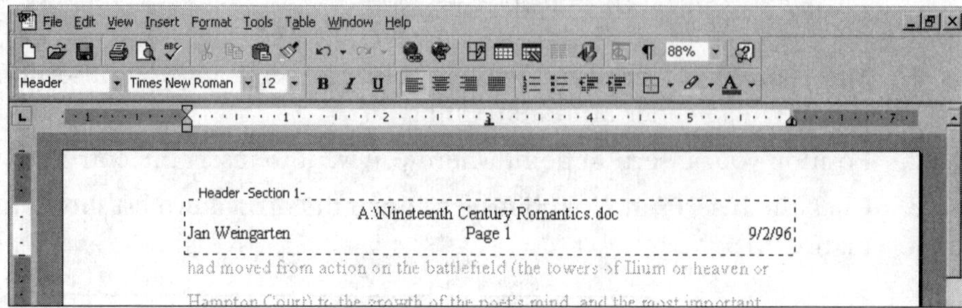

Figure 9.19 A header that uses an AutoText entry.

Creating a Different First Page Header

In most documents, the header or footer information doesn't need to appear on the first page. You may not want a header or footer at all on the first page, or you may want an abbreviated header or footer that contains only the information you want to appear on the first page.

Word takes care of that problem. You can format a section so the header or footer on the first page is treated differently from the header or footer for the rest of that section. You can have completely different information in the first page header or footer.

To change the contents of the header or footer on the first page:

1. Choose **Header and Footer** from the View menu.
2. Click the **Page Setup** button on the Header and Footer toolbar (the button that looks like an open book). When you choose **Page Setup** from the Header and Footer toolbar, the Page Setup dialog box opens with the **Layout** tab active, as shown in Figure 9.20.

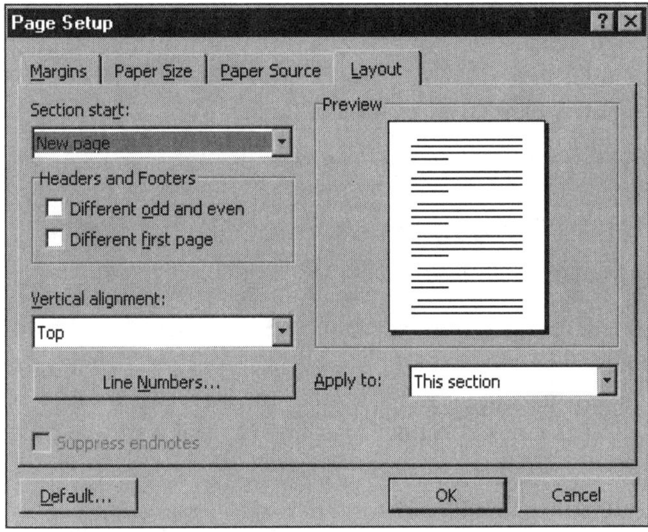

Figure 9.20 The ***Layout*** *tab in the Page Setup dialog box.*

3. Select the **Different first page** check box, then click **OK**. If the insertion point is anywhere past the first page of the section, Word displays the standard header. If the insertion point is in the first page of the section, Word displays the First Page Header editing box, as shown in Figure 9.21. You can move between the standard header and the first page header without returning to your document by clicking on the **Show Next** or **Show Previous** button on the Header and Footer toolbar.

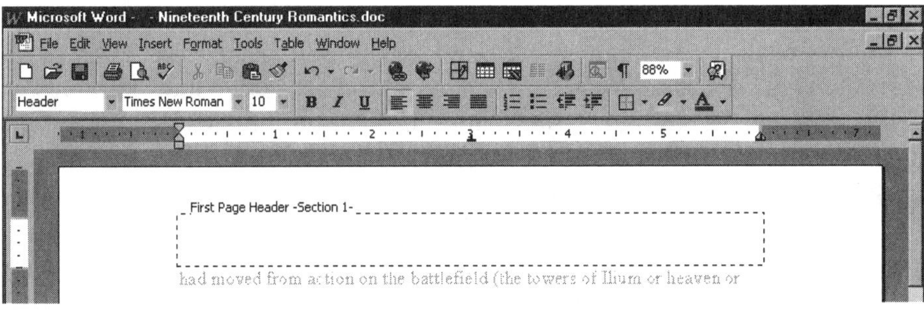

Figure 9.21 The editing box for a first page header.

4. Enter the text and formatting for the header, using any of the techniques discussed in this chapter. If you don't want any header or footer for the first page, follow step 4, but leave the header or footer editing area blank.
5. When you're done, click the **Close** button.

Using Different Headers or Footers for Odd and Even Pages

A simple page setup option lets you have different headers for odd and even pages. This allows you to do such things as always keep the page numbers on the outside of the page when the book is bound, add an extra level of navigation information such as chapter name on each pair of facing pages, or even skip page numbers on every other page.

To create separate headers or footers for odd and even pages:

1. Place your insertion point anywhere in the section you want to apply this option to (or anywhere in the document if you only have one section).
2. Choose **Header and Footer** from the View menu.
3. Click the **Page Setup** button on the Header and Footer toolbar.
4. Select the **Different odd and even** check box.
5. Select an option from the Apply To drop-down list. In most cases, you'll want to apply the odd and even headers or footers option to the whole document.
6. When you choose **OK** to close the dialog box, the header or footer editing box now tells you whether it's an odd or even page header. Once again, you can switch between the odd and even headers (and any other headers in your document by clicking the **Show Previous** or **Show Next** button on the Header and Footer toolbar.

Deleting a Header or Footer

There's no special delete key to get rid of a header or footer. What you have to do is open the header or footer you want to delete, select all the text and delete it. You can, however, quickly select everything in the header or footer in one keystroke: **Ctrl+A**. Then all you have to do is press the **Delete** or **Backspace** key.

Just keep in mind that when you delete a header or footer, it's gone throughout the document. You can't just delete the header on page 8 and expect it to remain on all the other pages. If you want to get rid of the headers for a particular part of a document, first create a separate section and then delete the headers in that section. The headers and footers in the other sections will stay put.

NUMBERING PAGES

As with many features in Word, page numbering couldn't be simpler as long as you let the computer do the work for you. You just saw how simple it is to add a page number code to a header or footer. But if you don't want to include a lot of text and formatting along with the page number, you can use the page numbering feature instead—it's no muss, no fuss. Just open the Page Numbers dialog box, pick a location, and you're done.

By default, page numbering is turned off. If you print a document, it won't have any page numbers. Even though you see page numbers on the Status Bar, you have to tell Word when you want the numbers to appear on the printed page.

This simplicity doesn't take away your flexibility. You still have the option of formatting your numbers as Roman numerals, resetting the page numbering in a certain section, or beginning page numbers from something other than 1. For information on inserting page numbers while editing a header or footer, see "Adding Page Numbers to a Header or Footer" earlier in this chapter.

When you use the Page Numbers dialog box to add page numbering, Word inserts the page number in a frame. Text boxes (discussed in more detail in Chapter 13), allow text or graphics to be positioned anywhere on the page.

To add page numbering using the Page Numbers dialog box:

1. Position your insertion point anywhere in the document (or anywhere in the section to which you want to add page numbers.
2. Choose **Page Numbers** from the Insert menu to open the Page Numbers dialog box shown in Figure 9.22.

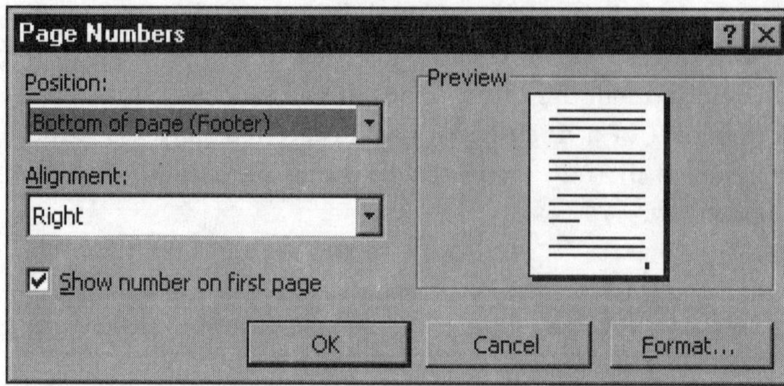

Figure 9.22 The Page Numbers dialog box.

3. From the Position list, select **Top of page (Header)** or **Bottom of page (Footer)**.
4. From the Alignment list, select a horizontal position for the page numbers. If you select **Inside**, the page number is on the left-hand side on odd-numbered pages and on the right-hand side on even-numbered pages, so it's on the inside when a book or document is bound. The **Outside** alignment option produces the opposite effect. **Left**, **Center**, and **Right** need no explanation. Notice that the results of your choices are reflected in the Preview area.
5. Clear the **Show number on first page** check box if you don't want page numbers to appear on the title page of a document or the first page of each section.
6. If you want to change any of the page numbering options, click the **Format** button to open the Page Number Format dialog box, shown in Figure 9.23.
7. Make the selections you want and click **OK**, then click **OK** again to close the Page Numbers dialog box:
   - To change the numbering format, make a selection from the Number format drop-down list.
   - To change the starting page number for the section, select **Start at** and enter a number in the accompanying text box.
8. Click **OK** to close the Page Number Format dialog box, then click **OK** again to close the Page Numbers dialog box.

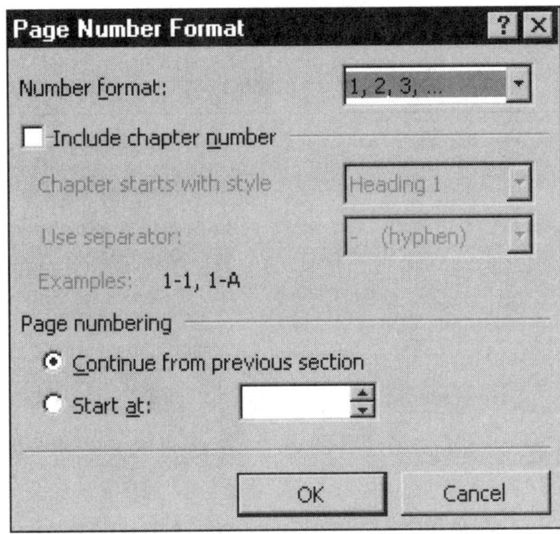

Figure 9.23 The Page Number Format dialog box.

NOTE

If you set up the first section of a book or report to use Roman numerals, remember to restart the numbering at page 1 with Arabic numerals in the section after the introductory section.

Removing Page Numbers

When you add page numbers directly into a header or footer, deleting them is simply a matter of selecting the page number and pressing the **Delete** key. When you insert page numbers using the Page Numbers dialog box the procedure is the same, but the process of selecting the page number is slightly different because it's in a frame.

To remove a page number inserted from the Page Numbers dialog box:

1. Click in the section where you want to remove page numbers.
2. From the View menu, choose **Header and Footer**.
3. Select the page number. Notice the diagonal shading around the page number. This means the page number field is in a frame.

4. Click anywhere in the diagonal shaded area to select the frame (see Figure 9.24).

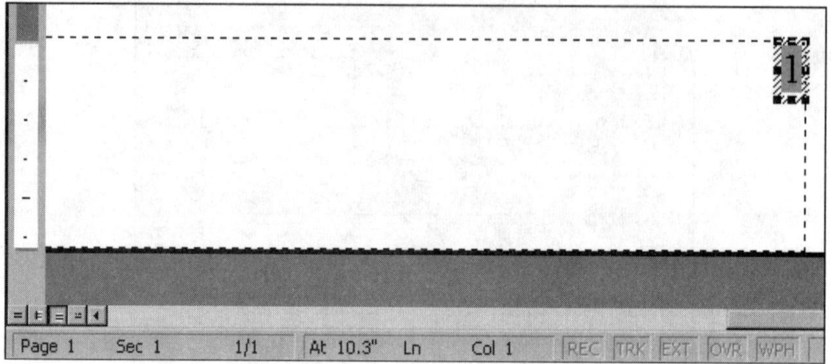

Figure 9.24 This page number is in a frame, and the frame is selected.

5. Press the **Delete** key to delete the page number and its frame.

Changing the Paper Size and Orientation

Not everything in the world is printed on 8.5x11-inch paper standing straight up. Everything we've done so far has been formatted for a standard 8.5x11-inch sheet of paper, with the text printed across the width of the page (called *portrait orientation*). That's Word's default, and it's probably what you'll use most of the time—but not always. What about envelopes? And what if you want the text to print across the long side of the page (called *landscape orientation*)?

It's easier than you might think. Word comes equipped with definitions for a bunch of different paper sizes, including legal-size paper and envelopes. You just pick the one you want and away you go. (You can also create your own custom paper sizes when you get really brave.)

The normal vertical orientation of a document is fine for most letters, reports, and the like, but some long tables, graphics, flyers, and other documents lend themselves to turning the page on its side, so the paper is wider than it is tall. You can adapt Word's paper and printing options to your needs, rather than vice versa.

Here are a few examples of documents that might be improved by using landscape orientation:

- A table with many columns. If the alternative is to make the columns uncomfortably narrow or switch the row and column labels so the information isn't organized naturally, it's probably better to switch to landscape.
- A folded brochure. A three-panel brochure, made from 8.5x11-inch paper turned on its side and folded twice, is a common format for advertising flyers or brochures.
- A calendar or other publication with wide graphics. For example, the Calendar Wizard gives you the choice of printing a calendar sideways. If you want to print a large picture that's wider than it is tall, you could shrink the picture or distort its proportions to make it fit on a portrait page. But for a better look, try landscape orientation.
- Advertising flyers. Because your audience sees so many documents printed portrait style, consider turning your flyer on its side to set it apart from the crowd.

To change the paper size or orientation:

1. Position your insertion point anywhere in the section where you want to change. If there's only one section in the document, the change applies to the whole document.
2. Choose **Page Setup** from the File menu and select the **Paper Size** tab, as shown in Figure 9.25.

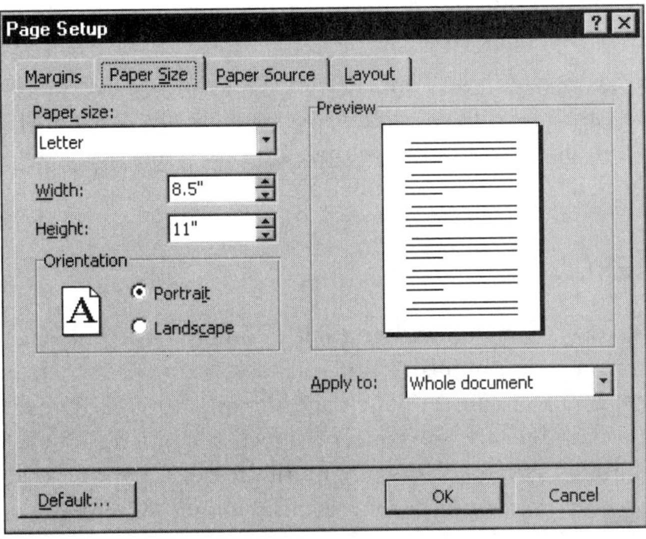

Figure 9.25 The ***Paper Size*** *tab in the Page Setup dialog box.*

3. To change the paper size, make a selection from the Paper size drop-down list.
4. To change the orientation, select **Portrait** or **Landscape**. Notice that the Preview box shows the results of your selections.
5. Make a selection from the Apply to drop-down list, then click **OK**.

When you switch to landscape orientation, you'll notice that the ruler changes. Your printable width of 6 inches or so suddenly expands to about 9. And in the other direction, you can enter only about two-thirds as many lines before Word inserts a page break. To get a birds-eye view of your new settings, choose **Print Preview** from the File menu.

NOTE

Remember that landscape orientation doesn't turn your text sideways. Your text still runs from left to right; it's just the blank page that's turned on its side.

By the way, if you normally use one of these other sizes of paper, such as 8.5x14 inches or the European A4 size, you don't have to change the setting every time you create a new document. Like the other page formatting settings in the Page Setup dialog box, you can select a size and use it as a default that's preset whenever you create a new document. Just change the settings so they match your standard documents and click the **Default** button. Word will ask you to confirm that you really want to change the default settings. If you do, click **Yes**; otherwise, click **No**.

In most cases, you won't mix paper sizes within the same document, although you can. The one case where you're likely to do so is when you want to print a letter along with an envelope. If that's what you want to do, Word will take care of it for you, so you needn't bother.

From Here...

At this point, you can create and edit fairly complex documents. You can add headers, footers, and page numbers (and you know how to keep them from printing on certain pages). You can set your page margins to complement paragraph indents, and you understand the concept of sections, which allows different areas of page formatting in the same document. In the next chapter, you'll learn techniques that will help you find your way around longer documents.

CHAPTER 10

Finding Your Way

Let's talk about:

- Finding text and formatting
- Replacing text and formatting
- Replacing word forms
- Getting to a specific page or location with **Go To**
- Using Bookmarks to mark your place

You've written your masterpiece. It's beautifully formatted. It has headers and footers, and there isn't a widow or orphan in sight. Now what? In my experience, a bunch of major editing changes. You need to add a sentence in that paragraph where you quoted Sally Swensen, but you can't remember what page that was on. You just found out that every place you used the word *hippopotamus*, it was supposed to be *antelope*. And your boss just said "Oh, by the way, all those italic headings need to be changed to bold." In the middle of all this, you get a frantic phone call. You have to leave for a while, but you want to be able to pick up where you left off when you come back.

We've been through enough by now that you probably realize this is all going to be a breeze. Yup. Just do a quick search for *Swensen*, replace *hippopotamus* with *antelope*, and replace the italic formatting with bold. And when you have to leave, stick an electronic bookmark in the document so you can get back to the same place.

Prep Work

Before you perform all these wonderful feats, type the following short paragraphs (I won't make you type a lot; we'll just pretend this is a long document) so we've got something to work with in this chapter:

```
As some of you may know from our last newsletter, our photographic
safari in search of the wild hippopotamus is selling out fast. I
never realized there were so many hippopotamus enthusiasts in our
small town! I am thrilled with the response and look forward with
great anticipation to this trip.
So hurry up if you want to be part of this hippopotamus happening. In
the words of Sally Swensen, who led our last excursion, "The opportu-
nity to see a hippopotamus up close is not to be taken lightly."
```

Make sure the last sentence (the one in quotes) is in italics. We're ready to go.

Find and Replace

With the Find and Replace features, you can quickly move to any text or formatting in your document. The Find and Replace dialog box has an assortment of options that allow you to zero in on what you want (and replace it with something else if you choose). Let's start by doing a simple text search and branch out from there.

To search for text:

1. Make sure your insertion point is located where you want the search to begin. (Actually, you'll soon discover some options that let you get around this, but for now, place your insertion point at the beginning of the sample text.)
2. Choose **Find** from the Edit menu (or press **Ctrl+F**). You'll see the **Find** tab of the Find and Replace dialog box, as shown in Figure 10.1.

*Figure 10.1 The **Find** tab in the Find and Replace dialog box.*

3. Enter the text you want to search for in the Find what text box. In this case, type **swensen**.

NOTE

It doesn't matter whether you enter the text in uppercase or lowercase. Find isn't case-sensitive by default; it finds anything that matches the characters in the text box. If you want an exact match, click the **More** button and select the **Match case** check box.

4. Choose **Find Next**.

The text that's found is selected. If you click anywhere in the document and start typing at this point, the selected text is replaced by whatever you type. If you don't want to type over the text, just click again to unselect it.

The Find and Replace dialog box remains on the screen so you can do a series of searches if you want. As soon as you click anywhere in the document window, the dialog box becomes inactive, but it doesn't go away. When you're finished using the dialog box, just click on its **Close** button.

Finding the Same Text Again

In the preceding example, **Find Next** took you right to *Sally Swensen.* But maybe you're not sure that's the only place you mentioned her. You want to find out if her name appears anywhere else in the document. With the Find and Replace dialog box still on-screen, just choose **Find Next** again and the search continues. You can keep clicking on **Find Next** until Word has found all occurrences of the word or phrase. When there aren't any more to find, you'll see the dialog box displayed in Figure 10.2.

Figure 10.2 *This dialog box appears when there are no more occurrences of your text.*

KEYBOARD

Shift+F4 is a great shortcut for searching for the next occurrence. You can let Word find the first place the word or phrase appears and then close the Find and Replace dialog box. Then just keep pressing **Shift+F4** until you've found all occurrences. Just remember that this shortcut doesn't work when the Find and Replace dialog box is active.

The Easiest Way to Find Formatting

Almost any formatting that can be included in a Word document can be included in a search string. You can search for formatting by itself or in combination with text. For example, if you know you turned on italics right before you used quotation marks, you could search for italic formatting and the quotation mark character.

With the Find and Replace dialog box active, look at the toolbars. All the buttons on the Standard toolbar (except the **Office Assistant** button) are dimmed, and so are several of the buttons on the Formatting toolbar. But notice the Standard toolbar buttons that are still active: the **Style**, **Font**, and **Font Size** buttons; the **Bold**, **Italic**, and **Underline** buttons; the **Alignment** buttons, and the **Highlight** button.

Clicking on any of these buttons when the Find and Replace dialog box is active adds that formatting item to your search. In Figure 10.3, I clicked on the **Bold** and **Center** buttons. Notice that my formatting choices are displayed just below the Find What box. Also notice that **swensen** is still selected in the Find What box. Whatever you searched for last remains in the box until you get rid of it. So if I click **Find Next** from Figure 10.3, Word will find the word *swensen*, but only if it's bold and part of a paragraph that uses center alignment.

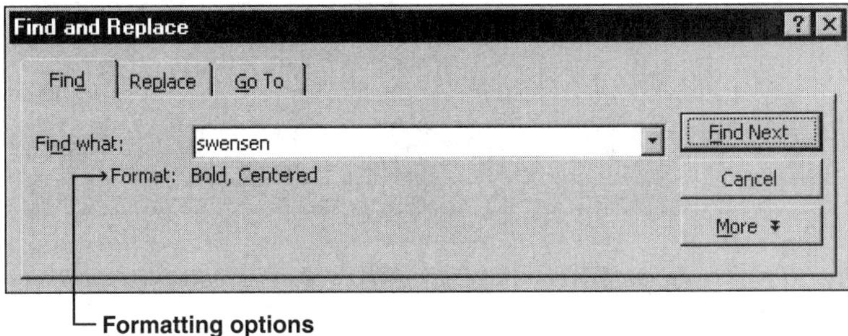

Figure 10.3 A search that includes character formatting.

And here's a cool trick—clicking on the **Bold**, **Italic**, **Underline**, or **Highlight** button once sets you up to search for those formatting options. But clicking a second time on any of these buttons lets you *exclude* a particular type of formatting. For example, clicking on the **Bold** button twice inserts *Not Bold* in the Find and Replace dialog box, and the search will find only text that's *not* bold.

Using the toolbar buttons is quick, but there are bunches of formatting options you can't access this way. So you need another way to find formatting:

1. Choose **Find** from the Edit menu (or press **Ctrl+F**), then click **More** to expand the Find and Replace dialog box.
2. Click on the **Format** button to display the list shown in Figure 10.4.

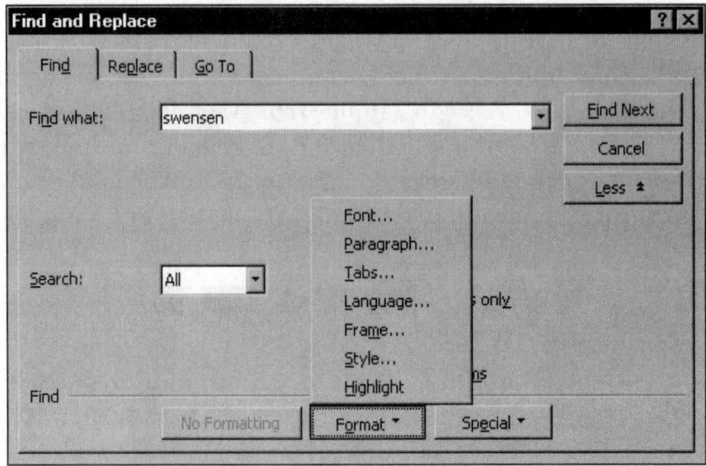

Figure 10.4 The expanded Find and Replace dialog box with the Format list opened.

3. Select the type of formatting you want to find from the Format list to open a dialog box that allows you to refine the search. For example, to get Figure 10.5, I selected **Tabs** from the Format list and typed **2** in the Tab stop position box. When I click **OK** to close the Tabs dialog box, Word will be ready for me to find a tab stop at 2".

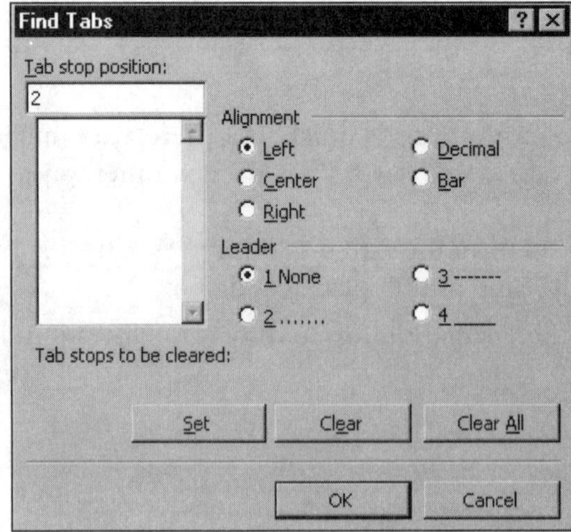

Figure 10.5 In the Tabs dialog box, I can tell Word which tab setting to search for.

4. You can add as many formatting options as you want. Just keep clicking on toolbar buttons or selecting options from the Format list until you've inserted all the items you want.
5. Before you continue, take a look at your search options. Make sure the Find What text box contains only the text you want to find and that the formatting and other options (just below the Find What text box) are correct.
6. When you're satisfied that the search is set up the way you want, click **Find Next**.

NOTE

If you want to get rid of all the formatting options in your search request, just click the **No Formatting** button.

Searching for Special Characters

It's easy to type letters, numbers, and punctuation marks into the Find What box, but what if you want to look for a paragraph mark? Or a tab? Or a graphic image? Just reach for the **Special** button.

NOTE

When you open the Find and Replace dialog box, the last thing you searched for will be in the Find text box. Because the text or special characters are selected, as soon as you start typing in the text box, the whole selection disappears—you don't have to delete it first.

To find special characters:

1. From the Find and Replace dialog box, click **More** to expand the dialog box. (If the button below the **Cancel** button says **Less**, the dialog box is already expanded.)
2. Place your insertion point where you want it in the Find What text box. For example, to insert a paragraph mark character after the word *swensen*, make sure your insertion point is just past *swensen* before you open the Special list.

If the text in the Find What box is selected when you open the Special list, the special character you select will replace what's in the Find What box instead of being added to it.

3. Click the **Special** button to open the list shown in Figure 10.6.

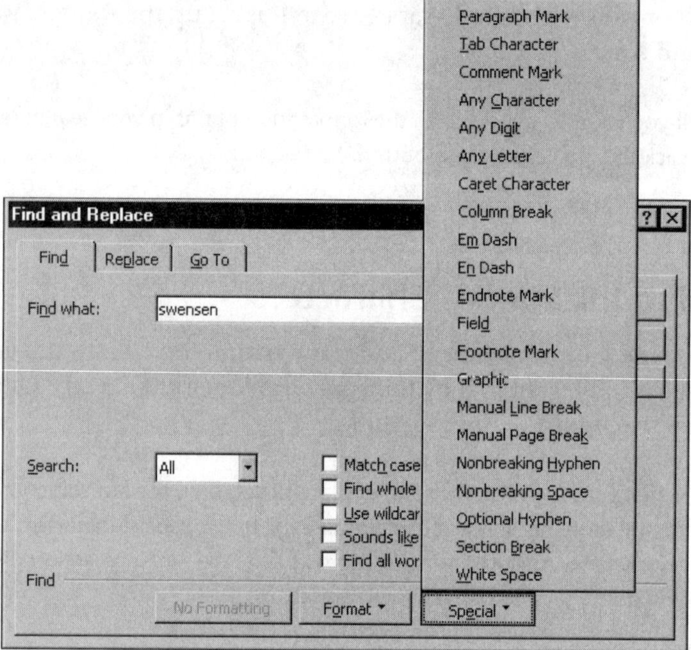

Figure 10.6 *The special character list.*

4. Click to select the type of character you want to find. As you can see in Figure 10.7, the Find What box displays a code that stands for the special character you select. I want to find the word *swensen,* but only if it's at the end of a sentence *and* at the end of a paragraph. So I entered **swensen** followed by a period, and then selected **Paragraph Mark** from the Special list. The code for a paragraph mark is `^p`.

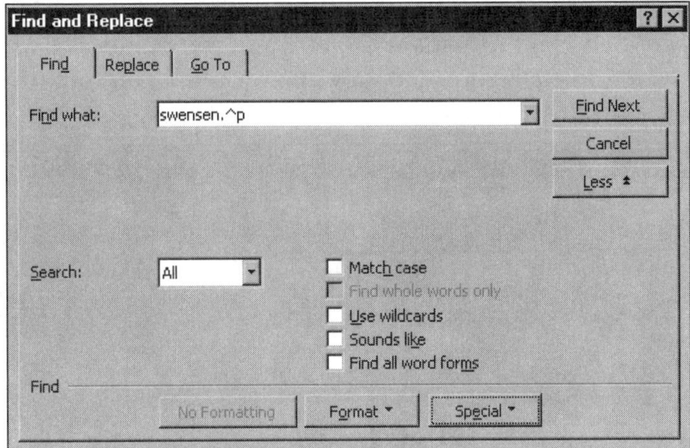

Figure 10.7 *A special character search.*

5. Click **Find Next** to initiate the search.

WARNING

If you perform a search and it doesn't look like Word has found anything, the Find and Replace dialog box might be covering what you want to find. You can move the box out of the way by dragging its title bar.

Using Wildcards

Word has special codes that can be used as wildcards. Wildcards can help if you don't know the spelling of a word. For example, you could use wildcards to replace the letters you're not sure of in *hippopotamus*:

- A question mark (?) takes the place of any one character.
- An asterisk (*) can take the place of any number of characters, including zero.

WARNING

You can't just use a regular asterisk or question mark. To tell Word to recognize these characters as wildcards, you must first check the **Use wildcards** check box in the Find and Replace dialog box. This goes for the other wildcard characters as well. If **Use wildcards** isn't checked, Word treats the question mark or other character as regular text.

Let's say you don't know whether there's one *p* or two, you have no idea what happens between the first *o* and the *m*, and you're not sure whether that last vowel is an *a* or a *u*. Figure 10.8 shows how you'd set up your search string.

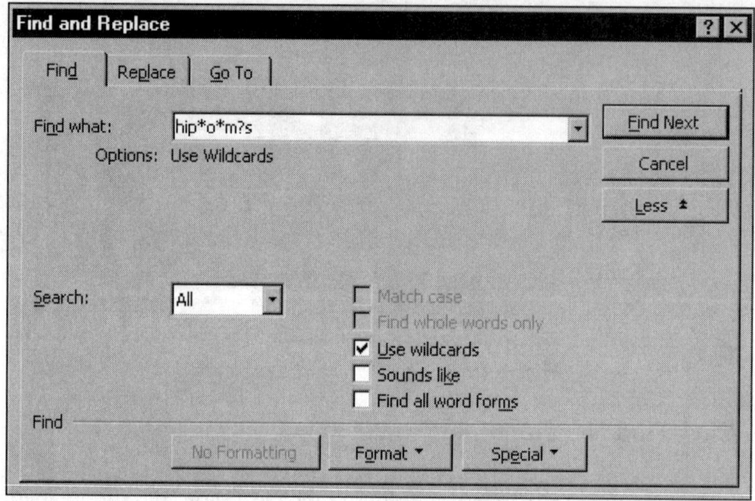

Figure 10.8 *This search string finds anything that starts with hip, has multiple (or no) letters between the p and the o and between the o and the m, and exactly one letter between the m and the final s.*

You insert wildcards in a search string by checking the **Use wildcards** check box in the Find and Replace dialog box and then choosing a wildcard item from the Special list. When you click the **Special** button with this check box selected, Word adds the wildcard items shown in Figure 10.9 to the top of the Special list.

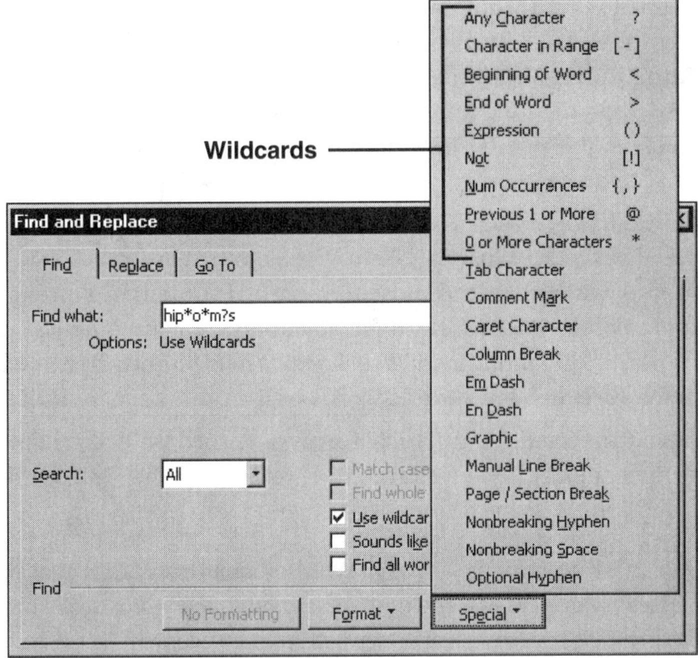

***Figure 10.9** The Special list with wildcards added.*

Refining the Search

You can set up some pretty fancy search strings. Now it's time to look at a few other options that can help you fine-tune your search.

NOTE

If you don't see the options I'm talking about in this section, click the **More** button in the Find and Replace dialog box.

- Select the **Match case** check box if you want to search for an exact match of the word or phrase in your search string. If **Case** isn't checked, a search for *COT* finds *cot*, *Cot*, and *COT*. With the option checked, only *COT* is found. When **Match case** is checked, the words `Options: Match Case` appear below the Find What text box.

- Select the **Find whole words only** check box if you want to make sure that the search finds whole words only. If this box isn't checked, a search for *cot* also finds *apricot*, *cottage*, and *ascot*—in other words, any word that has the letters *cot* in it. When **Find whole words only** is checked, the words `Options: Whole Words` appear below the Find What text box.
- To find a word when you're not sure of the spelling, select the **Sounds like** check box. With this option selected, Word takes a best guess at finding words that look close to the word you enter. For example, you can look for *ricipent* and still be able to find *recipient*, *paralel* will get you *parallel*, and *halaluja* finds *hallelujah*. When **Sounds like** is selected the **Match case** and **Find whole words only** options are unavailable.
- To search for all grammatical forms of a word, select the **Find all word forms** check box. For example, if you search for *go* with this option turned on, Word will find *go*, *goes*, *going*, and even *went*.

NOTE

What are *word forms*, anyway? Word programmers know that many words appear with different endings. For example, the words *walk*, *walks*, *walked*, and *walking* may all appear somewhere in your document. These are just different forms of the word *walk*. Suppose you're almost finished writing a lengthy article on the Key West Golf Club and you decide to replace the verb *walk* with *stroll*. The word forms option allows you to find and replace all forms of a word with the equivalent forms of another word. In your golfing document, you could open the **Replace** tab in the Find and Replace dialog box, select the **Find all word forms** check box, and type **walk** in the Find What text box and **stroll** in the Replace With text box. Clicking the **Replace All** button will replace all forms of *walk* with the appropriate forms of *stroll*.

Replace

Now you know how to use the Find and Replace dialog box to find text. But what about that *Replace* in the title? No problem. If you already know what you want to replace a set of text and formatting with, just open the **Replace** tab, type a replacement string in the Replace With text box, add any formatting options, and let Word do the work for you.

Let's make all the changes I talked about in the first paragraph of this chapter. No, you don't have to hastily shuffle the pages and reread the beginning of the chapter—I'll walk you through it. First we'll replace *hippopotamus* with *antelope* (and you don't even have to remember how to spell *hippopotamus*).

NOTE

Just about everything I covered in the Find section applies to replacing text. With only a few exceptions, if you can find it, you can replace it.

To find and replace text:

1. Choose **Replace** from the Edit menu (or press **Ctrl+H**).
2. Enter the text you want to search for in the Find What text box. For this example, use **hippopotamus**, and include wildcards for the parts you're not sure of.

   Notice that the text you entered in the Find What text box is still there when you open the **Replace** tab.
3. Enter the replacement text in the Replace With text box. Type **antelope** (see Figure 10.10).

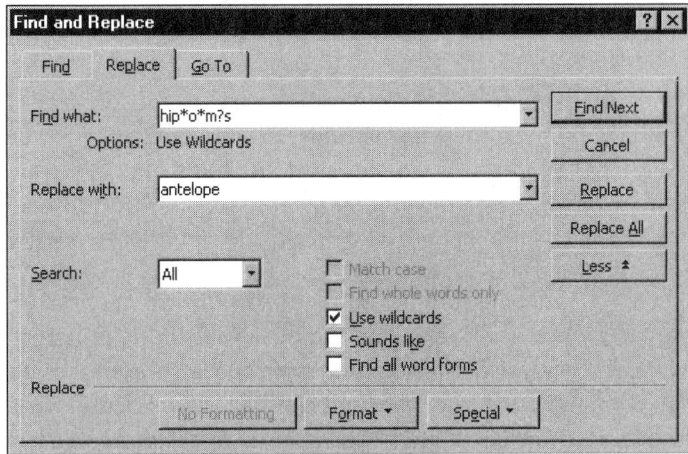

Figure 10.10 *The find and replace strings for our example.*

WARNING

Don't press **Enter** until you've finished entering your find and replace strings and made any changes you want on the menus. Notice that **Find Next** is the default button. As soon as you press **Enter**, Word tries to initiate a search whether you're ready or not. Click in the box you want to move to or press **Tab** to move among the text boxes.

4. Use the **Format** button to add formatting options to your search or replace request.
5. Use the **Special** button to add special characters to your search or replace request.
6. Choose any options you want from the check boxes. (If you don't see the check boxes, click the **More** button.)
7. Choose **Find Next**, **Replace**, or **Replace All**:
   - Choose **Find Next** to locate the first occurrence of the search string.
   - When you choose **Replace** the first time, Word simply finds the first occurrence of the search string. After that, choosing **Replace** replaces that item—clicking it again searches for and replaces the next item.
   - Choose **Replace All** to replace every occurrence of the search request in your document without stopping.

WARNING

When you're replacing one word with another, be sure you check **Find whole words only** or you could end up with some weird results. If you don't do this, every time Word finds the search string it'll replace it, even if the search string falls in the middle of another word. For example, you could enter **bed** as a replacement for *cot* and end up with *apribed*, *bedtage*, and *asbed*. Not a pretty sight.

NOTE

It's time-consuming to enter all that text. What if you have to suspend a search to run a search for something else? To return to your original task, do you have to retype and rearrange everything? Of course not. Word's right on top of this one. The Find What and Replace With text boxes have little down arrows next to them. If you click on one of these arrows, you'll get a history list that contains text you've already searched for. To reuse one of the items, select it from the list (use the scroll bar to move through the list if the item you want isn't visible). Keep in mind though, that Word doesn't keep track of any formatting or other options you used with the text.

NOTE

You can use **Replace** to get rid of repeated text or formatting. If you don't put anything in the Replace With text box and choose **Replace** or **Replace All**, Word finds whatever's in the search string and replaces it with nothing. In other words, it's gone. This is really nifty if you have to delete a particular word or code throughout your document. For example, if you want to delete all the bold formatting in a document, just click the **Bold** button on the Standard toolbar with your insertion point in the Find What text box, leave the Replace With text box blank, and choose **Replace All**.

Go To

Want to get quickly to page 162? Don't want to press **Alt+Ctrl+PageDown** 161 times? Use **Go To**. In addition to moving at breakneck speed to a specific page, this handy feature can whisk you to a bookmark, table (I know, you don't know about bookmarks or tables yet, but when you do, you'll know how to find them), or other Word object.

Locations that you go to can be either absolute or relative. For example, an *absolute* location is page 3 or the fourth table in a document. A *relative* location might be two pages beyond where you are now or the sixth table beyond the current table.

To use Go To:

1. Choose **Go To** from the Edit menu or press **Ctrl+G**. You'll see the **Go To** tab in the Find and Replace dialog box, shown in Figure 10.11. Of course, if you're already in the Find and Replace dialog box, you can just click on the **Go To** tab to open it.

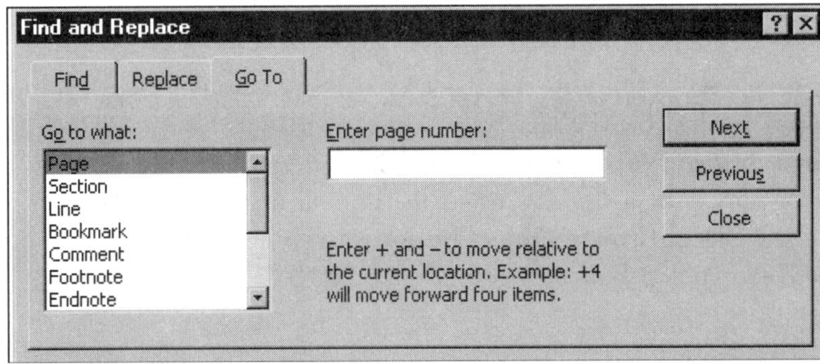

Figure 10.11 The ***Go To*** *tab in the Find and Replace dialog box.*

2. Select an option from the Go to what list.
3. Depending on the option you select, enter the necessary information in the text box. Following are a few examples of the items you can go to:
   - If you choose **Page**, enter the page number you want to move to in the text box.
   - If you choose **Section** or **Line**, enter the section or line number.
   - If you choose **Bookmark**, enter the bookmark's name in the text box or choose it from the drop-down list.
4. To go to a relative location, select an option from the Go to what list, then enter a plus (+) or minus (-) sign in the text box, followed by a number. For example to move forward six pages, select **Page** and type **+6** in the text box. This takes the place of steps 2 and 3.
5. Click the **Go To** button.

Earlier in this chapter you learned that pressing **Shift+F4** is a great shortcut for repeating the most recent **Find** command. That same shortcut applies to the **Go To** command. Whichever action you performed most recently—**Find** or **Go To**—is the one that's repeated when you press **Shift+F4**.

NOTE

Even though it's not part of the Go To dialog box, this is a good place to bring up the **Go To** key, **Shift+F5**, which keeps track of your last five locations. This can be a lifesaver when you accidentally move to another location in your document. Suppose you meant to press **Ctrl+Right Arrow** to move to the next word, but you pressed **Ctrl+End** by mistake. Now you're at the end of your document and you don't even remember where you were before. Just press **Shift+F5** and you're back where you started. Be aware, though, that once you've entered text or formatting anywhere, that's considered your last position.

Using the Browse Buttons

The browse buttons on the vertical scroll bar give you another tool for moving to different areas of a document—this time with just a mouse click or two. Click on the **Select Browse Object** button shown in Figure 10.12 to open the Browse Object dialog box shown in Figure 10.13.

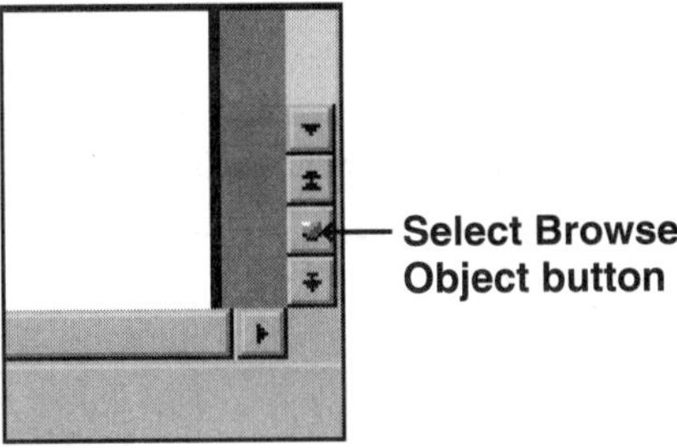

Figure 10.12 *The **Select Browse Object** button.*

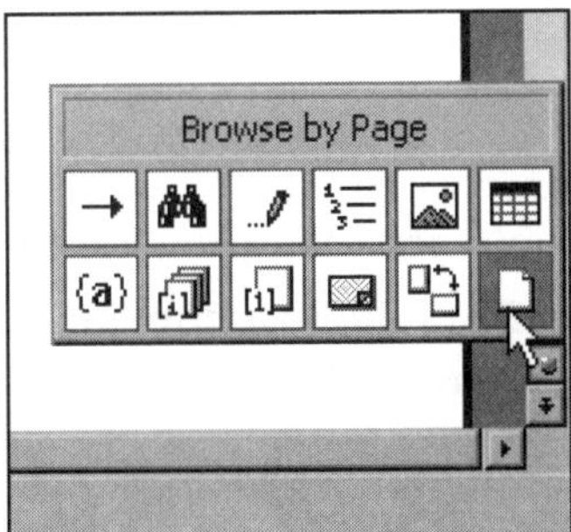

Figure 10.13 *The Browse Object dialog box.*

The little circle button between the double up and down arrow buttons at the bottom of the vertical scroll bar is the **Browse Object** button; it lets you tell Word what the double up and down arrows should do. As you move your mouse pointer over a button in the Browse Object dialog box, the title bar tells you what the button does. In Figure 10.13, my mouse pointer is on the button that looks like a piece of paper, and the title bar says `Browse by Page`. So if I click on this button, the double-arrow buttons will allow me to move through my document a page at a time.

NOTE

The **Go To** and **Find** buttons in the Browse Object dialog box take you directly to the **Go To** and **Find** tabs, respectively, in the Find and Replace dialog box.

Bookmarks

Remember that frantic phone call you got at the beginning of the chapter? Well, now you're back and you want to pick up where you left off. Forward-thinking person that you are, you stuck a bookmark in your document before you left, so you can quickly move to the right location. How did you stick a bookmark on a computer screen? Simple, with the magic of modern technology.

You can have as many bookmarks as you want. When you create the bookmark, you assign it a unique name, and then you can locate the bookmark by its name at any time (using the Go To or Bookmark dialog box). Bookmarks are great for marking areas in a document that need more work or information. For example, you could have a bookmark called `checkdate` that reminds you you still need to check the date for an event.

To create a bookmark:

1. Place your insertion point where you want the bookmark.
2. Choose **Bookmark** from the Insert menu to open the Bookmark dialog box shown in Figure 10.14.

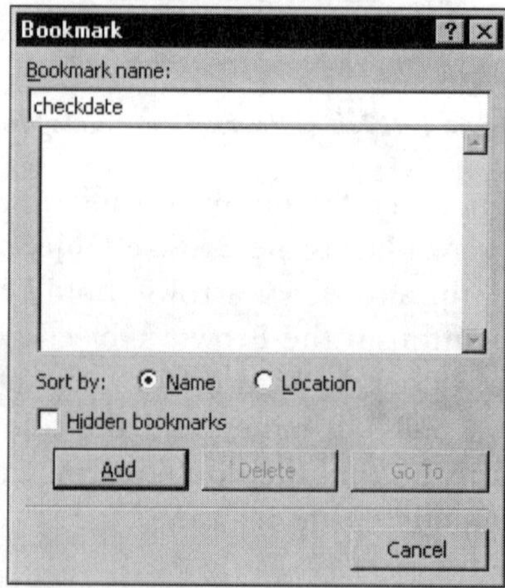

Figure 10.14 *The Bookmark dialog box.*

3. Enter a name in the Bookmark name text box and click the **Add** button. A bookmark name can't include any spaces. If the **Add** button dims while you're typing the bookmark name, that means your name is invalid.

That's all there is to it. Word saves your bookmark and closes the Bookmark dialog box. The bookmark is saved with the document, so it's accessible whenever the document is open. The next time you open the Bookmark dialog box from the document in which you created the bookmark, the bookmark will appear in the Bookmark list. It will also appear in the drop-down list when you choose **Go To** and select **Bookmark**.

Finding a Bookmark

There are two ways to find a bookmark: through the Bookmark dialog box or by using the **Go To** feature. To find a bookmark with **Go To**, use the instructions I gave you in the previous section and choose the bookmark you want from the Bookmark drop-down list.

To find a bookmark using the Bookmark dialog box:

1. Choose **Bookmark** from the Insert menu.
2. Select the bookmark you want to find from the Bookmark list.
3. Click on the **Go To** button (or press **Enter**).

Not much more to it. Bookmarks stay where they are until you delete them. A bookmark can be deleted by selecting it in the Bookmark list and clicking the **Delete** button.

FROM HERE...

Now that you can use **Find and Replace**, **Go To**, and bookmarks, you can get where you want to go with ease. Combine these features with all the techniques you learned earlier for moving your insertion point and navigating through documents, and you'll be able to find the most obscure nooks and crannies in your document.

In the next chapter, you'll learn about Word's proofreading tools. Before a document is complete, you have to make sure everything's spelled correctly and that your grammar will pass muster. And as a final finishing touch, you can use the thesaurus to fine-tune those word choices.

CHAPTER 11

Proofreading Tools

Let's talk about:

- Checking spelling
- Checking grammar
- Using AutoCorrect
- Using the Thesaurus

Without Word, proofreading can be a really tedious task. You print your document and try to read through it carefully as your eyes slowly glaze over. You puzzle over some unfamiliar words and try to find your dictionary in that pile of books and wonder how the heck you look something up when you don't know how to spell it. As a last resort, you call your mom to ask about the grammar in that one really funny-looking sentence.

With Word's writing and proofreading tools, you can let that dictionary molder away in the corner and give your mom some peace and quiet.

In Chapter 1, you got a little taste of Word's spell checking abilities. In this chapter, we'll explore more spelling and grammar options and check out automatic spell checking and AutoCorrect. Then we'll look at the Thesaurus, a great writer's tool that helps you find synonyms and antonyms

WARNING

All of these tools don't totally take the place of proofing the document yourself. As you saw in Chapter 1, a word can be spelled correctly and still be wrong for the document. And electronic grammar checkers are, at their best, fallible and subject to human interpretation. They give you choices, but you make the final decisions. If your document is important, don't assume it's perfect just because you've done a spelling and grammar check. These tools catch a lot of errors and make your proofing job much easier, but in the end, it's up to you to make sure it's right.

Checking Spelling and Grammar Automatically

I'm sure you've noticed the red and green squiggly underlines that keep cropping up whenever you type. Whenever you type something that Word doesn't recognize as a correctly spelled word, the word gets the squiggly red underline treatment, which is part of Word's automatic spell checking feature. The green underlines indicate possible grammatical errors.

This feature allows you to correct spelling and grammar mistakes as you type rather than waiting until you're done and then running a spelling and grammar check. To fix one of those squiggly underlined words, just right-click on it (or press **Shift+F10** with your insertion point anywhere in the word).

If it's a spelling error (a squiggly red underline), you get a shortcut menu, like the one in Figure 11.1, that contains a list of replacement words, along with a few other options.

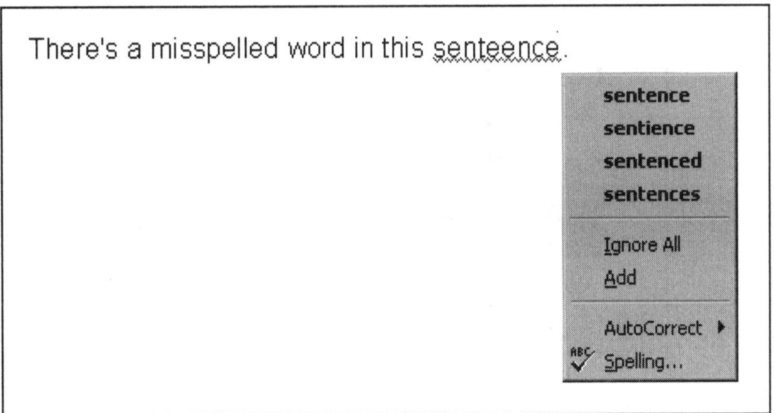

Figure 11.1 *You get a menu like this when you right-click on a word with a squiggly red underline.*

You have the following choices:

- If the word you want to use is listed in bold in the shortcut menu, just click on it.
- To add the word to your Custom dictionary, choose **Add**.
- To add the word to your AutoCorrect list and assign an automatic replacement for it, choose **AutoCorrect**, then click on one of the words in the AutoCorrect list.
- To tell Word that the word's okay in the current document, but that it should be flagged if it appears in another document, choose **Ignore All**.
- To open the Spelling dialog box for additional spelling options, choose **Spelling**.

If it's a grammatical error (a squiggly green underline), you get a shortcut menu, like the one in Figure 11.2, that lists some possible corrections.

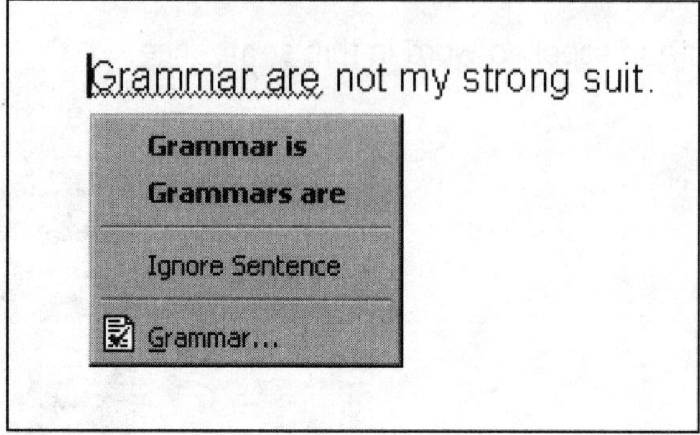

Figure 11.2 You get a menu like this when you click on a word with a squiggly green underline.

You have the following options:

- If the bold list contains the correction you want, just click on it.
- To ignore the underlined error, choose **Ignore Sentence**.
- To open the Grammar dialog box for additional options, choose **Grammar**.

You can quickly move to the next spelling or grammar problem by double-clicking on the **Spelling Status** button on the status bar (shown in Figure 11.3).

Figure 11.3 The status bar with the Spelling and Grammar Status button.

NOTE

In most cases, I find it more efficient to wait until I'm finished typing rather than stopping to right-click every time I see a squiggly line. Then, when I'm ready, I just double-click the **Spelling and Grammar Status** button on the Status Bar to quickly move from one word to the next and make any necessary corrections.

If you choose not to use automatic spelling or grammar checking, you can turn either of these options off from the **Spelling & Grammar** tab in the Options dialog box (choose **Options** from the Tools menu and select the **Spelling & Grammar** tab).

If you want to use automatic spelling or grammar checking, but you don't want all those squiggly underlines cluttering your document while you're working on it, just check the **Hide spelling errors in this document** check box in the **Spelling & Grammar** tab of the Options dialog box. Then, when you want to see the lines, go back to the **Spelling & Grammar** tab and uncheck the **Hide spelling errors in this document** check box.

Using the Spelling and Grammar Dialog Box

Word's spelling and grammar checker can check your whole document or specified portions of it.

NOTE

By default, Word checks grammar and spelling at the same time, but for the sake of clarity, we'll cover them separately in this chapter.

When you spell check a document (or a section), Word checks your text against its main dictionary. It can also check special supplementary dictionaries that you create and edit.

The easiest way to start a spell check session is by clicking the **Spelling and Grammar** button on the Standard toolbar. You can also choose **Spelling and Grammar** from the Tools menu or press **F7**.

The spell checker stops at and highlights the first word that's not in its dictionary, and the dialog box shown in Figure 11.4 is displayed.

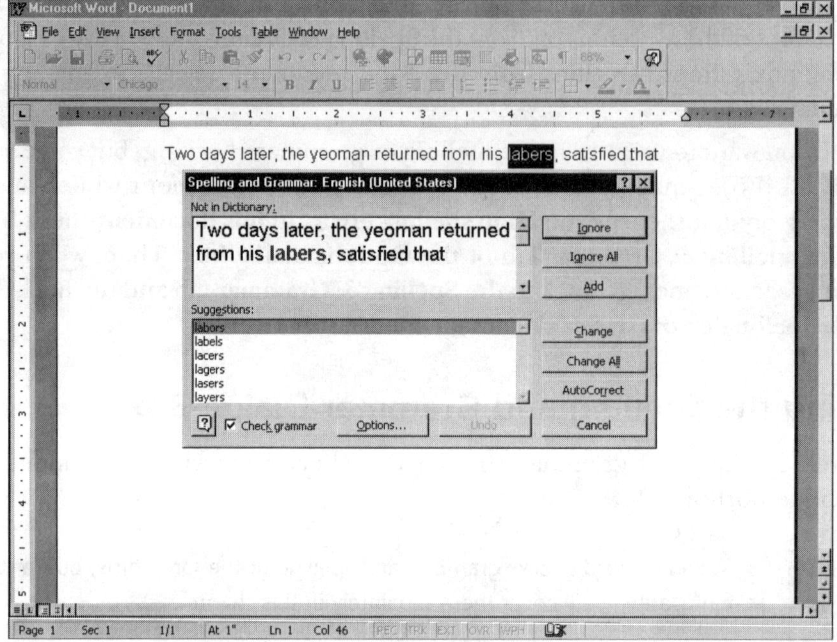

Figure 11.4 The Spelling and Grammar dialog box.

During a Spell Check

When you start a spell check, Word stops at the first word it finds that's not in its dictionaries and waits for you to do something. The misspelled word (or at least the word Word thinks is misspelled) is selected, and there's usually a list of words in the Suggestions list. In Figure 11.4, the spell checker has stopped and selected *labers*, and there are several alternatives in the Suggestions list.

What do you do next? That all depends on what you want to do about the word:

- If the word you want is in the Suggestions list, click on it (you may have to use the scroll bar to move through the list if you can't see all the words).
- Choose **Change** to replace the word in your document with the highlighted word in the Suggestions list.

- Choose **Ignore**, **Ignore All**, or **Add** if the word is spelled correctly but isn't in Word's dictionary. People's names often fall into this category, as do words that might be specific to your profession.
  - **Ignore** causes the spell checker to ignore the word, but if it finds it again in the document, it stops again. Suppose you're writing to a Ms. Snowe. *Snowe* is a good example of a word where you would choose **Skip Once**. It's a person's name, and it's spelled correctly, but it's so close to the spelling of a real word that you want to make sure the spell checker stops if it sees it again, just in case it's really supposed to be *snow* the next time.
  - **Ignore All** ignores the word during the current Word session. Suppose you're writing a letter to Mr. Bartesque. You know you'll never write to him again, so you don't want to add his name to your Custom dictionary. There's no possibility of his name being mistaken for a regular word, so choose **Ignore All** to bypass all occurrences.
  - **Add** is an option you will probably use a lot (at least you should). When you choose **Add**, the word is added to the Custom dictionary that you choose (more on how you do that in a bit). If your name is Sarita Sarelli, you would choose **Add** when the spell checker stops at *Sarita* and *Sarelli*. You no doubt sign your name to every letter, and you wouldn't want the spell checker to stop every time it encounters your name (you have enough to worry about already).
- Use the **AutoCorrect** button to add the word and its selected replacement from the Suggestions list to your AutoCorrect list so that the next time Word encounters this misspelling it will correct it automatically. (AutoCorrect is covered a little later in the chapter.)

Unless you specify otherwise, the spell checker stops at duplicate words and words with irregular capitalization. By default, it ignores words with numbers in them and words typed in all uppercase letters.

You can manually edit a word at any time by clicking in the document window. For this example, type **I ampride of my work**, then right-click on **ampride** and choose **Spelling** to open the Spelling and Grammar dialog box. Notice that the there aren't any words in the Suggestions list—Word doesn't have a clue what you want. To make a manual edit, just click in the document window. This temporarily pauses the spell check. Move your insertion point past the *m* and press the **Spacebar**. When you've paused a spell check, the **Ignore** button changes to **Resume**; click on **Resume** when you're ready to continue.

Don't forget to save your document every time you do a spell check. The changes you make during a spell check can be gone with the wind if anything happens to your computer before you save.

Choosing a Custom Dictionary

When you choose **Add** during a spell check, the spell checker adds the word to whichever Custom dictionary is active. To choose a different custom dictionary, click on the **Options** button in the Spelling and Grammar dialog box and make a selection from the Custom dictionary drop-down list.

Editing a Custom Dictionary

Words get added to a custom dictionary whenever you choose **Add** during a spell check. But you can also add your own words and do some other neat tricks by editing the word list.

To edit the Custom dictionary:

1. Click on the **Options** button in the Spelling and Grammar dialog box and choose **Dictionaries** to open the Custom Dictionaries dialog box shown in Figure 11.5.

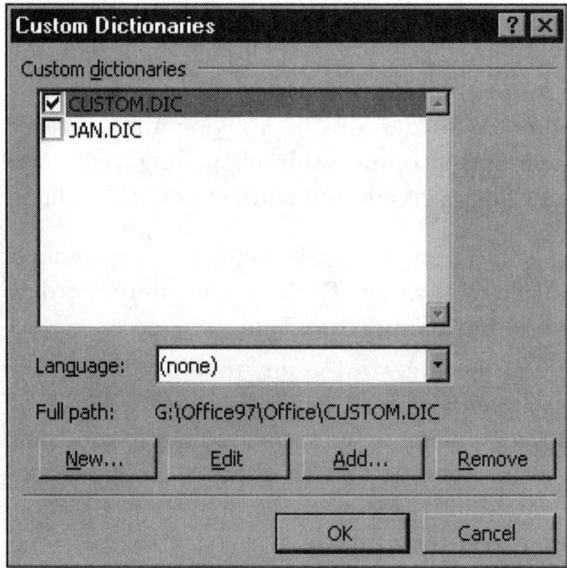

Figure 11.5 *The Custom Dictionaries dialog box.*

2. Select the dictionary you want to edit and click the **Edit** button. If automatic spell checking is turned on, you'll see the information box in Figure 11.6 after you click **Edit**. It tells you that Word will turn automatic spell checking off if you proceed, and it gives you instructions for turning it back on when you're finished editing the dictionary.

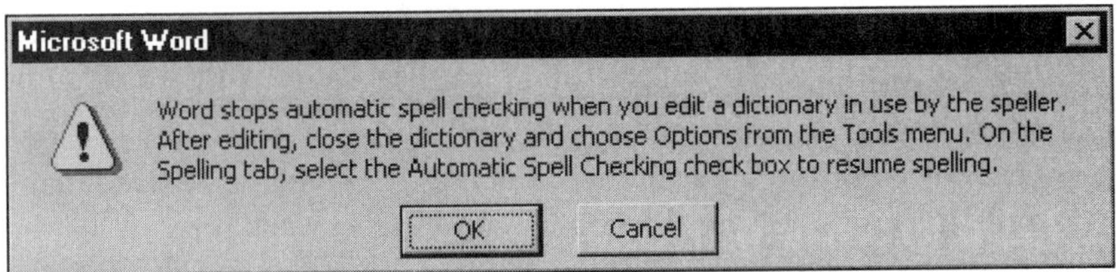

Figure 11.6 Pay attention to this information box.

3. Click **OK** to proceed with the edit or click **Cancel** to close the information box without editing the dictionary.
4. If you choose **OK**, Word opens the selected dictionary. As you can see, in Figure 11.7, it's just a list of words that you can edit any way you want.

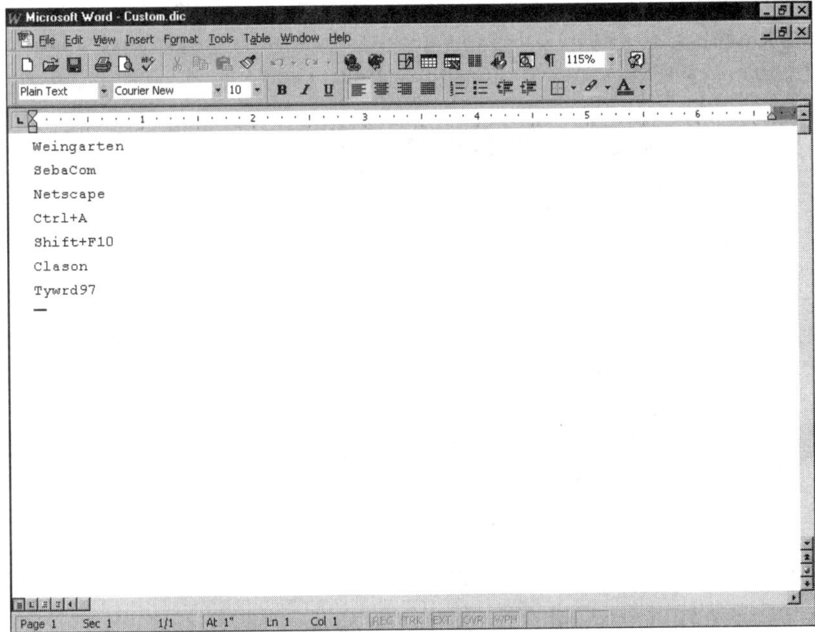

Figure 11.7 My Custom dictionary.

5. To add a word, just type it in the list. Make sure you put each word on a separate line.
6. To delete a word, select it and press the **Delete** key.
7. To change a word, use any text editing technique to add, delete, or move characters.
8. When you're finished editing, click the **Save** button on the Standard toolbar to save your changes, then press **Ctrl+F4** to close the document.
9. If you want to use automatic spell checking, turn it back on by choosing **Options** from the Tools menu, selecting the **Spelling & Grammar** tab, and checking the **Check spelling as you type** check box.

Go through your Custom dictionaries from time to time and check for unwanted or misspelled words. It's easy to sit there like a zombie and click that **Add** button during a spell check—you may add a misspelled word without noticing.

Changing Spelling Options

To change Word's default spelling options, choose **Options** from the Spelling and Grammar dialog box. If the Spelling and Grammar dialog box isn't open, choose **Options** from the Tools menu and click on the **Spelling & Grammar** tab. Figure 11.8 shows the **Spelling & Grammar** tab.

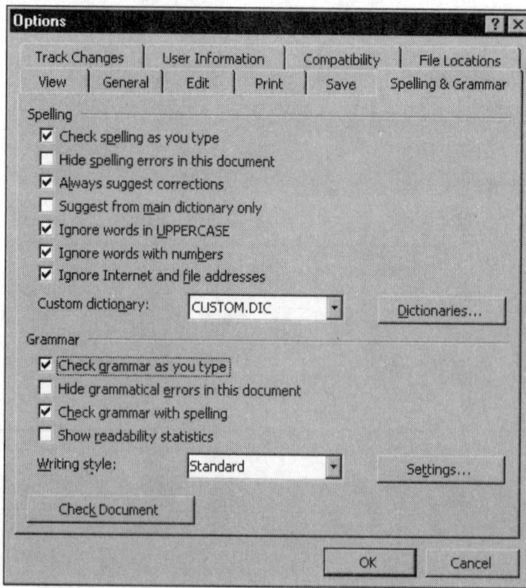

***Figure 11.8** The **Spelling & Grammar** tab in the Options dialog box.*

You have the following options:

- **Check spelling as you type** is the option that turns automatic spell checking on or off.
- **Hide spelling errors in this document**—when automatic spell checking is turned on, this option allows you to hide the squiggly underlines while you're working on a document. To view the errors caught by automatic spell checking, just deselect the **Hide spelling errors in this document** check box. This option is dimmed when the **Check spelling as you type** check box is deselected.
- **Always suggest corrections** is checked by default. This option tells Word to give you a list of possible corrections when you run a spell check.
- **Suggest from main dictionary only**—use this option if you want Word to check only the main dictionary during a spell check and to ignore any Custom dictionaries.
- **Ignore words in UPPERCASE**—when this option is checked, the spell checker won't stop on any words that are in all uppercase letters.
- **Ignore words with numbers** is checked by default, but I usually uncheck it. It's too easy to accidentally hit a number key in the middle of a word, and I need all the help I can get during a spell check. The only time I might disable this option would be in a document with a lot of codes that combine letters and numbers (like parts codes or serial numbers).
- **Ignore Internet and file addresses** tells the spell checker to ignore Internet addresses, filenames, and electronic mail addresses. This option is turned on by default.

NOTE

When you change any of these options, they stay changed until you change them again. It's not just for the current spell check session.

Checking Grammar

By default, Word checks grammar while it's checking spelling. The same procedure starts both a spelling and a grammar check—choosing **Spelling and Grammar** from the Tools menu. But let's take a closer look at Word's grammar checking options and see what happens when Word finds a grammatical error.

During a Grammar Checking Session

When you start a spelling and grammar session, Word checks your document against a built-in set of rules for grammar and writing style. (Later I'll show you how you can tell Word which set of rules you want to use.) Word stops at the first questionable word or phrase, gives you some options, and waits for you to make a choice. We'll use a few specific examples to see how grammar checking works.

For the first example, type **I am confident that I can write a good book.** Make sure you type the period and press the **Spacebar** after the sentence. Now, choose **Spelling and Grammar** from the Tools menu.

In Figure 11.9, notice that Word has highlighted the entire sentence in the document, and that the sentence is displayed in the Spelling and Grammar dialog box, with the suspect word in bold. Word lets you know which grammar rule it thinks is being violated. In this case, notice that it says *Commonly Confused Words.* Any suggested alternatives are displayed in the Suggestions list.

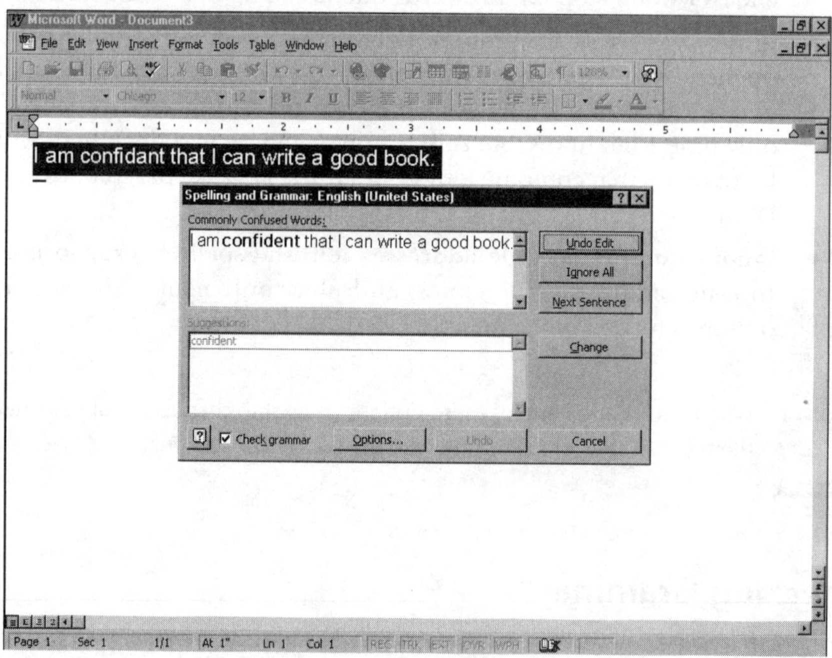

Figure 11.9 *The Spelling and Grammar dialog box stopped at a grammatical error.*

You have the following options:

- Choose **Change** to make the correction using the selected word or phrase in the Suggestions list.
- Choose **Ignore** to leave the highlighted error as it is (just because Word tells you it's an error doesn't mean it really is—remember, you're the final arbiter).
- Choose **Ignore All** if you want Word to ignore this particular error and any other errors that fail this grammar rule (in this example, Commonly Confused Words) during the current Word session.
- Choose **Next Sentence** to accept whatever changes you've already made to the current sentence, ignore any additional errors, and move on to the next sentence.

Now for a minilesson on why you shouldn't rely on a grammar checker. Take the following sentences that Word didn't flag. *This upset me a lot* should be *This upsets me a lot, This is a bad place for perfectionist like me* should be *for a perfectionist,* and *I am pride of my work* should be either *I am proud of my work* or *I take pride in my work.* These examples show, once again, that a grammar checker won't catch everything. It can't possibly know, for example, whether you meant for *upset* to be in the present or past tense.

A grammar checker can help, and you can maximize its usefulness by adjusting the options covered in the next section, but, as you've seen from this short sample, it's not magic. Are you getting tired of me repeating that yet? Good. Remember it.

Changing How Grammar Checking Works for You

From the Spelling and Grammar dialog box, click **Options**. If the Spelling and Grammar dialog box isn't open, choose **Options** from the Tools menu and select the **Spelling & Grammar** tab. Figure 11.10 shows the Grammar options in the **Spelling & Grammar** tab.

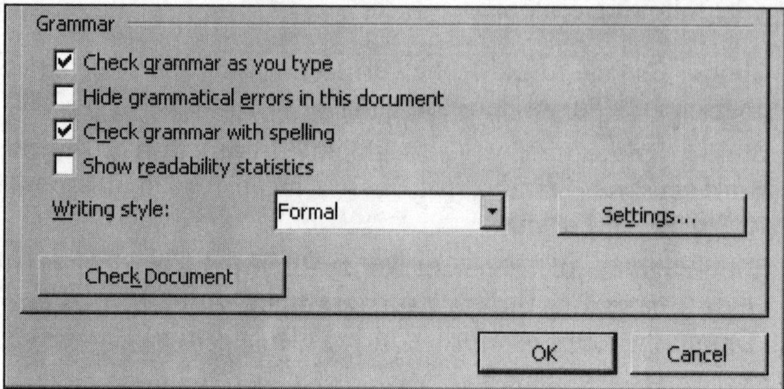

Figure 11.10 *Grammar options.*

The options in this tab are as follows:

- **Check grammar as you type** is the option that turns automatic grammar checking on or off.
- **Hide grammatical errors in this document**—when automatic grammar checking is turned on, this option allows you to hide the squiggly underlines while you're working on a document. To view the errors caught by automatic grammar checking, deselect the **Hide grammatical errors in this document** check box. This option is dimmed when the **Check grammar as you type** check box is deselected.
- **Check grammar with spelling** is turned on by default; it instructs Word to check grammar whenever you check spelling. If you want to check spelling without checking grammar, deselect this check box.

NOTE

You can turn grammar checking off for a particular session by deselecting the **Check grammar** box in the Spelling and Grammar dialog box.

- **Show readability statistics** is deselected by default. If you check it, Word displays a Readability Statistics dialog box, like the one in Figure 11.11, when a spelling and grammar check is completed.

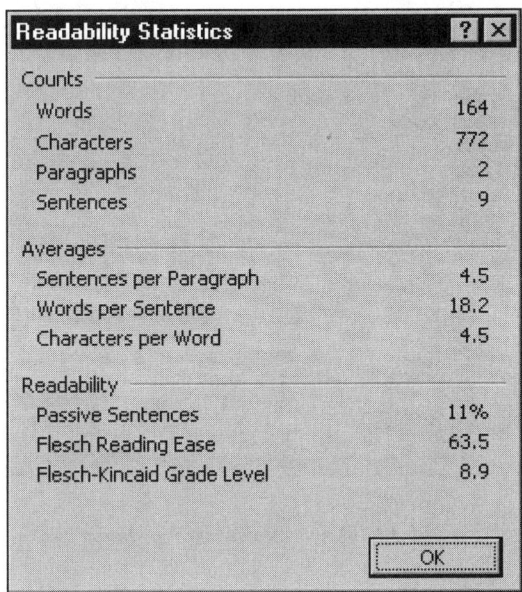

Figure 11.11 *The Readability Statistics dialog box.*

Choosing a Writing Style

You can turn the grammar checker into a more useful tool by setting its options to reflect your writing style as closely as possible. In Figure 11.10, notice that the selected writing style is **Formal**. You can pick a different style by selecting it from the Writing Style drop-down list, but let's take a closer look at this option by choosing **Settings**, which opens the Grammar Settings dialog box shown in Figure 11.12.

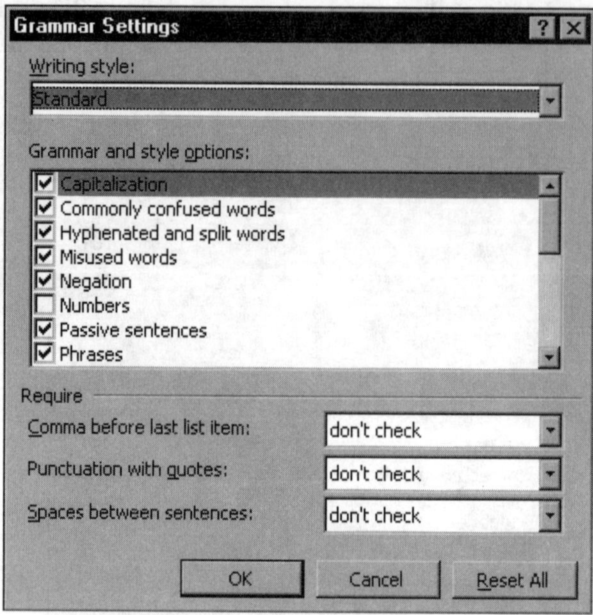

Figure 11.12 *The Grammar Settings dialog box.*

There are four writing styles to choose from: **Standard**, **Casual**, **Formal**, and **Technical**. In addition, you can create your own custom writing style. The writing style determines which rules the grammar checker will use. You can adjust and edit these styles to suit your preferences. You might want to choose different styles for different kinds of documents. For example, you could use the Technical style for your annual report and Casual for that short story you're writing during your lunch hours.

Editing a Writing Style

If you like a particular writing style but it still flags too many correct choices, you can edit it so that it flags only the rules you want it to.

To change grammar checking options:

1. In the Grammar Settings dialog box, select the writing style you want to edit.
2. Select or deselect check boxes to turn rules on or off.
3. Click **OK** to save the edited writing style.

To return all the grammar settings to their default options, choose **Reset All**.

AutoCorrect

The AutoCorrect feature can automatically correct your typing errors, expand abbreviations, and fix spacing and capitalization problems as you type. Word includes a whole bunch of the most common typing and spelling errors in the AutoCorrect dictionary, and you can edit the list to fit your needs.

You can also use AutoCorrect to change abbreviations for special characters, such as *(TM)*, into the actual typographic mark (™). In addition, Word can make some other useful typographical changes as you type. For example, you can automatically fix errors in capitalization (for example, *oREGON*).

Here's how it works. We all make certain mistakes as we type, and yours may not be as unique as you think. For example, many of us tend to type **hte** instead of *the* or **beleive** when we mean *believe.* It isn't that you don't know how to spell the word—your fingers just get in the way.

The AutoCorrect feature allows you to tell Word to watch your typing and correct common errors as you type. As you're typing and you type a pattern that AutoCorrect is looking for, Word makes the correction as soon as you finish the word. (A word ends when you type a space, a period, or a tab or hit the **Enter** key.)

Suppose you type the text shown in Figure 11.13.

In spite of the weight of both tradition adn|

Figure 11.13 *Oops—you misspelled and.*

Because the AutoCorrect list includes a correction for this mistake, AutoCorrect jumps in and corrects the misspelling as soon as you press the **Spacebar**, as shown in Figure 11.14.

In spite of the weight of both tradition and

Figure 11.14 AutoCorrect automatically fixes the spelling error.

It happens so fast that you may not even notice it, but the spelling is now correct.

NOTE

By default, AutoCorrect is turned on, which means that Word automatically makes any corrections from your AutoCorrect list as you type.

To turn AutoCorrect on:

1. Choose **AutoCorrect** from the Tools menu to open the AutoCorrect dialog box shown in Figure 11.15.

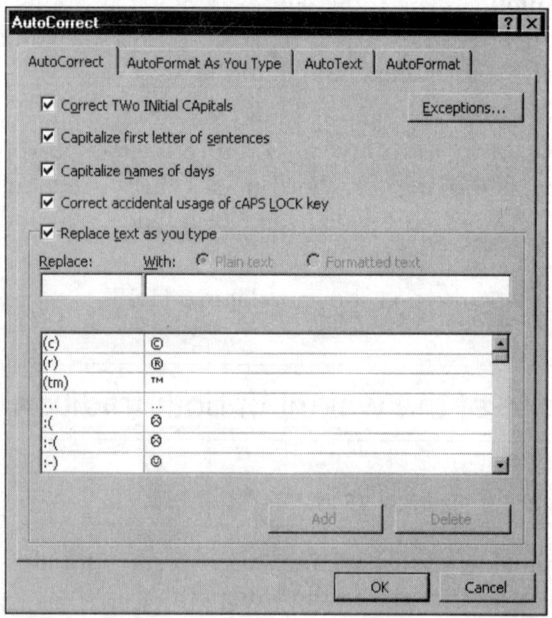

*Figure 11.15 The **AutoCorrect** tab in the AutoCorrect dialog box.*

2. If there isn't a check mark next to **Replace text as you type**, click to select it.
3. Unless you want to edit the AutoCorrect list at this point, click **OK** to close the dialog box.

AutoCorrect will now watch as you type and replace any of the words or phrases in the Replace list with their corrections in the With list.

NOTE

To turn AutoCorrect off, just remove the check mark from the **Replace text as you type** check box.

To add an entry to the AutoCorrect list:

1. Choose **AutoCorrect** from the Tools menu.
2. Type the word or phrase you want to replace in the Replace box. For this example, type **hte**. As you type, notice that Word scrolls through the entry list to display the part of the list that contains what you type, if it's there. You can see that *hte*, with its correction *the*, is already part of the list, so you don't need to add it. Now, delete the characters *hte* and type **isntall**. Notice that *isntall* isn't in the Replace list, so if you want to include it, you need to add it.
3. **Tab** over to the With box or click in it (don't press **Enter** or you'll be dumped back into the document).
4. Type the replacement word (for this example, type **install**).

NOTE

If you have text selected when you open the AutoCorrect dialog box, that text is automatically inserted in the With text box.

5. Choose **Add** (or press **Enter**—it's okay to use it here). Click **OK** when you've finished editing AutoCorrect entries.

To edit an AutoCorrect entry:

1. Open the AutoCorrect dialog box (choose **AutoCorrect** from the Tools menu).
2. Select the entry you want to change.
3. If you want to replace the entry's name (that's the text in the Replace list), click the **Delete** button. When you do this, the entry's name is selected in the Replace box.
4. Type a new name in the Replace box (the text you want Word to automatically change) and then click **Add**.
5. To change the replacement text, just **Tab** over to the With box and enter new text.

Create Exceptions to the AutoCorrect List

AutoCorrect does a great job of correcting common spelling and capitalization errors, but it can cause problems in some cases. Suppose you want to abbreviate the days of the week, so you type **Thurs.** for *Thursday*. Whenever Word sees a period, it thinks that's the end of a sentence and will automatically capitalize whatever comes next (unless **Capitalize first letter of sentences** is turned off). Word has already thought of this problem, and it includes a built-in Exceptions list that contains several common abbreviations (including *Thurs.*). When AutoCorrect encounters a word on the exceptions list, it knows not to capitalize the next letter.

To add your own exceptions:

1. From the AutoCorrect dialog box, click **Exceptions** to open the AutoCorrect Exceptions dialog box shown in Figure 11.16.

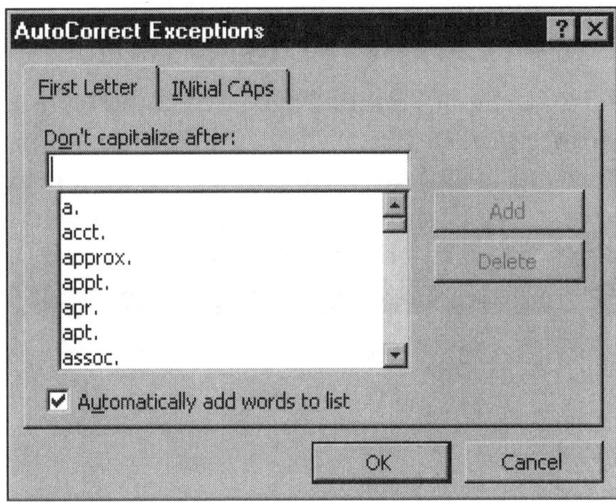

Figure 11.16 The AutoCorrect Exceptions dialog box.

2. Type the abbreviation (including the period) in the Don't capitalize after text box.
3. Click **Add**.

You can also create exceptions for words with two initial capitals by using the **Initial Caps** tab in the AutoCorrect Exceptions dialog box.

NOTE

You can automatically add an exception to your AutoCorrect list. When Word makes an AutoCorrect change you don't want, press the **Backspace** key and type over the correction. (If you use **Undo** instead, Word doesn't add the word to your Exceptions list.)

Using AutoCorrect to Expand Abbreviations

Suppose I'm writing a book about Microsoft Word 97 (gee, I am!), but I don't want to have to type the book's name over and over. No problem; I just create an AutoCorrect entry that inserts the book's name whenever I type **tyw**. I can even include formatting in the AutoCorrect entry. Here's how:

1. Type the text to which you want to apply an abbreviation. For this example, type **Teach Yourself Microsoft Word 97**.

2. Apply any text formatting you want. For this example, I chose the **BrushScript MT** font in **18 point** type and made it **bold**.
3. Select the text, then open the AutoCorrect dialog box and notice that *Teach Yourself Microsoft Word 97* is in the With text box. If you want the text formatting included in the entry, click the **Formatted text** radio button. Figure 11.17 shows my entry with **Formatted text** selected.

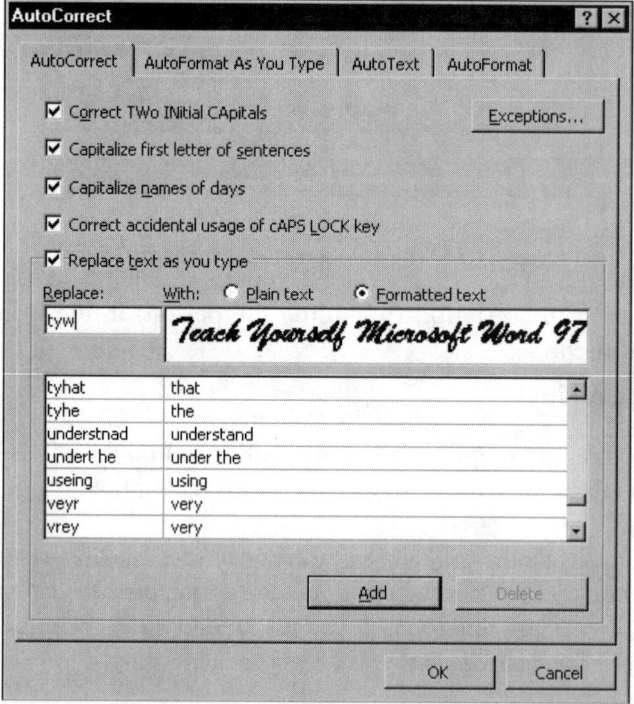

***Figure 11.17 Formatted text** has been selected.*

4. Type the abbreviation you want to use in the Replace text box. For this example, type **tyw**.
5. Choose **Add**.

Now, whenever you type **tyw** followed by a **space** or other punctuation, Word will automatically turn it into *Teach Yourself Microsoft Word 97*, complete with the appropriate formatting. The technique in this section (selecting text first) works for any AutoCorrect entry, whether it's an abbreviation or a correction.

NOTE

You can store paragraph formatting in an AutoCorrect entry by including the paragraph mark in your selection before you open the AutoCorrect dialog box.

Storing a Symbol or Special Character as an AutoCorrect Entry

The built-in AutoCorrect list includes shortcuts for several common symbols and special characters. For example, typing **(c)** inserts the standard copyright symbol, and typing **(tm)** inserts the trademark symbol. You can add AutoCorrect entries for additional symbols by doing the following:

1. Choose **Symbol** from the Insert menu to open the Symbol dialog box shown in Figure 11.18.

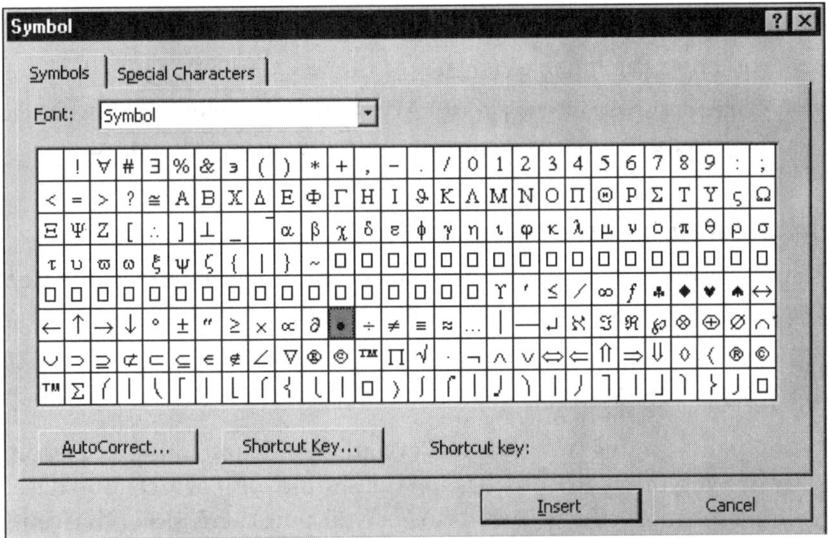

Figure 11.18 The Symbol dialog box.

2. Select the symbol you want and click the **AutoCorrect** button.

   Notice that the symbol you selected appears in the AutoCorrect list's With box, and **Formatted text** is selected.

3. In the Replace text box, type the abbreviation you want to use for the symbol, then click the **Add** button.

4. Click **OK** when you're finished.

Changing How AutoCorrect Treats Capitalization Issues

You can change the defaults for how AutoCorrect handles various capitalization problems. While in the AutoCorrect dialog box, select or deselect the following options to suit your needs (all of them are selected by default):

- **Correct TWo INitial capitals**—this option automatically changes the case of the second letter if you accidentally hold down the **Shift** key too long and type the first two characters of a word as uppercase text. With this option on, *WOrd* would automatically be changed to *Word.*
- **Capitalize first letter of sentences** automatically capitalizes the first letter of anything Word considers a sentence.
- **Capitalize names of days** automatically capitalizes the first letter when you enter the name of any day of the week.
- **Correct accidental usage of cAPS LOCK key** means just what it says. Uppercase letters are changed to lowercase and vice versa.

Turning Off AutoCorrect

If you don't want to use Word's AutoCorrect feature, just deselect the **Replace text as you type** check box in the AutoCorrect dialog box.

Using the Thesaurus

With the spelling and grammar checker and a little judicious proofreading of your own, everything in your document should be correct. But have you always used the most effective words to get your point across? For that finishing touch, use Word's Thesaurus.

To start the Thesaurus:

1. Place your insertion point anywhere in the word you want to look up. (For this example, type **work** and place your insertion point inside the word.)
2. Choose **Language** from the Tools menu and **Thesaurus** from the Language menu (or press **Shift+F7**).

The Thesaurus dialog box is displayed, as shown in Figure 11.19. Notice that *work* appears in the Looked Up box.

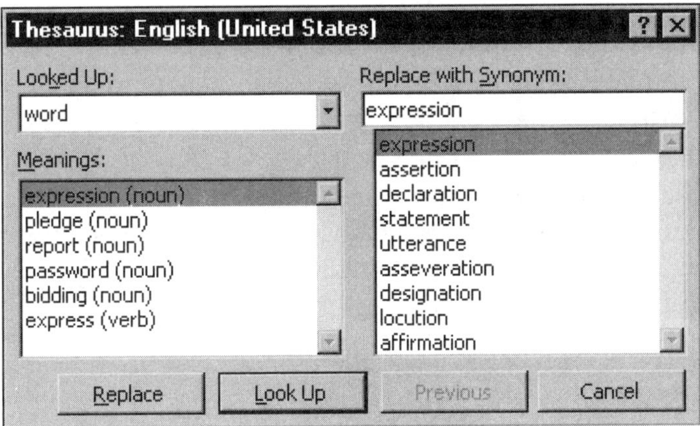

Figure 11.19 *The Thesaurus dialog box.*

You have the following options:

- The Looked Up box contains the currently selected word. As you use the Thesaurus, Word keeps track of the words you've looked up during this session, and you can go back to any word by choosing it from the Looked Up drop-down list.
- A word can have several meanings. The Meanings list shows words that describe the currently selected word, along with the parts of speech. When a word in the Meanings list is selected, a list of synonyms for that word is displayed under the Replace with Synonyms box.
- The word in the Replace with Synonym box is the one that will replace the selected word in your document if you choose **Replace**.
- The words below the Replace with Synonym list are additional synonyms for the currently selected meaning.

Replacing a Word

If you see a word you like better than the one in your document, Thesaurus can make the replacement for you:

1. Select the word you want from the Meanings list or the Replace with Synonym list. Notice that the selected word appears in the Replace with Synonym box.
2. Click the **Replace** button.

You can continue looking up as many words as you want while the Thesaurus window is open.

The Thesaurus is a great tool for playing "what if." If you want to find a more precise word for a particular situation, look it up. If you don't find what you're looking for right away, try looking up some of the other words in the Meanings list. You can often find the right word by probing down a few layers in Thesaurus.

From Here...

This chapter gave you a set of tools to check and fine-tune your writing. Just remember that none of them takes the place of your own proofreading efforts. Have I repeated that often enough yet? You'll avoid a lot of errors if you spell check every single document (and don't forget to save after spell checking). Then spell check whenever you make changes (remember, you don't have to check the whole document—you can easily check just the portion of the document you've changed). Use the grammar checker if it helps your writing efforts. Edit the writing styles and rules so that it's a help rather than a hindrance. And remember the Thesaurus for those agonizing word choices.

After all this heavy-duty proofreading stuff, it's time for some fun. In the next chapter, you'll get to cut loose and play around a little (or a lot). we'll look at all the different ways you can change the way your text looks. There's even a terrific feature, WordArt, that lets you change text into all sorts of strange shapes and styles.

SECTION III

Dressing Up: Fonts and Graphic Elements

CHAPTER 12

A Look at Fonts

Let's talk about:

- ✦ What are fonts?
- ✦ Inserting symbols and special characters
- ✦ Adding drop caps to text
- ✦ Having fun with WordArt

Let's make this a multiple choice quiz. My trusty *Webster's Dictionary* gives me two definitions for *font*. Which one do you think applies here?

1. A receptacle for baptismal or holy water.
2. An assortment of printing type of one size and style.

If you chose 2, step to the head of the class. (If you chose 1, go back to the beginning of the book and read every chapter twice.) Yes, we are talking about the text that you see on your screen and on the printed page. *Font* is just a fancy word for the size and shape of your text.

There's one more term you need to be familiar with before we move on: point size. The *point size* just tells you how tall the font is. A point is 1/72 of an inch, so a 12-point font (a standard size for business documents) would be 12/72 inch tall. You'll often see a font listed something like this:

Century Gothic Regular 12 pt

Century Gothic is the name of the font and describes a particular typestyle. *Regular* is what Word refers to as the *font style*. The same font can come in several different styles. For example, Century Gothic comes in regular, bold, italic, and bold italic. Twelve is the point size. There. Now you know how to decipher a font listing. You'll see a lot of these in this chapter. Figure 12.1 shows an assortment of fonts, styles, and point sizes.

Figure 12.1 *An assortment of fonts.*

NOTE

In word processing, margins, tabs, and page widths are usually measured in inches or centimeters. Fonts are measured in points. Theoretically, a point is 1/72 of an inch. However, there is some variation among different fonts, in the same way that shoe sizes from some manufacturers run a little loose or a little small. For example, the Times font runs slightly smaller than Palatino at the same point size. Body text in books, magazines, and reports tends to be between eight and twelve points.

Can I Do All This?

Yes, depending on your printer's capabilities. Word comes with about two billion fonts (I might be exaggerating slightly), and you might have even more that came with your printer or with other programs. You can do everything you see in Figure 12.1 and much, much more. You can change fonts whenever you want, and you can enhance their appearance by adding attributes like bold, double underline, and shadows.

NOTE

You can buy more fonts that come on either disks that you install or cartridges that you insert in your printer, but unless you have really specialized needs, the fonts you get with Word should be enough. I used to use extra fonts, but I never need them anymore.

Just keep in mind what I mentioned in Chapter 7 (when we played with bold, italic, and underline) about the ransom note school of design. With all these riches at your disposal, it's easy to get carried away with too many different sizes and styles. Be judicious—try to stick to one or two typestyles for a document, and be consistent and careful with sizes and attributes. (If you really are writing a ransom note, don't pay any attention to this advice.)

A Brief Primer on Good Taste

In Chapter 7, you learned how to apply character formatting to your text. Now it's time to focus on style. A typographer can wax rhapsodic over tiny, subtle differences in the angle of the leaning oval on an *o*, or the curl of the bar on a *Q*. Don't worry—I won't get into that kind of detail. Some basic guidelines are enough to produce attractive, readable documents.

Why Use Formatting?

Formatting is all about two things: readability and effect. Except for unusual circumstances like an avant-garde magazine ad or a poster whose intent is to attract attention rather than to inform, readability is the first issue. What you want to do with the document is communicate. The ideal is to reach readers almost transparently, so they don't notice all the details of formatting but they do get the overall effect you intend.

Variations in font size and thickness can set off headings from the longer blocks of text beneath them. Italic and bold formatting can add emphasis to words within sentences. The fonts you choose can harmonize together so that the page has that indefinable something that makes it, somehow, easy to read. Your readers will jump straight to the meaning you want to communicate.

Effect is the other half of formatting. Each choice of font you make sets a tone, creates an aura, and can either match or contradict the tone and effect of your words. For example, the Braggadocio font is bold and outgoing, Times New Roman is businesslike, and Desdemona is arty.

Types of Fonts

Fonts can be grouped into several categories. One division is between serif and sans serif fonts. A *serif* is the tiny decorative bar that extends from various parts of the characters in a font. Figure 12.2 shows an example of a few characters from a serif font, Times New Roman.

Figure 12.2 *A serif font.*

A *sans serif* font lacks these thin bars. Figure 12.3 shows an example in Arial, a common sans serif font.

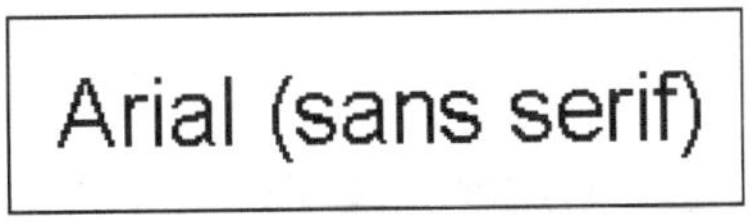

Arial (sans serif)

Figure 12.3 *A sans serif font.*

These differences between fonts may seem trivial, but when you're reading an entire page or an entire book of text, your mind grasps the difference immediately. In general, serif fonts such as Times New Roman or Century Schoolbook are best for body text—long stretches of text like you'd see in a novel or a report. Sans serif fonts, in general, are best for short stretches of text, such as labels in a diagram or subheadings in a chapter.

Another category of fonts can be used in situations like large newspaper headlines, banners, and the headings of ad copy. These are *display fonts.* They tend to be extra bold, or in typographical parlance, *black.* Examples of display fonts that are probably on your system are Arial Black and Haettenschweiler (see the examples in Figure 12.4).

Arial Black

Haettenschweiler

Figure 12.4 *Display font examples.*

The final category of fonts is *decorative.* These are used for special occasions for a particular effect. For example, Monotype Corsiva, shown in Figure 12.5, is the kind of font you might use for a formal invitation.

You are invited to a reception
at ten o'clock in the morning
on the 27th of December 1996
Regrets only

Figure 12.5 *A decorative font.*

Some decorative fonts have such a specialized function that you can't form words with them. That's because they consist purely of symbols. Numerous fonts contain what are called *printer's dingbats,* small symbols such as arrows or decorative bullets. Wingdings, shown in Figure 12.6, is one of these fonts.

Figure 12.6 *A dingbat font.*

How Can I Combine Fonts?

Any guideline can be broken by people who really know what they're doing, but here are some basic rules. A good safe limit on font combinations is two font families per page, a display or bold sans serif font for headings and a serif font for the body text. An upper limit for font variations, which would count different sizes of a font as separate variations, is about five or six. Beyond that, a page starts to look too confusing for the reader to easily sort out the meanings and effects of the various fonts and styles. Too many fonts can make a page look like a ransom note.

By all means, avoid Courier and other *monospaced* fonts where every character has the same width. There may be special occasions when one might be useful—for example, in a computer manual where you're distinguishing programming code from explanations—but for normal usage, it's a bad idea because monospaced fonts require more effort to read. Typewriter-style fonts were used for a long time because they were all we had. With the wealth of choices currently available, however, you can do much better.

Anything Else?

Here are a few suggestions of combinations of fonts for headings and body text that work well together: Arial bold and Times New Roman (a common but classic combination), Century Gothic bold and Century Schoolbook, Arial Narrow bold and Garamond MT. You can vary the size of the heading font to indicate the level of hierarchy in an outline or multi-level document.

If you think all this talk of fonts is just being fussy, consider the examples that follow. Figure 12.7 shows a page designed with one of the preceding combinations: Arial Narrow bold and Garamond MT.

A Guide to the Glen

Congratulations for selecting the newest hideaway in the Bay Resorts International family of vacation paradise: the Forest Glen. We hope that your stay in these luxurious surroundings brings only relaxation and pleasure. To make sure everything goes smoothly on your lost weekend, we have put together a brief guide to the amenities at the Forest Glen.

Comfort

The thermostat is just inside the Concert Hall to your right as you enter from the Grand Lobby. You may select any temperature you please: whatever gives you the deepest sleep and most comfortable waking hours.

The internationally famous mineral baths are shown on your map to the Forest Glen. When you start the baths, the mineral content will be optimum after the water runs a minute or two. Do not be alarmed if a little color remains even after running a bit. That comes from the minerals.

Figure 12.7 *A classical, simple mix of fonts.*

Notice how harmoniously the typefaces fit together, and how legible and approachable the page is. Now, for a bad example, consider a page with three or four different fonts that don't go together at all, as shown in Figure 12.8.

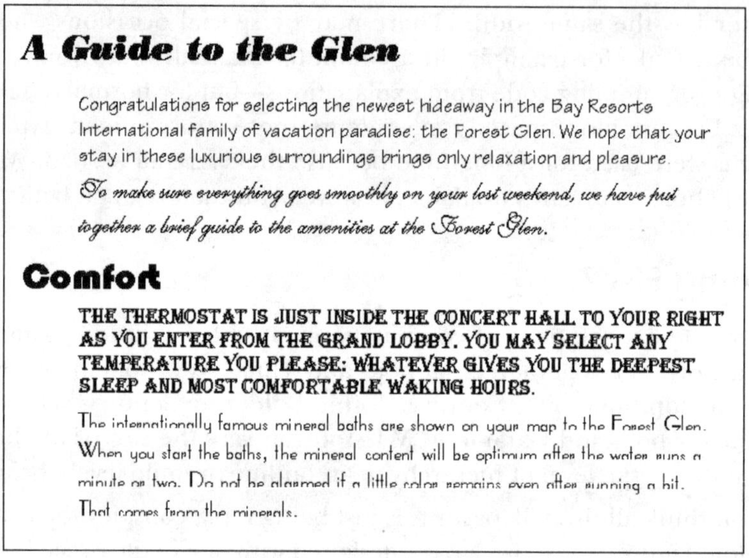

A Guide to the Glen

Congratulations for selecting the newest hideaway in the Bay Resorts International family of vacation paradise: the Forest Glen. We hope that your stay in these luxurious surroundings brings only relaxation and pleasure.

To make sure everything goes smoothly on your lost weekend, we have put together a brief guide to the amenities at the Forest Glen.

Comfort

THE THERMOSTAT IS JUST INSIDE THE CONCERT HALL TO YOUR RIGHT AS YOU ENTER FROM THE GRAND LOBBY. YOU MAY SELECT ANY TEMPERATURE YOU PLEASE: WHATEVER GIVES YOU THE DEEPEST SLEEP AND MOST COMFORTABLE WAKING HOURS.

The internationally famous mineral baths are shown on your map to the Forest Glen. When you start the baths, the mineral content will be optimum after the water runs a minute or two. Do not be alarmed if a little color remains even after running a bit. That comes from the minerals.

Figure 12.8 An ugly page with bad font combinations.

What About capital letters? You've probably gotten e-mail messages or memos from someone WHO HABITUALLY TYPES IN ALL CAPS LIKE THIS. Besides feeling like the writer was shouting, you probably thought there was something wrong with the appearance of the text but couldn't quite put your finger on it. There's a good reason for that feeling: text in all capitals is less legible. Tests have shown that capital letters are harder to read because they lack the visual cues that the combination of upper- and lowercase letters provide.

For example, consider the sentence shown in Figure 12.9.

THE DINNER BUFFET PRICE NORMALLY INCLUDES ICE CREAM AND FUDGE SAUCE.

Figure 12.9 *Text in all caps.*

If you hold this book a couple feet away from you and squint, you can begin to see, instead of individual letters, the basic shape of the words and the sentence. It looks like a block, a series of rectangles, and each of the letters is also like a square block. None of the letters extends below the baseline, as the lowercase letters *y* and *q* do, and all the letters are the same height at the top, too. Now look at the same sentence in a combination of upper- and lowercase letters.

The dinner buffet price normally includes ice cream and fudge sauce.

Figure 12.10 *Text in capital and lowercase letters.*

Hold the book back and squint at the sentence. Now you can distinguish shapes, letters that go above and below the line, different heights, and varying widths that give your eyes the information they need to tell letters apart. You've looked at so many printed words in your lifetime that your brain knows instinctively which letters are which. With these cues, your brain starts to guess what a word is before consciously putting all the individual letters together. This process is much more difficult with text that is in all capitals, because there's less visual information to grasp. With all capital letters, you have to work harder for the same result.

Missing Fonts

Sometimes you'll get a file that has text formatted with a font that isn't on your system. Without the font, the text doesn't appear as it did to the person who wrote the document, nor will it print that way. However, Word does automatically substitute another font—often Arial or Times New Roman—that should look at least roughly similar to the original font in the document. And if you don't need the document to look identical to its original version on someone else's machine, you can apply whatever fonts you like.

USING SPECIAL CHARACTERS AND SYMBOLS

In addition to all the regular font choices, Word comes with a bunch of special characters (everything from musical notes to the entire Greek alphabet) that act just like text and can be inserted anywhere in a document. It's really simple. Figure 12.11 uses a couple of these special characters.

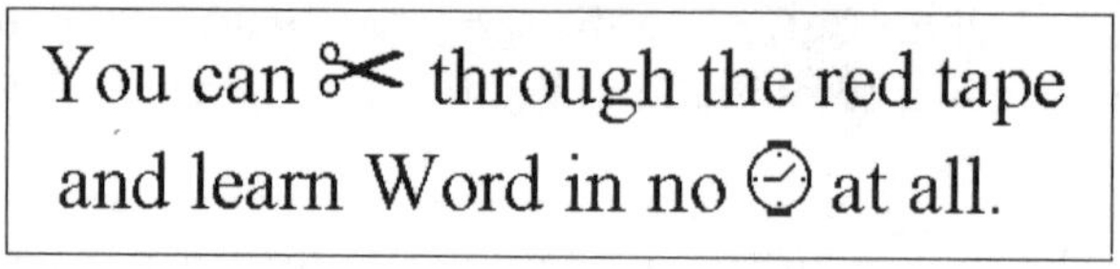

You can ✂ through the red tape and learn Word in no ⌚ at all.

Figure 12.11 Symbols and special characters can be inserted anywhere in a document.

Most of the TrueType fonts included with Windows 95 and Word contain special typographic characters that you used to have to approximate roughly, by typing such things as **(C)** for the © symbol or **(TM)** for the ™ symbol. The AutoCorrect features takes care of some of these for you. But the Symbol dialog box lists all these typographic marks in one place for easy insertion.

It's easy to know what to type when you need a *K*, but how do you know which key to press to get £ or a Greek letter? When you see them all together, you don't need to know the keystroke; you can simply select a character and insert it. And if you find a symbol character or typographic mark that you want to use regularly, you can assign your own shortcut key to it.

To insert a special character:

1. Place your insertion point wherever you want the special character.
2. Choose **Symbol** from the Insert menu.
3. Click the **Special Characters** tab (shown in Figure 12.12).

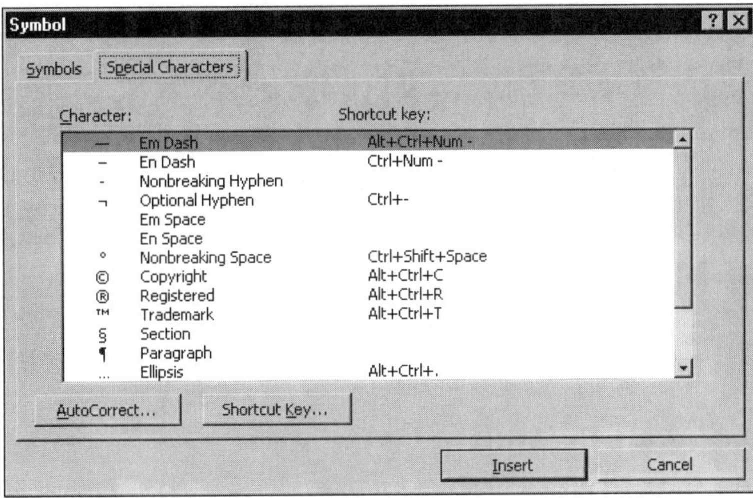

Figure 12.12 The ***Special Characters*** *tab in the Symbol dialog box.*

4. Select the item you want and click **Insert**. The dialog box remains open, allowing you to insert additional characters until you click **Close**.

Notice that most of these characters already have shortcut keys assigned. You can insert any character by typing the keyboard shortcut without going through the Symbol dialog box. For example, to insert a copyright symbol, just type **Alt+Ctrl+C**.

To insert a character from the Symbol font or other non-alphabetic fonts:

1. Place your insertion point where you want the symbol.
2. Choose **Symbol** from the Insert menu and select the **Symbols** tab (shown in Figure 12.13).

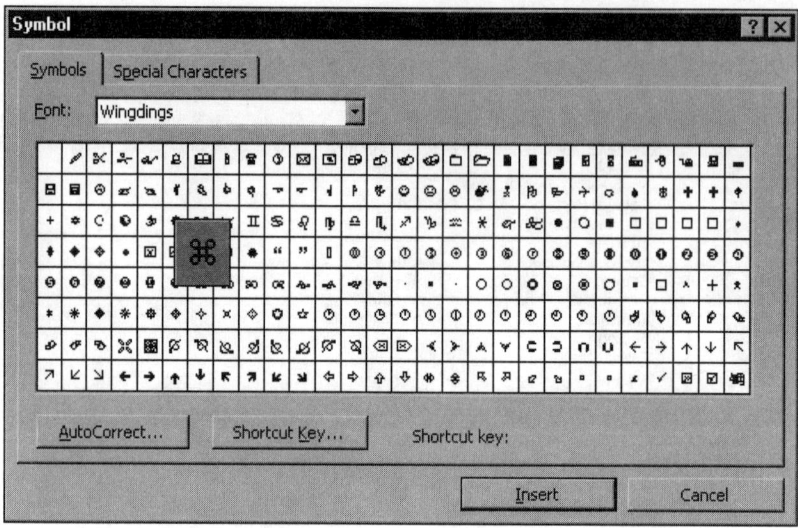

*Figure 12.13 The **Symbols** tab in the Symbol dialog box.*

3. From the Font list, select the name of the font containing the character you want to insert. The fonts that contain the most useful symbols are **Symbol**, **Wingdings**, and **Monotype Sorts**, but check out the other fonts when you get a chance.
4. Select a symbol and click **Insert**. The character is inserted in your document. The dialog box remains open, allowing you to insert additional symbols until you click **Close**. As you can see in Figure 12.13, when you click on a symbol you get a magnified view of it.

To assign your own shortcut key to a commonly used symbol:

1. Choose **Symbol** from the Insert menu.
2. Select the **Symbol** tab.
3. Select the symbol you want to use.
4. Click **Shortcut Key**. This opens the Customize Keyboard dialog box shown in Figure 12.14. Note that the selected symbol is displayed in the lower-right area of the dialog box.

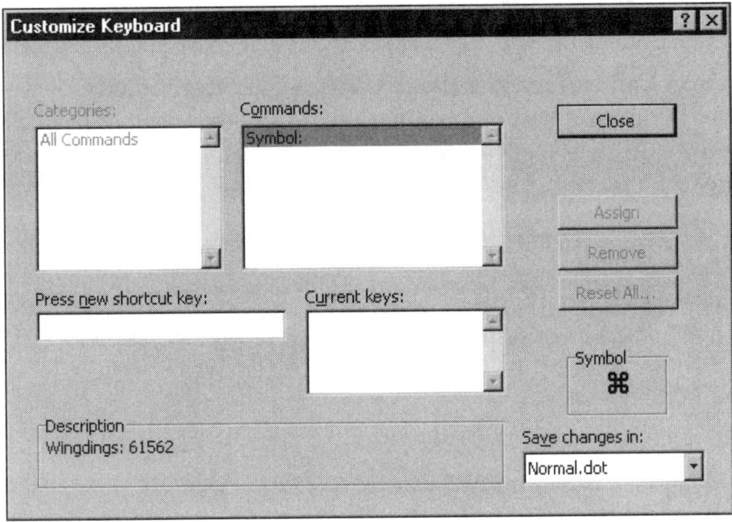

Figure 12.14 *The Customize Keyboard dialog box.*

5. Notice that your insertion point is already in the Press new shortcut key text box. Just type the characters for the shortcut key you want to assign.

   As soon as you enter your shortcut, Word lets you know whether that shortcut is already assigned to something else. If you can't seem to find an unassigned shortcut key, try holding down the **Alt**, **Ctrl**, and **Shift** keys while typing a character, or hold down the **Shift** and **Ctrl** keys while typing a number.

6. When you've found an available shortcut key, click **Assign**, then **Close**.

You might be tempted to press **Alt+A** instead of clicking on the **Assign** button. Even though this is a great technique for most dialog box buttons, it could give you unexpected results in this case. If your insertion point is still in the Press new shortcut key text box, pressing **Alt+A** (or any other keystroke combination) places that keystroke in the text box instead of executing the command.

Symbols and special characters act just like regular characters. If you choose a larger font size for your text, any special characters included in the text also change size.

WHAT'S A DROP CAP?

Use the **Drop Cap** feature to enlarge the first character, letters, or words of a paragraph. Drop caps are commonly used at the beginning of book chapters; they can also be an effective way to enhance announcements or stationery (see Figure 12.15).

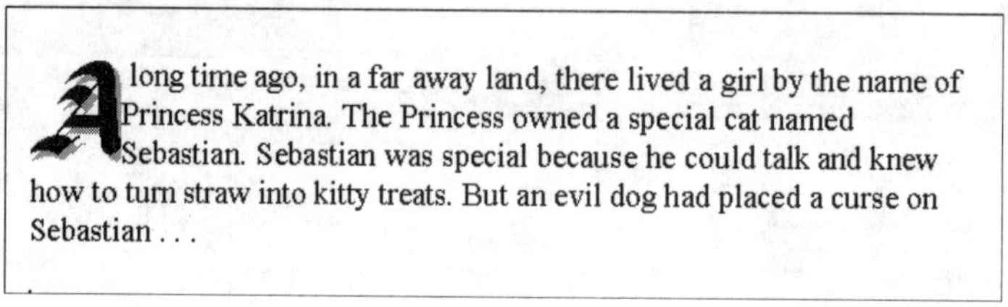

A long time ago, in a far away land, there lived a girl by the name of Princess Katrina. The Princess owned a special cat named Sebastian. Sebastian was special because he could talk and knew how to turn straw into kitty treats. But an evil dog had placed a curse on Sebastian . . .

Figure 12.15 Be creative with drop caps.

To create a drop cap:

1. Place your insertion point in the paragraph you want to add the drop cap to.
2. Choose **Drop Cap** from the Format menu to open the Drop Cap dialog box shown in Figure 12.16.

Drop Cap
Position
None
Dropped
In Margin
Options
Font:
EngrvrsOldEng Bd BT
Lines to drop:
3
Distance from text:
0"
OK
Cancel

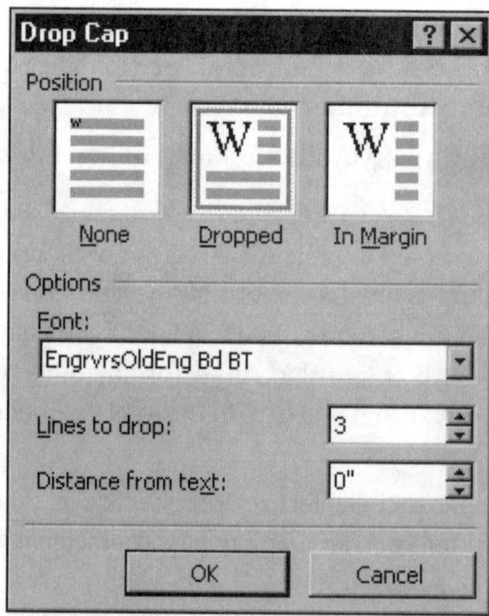

Figure 12.16 The Drop Cap dialog box.

NOTE

If **Drop Cap** is dimmed on the Format menu, you might have your insertion point in a paragraph that doesn't have any text. You can only apply the **Drop Cap** feature to a paragraph that already has text in it.

3. Click one of the Position options to determine the placement of the drop cap. Notice that **None** is selected when you first open the dialog box. If you click **OK** at this point, you don't get a drop cap; you must select one of the other two Position options.
4. Make a selection from the Font drop-down list. The drop cap character doesn't have to use the same font as the rest of the paragraph.
5. Enter a number in the Lines to drop box. This number tells Word how much space the drop cap will take up. If you specify three lines (the default), the drop cap extends down three lines from the first line of the paragraph.
6. Enter a measurement in the Distance from text box to tell Word how much horizontal space you want between the drop cap and the rest of the text.
7. When you've selected all the options you want, click **OK**.

To get rid of a drop cap:

1. Place your insertion point in the paragraph that contains the drop cap.
2. Choose **Drop Cap** from the Format menu.
3. Select **None** in the Position section.
4. Click **OK**.

Introducing WordArt

WordArt is a terrific feature that lets you perform amazing stunts and contortions on your text with the greatest of ease. Instead of spending a lot of time talking about it, look at Figure 12.17 to see what I mean. I did this in about two minutes. Really. I've used other programs that can do similar things with text, but none of them is as easy (or so much fun).

Figure 12.17 A small taste of WordArt's possibilities.

WordArt is really a graphics feature, so I should wait until the next chapter to show it to you, but it does relate to text and fonts, and it's too cool for words—I couldn't wait!

To use WordArt:

1. Right-click on any toolbar and choose **WordArt** to open the WordArt toolbar shown in Figure 12.18.

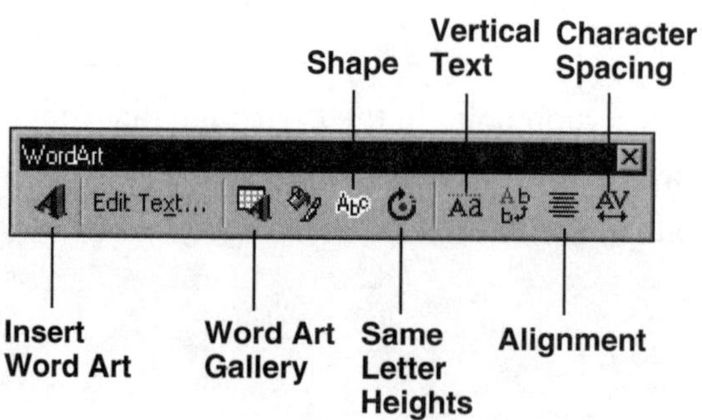

Figure 12.18 The WordArt toolbar.

NOTE

You can also choose **Picture** from the Insert menu and **WordArt** from the Picture menu. This takes you straight to the WordArt Gallery shown in Figure 12.19. If you use this technique, the WordArt toolbar isn't displayed until you complete step 7.

2. Click on the **Insert WordArt** button (the button on the far left with the letter *A*).
3. Select a style from the WordArt Gallery shown in Figure 12.19 and click **OK** to open the Edit WordArt Text dialog box shown in Figure 12.20.

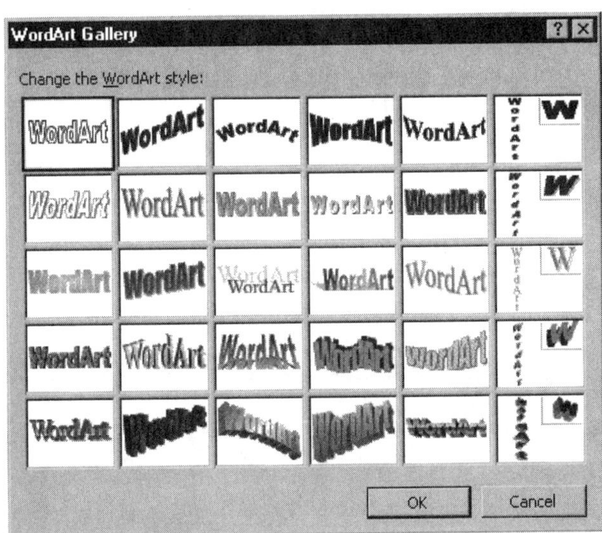

Figure 12.19 The WordArt Gallery.

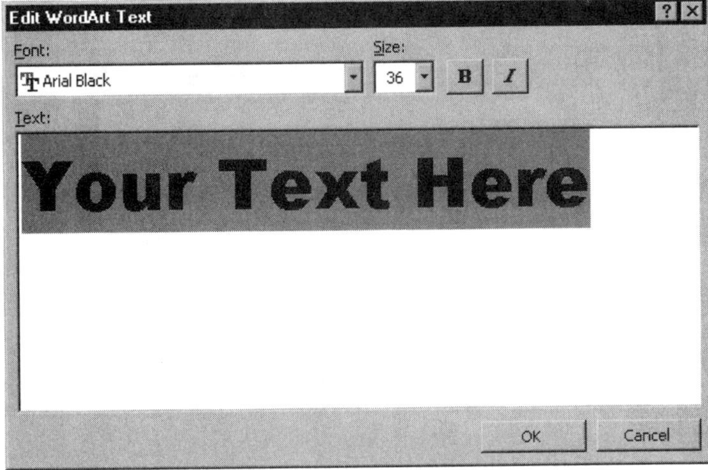

Figure 12.20 The Edit WordArt Text dialog box.

4. Type your text in the Text box. (For now, you can use the sample text *Your Text Here* that's already there if you want.)
5. Choose a font and point size from the Font and Size drop-down lists.
6. Click on the **Bold** or **Italic** button to make the WordArt text bold or italic.
7. Click **OK** to insert the WordArt in your document.

Notice that the WordArt toolbar is still open. You can use this toolbar to make all sorts of changes to your WordArt:

- Click on the **Format WordArt** button to open the dialog box shown in Figure 12.21. As you can see from the **Colors and Lines**, **Size**, **Position**, and **Wrapping** tabs, this dialog box contains options that let you change the appearance of your WordArt in just about any way you can imagine.

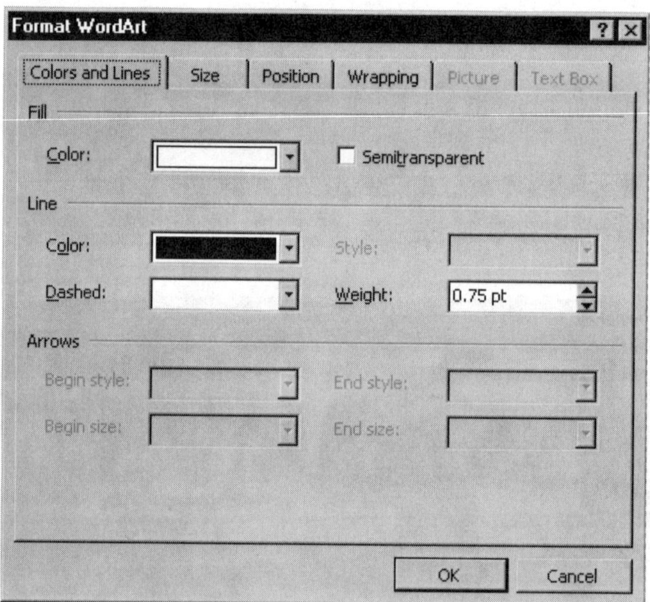

Figure 12.21 The Format WordArt dialog box.

- Click on the **WordArt Shape** button and make a selection from the palette shown in Figure 12.22 to change the shape of your WordArt text.

Figure 12.22 The WordArt Shape palette.

- You can rotate the text by clicking on the **Free Rotate** button and then dragging one of the green dots that appears at each corner of the WordArt object.
- You can make all the characters the same height by clicking on the **WordArt Same Letter Heights** button.
- Click the **WordArt Vertical Text** button to make the text vertical, as shown in Figure 12.23.

Figure 12.23 You can make your WordArt text vertical.

- Click the **WordArt Alignment** button and make a selection from the pop-up list to align the text inside its box.
- Adjust the character spacing by making a selection from the WordArt Character Spacing drop-down list.

Go ahead—play around here for a while. Choose different shapes and options and observe the results.

ROADMAP

As you'll see in the next chapter, there's a Drawing toolbar that gives you access to Word's drawing tools. If the Drawing toolbar is displayed, you can create a WordArt object by clicking its **Insert WordArt** button.

Exiting WordArt

Nothing to it. When you're finished with your masterpiece (for the moment anyway), just click anywhere outside the WordArt box.

It might not be the size you want, and it might not be in the right location, but it is a regular Word graphics object that you can size and move just like any other graphics object. The only problem is, you haven't learned how to do that yet. Patience, patience. We'll take care of that in the next chapter.

Changing the Default Font for New Documents

Here's one last bit of font information. When you start a new document, Word uses whichever font has been selected as the default font for the template on which the document is based. But you can assign any font you want as the default.

To change the default font:

1. Choose **New** from the File menu and select the template for which you want to change the default font. To change the default for standard documents, choose **Blank Document** from the **General** tab.
2. Choose **Font** from the Format menu to open the Font dialog box shown in Figure 12.24.

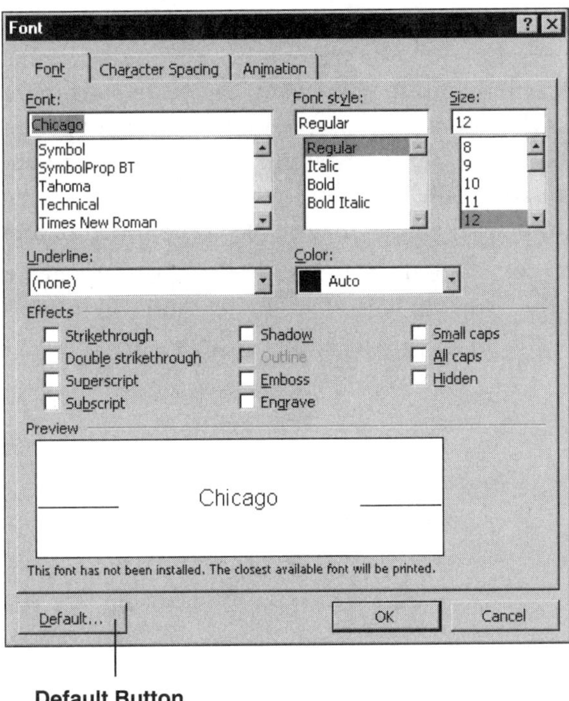

*Figure 12.24 The Font dialog box. Notice the **Default** button in the lower-left corner.*

3. Select all the font, size, and other character effect options that you want to be part of the default font.
4. Click the **Default** button. Word asks you to confirm the change, as shown in Figure 12.25.

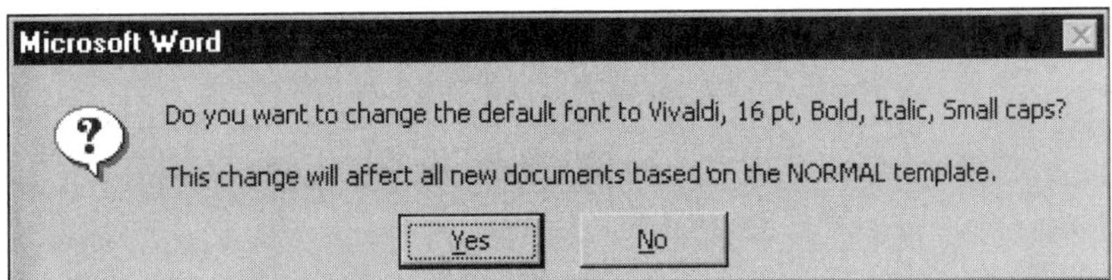

Figure 12.25 Confirming your default font change.

5. Click **Yes** to confirm the change.

FROM HERE...

With what you learned in this chapter, you can really start to wow your friends and colleagues with your expertise and ability to turn out professional-looking documents. Not only can you change fonts at will, you can use special characters and drop caps to add some flair. And you can perform incredible feats with text, twisting it into every shape imaginable at the touch of a button.

There's more to come. In the next chapter, you'll learn how to include graphic images (pictures) in your documents. And you don't even have to be an artist—Word graciously provides the pictures.

CHAPTER 13

Working with Graphics

Let's talk about:

- ✦ Inserting graphics
- ✦ Using the Clip Gallery
- ✦ Formatting and enhancing graphics
- ✦ Working with text boxes
- ✦ Adding AutoShapes

As you'll see in this chapter, the possibilities with graphics are almost unlimited. You can use graphics to get your newsletters, reports, and memos noticed. This doesn't mean that every document must include graphics, however. Like too many fonts on the same page, unattractive or poorly considered graphics in a document can detract from the meaning and lessen the effect of your words.

This chapter doesn't tell you everything you can do with graphics in Word—there's just too much. It does cut through the confusion and get you going quickly. And I'll point you in the right direction for further exploration.

Because Word's graphics features are smoothly integrated with the rest of the program, it's easy to use images to spice up your work. Support for many types of graphics images, built-in drawing tools, and commands that let you place a graphic anywhere on a page allow you to get just the right look.

In fact, some of Word's drawing features, such as adding special effects, using separate layers for graphics and text, and grouping drawing objects, are more flexible than in many desktop publishing programs. This chapter covers the basics of adding graphic images to your Word documents and creating your own graphics. I'll even get into some advanced features to show you the extent of Word's graphics capabilities.

Inserting Graphics

Word makes it easy to bring electronic images, called *clip art,* into your documents. The easiest way to insert graphics into a Word document is with the Clip Gallery.

Using the Clip Gallery

The Clip Gallery is actually a separate program that you can access from any Microsoft Office program. It lets you organize all the graphic clips, music clips, and video clips that are available on your system. You can view the clip art on your system and organize it by category and keyword.

To insert a graphic:

1. Position the insertion point where you want the picture.
2. Choose **Picture** from the Insert menu and **Clip Art** from the Picture menu. This opens the Microsoft Clip Gallery, shown in Figure 13.1.

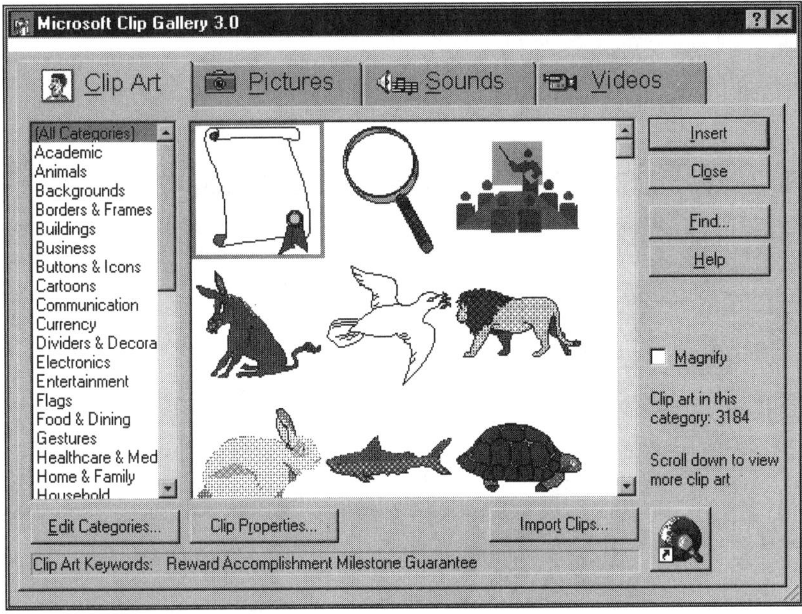

Figure 13.1 *Microsoft Clip Gallery 3.0.*

NOTE

If you are working in Normal view, Word automatically switches to Page Layout view when you open the Clip Gallery. Graphic images do not display in Normal view.

As you can see by scrolling through the pictures, there is quite a selection. These images were copied to your **Clipart** folder when you installed Word. Each picture is organized into a general category. The list of categories displays down the left side of the Clip Gallery dialog box. Later in this chapter you'll see how you can customize the Clip Gallery and search for specific types of graphics.

3. Click on a category name in the left column to display the pictures for that category. For this example, select **Cartoons**.
4. Click to select the graphic you want. For this exercise, select the weird-looking duck who's getting ready to smash his computer. (If you don't see this image, just select any image you want.)

NOTE

If you click to select the **Magnify** check box, Word gives you an enlarged view of each image as you click on it. Figure 13.2 shows an enlarged image of the mallet-toting duck, and you can also see the image's title: `hatecomp`.

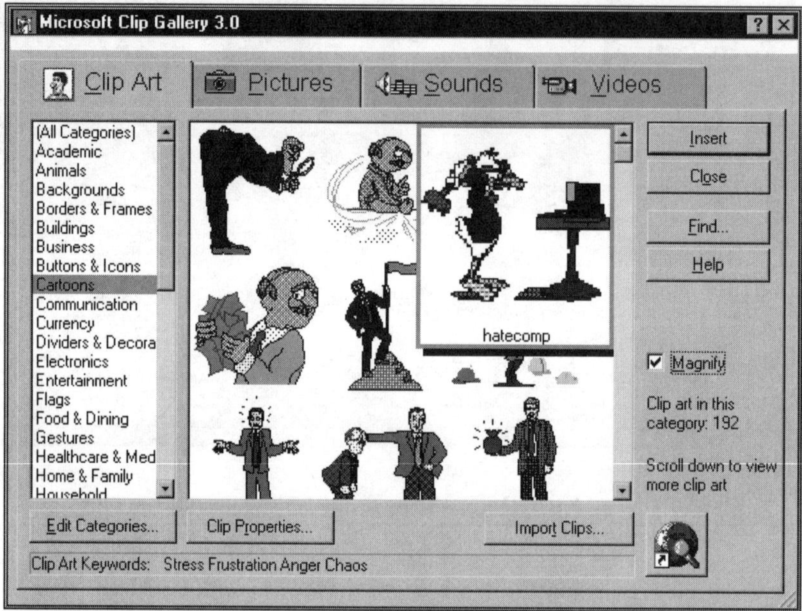

Figure 13.2 *With **Magnify** selected, you see an enlarged view of the selected image.*

Notice that `Clip Art Keywords` displays in the lower-left corner of the dialog box. *Keywords* describe the contents of each image you select. The keywords for our guy with the mallet are `Stress Frustration Anger Chaos`. In addition to identifying selected graphics, the keywords can be used to search through your clip art collection, as you'll see later in this chapter.

5. Click on the **Insert** button. Word places the image you selected in your document, as shown in Figure 13.3. Notice the little boxes around the picture—they're called *handles*, and they appear whenever an image (or any other graphic object) is selected. Later you'll use them to change the size of your picture.

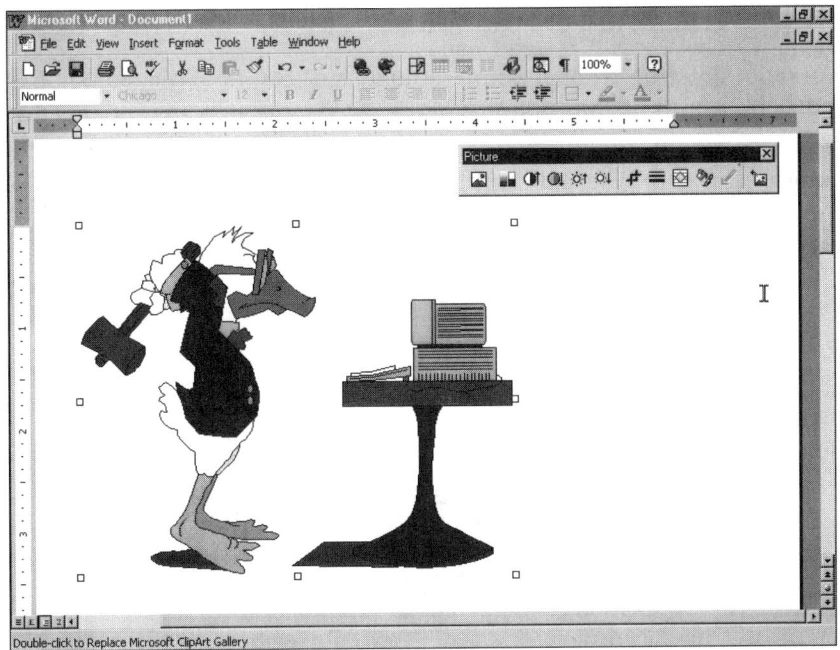

Figure 13.3 *The graphic image inserted in your document.*

6. Click anywhere outside the picture. The handles disappear, and the picture is part of your document. We'll play with it in a bit.

By the end of this chapter, we'll move, resize, and transform this image. You'll change its borders, its size, what's inside it, and just about everything else.

NOTE

If you see only a box on the screen where the graphic should be, you may have the **Picture Placeholders** option turned on. This allows faster scrolling through documents with many graphics by displaying a rectangle as a placeholder for a graphic. You can turn this option off by choosing **Options** from the Tools menu, clicking the **View** tab, and unchecking the **Picture Placeholders** check box.

NOTE

In addition to clip art, Word comes with an extensive collection of photographs, video clips, and sound clips that can be inserted in your documents just like clip art. Just select the **Pictures**, **Sounds**, or **Video** tab from the Clip Gallery dialog box, select the item you want, and choose **Insert**. Notice the **Play** button in the **Sounds** and **Videos** tabs. Click on it to get a sample of the selected sound or video clip before you insert it.

Finding the Image You Want

Remember those keywords I pointed out at the bottom of the dialog box? You can use them to find the right graphic, even if you don't know exactly what you want. Each image that came with Word contains at least one keyword. For example, the computer-killing duck you selected has the keywords *Stress, Frustration, Anger,* and *Chaos.*

To find a graphic using keywords:

1. Choose **Picture** from the Insert menu and **Clip Art** from the Picture menu.
2. Click on the **Find** button to open the Find Clip dialog box, shown in Figure 13.4.

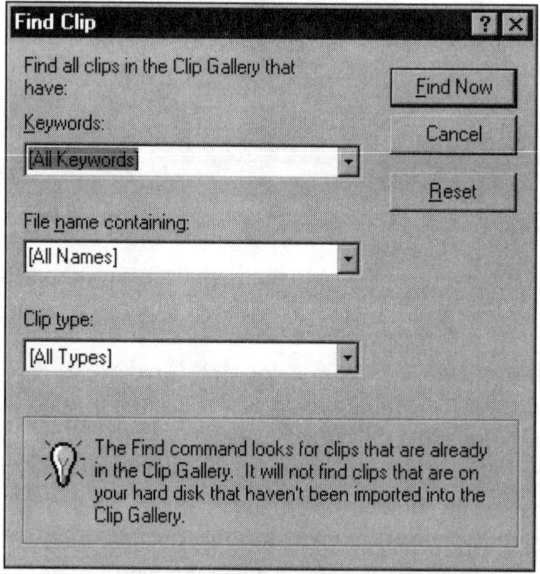

Figure 13.4 *The Find Clip dialog box.*

3. Type a word in the Keywords text box that describes, in general terms, the picture you want to find. For example, if I want to find pictures that represent the emotion anger, I type **anger** in the Keywords text box.

Leave the other items as they are, so that Word finds all files containing the keyword *anger*, regardless of the type of picture file or the name of the actual file.

4. Click on the **Find Now** button. Word finds any files for which *anger* is one of the keywords. You'll see that two files meet the search guidelines. Word created a new category, *Results of Last Find*, and added the two pictures to that category.

WARNING

The Results of Last Find category is temporary and is not available after you close the dialog box and reopen it. You must run a find operation again to display the Results of Last Find category. But it's easy to repeat a search. Just click on the drop-down arrow next to the keyword text box in the Find Clip dialog box to get a list of recent searches.

5. Click on the picture you want, then click on the **Insert** button to insert the picture into your document.

An Object Is an Object Is an Object

In addition to clip art, you can insert photographs, text boxes, scanned images, video clips, sound clips, and other items into documents. All of these items are called *objects*. We're focusing on clip art at the moment, but you use the same techniques to select, move, or delete any object.

Selecting and Deselecting Images

Selecting an image is the first step for almost anything you want to do with it. You select the image, then you do something to it. When you're done, you deselect the image.

- To select a graphic, click on the graphic you want to select. You can tell that a graphic is selected when it has handles (the little boxes) around it.
- To deselect a graphic, click anywhere outside the picture.

Moving an Image

Moving an image and changing its size are probably the two things you'll want to do right away with almost every picture you create, so let's get right to it. You'll be pleased to find that it's really easy.

To move an image:

1. Place your mouse pointer anywhere on the graphic. A four-headed arrow attaches itself to your mouse pointer.
2. Drag the picture wherever you want it and release the mouse button.
3. Deselect the picture.

That's all there is to it. As you drag you'll see a dashed outline, as shown in Figure 13.5.

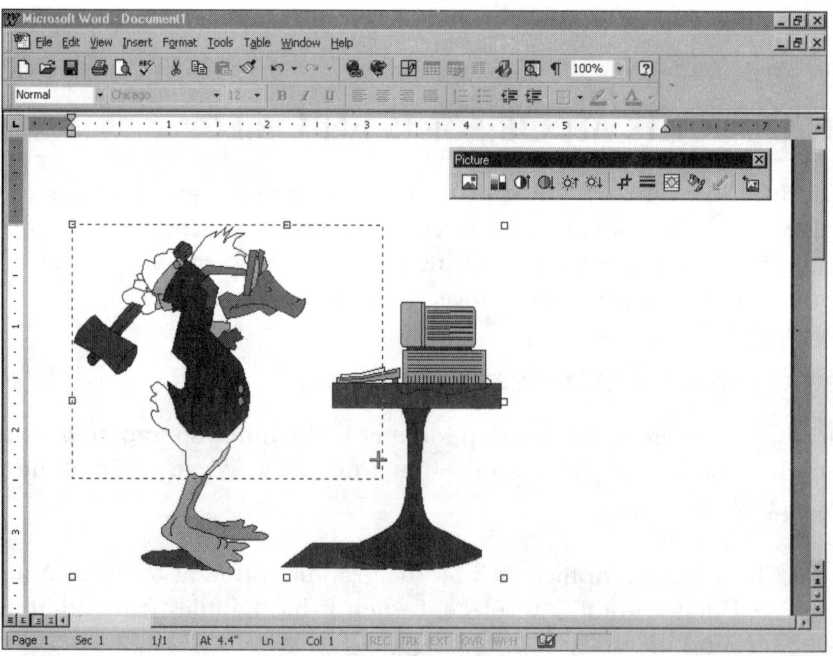

Figure 13.5 Image being dragged to a new location.

NOTE

If you want to be more precise in your movement, hold down the **Shift** key as you drag. This limits the movement to either a straight vertical line or a straight horizontal line.

WARNING

Make sure you don't grab a handle by mistake. You can tell you've got a handle because the mouse pointer is a two-headed arrow instead of a four-headed arrow. The handles are for resizing the picture, as you'll see shortly. If you accidentally resize or move the image, just click the **Undo** button before you do anything else.

Deleting a Picture

Of course, you can change your mind about the pictures in your documents; that's no problem with Word. Deleting graphics is simple.

To delete a picture, select the image you want to delete and press the **Delete** key. If you change your mind and want the picture back, simply click the **Undo** button before you do anything else.

Resizing a Graphic

You can make an image larger or smaller to suit your needs. Changing a picture's size is as easy as dragging a handle. Drag a corner handle to change the height and width at the same time without changing the proportions of the image. Drag a side handle to change the width of the graphic or a top or bottom handle to change the height of a graphic.

To resize a graphic:

1. Select the image you want to resize.
2. Move your mouse pointer over one of the corner handles. Notice that the pointer turns into a two-headed arrow.

WARNING

If you change just the height or width of a graphic, the image becomes distorted, giving you either a tall skinny image or a short fat one. Unless you're trying to achieve this effect, remember to resize using the corner handles rather than the top or side handles.

3. Drag the handle over, up, or down to make the box larger or smaller, then release the mouse button.
4. Deselect the image. Figure 13.6 shows the resized picture.

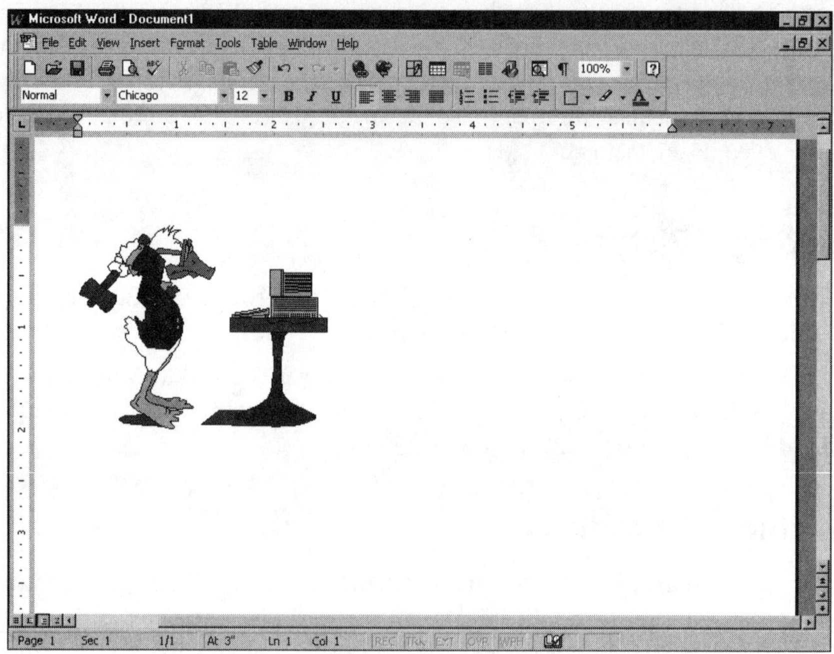

Figure 13.6 Resized picture.

If after playing with an image you don't like the result, it's easy to restore the image's original proportions. Then you can start the fun all over again.

To restore a resized picture to its original proportions:

1. Right-click on the picture you want to restore, click on **Format Picture** to open the Format Picture dialog box, then click on the **Size** tab (shown in Figure 13.7).

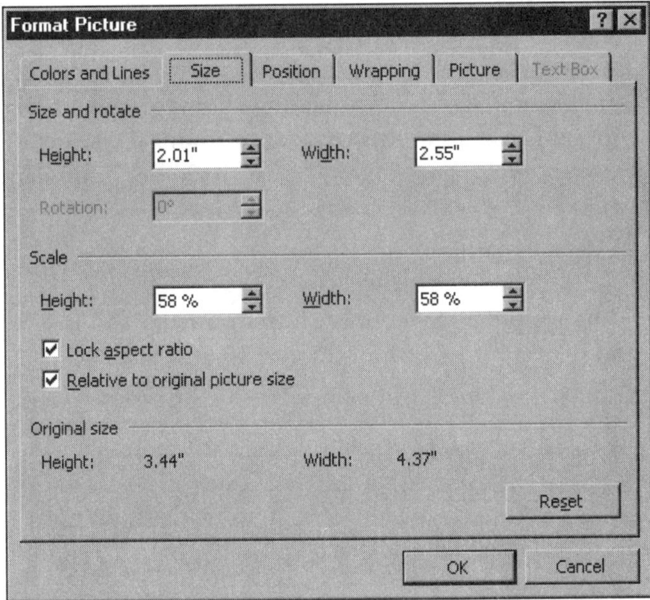

*Figure 13.7 The **Size** tab in the Format Picture dialog box.*

Notice that the original size displays at the bottom of the **Size** tab, just to the left of the **Reset** button.

2. Click the **Reset** button to return the picture to its original size.
3. Click **OK** to close the Format Picture dialog box and display the image in its original size.

Formatting and Enhancing Graphics

If you only want a basic image, you now have all the information you need. However, no one's ever satisfied with the original picture. You might want to hide a portion of the picture, add a caption, change how text flows around the image, add a border, change the background color, or change some of the colors. You can quickly make all these changes with Word.

Inserting Captions

Word makes it easy to insert your own captions under each picture in Word documents. You can either insert Word's default caption or customize the caption. The default caption is just a simple box, placed under the selected figure, that contains the text *Figure 1, Figure 2,* and so on. We'll begin now by inserting a default caption.

To insert a default caption:

1. Select the graphic, then choose **Caption** from the Insert menu. The Caption dialog box, shown in Figure 13.8, is displayed.

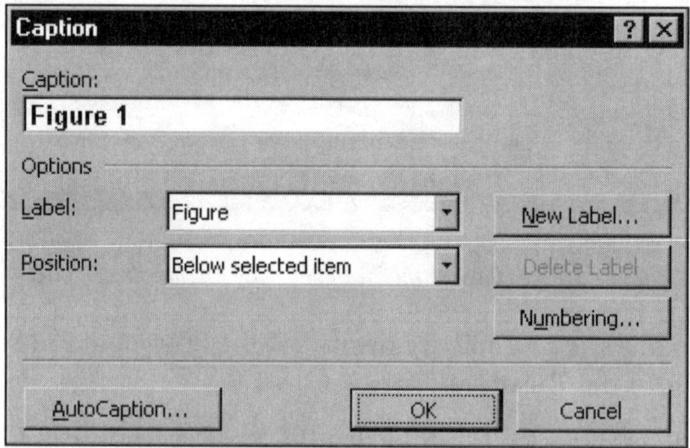

Figure 13.8 *The Caption dialog box.*

2. If you want the default caption to be displayed below the graphic, all you need to do is click **OK**.

The Text Box toolbar displays automatically after you insert a caption. When you deselect the caption, the toolbar automatically disappears. We'll talk about text boxes later in this chapter.

If you have hidden characters displayed, there are hatch marks around the caption box. These marks indicate the box margins, which let you know that you cannot add text inside that area.

The default caption doesn't provide much information, so let's change it. It's easy to add different text to captions, move them around, or change the print direction of the text inside the caption box.

Changing the Caption Text

Captions are supposed to tell readers something—*Figure 1* is not very descriptive. You'll probably want to add more text. For example, we could give our angry duck a caption like *Figure 1 Duck in need of major vacation.* If you like, you can even change or delete the word *figure.*

To change the caption text:

1. Select a graphic, then choose **Caption** from the Insert menu. Your blinking cursor is probably already in the Caption text box, just to the right of the words *Figure 1.* If not, you need to click in the Caption text box so you can add text after the words *Figure 1.*
2. Type the caption text.
3. Make a selection from the Position drop-down list if you want to change the caption's position.
4. Click **OK**. A graphic with a caption is shown in Figure 13.9.

SEASON'S GREETINGS

Figure 13.9 *A figure with a caption.*

NOTE

Word won't allow you to delete the word *Figure* or the number while you're in the Caption dialog box, but if you don't want to include them, you can delete them from the caption itself, just as you can delete any other text.

You can further customize your caption text by changing the caption label. *Figure* is the caption *label*. You can select one of the available options or create one of your own:

- In the Caption dialog box, choose a new label from the Label list.
- Click on the **New Label** button and enter a name in the Label text box to create your own label.

That's all the basic information you need to create captions. I just want to quickly point out one more thing—the **Numbering** button. You can number captions using letters, numbers, or Roman numerals, and you can even include chapter numbers.

THE PICTURE TOOLBAR

The Picture toolbar contains buttons that let you change just about anything on your graphic image. To display the Picture toolbar, do one of the following:

- Right-click on any graphic and choose **Show Picture Toolbar**.
- Right-click on any visible toolbar and choose **Picture**.

The Picture toolbar, shown in Figure 13.10, contains buttons you can use to further enhance your graphics.

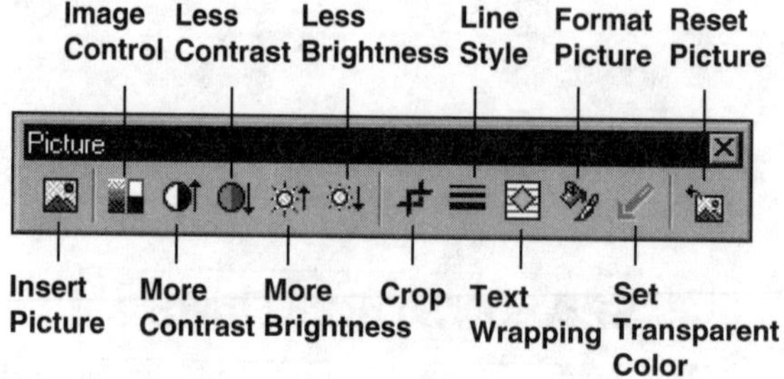

Figure 13.10 The Picture toolbar.

The following sections show how to use the Picture toolbar buttons to make all sorts of changes to your image.

Changing Image Control Options

One of the first things you need to decide about your graphic is how you want it to display and print. You can keep the automatic colors that display when you insert the graphic, you can change it to a grayscale or black-and-white image, or you can turn it into a watermark.

To select a new image type, click on the **Image Control** button in the Picture toolbar, then select an image type from the drop-down list.

Here's what the different options do:

- **Automatic** is the default setting, which can be either a full-color or black-and-white image, depending on how the image was originally created. If you have a color printer, it will print with the colors displayed on-screen. On a black-and-white printer, it will print in various shades of gray, regardless of the on-screen color.
- **Grayscale** gives you a high-resolution image that uses numerous shades of gray to create a three-dimensional image. The effect is similar to a black-and-white photograph.
- **Black and White** is a simple graphic with only two shades—black and white. It gives a one-dimensional effect.
- **Watermark** is a graphic that appears lightly in the background of a printed page. You can also place a watermark over the top of an existing graphic or text.

Adjusting Contrast and Brightness

The default shading might not always work for you. You can adjust the contrast and brightness of any image. *Contrast* is the difference between shades, and *brightness* is how brilliant or dim the object appears on the page. Contrast is most obvious in grayscale images; brightness is most important when working with watermarks.

There are two buttons for both contrast and brightness:

- Each click on the **Increase Brightness** button makes the selected image lighter, or brighter, on the screen and the printed page.

- Each click on the **Decrease Brightness** button makes the image darker, and more visible, on the screen.
- With each click on the **More Contrast** button, the whites become more white and the darker shades become darker.
- With each click on the **Less Contrast** button, the shades grow more similar and there is not as much contrast between light and dark.

If you make changes to the brightness and contrast of an image and later decide that you don't like the changes, you can reset the images to their original settings.

To reset the image to its original brightness and contrast settings:

1. Click the **Format Picture** button on the Picture toolbar, or right-click on the graphic you want to reset and select **Format Picture** from the shortcut menu.
2. Select the **Picture** tab (shown in Figure 13.11), and click on the **Reset** button. Note: If the Picture toolbar is active, you can just click its **Reset Picture** button. This replaces steps 1 and 2.

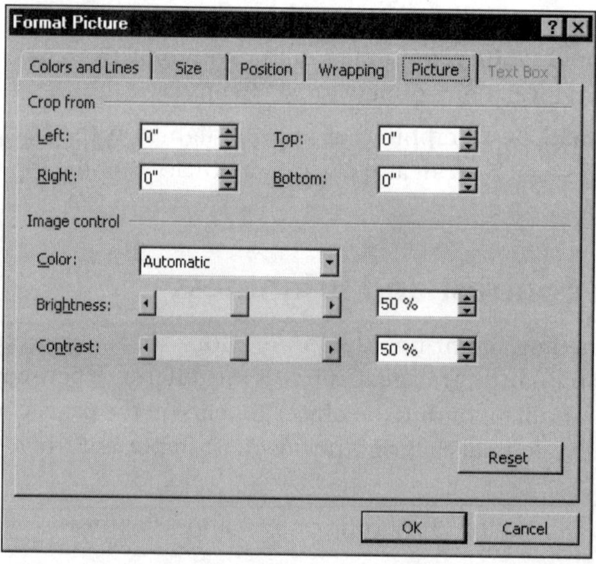

***Figure 13.11** The **Picture** tab in the Format Picture dialog box.*

NOTE

The **Picture** tab also contains cropping instructions (cropping is discussed in the next section). Choosing **Reset** from this tab also resets any cropping you may have done.

Cropping a Graphic

When you resized the graphic earlier, you made the entire image larger or smaller. But sometimes you want to hide part of the image without changing the size. *Cropping*, as in photography, refers to excluding parts of a graphic as if covering up parts of it with sheets of paper.

To crop an image:

1. Select the graphic you want to crop.
2. Click on the Picture toolbar's **Crop** button. Now, when you position your mouse pointer on one of the image's handles, a cropping icon attaches itself to your mouse pointer. The corner handles crop up and down at an angle. The side handles crop in from each side, and the top and bottom handles crop up and down at the top and bottom of the image.
3. Using the Cropping tool, drag the sizing handles to crop the image until only the part of the image you want to see is displayed. Figure 13.12 shows our dastardly duck without his computer (hmmm, his lower body also seems to have disappeared).

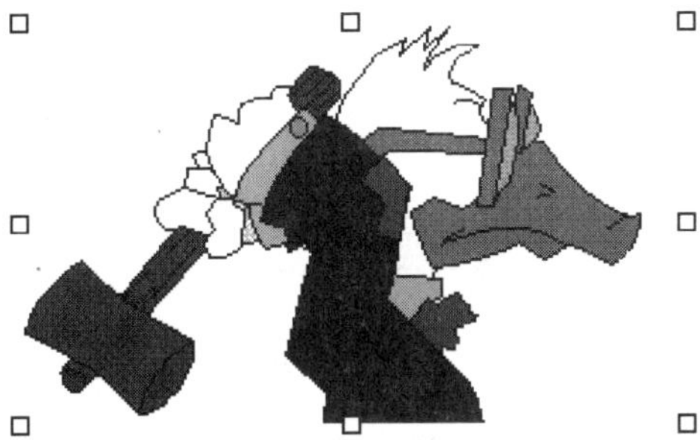

Figure 13.12 *The image has been cropped to show only the duck's upper body.*

For more precision in your cropping, you can enter specific cropping dimensions on the **Picture** tab in the Format Object dialog box. If you don't like what you've done, you can click the **Reset** button to display the whole picture again.

NOTE

Cropping is a great way to make plain graphics exciting. Crop pieces from several images and place them together in your documents to create unique new looks.

Changing How Text Wraps Around the Image

By default, text flows above and below a picture, with no text on the left or right side of the image. If your picture is at the top margin, the text will flow under it. The image in Figure 13.13 uses the default wrap options. The way the text flows is called *text wrap*.

First, a caveat: don't go to *The Dead* expecting to see zombies from beyond the grave ravage New York. The film is, on the contrary, an adaptation of a James Joyce story, the final one in *Dubliners*. From the nostalgic black-and-white opening credits in the beginning to the last snowflake, *The Dead* is a lovingly finished work that comes as close to Joyce as another medium can. It has almost none of the social relevance some reviewers crave, which doesn't matter at all. It's a beautiful film.

John Huston's last effort is almost a family project, with Tony Huston writing the screenplay and Anjelica Huston playing Gretta Conroy, whose husband Gabriel is the center of consciousness in the story. Properly

Figure 13.13 *The wrapping type for this picture is* ***Top and Bottom****.*

To change the way text wraps around your picture:

1. Select the picture, then click on the **Text Wrapping** button in the Picture toolbar to open the Text Wrap list shown in Figure 13.14.

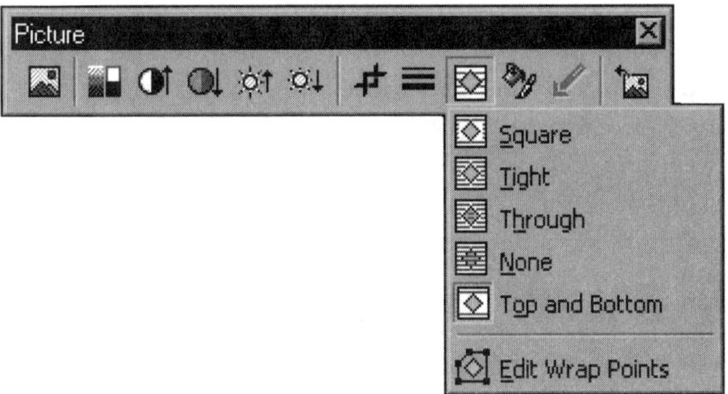

Figure 13.14 The Text Wrap list.

2. Select the wrap option you want. The pictures next to each option show you what the results will be. They're a little cryptic, so I'll explain:

   ✦ **Square** wrapping follows the borders of an invisible box, not the image itself. In a little bit, I'll show how you can choose to wrap text around the largest side, the left side, the right side, both sides, or through this box. Square wrapping is seen in Figure 13.15.

First, a caveat: don't go to *The Dead* expecting to see zombies from beyond the grave ravage New York. The film is, on the contrary, an adaptation of a James Joyce story, the final one in *Dubliners*. From the nostalgic black-and-white opening credits in the beginning to the last snowflake, *The Dead* is a lovingly finished work that comes as close to Joyce as another medium can. It has almost none of the social relevance some reviewers crave, which doesn't matter at all. It's a beautiful film.

John Huston's last effort is almost a family project, with Tony Huston writing the screenplay and Anjelica Huston playing Gretta Conroy, whose husband Gabriel is the center of consciousness in the story. Properly speaking, there is no story—Gabriel (Irish actor Donal McCann, excellently cast) and Gretta go to a family party in Dublin for the feast of Epiphany in 1904, they stay for dancing and dinner, and they go back to an inn that night. But the play of senses and feelings is so exquisitely done that you can't help empathizing with every character on the screen.

Figure 13.15 Square wrapping.

- **Tight** wrapping wraps text around the shape of the image. This one's the most fun, as you can see from Figure 13.16. As with the square wrap, you can choose a tight wrap around the largest side, the left side, the right side, or both sides of the image. The **Tight** wrapping option doesn't work if your image has a border.

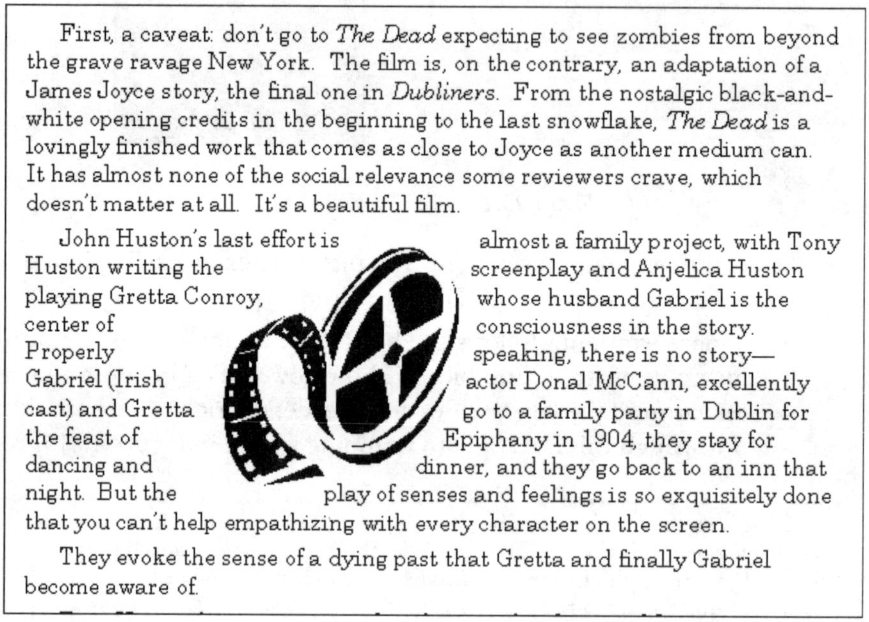

First, a caveat: don't go to *The Dead* expecting to see zombies from beyond the grave ravage New York. The film is, on the contrary, an adaptation of a James Joyce story, the final one in *Dubliners*. From the nostalgic black-and-white opening credits in the beginning to the last snowflake, *The Dead* is a lovingly finished work that comes as close to Joyce as another medium can. It has almost none of the social relevance some reviewers crave, which doesn't matter at all. It's a beautiful film.

John Huston's last effort is almost a family project, with Tony
Huston writing the screenplay and Anjelica Huston
playing Gretta Conroy, whose husband Gabriel is the
center of consciousness in the story.
Properly speaking, there is no story—
Gabriel (Irish actor Donal McCann, excellently
cast) and Gretta go to a family party in Dublin for
the feast of Epiphany in 1904, they stay for
dancing and dinner, and they go back to an inn that
night. But the play of senses and feelings is so exquisitely done
that you can't help empathizing with every character on the screen.

They evoke the sense of a dying past that Gretta and finally Gabriel become aware of.

Figure 13.16 Tight wrapping.

- **Through** wraps text through the open portions of an image, using the layering feature, which you will learn about later in this chapter.
- **None** prints text right through the box—it doesn't wrap at all. Be careful with this option, because your text can easily get lost behind an image, or the image can disappear behind the text. Figure 13.17 shows an image without wrapping.

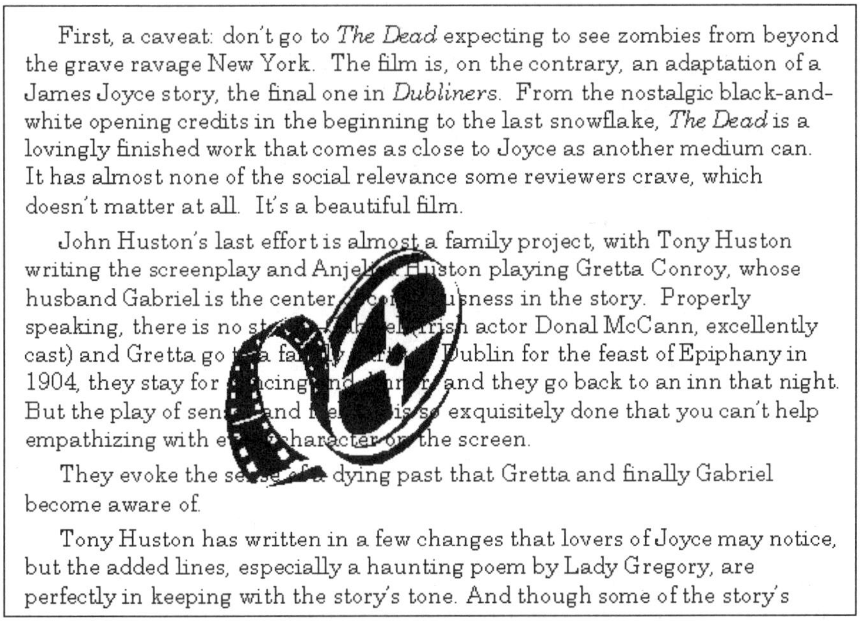

First, a caveat: don't go to *The Dead* expecting to see zombies from beyond the grave ravage New York. The film is, on the contrary, an adaptation of a James Joyce story, the final one in *Dubliners*. From the nostalgic black-and-white opening credits in the beginning to the last snowflake, *The Dead* is a lovingly finished work that comes as close to Joyce as another medium can. It has almost none of the social relevance some reviewers crave, which doesn't matter at all. It's a beautiful film.

John Huston's last effort is almost a family project, with Tony Huston writing the screenplay and Anjelica Huston playing Gretta Conroy, whose husband Gabriel is the center of consciousness in the story. Properly speaking, there is no story. When the Irish actor Donal McCann, excellently cast) and Gretta go to a family party in Dublin for the feast of Epiphany in 1904, they stay for dancing and dinner, and they go back to an inn that night. But the play of sense and feeling is so exquisitely done that you can't help empathizing with every character on the screen.

They evoke the sense of a dying past that Gretta and finally Gabriel become aware of.

Tony Huston has written in a few changes that lovers of Joyce may notice, but the added lines, especially a haunting poem by Lady Gregory, are perfectly in keeping with the story's tone. And though some of the story's

Figure 13.17 *No wrapping.*

- With **Top and Bottom** wrapping, text won't appear to the left or right of the box. It wraps from above the box to below, not around it.

As you can see in Figure 13.17, with no wrapping, the text can easily be obscured by the picture. A good use for no wrapping is as a watermark, where the figure is lightened and appears as a background to the text, as shown in Figure 13.18. To achieve this effect, click on the Picture toolbar's **Image Control** button and choose **Watermark**.

John Huston's last effort is almost a family project, with Tony Huston writing the screenplay and Anjelica Huston playing Gretta Conroy, whose husband Gabriel is the center of consciousness in the story. Properly speaking, there is no story—Gabriel (Irish actor Donal McCann, excellently cast) and Gretta go to a family party in Dublin for the feast of Epiphany in 1904, they stay for dancing and dinner, and they go back to an inn that night. But the play of senses and feelings is so exquisitely done that you can't help empathizing with every character on the screen.

They evoke the sense of a dying past that Gretta and finally Gabriel become aware of.

Tony Huston has written in a few changes that lovers of Joyce may notice, but the added lines, especially a haunting poem by Lady Gregory, are perfectly in keeping with the story's tone. And though some of the story's narration is turned into dialogue and part kept as a voiceover, Donal McCann's rich, gravelly voice could make it work even without words. It doesn't bother me that I can't entirely describe what my reaction to the movie

Figure 13.18 *No wrapping used as a watermark.*

You can further customize how text wraps around your images by using the options in the Format Picture dialog box. Open the Format Picture dialog box by clicking the Picture toolbar's **Format Picture** button and select the **Wrapping** tab (shown in Figure 13.19).

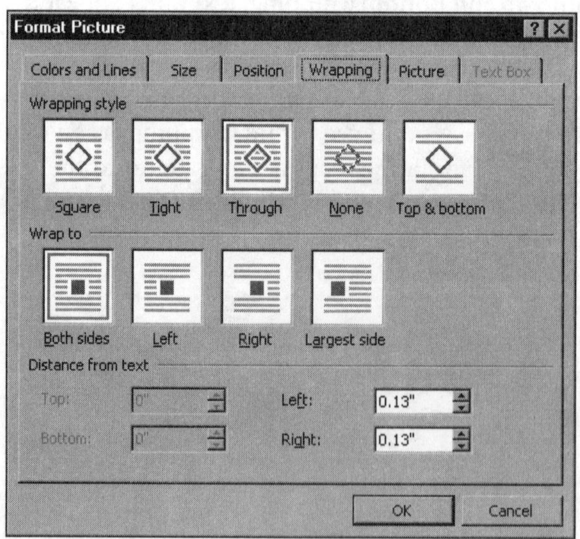

Figure 13.19 *The* ***Wrapping*** *tab in the Format Picture dialog box.*

The Wrapping style section contains the same options you can select from the **Text Wrapping** button on the Picture toolbar. The Wrap to options are not available from any other place, however. Notice that the wrap to options are available for all styles except **None** and **Top and Bottom**.

Select a wrapping style other than **Top and Bottom**, then select one of the Wrap to options:

- **Both Sides** wraps text completely around the image. The text begins on the left side of the image, breaks for the image by the space indicated in the Distance from text section, then continues on the right side of the image.
- **Left** wraps text around the left edge of the image. This option is useful if you have a graphic positioned closer to the right margin or if the image would be distorted by text on the right side.
- **Right** wraps text around the right edge of the image.
- **Largest side** wraps text around the largest edge of the image. In this way, if you move the graphic to the left, it wraps around the right side. If you move the image back to the right side of the page, the text wraps around the left side of the image.

Adding Borders to a Graphic

Like paintings in a museum, some pictures don't look complete without a frame or border.

You can apply the same border options to an imported graphic as to a paragraph or table. These include shadowed boxes, three-dimensional boxes, borders of different colors and widths, and different line styles.

To add a border to a graphic:

1. Select the image, then click on the **Format Picture** button in the Picture toolbar.
2. Click on the **Colors and Lines** tab. This tab, shown in Figure 13.20, lets you change the border and add color to the image's background. Notice that the defaults are **No Line** and **No Fill**.

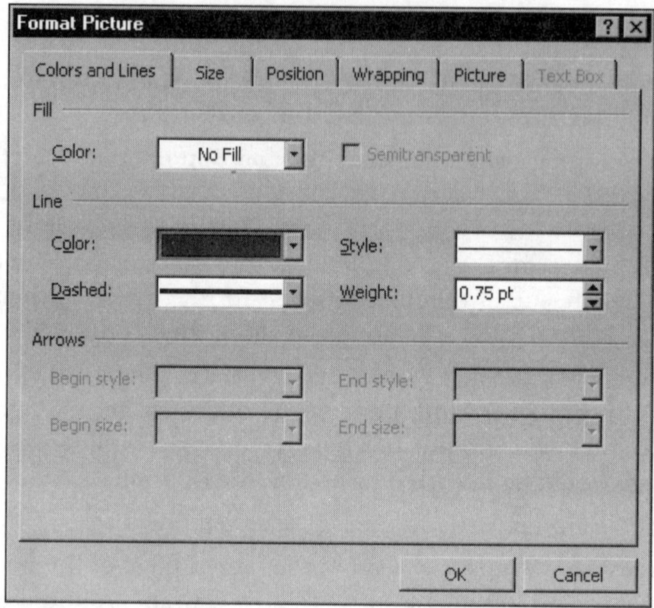

Figure 13.20 The ***Colors and Lines*** *tab in the Format Picture dialog box.*

3. In the Line section, choose a color from the Color drop-down list. After you select a color, the other options in the Line section—**Style**, **Dashed**, and **Weight**—become available.
4. Choose an option from the Style list.
5. Unless you want the border to be a solid line, choose an option from the Dashed list.
6. If necessary, enter a number in the Weight box. Word automatically selects a *weight*, or line thickness measured in points, when you select a line style, but you can retain the style and still make the border thicker or thinner by changing the point size of the line weight. Remember, the larger the point size, the thicker the border.
7. Click **OK** to accept the line options and add the border to your image.

Figure 13.21 shows an image with a 6-point, triple-line border.

Figure 13.21 *An image with a border added.*

NOTE

If you add a border to a figure that has tight wrapping, Word converts the wrapping to square.

Filling Objects

You can add background color, or *fill*, to a graphic. You can add a fill whether or not the border displays, because every image has an invisible box in which it displays. You add fill using the **Colors and Lines** tab in the Format Picture dialog box.

In addition to solid colors, there are gradients and textures you can use behind your images. Many of these features were once available only on complex desktop publishing programs. This is just one more feature that makes it even more difficult to distinguish between today's word processing and desktop publishing applications.

To add a fill to an image's background:

1. Select the image, then click on the Picture toolbar's **Format Picture** button.
2. Click on the **Color and Lines** tab, then select a color from the Color drop-down list in the Fill section. You can either close the Format Picture dialog box to fill the image using the selected solid color or add other effects to the fill.
3. If you want to customize the fill, choose **Fill Effects** from the Color list in the Fill section. You use the Fill Effects dialog box, shown in Figure 13.22, to turn the single color into a gradient or texture.

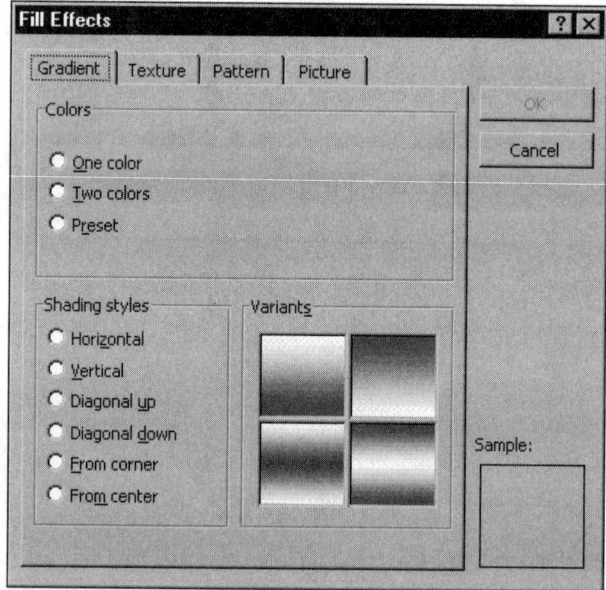

*Figure 13.22 The **Gradient** tab in the Fill Effects dialog box.*

The **Texture** and **Pattern** tabs, shown in Figures 13.23 and 13.24, allow you to choose from a variety of fill textures and patterns.

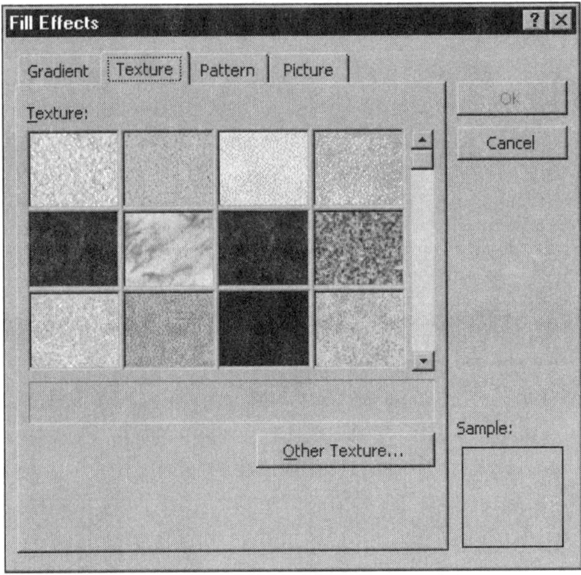

*Figure 13.23 The **Texture** tab.*

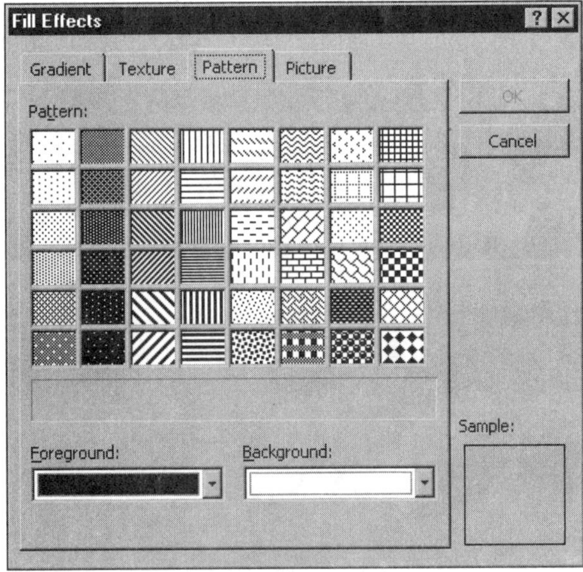

*Figure 13.24 The **Pattern** tab.*

Changing the Image

What happens if you spend hours creating a document, only to discover when it prints that the picture you chose looks terrible printed on your black-and-white laser printer? Not to worry. With a few clicks, you can pick a different picture.

Double-click on the unwanted graphic to open the Clip Gallery, select a new picture, and click the **Insert** button.

That's it!

POSITIONING IMAGES

You can link, or *anchor*, an image to a paragraph. Then, when you move the paragraph or add new text that causes the paragraph to flow to a new location, the image stays with it. Or you can tell Word to place the image a specified distance from the left margin. You can even lock an image's link, so the image always stays on the same page as its linked text.

To change the position of an image:

1. Select the image you want to position.
2. Right-click on the image and choose **Format Picture**, then select the **Position** tab (shown in Figure 13.25).

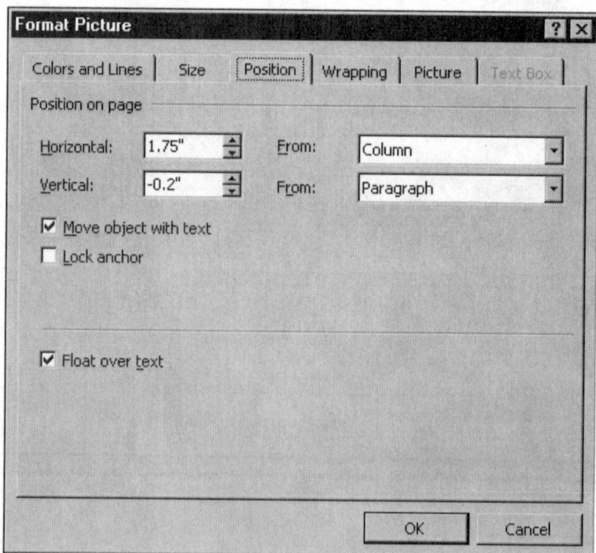

***Figure 13.25** The **Position** tab in the Format Picture dialog box.*

3. Change the settings you want and click **OK**.

Here's what the different settings do:

- Enter a measurement in the Horizontal box, then open the From drop-down list and choose **Margin**, **Page**, or **Column** to position the image a specified horizontal distance from the selected item.
- Enter a measurement in the Vertical box, then open the From drop-down list and choose **Paragraph**, **Margin**, or **Page** to position the image a specified vertical distance from the selected item.
- Select **Move object with text** if you want to anchor the image to its associated paragraph.
- Select **Lock anchor** if you want to make sure the image and its associated paragraph are always on the same page. If both items won't fit on a page, they're both pushed to the next page.
- Deselect **Float over text** if you want the image to be part of the current paragraph (Word calls this an *inline image*). An inline image flows with the paragraph that it's part of.

These positioning techniques aren't limited to clip art—you can use them with any type of drawing object.

WORKING WITH TEXT BOXES

When you worked with pictures, you saw how easy it is to move pictures around your documents; to add special effects, borders, and shading; and to make the picture smaller or larger. Wouldn't it be great if you could do that with some of your text? Word makes that possible with text boxes. A *text box* is a container for text. You can make the text box visible or hide it so that only the information inside the box shows. When you place text in a text box, you can then do some amazing things with what would otherwise be plain text.

Text boxes aren't just for text. The examples in this section use text, but you can insert just about anything into a text box, including graphic images, tables, and charts. Once an object is inserted in a text box, you can manipulate the text box using any of the available techniques.

Ever thought it would be convenient to insert a note in the margin of your papers? That's a great use for a text box. Need to position text over the top of a picture? Text boxes make that easy. Besides being able to move the text all over the screen when it's in a text box, you can add a fancy border, put a fill or texture behind the text, add three-dimensional effects, and add a variety of other special effects that I'll show you later in this chapter.

You used the Picture toolbar to work with pictures; now you'll use the Drawing toolbar to work with text boxes. To display the Drawing toolbar, right-click on any toolbar and click on **Drawing**. The Drawing toolbar is shown in Figure 13.26.

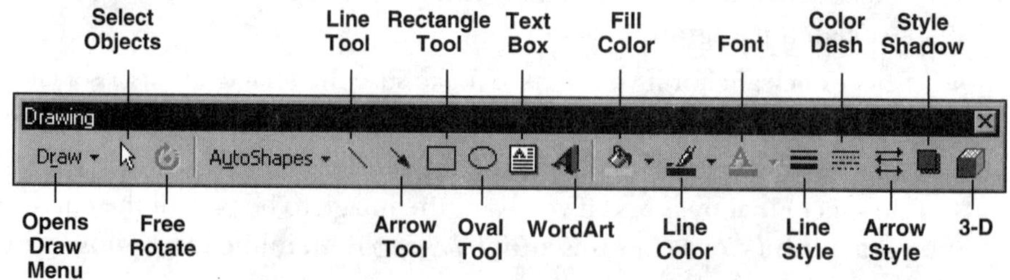

Figure 13.26 The Drawing toolbar.

You can also use the Picture toolbar to work with text boxes, so go ahead and display that too.

Creating Text Boxes

When you insert a text box into your document, it displays as a small square at the cursor position. You can either type new text into the text box or paste something else into it, such as a table, a block of text from another document, a picture, or a chart. There are several different ways to create text boxes. The easiest way is to use the Drawing toolbar.

To create a text box using the Drawing toolbar:

1. Click on the Drawing toolbar's **Text Box** button, then move the mouse pointer up into the document window. Your mouse pointer should display as a plus sign.
2. Click on the document window where you want the text box. Word places a 1-inch square in the document window, with a blinking insertion point inside the box.

Does the text box shown in Figure 13.27 look familiar? That's because the figure captions you created earlier in this chapter were actually text boxes.

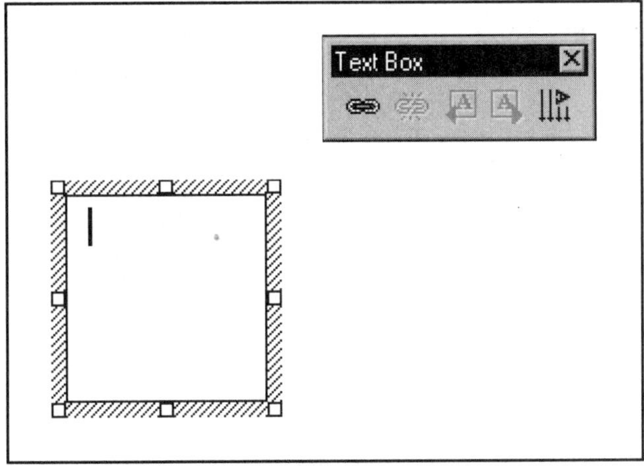

Figure 13.27 An empty text box.

Notice that the Text Box toolbar appears when you click to place the text box (if it doesn't, you can open it just like any other toolbar, by right-clicking on any toolbar and choosing **Text Box**). This toolbar contains buttons that help you work with the box itself. If you deselect the text box, the Text Box toolbar disappears. It displays again each time you select the text box.

You don't have to start with Word's default text box. After you click on the Drawing toolbar's **Text Box** button, just drag the mouse pointer until the box is the size you want before you release the mouse button. As you drag, you'll see an outline of the box.

NOTE

You can also insert a text box by choosing **Text Box** from the Insert menu and then clicking or dragging the insertion point in the document window.

After creating the box, you can use it for text, graphics, tables, and other data. I'll show you how to insert objects inside your text box and how to customize the text box by changing its shape, size, color, and borders; we'll also talk about some ways to use text boxes.

Inserting Text or Objects into Text Boxes

Text boxes are great for notes, captions, and sidebar information in the margin of your document. To add information to the text box, you can type new text, add text from a file, import a chart from another program, add a table, or insert a picture. Figure 13.28 shows one possible use for a text box.

First, a caveat: don't go to *The Dead* expecting to see zombies from beyond the grave ravage New York. The film is, on the contrary, an adaptation of a James Joyce story, the final one in *Dubliners*. From the nostalgic black-and-white opening credits in the beginning to the last snowflake, *The Dead* is a lovingly finished work that comes as close to Joyce as another medium can. It has almost none of the social relevance some reviewers crave, which doesn't matter at all. It's a beautiful film.

John Huston's last effort is almost a family project, with Tony Huston writing the screenplay and Anjelica Huston playing Gretta Conroy, whose husband Gabriel is the center of consciousness in the story. Prop- erly speaking, there is no story—Gabriel (Irish actor Donal McCann, excellently cast) and Gretta go to a family party in Dublin for the feast of Epiphany in 1904, they stay for dancing and dinner, and they go back to an inn that night. But the play of senses and feelings is so exquisitely done that you can't help empathizing with every character on the screen.

They evoke the sense of a dying past that Gretta and finally Gabriel become aware of.

Tony Huston has written in a few changes that lovers of Joyce may notice, but the added lines, especially a haunting poem by Lady Gregory, are

Figure 13.28 *A text box in a document.*

To enter text into a text box, make sure the insertion point is in the text box, then type your text. Notice that the text wraps in the box, as shown in Figure 13.29.

Figure 13.29 A text box with new text wrapped in the box.

Text in text boxes has the same characteristics as and can be edited just like normal text. Click anywhere outside the box to deselect it. Your text and text box are now part of your document.

You can also add pictures to your text boxes. One of the advantages of using a text box is that you can combine text and pictures in the same box.

To create a text box with text and a picture:

1. Click on the Drawing toolbar's **Text Box** button, then click in the document window to create a text box.
2. Type your text.
3. Make sure the insertion point is still in the text box, then choose **Picture** from the Insert menu and **Clip Art** from the Picture menu.
4. Select the picture you want in your text box, then click on the **Insert** button.
5. Resize the box to fit the graphic by dragging any of the handles.

The text box now has both text and a picture, as shown in Figure 13.30.

Figure 13.30 A text box with both text and a graphic.

You can also add text to a text box from an existing document, by either inserting an entire file or using the cut and paste feature to copy a block of text.

To insert a file into a text box:

1. Place your insertion point in the text box.
2. Choose **File** from the Insert menu.
3. Select the file you want and click **OK** (or just double-click on the file).

Word inserts the file's contents into the text box. The text retains its original paragraph and character formatting.

You can also paste text into a text box. Just use any of Word's selection and cut or copy techniques to place the text in the Clipboard, then move your insertion point into the text box and click the **Paste** button on the Standard toolbar (or press **Ctrl+V**).

Formatting Text Boxes

Working with text boxes is very much like working with pictures. You must select a text box before you can make any changes to the box or its contents. You can select the contents or the box itself. If there are other objects, such as pictures, inside the box, they can also be selected separately.

To select the contents of a text box, click anywhere inside the text box (except on a picture or other object). The sizing handles display, along with small hatch marks around the border, as shown in Figure 13.31.

Figure 13.31 A selected text box.

With the contents selected, you can enter new text or make enhancements to the existing text. You can also use any of the features in the Drawing or Picture toolbar.

To select the text box itself, click on any box border. You'll see the sizing handles and hatch marks. The only visible difference between selecting the box and selecting the box contents is that with the box selected, there's no insertion point inside the box.

If you press the **Delete** key with the box selected, the box and all its contents are deleted. If you press the **Delete** key with your insertion point inside the text box, only the character to the right of your insertion point is deleted.

Resizing and Moving Text Boxes

You use the same techniques to resize or move a text box that you already learned for resizing and moving pictures:

- To resize a text box, just drag one of the sizing handles.
- To move a text box, position your mouse pointer over one of the box borders (you're in the right place when a four-headed arrow attaches itself to your mouse pointer) and drag.

Enhancing Text Boxes

In addition to resizing, moving, and selecting text boxes, you can make changes to the text both inside and around the outside of text boxes. You can change text wrapping and alter the *internal margin* (the space between the text inside the box and the box border).

To change text wrapping, click anywhere in the text box, click on the Picture toolbar's **Text Wrapping** button, and select a wrapping style. The same options are available for both text boxes and pictures.

To adjust the spacing between the text and the box borders:

1. Right-click on any box border and choose **Format Text Box**.
2. Select the **Text Box** tab (shown in Figure 13.32).

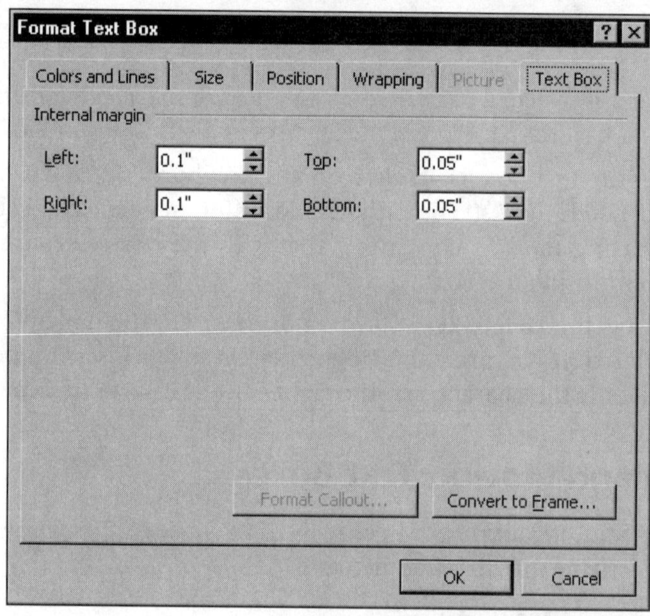

***Figure 13.32** The **Text Box** tab in the Format Text Box dialog box.*

3. Change any settings you want and click **OK**.

To rotate the text inside the text box, click anywhere in the text box to select it and then click on the **Change Text Direction** button in the Text Box toolbar. The text displays down the right side of the box, as shown in Figure 13.33.

Figure 13.33 Text positioned down the right side of the text box.

The next time you click the **Change Text Direction** button, the text moves to the left side of the box. Click again, and the text returns to its original horizontal orientation at the top of the box.

Customizing Borders

When you first create a text box, it has a single black line border. You can change the line weight, style, and color using the Drawing toolbar or the Format Text Box dialog box. The quickest way to customize borders is to use the Drawing toolbar.

To customize borders:

1. Click anywhere in the box, click on the Drawing toolbar's **Line Color** arrow, and select a color.
2. Click on the Drawing toolbar's **Line Style** button and pick a line style and weight.

Figure 13.34 shows a text box with a gray horizontal brick fill, black text, and a black 3-point line style.

Figure 13.34 *A text box with a customized border and fill.*

Adding Special Effects

The Drawing toolbar contains two special effects buttons you can use to make some fun changes to your text boxes and other objects: shadow and 3-D.

To add a shadow to your text box:

1. Click anywhere in the text box, then click on the Drawing toolbar's **Shadow** button. The Shadow pallette, shown in Figure 13.35, contains many shadow effects you can add to your box.
2. Click on a shadow effect. If you don't like the effect you chose, repeat the process until you find one that you like.

Figure 13.35 The Shadow pallette.

You can further customize your shadow effect by choosing **Shadow Settings** from the Shadow button palette and using the Shadow Settings toolbar to make the changes you want.

To add 3-D effects:

1. Click anywhere in the text box, then click on the Drawing toolbar's **3-D** button. The 3-D palette, shown in Figure 13.36, contains 20 different effects.

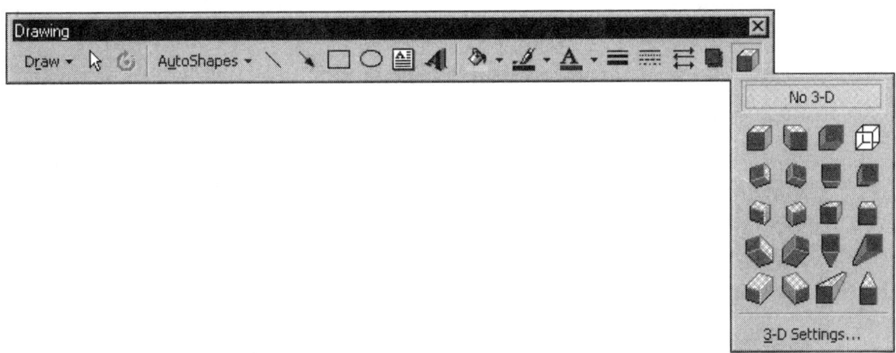

Figure 13.36 The 3-D palette.

2. Select the style you want. Figure 13.37 shows a text box with a 3-D effect.

Figure 13.37 A three-dimensional text box.

As with shadow effects, you can further customize the 3-D effects. Just choose **3-D Settings** from the 3-D palette and use the 3-D Settings toolbar to make the changes you want.

Linking Text Boxes

If you have ever used a page layout program like PageMaker, you know how text can flow from one area to another, making it simple to deal with articles that begin on one page and are continued later in a newsletter or magazine. Text flow is one of the last bastions that has traditionally separated word processing programs from page layout programs. Not anymore. By linking text boxes, you can achieve the same effect in Word.

To link text boxes:

1. Create the text boxes you want to link.
2. Select the first text box and click the **Create Text Box Link** button (the button looks like a piece of a chain-link fence) on the Text Box toolbar. The mouse pointer turns into a pitcher with a down arrow.
3. Click in the text box you want to link the first one with.

The link is complete. Text will automatically flow into the second text box when the first one is full.

Notice that the insertion point moves back into the first text box, the **Create Text Box Link** button is deactivated, and the **Break Forward Link** button is active. If you want to delete the link, just click the **Break Forward Link** button with the first text box selected.

NOTE

You can also create links between AutoShapes (covered in the next section) as long as they have text in them.

To move between linked text boxes, click the **Previous Text Box** or **Next Text Box** button on the Text Box toolbar.

What Happened to Frames?

If you used previous versions of Word or if you need to open documents created in previous versions, you will notice that there is no longer a reason to draw frames around every text box. In previous versions, you had to create a frame around any text box you wanted to drag to a new location on the document window. In Word 97, text boxes can do just about anything frames can do. The only time you must still use frames is when you want to include a footnote, endnote, or comment in a text box. Then you must convert a text box to a frame.

To convert a text box to a frame:

1. Click in the text box you want to convert, click on the Picture toolbar's **Format Text Box** button, and select the **Text Box** tab.
2. Click on the **Convert to Frame** button, then click **OK** when Word prompts you to do so.

The frame looks the same as your text box, but you can't change it using the Drawing or Picture toolbars. You can, however, still move the frame around the document by dragging it, and you can resize it using the resizing handles.

To make any other changes to the text wrapping, borders, or shading, you must use either the Format menu or the shortcut menu you get by right-clicking on the frame.

NOTE

If you use Word 97 to open an older Word document with frames, the frames are automatically converted to text boxes unless they contain a note reference mark or a comment mark, in which case the frames remain intact.

Using AutoShapes

How about spicing up a letter with a bright star shape, adding a banner across an advertisement, or putting a lightning bolt down the side of a sale flyer? Word 97 includes a set of ready-made shapes that you can use anywhere in a document, and you can add text to them just like regular text boxes. Other than the cool shapes, the only real difference between regular text boxes and AutoShapes is that you have to right-click on an AutoShape and choose **Insert text** before you can start typing. You can also draw ovals, squares, lines, and arrows, and you can add text to anything except a line or arrow.

To create an AutoShape:

1. Make sure the Drawing toolbar is displayed.
2. Click on the Drawing toolbar's **AutoShapes** button to display the menu shown in Figure 13.38.

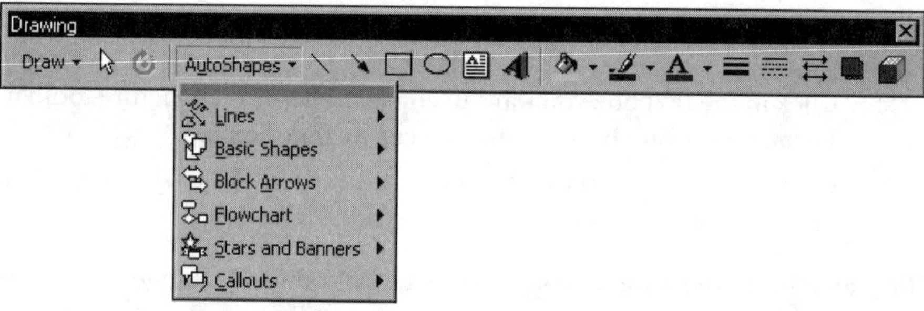

Figure 13.38 AutoShapes menu.

The AutoShapes menu contains six categories of shapes. As you move your mouse pointer over a category, it expands to display the available shapes for that category. Figure 13.39 shows the Stars and Banners palette.

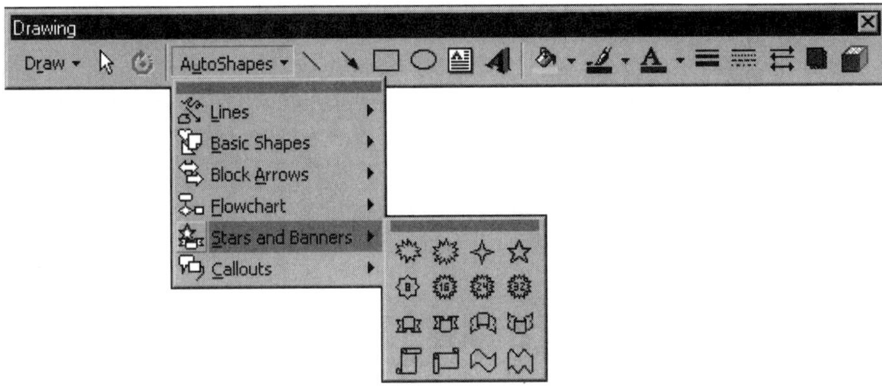

Figure 13.39 The Stars and Banners palette.

3. Click to select the shape you want. Your mouse pointer turns into a plus sign (+), just as it does when you insert a text box.
4. Click anywhere in the document window to insert the AutoShape at its default size or drag to size the shape before you release the mouse pointer.

Figure 13.40 shows an AutoShape inserted in a document.

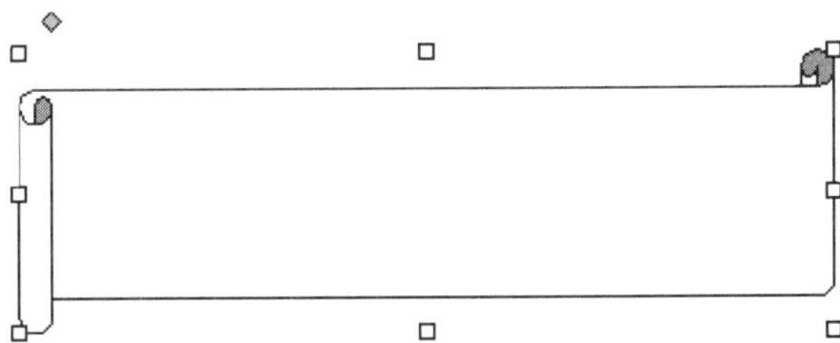

Figure 13.40 An AutoShape inserted in a document.

You can now move the AutoShape around the document like any other object. You can size it using the sizing handles; you can add borders, colors, line colors, shading, and 3-D effects. The only thing left to do is add some text.

- To add text to an AutoShape, right-click on the AutoShape, then click on **Add Text**.

This positions the insertion point inside the shape. By selecting the **Add Text** option, you permanently attach a text box to the AutoShape. Even if you don't add text right away, all you have to do to add or edit text later is click on the shape. Figure 13.41 shows the AutoShape from Figure 13.40 with text added.

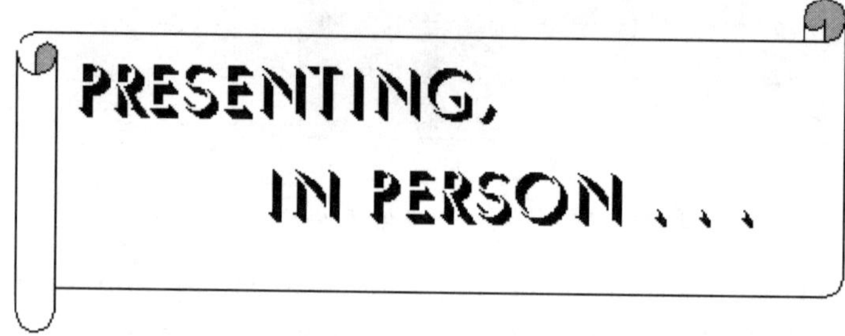

Figure 13.41 AutoShape with text.

If you already have a text box that you'd like to jazz up a bit, you can turn it into an AutoShape.

To change a text box to an AutoShape:

1. Select the text you want to change, click on **Draw** in the Drawing toolbar, and choose **Change AutoShape**. This displays the same list of AutoShapes you saw when you first created an AutoShape.
2. Select the shape you want from the list to change your text box to an AutoShape.

NOTE

You can create your own shapes by clicking on the **AutoShape** button and choosing **Freeform** or **Scribble** from the Lines category.

WORKING WITH MULTIPLE OBJECTS

You can group objects so that they act like one object, and you can arrange and align objects in relation to each other. The objects can be clip art, photographs, video clips, text boxes, or any other drawing objects.

To select multiple objects:

1. Click the **Select Objects** button on the Drawing toolbar (the button with a hollow arrow).
2. Drag to place a box around the objects you want to select, then release the mouse button. As you drag, a dashed outline shows the boundaries of the selection area. When you release the mouse button, any objects inside the selection area are selected. You can then work with all those objects at once.

To group objects:

1. Select the objects you want to group.
2. Click the **Draw** button on the Drawing toolbar and choose **Group**. Notice that the handles for the individual objects disappear, and there is one set of handles for the group. As long as the objects are grouped, they can be resized, moved, or deleted as if they were a single object.

To ungroup the objects, just select the group and choose **Ungroup** from the Draw menu on the Drawing toolbar.

To align objects:

1. Select the objects you want to align.
2. Click the **Draw** button on the Drawing toolbar, choose **Align or Distribute**, and select one of the alignment options shown in Figure 13.42.

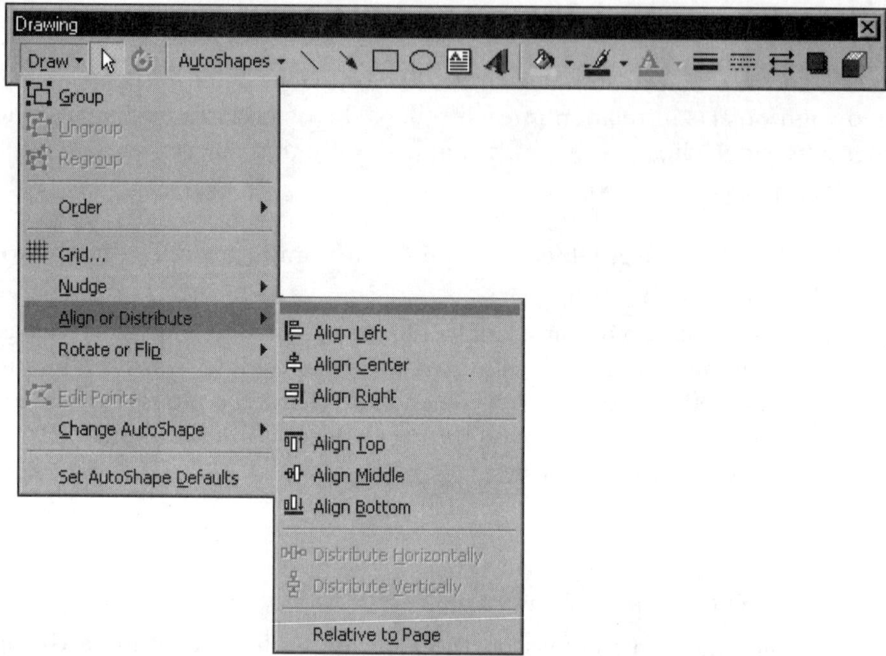

Figure 13.42 The Drawing toolbar's Align or Distribute menu.

The objects are aligned in relation to each other.

To arrange objects in layers:

1. Select the objects you want to arrange.
2. Click the **Draw** button on the Drawing toolbar, choose **Order**, and select one of the layer options shown in Figure 13.43.

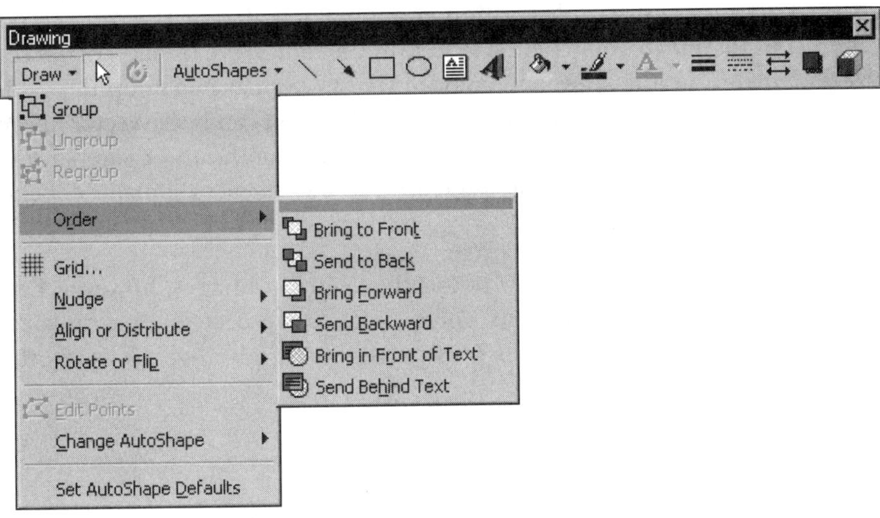

Figure 13.43 *The Drawing toolbar's Order menu.*

Graphics Miscellany

There! You've learned the basics of using graphics in Word 97. Is there more? Of course. There's plenty that we haven't covered, and before I leave you to your own devices, there are a few basic concepts I'd like to introduce.

Bitmap Images vs. Vector Images

There are basically two types of graphics used in today's word processing and desktop publishing programs: bitmapped graphics (*bitmaps*) and vector-based graphics, also called *object-oriented* or *draw* graphics:

- *Bitmap images* are stored on the computer as a collection of colored dots. That's also how they print. The Paint program included with Windows 95 creates bitmap graphics. Some common bitmap formats include BMP (Windows bitmap) and PCX.

- *Vector images* store information about the actual objects. For example, a vector image would define a circle by the radius, the position of the center, and the thickness and color of the stroke that makes up the circle. Because they are not made up of little dots, you can resize vector images without losing any detail. Circles remain smooth, and diagonal lines remain straight rather than jagged. Of course, the actual quality depends on your printer.

Vector images are not necessarily better than bitmap images, however. Each type of graphic has a specific use. Vector images are best for diagrams and illustrations, while bitmaps are the only possibility for photographs and other scanned images.

What Graphics Formats Can I Use?

Over the years, companies have developed a large collection of graphics formats. Some time during the history of the personal computer, someone developed each graphic format for a specific purpose. Whatever the original reason, we now have a multitude of formats available. Fortunately, Word ships with *converters* designed to understand the most popular graphic formats so you can use almost any of the images on the market today. In addition to the graphics that come with the various Microsoft products, including Word, you can purchase packages that contain nothing but graphics.

Among the bitmap formats that you can use with Word 97 are Tag Image File Format (TIFF), Windows bitmap (BMP), PC Paintbrush format (PCX), CompuServe GIF (Graphics Interchange Format) files, and JPEG or JPG (Joint Photographic Experts Group).

Word also supports a variety of vector images, such as Encapsulated PostScript (EPS) format, AutoCAD DXF format, CorelDraw images, Macintosh PICT images, and Windows metafile (WMF) images. The clip art images that ship with Word are in WMF format.

There are several other available graphics formats. If you didn't install those filters when you first installed Word, you can add them later by rerunning Word 97's or Office 97's setup program.

What is Linking and Embedding?

When we inserted pictures into our Word documents, we *embedded* them into the file. When a graphic is embedded, the actual graphic is stored in the Word document.

The other way you can use graphics is to *link* a graphic from its original location to a new location. A linked graphic maintains its connection to the original file on your disk. What's the use of this? If you later make changes to the original file, you can have those changes automatically updated in the copy of the graphic in Word without having to reinsert the object. Linking objects works well if you want to use a graph or chart in your documents. As you update the graph or chart in another program, it will also be updated the next time you display the Word document that contains the link to the graph.

To insert a linked object:

1. Choose **Picture** from the Insert menu, then choose **From File**.
2. In the Insert Picture dialog box, select the object you want to insert.
3. Click to select the **Link to file** check box, then click **OK** to insert the link in your document.

Importing Other Objects

In addition to the pictures in the Clip Gallery, you can insert other pictures, charts, files, and other data in your documents. You can insert pictures from other files on your system or from a floppy disk or you can insert pictures directly from a scanner.

To insert pictures that aren't in the Clip Gallery, choose **Picture** from the Insert menu. Then choose **From File**, select the picture or other object you want to insert, and then click on the **Insert** button.

NOTE

You can click in the **Link to file** check box to link the picture rather than embed it in your document. See the previous section on linking and embedding for more information on the advantages of linking.

How do I Customize the Clip Gallery?

Earlier in this chapter we used the Clip Gallery to find and insert pictures in documents. You can add items to the Clip Gallery, using it to organize all your graphic images, photographs, sound and video clips, and other objects. You can edit the categories, change clip properties of individual pictures, and import new clips into the Clip Gallery.

To add a new Clip Gallery category:

1. Open the Clip Gallery (choose **Picture** from the Insert menu and **Clip Art** from the Picture menu).
2. Click on the **Edit Categories** button to display the Edit Category List dialog box shown in Figure 13.44.

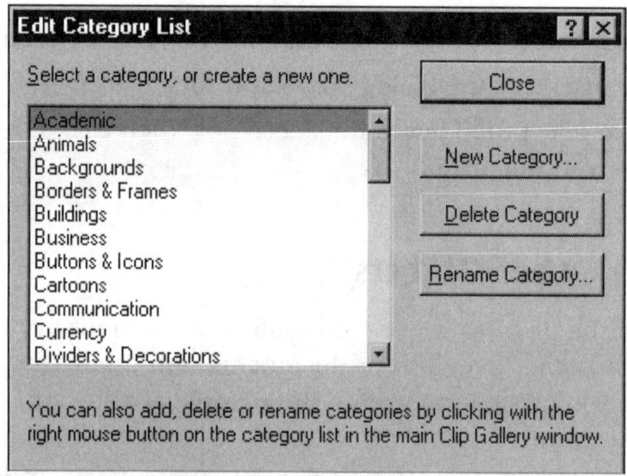

Figure 13.44 The Edit Category List dialog box.

3. Click on the **New Category** button, type the name you want to give your new category, and click **OK**.
4. Click **Close** to close the Edit Category List dialog box.

NOTE

You can change the name of any category by selecting it in the Edit Category List dialog box and clicking **Rename Category**.

You now have a new category, but it doesn't contain any clip art. Add items to categories by changing the clip properties for individual items.

To edit clip properties:

1. Select the clip you want to edit.
2. Click on the **Clip Properties** button to display the Clip Properties dialog box, shown in Figure 13.45.

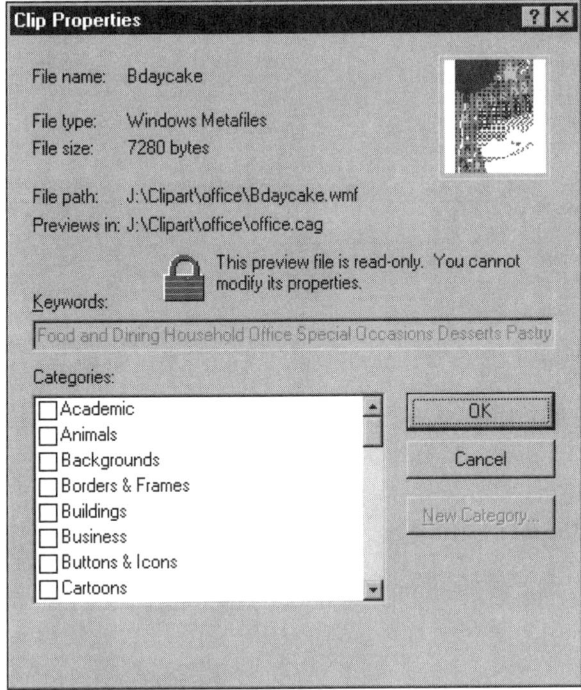

Figure 13.45 *The Clip Properties dialog box.*

3. Click to place check marks next to the categories you want the clip to be added to. A clip can appear in several different categories.

You are not making a copy of the actual picture; you are just creating an index entry for a graphic that already exists. It's kind of like making two entries for your bank in your address book: one under *B* for *bank* and another under *F* for *First National*. You can also add keywords so that you can quickly find pictures that are not in your favorites category.

To add clip art to the Clip Gallery:

1. Open the Clip Gallery and click on the **Import Clips** button to open the Add clip art to Clip Gallery dialog box shown in Figure 13.46.

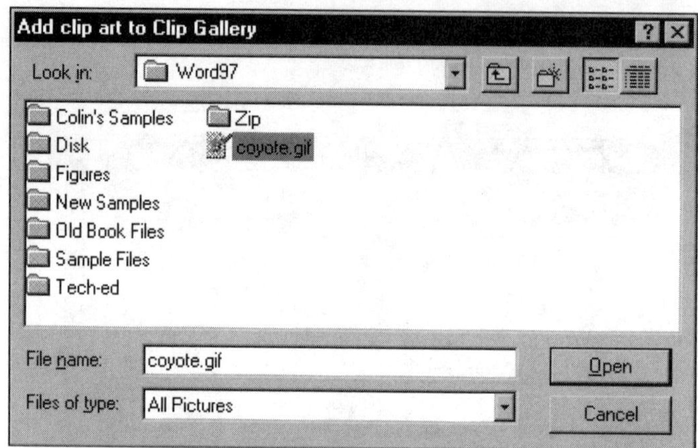

Figure 13.46 The Add clip art to Clip Gallery dialog box.

2. Use the Look in list to display the folder that contains the clip you want to import and select the appropriate file.
3. Click on the name of the file to import to the Clip Gallery, then click on the **Import** button.

You can import several files at once by pressing the **Ctrl** key as you select filenames.

You can use the preceding steps to add your own categories and organize the pictures using categories and keywords.

From Here...

This chapter gave you a taste of what you can do with graphics, but it's only the beginning. As you sharpen your skills, you'll continually discover more and more facets to this powerful feature.

In the next chapter, we'll get into managing and keeping track of your files. This might seem boring, but have you ever had a file that you knew was somewhere in your computer, but you couldn't find it? If that or any other file mishap has happened to you, read on. Learning to organize your files can be fun. Okay, maybe it's not exciting, but it will make your life (or at least the part of it that involves your computer) a whole lot easier.

SECTION IV

File Management and Printing

CHAPTER 14

Managing Files and Folders

Let's talk about:

- Understanding files, folders, and drives
- Creating folders
- Changing folders
- Copying, moving, and renaming files
- Deleting files
- Finding files

The more work you do on your computer, the more important it is to organize your files so that you can find what you want when you want it. There's an easy way to avoid having to deal with file management—don't create any files, and you won't have to bother with any of this stuff. If that's not an option, you should probably read this chapter.

Word uses most of the file management options and techniques that are used throughout Windows 95. If you're already comfortable with Windows 95 file management, you can skip most of this chapter. But even if that's the case, you might want to take note of some of the options available within Word. Sometimes it's easier to perform a file management chore if you don't have to leave the program you're working with.

What Is File Management?

When you pay your bills, do you throw all the receipts in a shoe box? And then throw the unmarked shoe box into a closet filled with a bunch of other shoe boxes and other stuff? If that's your system, how easy is it to find that one three-year-old bill from the TV repair place? (That's a rhetorical question—you don't have to answer.) You know what the solution is: Organize all those receipts in separate folders for utilities, rent, and so on. Well, it's the same deal with your computer files. The key is to put your files into groups that make sense to you so you don't waste time rummaging through that metaphorical messy closet whenever you need to work on something.

Understanding Files, Folders, and Drives

You've been working with files and folders throughout this book. Every time you save a document, you're creating or updating a *file*. The program that starts Word is a file. Every time you insert a graphic image, you're opening a file. And that document or image has to go to or come from somewhere, and that somewhere is called a *folder*. Your folders are all stored on a drive, which can be a hard disk, a CD-ROM, or a floppy disk drive.

Because we're talking about Word here, let's get right to it and use some Word dialog boxes to make all of this clear and show you how to move between files and folders.

You can do file management in Word through most dialog boxes that contain folder and file listings. For example, you get one of these dialog boxes whenever you choose **Open** or **Save As** from the File menu.

Figure 14.1 shows the Open dialog box with the **Clipart** folder that was created when I installed Office 97. It contains several subfolders for the various clip art categories.

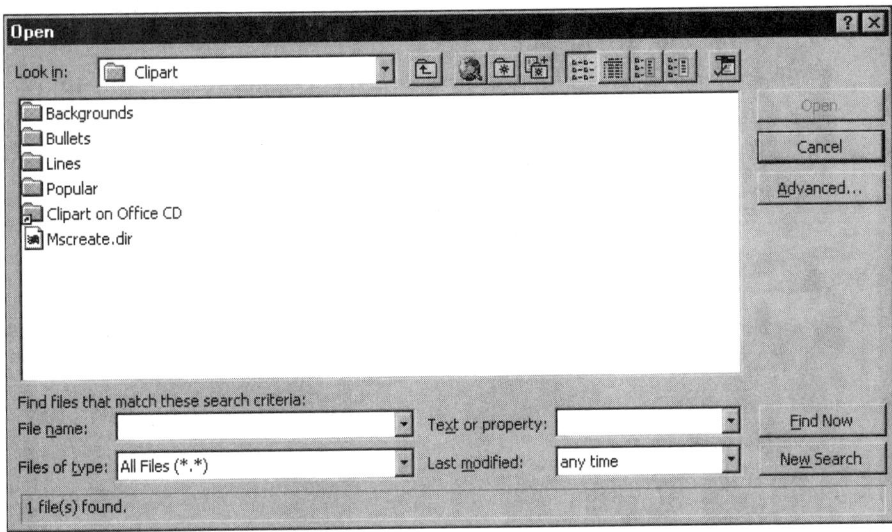

Figure 14.1 The Open dialog box.

Most file listing dialog boxes contain the same options. Everything that we'll do in this chapter is accessed from a dialog box like this.

Deciphering Paths

Windows 95 and Word make a lot of this path stuff transparent—you can safely skip this section without causing yourself irreparable harm. But it never hurts to know a little bit about what's going on behind the scenes. So here goes.

When you see a file listed, it often looks something like this:

```
C:\PROGRAM FILES\MICROSOFT OFFICE\CLIPART\POPULAR\DOVE.WMF
```

This is what this listing means:

- **C:** is the *drive name.* Anytime you see a letter followed by a colon in a folder listing or filename, that's the name of the drive. If you have one hard drive, it's always **C**. If you have more than one hard drive (or if your hard drive is broken down into sections or if you're on a network), the drives will be lettered from **D** on up. If you have one floppy drive, it's **A**. Your second floppy drive is **B**. (Lettering schemes can be rearranged, but most computers are set up something like this.) **C:** is also known as the *root* folder. That means all the folders on the **C:** drive branch off the **C:** folder.
- **PROGRAM FILES**, **MICROSOFT OFFICE**, **CLIPART**, and **POPULAR** are folders. They're also *subfolders,* because they're in other folders. A subfolder always has a parent and can sometimes have a child. The *parent* is the folder just above the subfolder—**MICROSOFT OFFICE** is the parent of **GRAPHICS**. A folder can have only one parent, but it can have many children. **POPULAR** is a child of **CLIPART**, but so are **BACKGROUNDS**, **BULLETS**, and **LINES** (seen in Figure 14.1).
- **DOVE.WMF** is the filename. The filename is always at the very end of the path.

Every file is part of a path, and every subfolder has a parent. You just learned the important part. The rest of this chapter gets into the gory details of maneuvering through paths and making sure your files and folders are organized how you want.

Selecting a File or Folder

To select a file or folder, just click it. It's easy to tell which is which. Folders all have those boring yellow folder icons next to them. The icons for files depend on the type of file. For example, if it's a Word file, there's a little Word logo; if it's a help file, there's a closed book. Depending on whether you select a folder or a filename, you have different options:

- If you select a file, you can click **Open** to open the file. You can also right-click on a filename to get a shortcut menu with the available file management options for that file.
- If you select a folder, choosing **Open** opens the folder and displays its contents (the files and subfolders contained in the folder).

All file listing dialog boxes include several other techniques for moving through your file and folder lists:

- Click the folder icon with a little up arrow inside it (just to the right of the Look in box) to quickly move to the parent folder of the folder that's currently open.
- Select a folder or drive from the Look in drop-down list to open that folder or drive.
- Type a path name in the File name text box and click **Open** or press **Enter** to open the folder specified in the path.

NOTE

You can also double-click on a folder or file to open it.

WARNING

Make sure you're in the folder you want to be in before you save a file. It's really easy to save files to the wrong folder without thinking about it.

Creating a New Folder

Creating folders is an important part of file management. Once you decide how you want your folders organized, you need to create folders for all your different file categories. In my case, I create a new folder for every book I work on. Then, depending on what's involved, I may create subfolders for different areas that relate to the project.

To create a new folder:

1. From any file management dialog box, display the folder in which you want to create a subfolder. For example, if I want to create a new subfolder under **C:\BOOKS**, I should have the **BOOKS** folder displayed, as shown in Figure 14.2.

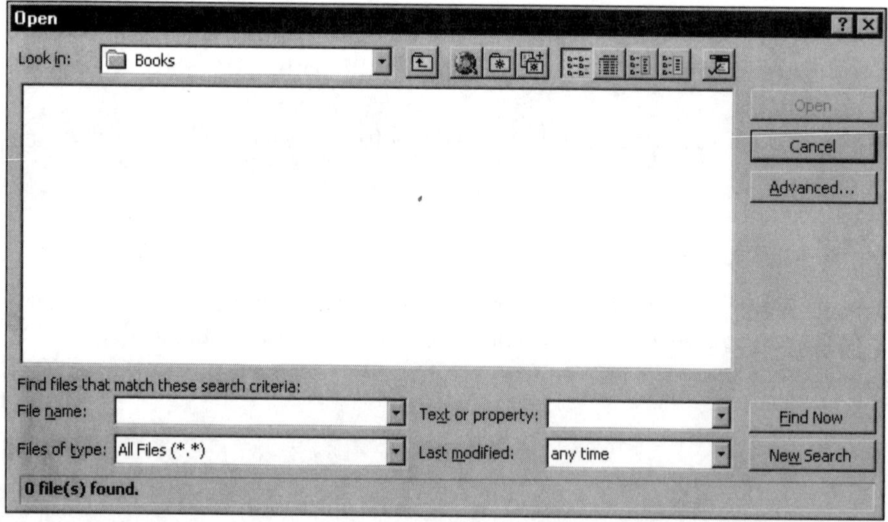

***Figure 14.2** I'm getting ready to create a subfolder under **C:\BOOKS**.*

2. Right-click on a blank area of the file/folder list area and choose **Explore** from the shortcut menu. This opens the Windows 95 Explorer with the current folder displayed, as shown in Figure 14.3.

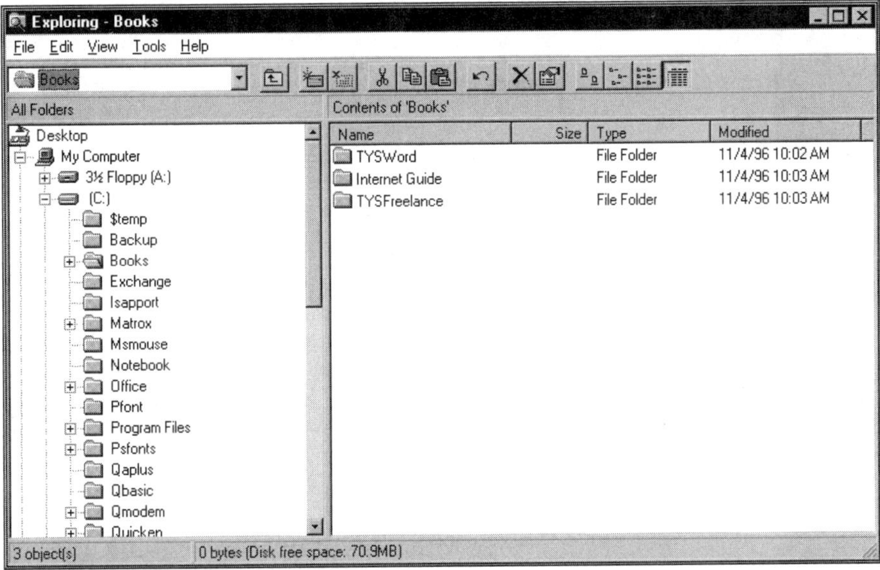

***Figure 14.3** The Windows 95 Explorer with **C:\BOOKS** displayed.*

3. Right-click on a blank area of the Contents pane and choose **New** from the shortcut menu, then choose **Folder**. As you can see in Figure 14.4, a new folder icon appears in your file list, with its default name selected.

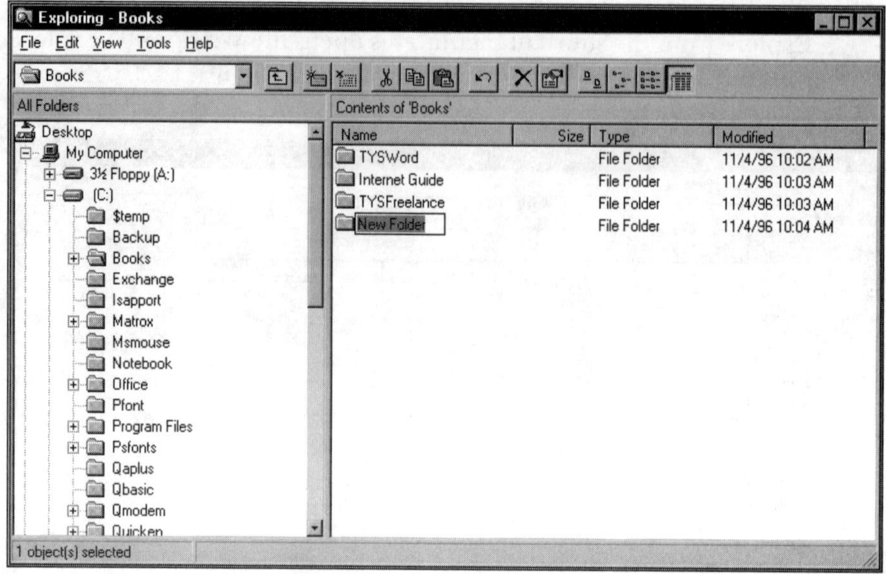

Figure 14.4 *Your new folder with a default name.*

4. To replace the default name with a name of your choosing, just type the name you want in the text box (your insertion point's already in there) and press **Enter**.
5. Click on the Explorer window's **Close** button to close Explorer and return to the Open dialog box.

Deleting Files and Folders

You can really get into trouble with this one if you space out. Word helpfully warns you before it proceeds, but it's not difficult to delete a folder and all the files in it. Pay attention to the dialog boxes that prompt you for responses. Read what they say before clicking or pressing a key.

Now that the warning is out of the way, I'll tell you how to remove files and folders. You might create a folder by mistake, or you might have a folder that's full of files you don't need anymore. Just be sure you *really* don't need any of those files before you continue.

To delete a file or folder, just select the file or folder you want to delete and press the **Delete** key (or choose **Delete** from the shortcut menu you get by right-clicking on the file or folder). Because deleting files and folders can have major consequences, I'm going to go into a bit more detail and include some warnings that can save you time and aggravation.

To delete files:

1. From any file listing dialog box, open the folder that contains the file you want to remove. The file you want to remove should be displayed in the file/folder list area.
2. Select the file you want to remove and press **Delete** (or right-click on the file and choose **Delete**).
3. The Confirm File Delete dialog box shown in Figure 14.5 gives you a last chance to change your mind.

Figure 14.5 *This is your last warning before the file is moved to the Recycle Bin.*

4. Choose **Yes** if you're sure you want to remove the file. If you proceed, the file will be deleted.

To delete folders:

1. From any file listing dialog box, open the parent of the folder that you want to remove. The folder you want to remove should be displayed in the file/folder list area.
2. Select the folder you want to remove and press **Delete** (or right-click on the folder and choose **Delete**).

When you delete a folder, any files and subfolders it contains are also deleted.

3. The Confirm Folder Delete dialog box shown in Figure 14.6 gives you a last chance to change your mind.

Figure 14.6 *This is your last warning before all files are moved to the Recycle Bin along with the folder.*

4. Choose **Yes** if you're sure you want to remove the folder. If you proceed, the folder and everything in it will be deleted.

There are ways to recover deleted files and folders, but they should only be used as a last resort. (I didn't even want to tell you about them until after I gave you all those warnings.) Anyway, Windows 95 has a Recycle Bin, and there are undelete utilities available.

NOTE

Remember how I told you at the beginning that you can use any file listing dialog box for file management? Well, instead of trying to figure out which dialog box to open every time you want to copy a file or create a folder, just pick one that you always use to do your file housekeeping. To simplify my life, I think of **Ctrl+O** (the shortcut for **File, Open**) as my file management key.

NOTE

The dialog boxes that you use for file management have other purposes. For example, the dialog box we've been using so far is the one you use for opening files. If you're using the dialog box for something other than the function described on its title bar, choose **Cancel** instead of **Open** or **OK** to close the dialog box. For example, if you click **Open** in the Open dialog box, Word thinks you're saying it's okay to open a file. It seems like **Cancel** would cancel whatever you've done, but it won't. If you've copied a file, it stays copied—**Cancel** just closes the dialog box.

Copying or Moving Files or Folders

It's easy to move or copy a file from one folder to another or to give a file a different name.

To move or copy a file:

1. From any file listing dialog box, open the folder that contains the file you want to move, copy, or rename.
2. Right-click on the file you want (don't double-click) and choose **Copy** from the shortcut menu. (Instead of right-clicking and choosing **Copy**, you can select the file and press **Ctrl+C**.) To move the file rather than copy it, choose **Cut** or select the file and press **Ctrl+X**.
3. Use any of the techniques I described in the section "Selecting a File or Folder" to open the folder into which you want to copy the file.
4. Right-click on a blank area in the file/folder list area and choose **Paste** from the shortcut menu. (Instead of right-clicking and choosing **Paste**, you can press **Ctrl+V**.)

That's it. The file is copied or moved to the new folder.

Renaming a File or Folder

To rename a file or folder, just right-click on the file or folder you want to rename and choose **Rename** from the shortcut menu. You can also select the file or folder and press **F2**. Either technique places your insertion point inside the name box, with the entire name selected. Type the new name and press **Enter**.

Selecting Groups of Files or Folders

Almost everything that you can do to one file or folder can be done to a group of files or folders. You can move, copy, delete, or print several files at once. You just select the files before you choose the command:

- To select files or folders that are next to each other in a list, drag the mouse pointer over the files you want to select. You can also hold down the **Shift** key while you press the **Up Arrow** or **Down Arrow** key.

- To select files or folders that aren't together in the list, hold down the **Ctrl** key while you click each file or folder. Keep doing that until all the files or folders you want are selected. Figure 14.7 shows a file list with several files selected.

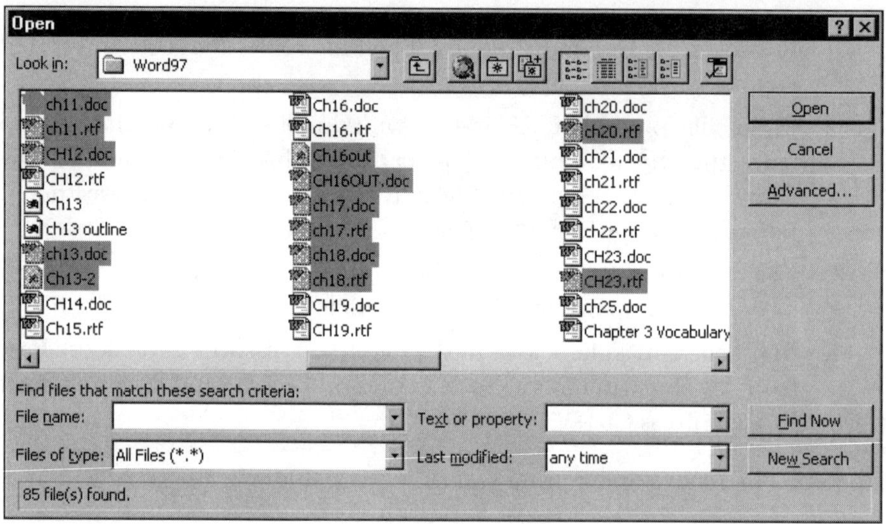

Figure 14.7 *The Open dialog box with several files selected.*

Once the files are selected, right-click on the selection and make a choice from the shortcut menu.

Printing from a File Listing Dialog Box

In the next chapter, we'll talk about all sorts of printing options. Most of them, however, have to do with printing one file (or part of a file) at a time. If you want to send several files to the printer at once, you can do it from a file listing dialog box. Simply select the files you want to print and choose **Print** from the shortcut menu.

Previewing Files

All file list dialog boxes have a **Preview** option that allows you to see what the file will look like before you open it. From any file listing dialog box, select a file and click the **Preview** button on the toolbar to open a Preview window, as shown in Figure 14.8.

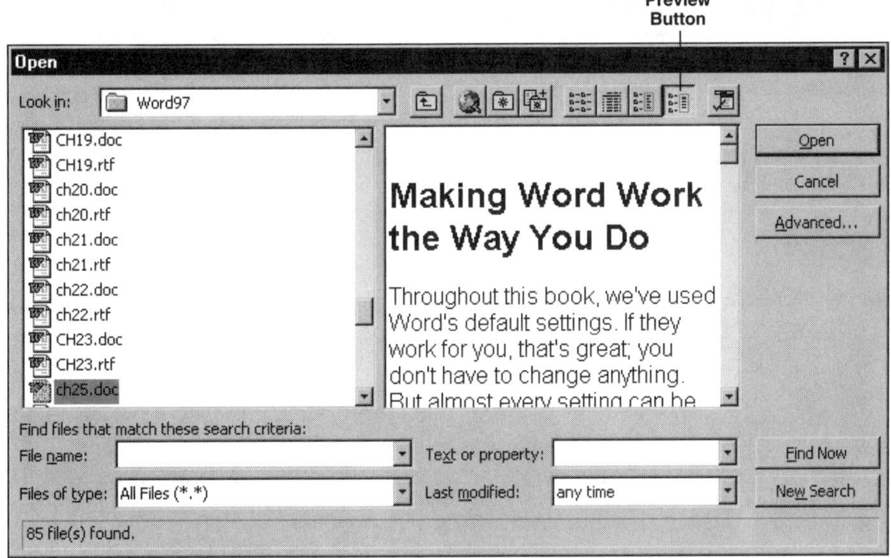

Figure 14.8 *The selected file is displayed in the Preview window.*

As you select different files, the file's contents are displayed in the Preview window. This can be a great way of browsing through a folder. Close the Preview window by clicking another file view button, such as **List** or **Details**. Note: You can't delete a file when the Preview window is open.

Other File Listing Options

Word gives you several different ways to display the information in file management dialog boxes. All of these options are accessed from the toolbar inside the dialog box:

- To display the files and folders as a textual list, click the **List** button (this is the default view; it's shown in Figure 14.9).

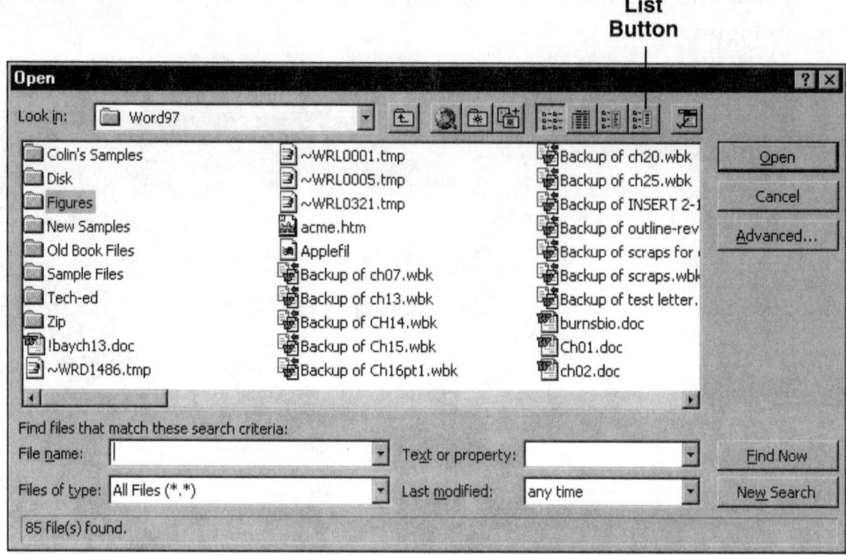

Figure 14.9 *List view.*

- To display the files and folders in a list that includes the file size, type, and date modified, click the **Details** button (a sample is shown in Figure 14.10).

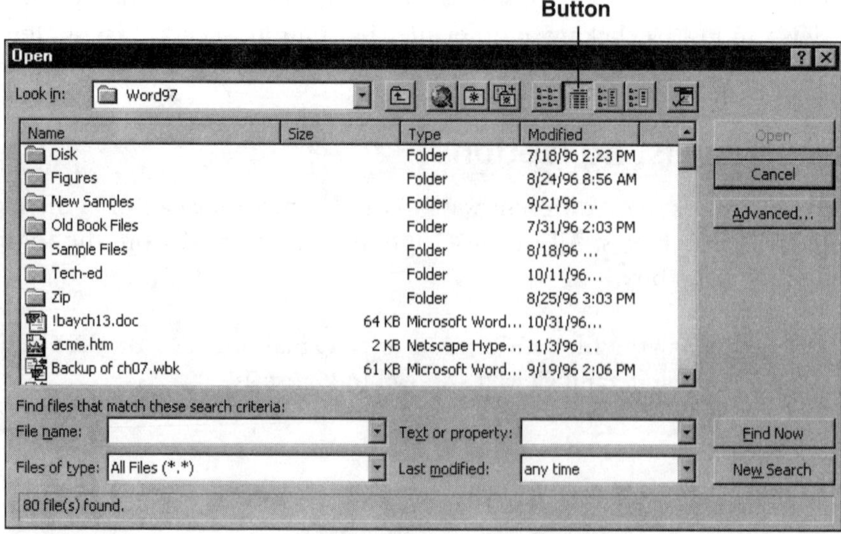

Figure 14.10 *Details view.*

- To display properties for the selected file, click the **Properties** button (a sample is shown in Figure 14.11).

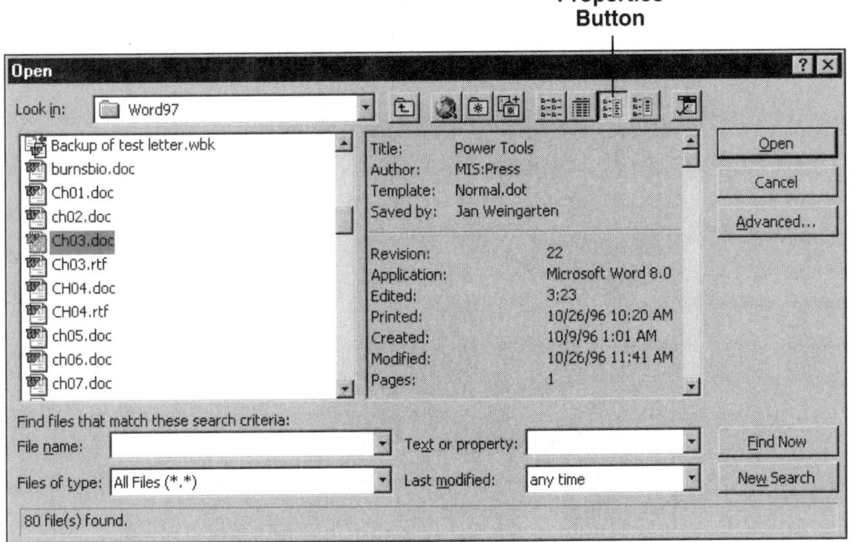

Figure 14.11 *Properties view.*

Opening a Document without Digging through Folders

Most of the time, when you open a document, you need to choose **Open** from the File menu, navigate to the folder that contains the document (or a shortcut to it), and then open the document. If, like most people, you often work with a group of documents during the day, you can take advantage of a built-in Word feature that keeps track of these documents.

By default, Word remembers the names and locations of the last four documents you opened from within Word. They're displayed at the bottom of the File menu.

To quickly open a recently used document:

1. Open the File menu.
2. Click on the file you want to open (see Figure 14.12).

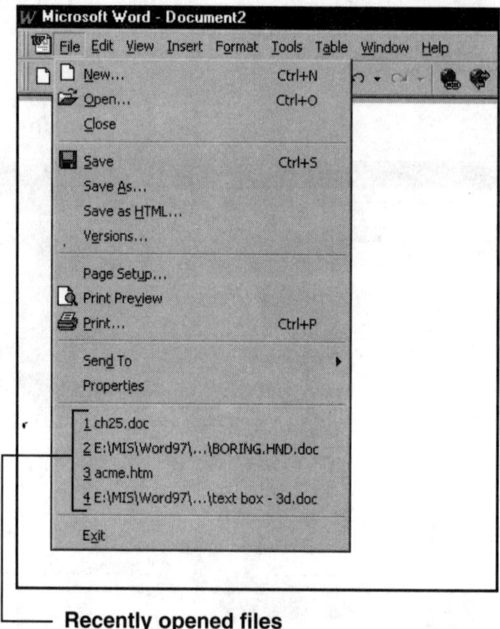

Figure 14.12 The File menu shows the four most recently opened files.

To increase the number of recently used files shown:

1. Choose **Options** from the Tools menu and select the **General** tab (shown in Figure 14.13).
2. Make sure the **Recently used file list** check box is selected.
3. In the entries box, enter the number of recently opened files that you want to show at the bottom of the File menu and click **OK**.

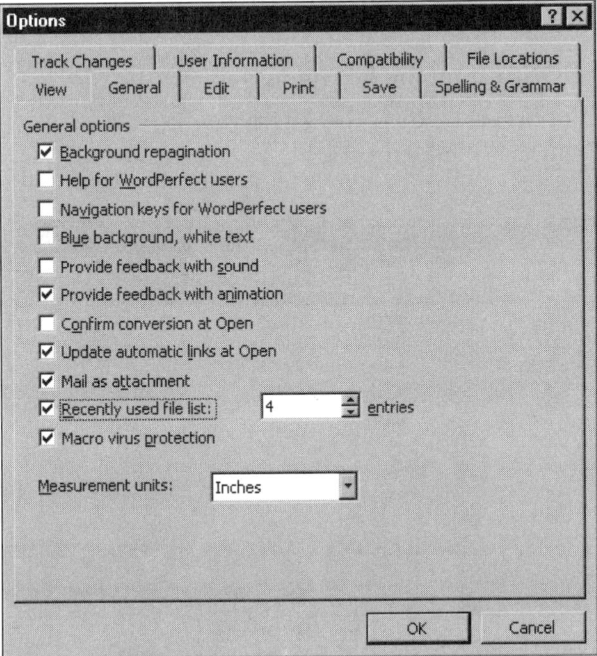

*Figure 14.13 The **General** tab in the Options dialog box.*

Reviewing Recently Used File Specifications

No matter how long the list of recently used files at the bottom of the File menu is, sometimes you're going to need to go through the Open or Save dialog box. When you do, you'll often find yourself looking for a particular group of files. For example, you may want to display a particular folder or all files with *trip* in the name.

When you use file specifications like these, Word saves you from having to retype them. The Open and Save dialog boxes can each display a list of several filename specifications that you've entered. If you want to return to displaying a certain set of files in the dialog box, you can pick the recent specification from the list rather than having to type it again.

To see a list of recently used file specifications:

1. Choose **Open** from the File menu.
2. Click the **arrow** next to the File name box to display recently used specifications (see Figure 14.14).

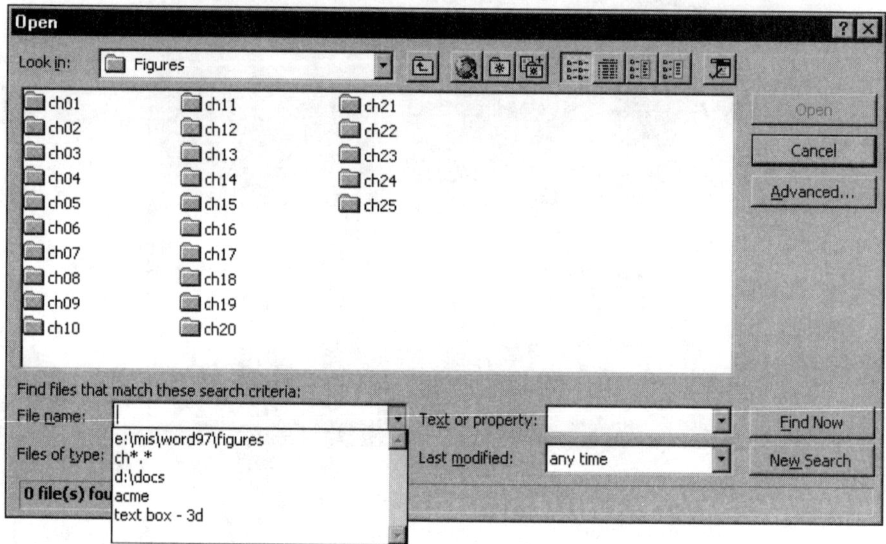

Figure 14.14 Recent file specifications list.

3. Select the item you want.

Setting a Convenient Default Folder

The Open dialog box displays the files in the default folder the first time you choose the **Open** command after starting Word. Normally, this is the **My Documents** folder. If you open a different folder in this dialog box, the next time you choose the **Open** command, that folder's contents will be displayed. However, when you exit Word and restart, the default folder appears again.

If there's a folder other than **My Documents** where you store most of your documents, you can set that folder to be the default folder. You can then spend less time on the repetitive process of navigating through disks and folders.

Similarly, the default folder for inserting a graphic using the **Picture** command on the Insert menu is the **Clipart** folder, which is inside the **Microsoft Office** folder. If you normally insert graphics from a different location, you can also specify that location as the default graphics folder.

To set default folders for documents and pictures:

1. Choose **Options** from the Tools menu and select the **File Locations** tab (shown in Figure 14.15).

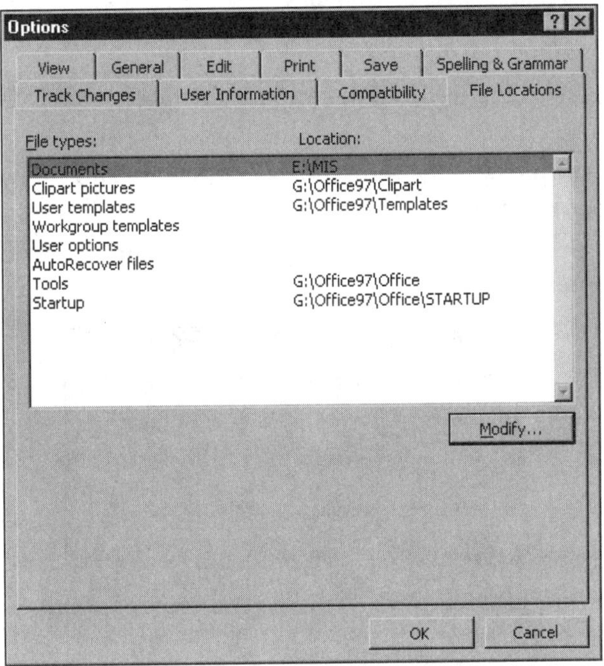

*Figure 14.15 The **File Locations** tab.*

2. Select either **Documents** or **Clipart pictures**, then click **Modify**.
3. In the Modify Location dialog box, navigate to the folder you want use as the default folder and click **OK**.
4. Back in the Options dialog box, click **Close**.

Finding the DOS Filename

You learned earlier in this book that Word 97 supports long filenames, up to a couple hundred characters. When you copy a file to a DOS floppy disk or move it to a computer that's running a previous version of Word under Windows 3.1, the file needs to have an old-style DOS filename. That means an eight-letter name and an optional three-letter extension. For this reason, Windows 95 maintains DOS-compatible filenames for each file. You can find out what this filename is by copying the file to a DOS disk, of course, but there's an easier way.

To see a document's DOS filename:

1. Choose **Open** from the File menu.
2. Navigate to the folder that contains the document you want to learn about.
3. Click the file with the right mouse button and choose **Properties** from the shortcut menu.
4. Click the **General** tab (see Figure 14.16) and look at the MS-DOS name item.

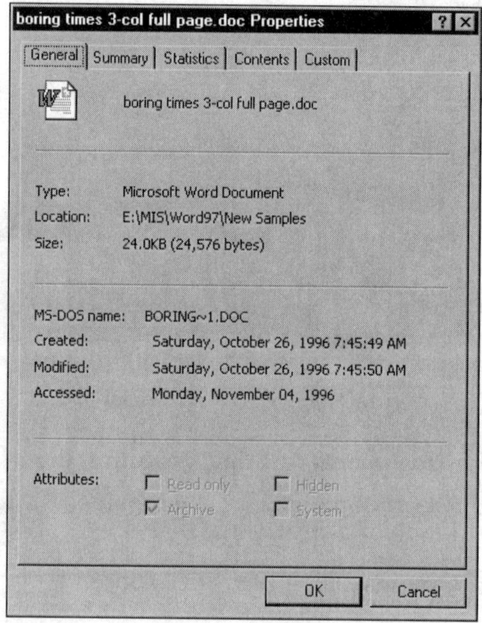

Figure 14.16 The DOS filename is in the Properties dialog box.

If the file is a Word 97 file, it has several tabs. For other files, you may only have a **General** tab.

Seeing Document Statistics

If you check the other properties of a Word document, you'll find a wealth of statistical information about the document. For example, you can see not only the date and time the file was last modified, but the day it was last opened, when it was printed, who saved it last, how many revisions it has gone through, and how much editing time was spent on it. You can also see all the information that you get when you choose **Word Count** from the Tools menu.

To see document statistics:

1. Choose **Open** from the File menu.
2. Navigate to the folder that contains the document in question.
3. Right-click on the file and select **Properties**.
4. Select the **Statistics** tab (shown in Figure 14.17).

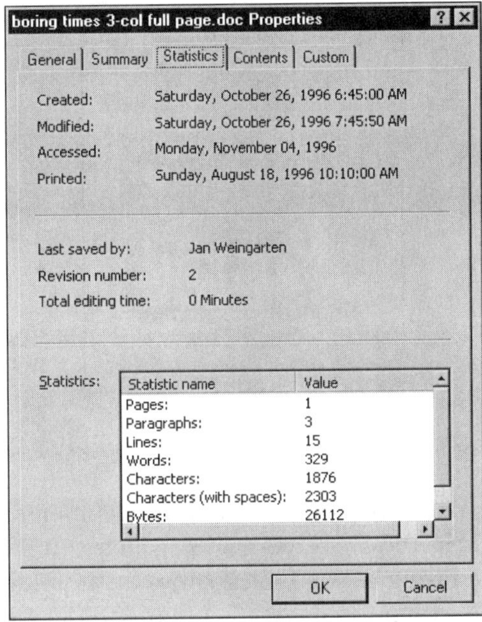

Figure 14.17 Document statistics.

Creating Shortcuts

Windows 95 introduced a new method of opening files or folders. A *shortcut* is an icon that stands in for a file or folder. For example, you might want to keep the actual document in the **My Documents** folder but still have quick access to it from the desktop. You can do this by creating a shortcut on the desktop. To do this, right-click on the file in any file listing dialog box and click **Create Shortcut**. Then use any cut and past technique to move the shortcut to your desktop. The shortcut is just a pointer to the document—when you double-click on the shortcut, the file or folder it references is opened.

You can have several different shortcuts to the same document or folder. If there's a folder or document that you work on or refer to frequently, you can put shortcuts to it in several places. That way, you have easy access to the folder or document without having to dig around and find it each time you want to open it. In Windows 95, the icon for a shortcut looks just like the icon for the folder or document it represents, except that a small shortcut arrow is added (see Figure 14.18).

***Figure 14.18** Shortcuts to a folder and a Word document.*

One useful place to collect shortcuts to various documents or folders is on the desktop. Another is in the **Favorites** folder, which you'll learn about in the next section. In file listing dialog boxes, shortcuts to folders and documents appear interspersed with normal documents and folders.

SPECIAL FOLDERS

A few folders have special significance and can make your work easier. One of these folders can make your work a little easier if you avoid it, because it's so big. The others provide convenient places for storing or getting access to your current work.

The Windows Folder

The **Windows** folder is where most of the Windows 95 operating system files are stored. Because this folder contains many files and is best reserved for operating system functions, you should avoid storing your documents here. You won't lose them forever or be unable to open them if you store them here, but it's an inconvenient place because the **Windows** folder is so crowded already. The **Windows** folder has a number of other folders inside it, which are also best avoided as storage places for your documents.

NOTE

Another reason to avoid the Windows folder is that it is likely to be overwritten when you install an update to your Windows software. For this same reason, it's better not to store files in any of your program folders—create new folders that won't be affected when you delete or update the software.

The My Documents Folder

The first time you start Word and save a document, the current folder that appears in the Save As dialog box is the **My Documents** folder. This folder is a convenient location for the documents you're currently working on. Rather than scatter them across the many folders on your disk, you may find it easier to store your working documents in the **My Documents** folder. You're not required to save any documents here, but it's a convenient location, at least until you come up with a better system. The **My Documents** folder is directly off the root of your **C:** drive (**C:\My Documents**).

As you become more familiar with Word and start creating more files, you'll probably want to create folders, divided into categories that reflect your needs. You can create extra folders within the **My Documents** folder or elsewhere on your disk. Creating new folders was covered earlier in this chapter.

The Favorites Folder

Windows 95 creates another folder, called **Favorites**, which is stored in the **Windows** folder (**C:\Windows\Favorites**). The **Favorites** folder, unlike the **My Documents** folder, normally stores shortcuts instead of documents. These can be shortcuts to folders or to documents. The actual folders and documents that the shortcuts point to can be stored anywhere. The **Favorites** folder simply groups in one place shortcuts that give you quick access to documents and folders in many places.

The **Favorites** folder is sort of like the Windows 95 Start menu in. From a single place, the Start menu, you can open programs and files from many locations on your disk. Similarly, from a single location—the **Favorites** folder—you can open documents and folders from anywhere on your disk or network or go straight to a site on the World Wide Web. There's nothing to keep you from actually saving documents in the **Favorites** folder, but it will be most useful if you restrict yourself to filing only shortcuts there.

Soon, you'll see how to get quick access to the **Favorites** folder. You'll also see how to add shortcuts to the **Favorites** folder without leaving Word.

Using Shortcuts in the Favorites Folder

As you just learned, the **Favorites** folder is a convenient gathering place for shortcuts to the documents and folders you use most. If you end up opening a document often, do yourself a favor by putting a shortcut to the document in the **Favorites** folder. You can do the same thing with a frequently used folder. This can be even more useful, because a folder shortcut gives you access to all the documents inside it, rather than just one file.

To add a document or folder shortcut to the Favorites folder:

1. Choose **Open** from the File menu.
2. Navigate to the folder that contains the folder or **document** for which you want to create a shortcut.
3. Select the folder or file.
4. Click the **Add to Favorites** button, as shown in Figure 14.19. Word saves a shortcut to the selected folder or document in the **Favorites** folder. The next time you want to open that item, you can quickly open it from the **Favorites** folder, rather than navigating through the hierarchy of files and folders on your disk.

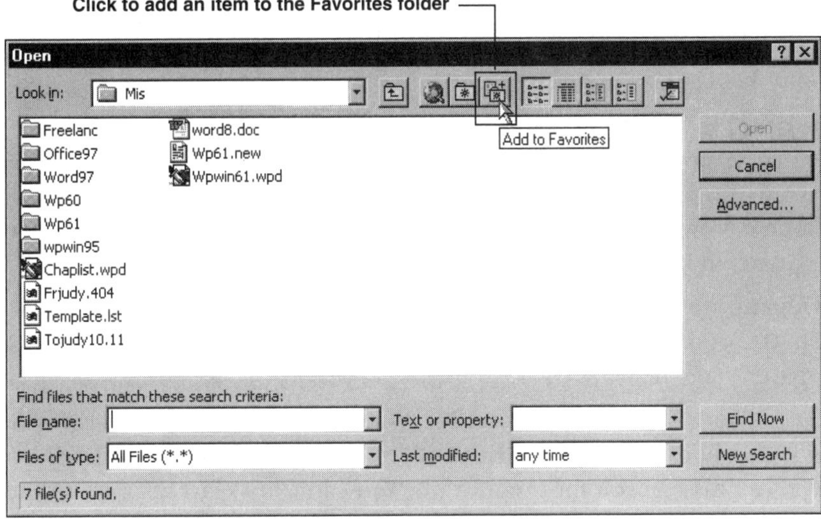

Figure 14.19 The **Add to Favorites** button.

To open the **Favorites** folder, from any dialog box, click the **Look in Favorites** button (see Figure 14.20).

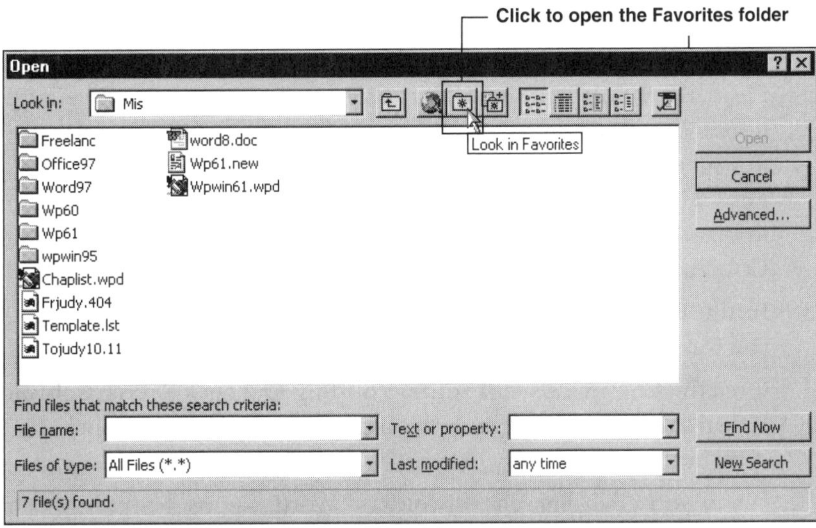

Figure 14.20 The **Look in Favorites** button.

You can open the **Favorites** folder from any file listing dialog box. To add shortcuts to the **Favorites** folder, you must use the **Open** dialog box.

Finding a Document

If the document you want to open isn't currently visible in the Open dialog box, one easy way to navigate to it doesn't require navigating at all—let the computer find it.

Depending on how many files you have and how wide you make the search, this could take a few extra seconds, but it requires much less work on your part.

In previous versions of Word for Windows, you could search for a file using DOS wildcards, such as **REPORT*.***. You can still search with wildcards, but you can also search more naturally. You can even search for text that's in the middle of a filename, which you couldn't do before. Now, if you do a filename search on *trip*, you'll find *Trip to Seattle*, *Trip.doc*, and even *Striped Shirt Invoice*.

To search for a document by name:

1. Choose **Open** from the File menu (although the Find features are available in other file listing dialog boxes, in most cases you want to find a file so you can open it).
2. From the Look in box, select a folder or disk that you're sure the document is inside. It's OK if the document is buried a few folders down, somewhere inside the folder you select. Word lets you search nested folders, not just one folder at a time. In fact, if the only piece of information you know is the disk drive, click the disk icon (for example, **C:**) to search the whole disk.
3. In the File name box, type part or all of the name of the document you want to find.
4. Click the **Commands and Settings** button, and click **Search Subfolders**. If **Search Subfolders** already has a check mark next to it, click the **Find Now** button.

   When you click **Search Subfolders**, Word begins searching, starting from the disk or folder you selected. When the search begins, the **Find Now** button changes to a **Stop** button. Click **Stop** to stop the search.

5. Any files that the search finds are displayed in the file/folder list. Select the document you want and click **Open**.

To search for files by type, click the **down arrow** next to the Files of Type box and select the type of file for which you want to search. Then proceed with the search as described earlier.

NOTE

When you pick a file type, only that type of file is displayed in the file/folder list area. For example, you can narrow the listing to show only Word documents, RTF (Rich Text Format) files, or other file types. If you want to see all the files in the current folder, select **All Files** from the Files of type list.

To find files based on their contents:

1. In the **Text or property box**, enter some text from the document you want to find. Your search will be most efficient if you can think of some text that is unique to that document. For example, the word *the* would locate many documents that you don't want. Searching for documents by specifying less common words, such as *dodecahedron*, will yield fewer false alarms.
2. Click **Find Now**.

NOTE

Word also includes advanced Find capabilities that allow you to use complex search criteria. To use these features, click **Advanced** from any file listing dialog box. To find out what the different options do, click the **What's This** button (the question mark in the upper-right corner), then click on the item you want to know more about.

FROM HERE...

Now that you can manipulate files and folders with ease, you have no excuse for dumping all your files in one folder. Get organized—manage those files. And use the **Favorites** folder to put frequently used files and folders at your fingertips. But if you do happen to lose a file, just use Word's file finding features to find it in a flash.

In the next chapter, we get into printing big time. You'll learn how to select the right printer, print selected pages of a document, cancel a print job, and much more. Stay tuned.

CHAPTER 15

Printing

Let's talk about:

- Selecting a printer
- Previewing a document
- Using the Print dialog box
- Selecting printer properties
- Using other print methods
- Canceling print jobs
- Printing envelopes

You've worked hard; your document looks great, and you want to show it off. You could have everyone crowd around your computer and stare at the screen, but your mom in Missoula doesn't drive. Hey, I've got it! How about printing it out and mailing her a copy?

You printed the document you created in Chapter 1, but that was just a quick introduction to printing. It's time to fulfill the promise I made to tell you more about Word's printing capabilities. By the end of this chapter, you'll be in total control of your print jobs.

SELECTING A PRINTER

Before you can print, Word has to know what kind of printer you have. And if you have more than one printer, you need to tell Word which one you want to use.

Do I Need to Select a Printer?

When you install and configure Windows 95 you also set up your printer. Word uses the system default printer you have selected for Windows 95. If you only have one printer, everything is set up (until you buy a new printer). How do you know if you need to select a printer? The Print dialog box, which you open by choosing **Print** from the File menu, displays the current printer selection. Take a look at Figure 15.1.

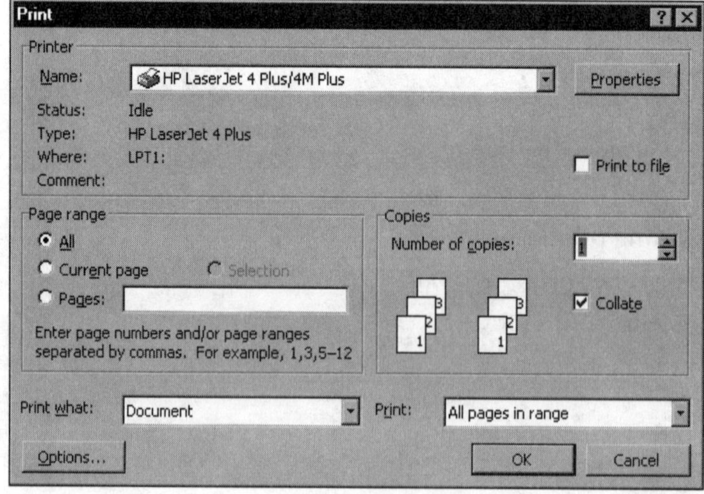

Figure 15.1 *The Print dialog box.*

If the name in the Name box is the printer you actually have and want to print to, you can move right ahead to printing. If there's no printer listed or if you want to choose a different printer, you have to make a selection.

To select a printer, click on the drop-down arrow next to the Name field and select the desired printer. If the printer you want to use is not listed when you click on the drop-down arrow, you will need to add the printer. For more information about adding a printer, see your Windows documentation.

NOTE

If you use more than one printer, glance at the Name box every time you print to make sure you're sending to the right printer.

Can I See My Document Before I Print It?

Absolutely! You can use Print Preview to check your document before you print. You can even get a bird's eye view of a whole page without seeing the actual words.

Although you cannot make changes to the text in Print Preview, you can display one, four, or even more complete pages at the same time. If you have questions about a particular section, you can use the magnifying glass to zoom in for a closer look.

To see a document in Print Preview:

1. Click on the **Print Preview** button on the Standard toolbar (the button has a piece of paper with a magnifying glass) or choose **Print Preview** from the File menu. When you first enter Print Preview, the mouse pointer changes to a magnifying glass with a plus sign, as shown in Figure 15.2. Notice that the Standard and Formatting toolbars are replaced by a special Print Preview toolbar.

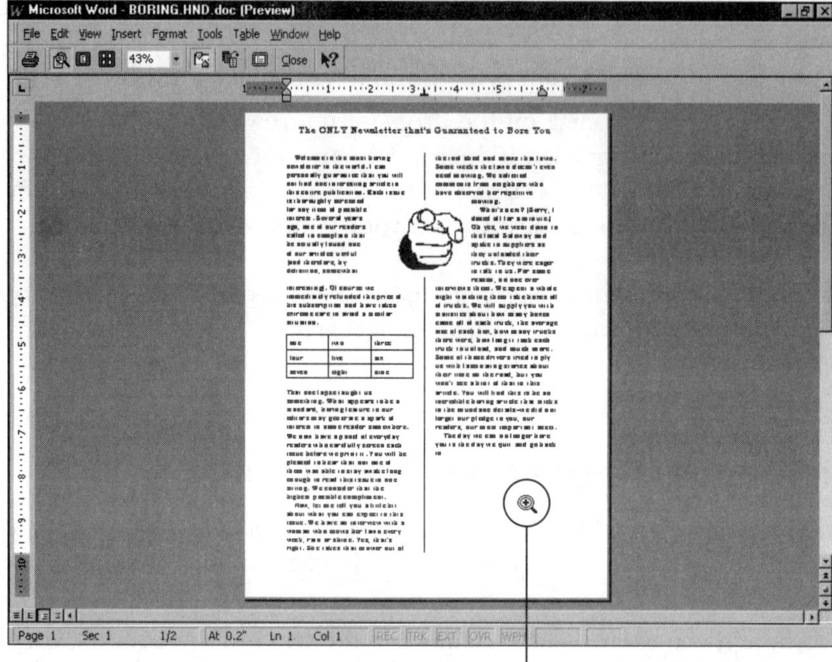

Figure 15.2 A document in Print Preview with the magnifying glass ready to zoom in on the document.

2. To zoom in on part of the document, click anywhere in the document. You will get a close-up view of the document, as shown in Figure 15.3.

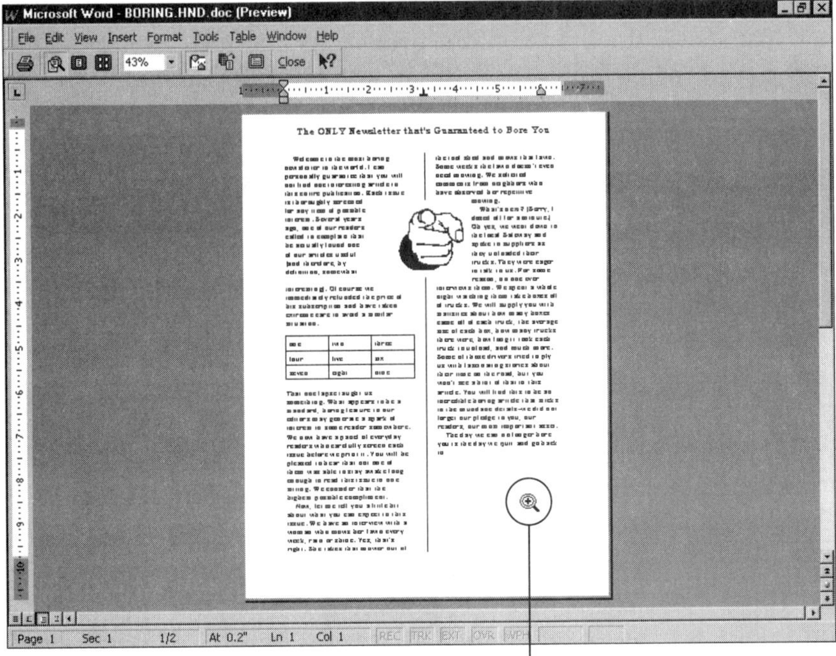

Figure 15.3 *Zoomed-in view of the document in Print Preview.*

To see multiple pages at once:

1. Click on the **Multiple Pages** button on the Print Preview toolbar. In the grid that appears, shown in Figure 15.4, you can select how many full pages you want to display.

Figure 15.4 *The multiple pages grid used to select the number of pages you want to see in the Print Preview window.*

2. Click in the grid and drag the pointer to the layout you want to see. The text at the bottom of the grid shows how many pages will be displayed. When you release the mouse button, that number of pages appears, as shown in Figure 15.5.

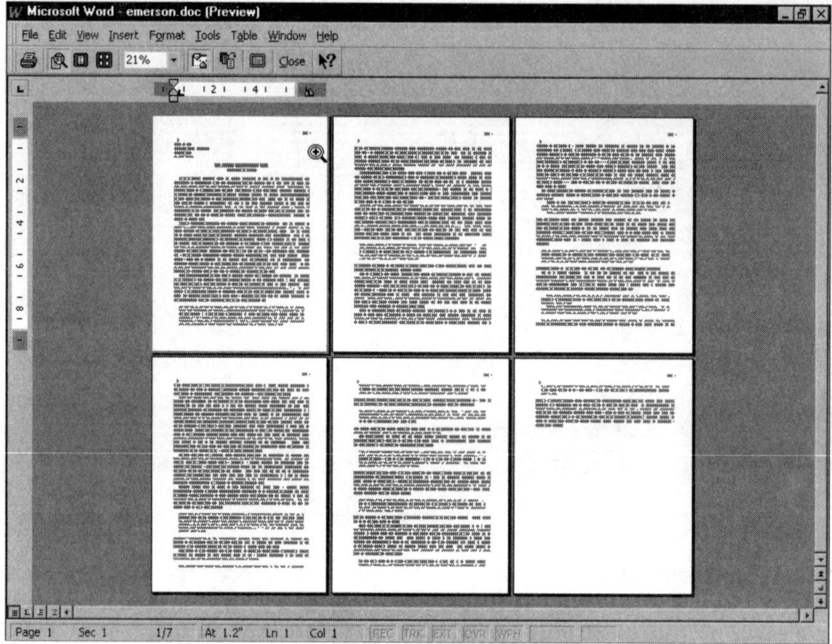

Figure 15.5 *Multiple pages in the Print Preview window.*

To leave Print Preview, press **Esc** or click on the **Close** button on the Print Preview toolbar to return to the document.

Shrinking and Magnifying the View

Word lets you change your view of a document to what helps you work best. You can change how big or small your document text appears on screen, without changing the actual printing size of the fonts. That means you can view your document at a smaller magnification and thus fit more on the screen at a time. Or you can increase the magnification and have the text appear larger and easier to read while you edit. Either way, the document prints at its normal size.

The **Zoom Control** button on the Standard toolbar is the tool that lets you work these wonders. To change the magnification of your document view in Print Preview:

1. Choose **Zoom** from the View menu. The Zoom dialog box, shown in Figure 15.6, displays.

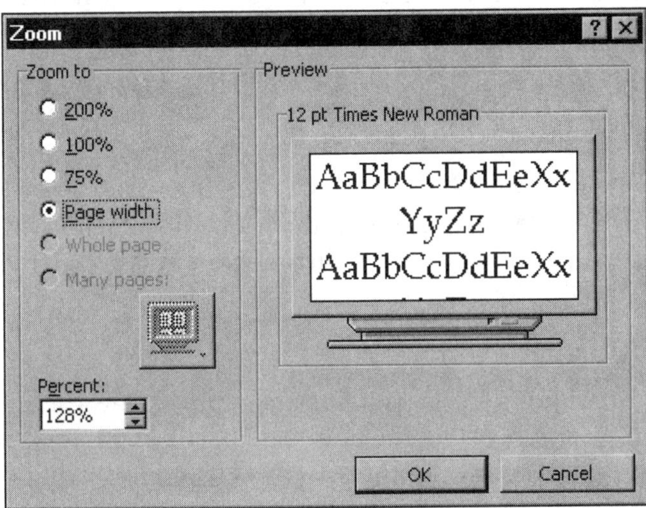

Figure 15.6 *The Zoom dialog box.*

2. Select the magnification you want to see. **100%** is actual size. Smaller percentages display the text at smaller sizes and fit more into your screen view. Larger percentages display the text at larger sizes, but less text will fit on the screen. If the view isn't exactly what you want, you can type in a different percentage.

Using the Print Dialog Box

You make most of your printing choices from the Print dialog box, which was shown in Figure 15.1.

To open the Print dialog box, choose **Print** from the File menu or press **Ctrl+P**.

Printing a Whole Document

This is the easiest choice—you don't have to do anything but click the **OK** button or press **Enter**. Printing the whole document is always the default, so all you have to do is open the document you want to print, open the Print dialog box, and click **OK**.

Clicking the **Print** button on the Standard toolbar sends the current document to the printer without going through the dialog box.

Printing the Current Page

This isn't much harder than printing the whole document. If you want to print the current page, just click on **Current page** in the Page range section before you click **OK**.

Printing a Selection

You might want to print only a specific paragraph or maybe a list from your document. Instead of selecting the information, copying it to another document, and printing the new document, you can select the information you want to print and print just that selection.

To print a selection:

1. Select the text you want to print, then choose **Print** from the File menu.
2. In the Page range section, click on **Selection**, then click **OK** or press **Enter**.

Printing a Range of Pages

Let's say you have a 50-page document, and you make corrections on pages 5 and 9, change the section from pages 21 through 28, and add three pages at the end. You don't want to reprint the whole document, and moving to and printing the changed pages one at a time would be difficult and time-consuming. The **Multiple Pages** option is the answer. You can specify exactly what portion of your document you want to print.

To print a range of pages:

1. Click in the **Pages** text box in the Page range section in the Print dialog box and specify the pages or labels you want to print.

2. Click **OK** to print the pages. Figure 15.7 is set up to print the pages I used in my example at the beginning of this section:
   - *5,9* means that pages 5 and 9 will print; the comma is like saying *and.*
   - *21-28* means that pages 21 through 28 will print; the hyphen is like saying *through.*
   - *48-* means that page 48 and all the pages that follow it will print. You can use a hyphen before or after a number to print a range from the beginning or to the end of a document. *48-* prints from page 48 to the end; *-10* prints from the beginning through page 10.

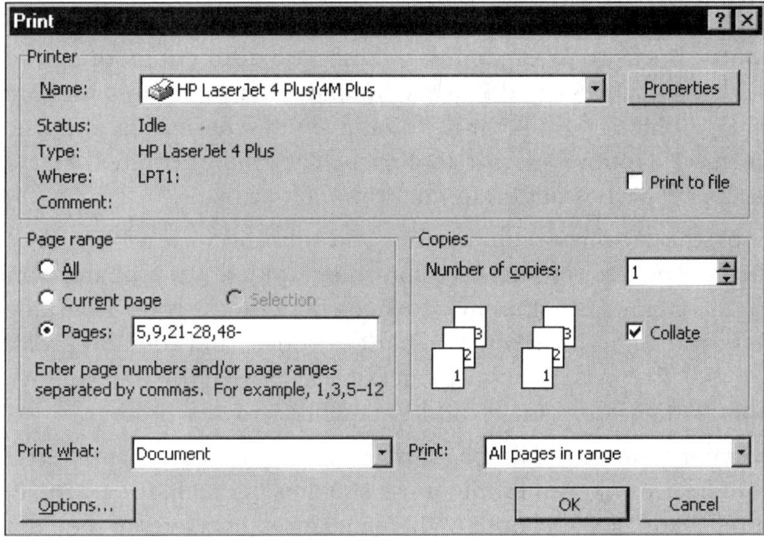

Figure 15.7 *The Print dialog box with multiple pages indicated for printing.*

Notice that the example in Figure 15.7 uses a combination of ranges. You can print exactly what you want by stringing together different page ranges.

Printing More than One Copy

If you need more than one copy of a document, you can do it through Word instead of printing the document and waiting in line at the copy machine. You don't even have to send the print job twice.

From the Print dialog box, type a number in the Number of copies text box (or use the incrementing arrows or the **Up** and **Down Arrows** on your keyboard to increase or decrease the number in the text box).

When you print multiple copies, Word automatically *collates* the pages. When you collate pages, Word prints the entire document from beginning to end and then starts over with the first page for the next copy. Deselect the **Collate** check box if you want to turn off the collating option. If you do not collate, Word prints as many copies as you specify of the first page, then it prints multiple copies of the second page, and so on.

Setting Printer Options

Each printer, based on its capabilities, can have a different set of options. For example, some printers can do *duplex printing*—that is, printing on both sides of the page. Others might print in color, print mirror images, and use other exotic features. Options specific to a particular kind of printer are available through the **Properties** button in the Print dialog box.

Among the most common options you will find in the Print Properties dialog box are printer resolution, color, and graphics. You probably want your finished document to look as good as possible. But as you're working on a document, you might print out several draft copies, and you don't really care what they look like; you just want them fast. That's what the **Resolution** option is all about: letting you print at different qualities to save time.

Resolution is measured in the number of dots per inch and is referred to in one of two forms: one printer might use 600 dots per inch, for example, while another refers to 720 x 720. Both of these measurements refer to the number of tiny dots in one inch of text. The higher the number, the better the resolution. Higher resolutions are better quality, but they take longer to print.

To set printer options for your printer:

1. Choose **Print** from the File menu to open the Print dialog box.
2. Click on **Properties** to display the Properties dialog box for your selected printer. You can select any of the options available for your printer in this dialog box. The dialog box changes depending on your printer.
3. Select the options you want and click **OK**.

Figure 15.8 shows the graphics options for one printer.

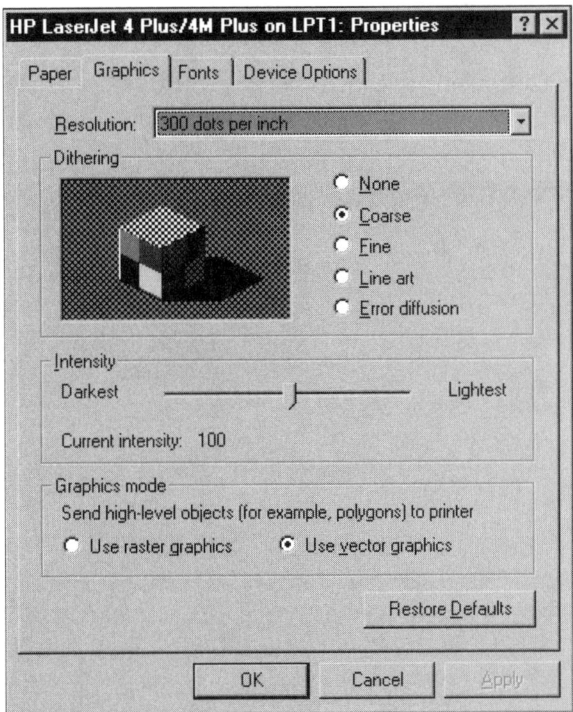

Figure 15.8 The graphics options for the HP LaserJet 4 printer.

Color printers include options for changing the quality of the output and the type of paper you use. In addition to resolution settings, many color printers let you change the print quality. **High Speed** prints the fastest but is the lowest quality output. This would be the suggested quality for drafts. **High Quality Text** prints text in the highest quality but graphics in a lower quality. **High Quality Graphics** is designed for documents with a lot of pictures. You can print the text in a regular quality, but print the graphics in a higher quality. **Photographic Quality** is the highest resolution available. It can be extremely slow to print documents in photographic quality, and this option uses the most printer ink or toner.

Changing Word's Printing Options

There are also printing options specific to Word that you choose by clicking on the **Options** button in the Print dialog box.

To set Word's printing options:

1. Choose **Options** from the Tools menu and select the **Print** tab (Figure 15.9). Or, if the Print dialog box is open, click on the **Options** button.

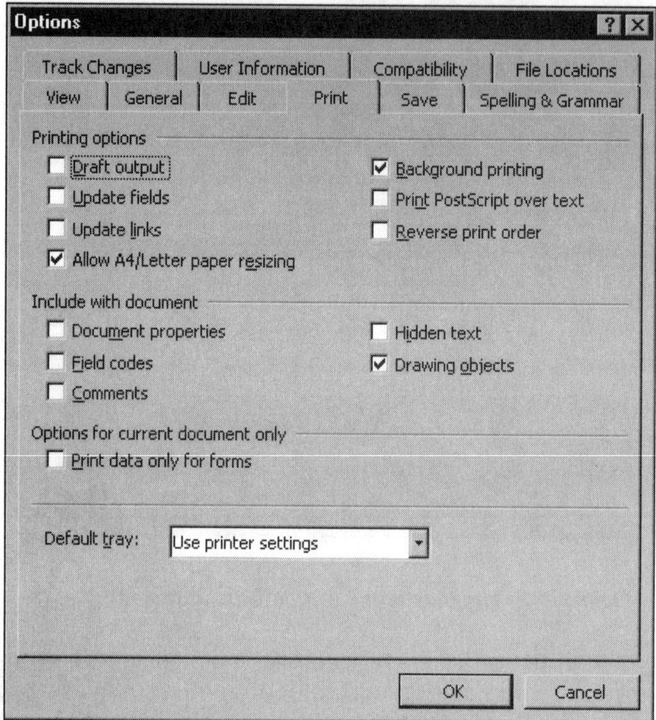

*Figure 15.9 The **Print** tab in the Options dialog box.*

The options you select in the Print dialog box remain in effect for future documents until you change the options again.

2. Select the printing options you want and click **OK**.

The printer options available to you are:

- **Draft output** prints the document without full formatting. This is the quickest way to print, but it does not include all the font and other formatting you may have applied. This is usually adequate for your own rough drafts.

- **Update fields** updates all fields before printing. This is useful when working with merged documents or forms. See Chapter 19, "Using Mail Merge," for more information on fields.
- **Update links** updates any linked information before printing the document. See the section in Chapter 13 on linking objects for more information about links.
- **Allow A4/Letter paper resizing** automatically adjusts documents formatted with A4 paper size (the standard size in some countries), for the standard paper size in your own country, such as Letter size. This affects only the printed copy of your documents, not the on-screen formatting.
- **Background printing** prints the document in the background so you can continue working while it prints. If you turn this option off, printing happens more quickly but it's longer before you can continue working.
- **Print PostScript over text** is used if you convert Word for Macintosh documents into Word 97 and those documents contain PostScript code.
- **Reverse print order** prints the document from the last page to the first. If your printer stacks printed pages so that they end up backwards, this option is useful. This option may be helpful if you need to take the pages off the printer and group them with pages from another source.

You can also use this dialog box to specify other options for printing. Your options are as follows:

- **Document properties** is the summary information stored by Word. You can change document summary information on the **Summary** tab by choosing **Properties** in the File menu. If you check this option, the document properties print on a separate page at the end of the document.
- **Field codes** prints the codes instead of results in fields. This applies mostly to merged documents, but it applies anywhere you insert a code, such as a code for the current date. For example, Word would print the code for the current date instead of inserting an actual date into the document.
- **Comments** can be added to any document; this option prints those comments on a separate page at the end of the document.
- **Hidden text** is text you add to a document for your eyes only. You can view it on screen, but it doesn't print unless you select this option.

- **Drawing objects** prints graphical objects placed in a document using Word's drawing tools. See Chapter 13 for more information about Word's drawing tools. Normally, you'll want to leave this option on. However, you can speed up printing by turning this option off. If you're just printing a draft so you can proofread it, you might not care about seeing your graphics. This option can save a lot of time, especially if you have a lot of graphics in your document. If you turn this option off, Word prints an empty box in place of the graphic.

There is one final option on this dialog box that applies only to the current document and needs to be selected each time you want to activate the option. You can turn on the **Print data only for forms** to print only data entered on a form, without printing the entire form.

What Else Can I Print Using the Print Dialog Box?

When you display the Print dialog box and click **OK**, Word automatically prints the document. In addition to printing the document, you can select other portions of the document to print.

To print other parts of the document:

1. Choose **Print** from the File menu.
2. Make a selection from the Print what drop-down list.
3. Click **OK**.

There are six options in the Print what list:

- **Document** is the automatic choice if you make no changes to the dialog box. This option prints the document on the screen, with any of the options you select.
- **Document properties** prints the properties for the current document. You can select this option to print just the properties without the entire document. You can view the document properties by choosing **Properties** from the File menu.
- **Comments** can be added to any document. You can choose to print the comments at the end of the document by making a selection in

the Options section, or you can choose **Comments** from the Print what list to print just the comments without the document.

- **Styles** are discussed in Chapter 20. You can select this option to print just the available styles for the current document.
- **AutoText entries** are discussed in Chapter 18. You select this option to print the AutoText entries you have available for the current document.
- **Key assignments** are discussed in Chapter 25. If you click on this option, you get a list of the special key assignments for Word. This is the only option not specific to a particular document.

Using Other Printing Methods

You don't always have to open the Print dialog box to print a document, and you don't always have to print a hard copy of the document. You can print documents automatically, print to a file, and print from the Open dialog box.

Printing Automatically

The easiest way to print documents is to print them automatically, using all the default settings, by clicking on the **Print** button in the toolbar. When you click on the **Print** button, Word automatically prints the entire document.

Printing an Unopened Document

You're working on another project when your boss buzzes you and wants you to bring her a printed copy of a specific document you typed last week. You can print the document she needs without opening it by displaying the Open dialog box.

To print a document from the Open dialog box:

1. Click the **Open** button on the standard toolbar.
2. Display the filename for the document you wish to print, then right-click on the filename.
3. In the shortcut menu, click on **Print**.
4. Click the **Cancel** button to close the Open dialog box.

Word automatically prints the document and you can continue working on your original document.

Printing to a File

You can also print to a file. This option is great if you want to print your document on a different printer from the one connected to your computer. For example, you can create your document using Word on your desktop system, print the document to a file, then print it on another machine with a higher-resolution printer, even if that machine doesn't have Word on it.

To print to a file:

1. Choose **Print** from the File menu to display the Print dialog box.
2. Select the printer you ultimately want to print your document, then set any options for the document and the printer.
3. Click in the **Print to file** check box, then click **OK**.
4. Choose a destination drive and folder, then name your document in the Print to File dialog box. You can now copy the file to a floppy disk and take it to any printer to print it. The only thing to keep in mind is that the printer must use the same printer language as the one you selected so that it can match the codes. You also need to make sure that the fonts you used are available on the other system.

Canceling a Print Job

You just sent that 200-page job to the printer and your boss (who just happens to be the president of the company) wants her memo printed now. You don't want to jeopardize that raise you're in line for by telling her she has to wait half an hour or so. What to do? Don't fret—there's an easy way out of this jam.

If you catch it before Word finishes sending the print job to your printer, you can double-click on the **Printer** icon in the Word status bar to automatically cancel printing. If the **Printer** icon no longer displays in the status bar, but now displays in the Windows 95 Taskbar, you can still stop the printing.

Once the job has gone to the printer, you can double-click on the **Printer** icon in the Taskbar to open the Windows 95 Print Status and History dialog box. Highlight the print job you want to cancel and choose **Cancel Printing** from the Document menu to stop the job. You can also choose **Pause Printing** from this menu. For more information on the Printer Status and History dialog box, see your Windows 95 documentation.

Depending on the speed of your computer, you might not be able to cancel the entire job before it is sent to the printer.

Printing an Envelope

With Word's envelope feature, it's a snap to address an envelope and send it to the printer. You don't have to do any fancy formatting; just enter the delivery and return addresses and Word takes care of the rest. It can even pull an address out of the document on your screen.

To print an envelope:

1. If you want to use the address from a document (like a letter), open the document.
2. Choose **Envelopes and Labels** from the Tools menu. The Envelopes and Labels dialog box displays, as shown in Figure 15.10. If the current document contains any addresses, the first address displays in the dialog box. If there's more than one address in your document, you can select the address you want before you open the Envelopes and Labels dialog box. The address you select is inserted in the Delivery address box.

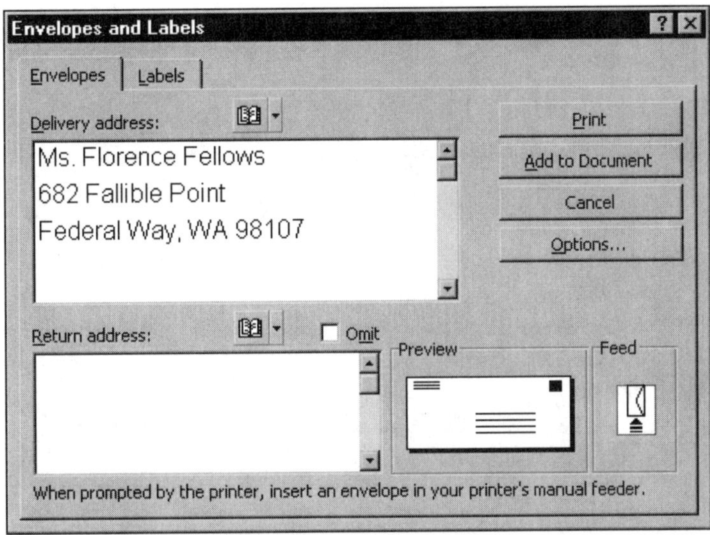

Figure 15.10 *The Envelopes and Labels dialog box. The address from my letter displays in the Delivery address box.*

3. It you inserted your address in the **User Information** tab of the Options dialog box, it shows up automatically in the Return address box. Or you can type the return address directly in the Return address box. If you have preprinted envelopes with your return address on them, you can click on the **Omit** check box to omit the return address. This option stays activated until you turn it off.
4. If Word didn't pull a mailing address from your document, type an address in the Delivery address box.
5. When you've entered all the address information and the preview display looks the way you want, click the **Print** button. (Make sure you insert an envelope in your printer first!) If you don't want to print the envelope right now, choose **Add to Document** instead of **Print**. This adds the envelope information to the end of your current document and allows you to save the envelope with the document and print it whenever you want.

That's about it, but there are a few more settings you can change. To change the envelope options, click on the **Options** button in the Envelopes and Labels dialog box to display the Envelope Options dialog box, shown in Figure 15.11.

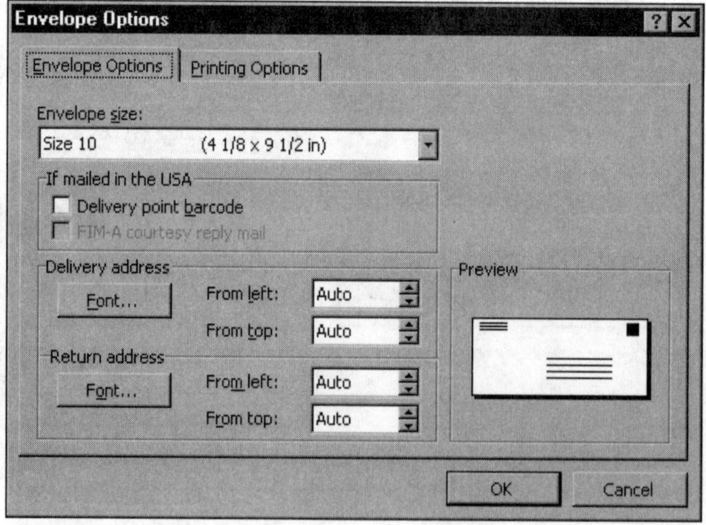

Figure 15.11 The Envelope Options dialog box.

You can choose from the following options to customize your envelopes:

- ✦ Click on the **Font** button in either the Delivery address or Return address area to display a Font dialog box. You can then tell Word how you want the addresses printed. You can print the return and delivery addresses in different fonts.
- ✦ By default, Word prints your addresses on a #10 envelope (that's standard business size). The Envelope size area shows which envelope form is selected. If you want to use a different envelope definition, you can choose from one of Word's predefined forms by picking it from the Envelope size drop-down list. You can also choose **Custom size** to set up a custom envelope definition.
- ✦ In the Delivery address and Return address sections, you can change the positions for the return and mailing addresses.
- ✦ In the If mailed in the USA section, you can tell Word to print a bar code above the mailing address by turning on the **Delivery point barcode** option. If you choose to add a barcode, you can also turn on **FIM-A courtesy reply mail** to add the courtesy reply symbols to your envelope.

NOTE

A bar code converts the ZIP Code into symbols that the post office uses to sort mail more quickly. You may get a discount on bulk mailings if you use bar codes.

You also have a few printing options available when printing envelopes. To display the printing options:

1. Select the **Printing Options** tab in the Envelope Options dialog box (shown in Figure 15.12).

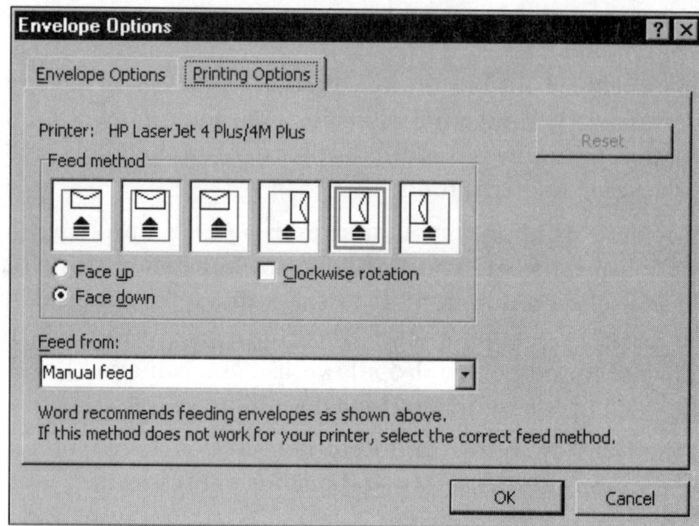

Figure 15.12 The ***Printing Options*** *tab in the Envelope Options dialog box.*

2. Select the options you want, then click **OK**.

You use the **Printing Options** tab to select such things as the feed direction and the method of feeding envelopes into the printer. Notice that for the feed method, Word assumes you will feed envelopes into the printer. If your envelopes are attached to the document or if you are using a special tray to feed envelopes, you can select the correct envelope tray in the Feed from drop-down list.

From Here...

At this point, you should feel in control of your print jobs. You can select which printer you want to use. You can print the whole document or any part of it, and you can change the number of copies and the print quality. You even know how to print a document without opening it. And printing envelopes will never be a hassle again.

In the next chapter, you'll get an introduction to Word's powerful Tables feature. At its most basic, it's a quick way to set up rows of text and numbers without using tabs. At its most powerful, a table can contain complex formatting and mathematical formulas.

SECTION V

Tables and Columns

CHAPTER 16

Working with Tables

Let's talk about:

- What is a table?
- Creating a table
- Editing a table's structure
- Formatting a table
- Using AutoSum to total a column of numbers
- Saving and deleting a table

Word tables make it easy to create charts, forms, and any other document that you want formatted in columns and rows. You could do many of the same things by setting tabs or using the Columns feature (which you'll learn about in the next chapter), but in most cases, tables are easier and more versatile.

You can change where a table is positioned on the page, adjust the width of table columns by dragging the mouse, and click a button to change the way numbers are formatted—and that's just the beginning.

The Tables feature has its own set of spreadsheet tools you can use to perform all sorts of complex calculations. If you've used a spreadsheet program like Excel or Quattro Pro, you'll be pleased to know that Word includes many of the same functions and capabilities. Depending on your needs, the Tables feature might keep you from having to learn a separate spreadsheet program.

This chapter introduces tables. You'll learn how to create a simple table, format it, and use a formula to total a column of numbers. And you'll get a glimpse of the powerful spreadsheet features—just enough to point you in the right direction. When you're comfortable with table basics, use Word's Help system to venture deeper into table territory.

Anatomy of a Table

Before you create a table, there's just one thing you need to know—what *is* a table? A *table* is just a bunch of rows and columns that contain text or numbers. You can even put graphic images inside a table. You only need to know three words to work with tables: *row*, *column*, and *cell*. Figure 16.1 shows how it works.

Column A	Column B	Column C	
Cell A1	Cell B1	Cell C1	Row 1
Cell A2	Cell B2	Cell C2	Row 2
Cell A3	Cell B3	Cell C3	Row 3
Cell A4	Cell B4	Cell C4	Row 4

Figure 16.1 *A sample table.*

A *table* is made up of rows and columns. The boxes that the rows and columns make when they meet are called *cells*. As you can see, *rows* go across and are identified by numbers, *columns* go down and are identified by letters, and cells get their names from their column and row location. So, a cell that's in the second row (row 2) of the far left column (column A) is named cell A2 (the column always comes first in the name).

Did I say you only needed three words? There's actually one more: *cell address*; that's what you call the cell location. In the example I used in the previous paragraph, A2 is the cell address. Now that the vocabulary/anatomy lesson is over, it's time to build a table.

How Can I Use Tables?

Tables are great for creating many different types of documents. You can create a simple table just to list data in nice even columns. But the fun begins when you use some of the formatting techniques you'll learn in this chapter. Here are just a few of the documents you'll be able to create using Word's Tables feature:

- Business invoices
- Resumes
- Crossword puzzles and word games
- Chore lists or to-do forms with daily check boxes
- Calendars
- Planner pages
- Requisition forms
- Expense sheets

The list is endless. In fact, many of the templates included with Word use complex tables. As you experiment with tables, you'll begin to see the possibilities.

Creating a Table

Okay, who's already noticed the **Insert Table** button on the Standard toolbar? You get a purple jelly bean. The rest of you, move your mouse pointer to the **Insert Table** button.

To create a table:

1. Click on the **Insert Table** button. The table grid displays.

2. Move the mouse pointer over the table grid. As you move, notice that the numbers in the box tell you how many columns and rows are selected (Figure 16.2).

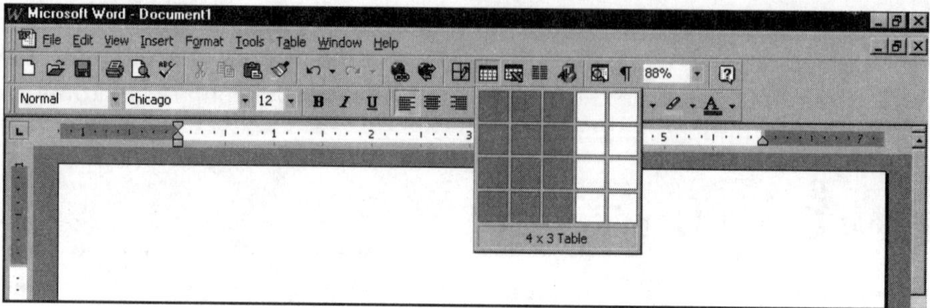

Figure 16.2 Just move the mouse pointer to select as many columns and rows as you want.

3. When you've selected the correct number of columns and rows, click the mouse button. For this example, click the mouse button when you have a table that is 3 columns by 4 rows. Your screen should look like Figure 16.3.

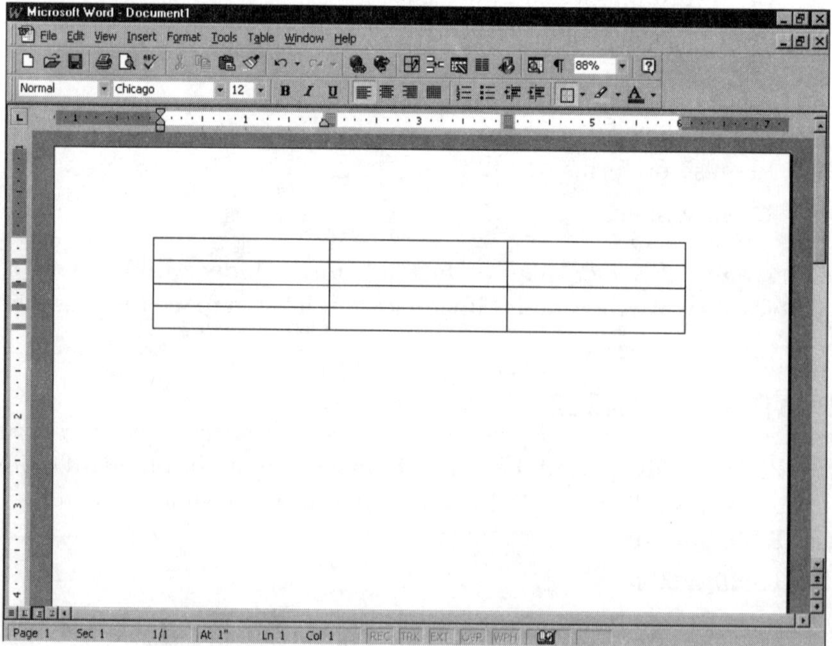

Figure 16.3 When you release the mouse button, the empty table displays on your screen.

You can also create a table by choosing **Insert Table** from the Table menu, entering the number of columns and rows you want in the Insert Table dialog box, and clicking **OK**. This dialog box also allows you to adjust column widths and use the AutoFormat feature to format the table. If you're creating a really large table, it can be faster and more efficient to use the Insert Table dialog box.

NOTE

It's a good idea to plan your table in advance, but don't worry too much about whether you have the right number of rows and columns. It's so easy to add and delete rows and columns (and change everything else about the table) that you can just sort of rough it out and work out the details as you go along.

Entering Text in a Table

Once you've created the basic table structure, you can type in any of the cells just like you would anywhere else in a document. When you first create a table, your insertion point is in the top-left cell (cell A1). If you want to enter text in that cell, just start typing. Otherwise, click in the cell where you want to enter text (or use an **Arrow** or the **Tab** key to move to a cell). Table 16.1 lists keyboard shortcuts for moving around in a table.

Table 16.1 *Keyboard Shortcuts for moving your insertion point in a table.*

KEYSTROKE	WHERE IT TAKES YOU
Tab	One cell to the right (if you're in the far-right cell of a row, it takes you to the first cell of the next row)
Shift+Tab	One cell to the left
Alt+Home	First cell in a row
Alt+Page Up	First cell in a column
Alt+End	Last cell in a row
Alt+PageDown	Last cell in a column
Up Arrow	Previous row
Down Arrow	Next row

NOTE

Because the **Tab** key works differently in tables, what do you do if you want to insert a regular tab while you're in a table? Just press **Ctrl+Tab**.

To enter text into a table (use Figure 16.4 as an example), use the **Tab** key to move from cell to cell or click in the cell you want.

Category	Last Year	This Year
Salaries	$152,334	$380,952
Telephone	$1,890	$2,590
Meeting and Seminar Refreshments	$250	$18,620

***Figure 16.4** Enter your text as shown here.*

NOTE

As you're entering text in a table, it's usually easier to press the **Tab** key to move to the next cell rather than reaching for the mouse.

Did you notice that the bottom row got taller when you typed **Meeting and Seminar Refreshments**? The height of a cell increases automatically when text wraps to the next line.

USING TABLE TOOLS

We're about to start messing with the table's format. To make that task easier, it's time to drag out Word's arsenal of table tools:

- First, there's the Tables and Borders toolbar, shown in Figure 16.5, which appears when you click on the **Tables and Borders** button in the Standard toolbar.

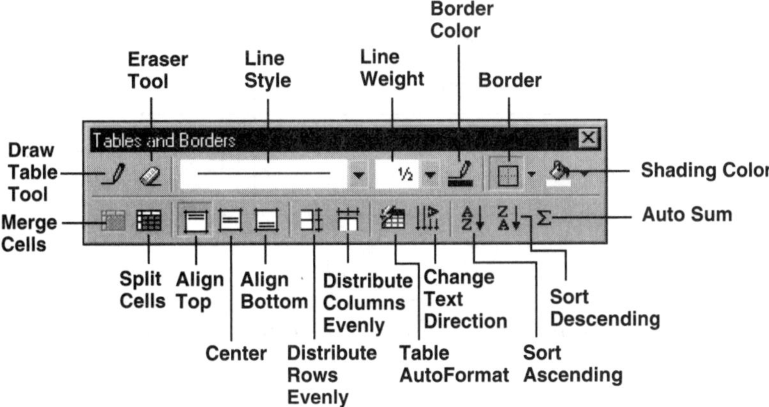

Figure 16.5 The Tables and Borders toolbar.

- The Tables menu also provides access to the Tables features. Notice that some of the features, such as inserting and deleting columns, rows, and cells, change as you select different parts of the table.
- Then there's the old familiar shortcut menu, but with a twist in Word 97. You get different shortcut menus depending on whether your insertion point is in an empty cell or on text and whether you have a cell, row, column, or the entire table selected. You get the various shortcut menus by clicking your right mouse button anywhere inside a table. If you don't see the option you are looking for, try clicking on another area of the table.

Inserting Rows, Columns, and Cells

You'll find plenty of reasons to add rows or columns after you create a table. In this case, we need a title row that explains the purpose of the table.

To add a title row at the top of the table:

1. Place your insertion point anywhere in the top row.
2. Choose **Insert Rows** from the Table menu or shortcut menu to insert one row above your insertion point location. Your table should look like Figure 16.6.

Category	Last Year	This Year
Salaries	$152,334	$380,952
Telephone	$1,890	$2,590
Meeting and Seminar Refreshments	$250	$18,620

Figure 16.6 *The new row appears above the row where your insertion point was located.*

You can also add multiple rows, columns, or cells to your table. Which options are available depends on what you select:

- Select the number of rows you want to insert into the table, then choose **Insert Rows** from the Table menu or shortcut menu. The specified number of rows is inserted above the insertion point.
- Select the number of columns you want to insert into the table, then choose **Insert Columns** from the Table menu or shortcut menu. The specified number of columns is inserted to the left of the insertion point.
- From inside the cell, select one or more cells, then choose **Insert Cells** from the Tables menu or the shortcut menu.

The Insert Cells dialog box, shown in Figure 16.7, displays.

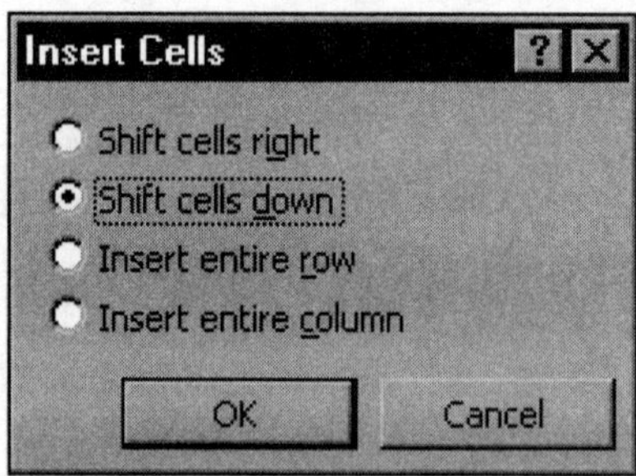

Figure 16.7 *The Insert Cells dialog box.*

In this dialog box, you have the following options:

- **Shift cells right** adds the cell or cells at the insertion point location, moving all other cells in the selected row, rows, column, or columns to the right.
- **Shift cells down** adds the cell or cells at the insertion point, moving all cells in the current column or columns down the inserted number of cells.
- **Insert entire row** inserts a row or rows above the insertion point.
- **Insert entire column** inserts a column or columns to the left of the insertion point.

Adding a Row as You Type

The procedure just described is the best way to add rows or columns except in one situation. You can add a row at the end of a table by pressing the **Tab** key with your insertion point in the very last cell.

To add a row as you type:

1. Move your insertion point to the last cell in the table.
2. Press the **Tab** key. A new row is created at the bottom. Leave the row empty for now—we'll use it later to add the columns of numbers.

This feature means that you can keep entering text and adding rows on the fly without having to know exactly how many rows you will need. It only works at the end of a table, though—you can't use this technique to add rows in the middle of a table (or to add columns anywhere).

Changing Column Widths

Let's increase the width of the first column so *Meeting and Seminar Refreshments* fits on one line. The fastest way to do this is to use the **AutoFit** option.

To change the column width using AutoFit:

1. Select the column you want to change.
2. Choose **Cell Height and Width** from the Table menu.

3. Click on the **Column** tab. Figure 16.8 shows the **Column** tab in the Cell Height and Width dialog box.

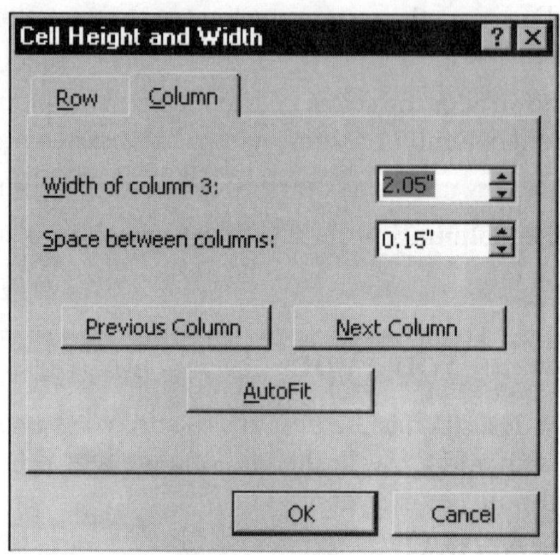

***Figure 16.8** The **Column** tab in the Cell Height and Width dialog box.*

4. Click on **AutoFit** to adjust the column width so all the text fits on one line.

Another way to increase your column width is to use the ruler. Figure 16.9 shows what the ruler looks like when your insertion point is inside a table. The squares are for the column width, and the indent markers are used to indent the cell text. You only see indent markers for the column where your insertion point is located (in Figure 16.9, the insertion point is in the first column, so the indent markers you see are for that column). You can drag the column markers to increase or decrease the width of a column or drag the margin markers to change the margins within a column.

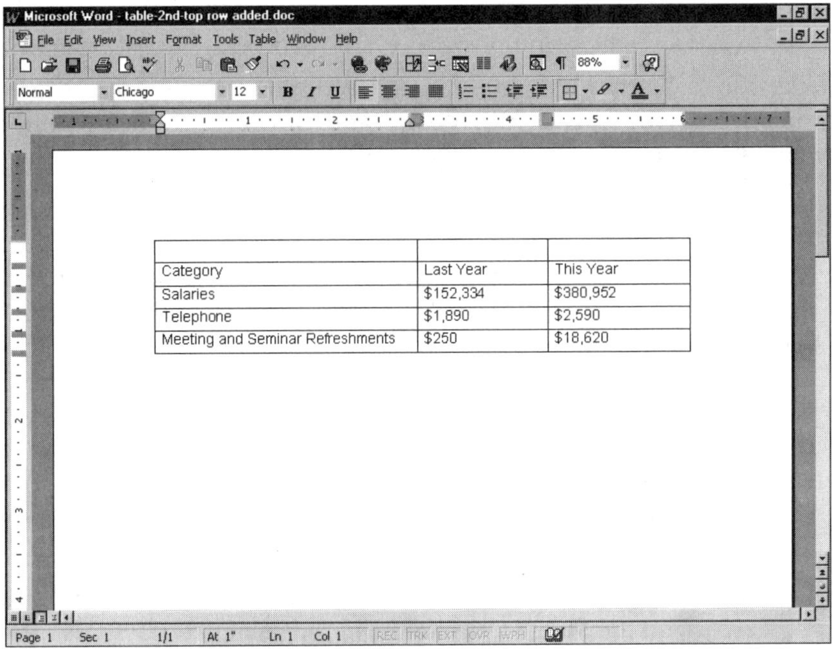

Figure 16.9 *Notice the column and indent markers on the Ruler.*

The easiest way to change column widths is to drag the table gridlines. Just position the mouse pointer over a column line until the mouse pointer changes into a double arrow and then drag the line to make the column wider or narrower.

Using any of these methods, make sure *Meeting and Seminar Refreshments* fits on one line before you proceed. You might have to experiment a little to get the right width. If the text isn't all on one line when you release the mouse button, or if you dragged too far and the column's too wide, try it again.

NOTE

Using the **AutoFit** option or the ruler to change column widths is quick and easy, but there might be times when you want to enter more precise measurements for column width (or to change the widths for several columns at once). You can do that by entering an exact measurement in the Width of column text box in the Cell Height and Width dialog box.

Another way to change column widths is to make all the column widths equal, or to *distribute* the column widths evenly between selected columns.

Select the columns you want to make even, then click on the **Distribute Columns Evenly** button in the Tables and Borders toolbar or choose **Distribute Columns Evenly** from the shortcut menu or Table menu.

MERGING CELLS

The top row is broken into three cells like all the other rows, but we want a title that spans all the columns. To do that, we need to turn the three cells into one. Sounds complicated, but it's not.

To merge cells:

1. Select the cells you want to merge by dragging the mouse pointer across them or using the **Shift** key with the **Arrow** keys. For this example, select cells **A1** through **A3** (all of the cells in the first row).
2. Choose **Merge Cells** from the shortcut menu or Table menu. You can also click on the **Merge Cells** button in the Tables and Borders toolbar. Cells A1 through A3 are now one big cell called A1, as you can see in Figure 16.10.

Category	Last Year	This Year
Salaries	$152,334	$380,952
Telephone	$1,890	$2,590
Meeting and Seminar Refreshments	$250	$18,620

Figure 16.10 *The cells in the top row are joined to create one cell.*

3. Type **Department Budget** in the top row.

There is another way to merge cells—you can use the **Eraser** tool on the Tables and Borders toolbar. We'll discuss the **Eraser** tool more in the section on using the table drawing tools.

You can also split a cell into more than one row or column by positioning the insertion point in the cell you wish to split or selecting the multiple cells to split and choosing **Split Cells** from the Table menu or the shortcut menu.

You can also click on the **Split Cells** button in the Tables and Borders toolbar. You then enter the number of columns or rows you want to create.

NOTE

If **Split Cells** is not an option on the shortcut menu, check the cells you have selected. You need to select the multiple cells from inside the table, not by dragging the mouse pointer on the outside borders.

SELECTING IN TABLES

When you're entering text in a table, you can use most of the formatting techniques you've already learned. You can center text on a line or use the **Bold**, **Italic**, and **Underline** buttons to change the appearance of a portion of text.

But what if you want all the text in one column centered? Or you want to change all your headings to bold text and be sure that any text you add to those cells will also be bold? You can apply formatting to any part of a table or the entire table by selecting the cells before you format. Table 16.2 shows a few ways to select items in a table.

Table 16.2 *Ways to select text, columns, and rows in tables.*

TO SELECT	DO THIS
A cell	Click the left edge of the cell just inside the cell's left border. The mouse pointer appears as a hollow arrow pointing up to the right.
A row	Click to the left of the row, just outside the table's left border. The mouse pointer appears as a hollow arrow pointing up to the right. You can also choose **Select Row** from the Table menu.
A column	Click on the column's top gridline or border, just above the table's top border. The mouse pointer appears as a small black arrow pointing down at the column. You can also click in the column's top or bottom cell, hold down **Shift**, and then press the **Up Arrow** or **Down Arrow** to move up and down the column, selecting part or all of the column. Finally, you can choose **Select Column** from the Table menu.

continued

Table 16.2 continued

To Select	Do This
Multiple cells	Use your mouse to drag across the cells, rows, or columns or select one cell, row, or column, then hold down **Shift** and click another cell, row, or column.
Text in the next cell	Press **Tab**.
Text in previous cell	Press **Shift+Tab**.
Select the entire table	Click anywhere in the table, then press **Alt+5** on the numeric keypad. **NumLock** must be off. You can also drag the mouse pointer down just outside the left border of the table to select the entire table. You can also choose **Select Table** from the Table menu.

You'll often select a group of cells before you edit a table's structure or format. For the most part, selecting in tables works the same as in document text, but there are a few things to be aware of.

Pay attention to the shape and direction of your mouse pointer before you start selecting. When you move the mouse pointer near any cell's left border or the table's left border, the pointer turns into a hollow arrow. To select cells, make sure the mouse pointer is a hollow upward-pointing arrow (but not the thin double-headed arrow you get when the mouse pointer's on a cell border—that's used for changing the column width).

NOTE

Selecting text in a table works slightly differently from selecting text in the rest of a document. Within a cell, you select text as you normally would. As soon as you move the mouse pointer outside of a cell, however, you begin selecting entire cells rather than the text they contain.

Formatting Tables and Cells

In the following sections, I'll go over the various options for formatting cells, rows, columns, and tables. For all of them, you'll use one of the selecting procedures discussed in the previous section before you format.

Formatting Cells

Formatting applies only to the cell where your insertion point is currently located or to the group of cells you select before formatting.

To format a cell or group of cells, you need to place your insertion point in the cell you want to format or select a group of cells. After selecting the cell or group of cells, you can make many changes:

- Use the **Alignment** buttons in the Formatting toolbar to align text in a cell in relation to the margins. As with any other text, you can right-align, left-align, center, or justify text in a cell.
- Choose the **Align Top**, **Center Vertically**, or **Align Bottom** buttons in the Tables and Borders toolbar to align text or numbers vertically in a cell.
- Click the **Change Text Direction** button in the Tables and Borders toolbar to rotate text within a cell. Use this option to print text vertically along either the right or left side of a cell. When you click on the **Change Text Direction** button the first time, it aligns it along the right side of the cell; click the button a second time and the text moves to the left side; a final click moves the text back to its original location.

Formatting Columns

You can add formatting options to an entire column instead of individual cells.

To format columns:

- Select the entire column by clicking just above the top of the column or columns you want to format.
- Use any of the toolbar buttons to format text in the selected column or columns.
- Choose **Cell Height and Width** from the Table menu. You can make precise adjustments to column widths or the space between columns by entering exact settings on the **Column tab**.

If you want several columns to have the same width, use the Cell Height and Width dialog box or click on the **Distribute Columns Evenly** button instead of adjusting the widths with the ruler or gridlines. Adjusting widths with the dialog box or the **Distribute Columns Evenly** button is much faster and more exact—with the ruler or gridlines, not only do you have to adjust each column separately, but it can be difficult to end up with exactly the same settings for several columns.

Formatting Rows

Formatting rows is similar to formatting columns. You can either format one row or multiple rows. Formatting multiple rows is different from selecting multiple cells. When you format rows, you need to make sure that you have selected the entire row, not just the cells in the row, because rows have different formatting options from cells. To select rows, click outside the table to the left of a row; drag to select additional rows.

Select the row or rows you want to format. Then you can either click on toolbar buttons to format text in the rows, or use the **Row** tab in the Cell Height and Width dialog box:

- Choose **Cell Height and Width** from the Table menu, then click on the **Row tab**. Figure 16.11 shows the **Row** tab.

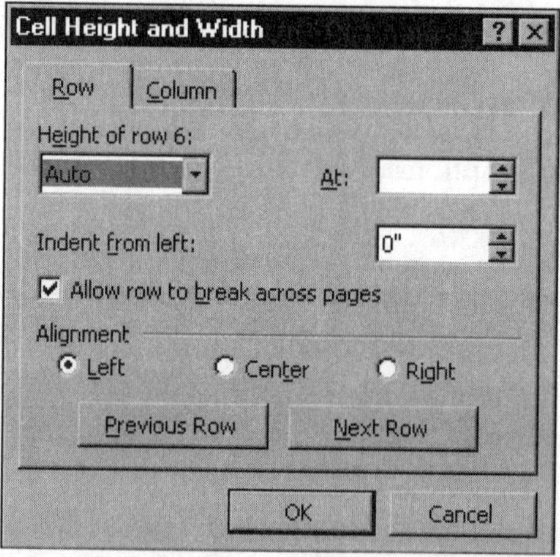

Figure 16.11 The ***Row*** *tab in the Cell Height and Width dialog box.*

- By default, you can enter as many lines of text as you want into a row; the height of the row automatically expands to fit the text. You can specify a row height or a minimum height by selecting an option in the **Height of rows** list and entering a number in the **At** text box.

- Enter a value in the **Indent from left** text box to adjust the left margin for the row or rows.
- By default, if a row won't fit on the current page, the entire row is pushed to the next page. If you want a row to behave like regular text when there's a page break, check the **Allow row to break across pages** check box.

You can designate one row as a heading. The *heading row* appears at the top of each page. To create a heading row:

1. Click in the row you want to appear at the top of each page. For this exercise, click in the first row.
2. Choose **Headings** from the Table menu.
3. Display the Table menu again. Notice that **Headings** is checked, indicating that you have turned on this feature. To turn the heading off, just click on **Headings** again; the headings disappear from your document.

Formatting Tables

Most of the choices here will look familiar to you from working with cells, columns, and even plain text. If you want a particular setting to apply to the whole table, select the entire table.

To format tables:

- Select the entire table, then use the toolbar buttons and menu commands to format text and the table. You can use any of the Formatting toolbar buttons, such as **Bold**, **Italic**, **Underline**, **Highlight**, and **Font Color**. You can also change the font and font size and add bullets or numbering.
- While the entire table is selected, you also have the shortcut menu options to distribute rows or columns evenly and merge cells.
- Use the Table menu to open the Cell Height and Width dialog box to adjust row height and column width for the entire table.

In addition to these routine functions, there are other formatting options that are only used when formatting the entire table:

- You can change table alignment without changing text alignment in individual cells by clicking on the **Align Left**, **Center**, and **Align Right** buttons. This indicates how you want the table placed on the page. These options only make a difference when the table does not stretch across the entire page from margin to margin.
- You can add a caption by choosing **Caption** from the shortcut menu to display the Caption dialog box, shown in Figure 16.12.

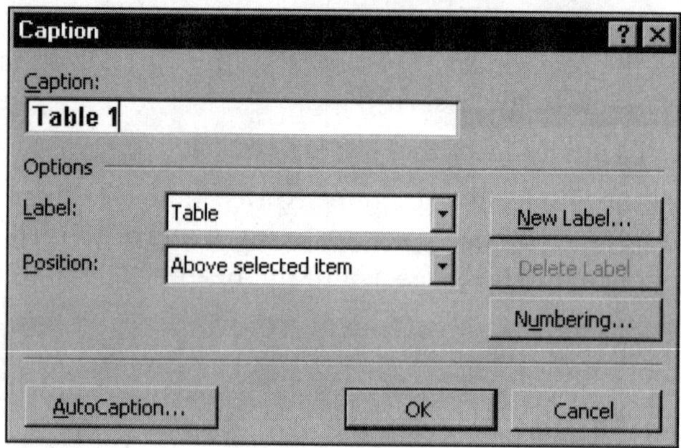

Figure 16.12 *The Caption dialog box.*

You can type additional text in the Caption text box to add a description to it. You can also change the position of the caption, putting it either above or below the table. Additional numbering options become available if you click on the **Numbering** button. You can use either regular Arabic numbers, Roman numerals, or letters for your caption numbers.

Now that you understand the different formatting options, make the following changes to the table you created:

1. Center all the row and column labels. Hint: Use cell formatting for the individual cells containing the text you want to center.
2. Make the top row a heading row. Hint: Use the Table menu.
3. Center the text in the top row. Hint: Format the cell by itself.
4. Change text in the top row to a larger size, and make it bold.

5. Add a caption above the table that includes the table number and the text **Department Budget**. Hint: Select the table and use the **Caption** command on the Table menu.
6. Right-align the cells containing the numbers. Hint: Use the Formatting toolbar.
7. Make the rows a bit taller. Hint: Use the Cell Height and Width dialog box.
8. Center the text vertically in all the cells. Hint: Use the Tables and Borders toolbar.

When you're finished, your table should look like Figure 16.13.

Table 1 Department Budget

Department Budget		
Category	Last Year	This Year
Salaries	$152,334	$380,952
Telephone	$1,890	$2,590
Meeting and Seminar Refreshments	$250	$18,620

Figure 16.13 The sample table with a caption and formatting.

The table is starting to look good. Just a few more touches, and it will be ready to go.

Changing the Border and Line Styles

You can change the borders, lines, and fill patterns for tables just like you did with graphics boxes. If you want, every cell could have a different line style (of course, that would look pretty silly, but it's technically possible).

When you change lines or borders, the changes affect the cell that your insertion point is in or the group of cells selected. The easiest way to change border and line styles is to use the buttons on the Tables and Borders toolbar. There are five basic steps to adding borders to cells, groups of cells, or the entire table:

1. Select a cell or cells.
2. Select a line style.
3. Select a line *weight,* or thickness.
4. Select a border color.
5. Select a border placement.

If you are using the Draw Table tool, which you'll learn about a little later in this chapter, you complete these basic steps before drawing.

To change border and line styles:

1. Place your insertion point in the cell you want or select a group of cells. If you want to place a line around the entire table or fill the table, select the whole table.
2. Display the Line Style list from the Tables and Borders toolbar or choose **Borders and Shading** from the Format menu, then choose a line style. For this exercise, choose the last line style in the list.
3. Display the Line Weight list and choose a line weight. For this exercise, choose **2 _ pt.**
4. Display the Border Color list and choose a border color. For this exercise, choose the dark gray color.
5. Display the Border list. For this exercise, choose **Outside Borders.** The descriptions for each border apply to the selection. For example, if the entire table is selected, **Outside** places a border around the whole thing, as in our example. If only one cell is selected, **Outside** places a line around the outside of the selection only.
6. You can display the Shading Color list to pick a color for the fill inside the selected cells.

In Figure 16.14, I selected the entire table and changed the outside lines. Then I changed the top and bottom lines for the second row to a double line. Finally, I selected the first row and added a 25% shading.

Table 1 Department Budget

Department Budget		
Category	Last Year	This Year
Salaries	$152,334	$380,952
Telephone	$1,890	$2,590
Meeting and Seminar Refreshments	$250	$18,620

Figure 16.14 The sample table with borders and shading applied.

If you want a table without any lines, select the whole table and choose **No Border**.

If you use a thick line style (as I did in Figure 16.14), you might have to adjust your column margins and line height. I had to increase the line height for the first and last rows and increase the column margin for the last column so the text wouldn't be crowded.

I think this table's just about done. Just one more thing: we need to total the columns.

PERFORMING CALCULATIONS ON A COLUMN OR ROW OF NUMBERS

This section serves as a brief (and I hope tantalizing) introduction to all the mathematical calculations you can perform in tables. You can insert complex formulas of your own or use the predefined functions to create forms and reports.

To total the numbers in a column or row:

1. Place your insertion point in the cell just below or to the right of the numbers you want to add. For the sample table, place your insertion point in cell **B6**, the empty cell under $250.00.
2. Click on the **AutoSum** button in the Tables and Borders toolbar.

Voilá! The numbers are totaled without further ado, as shown in Figure 16.15. The formula adds the dollar sign and commas to the number because the numbers above it contain that formatting.

Table 1 Department Budget

Department Budget		
Category	**Last Year**	**This Year**
Salaries	$152,334	$380,952
Telephone	$1,890	$2,590
Meeting and Seminar Refreshments	$250	$18,620
	$154,474.00	

Figure 16.15 *Sample table with the numbers in column B totaled with* ***AutoSum****.*

WARNING

Make sure your insertion point is in the right place before you choose **AutoSum**. If there's anything in the cell, the calculation replaces it. If that happens by mistake, just use the **Undo** feature before you do anything else.

Copying a Formula

To quickly recalculate the sum when any of the numbers change or to copy a formula to another cell and recalculate the correct value, you can recalculate the field.

To recalculate a field:

1. Copy **$154,474.00** and paste it into the next cell, under $18,620.00. Word copies the formula, the formatting, and the exact value. That amount is incorrect, but the cell contains a formula you can use to update the amount.
2. Right-click on the formula you just pasted in cell C6 and choose **Update Field** from the shortcut menu.

Anytime you change one of the numbers above the sum or add an extra row, you can update the field to recalculate the sum. The completed table is shown in Figure 16.16.

Table 1 Department Budget

Department Budget		
Category	**Last Year**	**This Year**
Salaries	$152,334	$380,952
Telephone	$1,890	$2,590
Meeting and Seminar Refreshments	$250	$18,620
TOTAL	$154,474.00	$402,162.00

Figure 16.16 *The completed table.*

AutoSum is one of many spreadsheet functions you can use in your table formulas. *Functions* are predefined math formulas. For example, there's a function called *ROUND* that can round a value up or down to the nearest whole value, and another called *MAX* that can find the largest number in a list. To get quick online help for formulas and functions when you're in a table, choose **Formula** from the Table menu, then press **F1** to access the online Help files.

Using Table AutoFormat

Using the **Table AutoFormat** feature is by far the easiest way to format a table. Once you've created a table and typed your data in it, you can sit back and let the computer do the work of formatting the table. Word includes a gallery of table styles that you can preview, one by one, until you see one you like. Word then applies those formats to your table, and it can even automatically adjust the widths of the columns to fit your text.

You can use Table AutoFormat either on a table with existing formatting or on a new table. Figure 16.17 shows our table with only text formatting applied.

Department Budget		
Category	Last Year	This Year
Salaries	$152,334	$380,952
Telephone	$1,890	$2,590
Meeting and Seminar Refreshments	$250	$18,620
TOTAL	$154,474.00	$402,162.00

Figure 16.17 Table with no formatting.

Let's format it:

1. Click anywhere in the table, then choose **Table AutoFormat** from the Table menu or shortcut menu. This opens the Table AutoFormat dialog box shown in Figure 16.18.

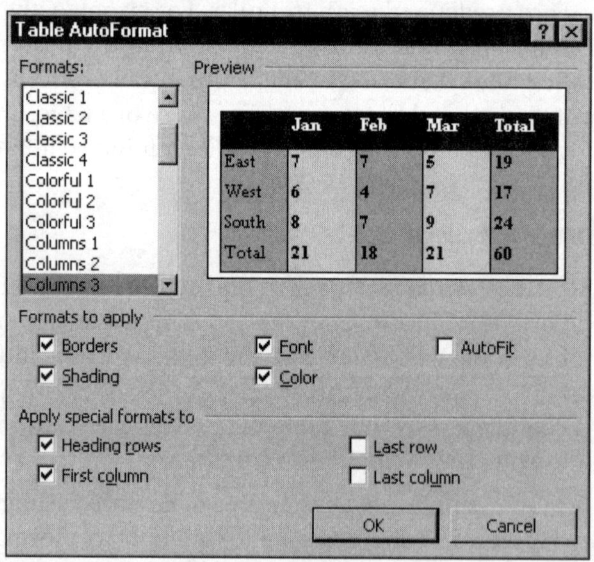

Figure 16.18 Choose a style in the Table AutoFormat dialog box.

Your choices are:

- ✦ You can preview the different styles by clicking on their names in the Formats list.
- ✦ If you want special formats in specific rows or columns, check the items you want to format in the Apply special formats to section. For example, if you check **Heading rows**, **First column**, and **Last row**, Word adds unique formatting to these areas of your document, as shown in the small onscreen preview.
- ✦ Check the options you want to add in the Formats to apply section.

2. After you choose a style and select the options you want, click **OK**. Figure 16.19 shows a table with the Columns 3 style applied.

Department Budget		
Category	Last Year	This Year
Salaries	$152,334	$380,952
Telephone	$1,890	$2,590
Meeting and Seminar Refreshments	$250	$18,620
TOTAL	$154,474.00	$402,162.00

Figure 16.19 *The table with the Columns 3 style applied.*

Using the Draw Tables and Eraser Tools

A terrific new feature in Word lets you draw tables and add individual lines. This is great for complex tables in which you need uneven lines and spaces. You can use the **Draw Tables** tool to draw whole tables, add lines to a new table, or add lines to an existing table.

To draw your own table:

1. Display the Tables and Borders toolbar and select a line style, weight, and color.

2. Click on the **Draw Table** button in the Tools and Borders toolbar, then drag from the location where you want the top-left corner of the table to be to where you want the bottom-right corner to create an empty table.
3. Position the **Draw Table** tool in the table, then click and drag from side-to-side or top-to-bottom to draw lines inside the box.
4. When all the lines are complete, click on the **Draw Table** button to turn off the **Draw Table** tool.

NOTE

Use the **Draw** tool with a regular table to add extra lines in the precise spots you want them.

Erasing Lines with the Eraser Tool

One of the advantages of using the **Draw Table** tool is that you can experiment with unusual line placement. The **Eraser** tool works with the **Draw Table** tool to make this possible.

To erase lines:

1. Click on the **Eraser** button in the Tables and Borders toolbar.
2. Position the eraser mouse pointer over the line you want to delete, drag to highlight the line, and then release the mouse button. You can delete all of a line or pieces of one line dissected by another.
3. Click on the **Eraser** button to turn off the **Eraser** tool. Figure 16.20 shows a table created with the **Eraser** and **Drawing** tools.

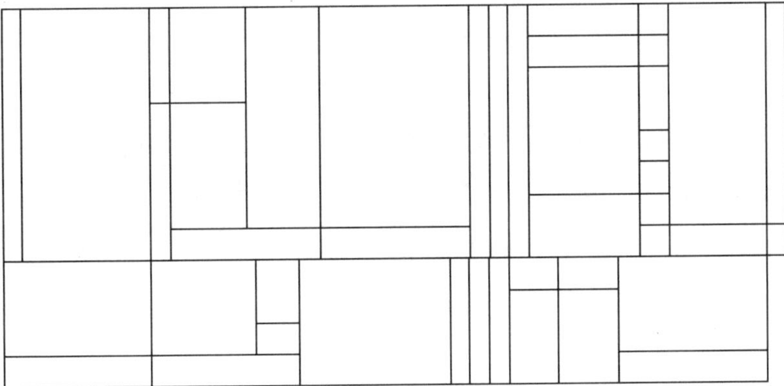

Figure 16.20 Table created with the ***Eraser*** *and* ***Drawing*** *tools.*

Sorting Tables

Word can sort information that's in table format, but a table sort can be a little tricky. In a basic table, you can click in the column you want to sort by, then click on the **Sort Ascending** button in the Tables and Borders toolbar. It couldn't be easier.

However, because tables can contain complex formatting, headers, split and joined cells, and many other elements, the results of a table sort can be unpredictable.

What's the solution? Always save before you try a table sort in case the sort goes bad on you. The real solution is to select the rows you want sorted before you perform the sort. Figure 16.21 shows the table (before sorting) with the middle three rows selected.

Department Budget		
Category	Last Year	This Year
Salaries	$152,334	$380,952
Telephone	$1,890	$2,590
Meeting and Seminar Refreshments	$250	$18,620
TOTAL	$154,474.00	$402,162.00

Figure 16.21 The table with the rows you want to sort selected.

To sort selected rows:

1. Select the rows to sort, then choose **Sort** from the Table menu. This displays the Sort dialog box, shown in Figure 16.22.

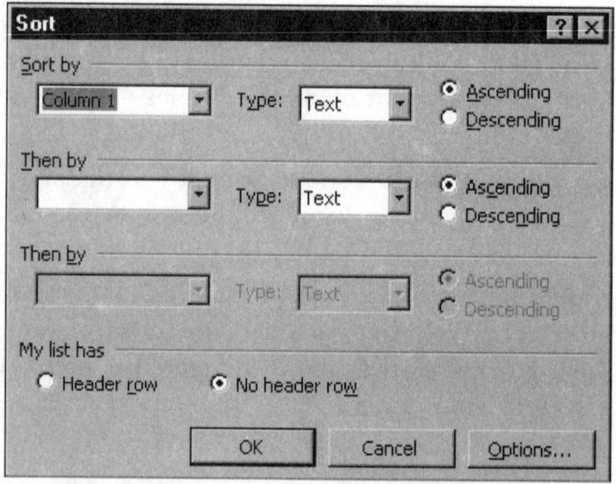

Figure 16.22 The Sort dialog box.

2. You want to sort by the text in column 1, so click **OK**. Word sorts the selected rows by column 1, as shown in Figure 16.23.

Department Budget		
Category	Last Year	This Year
Meeting and Seminar Refreshments	$250	$18,620
Salaries	$152,334	$380,952
Telephone	$1,890	$2,590
TOTAL	$154,474.00	$402,162.00

Figure 16.23 *The sorted table.*

Notice that only the selected rows were affected; everything else stayed put.

CONVERTING EXISTING TEXT TO A TABLE

Columns you've created and separated with tabs can be easily converted into Word tables. Why convert them? Once you've placed the rows of text in a table, it's much easier to adjust the widths of the columns, reshape the table, and apply formatting, such as gridlines, to separate the rows and columns of the table.

When you convert a selection of text into a table, Word automatically calculates how many rows and columns the table needs to incorporate all the text. When you specify the marker (usually a tab) that should divide each column of the table, Word figures out what the maximum number of columns needs to be and goes on from there.

To turn existing text into a table:

1. Select the text you want to turn into a table. Don't select the empty paragraphs before or after the text, or they will be included in the table as blank rows.
2. Choose **Convert Text to Table** from the Table menu. This displays the Convert Text to Table dialog box shown in Figure 16.24.

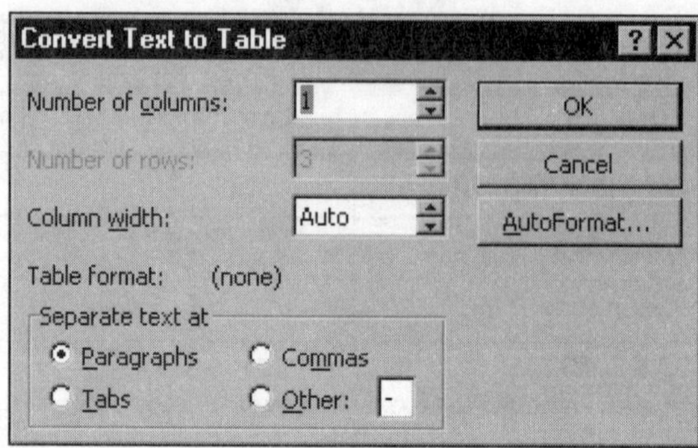

Figure 16.24 The Convert Text to Table dialog box.

In the dialog box, Word automatically selects the most likely candidate as the marker between columns. You can also separate columns with paragraphs, commas, or some other symbol you specify.

3. In the Separate text at box, select the punctuation mark used between columns, if it's different from Word's guess. Tabs between column items are most common, though some lists are separated by commas or spaces. If you select **Paragraph**, be warned that you'll probably end up with a single-column table.
4. Click **OK** to convert the text to a table.

If you want to accept Word's guesses for converting the text, you can skip the dialog box and just click on the **Insert Table** button on the Standard toolbar. Word then creates the table in a single step.

COPYING A TABLE

Copying a table or any portion of one is similar to copying regular text. Select the entire table or the cells you want to copy and choose **Copy** from the Edit menu or shortcut menu. You can also click on the **Copy** button in the Standard toolbar. After you copy a table, you can use the **Paste** command to paste the table at any location.

Deleting a Table (or Part of One)

Now that you've created this masterpiece, I'll tell you how to tear it apart or get rid of it. (If you want to keep the sample table, be sure you save it before you proceed.)

To delete an entire table:

1. Select the entire table.
2. Choose **Delete Columns** from the Table menu. The Table disappears. Remember, you can use the **Undo** command to retrieve deleted tables.

To delete the table contents while keeping the structure:

1. Select the entire table.
2. Choose **Clear** from the Edit menu or press the **Delete** key.

If you select a column or a row, choose **Delete Columns** or **Delete Rows** from either the Table menu or the shortcut menu to delete a column or row. Word resizes the table after the existing cells or columns are deleted.

If your insertion point is in one cell or if you have anything less than the entire table selected, choose **Delete Cells** from the Table menu or the shortcut menu. You'll get the Delete cells dialog box shown in Figure 16.25.

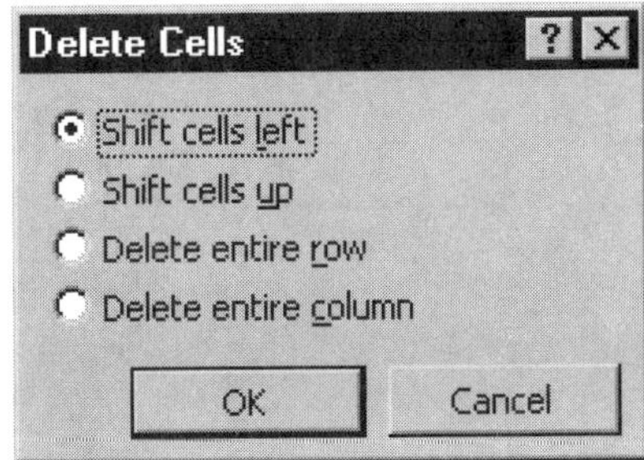

Figure 16.25 *The Delete Cells dialog box.*

You have the following options:

- Choose **Shift cells left** to delete the current column or selected columns and move existing cells to the left in the selected rows.
- Choose **Shift cells up** to delete the current row or selected rows and move existing cells up to fill in the blank spaces.
- Choose **Delete entire row** to delete the row in which the selected cells are located.
- Choose **Delete entire column** to delete all cells and data in the current column.

From Here...

As you've seen, Tables is an extremely powerful and multifaceted feature—and we hardly even scratched the surface in terms of the spreadsheet capabilities! As you work with tables, you'll continue to discover new uses. And if you discover that your spreadsheet needs to go beyond Word's capabilities, be sure to check out Microsoft Excel 97, which is included in the Microsoft Office 97 suite.

In the next chapter, we'll take a look at the Columns feature—another way of formatting text in rows and columns. And you'll learn how to set up automatically formatted bulleted and numbered lists.

CHAPTER 17

Columns and Labels

Let's talk about:

- ✦ Creating newspaper columns
- ✦ Creating mailing labels

In the last chapter, you learned about tables, one of Word's most powerful tools. But Word doesn't stop with just one feature for dividing a page into columns and rows; Columns and Labels give you different ways of breaking a page into smaller parts.

USING COLUMNS

You can become an instant desktop publisher by using multiple columns in your documents—as long as you use them where they add value rather than using them to impress. The type of columns Word lets you create are called *newspaper columns.* They get their name from (you guessed it) newspapers. Newspaper articles are usually laid out in two or more columns, and the text wraps from the bottom of one column to the top of the next. Newsletters are another common application for newspaper-style columns. With newspaper-style columns, the text flows to the bottom margin before it wraps to the next column.

Good uses for columns include long lists of short items (like name and address lists), indexes such as the one at the back of this book, and newsletters and newspapers. In general, good situations for using running columns are those that require quick skimming (such as newsletters and indexes) or long lists that would otherwise leave two-thirds of the page empty. Figures 17.1 through 17.3 show a few examples.

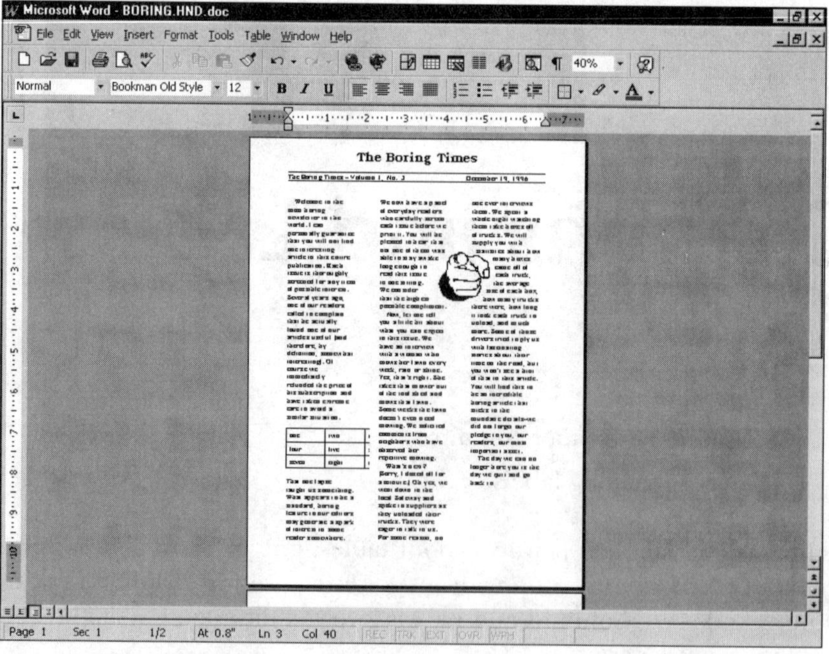

Figure 17.1 *A newsletter that uses columns.*

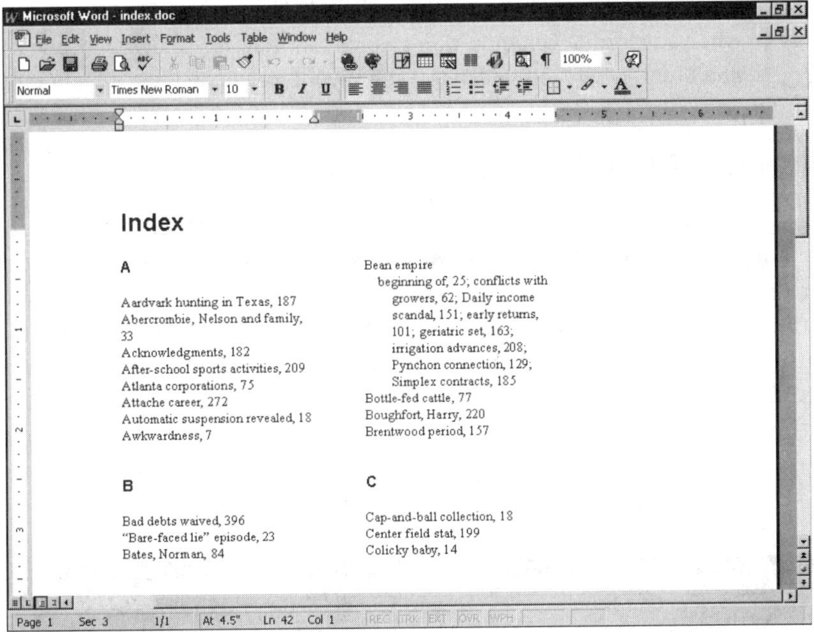

Figure 17.2 *A multicolumn index.*

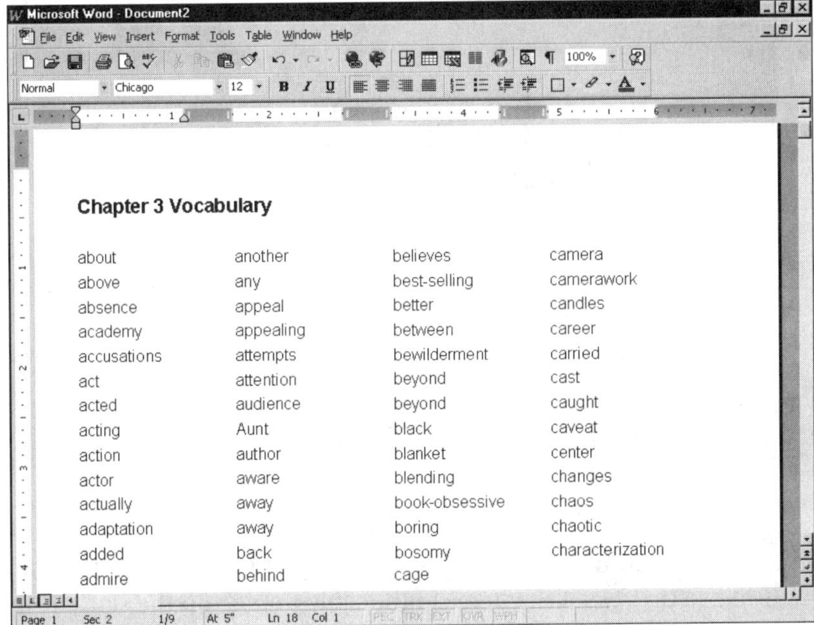

Figure 17.3 *A list broken down into columns.*

NOTE

If you're editing in Normal view and it looks like you've lost most of your page when you format columns, don't worry. Normal view shows only one column at a time—when you switch to Page Layout view, you'll see all your columns.

Columns versus Tables

Because tables also use columns, let's quickly go over the difference between table columns and newspaper columns. *Table columns* are groups of independent cells. You can move a column as a whole or trade its position with another column. Generally, however, each row of a table needs to stay together. If you delete an item from the first column and move everything else up, you may have suddenly assigned the Western region sales figures to the Northern region. While it is true that you can arrange several columns together in a table to look like newspaper columns, it's not very convenient. For example, consider the table shown in Figure 17.4.

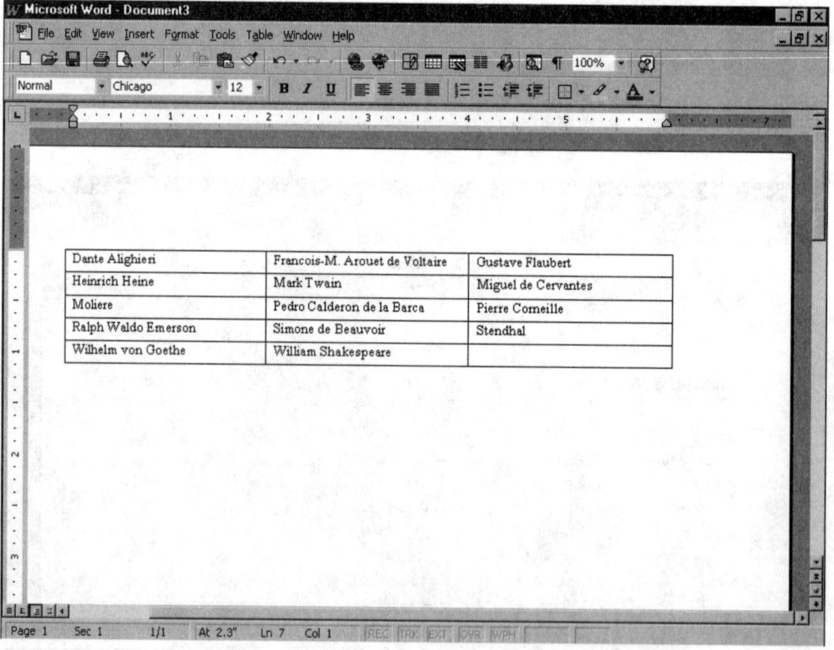

Dante Alighieri	Francois-M. Arouet de Voltaire	Gustave Flaubert
Heinrich Heine	Mark Twain	Miguel de Cervantes
Moliere	Pedro Calderon de la Barca	Pierre Corneille
Ralph Waldo Emerson	Simone de Beauvoir	Stendhal
Wilhelm von Goethe	William Shakespeare	

Figure 17.4 *This list shouldn't be formatted as a table.*

If you decide to add or delete an item in the middle of the table, you must manually move the rest of the items in the table to pick up the slack. If you do any editing, this will soon become frustrating. A table format works best when the corresponding items in each column—the rows—have a relationship to each other, as in Figure 17.5.

Redwood City	Walnut Creek	Portland	Houston	Minneapolis
1972	1978	1984	1989	1996
7 years	7 years	6 years	5 years	7 years

Figure 17.5 *A good use for a table.*

Running columns, on the other hand, don't come in rows. If one row of one column bears a relationship to the same row in a neighboring column, it's purely by chance. Use running columns where a single long column running down a page would mean no loss of information. Using narrower columns uses space more efficiently.

In Figure 17.4, adding and removing names from the list formatted as a table would be very tedious. In running columns, nothing could be easier (see Figure 17.6).

Dante Alighieri
Francois-M. Arouet de Voltaire
Gustave Flaubert
Heinrich Heine
Mark Twain
Miguel de Cervantes
Moliere
Pedro Calderon de la Barca
Pierre Corneille
Ralph Waldo Emerson
Simone de Beauvoir
Stendhal
Wilhelm von Goethe
William Shakespeare

Figure 17.6 *The name list formatted with the Columns feature.*

If you insert a line to type a new name or remove a name, Word automatically reflows the text through the columns so that you don't have to.

Arranging Text in Columns

Like the other page formatting options, you can apply column formatting to a whole document or to a selected part of it. If your document will contain a mixture of single- and multicolumn sections, it's easiest to select the text you want to arrange in running columns and apply column formatting to the selected text. That way, you don't need to insert section breaks manually.

To arrange text in running columns:

1. To see the section and column formatting, change to Page Layout view and click the **Show/Hide ¶** button on the Standard toolbar. Choose **Page Layout** from the View menu if you're not using that view already. Page Layout view lets you see what multiple columns will look like on a page, while the **Show/Hide ¶** button displays the section and column breaks on the page.
2. Select the text you want to format in columns, or place the insertion point anywhere in the section you want to format. If your document contains only one section, placing your insertion point anywhere in the document before you proceed will format the entire document.
3. On the Standard toolbar, click the **Columns** button and drag to select the number of columns you want, as shown in Figure 17.7.

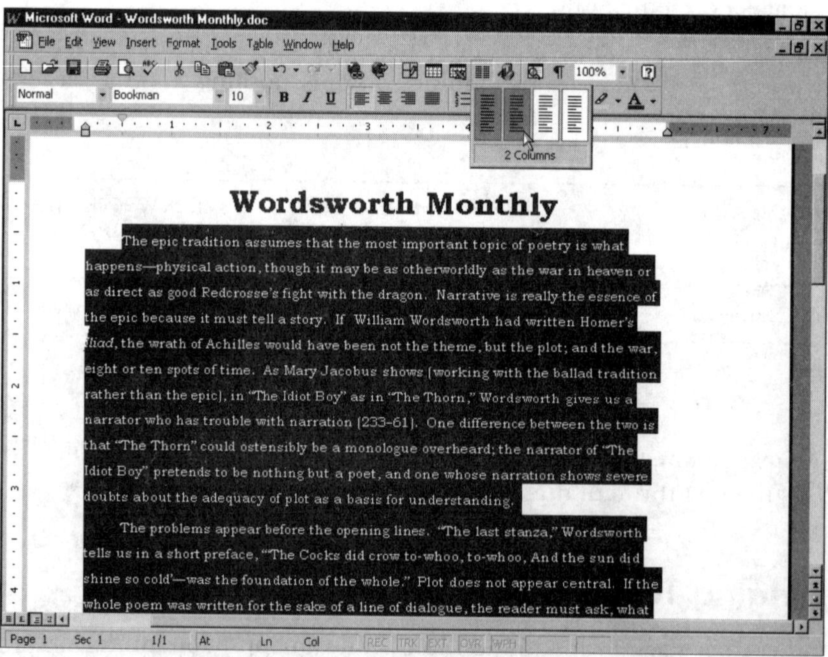

*Figure 17.7 Click the **Columns** button.*

Word inserts section breaks around the selected text and changes the column formatting, as shown in Figure 17.8.

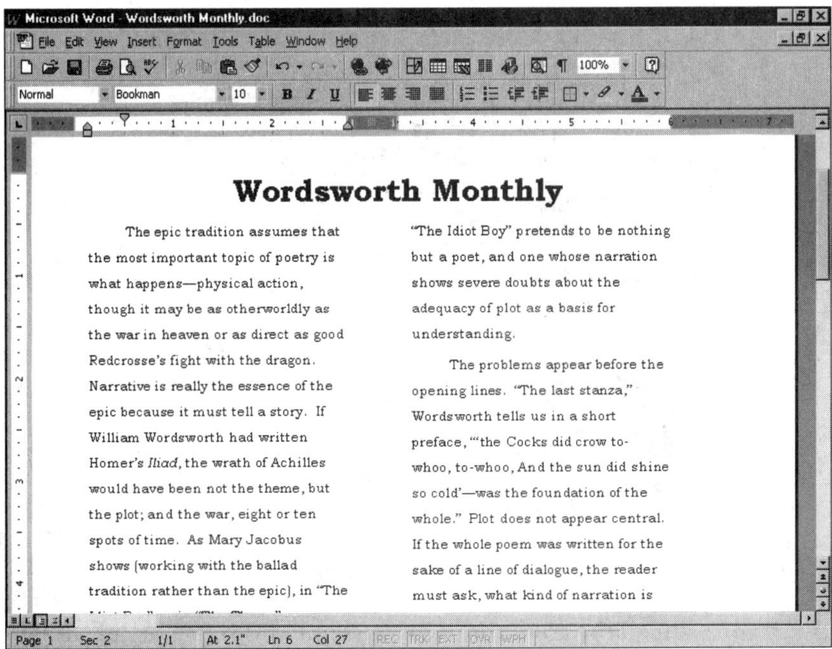

Figure 17.8 *Text formatted in two columns.*

If you want to undo the column formatting, click anywhere in the section, click the **Columns** button, and select **1 Column**.

Adjusting the Space between Columns

By default, Word leaves a minimum of half an inch of space between running columns on a page. If that seems too wide because of the font size you're using or too narrow because of a large font size or wide page margins, you can adjust the spacing between columns.

To adjust the space between columns:

1. Click anywhere in the columns without selecting any text. If you select text, Word will apply the settings only to the selected text rather than to the whole section of columns.

2. Choose **Columns** from the Format menu to open the Columns dialog box shown in Figure 17.9.

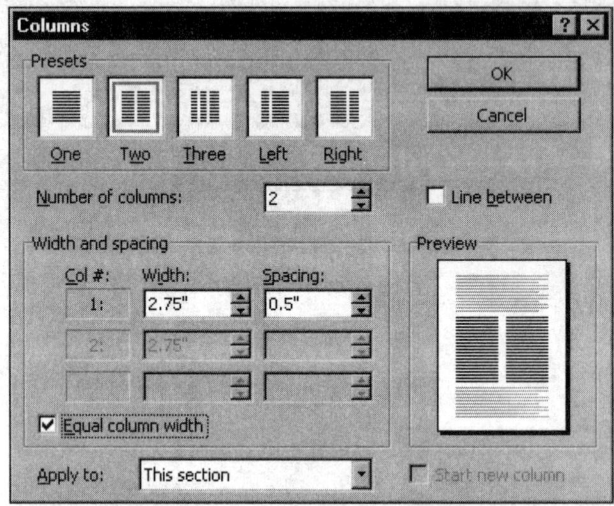

Figure 17.9 The Columns dialog box.

3. If you want all the columns to be the same width, make sure the **Equal column width** check box is selected.
4. In the Spacing box, specify the distance you want between columns and click **OK**.

Notice that the spacing you set is a minimum space between widths, not necessarily an exact one. If your columns are left-aligned (and thus have a ragged right edge), the space between columns will be slightly greater next to the lines that don't go all the way to the paragraph edge. If you format the paragraph as justified, the paragraph spacing will be exact. However, the narrower a justified column is, the more likely it is that some columns will have large chunks of white space in them to make the lines end evenly.

Making Columns an Unequal Width

In most cases, you'll use columns of equal width in running columns. The text looks better on the page and is easier to read when it's symmetrical. But for those times when you need the variety of unequal column widths, Word makes it easy for you.

To make running columns of unequal width:

1. Click anywhere in a section of multiple columns without selecting any text. If text is selected, only that text will have the new column formatting.
2. Choose **Columns** from the Format menu.
3. Clear the **Equal column width** check box. When this check box is deselected, you can adjust the width of any column.
4. Under Width, enter a width measurement for each column. As you change each width measurement, Word automatically adjusts the later column widths, keeping them in proportion. If you enter a width that's greater than the space remaining, Word borrows from previous column widths to make up the difference (see Figure 17.10).

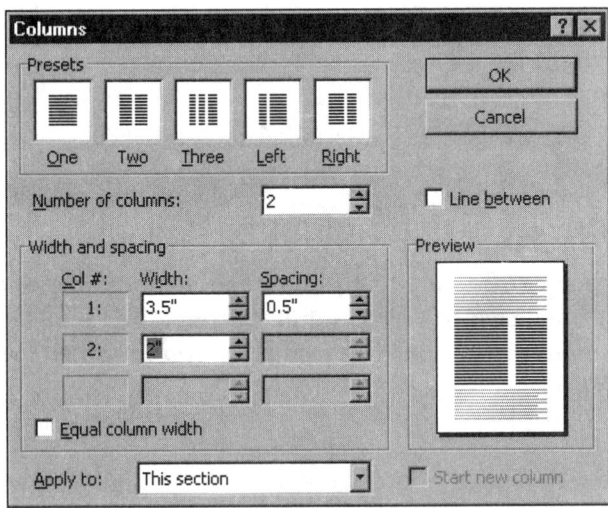

Figure 17.10 Defining unequal column widths.

5. Check the Preview box to see what your columns will look like and click **OK**. The result is shown in Figure 17.11.

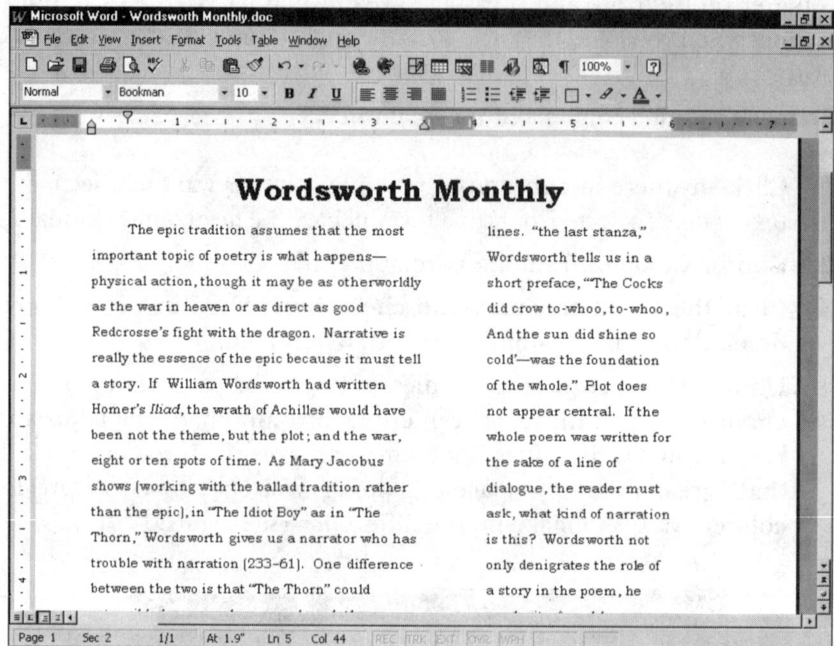

Figure 17.11 Columns with unequal widths.

Adding Lines between Columns

A vertical line between columns can add definition and focus to the page. To insert a vertical line between each column, just check the **Line between** check box in the Columns dialog box. The result is shown in Figure 17.12.

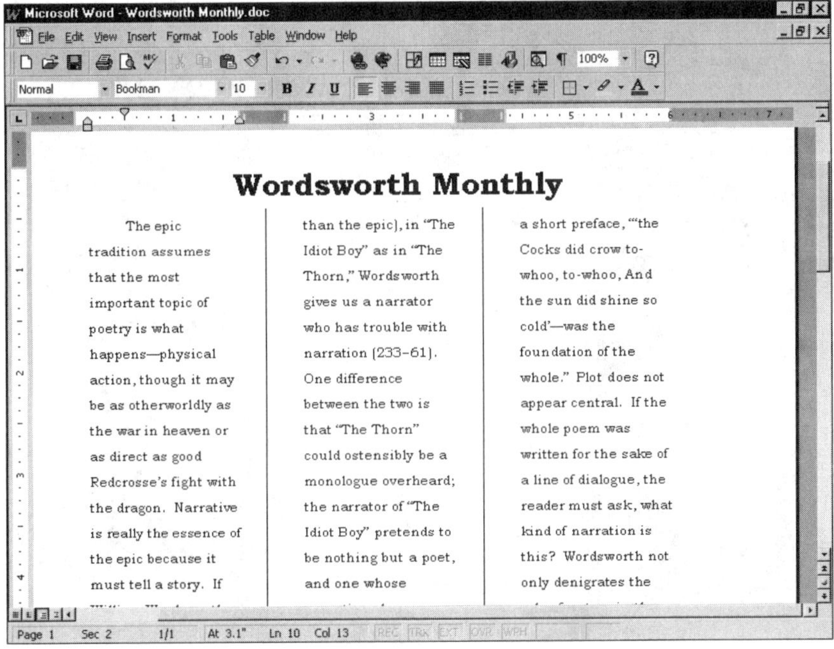

Figure 17.12 Vertical lines between columns.

Starting a New Column

To break a column before the end of the page, choose **Break** from the Insert menu and **Column Break** from the Break dialog box. This inserts a manual column break at the insertion point location and forces the remaining text to the beginning of the next column. This is useful in a newsletter, for example, if you want the story headline to always appear at the top of a column. If you insert a column break in a simple, one-column document, it has the same effect as a manual page break.

Balancing the Length of Columns

With regular newspaper-style columns, the text flows to the bottom margin before it wraps to the next column. This can result in uneven column lengths, as shown in Figure 17.13.

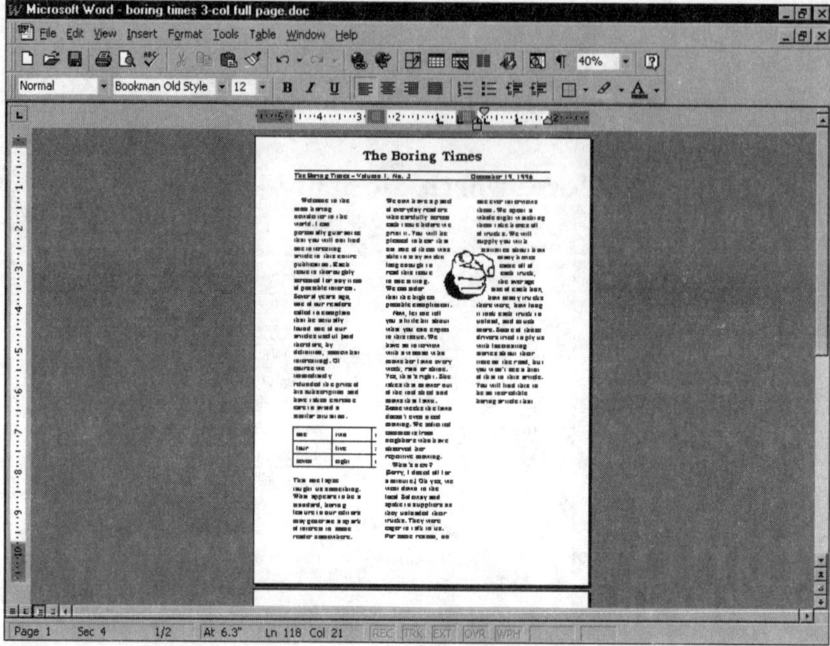

Figure 17.13 Newspaper columns with uneven column lengths.

To balance the text equally between columns:

1. From Page Layout view, place your insertion point at the end of the columns you want to balance.
2. Choose **Break** from the Insert menu to open the Break dialog box shown in Figure 17.14.

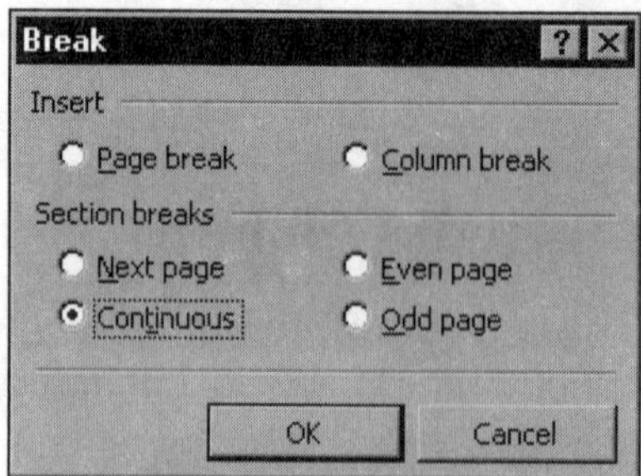

Figure 17.14 The Break dialog box.

3. Choose **Continuous** from the Section breaks section, then click **OK**. The section break that Word inserts forces the column text to balance equally among the columns, as shown in Figure 17.15.

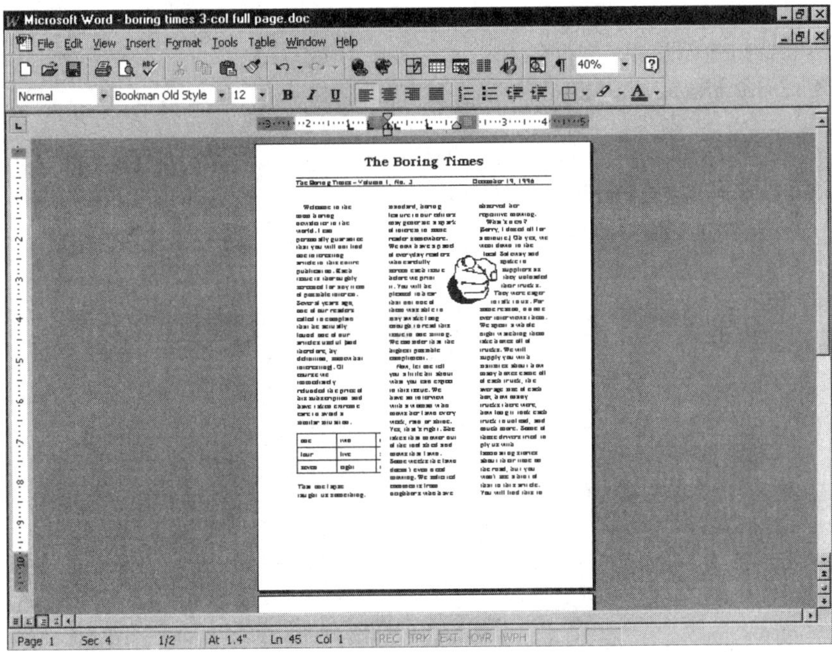

Figure 17.15 Balanced newspaper columns.

Creating Mailing Labels

As with envelopes, Word takes the calculating, measuring, formatting, and tedium out of printing sheets of labels. You can easily print a whole page of labels for a single commonly used address, create a table for typing in any set of addresses, or print a single label in a specified position on the page. Being able to print a single label is particularly useful. Because you don't always print entire pages of labels at the same time, many labels can be wasted. Word lets you specify the row and column of the next available label on a sheet and prints only on that label. This way, you can easily print one label at a time without wasting supplies.

You're not limited to address and shipping labels, by the way. Word includes preconfigured settings for not only the most common brands and sizes of address labels, but also file folder labels, name tags, videocassette tags, floppy disk labels, and others. Each type of label is identified by its product number, so when you buy labels at the store you can make sure that your printer will print them correctly.

To print a single label:

1. With a letter or any other document open, choose **Envelopes and Labels** from the Tools menu.
2. Click the **Labels** tab (shown in Figure 17.16).

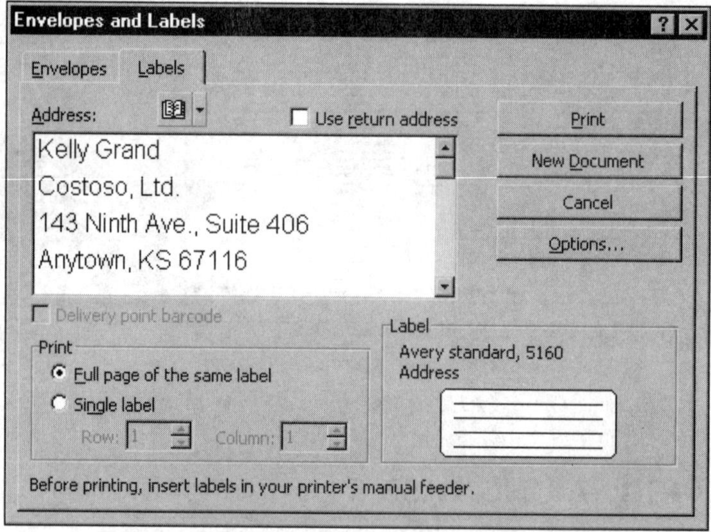

***Figure 17.16** The **Labels** tab in the Envelopes and Labels dialog box.*

3. In the Address box, type the information you want to appear on the label.
4. If you want to use your own address for a self-addressed envelope or mailer, select the **Use return address** check box.
5. Select the **Delivery point barcode** check box to insert a postal bar code on the label. This makes sense only if you're using an address label. If this option is unavailable, it's because the type of label you've chosen doesn't have room for a bar code.

6. Select **Single label** and specify the row or column of the next label you want to print.
7. Click **Options** to open the Label Options dialog box shown in Figure 17.17

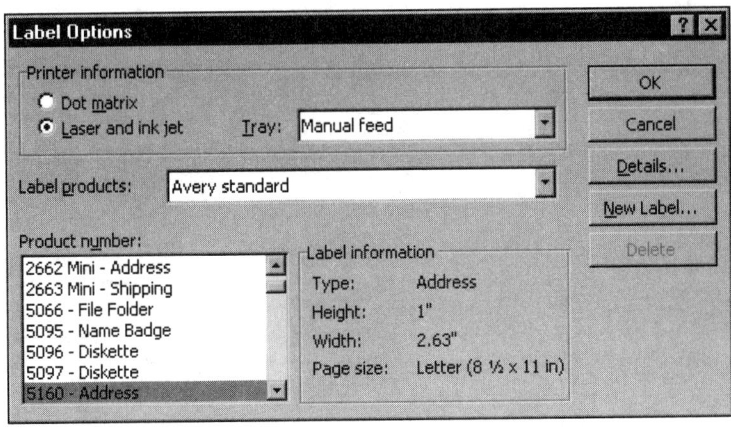

Figure 17.17 The Label Options dialog box.

8. Select your label type from the Product number list and click **OK** to return to the **Labels** tab.
9. Insert the page of labels in your printer tray and click **Print**.

To print a whole page of labels:

1. With any document open, choose **Envelopes and Labels** from the Tools menu.
2. Click the **Labels** tab.
3. In the Address box, type the information for the first label.
4. Select **Full page of the same label**.
5. Choose **Options**, select the label's product number, and click **OK**.
6. Click **Print** or **New Document**.

The **Print** button automatically prints a full page of identical labels. The **New Document** button creates a table with each label in a separate cell. If you want a page of different labels, you can edit the addresses or other information in the resulting table (see Figure 17.18).

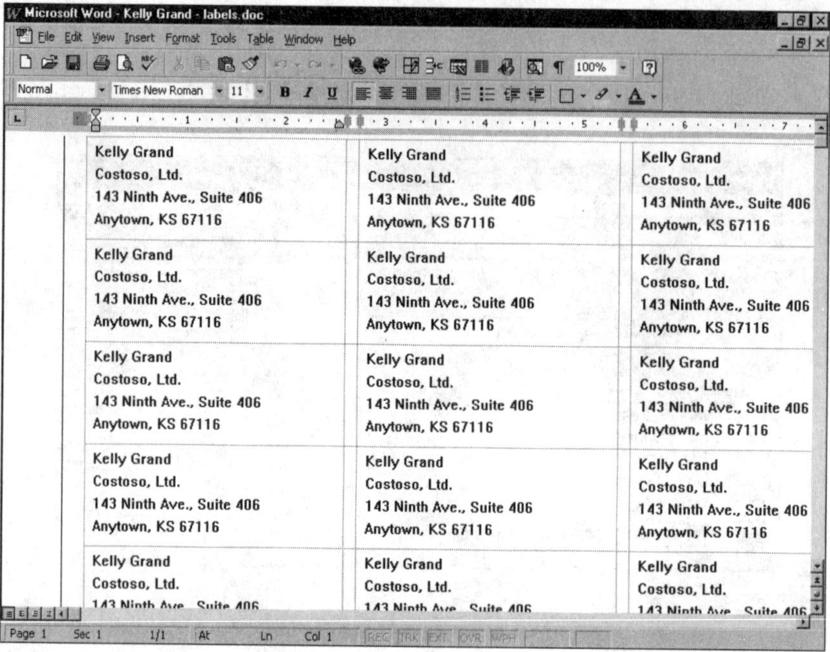

Figure 17.18 A page of identical labels that you can edit.

When you edit the table of labels, you don't need to worry about the height or width of cells, which is fixed. The left indent for each paragraph in the cell in the table is also preset. However, the first line in each label needs a specific Spacing Before paragraph setting. Before you edit the table, click in the first line, choose **Paragraph** from the Format menu, and look up the Spacing Before setting. When you're finished editing, apply that setting to the first line of each label.

Creating Mailing Labels from an Existing Address List

In the previous section, you learned how to create a page of identical labels and then edit the information on each label to create an address list. If you have a large list of mailing addresses or other information that's already in a document or database, you can avoid retyping all that information for your labels by using the **Mail Merge** feature.

This section gives you basic instructions for merging an address list to labels. For more specific information about Mail Merge, see Chapter 19.

To use Mail Merge to create labels:

1. From a blank document screen, choose **Mail Merge** from the Tools menu.
2. Click **Create**, then choose **Mailing Labels** from the list shown in Figure 17.19.

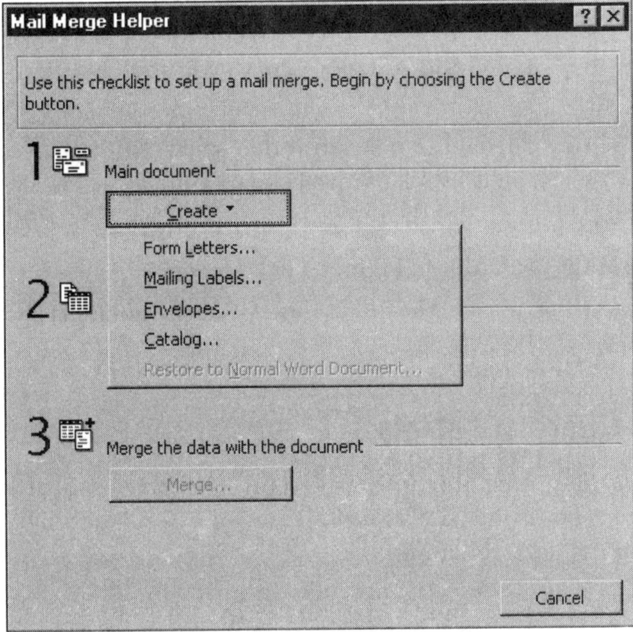

Figure 17.19 *The Create drop-down list in the Mail Merge Helper dialog box.*

3. Click **Active Window** to create the merge document in the current document window, or click **New Main Document** to open a new document window.

4. Click **Get Data** from the Mail Merge Helper:
   - If you already have a list of addresses you want to use, click **Open Data Source**.
   - If the addresses are in your Office address book, click **Use Address Book**.
   - If you need to create the address list from scratch, click **Create Data Source**.

NOTE

See Chapter 19 for instructions on creating a data source document and inserting merge fields in a main document.

5. After you specify the data source, click **Set Up Main Document**. Word opens the Label Options dialog box so you can choose the labels you want to use.
6. Choose your labels and make any other selections in the Label Options dialog box, then click **OK**. Word opens a Create Labels dialog box.
7. Insert the merge fields you want to use on the labels, then click **OK**.
8. Back in the Mail Merge Helper, click **Merge**.
9. Click **Printer** in the Merge to box to send the labels directly to the printer.

Creating Custom Labels

Word contains definitions for most common label types, but if the one you want isn't listed, no problem. You can create your own labels by telling Word how to format the label document.

1. Choose **Envelopes and Labels** from the Tools menu and select the Labels tab. The dialog box will say *New Custom laser* (Figure 17.20) or *New Custom dot matrix,* depending on which type of printer you have selected.

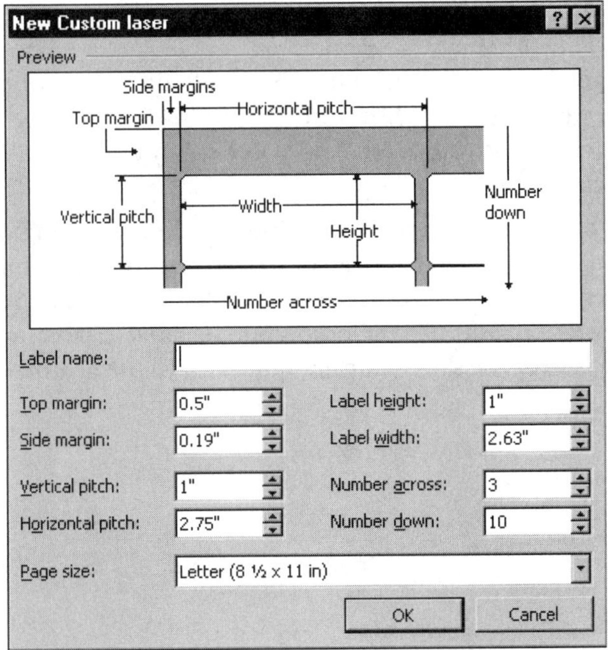

Figure 17.20 The New Custom laser dialog box.

2. Enter a name in the Label name box.
3. Enter the dimensions and other specifications for your label, then click **OK**.

The new label will be displayed in the Product number list and can be selected just like any other label.

If you don't see the exact labels you have in the product list, you can often substitute another definition that matches your labels. For example, your labels might not be Avery, but if they have the same dimensions as the Avery 5160 labels, you can use that label.

From Here...

It just keeps getting better and better. Not only do you have the power of tables to work with, you know how to use columns for those occasions when tables aren't quite what you need. And you can whip out a sheet of mailing labels in a flash.

The next chapters begin a journey into new and exciting territory: the world of automation tools. In a way, all of Word's features are automation tools, but the features in the next section are specifically designed to speed and automate word processing tasks. The first two, AutoText and macros, are among the most powerful, and at the same time are quite easy to use at a basic level.

SECTION VI

Automation Tools

CHAPTER 18

An Introduction to AutoText and Macros

Let's talk about:

- Recycling your work with AutoText
- Creating an AutoText entry
- Inserting AutoText
- Using AutoComplete
- Recording a simple macro
- Editing macro text
- Pausing during macro recording

Recycling Your Work with AutoText

In any kind of writing, we type some of the same phrases, format some of the same sentences, and insert some of the same pictures time after time. Think of how often you've typed your company name, a product name, the closing to a letter. Wouldn't it be great to skip some of that repetitive typing?

That's what the AutoText feature is for. AutoText, known as the *glossary* in earlier versions of Word, lets you assign abbreviations to frequently used passages of text (whether formatted or unformatted), graphics, tables—virtually anything you can insert in a Word document. Once an AutoText entry has been defined, you just type your abbreviation and press **F3** to insert the whole entry, replacing the abbreviation.

With AutoText entries defined, you could merely type **AML** to get *Amalgamated Manufacturing Limited*, type a few characters to insert your company's graphic logo, or insert a preformatted table with just a few keystrokes.

To create an AutoText entry:

1. Select the text, table, picture, or other object that you want to store for re-use. If you want to include the paragraph formatting in the AutoText entry, be sure to select the paragraph mark.
2. Choose **AutoText** from the Insert menu and **New** from the AutoText menu (or press **Alt+F3**) to open the Create AutoText dialog box shown in Figure 18.1.

   Word takes part of the selected text and places it in the text box as the suggested name.
3. If you don't like the name Word suggests, type an abbreviation or short word in the text box. Don't make this word too long, because the idea is to save time. This is the abbreviation you'll type in a document to insert this entry.
4. Click **OK**.

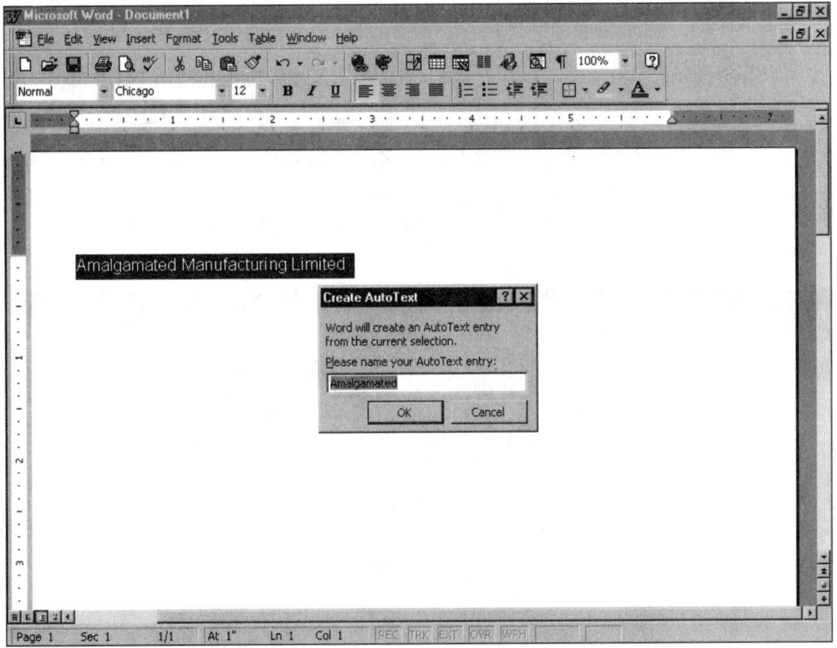

Figure 18.1 The Create AutoText dialog box.

The AutoText entry you just added is now available for use. In this document or another document based on the same template (usually the Normal template), you can type this abbreviation and press **F3**. You can define many different AutoText entries. Because they're saved in the template, they're still available after you exit and restart Word.

To insert an AutoText entry with a keystroke:

1. Type the abbreviation you defined for an AutoText entry. As you type, a prompt will pop-up displaying the entry.
2. Press **F3** or **Enter**. The AutoText entry you specified is inserted in the document, replacing the abbreviation you typed. If the computer beeps and doesn't insert anything, then the abbreviation you typed is not the name of an available AutoText entry.

To insert an AutoText entry from a list:

1. Place your insertion point where you want to insert the AutoText entry.
2. Choose **AutoText** from the Insert menu and select the entry you want from the list shown in Figure 18.2. Notice that the entries are broken down by category. As you point to a category, it expands to display a list of entries—just find the entry you want and select it.

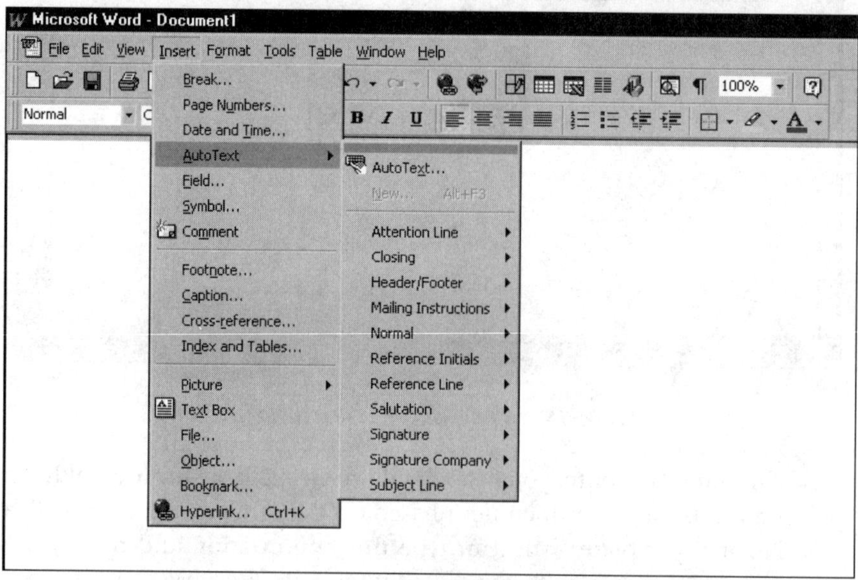

Figure 18.2 *You can insert AutoText entries directly from the Insert menu.*

To insert an AutoText entry from the dialog box:

1. Click to place the insertion point where you want to insert the AutoText entry.
2. Choose **AutoText** from the Insert menu and choose **AutoText** again from the AutoText menu. This displays the **AutoText** tab in the AutoCorrect dialog box, as shown in Figure 18.3.

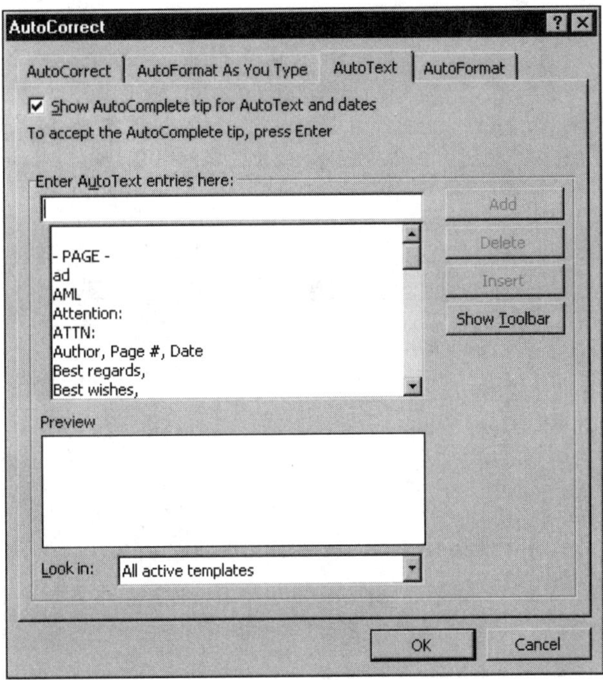

Figure 18.3 *The AutoCorrect dialog box.*

3. Select the name of the AutoText entry you want. The Preview box displays part of that item's contents, as shown in Figure 18.4.

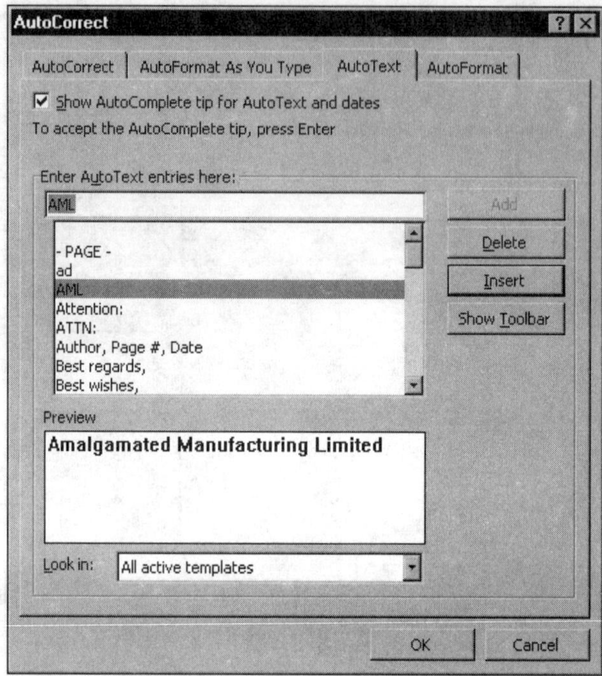

Figure 18.4 When an entry is selected, its contents are displayed in the Preview box.

4. Click **Insert**. Word inserts the selected entry at the insertion point. If text is already selected when you insert the AutoText entry, the AutoText entry replaces the selected text.

To insert an AutoText entry with AutoComplete:

1. First, make sure **Show AutoComplete tip for AutoText and dates** is checked in the **AutoText** tab.
2. Type the first few characters of the entry. A prompt will appear above your insertion point that contains the text for the entry.
3. To insert the entry, press **Enter** or **F3**. If you don't want to insert the entry, just keep typing, and Word will ignore the AutoText prompt.

AutoComplete only works if the abbreviation you use for the AutoText entry contains at least four characters.

To delete an AutoText entry:

1. Display the **AutoText** tab in the AutoCorrect dialog box.
2. Select the entry you want to delete and click **Delete**.

You can't use **Undo** to get back an AutoText entry that you've deleted by mistake. If this happens, you have to re-create the entry from scratch.

Using the AutoText Toolbar

Word has an AutoText toolbar that places all the AutoText entries and commands a mouse click away.

- To display the AutoText toolbar (shown in Figure 18.5), choose **Show Toolbar** from the **AutoText** tab in the AutoCorrect dialog box, or right-click on any toolbar and choose **AutoText** from the Toolbar list.

Figure 18.5 *The AutoText toolbar.*

- The **AutoText** button on the far left opens the **AutoText** tab, which gives you access to all AutoText options.
- The **All Entries** list contains all the currently available AutoText entries. To insert an entry, just select it from the list.
- The **New** button is for creating new AutoText entries. This button is only active when text or some other object is selected.

Printing AutoText Entries

It can be difficult to keep track of which AutoText entries are available where. So Word gives you a way to print a list that contains the names and contents of all the AutoText entries attached to the current document.

To print a list of AutoText entries, open the document for which you want the list. Choose **Print** from the File menu to open the Print dialog box, choose **AutoText entries** from the Print what drop-down list, and click **OK**.

Recycling Your Work with AutoCorrect

In Chapter 11, you learned about using AutoCorrect to fix typographical errors as you type. If you're a big fan of automation, you can use AutoCorrect the same way you use AutoText. Instead of pressing **F3** after typing an abbreviation, you can just continue typing and the abbreviation will be changed automatically.

When you use AutoCorrect this way, there's a subtle difference from AutoText you should be aware of. If you pick a normal word with AutoText, it's okay because nothing happens until you press **F3**. But if you pick a common word with AutoCorrect, every time you type that word—whether you mean to expand it or not—the word is changed to the AutoCorrect entry you defined.

But with that caveat, AutoCorrect is a great way to quickly expand abbreviations and insert common graphics, formatted tables, and other objects in a document.

To define an AutoCorrect entry:

1. Select the text, table, graphic, or other object you want to re-use.
2. Choose **AutoCorrect** from the Tools menu. Figure 18.6 shows the **AutoCorrect** tab in the AutoCorrect dialog box.

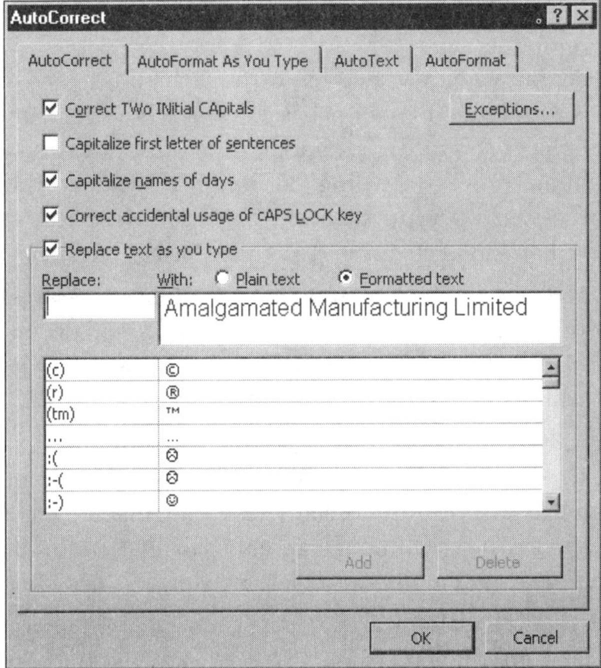

Figure 18.6 The ***AutoCorrect*** *tab in the AutoCorrect dialog box.*

The selected text appears automatically in the With box.

3. In the Replace box, type the abbreviation or short name you want to use for this item.
4. Click **Plain Text** or **Formatted Text** to determine how the entry will be inserted. For a graphic, this choice isn't available.
5. Click **Add** to add the entry.
6. Make sure the **Replace text as you type** check box is selected and click **OK**. The entry you added is now available and will appear automatically as you type.

To insert an AutoCorrect entry in a document, type the abbreviation for the AutoCorrect entry and keep on typing. The entry appears automatically as you continue to type.

Working with Macros

AutoText is great, but when you need to turn up the power, it's time to turn to macros. What is a macro? At its most basic, a *macro* is a shortcut that uses one command to replaces several keystrokes, commands, or actions. You can use macros to eliminate repetitive typing (although if that's all the macro does, you're probably better off with AutoText or AutoCorrect) or to replace any series of actions that you perform on a routine basis.

In this chapter, you'll create a simple recorded macro—sort of like turning on a tape recorder and letting Word record everything you do. You'll learn how to create, play back, and edit a macro. I'll even show you how to pause in the middle of recording a macro.

But macros are much more than a simple recording device. The macros feature includes a complete programming language, Visual Basic for Applications, that can be used to perform almost any task imaginable. For example, you could use the different programming commands to set up a complete data-entry system with its own custom menus and dialog boxes. You can even write macros that control other programs.

We won't get quite that fancy here. The goal of this chapter is to help you understand the basics of macros. When you're ready, look at Word's online help, especially the modules on macro programming.

Recording and Playing a Simple Macro

Don't underestimate a macro just because it's simple—even the most basic macro can save hours of typing the same thing over and over. Let's say that every time you finish a letter, you type **Sincerely,** then you press the **Enter** key three times, type your name, press the **Enter** key again, and type your title. So far, this could be accomplished with AutoText or AutoCorrect. But then you have to print a copy of the document properties, then print the entire letter, and finally, you must close the document. Of course, before you start the process, you save the document one last time (even though you already saved it several times as you worked on it). Here are the steps you'd have to go through to complete the process:

- Type the signature information.
- Choose **Save** from the File menu.

- Open the Print dialog box, choose **Document properties** from the Print what drop-down list, and click **OK**.
- Open the Print dialog box again and print the document.
- Choose **Close** from the File menu to close the document.

All these steps are easy, but they can get pretty tedious after a while, especially when there's no reason to go through them. Macros can take the tedium out of repetitive typing and/or commands, just like AutoText and AutoCorrect can take the tedium out of repetitive typing.

To record a macro:

1. Choose **Macro** from the Tools menu, then choose **Record New Macro** from the cascading Macro menu. The Record Macro dialog box is displayed, as shown in Figure 18.7.

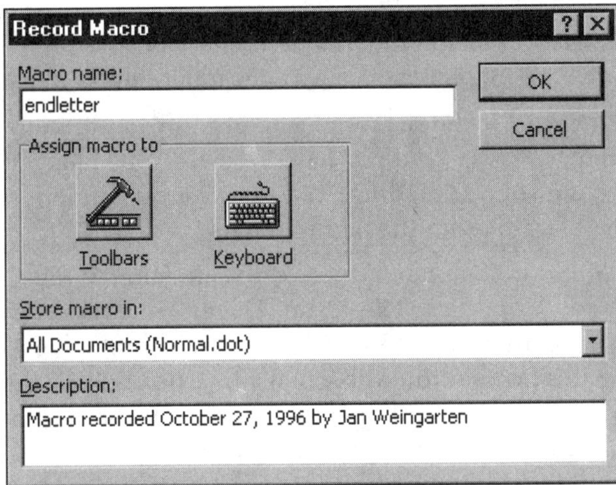

Figure 18.7 *The Record Macro dialog box.*

2. Enter a name for the macro in the Macro name text box. You might call the sample macro I described **endletter** because it's used at the end of every letter.

   You can use up to 80 characters for the macro name. The name can include numbers, but the first character must be a letter. The name can't include any spaces or symbols.

3. Make a selection from the **Store macro** in list to tell Word where to put the macro. If you store the macro in the Normal template, it will be available whenever you create a document that uses that template. If you store the macro in the current document, you can only use the macro for that document.

NOTE

At this point, you can assign the macro to a toolbar for easy access or to a keystroke shortcut so you can run the macro by pressing a couple of keys. I'll show you how to do that in a separate section in this chapter.

4. If you want to, enter a description in the Description box.
5. When you're ready, click **OK**. Notice that the **REC** button on the status bar is active, a Macro toolbar with two buttons is displayed, and a little audio cassette icon (*recorder*, get it?) attaches itself to your mouse pointer.

   While you're recording a macro, you can use your mouse to make selections from menus and dialog boxes, but you can't use it to move your insertion point or select text—you have to use the keyboard.
6. Type the text for the signature line just as you normally would. Type **Sincerely,** followed by three hard returns, your name, another hard return, and your title. Figure 18.8 shows my document screen during macro recording with the text entered.
7. Complete the commands to save the document (**File**, **Save**); print document properties (**File**, **Print**, **Document Properties**, **OK**); print the document (**File**, **Print**, **OK**); and close the file (**File**, **Close**). During this process you will actually be executing all the commands: the Print dialog box will open, you will print the document, you will clear the document from your screen, and so on.
8. When you're finished, click the **Stop Recording** button on the Macro toolbar (the one shaped like a square), or double-click the **REC** button on the Status Bar.

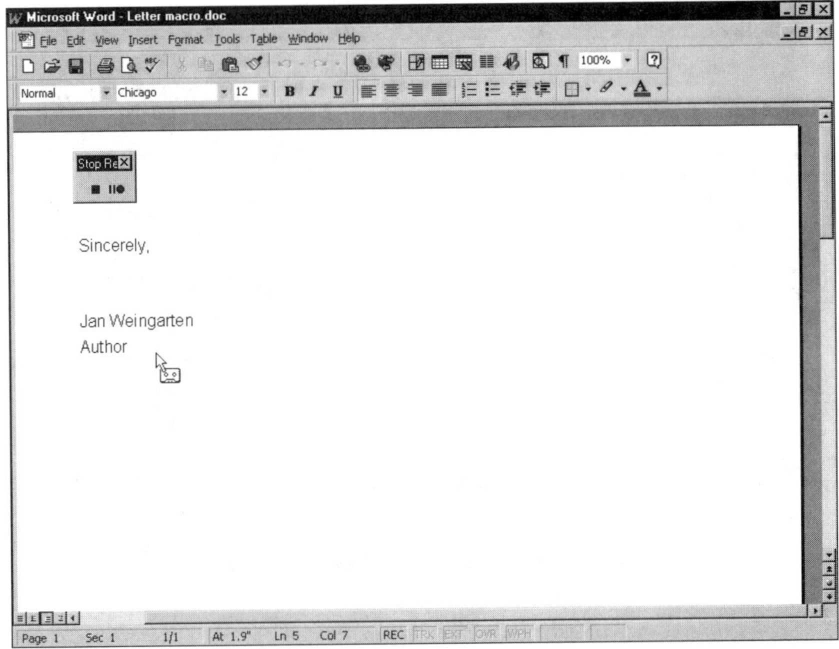

Figure 18.8 *I've entered the text for the macro.*

Notice that the cassette icon disappears from your insertion point, the Macro toolbar closes, and the **REC** button on the Status Bar becomes inactive.

You just recorded your first macro! Let's prove it by playing it back.

Because one of the things this macro does is save the current document, before you run the macro, make sure you have a sample document on your screen that's already been saved.

To run a macro:

1. Choose **Macro** from the Tools menu, then choose **Macros** from the cascading Macro menu (or press **Alt+F8**). The Macros dialog box shown in Figure 18.9 is displayed.

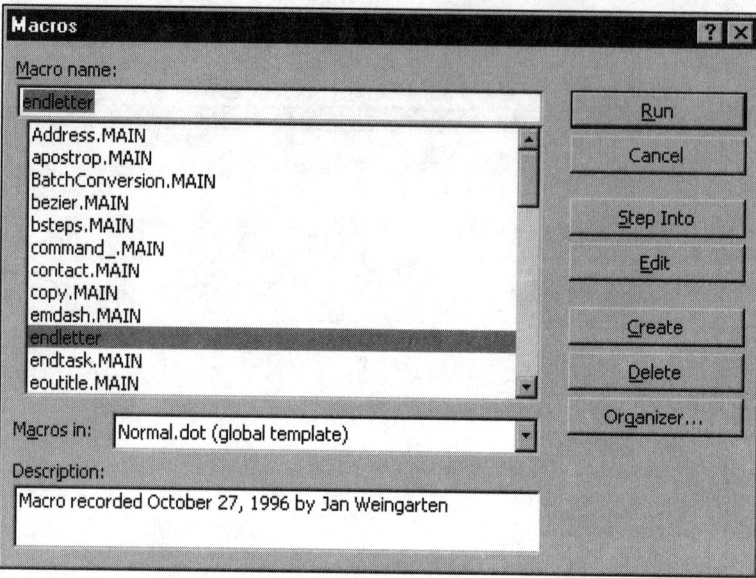

Figure 18.9 The Macros dialog box.

2. Select the macro you want to run (in this case, **endletter**.
3. Choose **Run** (or press **Enter**).

The text you just typed should magically appear on your screen. Then the macro will save the document, print both the document properties and the actual document, and close the file. Now, whenever you finish a letter, all you have to do is run the macro.

Assigning a Macro to a Toolbar or Keystroke

One of the main reasons to use a macro is to save time. So why go through the hassle of opening the Macros dialog box and selecting the macro you want every time you want to run a macro? Why not just click on a toolbar button or press a couple of keys? Depending on your preferences, you can easily assign a macro to a toolbar or give it a keyboard shortcut.

NOTE

The best time to assign a macro to a toolbar or keystroke is when you initially create the macro, by clicking the **Toolbars** or **Keyboard** button in the Record Macro dialog box. If you decide to do it after the fact, you have to do it through the Customize dialog box, which is covered in Chapter 25.

Once you assign a macro to a toolbar or keystroke, it becomes just like any other toolbar button or keystroke shortcut. Run the macro by clicking the toolbar button or pressing the keystroke combination.

To assign a macro to a toolbar:

1. From the Record Macro dialog box, click the **Toolbars** button. This opens the **Commands** tab in the Customize dialog box. As you can see in Figure 18.10, an Office Assistant pops up at this point to see if you need additional help. If you want help, click the **Yes** button. Otherwise, you can just ignore the Office Assistant and proceed.

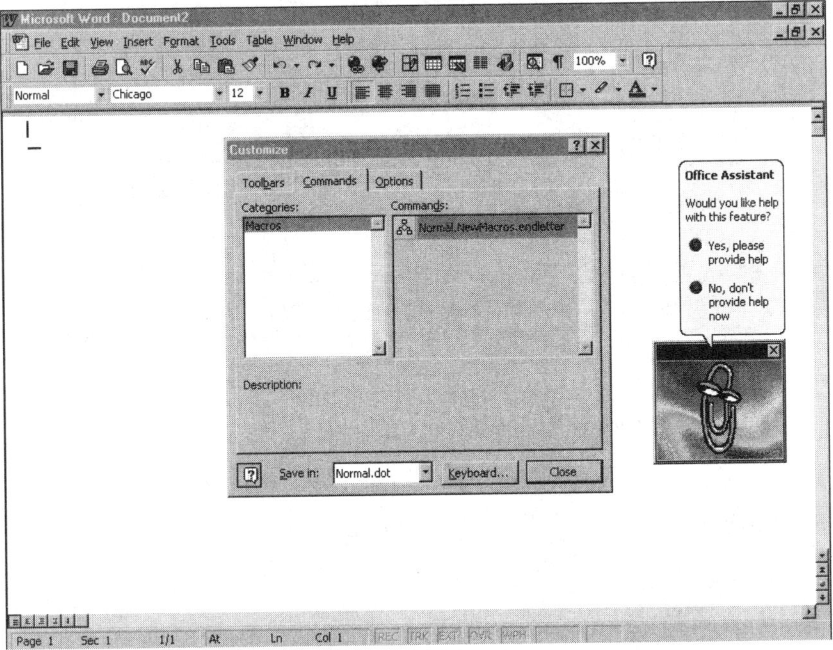

*Figure 18.10 The **Commands** tab in the Customize dialog box.*

2. Select the macro and drag it to the toolbar or menu you want to assign it to. If the toolbar you want to assign the macro to isn't visible, click the **Toolbars** tab and select the toolbar you want, then go back to the **Commands** tab and drag the macro to the toolbar.
3. Click **Close** to begin recording the macro.

To assign a macro to a keystroke:

1. From the Record Macro dialog box, click the **Keyboard** button. This opens the Customize Keyboard dialog box (shown in Figure 18.11) with your macro selected in the Commands list.

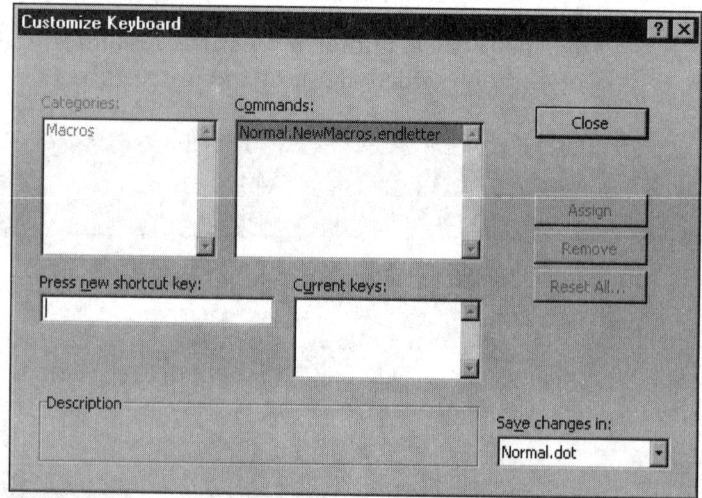

Figure 18.11 *The Customize Keyboard dialog box.*

2. Type the keystroke combination in the **Press new shortcut key** box.
3. Click **Close** to begin recording the macro.

Editing a Macro

Unless you're familiar with Visual Basic for Applications, you're probably better off redoing a simple macro rather than trying to edit macro commands. But if all you want to do is change some of the text in the macro, that's not too big a deal. A macro file can be edited like any Word file, but as you'll see, there are a few things to watch out for. We'll edit the macro you just created to change *Sincerely* to *Yours truly*.

To open a macro file:

1. Choose **Macro** from the Tools menu, then choose **Macros** from the cascading Macro menu.
2. Select the macro you want to edit and choose **Edit**. Your macro appears in a Visual Basic editing window, as shown in Figure 18.12.

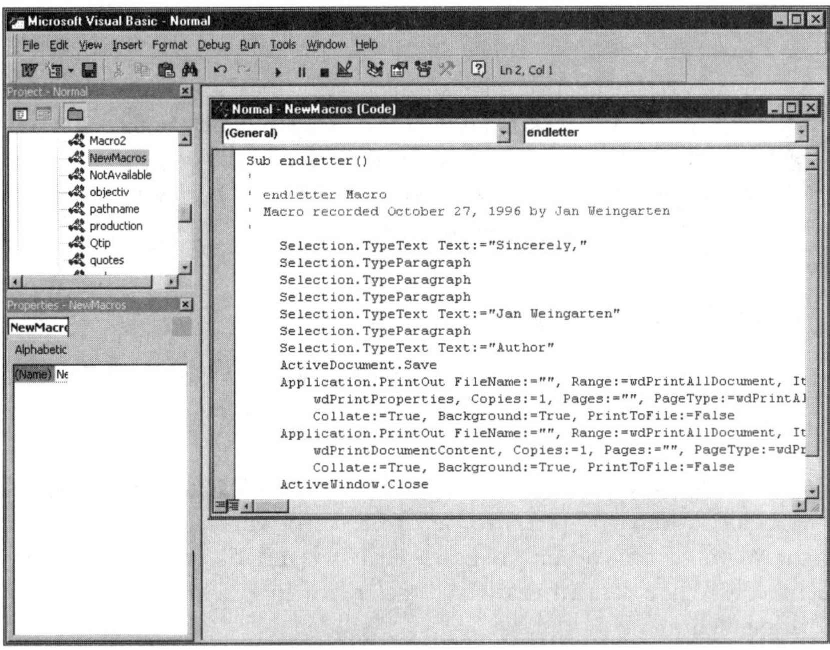

Figure 18.12 *Your endletter macro as it appears in the Visual Basic Editor.*

The lines that start with `Selection.TypeText` tell Word that the text between the quotation marks should be inserted in the document when the macro is played. Notice that *Sincerely*, my name, and the word *Author* are all inside quotation marks. `Selection.TypeParagraph` is the code that tells Word to insert a hard return in the document when the macro is played. You pressed the **Enter** key three times between *Sincerely* and your name, so there are three `Selection.TypeParagraph` codes.

To change the text in a macro:

1. Move your insertion point past the first quotation mark on the line that contains the word *Sincerely*.
2. Delete the word *Sincerely*, and type **Yours truly**, but make sure you leave the quotation marks.
3. Choose **Close and Return to Microsoft Word** from the File menu to update the macro and return to Word.

It's easy to edit the text in a macro. Just add or change any of the text between the quotation marks.

Be very careful not to change anything else in the macro file, unless you know what you're doing. Except for the text between quotation marks, everything is a code or command. For this macro, make sure you only change text inside the quotation marks. If you change something else by mistake, choose **Undo** from the Edit menu right away.

Pausing While You Record a Macro

You might need to pause to do something else while you're in the middle of recording a macro. To do this, just click the **Pause Recording** button on the Macro toolbar.

When a macro is paused (when this happens, the **Pause Recording** button on the Macro toolbar appears to be pressed in), you can do whatever you want in Word or any other program and it won't be recorded as part of your macro. When you're ready to start recording again, just click **Pause Recording** again.

Word's Help system includes in-depth online macro information. To see brief descriptions of all the macros included with Word, choose **Contents and Index** from the Help menu, select the **Index** tab, type **macro**, and then select **built-in macros**. As you dig deeper into the world of macros, you'll find the online macro information a valuable resource; it contains a comprehensive reference of all macro commands and features.

From Here...

You've learned how to work with AutoText and AutoCorrect, and you created and edited a simple macro. The best way to get familiar with macros is by playing with them. Just start creating and using macros for tasks you do on a regular basis. Pretty soon you'll wonder how you ever got along without them.

The next chapter continues the automation theme by showing how you can use the mail merge feature to streamline the task of creating form letters and similar documents.

CHAPTER 19

Using Mail Merge

Let's talk about:

- ✦ Understanding data source and main document files
- ✦ Using the Mail Merge Helper
- ✦ Creating a data source file
- ✦ Creating a main document file
- ✦ Performing the merge

Have you ever gotten one of those form letters that sounds like it was meant just for you, but you know the same letter went to several thousand other people? Ever wonder how they include your name and all that specific information without making it look like it's pasted in? Well, they probably have a program like Word that lets them merge a list of names, addresses, and other variable information into a form letter.

In this chapter, we'll go through a basic form letter merge. Merges can be used in lots of different ways, but this introduction will give you a basic understanding of how merges work so that you have the essential exploration tools when you're ready to delve deeper into merge territory.

Understanding Data Source and Main Document Files

You need to have two files before you can perform a merge: a data source file and a main document file. The *data source file* contains the list of variable information—using the form letter example, the data source file would be the list of names and addresses. The *main document file* is the letter itself—you insert place markers (Word calls them *fields*) into the main document file to tell Word where the information from the data source file should go when the two are merged.

This will all make sense after you've created your own data source and main document files.

Using the Mail Merge Helper

Word's Mail Merge Helper leads you through the entire mail merge process: from creating your main document and data source files to performing the actual mail merge.

To start the Mail Merge Helper:

1. Choose **Mail Merge** from the Tools menu to open the Mail Merge Helper dialog box shown in Figure 19.1.

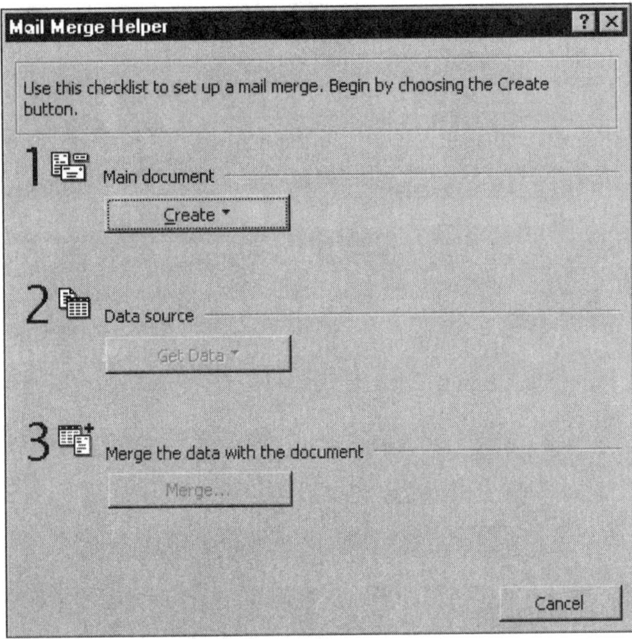

Figure 19.1 *The Mail Merge Helper.*

Take a look at the top of the dialog box (just under the title bar). It says `Use this checklist to set up a mail merge. Begin by choosing the Create button.` As you work with the mail merge feature, keep an eye on this part of the dialog box. If you're not sure what to do next, the checklist area is there to point you in the right direction. Let's do what it tells us.

2. Click the **Create** button and make a choice from the list shown in Figure 19.2. For this example, choose **Form Letters**.

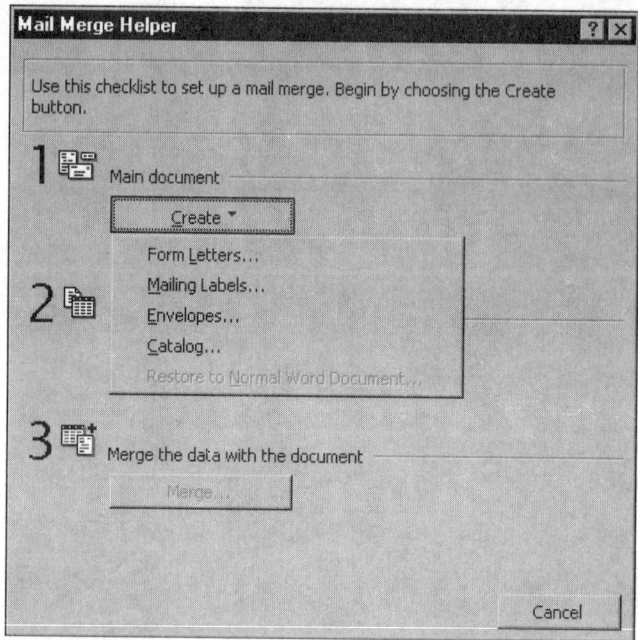

Figure 19.2 Choose which type of main document you want to create.

3. After you choose which type of document you want to create, the dialog box shown in Figure 19.3 appears. If you already have a document on-screen that you want to use for your main document, choose **Active Window**. If you want to start from scratch with a blank document, choose **New Main Document**. For this example, choose **New Main Document**.

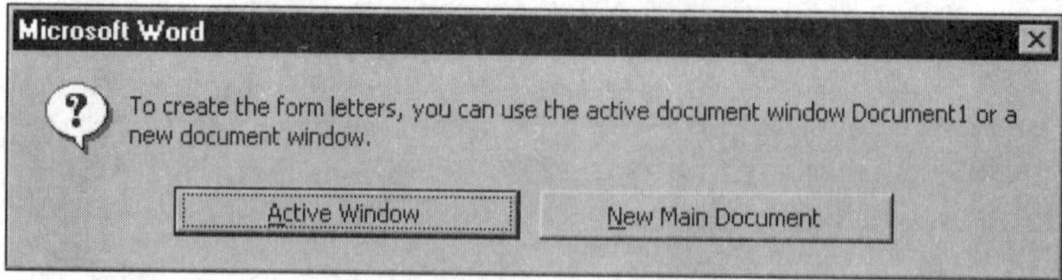

***Figure 19.3** Choose **Active Window** or **New Main Document** from this dialog box.*

4. As soon as you make a selection, you're returned to the Mail Merge Helper. Notice that the checklist area is telling you that `The next step in setting up the mail merge is to specify a data source. Choose the Get Data button`, and the **Get Data** button is now active.

So that's what we'll do. But first, let's preview the data source file you're going to create.

Creating the Data Source File

You're going to create a data source file that contains the following information:

```
Charity Chambers
Casual Corner
300 Cherry Lane
Chehalis, WA 98111
Charity
$92,000

Mary Masterson
PO Box 8935
400 Juniper Alley
Jumping Frog, GA 98778
Mary
$84,000,000

Kim Klaster
Kustom Karpets
500 Kiplinger Korner
Kalamazoo, KY 88888
Kim
$150,000
```

The data source file is made up of fields and records. A *field* is one piece of information. For example, *Kim Klaster* is one field. A *record* is a group of related fields—all the information for Kim is one record.

To create a data source file:

1. Choose **Get Data** from the Mail Merge Helper dialog box and make a selection from the list shown in Figure 19.4. For now, choose **Create Data Source**.

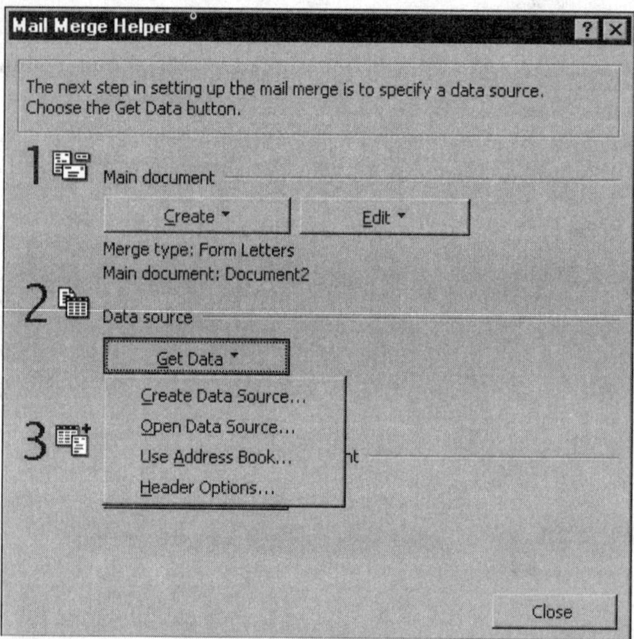

Figure 19.4 Make a selection from the Get Data drop-down list.

At this point, the Create Data Source dialog box, shown in Figure 19.5, should be on your screen. Use this dialog box to name your fields.

The Field name list contains a bunch of commonly used field names. You can use the field names provided by Word or add your own. We'll do a little of both, and we'll get rid of the field names we don't need in this file.

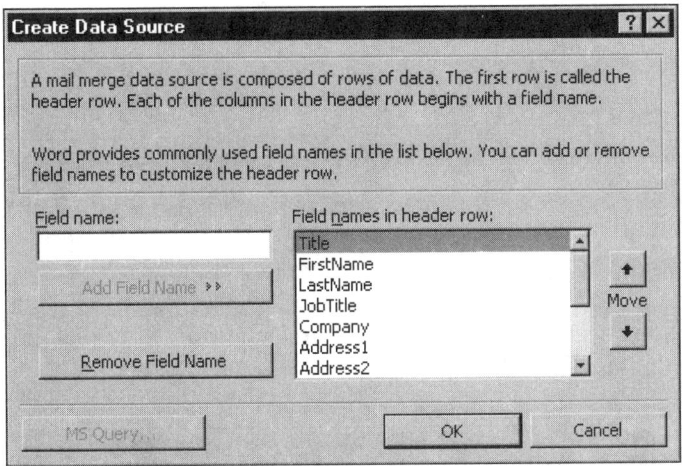

Figure 19.5 The Create Data Source dialog box.

2. To delete a field name, select it and click on the **Remove Field Name** button. In this data source file, we don't need the Title, Job Title, Country, HomePhone, or WorkPhone fields, so go ahead and remove them.

NOTE

When you remove a field name, its name is displayed in the Field name text box. If you removed the name by mistake, just choose **Add Field Name** to put the name back in the Field names list.

3. To add a field name, type the name you want in the Field name text box, then click the **Add Field Name** button or press **Enter**. For this example, add fields called **Salutation** and **AmountWon**.
4. To change the position of field names in the list, select the field you want to reposition and use the up or down Move arrow. For this example, place the field names in the following order:

   FirstName

   LastName

   Company

Address1

Address2

City

State

PostalCode

Salutation

Amount Won

When you're finished, your Create Data source file dialog box should look like Figure 19.6.

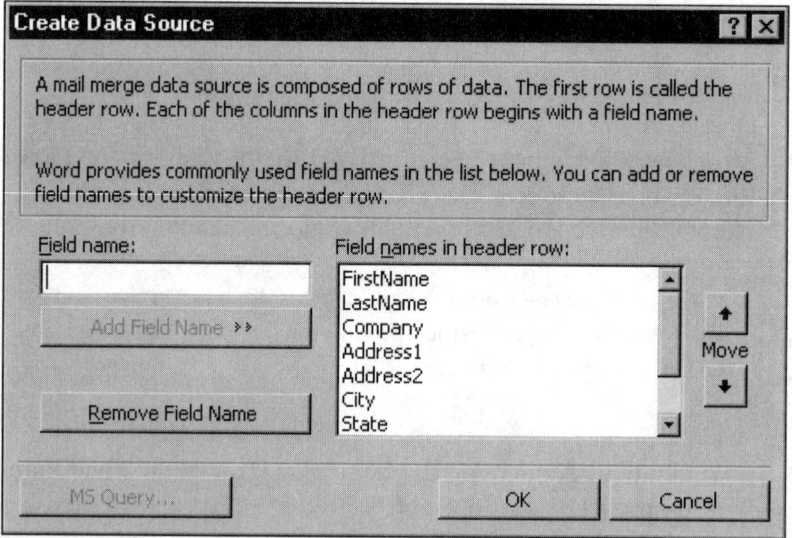

Figure 19.6 The completed Field names list.

5. Click **OK** when your Field names list is complete. Word opens a Save As dialog box—it expects you to save the data source document at this point even though it doesn't contain any real data yet.
6. Enter a name for the file in the File name text box, then choose **Save**. Word displays the dialog box shown in Figure 19.7.

Figure 19.7 *Tell Word whether you want to add records to the data source or work on the main document.*

7. Choose **Edit Data Source** to begin adding records to your data source file.

NOTE

If you want to work on the main document before you put data in the data source document, choose **Edit Main Document**.

At this point, Word displays the Data Form dialog box shown in Figure 19.8.

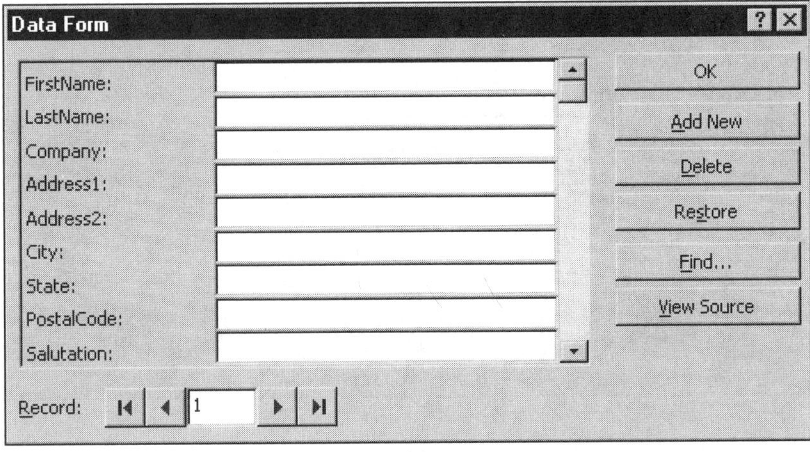

Figure 19.8 *The Data Form dialog box.*

This is where you enter the specific information for each record. All you have to do is type in the appropriate text box and press **Enter** to move to the next field. When you press **Enter** from the last field (in this example, Amount Won), the current record is entered in your document and the text boxes clear so you can enter the information for the next record.

8. Enter all the information for Charity (found at the beginning of this section): her name in the FirstName and LastName boxes, the name of her company in the Company text box, etc. You can move to any field by clicking in its text box. And of course, just like in any dialog box, you can press **Tab** or **Shift+Tab** to move among the fields and buttons.
9. When you've entered all the data for Charity, choose **Add New** (or press **Enter** if your insertion point is in the last field) and continue until you have completed all three records. Notice that there's no company name for Mary Masterson. Just leave her Company text box blank. Before you move to the second record, your Data Form dialog box should look like Figure 19.9.

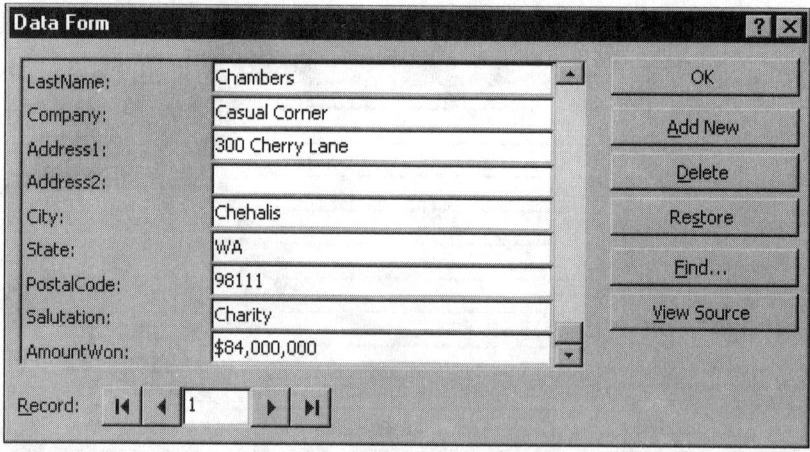

Figure 19.9 The Data Form dialog box with one record entered.

You can use the **Record** buttons at the bottom of the Data Form dialog box to move among the records in your data source file. The arrow buttons with vertical lines move you to the first or last record, respectively, and the plain arrow buttons move you to the next or previous record.

So far, all you've saved is the field name information. Now it's time to save the data you entered.

1. When you're finished entering records, choose **View Source**. Word displays your data source information as a table, as shown in Figure 19.10. Notice that the first row contains the field name information.

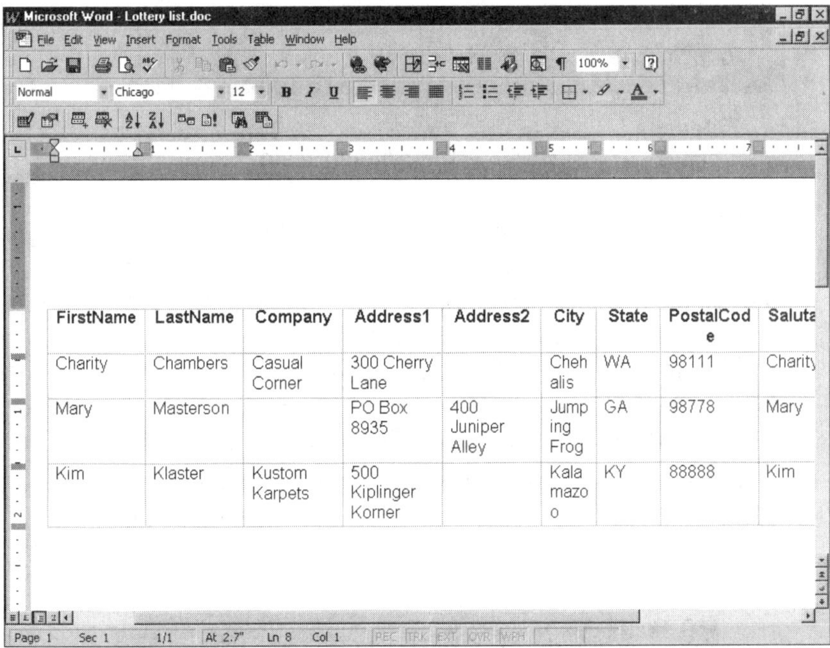

FirstName	LastName	Company	Address1	Address2	City	State	PostalCode	Saluta
Charity	Chambers	Casual Corner	300 Cherry Lane		Chehalis	WA	98111	Charity
Mary	Masterson		PO Box 8935	400 Juniper Alley	Jumping Frog	GA	98778	Mary
Kim	Klaster	Kustom Karpets	500 Kiplinger Korner		Kalamazoo	KY	88888	Kim

Figure 19.10 *The completed data source file.*

You don't have to save right now, but it's a good idea. You wouldn't want to have to re-create what you just did, would you? And that's just what could happen if the power were to go out before you save.

2. Choose **Save** from the File menu. The data source file is a regular document. You should save it frequently as you're working, just as you would with any other file.

THE DATABASE TOOLBAR

Hey, there's a new toolbar (shown in Figure 19.11) just above the Standard toolbar. This one takes the work out of working with mail merge files.

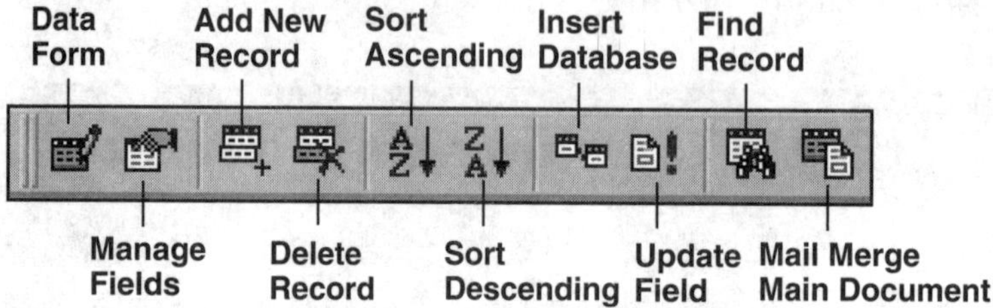

Figure 19.11 The Database toolbar.

- The **Data Form** button on the far left opens the Data Form dialog box. You can edit your data source records by making changes to the table, but if you find it easier to add or edit records through the Data Form dialog box, just click this button. To edit an existing record, place your insertion point anywhere in that record and click the **Data Form** button.
- The next button, **Manage Fields**, opens the Manage Fields dialog box shown in Figure 19.12. Use this dialog box to make changes to your field names.

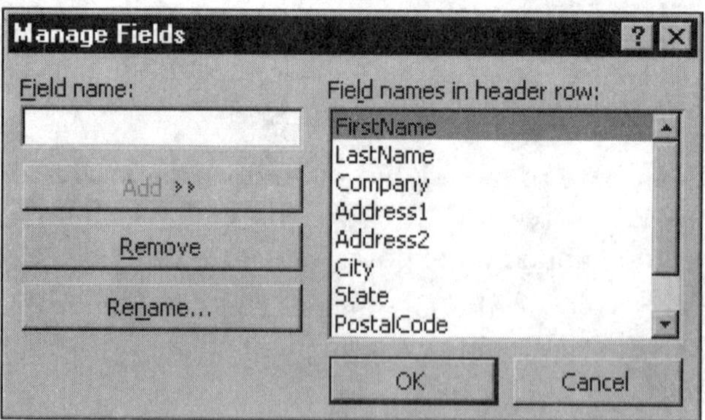

Figure 19.12 The Manage Fields dialog box.

- The **Add New Record** button adds a new row at the bottom of the table. You can enter data directly into the table or use the Data Form dialog box to insert new records.
- The **Delete Record** button deletes the record that your insertion point is in. If you delete a record by mistake, choose **Undo** before you do anything else.
- The **Sort Ascending** and **Sort Descending** buttons are for sorting the records in the table. We'll talk about sorting later in this chapter.
- The **Insert Database** button allows you to bring in data from another source (for example, an Excel spreadsheet).
- The **Find Record** button opens the Find in Field dialog box shown in Figure 19.13. It allows you to search for specific data in your data source file.

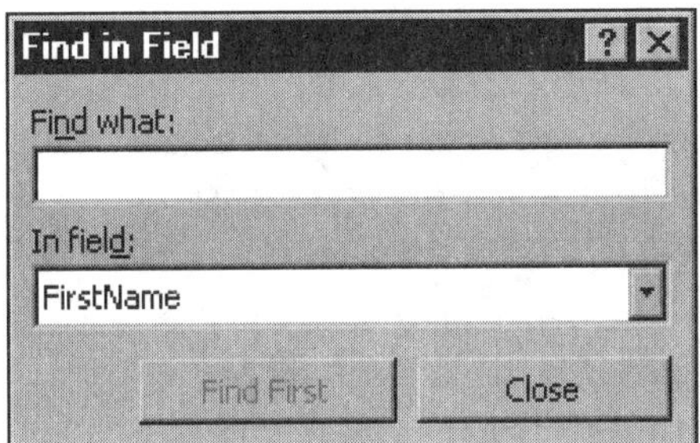

Figure 19.13 The Find in Field dialog box.

- The **Mail Merge Main Document** button switches you to the main document that's associated with this data source file.

Okay, you have your data source file, and you know how to edit it. It's time to create the main document file.

Creating a Main Document File

A main document file is just a regular document with codes wherever you want to enter variable information from the data source file. Take a look at the following letter:

```
Charity Chambers
Casual Corner
300 Cherry Lane
Chehalis, WA 98111

Dear Charity,

We are pleased to inform you that you are the lucky winner of
$92,000. Please contact the Lottery Office by 5 p.m. on November 15
to claim your winnings.
Sincerely,

Marla Millions
Lottery Administrator
```

What's the variable information? Well, the name and address for a start. Instead of Charity's name and address, we need a code that tells Word to use the information from the data source file when we run the merge. We also need codes instead of the salutation (otherwise all the letters would say *Dear Charity*) and the amount. Let's do it.

When you created the data source file, you created a blank main document file. From the data source file, click the **Mail Merge Main Document** button on the Database toolbar to switch to the blank main document associated with the data source file.

You should be in a blank document window, and the Database toolbar is replaced by the Mail Merge toolbar shown in Figure 19.14. This toolbar helps you create the main document file.

Figure 19.14 *The Mail Merge toolbar.*

The following steps are specific to the sample letter, but they'll familiarize you with the procedures you can use to enter text in any main document file:

1. Make sure your insertion point is at the top of the document and type today's date. Or choose **Date and Time** from the Insert menu to insert a date field that will automatically be updated whenever you open the document.
2. Press the **Enter** key twice. This is where you would usually type in the person's name and address. Instead of an actual name and address, we'll use field codes.
3. Click on the **Insert Merge Field** button on the Mail Merge toolbar to open the list shown in Figure 19.15. This list takes all the guesswork out of inserting field codes in your main document file.

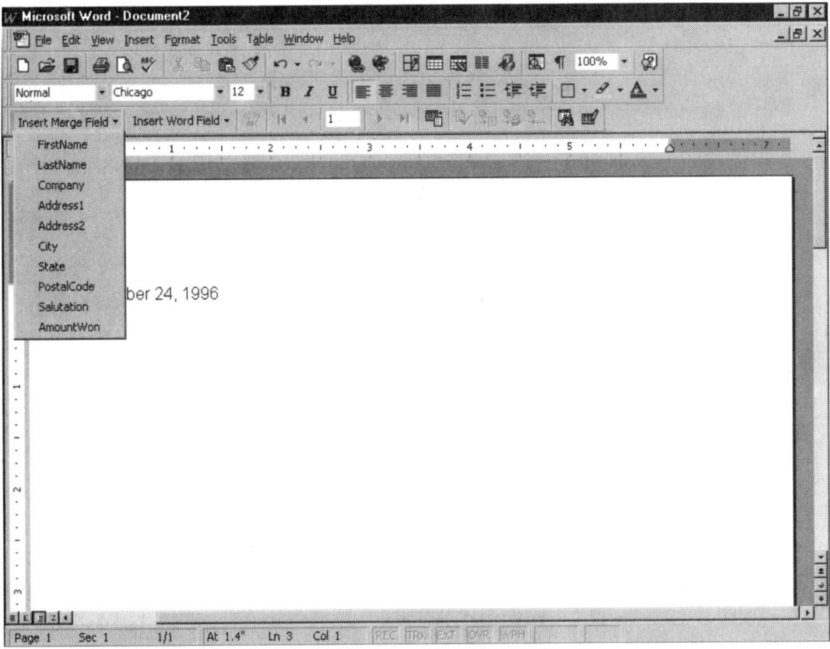

Figure 19.15 *This list contains all the field names from your data source file.*

4. Click on **FirstName** to insert the FirstName field at your insertion point location, then press the **Spacebar** and choose **LastName** from the Insert Merge Field list. As you can see in Figure 19.16, Word inserts field codes in double brackets, separated by a space. The `<<FirstName>>` and `<<LastName>>` fields will be replaced by the actual names in the data source file when you complete the merge.

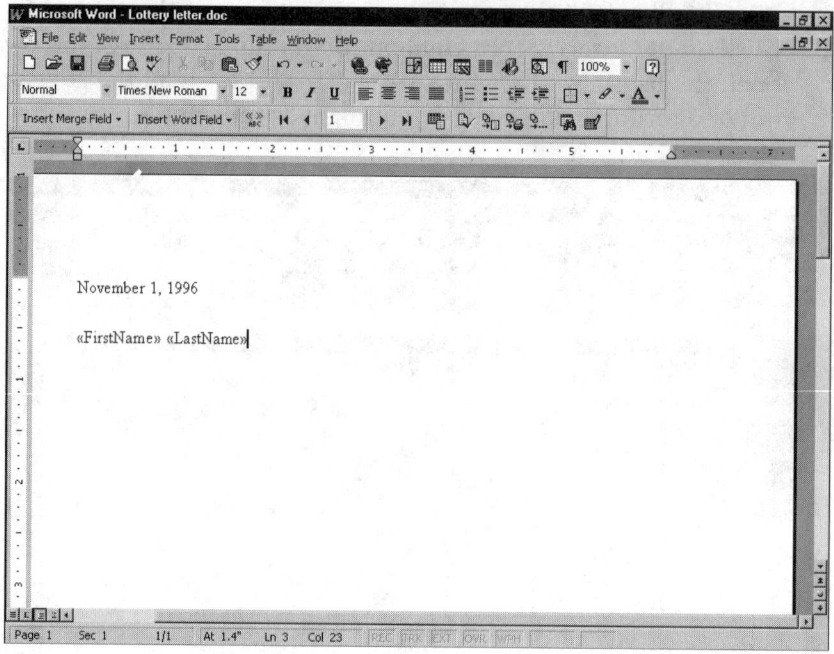

***Figure 19.16** Beginning of the main document.*

5. Press the **Enter** key to move to the next line and use the Insert Merge Field list to add Company, Address1, Address2, and City, State, and PostalCode fields. Use the spacing and punctuation you normally would when entering these fields. For example, put the City, State, and PostalCode fields on one line, with a comma and space after City, and a space after State.
6. Press the **Enter** key twice to move to the salutation line.
7. Type **Dear** and press the **Spacebar**.
8. Choose **Salutation** from the Insert Merge Field list. Then, with your insertion point directly after the Salutation field code, type a comma and press the **Enter** key twice.

9. Type **We are pleased to inform you that you are the lucky winner of** .
10. Make sure you press the **Spacebar** after the word *of,* then insert the **Amount Won** field code and type an exclamation mark.
11. Enter the rest of the text: **Please contact the Lottery Office by 5 p.m. on November 15 to claim your winnings.**

    Sincerely,

    Marla Millions

    Lottery Administrator

    Your screen should look like Figure 19.17.

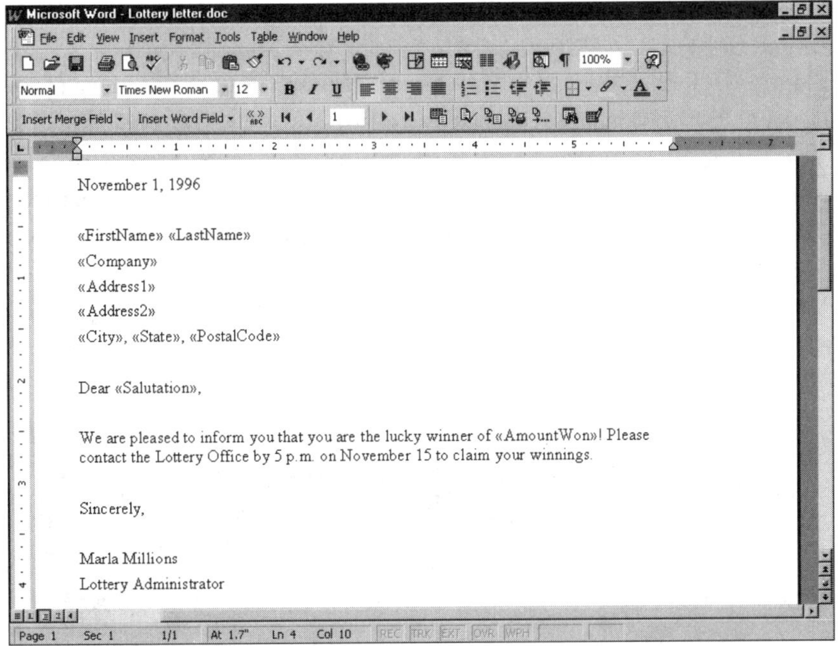

Figure 19.17 *The completed main document file.*

12. Save the file as **Lottery Letter** and leave it on your screen.

Be sure you spell check and proofread your main document file before you perform a merge. Otherwise you could end up with the same error repeated on every letter. If you do discover a mistake after performing a merge, just close the merged file without saving and run the merge again. That's much easier than making corrections on each letter.

That's it. You just created a data source file and a main document file. All that's left is to bring them together.

Performing the Mail Merge

This is a piece of cake if you start with your data or main document file on-screen. And it's not even hard if you start from a blank screen—it just means that you have to specify which data and main document files you want to use.

For these steps, I'm assuming that **Lottery Letter** is still on-screen and the Mail Merge toolbar is visible. If the Mail Merge toolbar isn't displayed, right-click on any toolbar and choose **Mail Merge** from the Toolbar list.

To merge the main and data source documents, click the **Merge to New Document** or **Merge to Printer** button on the Mail Merge toolbar or open the Mail Merge Helper (by clicking **Mail Merge Helper** on the Mail Merge toolbar or choosing **Mail Merge** from the Tools menu) and click on the **Merge** button.

The **Merge to New Document** button automatically performs the merge and sends the output to a new Word document, which you can save, print, or edit like any other document. The **Merge to Printer** button sends the merged documents directly to the printer.

If you choose **Merge** from the Mail Merge Helper, you get the dialog box shown in Figure 19.18, which allows you to set several options before performing the merge. I'll discuss the Merge dialog box in a bit. For now, if you choose this method, just click on the **Merge** button in the Merge dialog box.

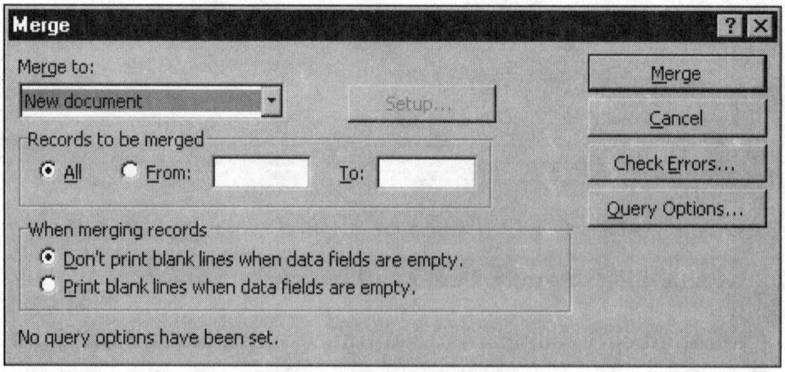

Figure 19.18 *The Merge dialog box.*

Quick as a flash (it might take a few flashes if you're using a long data source file), the merged documents are displayed on your screen, with the insertion point at the top of the document. Scroll down to take a look at your other records. You should have three letters, with all the right information in the right places. Wherever you inserted a code in the main document file, you now have the specific information for each addressee.

Now let's take a look at Mary Masterson's letter (Figure 19.19). Remember, we left the Company field of her data record blank. So how come there's no blank line after Mary Masterson's name? Any why aren't there extra blank lines for Charity's and Kim's addresses—neither of their records use the Address2 field. Explanation coming right up.

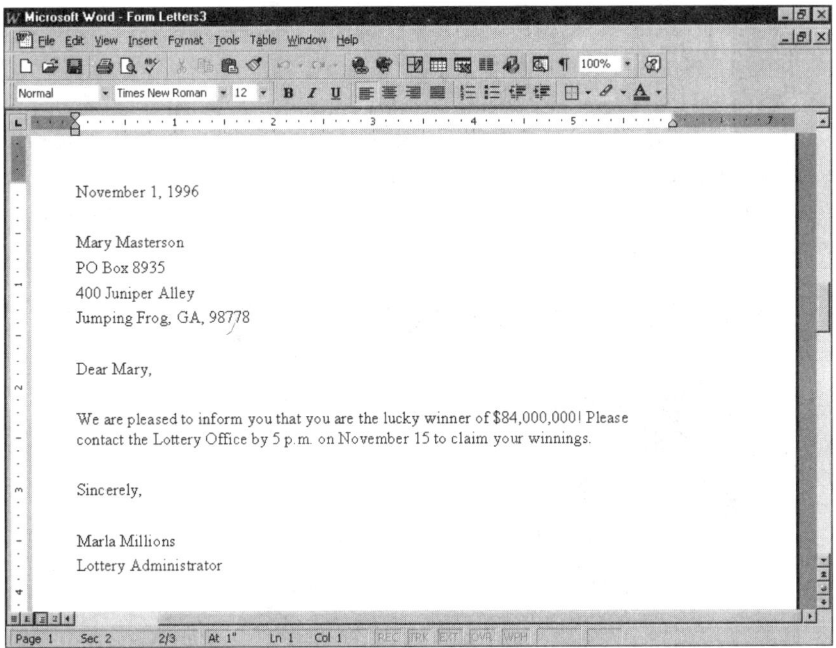

Figure 19.19 *The merged record for Mary Masterson.*

In most cases, you don't need to save the completed merge file. You can always re-create it by merging the main document and data source files—saving the completed merge is usually a waste of disk space.

CHANGING MERGE OPTIONS

The Merge dialog box (Figure 19.18) lets you control the results of the merge. This dialog box is displayed when you choose **Merge** from the Mail Merge Helper or **Mail Merge** from the Mail Merge toolbar.

Notice that the default for When merging records is **Don't print blank lines when data fields are empty**. That's why you didn't end up with a blank line in Mary's record. If you actually want the blank line to appear, choose **Print blank lines when data fields are empty**.

This dialog box contains some other useful options:

- By default, Word merges all the records from the data source file. If you want to merge only certain records, enter a range of numbers in the From and To text boxes.
- You can test your merge before you actually perform it. This option is especially useful if you plan to merge directly to a printer—you can make sure everything works the way it should without wasting paper. Click on the **Check Errors** button to open the dialog box shown in Figure 19.20.

Figure 19.20 *The Checking and Reporting Errors dialog box.*

- The Query Options dialog box, shown in Figure 19.21, contains options for filtering and sorting records. Getting into all the query options is beyond the scope of this book, but if you press **F1** from the Query Options dialog box, the Office Assistant will point you to areas where you can get help on this topic.

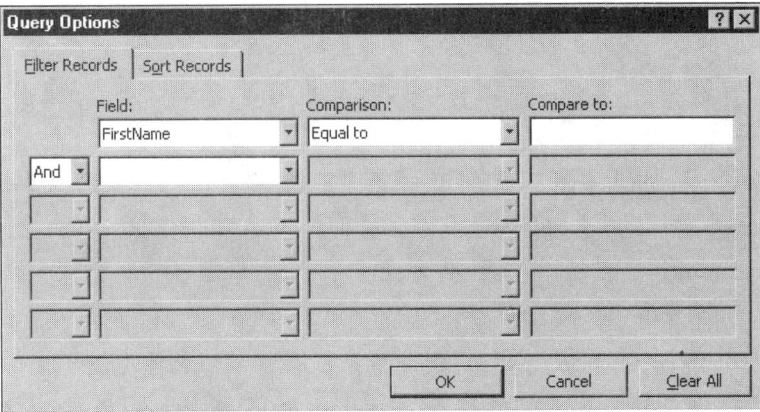

Figure 19.21 The Query Options dialog box.

FROM HERE...

As you work with mail merges, you'll find them invaluable. This chapter just scratched the surface—once you create a data source file, you can merge it with any number of main document files. For example, you could use the same mailing list to create letters, labels, envelopes, and a phone list.

Coming up: styles. No, *not* the new fall fashions—Word Styles, a powerful tool that can help you achieve consistency in your formatting. We'll also talk about Word's automatic formatting feature, where you can just sit back and let Word do all the heavy lifting.

CHAPTER 20

Working with Styles and Automatic Formatting

Let's talk about:

- Why use styles?
- How styles work
- Where styles are saved
- Applying styles
- Creating a style from scratch
- Modifying styles
- Creating style templates
- Using AutoFormat

Isn't it great to be in style? You're lookin' good, and you know you haven't forgotten any of those ever-so-essential accessories. Well, you can give your Word documents that same secure, stylish feeling with the Styles feature. A style is just a way of applying formatting in a consistent manner. You put all the formatting codes into a style, and then you apply the style to a section of text.

Why Use Styles?

So far, styles sound kind of like AutoText and macros, don't they? Well, in a way they are. You could write an AutoText entry that contains formatting codes and insert it wherever you want to apply the formatting to a section of text. So why create a style? Here's the scoop: Styles have one big advantage over macros and AutoText for formatting text—they let you change your mind. And, in matters of style, it's always important to change with the times.

Say you write a macro that centers and bolds text for a heading, and you apply that macro to headings throughout a document. Everything's great—until you decide that you want all those headings to be at the left margin and in a different point size. Oh, and you want the **Keep with Next** option turned on for each heading to make sure you don't end up with headings dangling alone at the bottom of a page.

Hmmm, what to do? You could write another macro that does all the new stuff and deletes the old codes. The macro could even search through your document to find the old formatting codes. But there would be quite a few steps involved. And besides, you've used the same macro to format 50 other documents. You'd have to open each document and run the new macro.

Here's the beauty of styles: If you edit a style, every place you've applied that style is automatically updated to reflect the change. Using the preceding example, if you had used a style instead of a macro, all you would have to do is edit one style—delete the formatting you no longer want and add the new options. That's it.

Here are a few things styles can do for you:

- Save hours of repetitive reformatting work.
- Provide visual consistency within a document or across a set of documents.
- Create a consistent structure for tables of contents and outlines.
- Allow a group of people to quickly create documents that have the same look.

In this chapter, you'll learn how to apply, create, modify, and organize styles. And in the next two chapters, you'll put your style knowledge to use as you use Word's predefined styles for three time-saving features that are useful with longer documents: outlines, tables of contents, and indexes.

First I'll show you how to use the styles that come with Word; then you'll learn how to create your own styles.

How Styles Work

A style is a collection of character or paragraph formats stored in a Word document or template. For example, a style can contain font, font size, indent, tab, and line-spacing instructions, which can be applied to a paragraph in a single step. A style can also apply font formatting to only a word or sentence. A set of formats applied to an entire paragraph is called a *paragraph style.* A set of formatting applied to only selected text is called a *character style.*

You can have many paragraph styles in a document, but only one style per paragraph. Every paragraph in Word has a paragraph style applied to it. If you open a new document and start typing, Word automatically applies the Normal style to each paragraph in your document. The Normal style is the basis for many other styles built into Word.

But don't think that styles tie your hands, preventing you from making exceptions. For example, you may want to make a single sentence within a paragraph italic, although the font for the paragraph style is defined as plain text. No problem; simply select the piece of text and format it as italic. Word remembers that this selection should be italic and leaves it that way, even if you modify the style's font later.

Where Styles are Saved

Styles are saved in documents and templates. Each time you create a document based on a template, you have access to the styles saved in that template. A special template called the *Normal* (or *Blank Document*) template is attached to new Word documents created by clicking the **New** button on the Standard toolbar. And in the Normal template, there's a paragraph style called *Normal* that is applied to all paragraphs until you specify a different style.

We'll get into templates more later. For now, just remember that the styles you create can be saved in the Normal template or in a template of your choosing, and thus they can be available whenever you use a particular template. If you send your template to other people, they'll have access to the styles it contains.

Applying a Style

Now we'll apply styles to a document to see how they work. As you learned earlier, each paragraph in a Word document has a style applied to it. You can tell which style is applied to the current paragraph by looking at the Style box at the far left of the Formatting toolbar. But this only shows the style for one paragraph at a time. Remember, you can't always tell which style has been applied just by looking at the formatting. If you want to review the styles in a document, you can display a special bar in the margin area that shows all the styles at once. This takes up extra screen space, but it is worthwhile when you're learning about styles or working in a document with complex style formatting. Note that this feature only works when you're in Normal view.

To view the styles applied in a document:

1. Switch to Normal view (choose **Normal** from the View menu).
2. Choose **Options** from the Tools menu and select the **View** tab (shown in Figure 20.1).

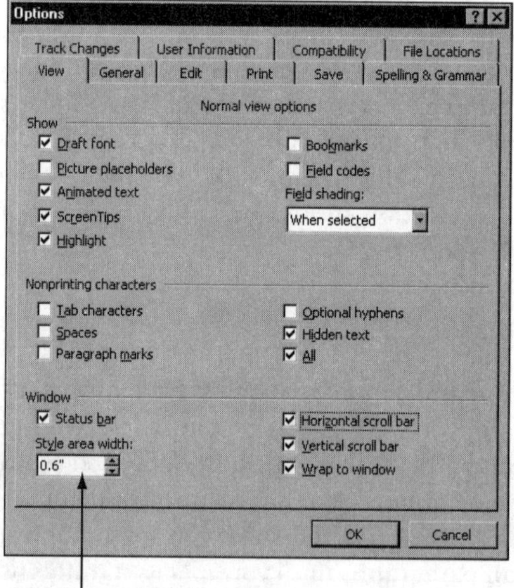

20.1 The View tab in the Options dialog box.

3. Enter a measurement in the Style area width box (.5–.8 inches should provide enough space in most instances) and click **OK**.

The Style bar appears along the left side of the screen, as shown in Figure 20.2. Each style name represents a separate paragraph. Here you can see that the Normal style is applied to each paragraph by default.

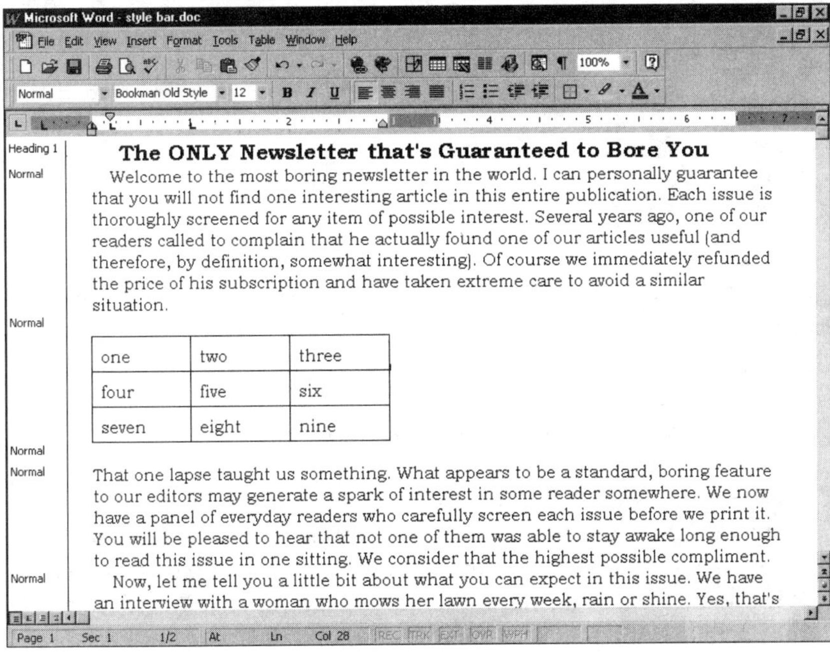

Figure 20.2 A document in Normal view with the style bar visible.

NOTE

You can adjust the width of the style bar by positioning your mouse pointer on the line that separates the style bar from your text and dragging the mouse pointer to make the bar wider or narrower. You can tell when the mouse pointer is properly positioned because it changes into a vertical line with solid horizontal left and right arrows.

To apply a style to a paragraph:

1. Display the Formatting toolbar.

2. On the Formatting toolbar, click the arrow next to the Styles box. The Style list shown in Figure 20.3 contains the styles available in the current document. As you can see, the items in the Style list show samples of the character formatting included in each style. Each style has its own collection of paragraph and character formats.

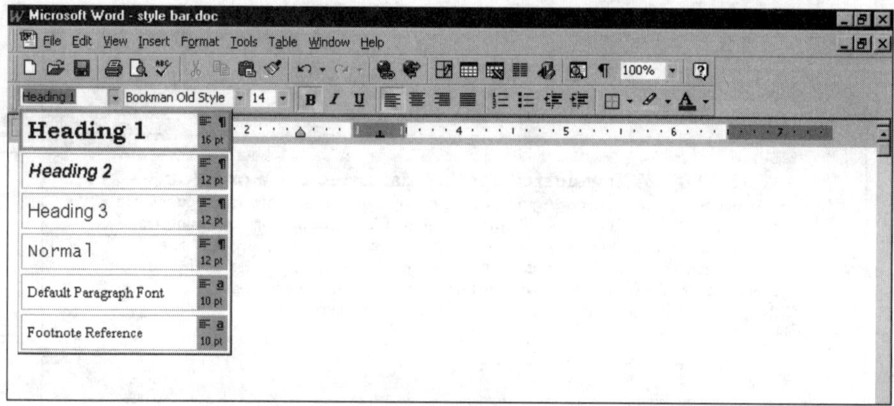

Figure 20.3 The Style list.

3. Click a style name. For this example, click **Heading 2**. The paragraph changes font and font size. If you display the Paragraph dialog box, you can see that the spacing before and after the paragraph changes. If the style bar is displayed, it shows that the style has changed from Normal to Heading 2, as shown in Figure 20.4.

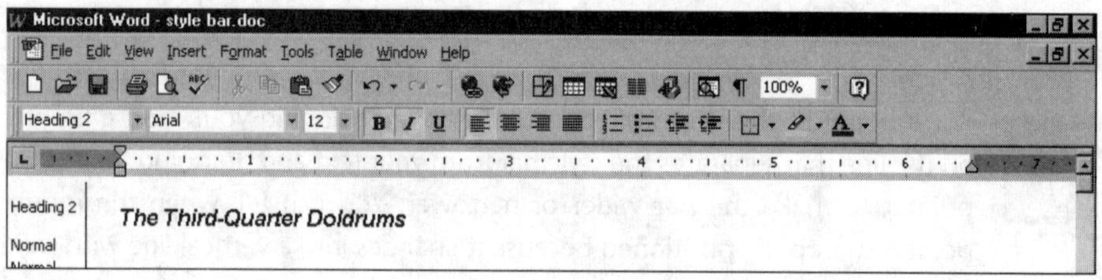

Figure 20.4 The style changes to reflect your selection.

Consider the steps you would have had to take to change the formatting manually. You would have had to change the font attributes one at a time and then open the Paragraph dialog box to change the spacing before and after the paragraph.

By applying a style, you accomplished the formatting tasks with one step. And you didn't even have to create the style—Word did the work for you. But what happens when you can't find a predefined style that suits your need? It's time to define a style of your own.

Creating Your Own Styles

When the predefined styles don't provide the formatting solutions you require, you can either modify the built-in styles or create your own. You can create a style for each paragraph formatting situation that should be kept consistent, giving each style a descriptive name. For example, you might define Letter Closing, Note, Indented Graphic, and Long Quotation styles. Each time you run into that kind of paragraph, just apply the style to take care of all the formatting at once.

Let's say you want to create a paragraph that is set off from the normal flow of text to emphasize a quotation. Creating a style that's indented on the left and right and has an italic font should serve your purpose. The first time you create the paragraph, you'll have to format it manually and create a new style. The next time a quotation paragraph comes up, all you need to do is apply the style.

To define a style:

1. Apply font and paragraph formatting to a sample paragraph. The style you create will use this formatting.
2. In the Style box on the Formatting toolbar, type a new style name and press **Enter**.

That's all it takes. You've just created a new style that now appears in the Formatting toolbar's Style list for this document. If you click in another paragraph and apply the style, the paragraph and font formatting you defined for the style will be applied instantly.

Modifying an Existing Style

Modifying a style is similar to creating a style. When you modify an existing style, Word automatically reformats all the paragraphs in your document that have that style applied to them. By changing one style, you can make hundreds of tedious changes at once. Because it's so easy to modify a style, you can try several fonts, sizes, and other options in a few seconds. This shortens the trial-and-error process of refining your document's appearance and size.

Suppose you decide the Quotation style is a little overpowering and you'd like to reduce the point size. Here's all you have to do.

To modify a style:

1. Select a paragraph that uses the style you want to change.

Make sure the name of the style you want to change is displayed in the Formatting toolbar's Style list (or in the style bar if it's turned on).

2. Reformat the paragraph to use the options you want.
3. On the Formatting toolbar, click in the Style box and press **Enter**. Word opens the Modify Style dialog box shown in Figure 20.5.

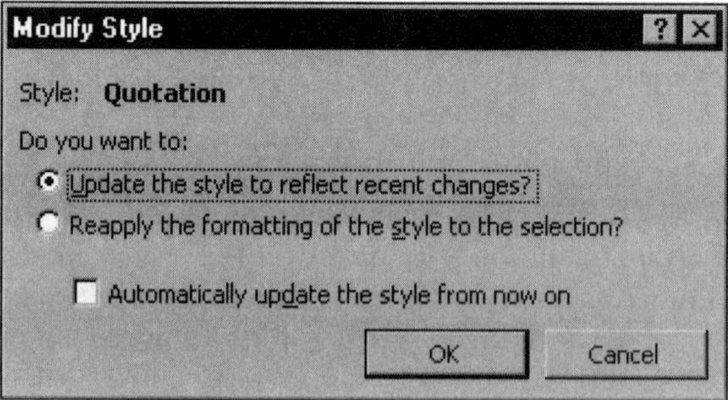

***Figure 20.5** The Modify Style dialog box.*

Word asks if you want to update the style or return the paragraph to the existing style. If you reapply the style, your formatting changes to the paragraph are discarded.

4. Click **OK**. Word redefines the style using the currently selected text as the basis for the style. If you had changed a paragraph formatting attribute (such as an indent), Word would have saved that change also.

Modifying Other Style Options

Besides formatting, there are a few other options you can select when creating or modifying a style. Two of these (**Based On** and **Style for Following Paragraph**) link a style with other styles, and a third option (**Add to Template**) determines where styles are saved.

Basing a style on another style allows you to change a whole series of styles by changing only the style they're based on. If you change the Normal style so it uses the Bookman font, for example, the TOC (table of contents) styles also change to Bookman because they're based on the Normal style.

Another useful option defines a style for the next paragraph. When you press **Enter**, this option determines what style is automatically applied to the next paragraph. Normally the same style continues, but it doesn't have to. For example, notice the headings in this book. In every case, the paragraph after a heading is plain body text. Rather than manually apply the body style after typing each heading, I set the style of the next paragraph to Body so it changes automatically as soon as I press **Enter**.

The **Add to Template** option determines if a style is saved only in the current document. Selecting this option saves a style in the template on which the document is based. This lets you re-use the styles in other documents and enables you to share the style with other people by giving them a copy of the template.

To apply other style options:

1. Choose **Style** from the Format menu to open the Style dialog box shown in Figure 20.6.

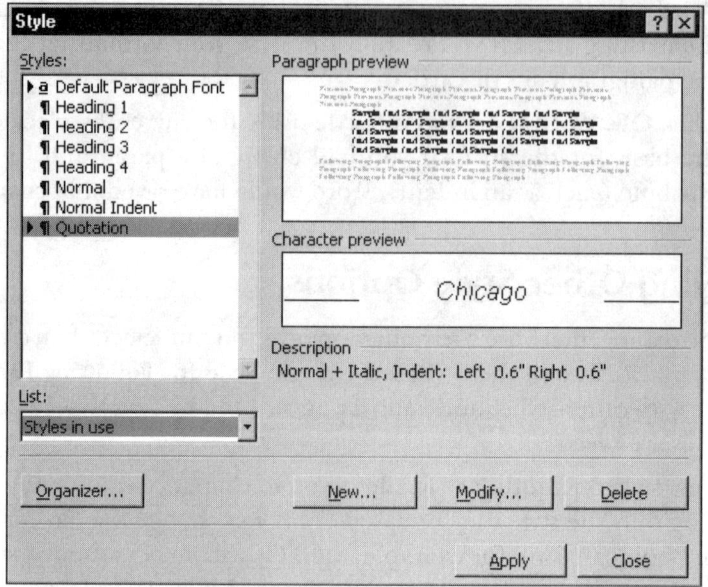

Figure 20.6 The Style dialog box.

2. Select the style you want to change and click **Modify** to open the Modify Style dialog box shown in Figure 20.7.

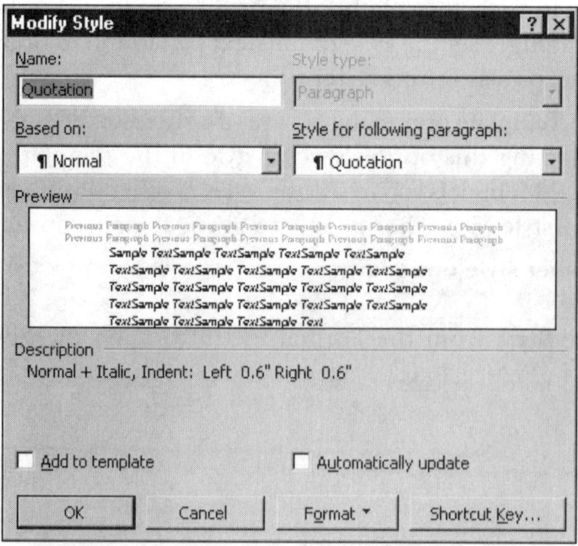

Figure 20.7 The Modify Style dialog box.

You can change any of the formatting options for the style by making selections from the Format drop-down list.

3. From the **Based** on list, select a style whose changes you want this style to inherit.
4. From the **Style for following paragraph** list, select a style to apply automatically when you press **Enter** after typing in this style.
5. Select the **Add to template** check box to make this style available for other documents.
6. Click **OK** and then click **Close** in the Style dialog box.

Deleting a Style

As you create more styles, you're bound to end up with some that don't work for you anymore. If you aren't going to use them, they're just cluttering up the Style list on your toolbar. You can clean house to keep your style list down to a manageable length.

To delete a style:

1. Choose **Style** from the Format menu.
2. Select the style you want to delete and click the **Delete** button. Word asks you to confirm the action, as shown in Figure 20.8.

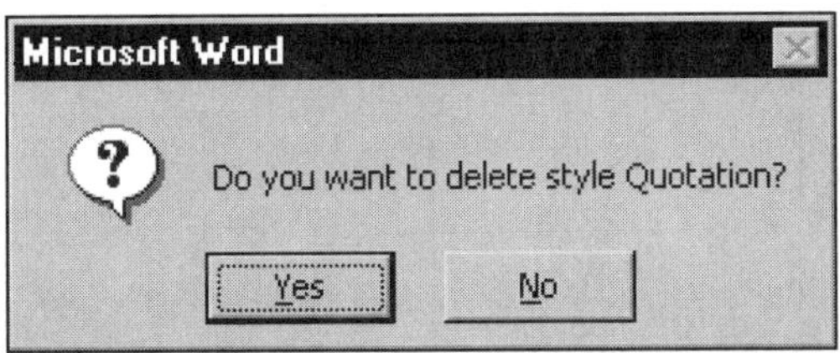

Figure 20.8 *Word displays this dialog box to make sure you really want to delete the style.*

3. Choose **Yes** to delete the style.

If you change your mind and want the style back, just use the **Undo** command as soon as you close the Style dialog box.

Not all styles can be deleted. Word has a set of default styles that always remain in any template you're using. These include the Normal, Heading 1,

Heading 2, and Heading 3 styles. If you click a style and the **Delete** button is dimmed, that's why.

Using Predefined Styles from the Style Gallery

Word comes with hundreds of predefined styles in its numerous templates. Often you can find a predefined set of styles to suit your needs, saving you the trouble of creating styles yourself.

To use the styles in the style gallery:

1. Choose **Style Gallery** from the Format menu to open the Style Gallery dialog box shown in Figure 20.9.

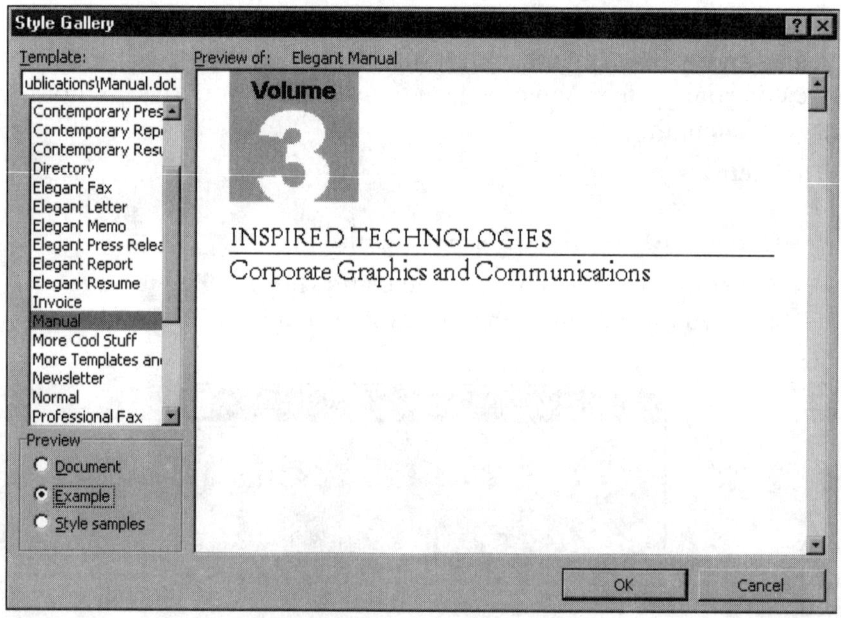

Figure 20.9 *The Style Gallery.*

Notice the three Preview options just below the template list. When **Document** is selected, the Preview box shows how your own document would look with the template styles. **Example** shows a document with sample text in each style. **Style Samples** shows the names and samples of all the styles in the template.

2. Select an item from the Template list.
3. If you like what you see in the Preview box and you want to use the styles in your document, click **OK**. The styles from the selected template are applied to all your paragraphs that have the same style names. Any unused styles from the template are also available for applying to other paragraphs in your document.

Styles and Templates

In Chapter 3, you learned that a template supplies the tools you need to shape a new document. So far in this chapter, you've learned about styles, the most important information in a template. By putting the two features together, you end up with a handy way of organizing styles so that just the ones you need are available for particular documents.

Creating academic reports may require a special set of formatting functions, such as double-spaced paragraphs, while creating a brochure may require paragraphs with narrow margins. Each of these documents requires a set of styles to perform the formatting functions you need. This is where templates become important in organizing your styles effectively. If all your styles were available in every document, the sheer number could become confusing and distracting. A long list of styles can make it hard to remember which styles you should use for your academic report and which for brochures.

By using individual templates, you can localize a set of styles to a specific template. Your Academic Report template can contain only the styles needed for that purpose, your Brochure template would contain brochure styles, and so on. However, this method of using templates introduces its own inefficiencies. What if you want to use the styles you created in one template in another template? Fortunately, you can copy styles from one document or template to another.

Copying Styles Between Documents or Templates

In the previous section, you learned to copy styles from different templates into a document by using the Style Gallery. However, using the Style Gallery copies all the styles from a template into a file. This leaves you with the same problem you just had: too many styles from which to choose. Word solves this problem with the Organizer. The Organizer allows you to copy individual styles between any two documents or templates.

As you'll see from the other tabs in the Organizer, you can also use this feature to copy AutoText entries and custom toolbars.

To use the organizer to move styles:

1. Choose **Style** from the Format menu.
2. Click the **Organizer** button in the Style dialog box. This displays the **Styles** tab in the Organizer dialog box, as shown in Figure 20.10.

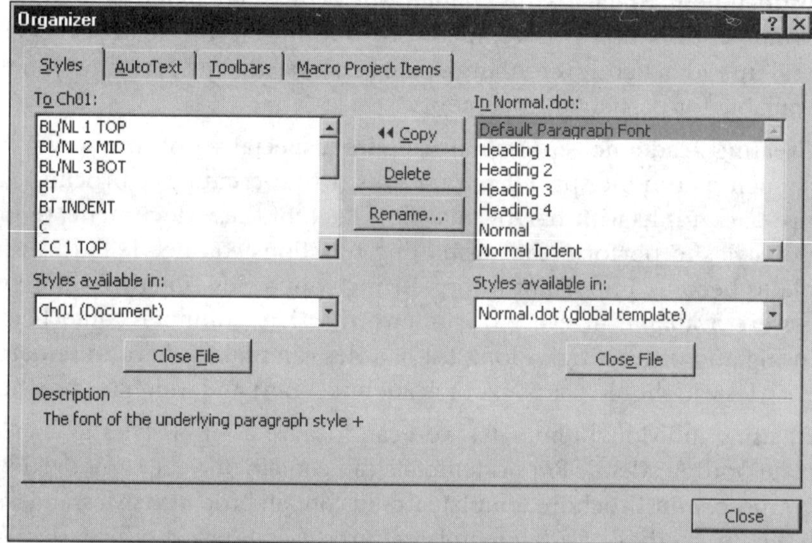

***Figure 20.10** The **Styles** tab in the Organizer dialog box.*

When the Organizer first opens, the styles from your document or template are displayed on the left. On the right are the styles from the Normal template. You can display a different set of styles in either location. If you want to copy styles *from* a different file or template (other than the one that's currently displayed), pick a different file for the left side of the dialog box from the **styles available in** list. If you want to copy styles *to* a different file or template, pick a different file for the right side of the dialog box.

3. To close the file that's currently displayed in either list, click the appropriate **Close File** button.
4. Click the **Open File** button, select the file (DOC) or template (DOT) you want to use from the Open dialog box, and choose **Open**. If necessary, use the Look in list to move to the folder that contains the file or template you want.
5. From the list on the left, select the style you want to copy.
6. Click the **Copy** button. The style is copied to the other open document or template.
7. Click **Close**. Be sure to save the document or template that you copied the style to.

If you want to delete a style from a particular template or document, display the template or document in the left side of the dialog box, select the style you want to delete, and click the **Delete** button.

Creating Your Own Template

In Chapter 3, you saw examples of creating a new document based on a template. The templates shown in that chapter contained text, but even templates with no text can contain something valuable: styles. If you create a template and copy your own styles into it, then new documents based on that template will have the same styles available.

This lets you re-use styles more easily without mixing up invoice styles with proposal styles. And you can give the resulting template to other people you work with, making the whole group's formatting consistent.

To create a template with your styles:

1. Choose **New** from the File menu.
2. Select the **General** tab and select **Blank Document**. The **Blank Document** icon represents the Normal template. Word calls it *Blank Document* to make it sound more user-friendly.
3. Click on **Template** in the Create New area in the lower-right corner of the dialog box, then click **OK**.
4. Open the Organizer (choose **Style** from the Format menu and click the **Organizer** button) and use the techniques from the previous section

to copy the styles you want from another document or template. (You can also create styles from scratch in the template, as if it were any other document.)

5. Delete any text you may have typed in the template. The reason for this is that we want only styles in the template, not boilerplate text. If you leave the text in, each new document based on the template will begin with this same text.
6. Choose **Save** from the File menu to open the Save As dialog box. The folder you open determines which tab of the New dialog box will display your template. If you use the main **Templates** folder (the default), your template will appear with the **Blank Document** icon (the Normal template) in the **General** tab.
7. Type a name for the template and click **Save**. The styles in this template will now be available when you choose **New** from the File menu and create a new document based on this template.

USING AUTOFORMAT

Now that you've learned how to work with styles, here's a feature that makes formatting even easier. Word's AutoFormat feature can make you look like you spent hours refining your formatting when what you really did was—nothing. This feature uses IntelliSense technology that actually makes educated guesses about the kind of formatting you might want, based on how you type a document.

For example, if a one-line paragraph starts with a capital letter and blank paragraphs before and after it, Word assumes the paragraph should be a heading. AutoFormat can also clean up extra paragraphs, turn double hyphens into true typographical dashes, turn a long group of spaces into tabs with appropriate tab settings, and a host of other stuff. It's like having an expert graphic designer at your side while you work.

AutoFormat is flexible, too. You can have AutoFormat watch in the background and format your document while you type, or you can have AutoFormat analyze and format an existing document that's already been typed. In either case, you have the option of accepting or rejecting each formatting change individually or accepting everything wholesale.

Should you use AutoFormat? If you're following a strict style sheet and all the decisions about formatting have already been made in your workgroup, then probably not. But if you don't have a clue about formatting, or you just don't want to be bothered with it, AutoFormat is a great idea. It can smooth out the formatting and typing glitches that could otherwise cause eyestrain and readability headaches.

Formatting as You Type with AutoFormat

If you let AutoFormat take care of the formatting while you type, it's easier to concentrate on the content of your document and worry about its appearance later. Even if the formatting isn't exactly what you want, it can give you a good head start.

By default, **AutoFormat As You Type** is turned on. Some of the changes can be confusing—and may even cause drastic changes to your carefully planned formatting. I prefer to work with **AutoFormat As You Type** turned off. That way I can control my own formatting and still have the freedom to use the AutoFormat feature when *I* want it. To turn off **AutoFormat As You Type**, choose **AutoCorrect** from the Tools menu and select the **AutoFormat As You Type** tab. Deselect (click on the item to remove the check mark) any items you don't want Word to handle automatically.

With **AutoFormat As You Type** turned on, AutoFormat watches in the background while you type a document. When you type something that looks like it could be formatted in a typical way, AutoFormat jumps in and makes the change.

If you decide to use **AutoFormat As You Type**, make sure the **Office Assistant** is turned on. If it's not, you won't get any warning or notification when Word makes an AutoFormat change.

Unless you've changed Word's default options, Word is already set up to use the **AutoFormat As You Type** feature. If you follow the examples in this section and nothing happens, choose **AutoCorrect** from the Tools menu and select the **AutoFormat As You Type** tab. Any of the items that don't have check marks are turned off. To turn them on, just click on the item to place a check mark in its box.

Make sure the Office Assistant is visible. If it's not, click the **Office Assistant** button on the Standard toolbar (the question mark at the right end). This isn't required, but the Office Assistant provides valuable information while you're using **AutoFormat As You Type**.

Here's an example of formatting while you type. Press the **Enter** key once, then type a short phrase that begins with a capital letter, and press **Enter** twice. After the first time you press **Enter**, the line looks like Figure 20.11.

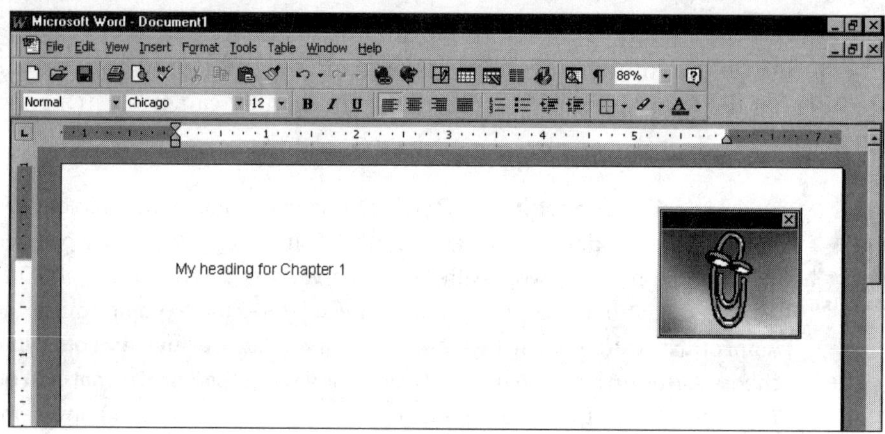

***Figure 20.11** A line of text before AutoFormat is applied.*

When you press the **Enter** key the second time, AutoFormat guesses that this line should be a heading and applies the heading format. The Office Assistant tells you what just happened and gives you some options, as shown in Figure 20.12.

At this point, you can just ignore the change and keep on typing. If you don't like or don't understand the change, you can use the Office Assistant to undo the formatting change or turn the option off.

To undo the Autoformat change, click **No, change it back to how it was** in the Office Assistant.

If you undo an AutoFormat change, the Office Assistant gives you the option of changing your mind yet again. If you decide you were too hasty in undoing the change, click **Yes, please do it** to reapply the suggested formatting.

To turn off an automatic formatting option, click **Explain how to turn this option off** in the Office Assistant. When you do this, Word slowly moves the mouse pointer for you as it opens the AutoFormat As You Type tab dialog box to show how you can change the option to keep this formatting change from happening in the future.

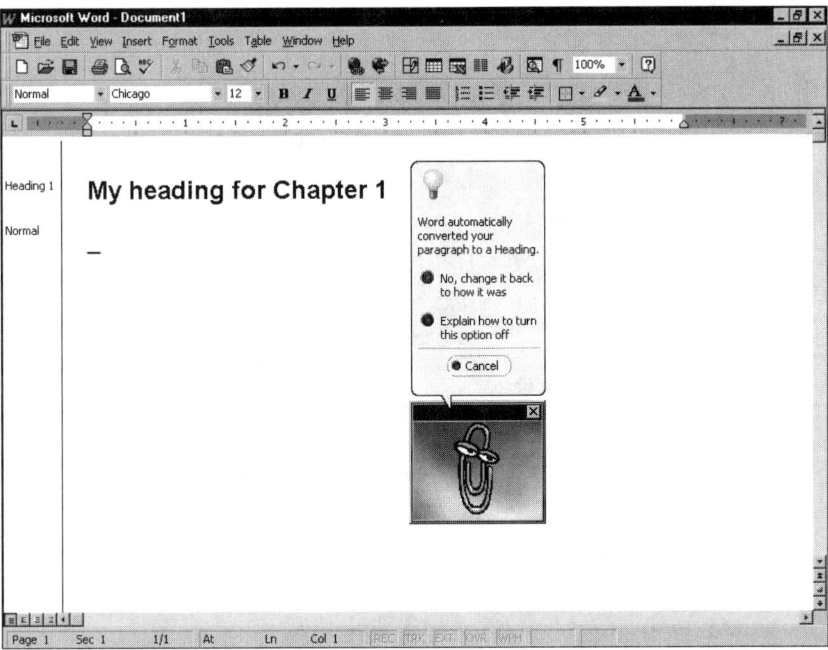

Figure 20.12 The line is reformatted, and the Office Assistant describes the formatting change.

Formatting Existing Text with AutoFormat

As I mentioned earlier, using **AutoFormat As You Type** isn't always the best way to go. And you probably have many existing documents already. Using AutoFormat on existing documents is an easy way to make text files more readable and apply formatting all at once to normal Word documents that you've already typed.

When you use AutoFormat to format a document that's already typed, you're not giving up control. You'll still have the option of accepting some changes, rejecting others, accepting all the changes at once, or rejecting all the changes. It's up to you.

To format a document with autoformat:

1. Open a document you want to format.
2. Choose **AutoFormat** from the Format menu to open the AutoFormat dialog box shown in Figure 20.13.

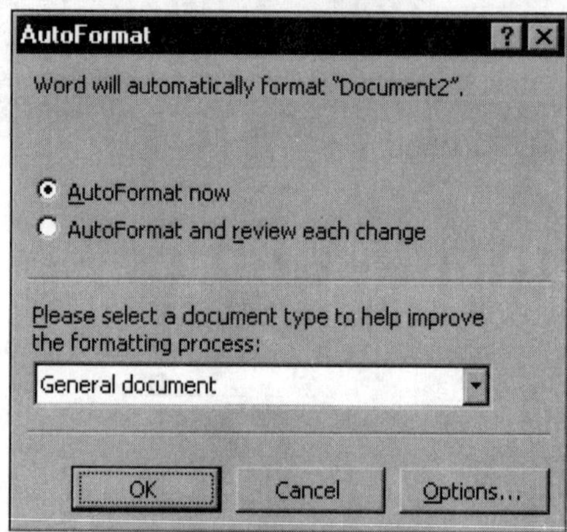

Figure 20.13 The AutoFormat dialog box.

3. Select the options you want and click **OK**.

- If you choose **AutoFormat now**, Word formats the document without any input from you. Of course, if you select this option and are unhappy with the result, you can use the **Undo** option to reverse the formatting changes.
- If you choose **AutoFormat and review each change**, Word stops at each proposed change and lets you decide what to do.
- The AutoFormat choices Word makes are dependent on the type of document. Make a selection from the document type drop-down list that most closely matches your document.
- If you click the **Options** button, Word takes you to the **AutoFormat** tab in the AutoCorrect dialog box, where you can specify which kinds of formatting changes you do and don't want AutoFormat to make.

Here's what happens during the process if you select **AutoFormat and review each change**: Word formats the document and displays the dialog box shown in Figure 20.14.

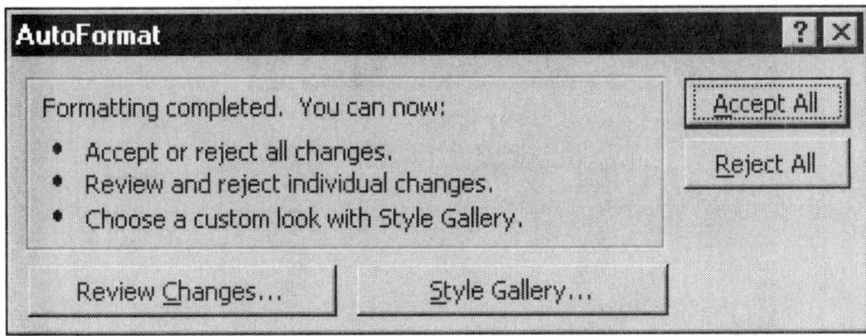

***Figure 20.14** At this point, you can accept or reject the formatting changes.*

Click **Review Changes** to see each formatting change one at a time.

You can also click **Accept All** or **Reject All** to accept or reject all the changes at once without reviewing them, and you're done. If you choose to review the changes, the dialog box shown in Figure 20.15 appears.

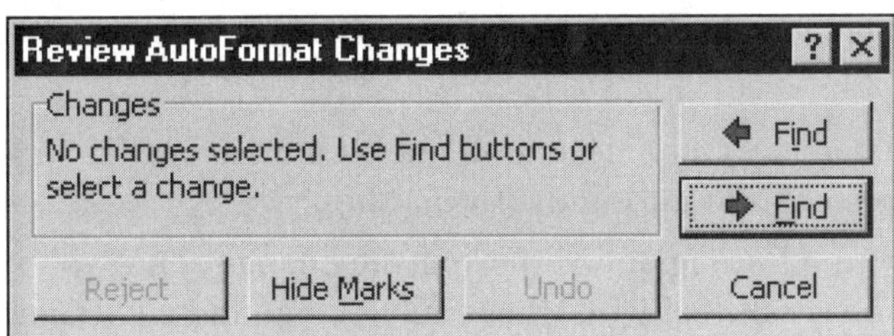

***Figure 20.15** Click one of the **Find** buttons to select a formatting change to review.*

Click the **Find** button with the right arrow to see the first formatting change. Word highlights the changed text, and the Changes box tells you what formatting change was made (as shown in Figure 20.16).

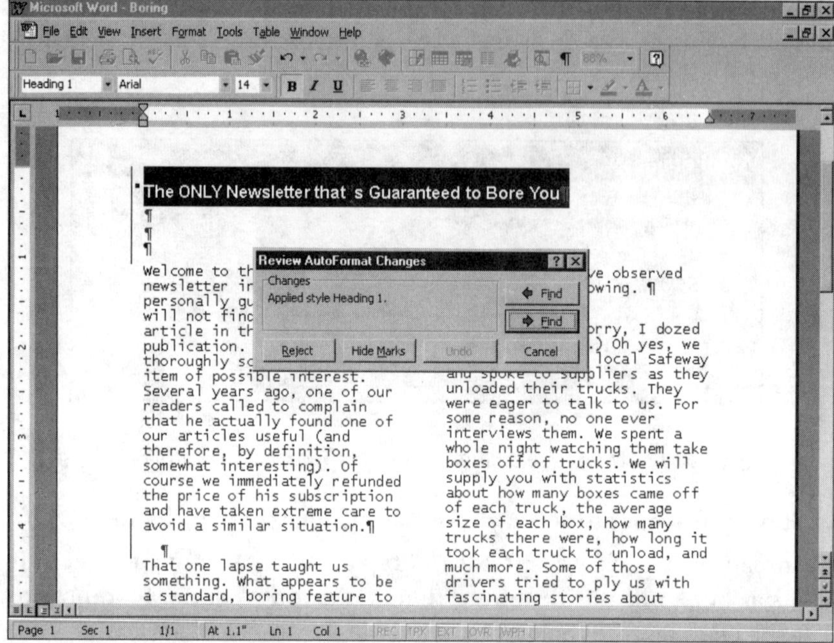

Figure 20.16 Word highlights the changed text and explains the change.

1. Click **Find** again to move to the next change, or click **Reject** to return the selection to its original formatting.
2. Continue finding and reviewing the changes until you've seen them all or are satisfied with what you've seen, and click **Cancel** or **Close**. You now have another chance to accept the changes you've approved or to reject them all. If you click **Accept All**, you're not accepting all the original changes—just the ones you didn't reject individually.
3. Click **Accept All** or **Reject All**.

As you read over this procedure, it may look a little complicated; it really isn't. AutoFormat is one of those features that looks intimidating on paper but flows very naturally on the screen when you use it. It's harmless, too. If you mistakenly accept all the changes when you don't really want them, you can click the **Undo** command once or twice to go back to your original formatting.

From Here...

No more excuses for inconsistent formatting—you know how to use styles and AutoFormat to help you achieve consistent formatting in your documents. And you know that by using styles, you can quickly make changes throughout a document just by editing a style.

This chapter completes the section on automation tools. The next section covers organizational and referencing tools. You'll learn about features that will help you work with large documents, and I'll show you how to work with several documents at one time. In the next chapter, you'll see how easy it is to create bulleted and numbered lists and to organize your thoughts with the outline feature.

SECTION VII

Organizational and Reference Tools

CHAPTER 21

Creating Lists and Outlines

Let's talk about:

- Creating bulleted and numbered lists
- Creating outlines
- Collapsing and expanding the outline
- Printing outlines

If only I could organize my thoughts as easily as Word can organize my lists and outlines! With Word's Outline view, I never have to remember which number comes next or which level I'm supposed to be in (but I still have to come up with the ideas to put in the outline—maybe they'll have a solution for that by the next version). I can collapse the outline to see only the major headings. When I move an entire "family" of outline text to a new location, it automatically renumbers. But before we get to all the fancy outline stuff, there's an even easier feature for creating a quick bulleted or numbered list.

Creating a Bulleted or Numbered List

Bullets can add pizzazz to what might otherwise be a boring list. But consider the steps you'd have to go through by yourself to create a bulleted list: find out how to create a bullet character, press **Tab**, type some text, add a tab setting for where the text should start, then set the left indent to where the following line should start. That's a lot of work.

There's a much easier way: click one button and type your text. That's all. There's even a way to have Word format your lists automatically without using the toolbar. Either way, you'll never have to look up a bullet character or go back and renumber your list three times after you've added or deleted numbered items.

With hardly any effort, your numbered and bulleted lists will look like those in Figure 21.1.

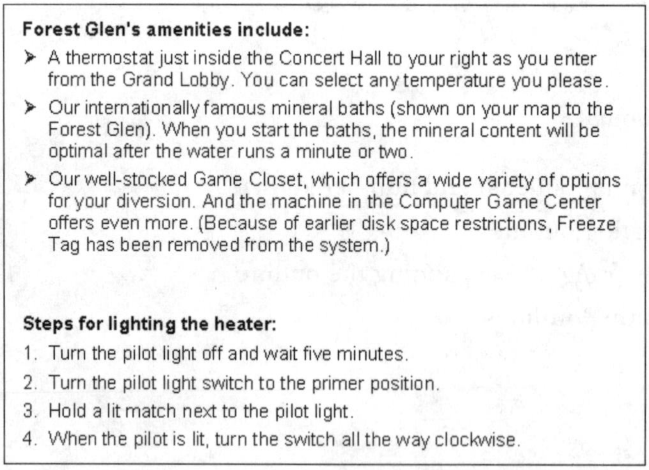

Forest Glen's amenities include:

➤ A thermostat just inside the Concert Hall to your right as you enter from the Grand Lobby. You can select any temperature you please.

➤ Our internationally famous mineral baths (shown on your map to the Forest Glen). When you start the baths, the mineral content will be optimal after the water runs a minute or two.

➤ Our well-stocked Game Closet, which offers a wide variety of options for your diversion. And the machine in the Computer Game Center offers even more. (Because of earlier disk space restrictions, Freeze Tag has been removed from the system.)

Steps for lighting the heater:

1. Turn the pilot light off and wait five minutes.
2. Turn the pilot light switch to the primer position.
3. Hold a lit match next to the pilot light.
4. When the pilot is lit, turn the switch all the way clockwise.

Figure 21.1 *Sample bulleted and numbered lists.*

Creating a Numbered List

Numbered lists are best for items that have an implied sequence, such as instruction steps, or where the numbers are significant, as in a Top Twenty list. For other collections of items, a bulleted list is better.

To create a numbered list:

1. Click the **Numbering** button on the Formatting toolbar.
2. Type the items in the list, pressing **Enter** after each one.
3. When you're finished, click the **Numbering** button again to turn off numbering for subsequent paragraphs.

If you add new lines in the middle of the list or delete existing lines, the list is automatically renumbered to take your changes into account. You can't select the numbers themselves because they are part of the paragraph formatting.

To create an automatic numbered list:

1. On a blank line, type **1** followed by a **period**, and press the **Tab** key.
2. Type the first item in your numbered list and press **Enter** (as shown in Figure 21.2).

```
1.    Choose Shut Down from the Start menu|
```

Figure 21.2 *The first numbered item.*

As soon as you press **Enter**, Word recognizes that you're starting a numbered list and immediately applies the formatting and numbers the next paragraph for you, as shown in Figure 21.3.

```
1.    Choose Shut Down from the Start menu.
2.    |
```

Figure 21.3 *The list after pressing **Enter**.*

3. Add your other list items, pressing **Enter** after each one.

4. When you're finished with the list, press **Enter** to add a new numbered line, then press **Backspace** or click the **Numbering** button on the Formatting toolbar. Either action returns the paragraph to normal formatting without numbers.

Creating a List of Bulleted Items

Creating a list where each item is marked with a bullet is almost exactly the same as creating a numbered list. As with numbered lists, you can't select the bullet character because it's part of the paragraph formatting.

To create a bulleted list:

1. Click in the paragraph you want to format.
2. Click the **Bullets** button on the Formatting toolbar.
3. Type the items in your list, pressing **Enter** after each one.
4. When you're finished, click the **Bullets** button again.

To create an automatic bulleted list without using the toolbar:

1. On a blank line, type an **asterisk (*)** and press **Tab**.
2. Type the first item in the bulleted list and press **Enter** (as shown in Figure 21.4.

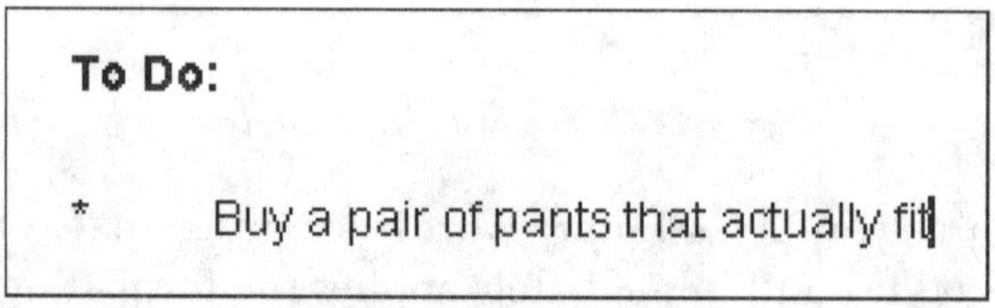

To Do:

*   Buy a pair of pants that actually fit

Figure 21.4 *The first bulleted item.*

As soon as you press **Enter**, Word figures out that you're starting a bulleted list and applies bulleted formatting, as shown in Figure 21.5.

To Do:

- Buy a pair of pants that actually fit
- |

Figure 21.5 When you press ***Enter****, Word automatically inserts a bullet and a tab.*

NOTE This option uses the **AutoFormat As You Type** feature. If **Automatic bulleted lists** isn't checked in the **AutoFormat As You Type** tab of the AutoCorrect dialog box, the steps described in this section won't work. The same goes for the earlier instructions for creating a numbered list, if **Automatic numbered lists** isn't checked.

3. Type the entries in your list, pressing **Enter** after each one.
4. When you're finished, press **Backspace** or click the **Bullets** button on the Formatting toolbar.

Changing the Bullet or Number Style

Word uses simple defaults for bulleted and numbered lists. The bullets are simple filled circles, and the numbering uses Arabic numerals (1,2,3) followed by a period. You can change these options for different effects.

To change bullet and numbering options:

1. Select all the items of the list that you want to format.
2. Choose **Bullets and Numbering** from the Format menu.
3. Select the **Bulleted** or **Numbered** tab (shown in Figures 21.6 and 21.7), depending on the type of list.
4. Click on the format you want to use, then click **OK**.

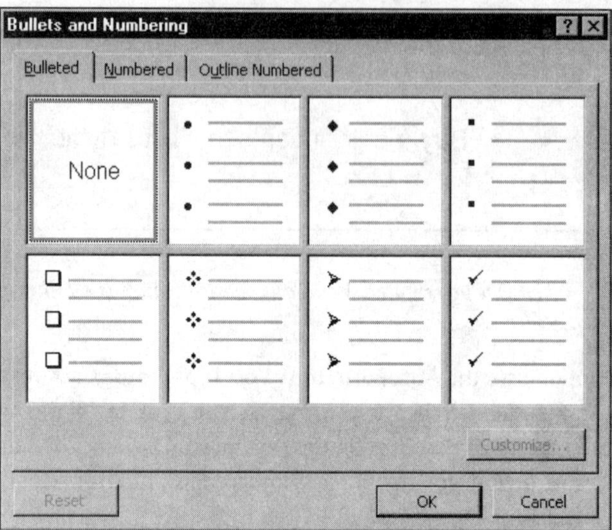

*Figure 21.6 The **Bulleted** tab in the Bullets and Numbering dialog box.*

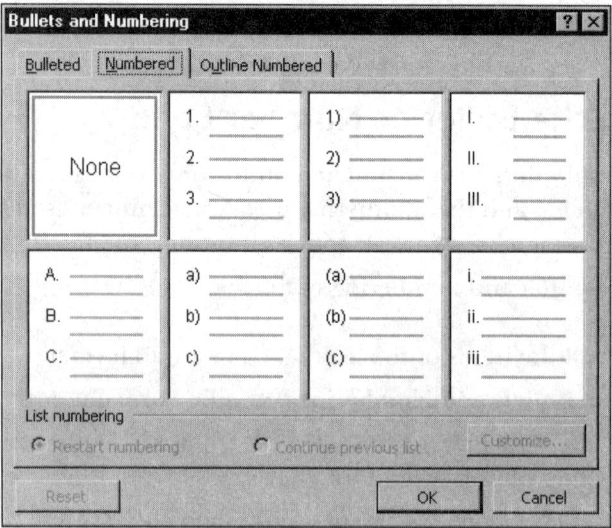

*Figure 21.7 The **Numbered** tab in the Bullets and Numbering dialog box.*

The formatting is applied to the selected items (not the entire list).

You can access additional options by clicking the **Customize** button from either the **Bulleted** or **Numbered** tab. Figure 21.8 shows the Customize Bulleted List dialog box.

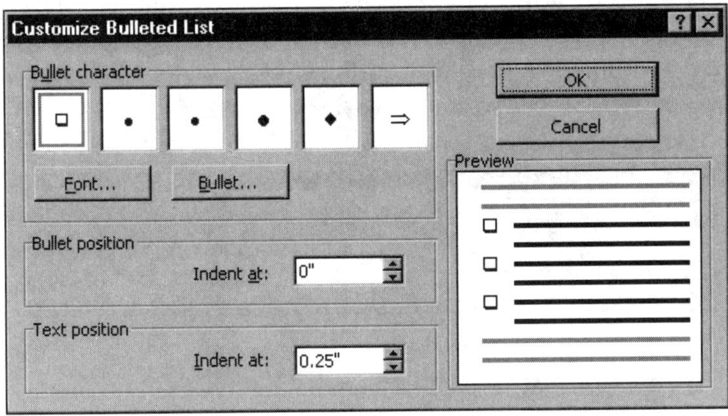

Figure 21.8 The Customize Bulleted List dialog box.

NOTE

You can turn existing text into a bulleted or numbered list by selecting the paragraphs you want and then clicking the **Numbering** or **Bullets** button on the Formatting toolbar. You can even change a bulleted list to a numbered one or vice versa. For example, if you have a bulleted list that you want numbered, just select the list and click the **Numbering** button.

If you decide you don't want the bullets or numbers anymore, no problem. Just select the list and click the **Numbering** button if it's a numbered list or the **Bullets** button if it's a bulleted list.

OUTLINES

Okay, bullets and numbers are pretty cool for a quick list, but what about a real outline? Creating your outline can be as simple as turning on Outline view and typing your text, but the feature contains enough power to manipulate your outlines in almost any way you desire.

Understanding Outline Levels

An outline usually contains items grouped according to their relation to a main topic. A main topic could have several subordinate topics, and each subordinate topic could have its own set of subcategories. In outline terminology, each group or subgroup is a *level*, and an entry and all its subordinate levels are considered a *family*. In a standard outline, subordinate levels are indented under their parents, as shown in Figure 21.9.

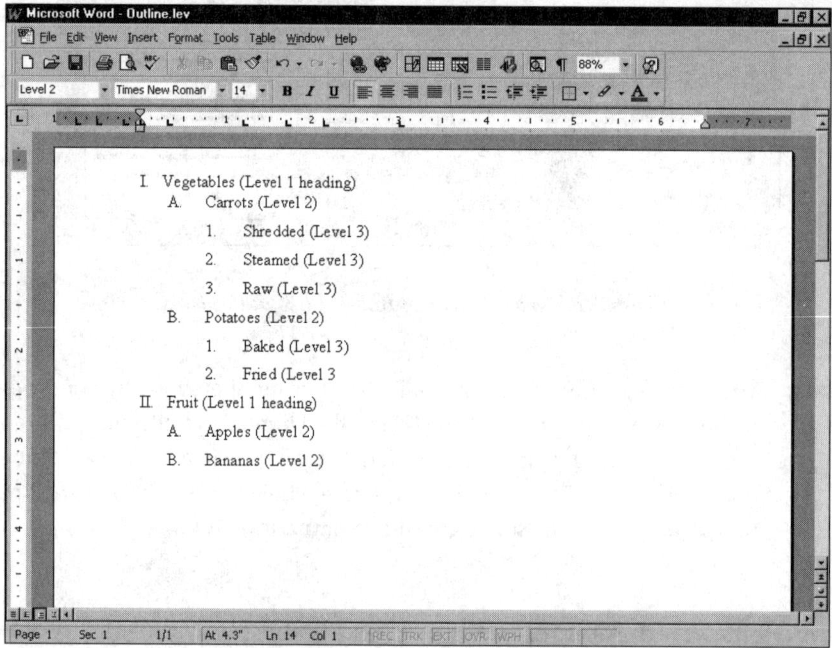

Figure 21.9 *A sample outline with three levels.*

In the figure, vegetables is a major category, so it's a first-level item at the left margin. Carrots and potatoes are second-level items that are part of the vegetables family. The different carrot classifications belong to both the carrots family and the vegetables family. The family concept will become important when you start moving outline groups around.

The second-level items are indented one tab stop under the first-level items. As you add levels, each level is indented one tab stop to the right and given a different numbering style. You can choose from several predefined outline styles or create your own. We'll talk about the different styles later, but I wanted you to have a basic understanding of outline levels before you create your own outline.

Displaying a Document in Outline View

Outlines make use of Word's built-in heading styles, so if you have a document that uses these styles, you already have the basis for an outline. When you're looking at one page at a time in Normal or Page Layout view, it can be difficult to get a feel for whether the sequence of chapters and sections in your work makes sense. This is the main advantage of Outline view—it lets you view and modify the organization of your document.

To display a document in Outline view, just choose **Outline** from the View menu or click the **Outline View** button in the lower-left corner of the document window.

In Outline view, you can work with any level of detail in the document. You can see only the top level or two of your headings, add a few lower-level headings, or see the entire document, including body text. You can use this hierarchical view to see and organize an existing document, or you can compose your entire document this way. You can also use Outline view as a quick way to move or rearrange large chunks of a document by dragging rather than cutting and pasting.

A final advantage of Word's Outline view is that as you choose a heading level, Word automatically applies the appropriate heading style for you. With these headings assigned, modifying heading styles or generating a table of contents takes only a few seconds. If you plan to create a table of contents, you should definitely look at your document in Outline view.

Using Heading Styles

Outline view is based on the built-in heading styles—Heading 1, Heading 2, and so on. As you promote or demote headings to higher or lower levels in your outline, Word applies the corresponding heading style. For example, I organized this book in Outline view. Chapter names are Heading 1, the main headings in each chapter are second level (Heading 2), and subheadings go down from there. But you can start with any level you like. For example, you could have a special Chapter style for the chapter name, then use Outline view, and begin with Heading 1 for the headings within each chapter.

Remember that if you don't like the default fonts and paragraph formatting assigned to the built-in heading styles, you can modify them. If you leave the Formatting toolbar displayed while working in Outline view, you can see the style applied to any selected heading. You can also turn on the style bar in Outline view so you can see the styles for all of your paragraphs at once (choose **Options** from the Tools menu, select the **View** tab, and enter a measurement in the Style area width box).

Understanding Outline View

When you change to Outline view, the appearance of your document changes. Paragraphs are displayed at different levels of indentation from the left margin, depending on the heading style, if any, applied to the paragraph. A new toolbar also appears, as shown in Figure 21.10.

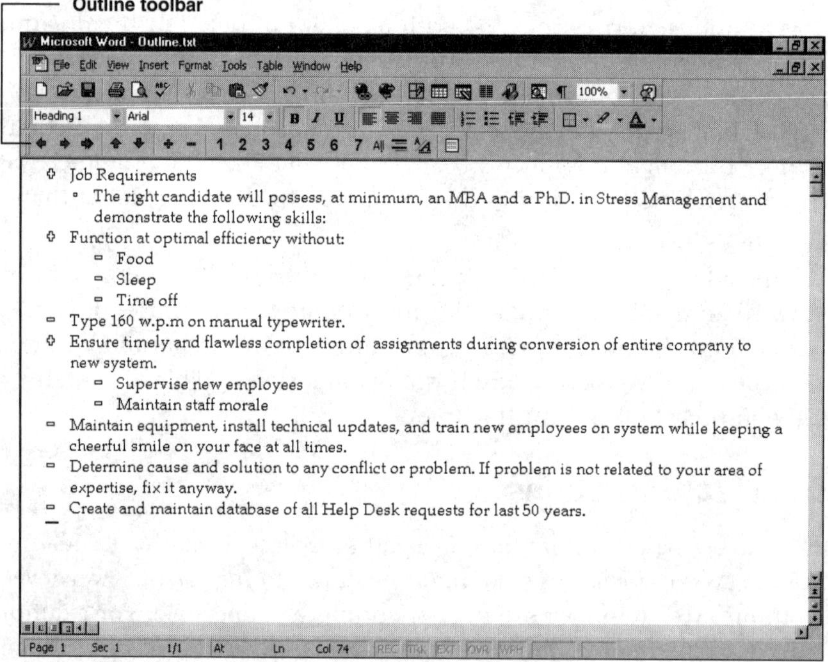

***Figure 21.10** Outline view with the Outline toolbar.*

The buttons on the Outline toolbar allow you to promote and demote headings, rearrange text, expand and collapse the text under a heading, and display different levels of detail. Each heading has a + or - icon, showing that it contains subheadings or body text (+), or has no text under the heading (-).

Inserting Text in Outline View

When editing the existing text in a heading or body paragraph displayed in Outline view, you can type as you normally do. However, whenever you press **Enter** to create a new paragraph, the new paragraph appears at the same level as the preceding paragraph, no matter how the styles are defined. For example, if you add a paragraph after a level 3 heading, the new paragraph is also a level 3 heading. This allows you to quickly assign heading levels for easy rearranging of your outline as you type.

You can also apply font formatting from dialog boxes or from the Formatting toolbar, but paragraph formatting must wait until you're working in Normal or Page Layout view. This lets you concentrate on the content and organization of your document rather than on its appearance.

Assigning a Heading

When you want to change the heading level of a paragraph you can either use buttons on the Outlining toolbar or assign headings visually by dragging the icon to the left of the paragraph. If you move the heading to the left, it is promoted, or changed to a higher heading level (for example, from Heading 2 to Heading 1). If you move a heading to the right, it's demoted. If you demote a paragraph all the way to the right, it ceases to be a heading and becomes a body paragraph with the Normal style.

If you select a group of paragraphs, heading levels change relative to each other. For example, if you demote a selection that includes heading levels 1, 2, and 3, they change to heading levels 2, 3, and 4. Body text retains its original style.

To assign a heading level to a paragraph:

1. Select the paragraph or paragraphs you want to promote or demote.
2. Drag the paragraph's heading icon to the left or right. A dashed vertical line shows where the headings will end up, as shown in Figure 21.11. You can also click the **Promote** or **Demote** button on the Outlining toolbar to change one heading level at a time.

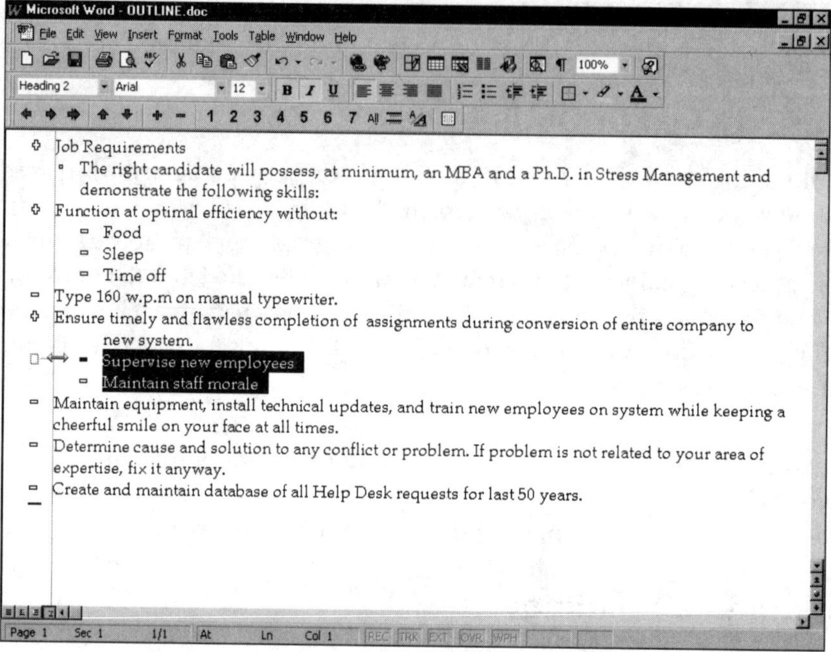

Figure 21.11 *A level 2 heading being promoted to level 1.*

To change a heading to body text:

1. Place the insertion point in the paragraph you want to change to body text.
2. Drag the paragraph's heading icon all the way to the right. The dashed vertical line that shows the heading level moves all the way to the right, then jumps to the left, where the other body paragraphs appear. You can also use the **Demote to Body Text** button on the Outlining toolbar to change a heading to body text.

Expanding and Collapsing Headings

When you're working on an outline, sometimes it helps to be able to see only certain portions of it. For example, you might want to hide everything but the first-level headings to make sure you've covered all your major points. With the plus (+), minus (-), and numbered **Show Heading** buttons, you're in the driver's seat. You can use the buttons on the Outlining toolbar to display as much or as little of your outline as you want:

- Click on the - button to hide all the levels in the current family below the one your insertion point is in.
- Click on the + button to show all the levels of the current family.
- Use the **Show Heading** buttons to display a specified number of outline levels. For example, if you click on **1**, only first-level items are visible; if you click on **7**, all the outline levels down to Heading 7 are visible.
- Click the **All** button to view the entire outline, including any body text.
- Click the **Show First Line Only** button to display all the heading levels and the first line of any body text paragraph.

To fully expand or collapse a heading:

1. Click in the heading paragraph you want to expand or collapse.
2. Click the **Expand** (+) button on the Outlining toolbar or double-click the + icon next to the heading. The paragraph alternates between fully expanded and fully collapsed if you double-click again.

To expand or collapse a heading one level at a time:

1. Click in the paragraph you want to expand or collapse.
2. Click the **Expand** or **Collapse** toolbar button.

Displaying Different Levels of Detail

Before you start working with part of a document, you'll often want to see the organization of the document as a whole. You can quickly adjust how much information is displayed in Outline view to work in as general or as detailed a view as you'd like. One way to do this is to specify how many heading levels are displayed. If you show down to Heading 3, for example, only heading levels 1, 2, and 3 appear in Outline view.

You can simplify the screen display even further by showing only the first line of any paragraph in Outline view. This is especially helpful when you're displaying body text, which is likely to be in paragraphs that are longer than one line. You can also choose to display all text without the font formatting that appears in Normal and Page Layout view. This focuses your attention further on the content of your document and usually means that more text can fit on your screen at one time.

To view your whole document at a limited level of detail, click one of the number buttons on the Outlining toolbar. As you'd expect, the **All** button displays every paragraph in the document.

To show only the first line of each paragraph, click the **Show First Line Only** button on the Outlining toolbar. Paragraphs that would otherwise take more than one line are marked with an ellipse (...) at the end of the line. In most cases, this affects only body text.

To hide or display font formatting, click the **Show Font Formatting** button on the Outlining toolbar.

Moving Outline Text

Even if you aren't applying heading styles scrupulously, Outline view provides a convenient way of moving text anywhere in a document. When you move text, you can drag it and drop it as you normally do, or you can drag the heading icons. When you drag the heading icon, you automatically move all the headings and text subordinate to that heading (the entire family). This makes it easy to rearrange a document to get the organization just right.

You can also use the **Move Up** and **Move Down** toolbar buttons to move selected text up or down, one paragraph at a time, in a document. However, these buttons move only the selected text—not any subordinate headings or body text.

To move selected text anywhere in a document:

1. Select the paragraphs you want to move.
2. Click in the middle of the selected text and drag to the new location. When you release the mouse button, the selected text is inserted at the insertion point.

To move a heading and its subordinate text:

1. Click the icon next to the heading you want to move to select the heading along with any subordinate headings and text, as shown in Figure 21.12.

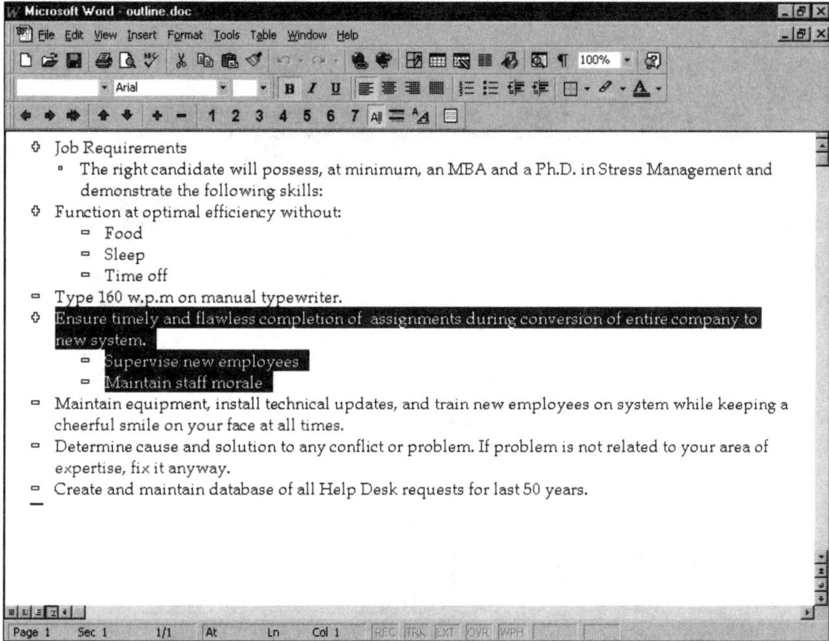

Figure 21.12 *Click a heading icon to select the entire heading family.*

2. Drag the heading icon up or down to its new location in the document. A dashed vertical line attaches itself to your mouse pointer and shows where the text will be inserted when you release the mouse button.

To move selected paragraphs up or down:

1. Click anywhere in the paragraph or select multiple paragraphs.
2. Click the **Move Up** or **Move Down** button on the Outlining toolbar. The selected paragraphs move up or down in the document, one paragraph at a time.

Customizing Outline Numbering Styles

Just as with numbered lists, you can change the numbering style for your outline. To do so, choose **Bullets and Numbering** from the Format menu and select the **Outline Numbered** tab (shown in Figure 21.13).

Select the style you want and click **OK**, or click the **Customize** button for more options.

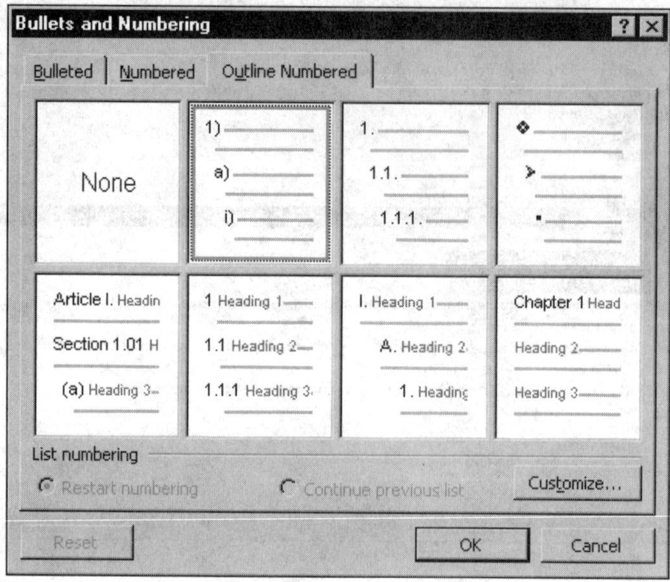

Figure 21.13 The ***Outline Numbered*** *tab in the Bullets and Numbering dialog box.*

Printing an Outline

If you print from Outline view, only the outline headings shown on the screen will be printed. This makes it easy for you or others to review the organization of a document without regard to the formatting or contents of the individual paragraphs.

To print an outline:

1. Adjust the display of Outline view to show only the headings and information you want to print.
2. Choose **Print** from the File menu and click **OK**.

From Here...

You can use bulleted or numbered lists to add emphasis to your reports and presentations without breaking a sweat. And if you have ideas to organize, Word can help you put them in order. You can do your thinking on-screen, moving families and levels around as much as you please.

In the next chapter, we'll make short work out of long documents. You'll learn to generate a table of contents or an index and to cross-reference items in different locations.

CHAPTER 22

Working with Long Documents

Let's talk about:

- Creating a table of contents
- Creating an index
- Cross-referencing index entries
- Updating indexes and tables of contents

Creating a Table of Contents

Creating a table of contents used to mean a lot of work. It could take hours of paging back and forth to find headings, look up page numbers, and format all the information properly. When the book changed and the table of contents had to be updated, it was even more work. In Word, the computer does almost all the work. Once heading styles are applied to headings in your document—either by applying them as you type, or by using Outline view—all you have to do is select a few options to decide how you want the table of contents displayed. Word does the rest.

Updating a table of contents is even easier. All you have to do is select the table and press a key. Word re-creates the table of contents, picking up any added headings and changed text; or, if you choose, Word can update only the page number for each heading.

Word also takes care of formatting, automatically applying built-in styles for each heading level that you include in the table of contents. The only thing you have to do is to add a title before the table of contents.

How a Table of Contents Is Generated

Word creates a table of contents based on the styles assigned to the paragraphs in your document. Generally, you'll assign the styles Heading 1, Heading 2, and so on, to the different levels of headings in your documents. Word searches through the document for paragraphs with these styles, notes the heading level and page number for each, and compiles them into a table of contents. The table of contents itself is a single field. Like page number fields, the table of contents can be updated with a single keystroke.

In spite of it being a field, a table of contents can be formatted one paragraph at a time—or even a character at a time. If you choose to update only page numbers, any manual formatting you apply is preserved. However, if you update the entire table of contents, formatting changes you made may be lost. You can avoid this by modifying the built-in styles TOC 1, TOC 2, and so on. Word uses these styles when formatting the table of contents.

Preparing for the Table of Contents

Your first task in preparing for a table of contents happens when you're composing the document. Because the table of contents is based on styles, each heading you want to display in the table of contents must have a style consistently applied. If you use Outline view to organize your document, your document styles are already consistent.

The other thing you can do to prepare to build a table of contents, if you wish, is to change to Outline view. Here you can decide what level of detail you want to include in the table of contents. For example, you can have a table of contents display only down to second-level headings. By clicking the **Show Heading 2** button on the Outlining toolbar, you'll see which headings the table of contents would include.

Building a Table of Contents

Once you've decided how much detail you want to show in a table of contents (although that step is not required), you're ready to have Word generate the table. You can select from a variety of formatting options often used in tables of contents. For example, you can exclude page numbers, change the way page numbers are displayed, and see previews of a variety of formatting styles.

If your document is consistently formatted with styles but they aren't built-in outlining styles such as Heading 1, you can specify any other style for each level of heading in the table of contents. In most cases, however, you'll have heading styles applied and you can generate a professional-looking table of contents without selecting any options at all.

To build a table of contents:

1. Click where you want to place a table of contents in the document. Because the entire table of contents will be inserted at the insertion point, you may want to insert page breaks before and after that point to make sure the table of contents text is on its own page or pages at the beginning of your document.
2. Choose **Index and Tables** from the Insert menu.
3. Select the **Table of Contents** tab (shown in Figure 22.1).

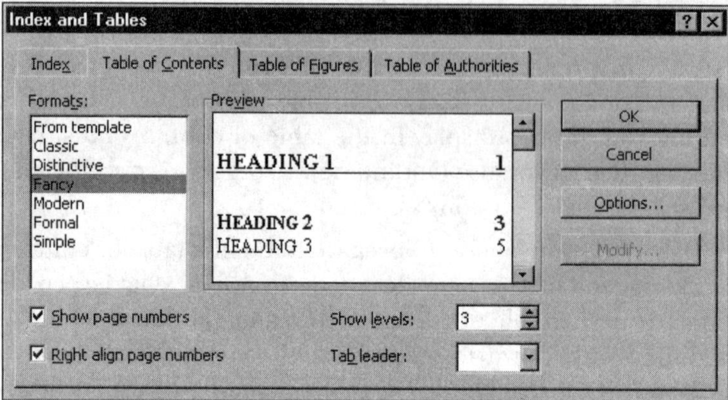

Figure 22.1 The ***Table of Contents*** *tab in the Index and Tables dialog box.*

4. In the **Show levels** box, enter the number of heading levels you want to include in the table of contents.
5. Select the page number and tab leader options you want. Notice that the effects of your choices appear immediately in the Preview box.

- **Show page numbers** displays the page number for each heading. You can turn this option off to show the organization of headings but not their location.
- **Right align page numbers** aligns page numbers at the right margin for each paragraph in the table of contents. With this option off, the numbers are placed right next to the heading text.
- **Tab leader** inserts a row of periods, dashes, or underlines between each heading and its page number. This option is available only if the other two options are selected.

6. Select a set of table of contents style from the Formats list and click **OK**. The **From Template** option uses the table of contents styles in the template on which your document is based (usually **Normal.dot**).
7. When you've selected all your options, click **OK**. Figure 22.2 shows a completed table of contents.

NOTE

The entire table of contents is a field. When you click anywhere inside it, the whole thing is highlighted with a gray background, but you can still select and edit portions of the table.

COMMON PLUMBING PROBLEMS..1

Clogged shower drains..1

Burst pipes..2
Under the house..5
In the basement..5
Under the lawn..7
Between walls..7

Leaks under sinks..9
Finding the source..9
Turning off the water supply..12

Water running in toilets..12

ELECTRICAL REPAIRS..13

Fuse replacements..13

Circuit breakers..13

Light fixtures..13

Figure 22.2 The completed table of contents.

By default, the table of contents is based on Heading 1, Heading 2, and so on. If you have other styles assigned, click **Options** from the **Table of Contents** tab to open the Table of Contents Options dialog box shown in Figure 22.3 and specify which style goes with which heading level.

Table of Contents Options

Build table of contents from:
Styles
Available styles: TOC level:
Heading 1 1
Heading 2 2
Heading 3 3
Heading 4
Heading 5
Heading 6
Table entry fields

OK
Cancel
Reset

Figure 22.3 The Table of Contents Options dialog box.

Formatting the Table of Contents

Although the table of contents is a field that can be updated, you can still format the characters and paragraphs as you would any other text in your document. You can change fonts, apply paragraph styles, change spacing, and so on.

As you learned from reading about styles in Chapter 20, the easiest way to change the formats in the table of contents is to modify a style. That way, all the appropriate paragraphs in the table of contents are reformatted at the same time. The styles used are TOC 1, TOC 2, and so on, corresponding to the heading levels shown in the table of contents.

Any individual formatting other than what you apply with styles may be lost when you update the table of contents. That's another good reason to modify the table of contents styles, rather than formatting the text directly.

Updating a Table of Contents

This is the greatest reason to use Word's table of contents feature. A task that could take hours—scouring through hundreds of pages of a reformatted book to find new page numbers for each heading—requires no work at all. Because the table of contents is a field, it can be updated automatically. The computer does the work.

When you update a table of contents, you can do it the quick way or the thorough way. The quick way is to refresh only the page numbers, which assumes that the headings haven't changed. If you've changed the organization of the document or reworded some of the headings, then you should update the entire table of contents rather than just the page numbers.

To update the table of contents:

1. Click anywhere in the table of contents to select the field.
2. Press **F9**. Word lets you specify how much of the table of contents you want to update (see Figure 22.4).
3. Select the option you want and click **OK**. Word passes through the document, updating the information in the table of contents field.

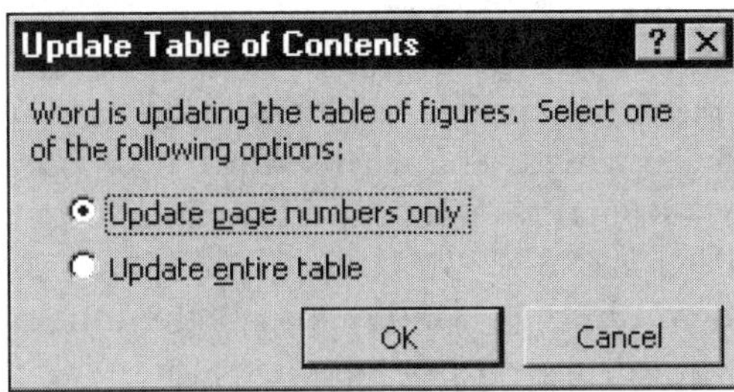

Figure 22.4 *You can update the entire table of contents or just the page numbers.*

Creating an Index

As laborious as it is to create a table of contents by hand without a table of contents feature, creating an index by hand is even harder. In a table of contents, at least it's clear where the headings are, and it's simple to decide which headings to include. Not so with an index. You must decide which words to index, how to phrase the index entry, and what synonyms to use for it in other entries. You must type those phrases for the index, track down all the page numbers for the appropriate pages, and keep everything updated. Word removes some of the drudgery from this process.

Notice that I said *some* of the drudgery is removed. You should know before you proceed that indexing is hard work. Creating a bad index is easy. The hardest part of creating a good index is reviewing the entire document, one page at a time, putting yourself in the reader's shoes to consider what entries might be useful, and wording them in a consistent way. A multilevel index, where an individual entry such as *Aircraft* lists entries for particular types of airplanes underneath it, is even harder. Indexing is an art, not a science.

But whether you're making a good index or a bad one, Word does the dirty work, leaving the mental exertion to you. The index feature gathers index entries with the same heading, applies formatting styles, arranges the index in multiple columns, and keeps track of the page numbers for each entry. You decide what to index and how to word each entry. Is it worth it? If you remember how frustrated you were the last time you used a poor index, you'll want to make a good one.

How Indexing Works in Word

After working with page numbers and tables of contents, you won't be surprised to learn that an index is a field. This allows Word to keep track of its items and page numbers for automatic updating. How do you get an item into the index? You go to the page in the document containing the information you want to index, and you insert an index entry. The index entry, also a field, contains the text that will appear in the index, along with the page number.

If you select text before marking an index entry, the selected text is automatically inserted in the index entry, so you don't have to type it again. You can also choose to rephrase the text to make it consistent with other entries in your index. That's where the hard work comes in. When you've finished marking all the index entries in a document, you can build the index, choosing among the most common formatting options for a professional-looking index.

Marking Items for the Index

When you mark text as an index entry, Word inserts a field containing the information about the index entry. A typical index entry in the body of your document looks like Figure 22.5.

Figure 22.5 *An index entry field.*

The *XE* identifies the field as an index entry, the text that will appear in the index is *River Barges,* and the *\i* at the end means that the page number will be shown in italic in the finished index. If you've specified other formats for the index entry, such as a bold page number, those options appear in the field. You can edit the River Barges text to change the entry, but don't edit anything in the field except the text between quotation marks. If you want to change other options, it's best to delete the field and re-insert the index entry.

Normally, field codes like this are not visible in a Word document. But because you need to see what you've indexed, Word marks them as hidden text and turns on the display of hidden text and other hidden characters as soon as you mark an index entry. You can turn the display of index entries on and off by clicking the **Show/Hide ¶** button on the Standard toolbar.

Marking a Simple Index Entry

In shorter documents, most of your index entries are likely to be simple, single-level entries (for example, *Lawn sprinklers, 225*). After you insert an entry, you can add other entries for the same location without any further commands. This lets you add synonym terms easily (for example, *Sprinklers, lawn*).

To mark an item as a main index entry:

1. Go to the page in your document with the information you want to index and select a word or phrase for the index entry. Don't worry if this isn't exactly the text you want to use. You can edit the text in the dialog box.
2. Press **Alt-Shift-X**. Or choose **Index and Tables** from the Insert menu, go to the Index tab, and click **Mark Entry**. The Mark Index Entry dialog box shown in Figure 22.6 is displayed.

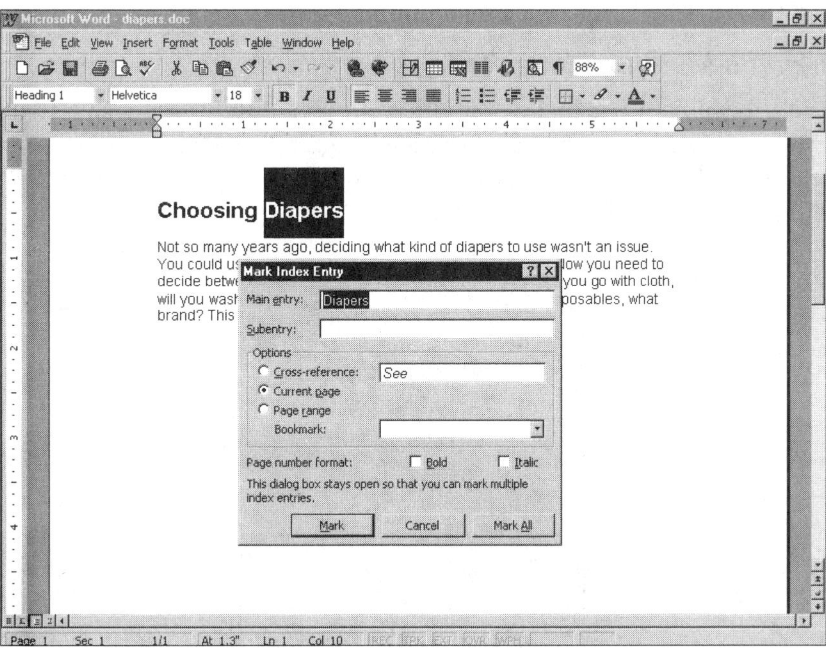

Figure 22.6 The Mark Index Entry dialog box.

3. If necessary, edit the text in the Main entry text box.

4. Select the **Bold** and/or **Italic** check box if you want to format the page numbers. It's sometimes useful to mark as bold the most important of several page numbers in an entry. Some indexes use italic to mark pages with illustrations or some other special meaning.
5. Click **Mark**, then click **Close**. The index entry is inserted in your document. If nonprinting characters weren't already displayed, they are now, as shown in Figure 22.7.

Choosing·Diapers{·XE·"Diapers"·}¶

Not·so·many·years·ago,·deciding·what·kind·of·diapers·to·use·wasn't·an·issue.· You·could·use·cotton,·or·you·could·use·cotton.·That·was·that.·Now·you·need·to· decide·between·cotton·cloth·diapers·and·disposable·diapers.·If·you·go·with·cloth,· will·you·wash·them·yourself·or·use·a·service?·If·you·go·with·disposables,·what· brand?·This·article·will·offer·some·guidance.¶

Figure 22.7 *A paragraph with an index field displayed.*

Marking a Multilevel Index Entry

You can specify a subentry for a multilevel index entry when a simple index entry would result in more than five or six page references in the final index. The index in Figure 22.8 shows a single-level entry, followed by several multi-level entries.

Comb, 2
Crib
    adjusting height, 52
    safety issues, 51
    selecting, 11
    sheets, 11
Crying
    causes, 2
    length, 4
    recognizing types of, 4
    solutions to try, 3

Figure 22.8 *A multilevel index.*

The key tip here is to be consistent in how you word the main entry for each index item. For example, you wouldn't want entries for *Crib* and *Cribs* in the same index.

To create a multilevel index entry:

1. Select text and press **Alt-Shift-X**.
2. In the Main entry and Subentry boxes, type the main and subordinate title (if any) for the index entry and click **Mark**.
3. When you've completed your entries, click **Close**.

If you need subheadings beyond two levels, insert a colon between each added heading in the Subentry box (for example, *Baby:care of:navel*).

Creating Many Index Entries at Once

Marking too many index entries in your document for a single term can result in a hard-to-use index. Think of how daunting it would be to find a reference like this: *Basketball, 2, 6–7, 8, 11, 15, 22, 35, 48, 51–60, 85, 105.* That's the danger of using the **Mark All** feature when indexing.

However, for important words that you're sure appear only a few times in a document, using this feature can save time.

To create index entries for every instance of a word or phrase:

1. Select the first instance of the word or phrase in the document and press **Alt-Shift-X**.
2. In the Main entry and Subentry boxes, type the main and subordinate title for the index entry and click **Mark All**.
3. Click **Close**. Word inserts index fields every place in the document where the main entry or subentry text appears.

Creating Cross-References in an Index

Where a reader may think of an idea one way and you've indexed it another way, use a cross-reference to point the reader to the full index entry. Cross-references don't appear with page numbers; the entry they refer to should contain the page numbers. Be certain that your cross-reference points to a real index entry. Figure 22.9 shows a typical index cross-reference.

Binky. See Pacifier

Figure 22.9 *A cross-referenced index entry.*

To create a cross-referenced index entry:

1. Select the first instance of the word or phrase in the document and press **Alt-Shift-X**.
2. In the Main Entry box, type the text that the cross-reference will be listed under.
3. Click in the **Cross-reference** text box and type the exact text of the index entry you want to refer to.
4. Click **Mark**, then click **Close**. The **Mark All** button isn't available for cross-referencing because you need to mark a cross-reference entry only once.

Including a Range of Pages in the Index

Where you discuss a topic for several pages in a row, a series of individual page numbers in the index isn't useful. It's easier to make sense of *5–9* than *5, 6, 7, 8, 9.* To create an index entry for such a range, you first select the series of pages and create a *bookmark*—a selection that Word remembers by name. The resulting entry in the index shows the range of pages covered by the bookmark (as shown in Figure 22.10).

Postpartum blues, 30-37

Figure 22.10 *An index entry for a range of pages.*

To mark an index entry for a range of pages:

1. Select the pages of text that you want to include a single index entry for.
2. Choose **Bookmark** from the Insert menu to open the Bookmark dialog box shown in Figure 22.11.

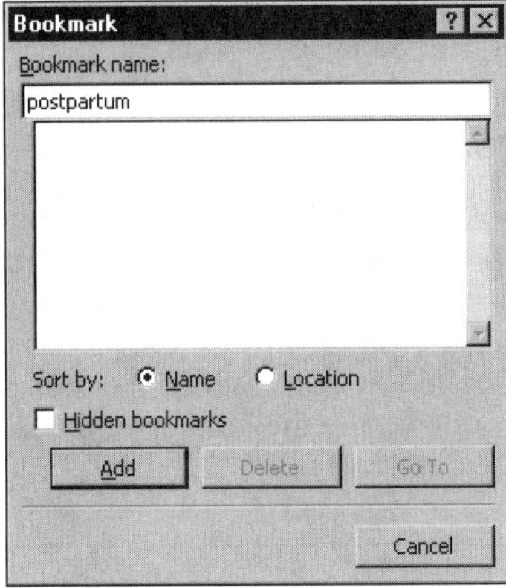

Figure 22.11 *The Bookmark dialog box.*

3. Type a name (without spaces) that describes the selection and click **Add**. This creates a bookmark that Word can associate with the index entry.
4. Press **Alt-Shift-X** while the pages are still selected.
5. In the Main entry and Subentry boxes, type the text for the index entry.
6. Select the bookmark you just created from the Bookmark drop-down list, as shown in Figure 22.12.

Mark Index Entry
Main entry: Postpartum blues
Subentry:
Options
Cross-reference: See
Current page
Page range
Bookmark: postpartum
Page number format: Bold Italic
This dialog box stays open so that you can mark multiple index entries.
Mark Cancel Mark All

Figure 22.12 *The Mark Index Entry dialog box with a bookmark pointing to a page range.*

7. Click **Mark**, then **Close**. In the final index, the index item displays the range of pages defined by the bookmark.

Building an Index

Most of the hard work is over now. When you build an index, you have several formatting options. Chief among these is the type of index: indented or run-in. An *indented* index is easier to read because each index entry has its own line. If you're short on space, a *run-in* index takes fewer pages because several entries can run together in a single paragraph below each main index entry. Figure 22.13 shows part of an indented index on the left and a run-in index on the right. Each index begins with the same index entries in the document.

Baby
  calming
    ideas, 7
    not always possible, 8
  curiosity, 9
  getting to know, 7
  sleep habits, 8
  stages of development, 9
  talking baby talk, 7
  types of sleep, 9
Bath
  before umbilical falls off, 53
  safety during, 53
  soap and shampoo for, 54
  sponge, 53
Binky. *See* Pacifier
Bottle
  proper temperature, 56
  sterilizing, 56

Baby: calming; ideas, 7; not always possible, 8; curiosity, 9; getting to know, 7; sleep habits, 8; stages of development, 9; talking baby talk, 7; types of sleep, 9
Bath: before umbilical falls off, 53; safety during, 53; soap and shampoo for, 54; sponge, 53
Binky. *See* Pacifier
Bottle: proper temperature, 56; sterilizing, 56; tooth damage, 56; types, 56; when to start, 56
Breast: care, 58; examinations, 58; lumps not unusual, 59; signs of mastitis, 59
Breastfeeding: benefits, 57; colostrum, 57; frequency, 58; immunity, 57; organizations, 57; preparation, 58
Burping: after feeding, 54; other times, 54

Figure 22.13 *An indented index on the left; a run-in index on the right.*

As with the table of contents, you can select from several sets of styles, each of which you can preview, and apply them to your index. Word automatically applies the built-in index styles to the index. These include Index Heading for alphabetic headings, Index 1 for main entries, Index 2 for the first subentries, and so on. As with tables of contents, if you redefine these styles, you'll automatically reformat the index.

For convenience, Word automatically inserts section breaks before and after the index. After the index is generated, you can always click in the index and choose **Page Setup** from the File menu to change the page formatting for the section. For example, you may want to change the Section Start from **Continuous** to **New Page**. You can review page setup options in Chapter 9.

To build an index:

1. Click in the document where you want the index to be inserted.
2. Choose **Index and Tables** from the Insert menu.
3. Select the **Index** tab (shown in Figure 22.14).
4. Select **Indented** or **Run-in** in the Type area.
5. Select the column and page number options you want:
   - **Columns** specifies the number of running columns for your index. Because most index entries aren't very wide, you'll use the page more efficiently if you format the index in two or three columns.

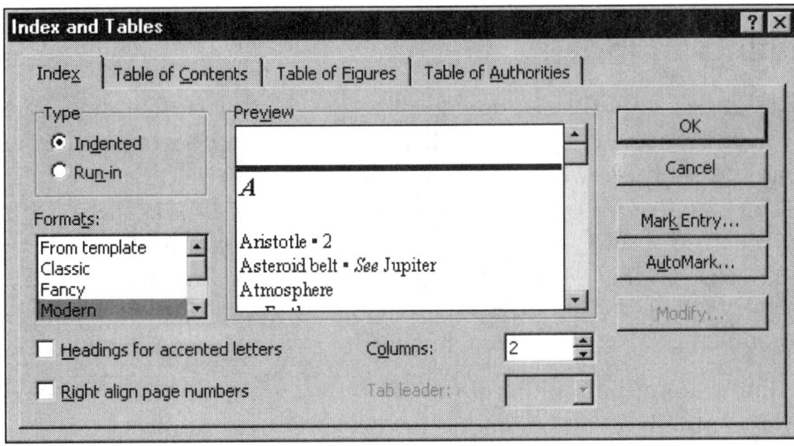

*Figure 22.14 The **Index** tab in the Index and Tables dialog box.*

   - **Right align** places the page numbers at the right margin of each column or paragraph. With this option off, the numbers appear immediately after the index entry, separated by a comma. At the right margin, page numbers are a little harder to associate with the index entry.
   - **Tab leader** inserts a row of periods, dashes, or underlines between the index entry and the page number, if the **Right align page numbers** check box is selected. This helps identify page numbers with the index entry but can make the page visually confusing.

6. Make a selection from the Formats list.
7. Check the Preview box to see the effect of your options, then click **OK**. Word goes through the document, collecting information from index entries, and inserts the finished index at the insertion point.

Formatting an Index

Like a table of contents, you can apply font and paragraph formatting to the finished index. However, it is unwise to do so. When you update the index—and remember, documents always change—all your formatting and text changes will be lost. To change the formatting so that it will stay, modify the index styles or format the text in individual entries back in the body of your document.

Updating an Index

Any good index should be updated at least once or twice. The first time you build it, you'll probably notice duplicate entries, neighboring entries whose wording doesn't quite work, multilevel entries that should be turned into a single entry, and other problems. You may be tempted to fix these problems in the index itself—but don't. You'll lose the information in the next update. Instead, return to the index entries in the body of the document and make your changes there. When you update the index next time, your changes will be included.

To understand the multilevel problem, look at Figure 22.15. The first set of entries is multilevel but shouldn't be, because there's only one item under the main entry. The next indexed entry shows how the problem could be repaired. The third set of entries shows a main entry with more than one subentry, which is correct for a multilevel entry.

To fix this problem, edit the marked index entries in the body of the document. Figure 22.16 shows the first two index entries that produced the index in Figure 22.15. You can change the unnecessary multilevel heading to a single-level entry by editing the text directly and removing the colon character.

Electric appliances
    humidifier, 6

Electric humidifier, 6

Evaporation
    and humidifiers, 18
    cause of dehydration, 43
    cooling effect, 51

Figure 22.15 Problems and solutions.

{XE "Electric appliances:humidifier"}

{XE "Electric humidifier"}

Figure 22.16 A multilevel entry changed to a simple entry.

As you can see, the real work of updating an index isn't assembling the current index entries and page numbers, which you can do with a keystroke. The real work is in finding and fixing the problems that keep it from being a good index.

To update an index:

1. Click anywhere in the index.
2. Press **F9**. Word pages through the document and recompiles the index entry information. Any formatting or text changes you made to the index itself is lost. Changes to marked index entry fields are incorporated in the updated index.

From Here...

Even though Word can't take all the work out of writing long documents, it can sure make it easier to organize and format them. Word's table of contents and indexing features make short work out of potentially complex tasks.

Now that you can work with really long documents, how about learning how to juggle nine documents at once? Yes, that's right, Word allows you to work with several open documents at the same time. Why would anyone want to do that, you might ask? For the answer to that riveting question, you'll have to read the next chapter.

CHAPTER 23

Working with Multiple Documents

Let's talk about:

- Opening multiple documents
- Switching between documents
- Arranging document windows
- Sizing document windows
- Minimizing documents
- Cutting and pasting between documents
- Switching between applications

Now that you can do just about anything you want to a Word document, what's left? Doing stuff to several documents at once! And now for the answer to the burning question I left you with at the end of the last chapter: why would anyone want to juggle a whole bunch of documents (or even two)?

When you're working on a project, it's often helpful to be able to refer to another portion of it. I had Chapter 22 (the previous chapter) open while I wrote this chapter. That way, I was able to quickly switch to it and double-check the question I asked at the end. Switching back and forth between open documents is much quicker and easier than closing the document you're working on, opening the one you want to look at, closing it, and then reopening the first one.

Being able to open more than one document at a time also means that you can switch gears in midstream without losing momentum. If your boss runs in and asks you to make a quick change to the report you completed yesterday, you don't have to quit what you're doing. Just leave your document on-screen, and open the report in a new document window. When you finish and close that document, your document's sitting right where you left it. No wasted steps.

Last, but most definitely not least, having several documents open makes it easy to move and copy information between them. Suppose you used a table in last month's report and you want to include it in another document. Just open both documents—as you'll soon see, you can even arrange it so you can see both of them at once. Using the techniques you've already learned for cutting and pasting, just copy the table from one document to the other.

Opening Multiple Documents

Whenever you open a document, it is displayed in a document window. By default, the current document window is *maximized*, which means that it takes up all the space in the Word window. When you open another document (or start a new one), it is displayed in its own maximized window. Let's work through this together so you can see what I mean.

To open multiple documents:

1. Open Word and type **This is Document 1** in a blank document window. Notice that the title bar for the new document says *Microsoft*

Word - Document1. Until you save a document, it's identified by its document number.

2. Open any document by clicking the **Open** button on the Standard toolbar and choosing any document you've already created from the file list. (You can also press **Ctrl+O** or choose **Open** from the File menu.)
3. Without closing the first or second document, use the procedures in step 2 to open a third document.

In Figure 23.1, I have the first document on-screen, and I've pulled down the Window menu.

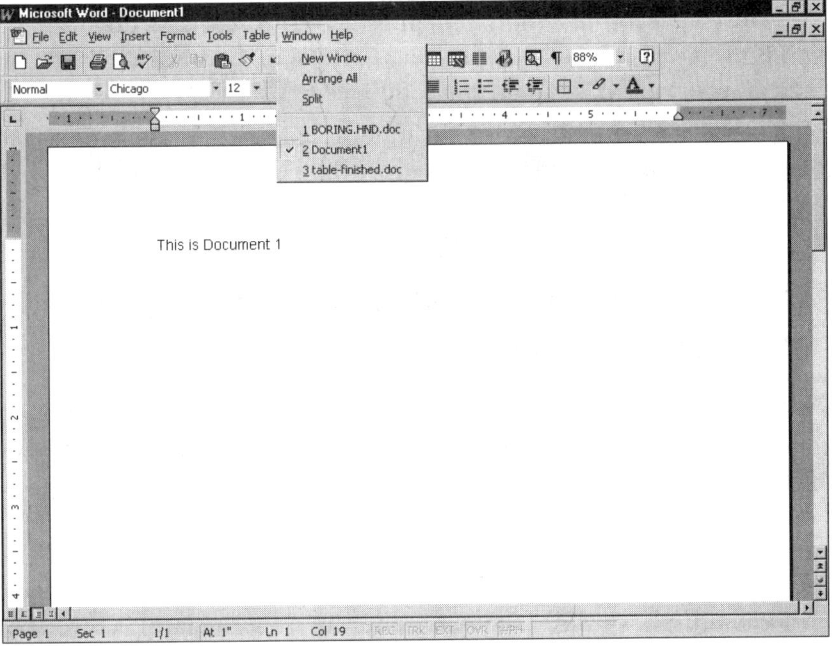

Figure 23.1 *The Window menu lists the three open documents.*

You're still only seeing one window at a time. As you open document windows, the other windows get hidden behind the current one, but they're still there. Word lists them at the bottom of the Window menu.

Switching between Document Windows

There are two ways to move between document windows when you only have one window displayed:

- ✦ Choose the file you want from the Window menu by choosing **Window** and clicking on your choice. If you're using the keyboard, you can type the number next to your choice in the Window menu.
- ✦ Press **Ctrl+F6** to cycle forward through your open documents or **Ctrl+Shift+F6** to cycle backward.

Try it. Notice that the document you choose from the Window menu instantly appears on your screen. When you press **Ctrl+F6**, the last document you opened is displayed. If you keep pressing **Ctrl+F6** or **Ctrl+Shift+F6**, you move through all your open documents in sequence.

Now you can work with several documents at once and instantly switch to the one you want. But what if you want more than one document displayed on your screen?

Displaying and Arranging Multiple Document Windows

Unless you specify otherwise, every new or opened document is displayed in a maximized window, which means that it hides any other open documents you might have. Well, let's specify otherwise.

Using the Restore Button

When a document window is maximized (the default state), there are six buttons in the upper-right corner of your computer screen. The top buttons work with the Word program as a whole (more about that in a minute). The one we want, though, is the middle button in the second row that looks like two cascading pages. This is the document's **Restore** button. When you click the **Restore** button in a maximized window, the window is restored to a smaller size within the Word window. Figure 23.2 shows a maximized Word document window, and Figure 23.3 shows the same document after clicking on the document's **Restore** button.

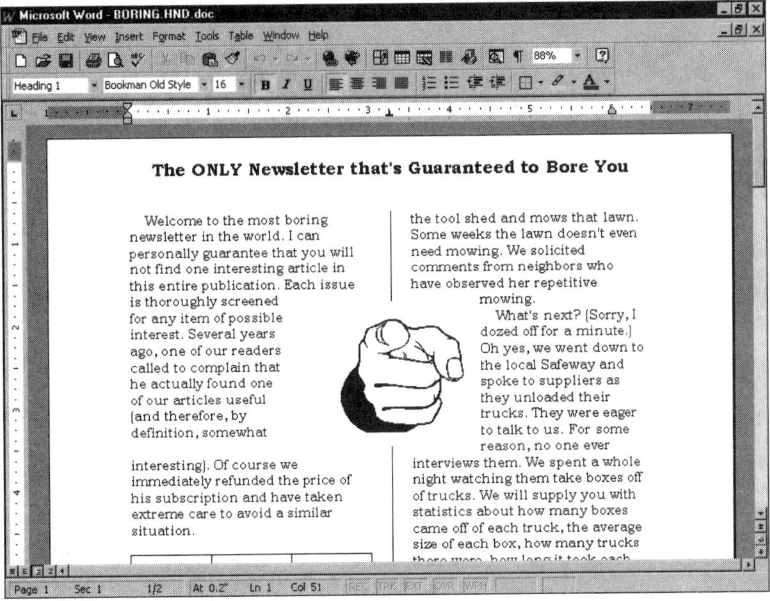

Figure 23.2 A maximized Word document window.

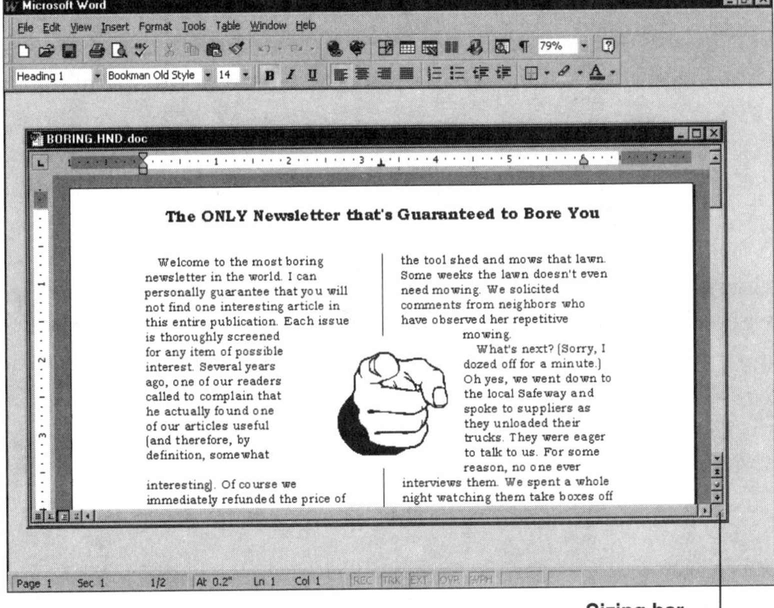

Figure 23.3 A document restored to "normal" size.

In Figure 23.2, notice that there are two **Restore** buttons, one above the other. The button on the very top is for Word itself, and so are the **Minimize** and **Close** buttons on each side. If you click Word's **Restore** button instead of the **Restore** button for the document window, the Word program window changes size and the **Restore** button turns into a **Maximize** button. If this happens, just click on the **Maximize** button to get Word back the way it was.

In Figure 23.3, notice that the document's **Restore** button changed to a **Maximize** button. You can click on this **Maximize** button to return the document window to full size (or double-click on the document's title bar).

Sizing Document Windows

Sizing a document window is very much like sizing a graphics box:

1. Make sure the window you want to size is active (the active window is the one with the highlighted title bar). If the window is already maximized, you can't resize it. You'll have to first use **Restore** or **Arrange**.

   If you can see any part of an inactive window, a quick way to switch to that window is to click anywhere in the part of that window that is visible.
2. Move your mouse pointer over one of the window borders until the pointer turns into a double-headed arrow.
3. Drag the mouse in the direction you want to size the window. As you drag, a shaded outline shows what's happening to the size of the window.
4. Release the mouse button when the window is the size you want.

If you want to change the height and width at the same time, position your mouse pointer over a corner border until the pointer turns into a diagonal double-headed arrow. There's even a special sizing bar (shown in Figure 23.3) in the lower right corner of the document window that makes an especially easy target. Then click and drag as earlier.

If you don't have a mouse (or if you aren't fond of small furry rodents), try this: press **Alt+ -** to activate the document's Control menu, then choose **Size**. Use the **Up Arrow** and **Down Arrow** keys on your keyboard to make the window taller or shorter. Use the **Left Arrow** or **Right Arrow** to change the window's width. If you want to fine-tune your window's size, hold down the **Ctrl** key while using the **Arrow** keys. Press **Enter** when the window is the size you want.

MOVING A DOCUMENT WINDOW

Moving a document window is exactly like moving a dialog box. Just position your mouse pointer over the title bar and drag the window wherever you want it.

To move a document window with the keyboard, make sure the window you want to move is active, and press **Alt+ -** to activate the window's Control menu. Choose **Move**, then use the **Arrow** keys on your keyboard to move the window in the direction you want. If you want to fine-tune your window's position, hold down the **Ctrl** key while using the **Arrow** keys. When you're finished press **Enter** to anchor the window in its new location.

Arranging Windows Automatically

Word's Window menu has a command that automatically displays and arranges all your open document windows. Strangely enough, this command is called **Arrange All**.

When you choose **Arrange All** from the Window menu, your open documents are displayed one on top of the other as shown in Figure 23.4. You can see a portion of each document, and they're arranged like floor tiles, with none of the windows overlapping.

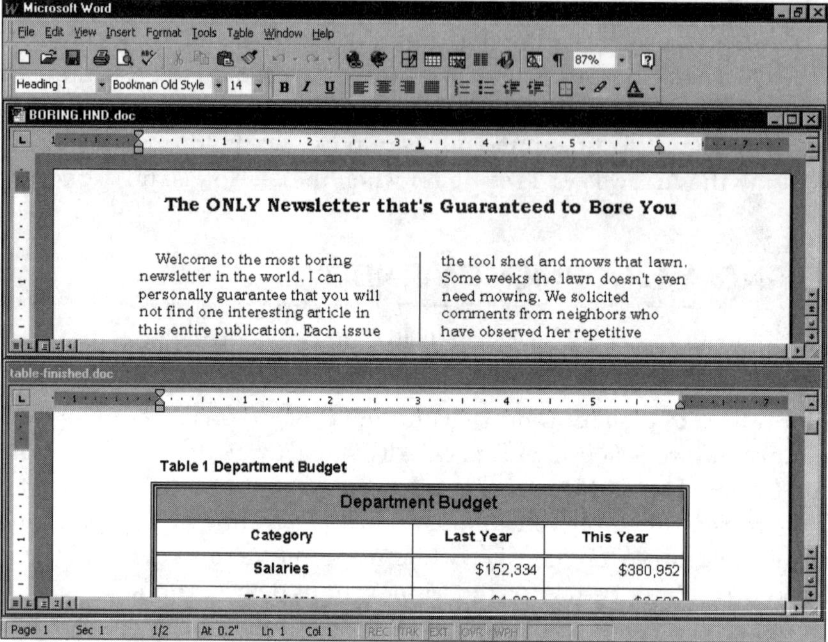

Figure 23.4 Two open documents.

Word tries to give each document window an equal amount of space. If there are two or three open documents, the documents are arranged horizontally. When you have more than three open documents, Word does its best to divide the documents into the available workspace, as shown in Figure 23.5, which has five open documents.

You can click anywhere in a document window to make that document active. And of course, you can use the Window menu or keyboard to switch between documents.

Arranging is a quick way to display your open documents and see what you have. If you move and size several document windows, however you can end up with a fairly confused (and confusing) arrangement, with some document windows hidden and others taking up too much space. Just choose **Arrange All** to force some order into the situation.

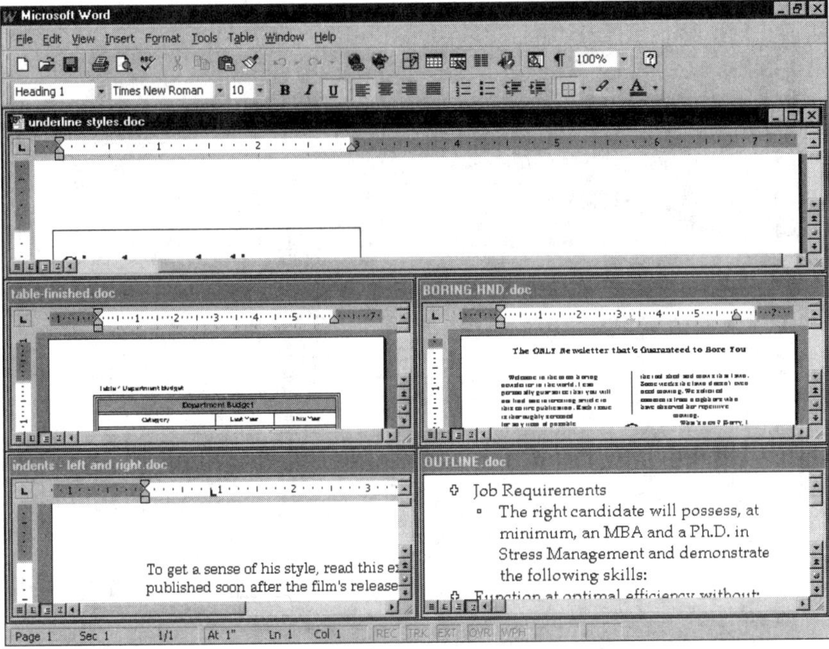

Figure 23.5 Five open documents.

Minimizing Document Windows

You can minimize any document window that's been sized, restored, maximized, or arranged. Just click on the **Minimize** button (the first of the three buttons in the upper-right corner of the document window, it has a horizontal line at the bottom of the button). *Minimizing* shrinks the document to a button that displays the document name (or number if it has not been saved and named yet). In Figure 23.6, I show four minimized documents below an open document. Notice that the minimized documents still show up on the Window menu, so you can easily switch to any of them.

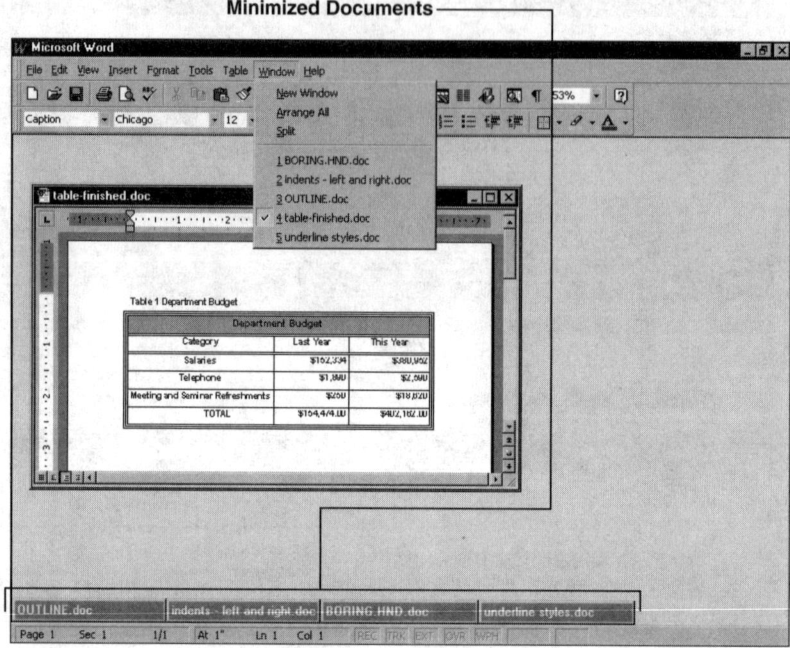

***Figure 23.6** Minimizing shrinks documents to icons. The minimized documents are still listed on the Window menu.*

If you have a document window maximized, you will not be able to see the icons for the minimized document windows. Just choose **Arrange All** from the Window menu to see them again. Minimized documents aren't included when you choose **Arrange**, but Word sees to it that the arranged document windows don't cover up any minimized document icons.

Restoring Minimized Documents

You can restore a minimized document to whatever size and position it had before it was minimized in several ways:

- Double-click on its title bar.
- Select the document icon and click its **Restore** button.
- Select the document icon by pressing **Ctrl+F6** until the document's title bar is highlighted, press **Alt+ -** to activate its Control menu, then choose **Restore**.
- Choose the document from the Window menu.

Cutting and Pasting between Documents

In Chapter 6, "Moving and Copying Text," you learned how to select blocks of text and move or copy them to the Clipboard. Once the text is in the Clipboard, you can paste it to a new location. Well, that new location isn't limited to your current document—text or objects in the Clipboard can just as easily be pasted into a different document.

Whatever you cut or copy to the Clipboard stays there until you cut or copy something else, so you can cut something from one document, open another document, and then use the **Paste** command to bring the information into the new document.

The easiest way to cut and paste small amounts of material between documents, however, is to have both documents on your screen at the same time. That way, you can zip back and forth between the documents by clicking anywhere in the document window. Cut or copy something from one document, then click in the other document, move your insertion point to the location you want, and choose **Paste**. It's as simple as that. Figure 23.7 shows one example of a screen arrangement that would make it easy to work with two documents at once. I opened both documents, then moved and sized the document windows. I can click in either document to activate it and use the scroll bars to move wherever I want.

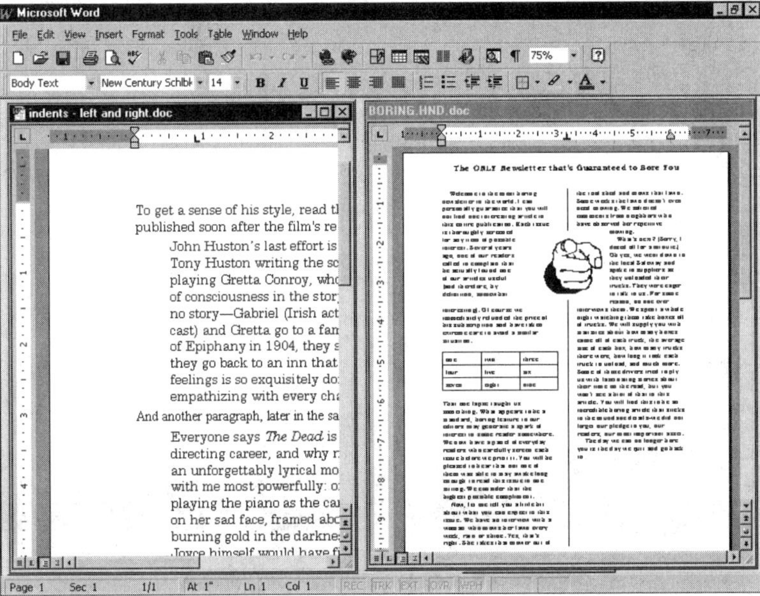

Figure 23.7 Two document windows side by side.

SWITCHING BETWEEN APPLICATIONS

In this chapter, we've been talking about displaying and working with multiple documents in Word. But Windows 95 also allows you to work with more than one program at the same time. You can switch between programs as easily as you can between Word documents.

The Start Button

The **Start** button located at the bottom-left corner of your screen allows you to quickly start other programs right from within Word. When you click on the **Start** button you'll see a menu like the one in Figure 23.8. From the Start menu, choose **Programs** and then select the program you want to start. (How many programs you can have open at one time depends on the size of your hard disk and how much memory you have.) You can also use the other commands on the Start menu from within Word. See your Windows 95 documentation for more information on the commands listed on the Start menu.

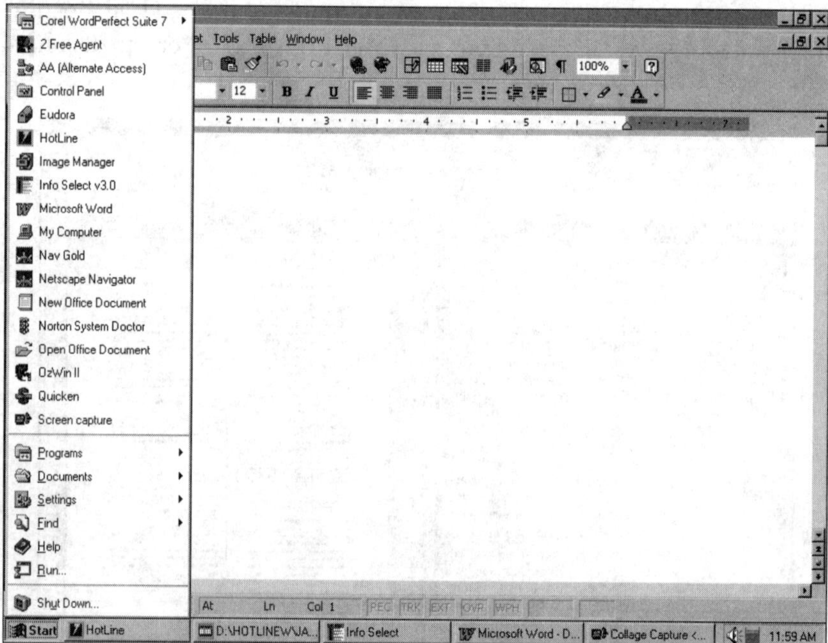

Figure 23.8 The Windows 95 Start menu.

The Taskbar

The Windows Taskbar is a handy tool that you can use from any place in Windows. It lets you quickly switch to an open program or window by clicking on a button. By default, the Taskbar displays at the very bottom of your screen, below your Word Status Bar. The Taskbar displays a button for all open programs and windows. If you only have Word open you will only see a button for Word. Figure 23.8 shows the Taskbar with several buttons representing open programs. You can close a Windows program from the Taskbar by right-clicking on its button and then choosing **Close**.

Alt+Tab

Alt+Tab is the magic key combination that takes you back and forth between programs. If you have more than two programs open, hold down the **Alt** key while you tap the **Tab** key. As you press the **Tab** key, the names of your open programs are displayed in sequence in the middle of your screen. When you see the name of the program you want to switch to, release the **Alt** key.

Refer to your Windows documentation for more detailed information about working with multiple applications.

FROM HERE...

Well done! You're well on your way to becoming a Word wizard. As you keep working with the program, more and more of the features will start to become second nature, and you'll find yourself experimenting with new ways to approach your tasks.

The next chapter introduces you to Word's features that work hand-in-hand with the Internet. If you already have an Internet connection, you can get support from Microsoft's Web site with the click of a button. Want to create your own Web page? Word has everything you need to get going.

SECTION VIII

Word and the Internet

CHAPTER 24

Word's Internet Connection

Let's talk about:

- ✦ Getting on-line help
- ✦ Creating Web documents in Word
- ✦ Using the Web Wizard
- ✦ Editing Web documents
- ✦ Getting free stuff from the Web

Word 97 is tightly integrated with the Internet. You can connect to the 'Net directly from Word, add links to Web sites in your Word documents, turn Word documents into Web documents, create new Web, and much more. This chapter gives you a brief look at the Internet offerings you get with Word.

To make use of the features in this chapter, you must have a modem, an Internet connection, and a Web browser. If you have the modem but not the browser, you're in luck. Your Word CD comes with Internet Explorer, one of the top Web browsers.

This chapter assumes that you're already hooked up to the 'Net and are somewhat familiar with the Internet and the World Wide Web. If this is all totally new to you, take a look at *Internet Explorer Virtuoso* or *Netscape Virtuoso* by Elissa Keeler and Robert Miller (MIS:Press) for more information about the 'Net.

Go Straight to the Web from Word

There's a **Web Toolbar** button on the Standard toolbar (the button's a globe with two arrows on it). Just click it to open the Web toolbar shown in Figure 24.1. From there, you can click any button to open your Web browser and initiate your Internet connection.

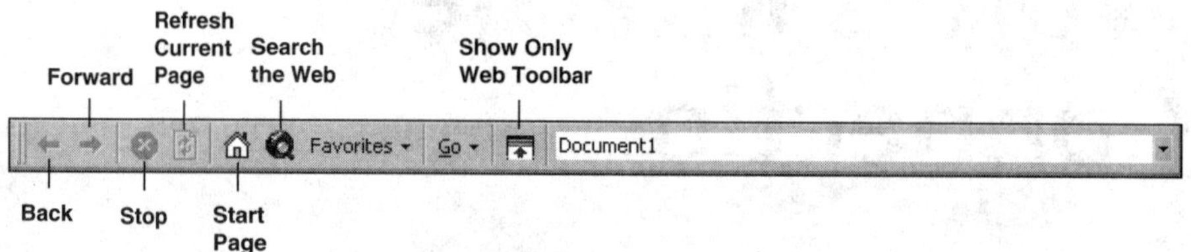

Figure 24.1 The Web toolbar.

Opening an HTML Document from Word

If you have Web page URLs or shortcuts stored on your computer, you can go to any of them from Word's Open dialog box. Just display the Open dialog box, find the shortcut or URL you want, and double-click on it. Word automatically opens your Web browser and initiates your Internet connection.

Get Online Help

When you choose **Microsoft on the Web** from Word's Help menu, you get the menu shown in Figure 24.2.

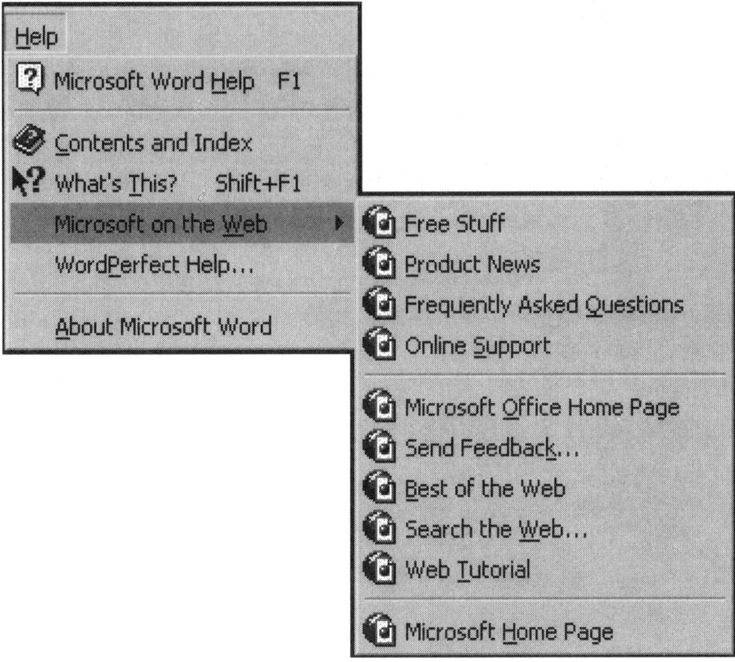

Figure 24.2 The Microsoft on the Web Help options.

Just select one of the options to open your Web browser, initiate your Internet connection, and go directly to the specified page. All these options connect you to different areas on Microsoft's site on the World Wide Web, which contains tips, demos, technical information documents, and a complete reference center.

NOTE

If you're new to the Web, be sure to check out Microsoft's Web tutorial. It will answer lots of your basic questions and it provides a great introduction to the Web. Just choose **Web Tutorial** from the Help menu's Microsoft on the Web menu.

Create Web Documents in Word

Creating your own Web page has never been easier. With Word's Web Wizards you can create Web documents without learning a bunch of complex codes. You can also easily format a Web document for use in Word or take a Word document and turn it into a Web document.

Using Web Wizards

You don't have to know anything about HTML or recite a secret password to create a slick-looking Web page without leaving Word. As with Word's other Wizards, Web Wizards take you step by step through the process of creating and formatting a Web page, even providing sample text that you can replace with your own.

To use a Web Wizard:

1. Choose **New** from the File menu and select the **Web Pages** tab (shown in Figure 24.3).

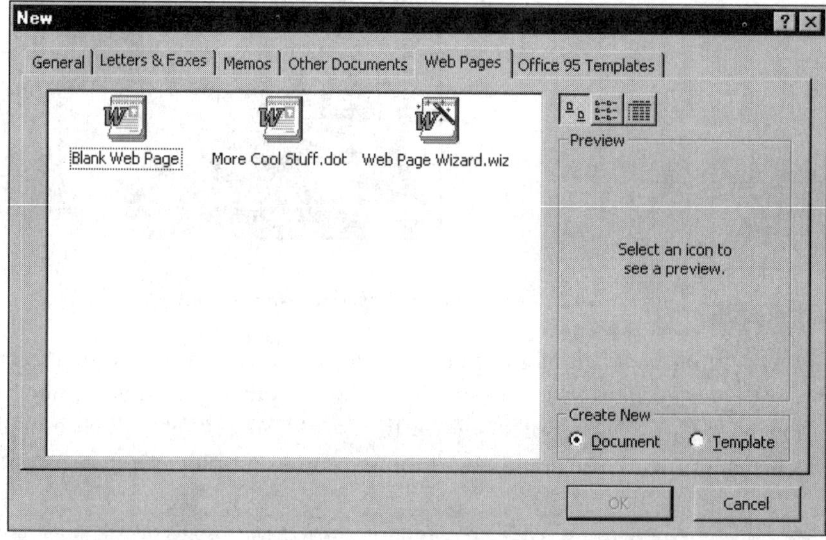

Figure 24.3 The ***Web Pages*** *tab in the New dialog box.*

2. Double-click on **Web Page Wizard.wiz** (or select it and click **OK**) to open the Web Page Wizard dialog box shown in Figure 24.4.
3. Select the type of page you want to create, then click **Next**. As you select different page types, notice that the selected layout appears on your screen, so you can see what the result will be before you click **Next**.

Figure 24.4 *The first Web Page Wizard dialog box.*

4. Select a style from the dialog box shown in Figure 24.5 and click **Finish**. Once again, the style changes are displayed on-screen as you scroll through the options.

Figure 24.5 *Choose a style from this list.*

After you click **Finish**, the sample page is displayed on your screen. All you have to do is replace the sample text with your own pearls of wisdom to end up with a beautifully formatted Web page that you can show off to your friends.

The Web Page Wizard is a great way to get started with Web publishing. You don't have to worry about fancy codes and other arcane stuff—just pick your options and enter the text you want. Figures 24.6 through 24.10 show a few examples of the different pages you can create with the Wizard.

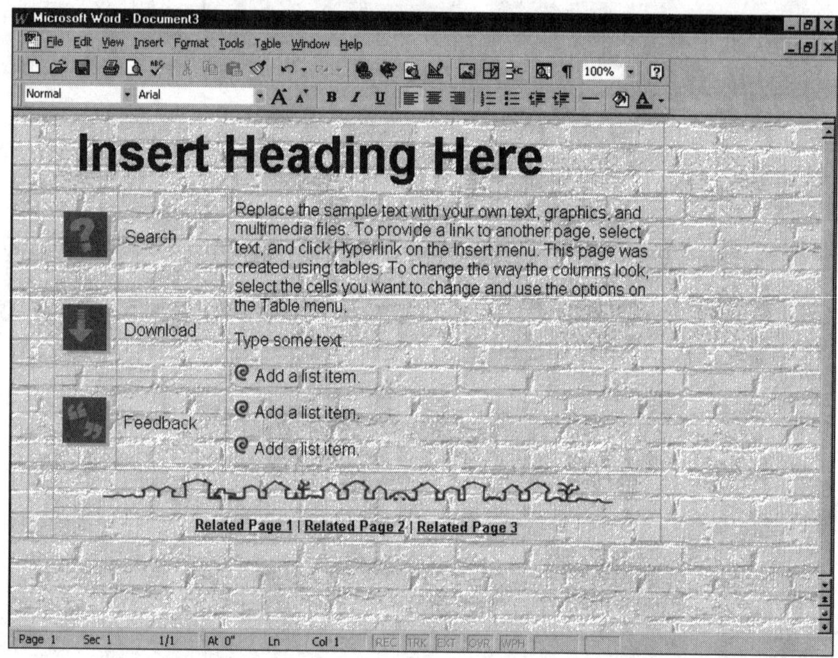

Figure 24.6 A two-column layout that uses the Community style.

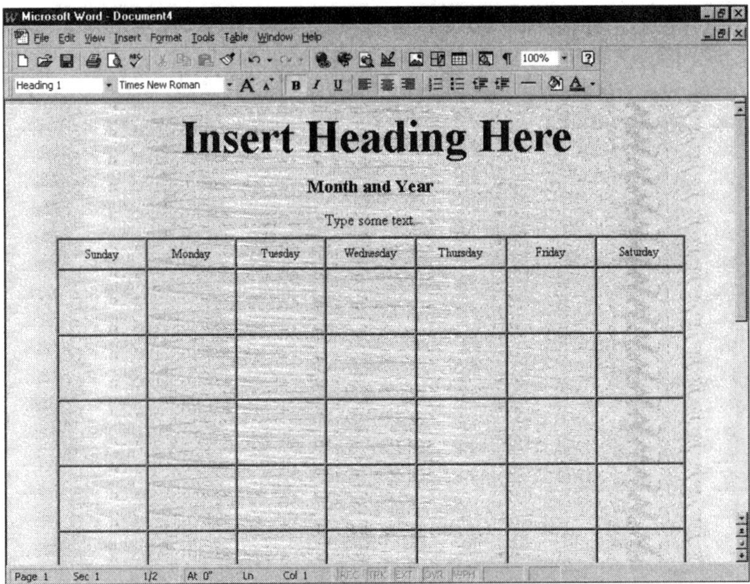

Figure 24.7 *A calendar that uses the Contemporary style.*

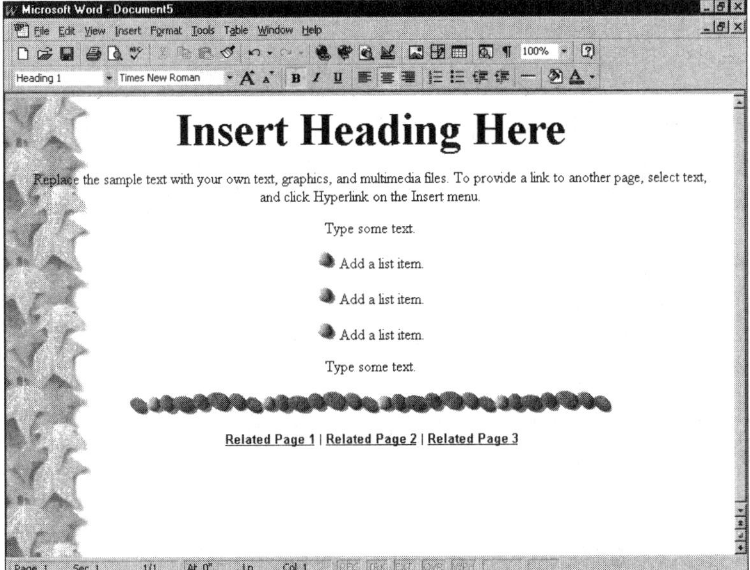

Figure 24.8 *A centered layout that uses the Outdoors style.*

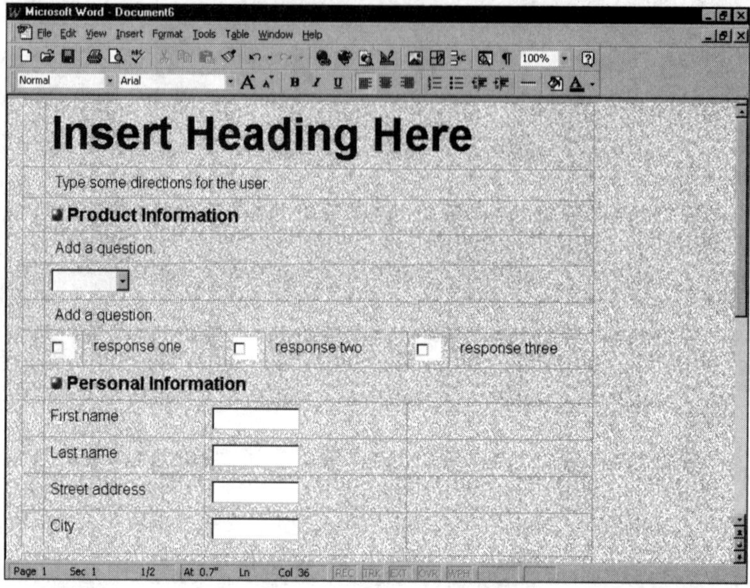

Figure 24.9 A registration form that uses the Professional style.

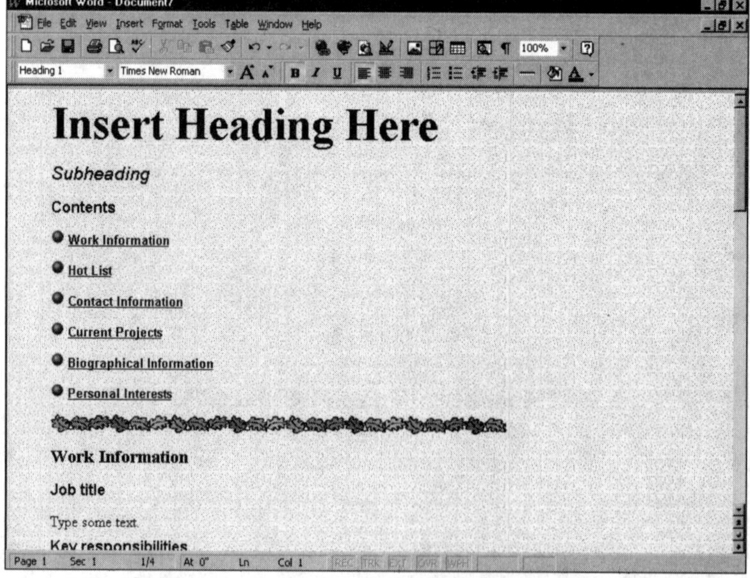

Figure 24.10 A personal home page that uses the Harvest style.

Creating a Web Page from Scratch

The Web Wizard can be a good starting point, but if you're a do-it-yourself kind of person, you can design your own Web page, using most of the Word tools you've already learned about.

To create a Web page from scratch:

1. Choose **New** from the File menu and select the **Web Pages** tab.
2. Double-click on **Blank Web Page** (or select it and click **OK**). This takes you to a blank editing screen.
3. Add text, tables, graphics, and other items using the Word features you're already familiar with.

ROADMAP

You may notice a few different buttons on the Standard and Formatting toolbars. When you create a Web document, some Word features become unavailable and some new options are added. These changes are covered in the section "Editing Your Web Page."

Saving Your Web Page

At this point, you can do all sorts of stuff to your page. I'll get into some of the more common options, but because many of them require or request that you save your Web page first, let's start there. You save a Web page the same way you save any other document—it just uses a different extension that tells Word and your Web browser to treat the document as a Web page.

To save your Web page:

1. Choose **Save As** from the File menu.
2. Use the Save in list to navigate to the drive and folder in which you want to save the file.
3. Enter a name in the File name box. You don't have to type in the extension—Word automatically assigns an extension of **HTML** to all Web documents.
4. Click **Save**.

Editing Your Web Page

Whether you start with a Web Wizard or a blank page, you can do almost anything to a Web page that you can to a Word document. This section is a brief introduction to some of the tools you can use to create your Web page.

Differences between Editing Word Documents and Editing HTML Documents

The first thing you'll notice is that some of the buttons on the Standard and Formatting toolbars are different. I'll cover the additions in a minute, but here's what happened to a couple of old standbys:

- The **Columns** button is missing because HTML doesn't support newspaper-style columns. To get a column effect, use tables.
- The Ruler isn't displayed because margins, indents, and tabs don't have the same relevance in HTML documents. If you want to see the ruler, slide your mouse pointer slowly over the shaded area at the top of the editing screen. The ruler slides into view, then disappears as soon as you move your mouse pointer from the area.

Figures 24.11 and 24.12 show the new buttons on the Standard and Formatting toolbars.

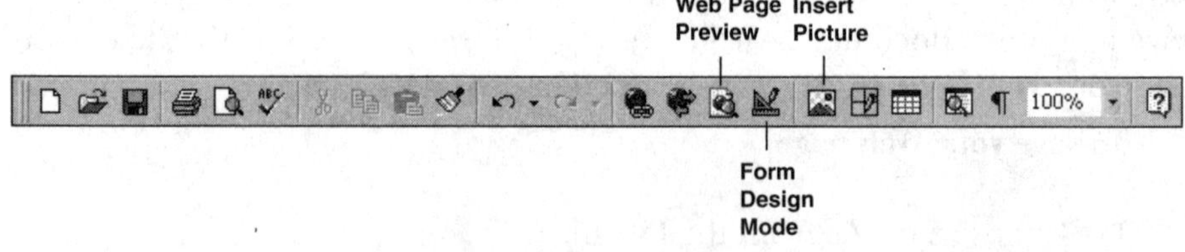

Figure 24.11 The Standard toolbar.

Figure 24.12 The Formatting toolbar.

The new buttons on the Standard toolbar are:

Web Page Preview Opens your Web browser and displays the current document.

Form Design Mode Used for designing forms, an advanced feature that's not covered in this book.

Insert Picture Opens the Insert Picture dialog box so you can add images to your document. If you want to use the Clip Gallery instead, choose **Picture** from the Insert menu and **Clip Art** from the Picture menu.

The new buttons on the Formatting toolbar are:

Increase/Decrease Font Size Incrementally increases or decreases the size of selected text.

Horizontal Line Adds a horizontal line in the style that's currently selected in the Horizontal Line dialog box.

Background Opens the Background color palette so you can add a background to your page. To add a textured background, click **Fill Effects**.

Changing Text Color

In a Web document, the main text is usually one color, *hyperlinks* (the colored text you click on to go to a different page) are another color, and hyperlinks that you've already visited are in a third color. By default, Word makes body text black, hyperlinks blue, and followed hyperlinks violet.

To change the default text colors, choose **Text Colors** from the Format menu and select your options from the dialog box shown in Figure 24.13.

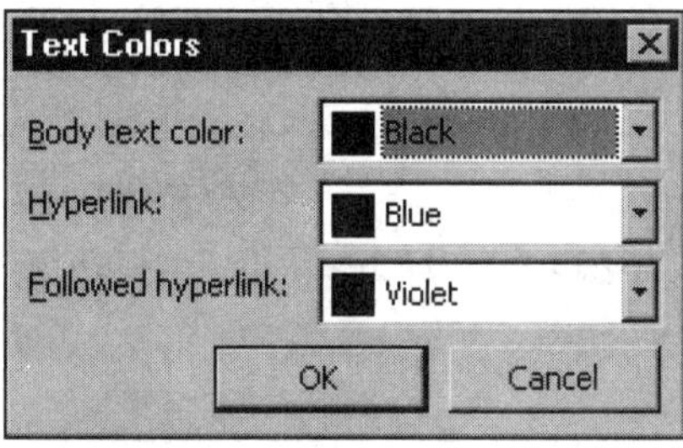

Figure 24.13 *The Text Colors dialog box.*

The colors you choose are used as the default, but you can change the color of selected text by clicking the **Font Color** button on the Formatting toolbar.

Assigning a Title

The *title* is different from the heading you put at the top of your Web page and from the document's filename. In an HTML document, the title is what shows up in the title bar when you display the page. The title is also used when the document is added to a History or Favorites list. If you don't give your document a title, the filename (which can be a long, ugly string of characters) shows up on the title bar instead.

To assign a title to your Web page, choose **Properties** from the File menu and fill in the Title box. The Document Properties dialog box is shown in Figure 24.14.

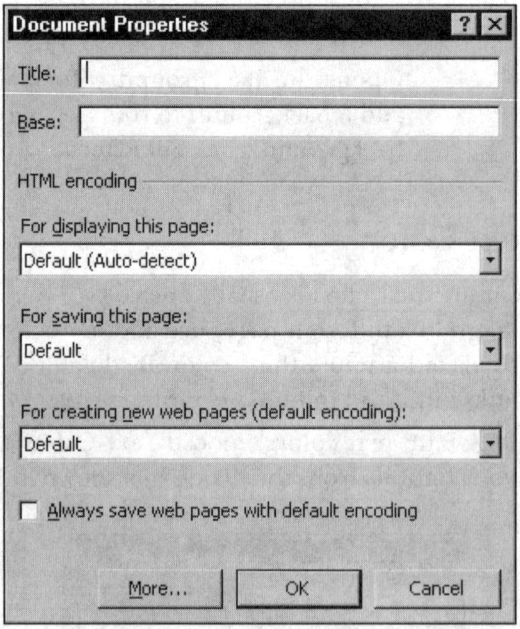

Figure 24.14 The Document Properties dialog box.

Adding Horizontal Lines

In Web pages, horizontal lines are commonly used to separate sections. To add a horizontal line, choose **Line** from the Insert menu, select a line style from the dialog box shown in Figure 24.15, and click **OK**.

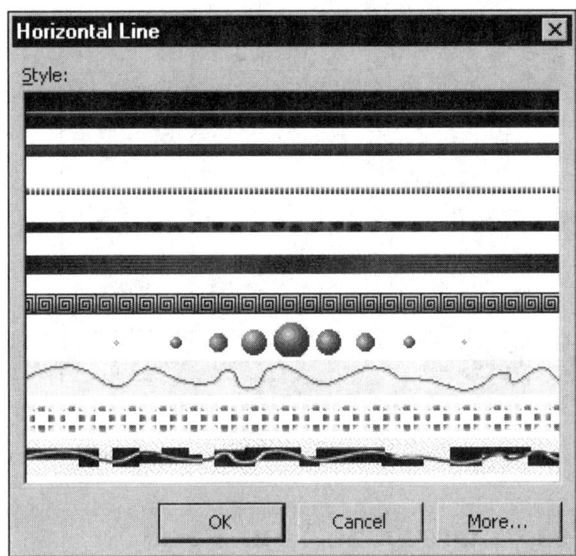

Figure 24.15 The Horizontal Line dialog box.

If you click on the **More** button, Word opens the Insert Picture dialog box so you can choose among additional graphic lines.

The **Horizontal Line** button on the Formatting toolbar inserts a line using the style that's currently selected in the Horizontal Line dialog box. Once you've picked a line style, you can quickly insert additional lines using the same style by clicking the **Horizontal Line** button.

Creating Bulleted and Numbered Lists

You can usse the techniques covered in Chapter 21 to create bulleted and numbered lists. The main thing to be aware of with lists on Web pages is that you can use graphic images for your bullets. When you choose **Bullets and Numbering** from the Format menu, you get the dialog box shown in Figure 24.16, which allows you to select from several snazzy graphical bullets.

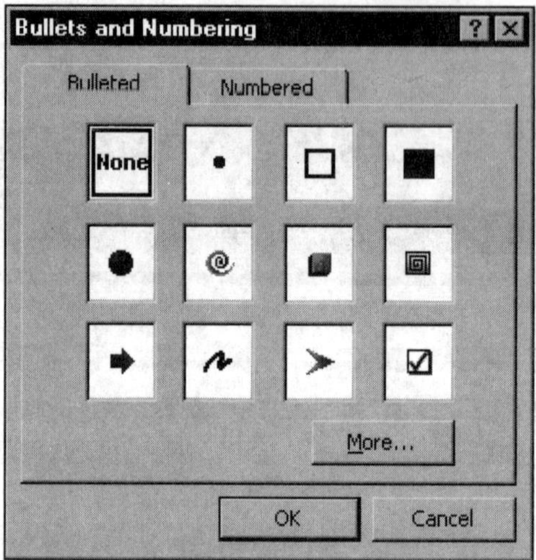

Figure 24.16 *The Bullets and Numbering dialog box.*

Using Tables to Organize Your Page

Tables are a great way to organize the layout of your Web page. Use the table drawing tool and all the other table techniques you learned about in Chapter 16.

Adding Backgrounds

You can add a colored or textured background to your Web page. This is a great way to add interest to your page. But be careful—it's easy to go overboard and end up with a background that overpowers or even obscures your text.

To add a solid background, choose **Background** from the Format menu and select a color. To add a textured background, choose **Background** from the Format menu, choose **Fill Effects**, and make a selection from the Fill Effects dialog box. For additional background choices, choose **Other Texture** to open the Select Texture dialog box.

Working with Styles in Web Documents

You apply styles to Web documents the same way you do to regular Word documents: make a selection from the Style list on the Formatting toolbar or use the Style dialog box. The only thing you need to know is that Word gives you several HTML-specific styles that correspond directly to HTML tags. To get a particular effect, just apply the style you want. Here's what the most important special styles are for:

- The `H1` through `H6` styles are the standard heading levels supported in HTML.
- `HTML Markup` is used to identify raw HTML code in your document. If you don't use this style, the code is interpreted as regular text.

NOTE

When you use the Web Wizard, Word automatically applies the necessary styles.

Working with Graphics

You can insert graphics into your Web document using the Clip Gallery, WordArt, AutoShapes, or any other technique you've learned about in this book. Word converts all Web graphics to GIF or JPG format.

Adding Hyperlinks

You can use *hyperlinks* to jump to a different location on your page, to a different page, even to sound or video files.

The easiest way to create hyperlinks is with Word's AutoFormat As You Type feature:

1. Choose **AutoCorrect** from the Tools menu and select the **AutoFormat As You Type** tab.
2. In the Replace as you type section, select **Internet and network paths with hyperlinks**.

Now, when you type a filename or Internet address, Word automatically converts the address to a hyperlink.

The AutoFormat features require you to enter the address manually. If you need to browse for it, use the Insert Hyperlink dialog box (shown in Figure 24.17). To access it, click the **Insert Hyperlink** button on the Standard toolbar (the button's a globe with a piece of chain link fence attached to it) or choose **Hyperlink** from the Insert menu.

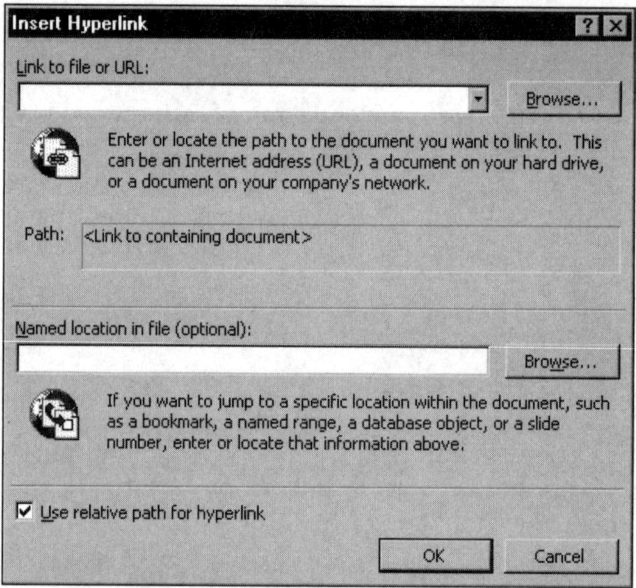

Figure 24.17 *The Insert Hyperlink dialog box.*

Previewing Your Web Page

Word's Web editor is a semi-WYSIWYG environment, but it doesn't show *exactly* what your page will look like in a Web browser. For that, you have to view the document in the browser itself.

To preview your Web page, choose **Web Page Preview** from the File menu. Word opens your Web browser and displays the current document.

Viewing the Source Code

As you create your Web page, Word busily converts all your formatting to HTML tags. When you open an HTML document in a Web browser, the HTML tags tell the browser how to format the document. If you want to see what's going on behind the scene, choose **HTML Source** from the View menu to see the code.

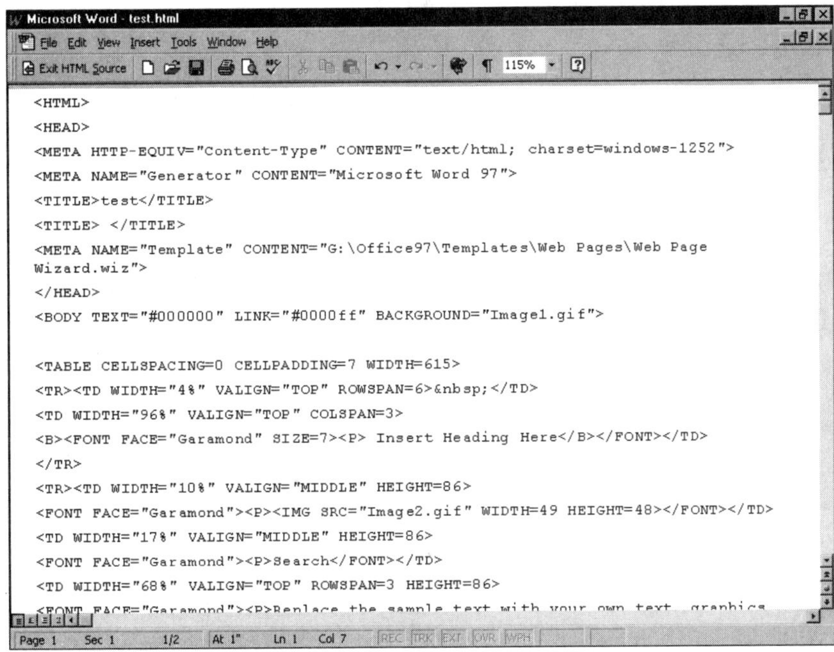

Figure 24.18 The HTML source for a sample document.

Inserting Raw Code

If you prefer not to deal with HTML code at all, that's fine. You really don't need to. But if you get to a point where you want to include some raw code in your Web document, here's how. Just insert an HTML tag into your document by typing the code, selecting it, and applying the special HTML Markup style to it.

NOTE

Delving into the mysteries of HTML is beyond the scope of this book. If you're interested in learning more about it, check out some of the resources on Microsoft's Web page or look at the books referenced earlier in this chapter. A good way to dip your toe into the HTML pond is to use Word's tools to create your pages and use the **View/HTML Source** option to study the resulting code.

Convert a Word Document to HTML Format

You can easily convert a Word document to HTML format. Just choose **Save as HTML** from the File menu and specify a file and path name.

When you save a document in HTML format, Word converts all of the formatting that it can. Any formatting that's not supported by HTML is lost.

NOTE

Make sure you preview your document in your Web browser. Not all Word features are supported by HTML, so some of your formatting may be lost or changed. With the Web document on-screen, click the **Web Page Preview** button on the Standard toolbar.

Save a Web Document in Word Format

To covert an HTML document to Word format, just open the document and choose **Save as Word Document** from the File menu.

More Cool Stuff

Want more Wizards? Want software to help you post documents on the Web? Want it now? Want it free? Okay, here's the deal. Microsoft's Web site contains all sorts of cool stuff—all you have to do is download it. In addition, your Word CD includes several useful Web tools, some of which you may not be aware of.

To get to these riches, choose **New** from the File menu, select the **Web Pages** tab, and click on **More Cool Stuff** to open the page shown in Figure 24.19.

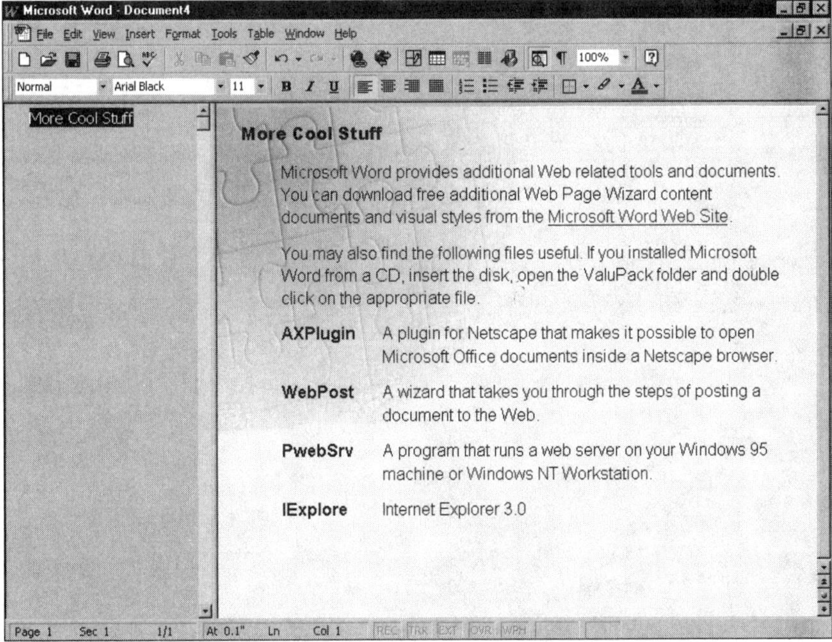

Figure 24.19 *More cool stuff.*

To go to the Web site that contains the freebies, click on the **Microsoft Word Web Site** hyperlink to open your Web browser and initiate an Internet connection. If you want to access the stuff on your CD, just follow the instructions on the More Cool Stuff page.

FROM HERE...

How's that for a whirlwind Web intro? Word gives you a bunch of cool tools for exploring and working with Web documents. If you want to quickly create a page without any hassle, use the Web Wizard. If you want to dig deeper and get into more complex Web page formatting, you'll find that Word's Web tools will support you every step of the way.

The next and final chapter is devoted to the ways in which you can customize Word to make it fit your working style.

SECTION IX

Customizing Word

CHAPTER 25

Making Word Work the Way You Do

Let's talk about:

- Customizing the toolbar
- Customizing menus
- Customizing the keyboard
- Changing Word's default options

Throughout this book, we've used Word's default settings. If they work for you, that's great; you don't have to change anything. But almost every setting can be customized to meet your needs. Do the Office Assistant's incessant sounds annoy you? No problem—just turn them off. Do the scroll bars just take up screen space, and do you find that you don't really use them anyway? Fine—just get rid of them.

Is there a command that you use all the time? If it's not easily accessible from a toolbar button, would you like it to be? Get ready to learn how to add and remove commands from both toolbars and pull-down menus and select your own shortcut key combination for almost any Word command or option.

By the end of the chapter, you'll be well equipped to adapt Word to the style of typing, editing, formatting, and printing you prefer. Commands that you use often can be near; other commands can be hidden or removed.

Changing the Appearance of Toolbars

Before we get into adding toolbar buttons, let's talk about adjusting the appearance of the toolbars you already have. You can adjust the Word workplace to your liking by deciding which toolbars to display and where. You can also adjust the appearance of both toolbars and the ScreenTips that identify each button.

Moving and Resizing a Toolbar

If you've used drawing and paint programs, you're familiar with the idea of a *palette*—a collection of tools in a box that can be moved anywhere on the screen. Although it isn't widely known, Word's toolbars can behave like palettes (Word calls them *floating toolbars*). They can also be anchored to the top, bottom, or sides of the Word window (like the Standard and Formatting toolbars that you've been using throughout this book (Word calls them *docked toolbars*).

For example, you can move the Standard toolbar to the bottom of the screen, the left side, or the right side. You can display it as a floating palette in the middle of the screen. And you can resize it into a block of two, three, or more rows of buttons.

Figure 25.1, though unrealistic for everyday use, shows a possible arrangement of several of Word's toolbars.

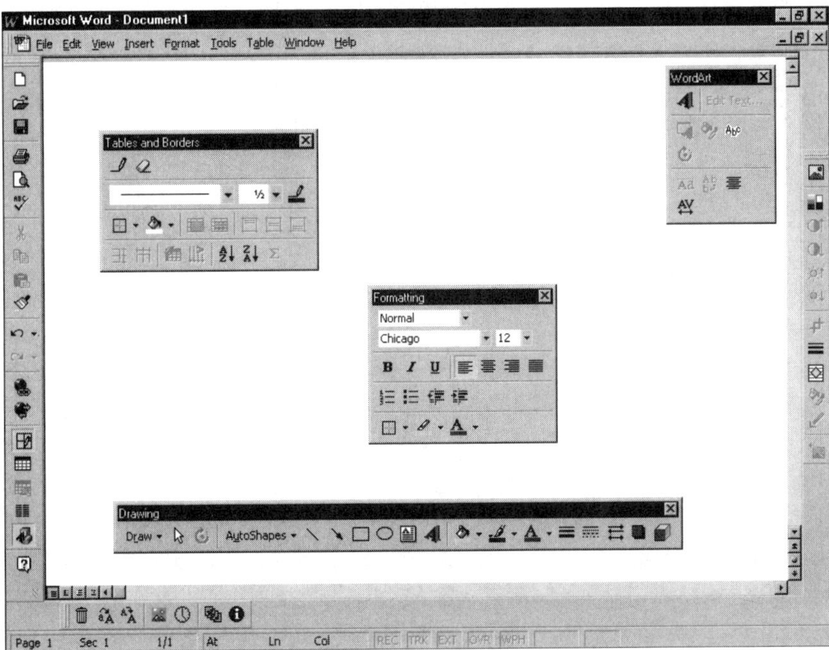

Figure 25.1 Toolbars can appear anywhere on the screen.

If a toolbar is *docked* (anchored to the top, bottom, or side of the screen), position your mouse pointer on the move handle at the far left end of the toolbar (the *move handle* consists of the pair of vertical lines and the small blank area to the left of the lines, as shown in Figure 25.2. With your mouse pointer on the move handle, just drag the toolbar wherever you want it.

Figure 25.2 The mouse pointer positioned on a move handle.

If a toolbar is floating, position your mouse pointer on the toolbar's title bar and drag the toolbar to a new location.

As you drag, a gray outline shows what the shape and location of the toolbar will be when you release the button. To anchor the toolbar to the left, right, top, or bottom of the screen, drag until the mouse pointer (not just the toolbar outline) is all the way at the edge.

To resize a toolbar, move the mouse to one of the toolbar's borders. You'll know you're in the right position to resize the toolbar when the mouse pointer turns into a double-headed arrow. At that point, just drag to resize the toolbar.

Once again, a shaded outline shows what the shape of the toolbar will be when you release the mouse button.

You can't resize a docked toolbar. But you can turn a docked toolbar into a floating toolbar by dragging it to a new location, at which point you can resize it if you want.

Changing Toolbar Options

You can change the appearance and function of your toolbars in several ways. You can increase the size of the icons and display or hide ScreenTips. If you're showing ScreenTips, you can also choose to have them display any shortcut key assigned to the command. You can even apply animation effects to your menus.

To change toolbar options:

1. Double-click on the blank area (where there aren't any buttons) of any toolbar to open the Customize dialog box.
2. Select the **Options** tab (shown in Figure 25.3).

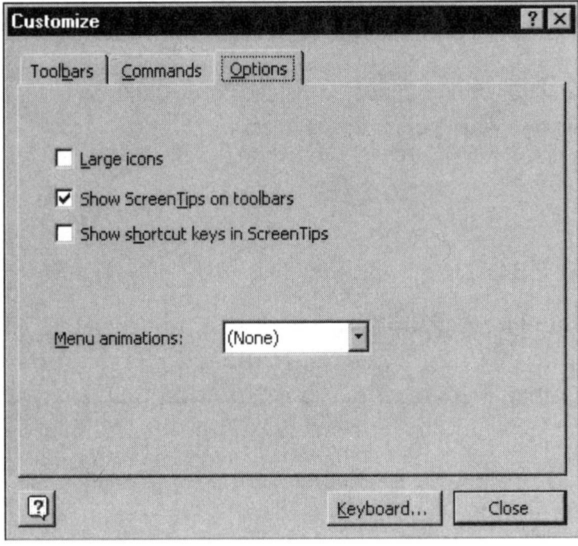

*Figure 25.3 The **Options** tab in the Customize dialog box.*

3. Select the options you want and click **OK**.

Removing and Rearranging Toolbar Buttons

You've already learned how to do some simple customizing of toolbars by changing their options, moving them around the screen, changing their size, and determining which toolbars will be displayed. You can go much further.

You can remove buttons from toolbars, add other commands and features, and create your own toolbars.

Using the mouse, you can rearrange a toolbar by moving buttons from one place to another, increasing the space between them, or removing buttons from the toolbars altogether. None of these changes requires you to open a dialog box. You can even move buttons from one toolbar to another.

If you plan to move a button from one toolbar to another, make sure both toolbars are displayed before you proceed:

1. Hold down the **Alt** key and click a toolbar button. A shaded box around the button shows that it can now be moved.
2. Drag the button to a new position on the toolbar (or another visible toolbar) to move it, or drag it off the toolbar entirely to remove it.

NOTE

You can copy a toolbar button instead of moving it by holding down the **Ctrl** and **Alt** keys while you drag the button.

Resetting a Toolbar

OK, suppose you played around with a toolbar and turned it into a complete mess. Before we go much further, you'll probably want to know how to restore that mess, er, toolbar, to its original state. Knowing that you can reset the toolbar allows you to experiment more freely to find the toolbar setup that works best for you.

To reset a toolbar to its default settings:

1. Open the Customize dialog box (double-click on any blank toolbar area or open the View menu and choose **Toolbar**, then choose **Customize** from the Toolbars menu).
2. Display the **Toolbars** tab.
3. Select the toolbar you want to reset and click **Reset**. Word prompts you for confirmation (Figure 25.4).

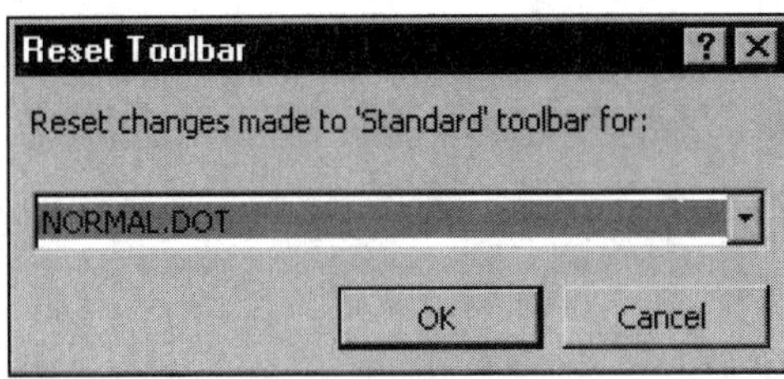

Figure 25.4 The Reset Toolbar Confirmation dialog box.

4. Click **OK**, then choose **Close** in the Customize dialog box.

The toolbar returns to its original settings.

Adding Toolbar Buttons

You can get easy access to the Word features you use the most by placing them in easy reach on a toolbar. If you generally use the mouse to choose commands from menus and select options from dialog boxes, you're the ideal candidate for putting commonly used commands on the toolbar. The advantage of toolbar buttons over menu commands and shortcut keys is that they're always visible. You can add buttons to an existing toolbar, or you can create a new toolbar.

To add a button to a toolbar:

1. Display the toolbar you want to customize.
2. Open the Customize dialog box (double-click on any blank toolbar area or open the View menu and choose **Toolbar**, then choose **Customize** from the Toolbars menu).
3. Select the **Commands** tab (shown in Figure 25.5).

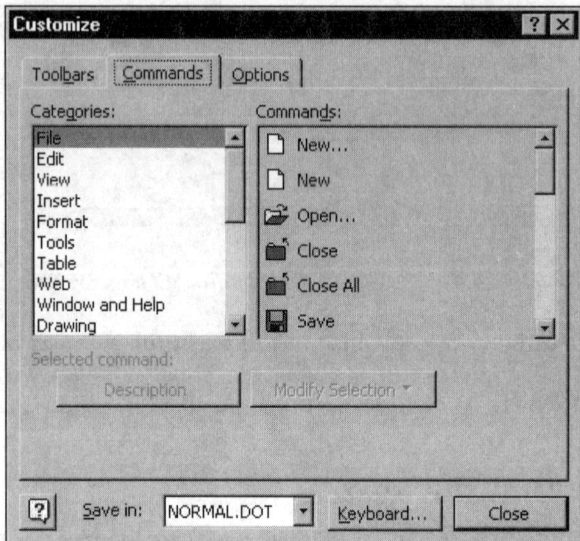

***Figure 25.5** The **Commands** tab in the Customize dialog box.*

4. From the Categories list, select a category to display the commands in that category. If you're not sure which category a command might be in, select the **All Commands** category.
5. From the list of commands or buttons, click the item you want to add to a toolbar.
6. Click the **Description** button if you want to see what the selected command does. A description box for the selected item appears at the bottom of the dialog box, as shown in Figure 25.6. Click anywhere except on the **Description** button to close the description box.
7. Drag the command to the toolbar you want it to appear on. As you drag, a little bar and an *x* attach themselves to your mouse pointer. When you see the *x*, it means you're not in a position where you can drop the command. When your mouse pointer is in the right position (on a toolbar or menu), the *x* changes to a +.

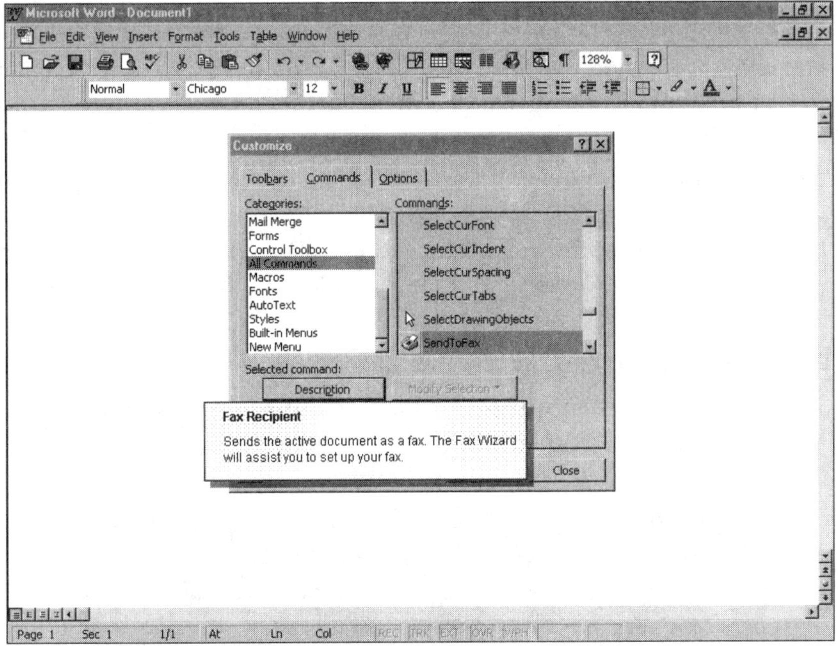

Figure 25.6 ***SendToFax*** *is selected in the Commands list, and the Description box shows what the command does.*

NOTE

The button doesn't have to end up in exactly the right position—remember, you can move a toolbar button anywhere you want it.

If the item you add has a picture next to it in the Commands list, that picture is what ends up on the toolbar button. If you choose a command that doesn't have a button assigned, the button displays the text for the command. The next section shows how to assign a picture to a button.

8. Choose **Close**. Your new button now appears on the toolbar you moved it to. You can change the position of the button or remove it by holding down the **Alt** key while you drag the button.

Changing Button Options

OK, you know how to add buttons to a toolbar. But there's more: You can change a bunch of the button's options, including its name, the picture assigned to it, and whether the button displays text only or an image with the text.

To change button options:

1. Open the Customize dialog box (double-click on any blank toolbar area or open the View menu and choose **Toolbar**, then choose **Customize** from the Toolbars menu).
2. Display the toolbar that has the button you want to change.
3. Right-click on the button to display the shortcut menu shown in Figure 25.7.

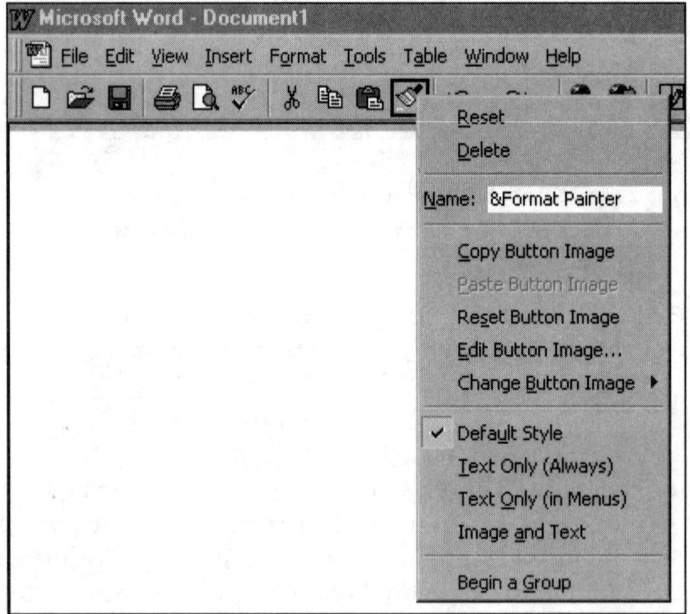

Figure 25.7 *This shortcut menu lets you change button options.*

4. Change any of the options you want.

Here's what some of the options do:

Reset Gets rid of any changes you've made to the buttons and returns it to its original settings.

Delete Deletes the button.

Name Allows you to change the button's name. Just enter the name you want in the text box. This is discussed in a bit more detail in the section on adding commands to menus.

Edit Button Image Opens the Button Editor shown in Figure 25.8. By choosing different colors and clicking in the Picture area.2, you can totally redesign the button. Play around with this option to get a sense of what's possible.

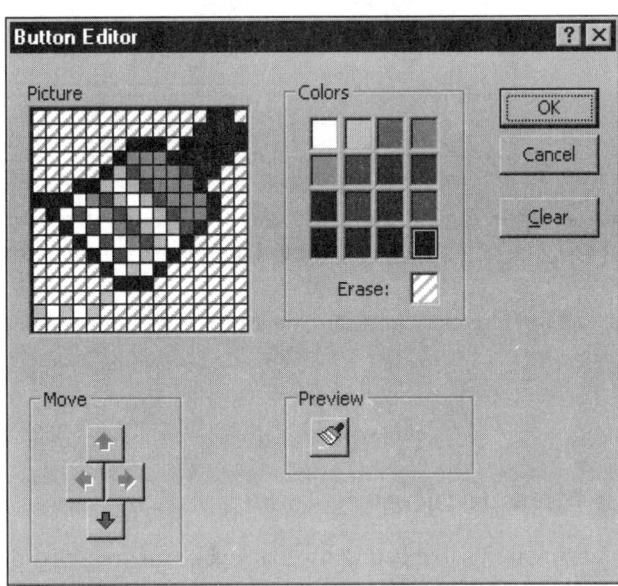

Figure 25.8 The Button Editor dialog box.

Change Button Image Opens the palette shown in Figure 25.9. Just click to assign one of the pictures to your button.

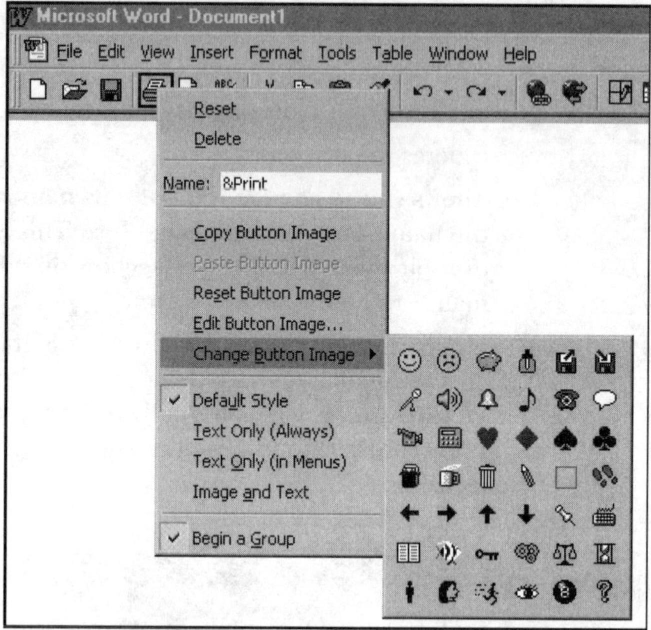

Figure 25.9 The Change Button Image palette.

Text and image options	Allow you to determine whether the button displays an image with the text or text only.

NOTE

These options also work for changing items on pull-down menus.

Creating a New Toolbar

In addition to adding items to existing toolbars, you can create your own toolbar from scratch.

To create a new toolbar:

1. Open the Customize dialog box (double-click on any blank toolbar area or open the View menu and choose **Toolbar**, then choose **Customize** from the Toolbars menu).
2. Select the **Toolbars** tab.
3. Click the **New** button.
4. Type a name in the **Toolbar name** box.
5. From the **Make toolbar available to** list, pick the template or document that you want to save the toolbar in.
6. Click **OK**. Word displays your new, empty toolbar.
7. Select the **Commands** tab in the Customize dialog box.
8. Drag the commands you want to your new toolbar.

Customizing the Keyboard

If you like using the keyboard as much as possible, this section is for you. There are many commands in Word that aren't available with a single keyboard combination if you keep Word's default settings.

However, there's nothing to keep you from assigning a shortcut key to nearly any command you can think of. If you use certain commands frequently, it's definitely worth assigning a few of your own shortcut keys.

Adding a Shortcut Key

You can use this procedure to assign a shortcut key of your choice to a command in Word. If you just want to see what shortcut keys are already assigned to a certain command, you can follow the first four steps until you see the current shortcut key assignments. Then close the dialog box without assigning any new ones.

To assign a shortcut key to a command:

1. Open the Customize dialog box (double-click on any blank toolbar area or open the View menu and choose **Toolbar**, then choose **Customize** from the Toolbars menu).

2. Select the **Commands** tab.
3. Click the **Keyboard** button to open the Customize Keyboard dialog box shown in Figure 25.10.

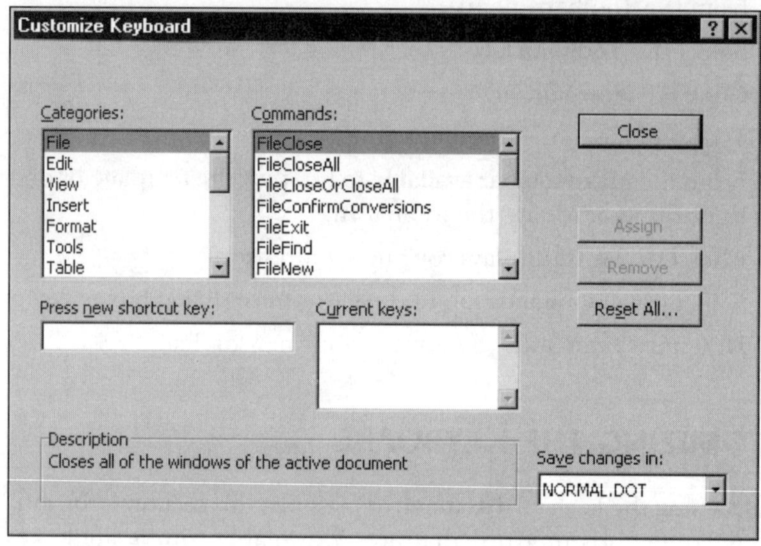

Figure 25.10 The Customize Keyboard dialog box.

4. Select a category, then select a command from that category. If any shortcut keys are already assigned to the command, they appear in the Current keys list.
5. Click in the **Press new shortcut key** box and type the key combination you want to assign. You can use any combination of the **Ctrl**, **Alt**, and **Shift** keys, function keys, or any characters on the keyboard.

   After you enter the key combination, look below the Press new shortcut key box to see if the combination you typed is already used by another command, as shown in Figure 25.11.

   If it's used by a command for which you don't need a shortcut key, go ahead and replace it. Otherwise, try a new key combination. Word hasn't assigned many **Ctrl+Alt+Shift** combinations or **Ctrl+Shift+number** combinations, so you should be pretty safe with these.

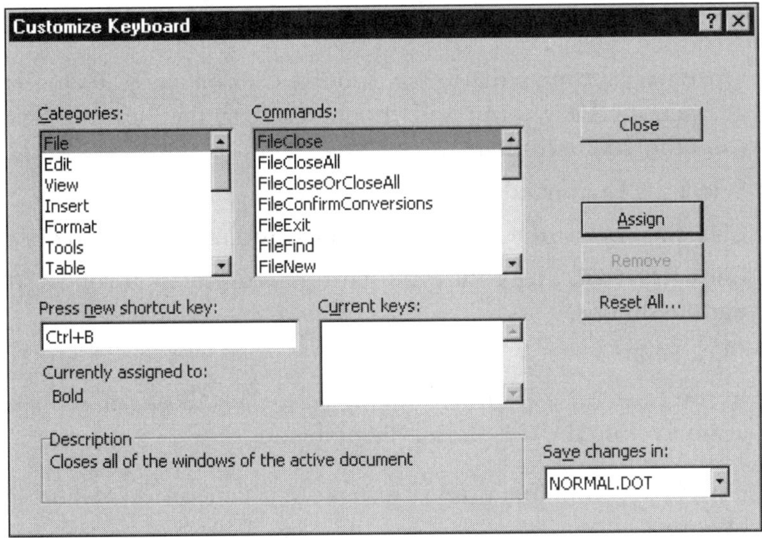

Figure 25.11 The shortcut key you typed is already in use.

6. Click **Assign**. If you forget the assigned shortcut key, you can return to the dialog box and look at the current keys for any command you select.

NOTE

If you select a keystroke combination that's already used by one of the pull-down menus, Word won't warn you. Don't ask me why—this is just one of those little program quirks. For example, if you enter **Alt+F** in the **Press new shortcut key** box, Word tells you that the key is currently unassigned. But **Alt+F** is the keystroke that opens the File menu, and if you assign it to another command, it won't work anymore to open the menu. If you're not aware of this, you can end up with some nasty surprises when you press a trusty old key to open a menu.

Returning Keyboard Shortcuts to Their Original Settings

Over time, you can end up with too many keyboard shortcuts. Maybe someone else will be using your computer and you don't want to confuse them with some of the unpredictable keystrokes you've assigned. No problem—Word lets you reset all your shortcut keys at once. You can also remove shortcut keys one at a time, as you'll learn in the next section.

To reset all shortcut keys to their defaults:

1. Open the Customize dialog box (double-click on any blank toolbar area or open the View menu and choose **Toolbar**, then choose **Customize** from the Toolbars menu).
2. Select the **Commands** tab.
3. Click the **Keyboard** button to open the Customize Keyboard dialog box.
4. Click **Reset All**. The Office Assistant pops up to ask if you're sure you want to do this.
5. Click **Yes**.
6. In the Customize Keyboard dialog box, click **Close**, then click **Close** again to close the Customize dialog box.

All the shortcut key combinations are now set to what they were when you first installed Word.

Removing Keyboard Shortcuts

As you've seen, you can remove a keyboard shortcut from a command simply by assigning it to another command. You might also want to remove a shortcut key if you find yourself often pressing it accidentally, making an unwanted change.

To remove a shortcut key:

1. Open the Customize dialog box (double-click on any blank toolbar area or open the View menu and choose **Toolbar**, then choose **Customize** from the Toolbars menu).
2. Select the **Commands** tab.
3. Click the **Keyboard** button.
4. Select the category and command with the shortcut key you want to delete. The shortcut keys assigned to the selected command appear in the Current Keys box.
5. Select a shortcut key combination from the Current Keys box and click **Remove**.
6. Click **Close**, then click **Close** again in the Customize dialog box.

Customizing Menus

As you can tell by the arrangement of items in the Customize dialog box, the same commands that are available for toolbar buttons and shortcut keys can be assigned to pull-down menu commands. You can add your own menu commands or remove commands you never use.

The main advantage of removing items from menus is simplification. Some of the menus, especially the Insert and Format menus, are quite long. It would be easier to see what's there if you removed the items you don't use. However, removing commands from the menu puts them out of your mind; if you need them sometime in the future, you might not remember that they were ever available. A good compromise is to wait until you've used Word for a few months and then remove the commands you haven't used.

Menus are somewhat different from toolbar buttons and shortcut keys in that the commands take two steps to perform: one to open the menu and the other to choose the command. But when you open the menu, you can always see the name of the command. You don't need to rely on memory for a shortcut key or the appearance of a toolbar icon.

Commands that are a little more involved or that need more text for you to recognize are good candidates for adding to a menu.

Removing Commands from a Menu

Streamlining your menu choices can make it easier to find the commands you want to use. As with other options you customize, remember that you can always reset the menus to their original configuration if you don't like what you've done. An easy shortcut key allows you to delete items from menus without ever opening the Customize dialog box.

To remove a command from a menu:

1. Press **Ctrl-Alt-Hyphen** (-). The mouse pointer changes to a thick minus sign.
2. Open a menu and click the command you want to remove.

When this particular mouse pointer is active, the next pull-down or shortcut menu item you select is deleted. Be careful with this.

You can also remove menu commands by opening the Customize dialog box. When the Customize dialog box is open, you can just drag a menu item off the menu to delete it. The advantage to this technique is that you don't have to remember the keyboard shortcut.

Resetting All Menu Changes

It's possible that you'll make some mistakes while customizing the menus—perhaps by deleting commands that you didn't mean to. You can reset the menus in the same way that you learned to reset all the shortcut keys.

To return menus to their default settings:

1. Open the Customize dialog box (double-click on any blank toolbar area or open the View menu and choose **Toolbar**, then choose **Customize** from the Toolbars menu).
2. Select the **Toolbars** tab.
3. Select **Menu Bar** to reset all the pull-down menus or select **Shortcut Menus** to reset all the shortcut menus.
4. Click **Reset**.
5. Click **OK** when prompted.
6. In the Customize dialog box, click **Close**.

Renaming Menu Commands

Because different people come from different backgrounds, they don't always refer to things the same way. There may be some commands in Word that sound foreign to you. If it helps you identify commands (or even just for fun), you can rename any of the menu commands in Word. The drawback is that if you make too radical a change, you may no longer recognize references to the command in the online Help or in this book.

To rename a menu command:

1. Open the Customize dialog box (double-click on any blank toolbar area or open the View menu and choose **Toolbar**, then choose **Customize** from the Toolbars menu).
2. Right-click on the menu item you want to rename.

3. Type the name you want in the Name text box in the shortcut menu (shown in Figure 25.12).

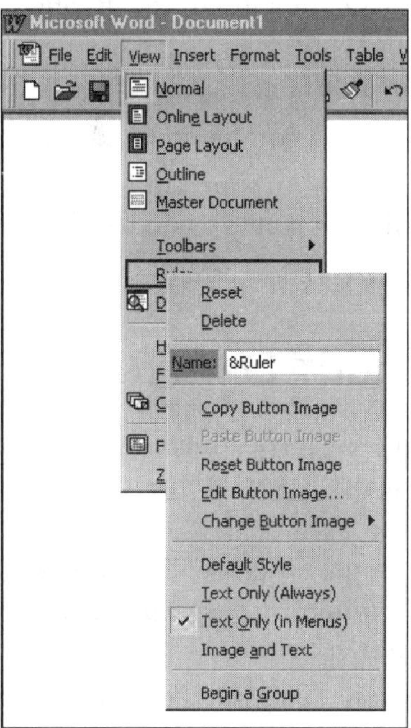

Figure 25.12 Enter a new name for the menu item.

NOTE

The ampersand (&) indicates which character will be underlined in the menu. As you know, you can select an item from a menu by pressing the underlined character (along with the **Alt** key if it's a top-level menu command) instead of clicking the item with the mouse. So make sure the ampersand is in front of the character you want to use as a keyboard shortcut for that item.

Adding Commands to a Menu

When you customize the menus in Word by adding commands that you want visible access to, you have dozens and dozens of commands from which to choose. If you add many commands, however, remember that a menu may become so long that it becomes unwieldy to use. Other commands may be best added to a toolbar or given shortcut keys for even quicker access.

To add a command to a menu:

1. Open the Customize dialog box (double-click on any blank toolbar area or open the View menu and choose **Toolbar**, then choose **Customize** from the Toolbars menu).
2. Select thc **Commands** tab.
3. Select a category and a command to add to a menu.
4. Drag the item to the menu you want. A horizontal line shows you where the command will be inserted when you release the mouse button.
5. Close the Customize dialog box.

SELECTING THE RIGHT OPTIONS

If you've been following the procedures in this book, you've already run across the Options dialog box several times. You open it by choosing **Options** from the Tools menu.

Among the ten tabs in the Options dialog box are more than 100 options. These options let you do things from specifying centimeters as your measurement unit to printing hidden text.

All these options are essentially ways you can further customize your environment in Word. Some deal only with appearance, others with the behavior of the program, and still others with the contents of files. It can be intimidating to be faced with this plethora of options. This section will point out some specific options that are likely to be useful in customizing the way Word works with you. The suggestions are grouped according to their tab in the Options dialog box.

NOTE

This section doesn't cover every single option—there are just too many. If you see an option that looks interesting but you're not sure what it does, click on the **What's This** button (the question mark in the upper-right corner of the Options dialog box), then click on the option you want more information about.

The View Tab

The appearance of your workspace in Word is the most noticeable customizing change you can make from the Options dialog box. There are several easy ways in which you can create more room to work so that you can see more of a document at one time. You can simplify the screen and speed up scrolling to allow you to concentrate better on the text, on the one hand, or you can add more information to make it easier to see your formatting.

By the way, there's one thing you may not have noticed yet about the **View** tab: there are three versions of it. If you change to Page Layout view and then open the Options dialog box, the **View** tab has a couple of options that aren't available when you're in Normal or Outline view. Normal and Outline views also have an option (**Style Area Width**) that is not available in Page Layout view. Figure 25.13 shows the **View** tab for Normal view.

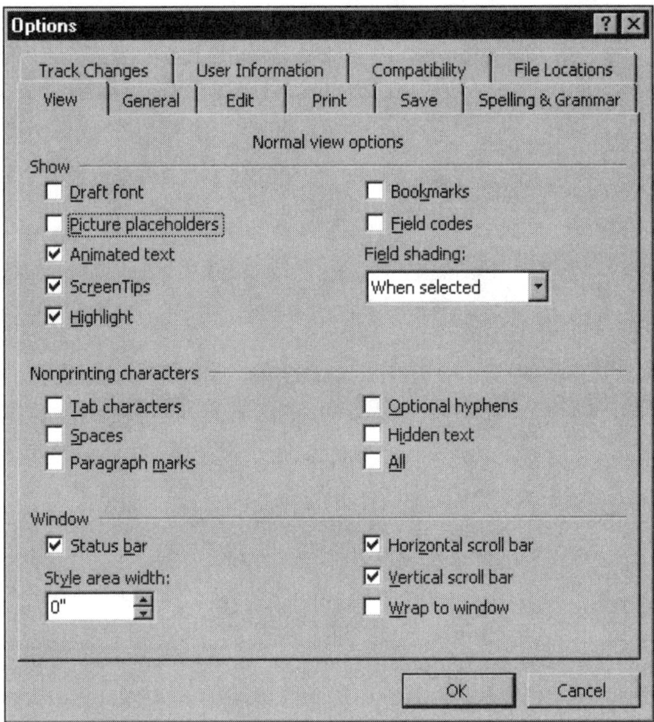

*Figure 25.13 The **View** tab for Normal view.*

Making More Space to Work In

You know how to turn toolbars on and off to balance a larger workspace with fewer easily accessible commands. Parts of the screen can also be hidden to give you more room to work (Table 25.1).

Table 25.1 Options that can be adjusted to maximize screen display.

THIS OPTION	DOES THIS
Status Bar	Displays measurement information about the position of the insertion point along the screen along with the status of several advanced features. If you don't care what page you're on and don't need to see any status information, you can create a little more workspace by turning this off.
Horizontal Scroll Bar	Scrolls the document window from side to side. If the entire width of your document fits horizontally on the screen, you can turn this option off. However, if the document is wide, not being able to scroll can be inconvenient.
Vertical Scroll Bar	Scrolls vertically through a document and shows you, by the position of the scroll box, how far into a document you are. Without the vertical scroll bar, you can still move through a document using the **Page Up** and **Page Down** keys, the **Find** command, and so on. In short documents, this is easy. In longer documents, you may feel hamstrung by not having the vertical scroll bar.
Style Area Width	In Normal and Outline views (but not Page Layout view), this displays a column on the left side of the window listing the style applied to each paragraph. If you're not a user of styles, you should definitely turn off this option by setting the width to zero. If you do use styles, you can always see the style of a selected paragraph on the Formatting toolbar, but the style area lets you see styles of multiple paragraphs at one time.

NOTE

Don't forget that there's another simple way of showing more of a document on the screen at one time: click the **Zoom** arrow on the Standard toolbar and lower the magnification of the document (for example, to **75%**). You can strike your own balance between showing more of the document and displaying the text in sizes too small to read.

Showing Nonprinting Characters

Earlier in the book we discussed using the **Show/Hide ¶** button on the Standard toolbar to show or hide all nonprinting characters, such as paragraph marks, spaces, and tabs. But it doesn't have to be all or nothing—you can display certain nonprinting characters but not others.

For example, seeing a mark on the screen for every space character can be visually distracting if you're not used to it. You can hide the marks for spaces but continue to show tab characters and paragraph marks (Table 25.2).

Table 25.2 *Options to control the display of non-printing characters.*

Tab Characters (a right-pointing arrow)	Tabs used in simple columns, indents, and elsewhere. If you have a document that has several tabs in a row, reformatting can make lines break at the wrong places, change text alignment, and so on. Displaying tab characters lets you catch these problems.
Spaces (displayed as dots)	Space characters between words and (in poorly formatted documents) in long strings used instead of tabs or indents. It may be useful to display space characters if you have a very small font that makes it hard to see if you've typed a space between words.
Paragraph Marks	The paragraph mark, which contains paragraph formatting information, at the end of every paragraph in a document. These are useful to display because you can see when you've used extra returns instead of proper paragraph formatting, and seeing the marks makes it easier to copy and paste paragraph marks.
Optional Hyphens (displayed as a dash with a little doohickey on the right end)	Suggested places for a break in a word, if hyphenation is turned on. The optional hyphenation takes effect only if that particular word falls near the end of a line. If there's no hyphenation command on the Tools menu, you didn't select this option when installing.
Hidden Text (text displays with a dotted underline)	Text with the Hidden attribute applied. With this option turned off, you won't even know that hidden text is there. With this option turned on, there's no visible change to the screen except where hidden text appears.

continued

Table 25.2 continued

THIS OPTION	REPRESENTS THIS
All	All of the marks including those described above. Selecting this option has the same effect as turning on the **Show/Hide ¶** button on the Standard toolbar.

The Edit Tab

By default, several of the options on the **Edit** tab are turned on. You may have assumed that Word always works this way, but these can actually be turned off. If you notice editing mistakes occurring because of one of these options or if you find yourself getting confused about how Word will react in a given editing situation, you may want to change some of these options. See Figure 25.14.

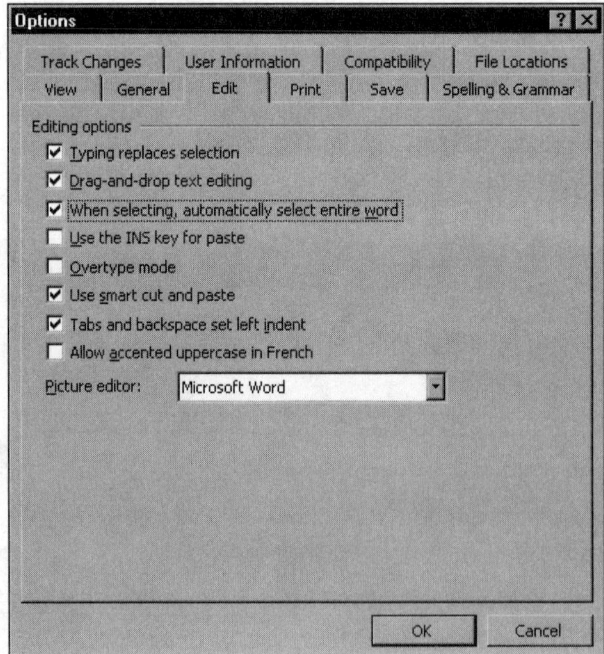

Figure 25.14 *The **Edit** tab.*

Even if you don't change any of these default options, it's good to know that the features are available. Table 25.3 summarizes the most useful of the editing options.

***Table 25.3** Editing options.*

THIS OPTION	DOES THIS
Typing replaces selection	As you've seen throughout this book, selected text is automatically deleted when you start typing. This is standard Windows 95 behavior, so you might want to get used to it if you plan to work with many other programs. But if you really can't stand it, turn off this option. When it's turned off, the new text is inserted in front of the selected text and the selected text stays where it was.
Drag-and-drop text editing	Lets you move a selection by clicking in the middle of the selected text and dragging to a new location. If you often move text accidentally and then look back and see that you've garbled up a paragraph, you may want to turn this option off.
When selecting, automatically select entire word	As you drag the mouse, Word begins selecting complete words at a time, as soon as you drag past the beginning or end of a word. If not being able to select parts of two neighboring words is frustrating, you can turn this option off. You can get the same result with this option on, however, by holding down the **Shift** key while pressing the **Right** or **Left Arrow** key. This lets you select text one character at a time.
Use the INS key for paste	Assigns the **Ins** key on the keyboard to the **Paste** command. This has two effects: you can paste more easily, and it becomes less likely that you will accidentally type over text in a document. Why? Normally, the **Ins** key turns on Overtype mode. The downside is that you might accidentally paste text if you press the **Ins** key by mistake.

continued

Table 25.3 continued

THIS OPTION	DOES THIS
Overtype Mode	When no text is selected and you type a character, deletes the next character. This is best turned off, as it makes it very easy to inadvertently delete text.
Use smart cut and paste	Adds or removes spaces when you cut and paste words. If you're cutting a word from one sentence and pasting it into another, you would otherwise have to worry about selecting the correct space before or after the word and having two spaces in a row or two words jammed together. With this option, Word leaves exactly one space between words in the text that you cut and paste.
Tab and backspace set left indent	Automatically increases or decreases indent for the current paragraph when you press the **Tab** or **Backspace** key.

The User Information Tab

The **User Information** tab of the Options dialog box stores your name, initials, and mailing address (see Figure 25.15). This information can then be used by several features in Word.

The mailing address is the information you're most likely to want to update. Your name and initials don't change much, but your mailing address may. The address you supply here is used as your return address when you have Word automatically create an envelope for your correspondence.

The name entered here is used to identify you as the author when you create a new document. You can see this and other document summary information by opening a document and choosing **Properties** from the File menu. The initials are used in some advanced features of Word, such as revisions and annotations.

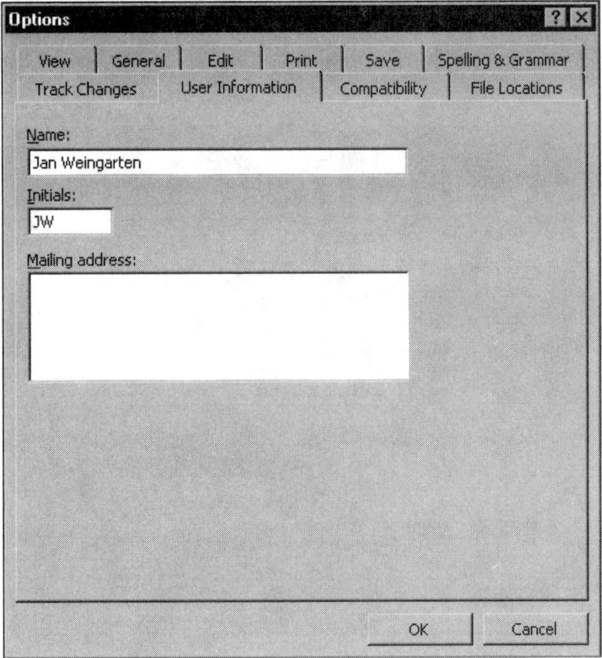

Figure 25.15 *The* ***User Information*** *tab.*

The Save Tab

One of the ways you can customize Word's operation is by determining whether Word will save your documents automatically, and, if so, how often. This adds a measure of security to your work. You can also speed up the process of saving long documents by selecting an option that tells Word to save added information at the end of a document rather than rewriting the entire document to the disk. This makes for faster saving but slightly larger files. You can also have Word create a backup copy of your most recent version of the document each time you save. If you're using TrueType fonts, you can choose to save, in the document, a copy of the fonts used. This allows all your readers to see the full formatting even if they don't already have these fonts on their systems, but it increases the file size. See Figure 25.16.

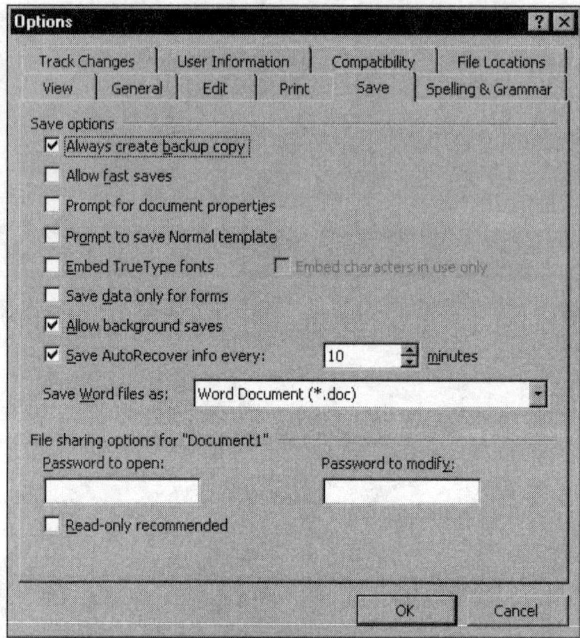

Figure 25.16 *The* ***Save*** *tab.*

Table 25.4 shows what a few of the more useful options do.

Table 25.4 *Save options.*

THIS OPTION	DOES THIS
Always create backup copy	Whenever you save, keeps the old copy of the document in the same folder with the current document. The backup document is named **Backup of *document name*.** This option and the **Allow Fast Saves** option can't both be selected.
Allow Fast Saves	Saves documents more quickly but doesn't use disk space quite as efficiently. If you're working on a very long document, saving without this option can take several seconds.

Embed TrueType fonts	Saves a copy of each TrueType font used in the document. If you have text in the Playbill font, for example, you can select this option and send the document to somebody who doesn't have the font. They will still be able to see text formatted with the included font. File size increases, however.
Save AutoRecover info every	Saves a copy of your document at the interval you specify. This copy doesn't commit you to the changes you've made, nor does it interfere with backup copies that you create. It's used only for recovery in case your computer goes down while you're in the midst of working on a document.

The Compatibility Tab

If you've switched to Word 97 from another word processing application, such as Word for DOS or WordPerfect, you're probably already familiar with the quirks and idiosyncrasies of your old program. These might include such things as wrapping spaces at the end of a line to the beginning of the next line or allowing you to condense the spacing between the letters of a word only by whole points rather than by fractions of points. Word 97 lets you select sets of compatibility options (see Figure 25.17) so that your documents look as much as possible like they did in the previous program.

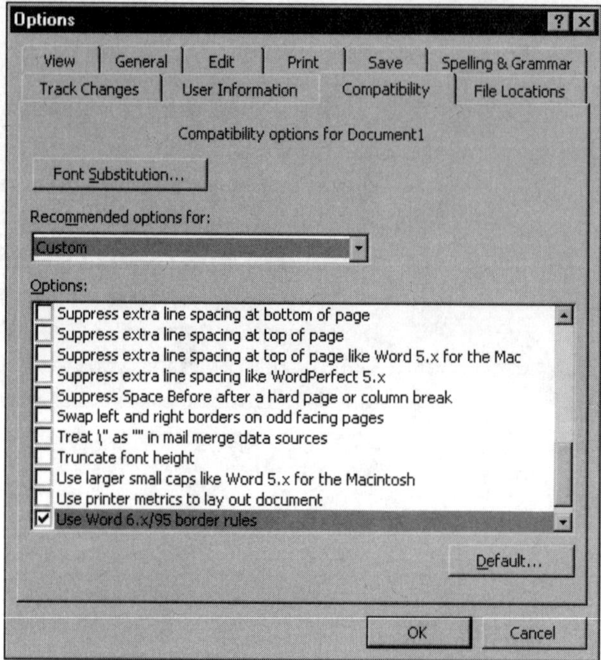

Figure 25.17 *The* ***Compatibility*** *tab.*

When you need to re-create the appearance of a document precisely, these options are helpful. However, they can also be helpful if you notice a specific change in line spacing, treatment of hanging indents, or another cosmetic change that you don't understand. Instead of whole sets of compatibility options, you can select them one by one.

There are too many compatibility options and too many possible needs to describe them all here. However, if something bothers you about the way the program displays or formats certain features, it's worth coming to this list and scanning the items to see if something solves your problem.

For example, suppose you format a paragraph to have a hanging indent. Normally, Word automatically sets an invisible tab at the location of the indent. On the first line of a paragraph with a hanging indent, pressing **Tab** takes you to the point where the second and other lines will begin; this is convenient. However, you may be accustomed to indents working in a different way or you may want to set a tab elsewhere. Looking at the list of options in the **Compatibility** tab, you find an option called **Don't add automatic tab stop for**

hanging indent. When you select this option, the hanging indent feature now works just as you want it to.

From Here...

In this chapter, you've learned how to tailor the appearance and behavior of Word 97 to your own working style. You can display only the toolbars that you need in the shape, position, and style that you prefer. You've learned how to simplify toolbars by removing unneeded buttons and to add buttons for commands you use frequently. You can also add and remove items from the menus in Word and assign personalized shortcut keys to save you time executing commands. Finally, you know how to focus on some of the more practical options available for customizing the Word environment. In all, you can now make Word 97 work the way you do.

We've reached the end of the road. But the end of this road is really just an on-ramp. Word is an incredibly rich program—there's much more depth and many more features than could possibly be covered in a book this size. It's time for you to make Word work for you. Use and master the features that fit your needs. Explore, explore, explore. As you gain experience with a particular feature, you'll continue to discover new shortcuts and possibilities.

Enjoy!

INDEX

Q

R